THE WRITER'S HANDBOOK

THE WRITER'S HANDBOOK

Edited by
A. S. BURACK
Editor, The Writer

Boston
THE WRITER, INC.
Publishers

FOREWORD

The one hundred chapters in this new edition of THE WRITER'S HANDBOOK, forty of which appear here for the first time, offer a comprehensive introduction to a wide variety of literary forms and fields. Part IV, *The Writer's Markets*, is brought up to date regularly, and includes the addresses, editors' names, and editorial requirements of 2,500 publishing markets for fiction, nonfiction, poetry, fillers, juveniles, and other special fields, in magazine or book form, as well as stage and television plays.

The chapters in this book originally appeared as articles in *The Writer* magazine, and this comprehensive selection, made after careful consideration from the hundreds available, presents aspiring as well as practicing writers with the techniques, approaches, and insights that will help them turn their creative ideas into salable manuscripts. The market lists give detailed information to help writers increase their chances of publication.

I wish to thank the authors who have generously granted us permission to reprint their articles as chapters in this book. It is my hope that THE WRITER'S HANDBOOK will continue to be a source of instruction and inspiration to writers.

Boston   A. S. BURACK

CONTENTS

PART I—BACKGROUND FOR WRITERS

PART II—HOW TO WRITE: Techniques

FICTION

NONFICTION

POETRY

PART III—THE EDITORIAL AND BUSINESS SIDE

PART IV—THE WRITER'S MARKETS

Where to Sell

PART I

BACKGROUND FOR WRITERS

1

CREATIVE TRUST

By John D. MacDonald

The writer and the reader are involved in a creative relationship. The writer must provide the materials with which the reader will construct bright pictures in his head. The reader will use those materials as a partial guide and will finish the pictures with the stuff from his own life experience.

I do not intend to patronize the reader with this analogy: The writer is like a person trying to entertain a listless child on a rainy afternoon.

You set up a card table, and you lay out pieces of cardboard, construction paper, scissors, paste, crayons. You draw a rectangle and you construct a very colorful little fowl and stick it in the foreground, and you say, "This is a chicken." You cut out a red square and put it in the background and say, "This is a barn." You construct a bright yellow truck and put it in the background on the other side of the frame and say, "This is a speeding truck. Is the chicken going to get out of the way in time? Now you finish the picture."

If the child has become involved, he will get into the whole cut-and-paste thing, adding trees, a house, a fence, a roof on the barn. He will crayon a road from the truck to the chicken. You didn't say a word about trees, fences, houses, cows, roofs. The kid puts them in because he knows they are the furniture of farms. He is joining in the creative act, enhancing the tensions of the story by adding his uniquely personal concepts of the items you did not mention, but which have to be there.

Or the child could cross the room, turn a dial and see detailed pictures on the television tube. What are the ways you can lose him?

3

You can lose him by putting in too much of the scene. That turns him into a spectator. "This is a chicken. This is a fence. This is an apple tree. This is a tractor." He knows those things have to be there. He yawns. And pretty soon, while you are cutting and pasting and explaining, you hear the gunfire of an old western.

You can lose him by putting in too little. "This is a chicken," you say, and leave him to his own devices. Maybe he will put the chicken in a forest, or in a supermarket. Maybe the child will invent the onrushing truck, or a chicken hawk. Too much choice is as boring as too little. Attention is diffused, undirected.

You can put in the appropriate amount of detail and still lose him by the way you treat the chicken, the truck, and the barn. Each must have presence. Each must be unique. *The* chicken. Not *a* chicken. He is eleven weeks old. He is a rooster named Melvin who stands proud and glossy in the sunlight, but tends to be nervous, insecure and hesitant. His legs are exceptionally long, and in full flight he has a stride you wouldn't believe.

If you cannot make the chicken, the truck, and the barn totally specific, then it is as if you were using dingy gray paper for those three ingredients, and the child will not want to use his own bright treasure to complete the picture you have begun.

We are analogizing here the semantics of image, of course. The pace and tension and readability of fiction are as dependent upon your control and understanding of these phenomena as they are upon story structure and characterization.

Here is a sample: The air conditioning unit in the motel room had a final fraction of its name left, an "aire" in silver plastic, so loose that when it resonated to the coughing thud of the compressor, it would blur. A rusty water stain on the green wall under the unit was shaped like the bottom half of Texas. From the stained grid, the air conditioner exhaled its stale and icy breath into the room, redolent of chemicals and of someone burning garbage far, far away.

Have you not already constructed the rest of the motel room? Can you not see and describe the bed, the carpeting, the shower? O.K., if you see them already, I need not describe them for you. If I try to do so, I become a bore. And the pictures you have composed in your head are more vivid than the ones I would try to describe.

No two readers will see exactly the same motel room. No two children will construct the same farm. But the exercise of the need to create gives both ownership and involvement to the motel room and the farm, to the air conditioner and to the chicken and to their environments.

Sometimes, of course, it is useful to go into exhaustive detail. That is when a different end is sought. In one of the Franny and Zooey stories, Salinger describes the contents of a medicine cabinet shelf by shelf in such infinite detail that finally a curious monumentality is achieved, reminiscent somehow of that iron sculpture by David Smith called "The Letter."

Here is a sample of what happens when you cut the images out of gray paper: "The air conditioning unit in the motel room window was old and somewhat noisy."

See? Because the air conditioning unit has lost its specificity, its unique and solitary identity, the room has blurred also. You cannot see it as clearly. It is less real.

AND WHEN THE ENVIRONMENT IS LESS REAL, THE PEOPLE YOU PUT INTO THAT ENVIRONMENT BECOME LESS BELIEVABLE, AND LESS INTERESTING.

I hate to come across a whole sentence in caps when I am reading something. But here, it is of such importance, and so frequently misunderstood and neglected, I inflict caps upon you with no apology. The environment can seem real only when the reader has helped construct it. Then he has an ownership share in it. If the air conditioner is unique, then the room is unique, and the person in it is real.

What item to pick? There is no rule. Sometimes you can use a little sprinkling of realities, a listing of little items which make a room unique among all rooms in the world: A long living room with one long wall painted the hard blue of Alpine sky and kept clear of prints and paintings, with a carved blonde behemoth piano, its German knees half-bent under its oaken weight, and with a white Parsons table covered by a vivid collection of French glass paperweights.

I trust the reader to finish the rest of that room in his head, without making any conscious effort to do so. The furnishings will be appropriate to his past observations.

How to make an object unique? (Or where do I find the colored paper for the rooster?) Vocabulary is one half the game, and that can come only from constant, omnivorous reading, beginning very early in life. If you do not have that background, forget all about trying to write fiction. You'll save yourself brutal disappointment. The second half of the game is input. All the receptors must be wide open. You must go through the world at all times looking at the things around you. Texture, shape, style, color, pattern, movement. You must be alert to the smell, taste, sound of everything you see, and alert to the relationships between the aspects of objects, and of people. Tricks and traits and habits, deceptive and revelatory.

There are people who have eyes and cannot see. I have driven friends through country they have never seen before and have had them pay only the most cursory attention to the look of the world. Trees are trees, houses are houses, hills are hills—to them. Their inputs are all turned inward, the receptors concerned only with Self. Self is to them the only reality, the only uniqueness. Jung defines these people in terms of the "I" and the "Not I." The "I" person conceives of the world as being a stage setting for Self, to the point where he cannot believe other people are truly alive and active when they are not sharing that stage with Self. Thus nothing is real unless it has a direct and specific bearing on Self.

The writer must be a Not-I, a person who can see the independence of all realities and know that the validity of object or person can be appraised and used by different people in different ways. The writer must be the observer, the questioner. And that is why the writer should be wary of adopting planned eccentricities of appearance and behavior, since, by making himself the observed rather than the observer, he dwarfs the volume of input he must have to keep his work fresh.

Now we will assume you have the vocabulary, the trait of constant observation plus retention of the telling detail. And at this moment—if I am not taking too much credit—you have a new appraisal of the creative relationship of writer and reader. You want to begin to use it.

The most instructive thing you can do is to go back over past work, published or unpublished, and find the places where you described something at length, in an effort to make it unique and special, but somehow you did not bring it off. (I do this with my own work oftener than you might suppose.)

Now take out the subjective words. For example, I did not label the air conditioner as old, or noisy, or battered, or cheap. Those are evaluations the reader should make. Tell how a thing looks, not your evaluation of what it is from the way it looks. Do not say a man looks seedy. That is a judgment, not a description. All over the world, millions of men look seedy, each one in his own fashion. Describe a cracked lens on his glasses, a bow fixed with stained tape, tufts of hair growing out of his nostrils, an odor of old laundry.

This is a man. His name is Melvin. You built him out of scraps of bright construction paper and put him in front of the yellow oncoming truck.

The semantics of image is a special discipline. Through it you achieve a reality which not only makes the people more real, it makes the situation believable, and compounds the tension.

If a vague gray truck hits a vague gray man, his blood on gray pavement will be without color or meaning.

When a real yellow truck hits Melvin, man or rooster, we feel that mortal thud deep in some visceral place where dwells our knowledge of our own oncoming death.

You have taken the judgment words out of old descriptions and replaced them with the objective words of true description. You have taken out the things the reader can be trusted to construct for himself.

Read it over. Is there too much left, or too little? When in doubt, opt for less rather than more.

We all know about the clumsiness the beginning writer shows when he tries to move his people around, how he gets them into motion without meaning. We all did it in the beginning. Tom is in an office on one side of the city, and Mary is in an apartment on the other side. So we walked him into the elevator, out through the foyer, into a cab, all the way across town, into another foyer, up in the elevator, down the corridor to Mary's door. Because it was motion without meaning, we tried desperately to create interest with some kind of ongoing interior monologue. Later we learned that as soon as the decision to go see Mary comes to Tom, we need merely skip three spaces and have him knocking at Mary's door. The reader knows how people get across cities, and get in and out of buildings. The reader will make the instantaneous jump.

So it is with description. The reader knows a great deal. He has taste and wisdom, or he wouldn't be reading. Give him some of the vivid and specific details which you see, and you can trust him to build all the rest of the environment. Having built it himself, he will be that much more involved in what is happening, and he will cherish and relish you the more for having trusted him to share in the creative act of telling a story.

2

SHOULD I BE A WRITER?

By Joe Gores

I MAKE my living writing, not talking, but like most professionals I am periodically asked to speak about my craft. Certain questions always pop up in the cat-and-mouse sessions which follow. Since they seem to reflect genuine concerns of beginning writers, and since I presume my answers reflect the attitudes of the average pro, I list herewith a few exchanges of possible value.

I have a good job, but I have always wanted to write. Should I be a writer?

I believe it's more a question of *must* you be a writer. It chooses you, not the other way around. Keep your job and write in your spare time until you find out whether you can make it or not. Try to avoid professions which leave your creative faculties dulled at the end of the day, such as teaching, writing for a newspaper, or doing ad agency copy. Writing is not a "second profession"—it demands as much time as you can give it, preferably a lifetime. Nor is professional writing therapy, an outlet for creative energies, or a hobby. Dorothy Parker once wryly commented, after mentioning certain writing-is-fun writers, "And there was that poor sucker Flaubert, rolling around on his floor for three days looking for the right word."

The day before I graduated from Notre Dame, I asked my creative writing teacher, Richard Sullivan, whether I should be a writer. I have never forgotten his answer. "It's very easy, Joe," he said. "Go to a big city and get a little room with a table and a chair in it. Put your typewriter on the table and your backside on the chair, and start typing. When you stand up ten years later, you'll be a writer."

9

I am interested in the creation of literature, so why should I have to demean my art by writing for money?

Don't knock it until you've tried it. And who told you writing is an art? It's a craft. Unless you are making a living from your writing, or are trying to, you are just kidding yourself. Ernest Hemingway stated, "I write hardcover books for money." William Faulkner often said that when he got a letter he turned the envelope upside down and shook it. If a check fell out, he read the letter.

I find it unusually interesting that the proliferation of university and foundation grants-in-aid to writers has not produced anyone with the enduring stature of a Hemingway or a Faulkner. Writing is grueling work, and most of us would rather make excuses than stories. But when your food and rent come out of the typewriter, you tend to give it regular exercise. I doubt if most non-professionals have any idea of the amount of work a pro regularly turns out. In a typical year, for example, I have written three novels, two screenplays, a nonfiction book proposal (fifty pages and a detailed outline), and several short stories and articles: two thousand typed manuscript pages, including revision drafts. And I am light years away from being the most prolific pro around.

Geoffrey Household, British master of suspense, put it this way:

If you cannot live by your writing, the translation into words of your own manner of thinking cannot be effective, for your whole aim and object is to be so completely good that the maximum number of people, whether they approve or not, will have to pay money to read you. The market is the ultimate test for the craftsman. That it should also be the first and only test for the hack is unimportant.

Isn't professional writing merely hack writing anyway?

All hacks are by necessity professionals, but not all professionals are hacks. The hack works *only* for money, invariably subordinating artistic considerations to the buck. The professional can take on almost any writing chore, as long as he involves himself in the project and does the best job he can, without descending to mere hack work. Our business is to write, exactly as a bricklayer's business is to lay bricks. I have yet to hear someone accuse a bricklayer of being a hack because he laid bricks for a sewage disposal plant instead of waiting around (while his family starved) to lay bricks for a cathedral.

How long will it take me to become a professional writer?

If we assume a modicum of talent and a lot of drive (ten percent ability, ninety percent determination, according to W. Somerset Maugham), Professor Sullivan's figure is about right: ten years to learn the craft well enough (and to make a sufficient percentage of your living from it) to consider yourself a professional. You never stop learning, of course. Nothing you will ever write will be quite as good as it *could* be. Faulkner once said of the writer in relation to his work, "Once he matched the work to the image, the dream, nothing would remain but to . . . jump off the other side of the pinnacle of perfection into suicide."

Can you break it down into dollars and cents?

When I began selling, I made a penny per hour at the typewriter. It took me four years, averaging three hundred rejection slips a year, to make my first story sale. During the next six years, my writing income averaged $354.50 a year. If you can live on that, hop to it. I'd guess that the pro with those necessary ten or fifteen years behind him will be making between $5,000 and $15,000 a year, with the norm between $7,000 and $12,000.

Will writers' courses help me become a good writer?

No. Writing will help you become a good writer. The single most important thing for a writer is to write. The second is to rewrite. Writers' courses *do* make the beginning or amateur writer write and provide him with criticism of his work.

One of the big arguments advanced for such courses is that they help dispel the loneliness. If you can't stand being alone, find another line of work. Punch tickets in the subway or something. Nobody can write it for you, nobody can help you write it (my cat tries, he sleeps on my desk as I work and talks over plots with me). Being solitary is not being lonely. Watching a host of heroes and villains and lovers and haters emerge from the typewriter is not being lonely. Working on a novel the other day, I had to sit by in astonishment while a couple of guys I've written about in short stories for years got into a devil of a row. I had no idea they were going to do that. I'd always thought of them as close friends.

Write. And write, write, write. And submit. Take your lumps and your rejection slips. When your work gets good enough, you will start getting the occasional editorial reaction along with the printed confetti, and you will be on your way.

How can I determine the correct markets for my material?

Use common sense, first of all. In *Playboy*, Jack and Jill don't go up the hill *just* to fetch a pail of water; in *Good Housekeeping*, the heroine does not smoke pot and have a live-in boyfriend. *Read the magazines*. And I mean read (or skim) *everything* in them, especially the advertising. Reading the ads will help you judge whether your work is calculated to grab the reader of that particular magazine.

Novelists should read a lot of novels, especially those from the current lists of publishers they favor. If the publishers' editorial tastes vary wildly from your own, start considering a different publishing house. And do not be discouraged when, after all of this, the inevitable rejection slips pile up. Even some major best sellers have collected a dozen or more rejections before a publisher finally took them.

As a beginner, should I stick to shorts or try the novel?

Each form has much to offer. The short story usually deals with a single incident or point in time which radically and instantly changes the protagonist's life. The short is the great teacher, forcing you to be parsimonious with words, to write compelling and revealing dialogue, and to be selective in your use of description.

The novel usually is marked by the impact of time on its characters, and shows gradual significant change or development in them —a war, say, rather than a single battle. Unlike the short story, the novel forgives many errors, but you have to *write* the darned thing. Pages and pages, thousands and thousands of words, weeks, months, sometimes years, with no money coming in and little assurance of any even when it is finished. You have to stick to the novel, yet most amateurs remain amateurs precisely because they *don't* have sticking power. They'd rather play golf.

Whatever you write, be aware of the market. In the thirties, a

10,000-word short story was acceptable; by the fifties the optimum word length had dropped to 5,000 words. Today it's about 3,500; we live in a faster age. Novels should range between 55,000 and 85,000 words, with 60,000 to 70,000 optimum. Too short, the reader feels cheated; too long, the printing costs become prohibitive. Herman Wouk and Harold Robbins write 900-page books which sell for $10.00; you and I don't. Why? For the moment, at least, we aren't going to sell like Wouk or Robbins.

Do I need an agent?

No. Beginning writers not only don't need an agent, most of them aren't going to get one, not a reputable agent. Why *should* he take you on? Ten percent of almost nothing leads to forced sales of his office furniture. He wants writers who not only can sell, but who also can *produce,* can meet deadlines, can absorb criticism, can function, in short, in a professional manner.

Contrary to popular belief, an agent is not going to sell your book any faster than you are, not if it is a salable book. If it isn't, he's not going to sell it at all. Editors buy books, not somebody's boyish good looks. It is after you are offered a contract that you need an agent, and you can then probably get a reputable one.

He will know why clauses can be blue-penciled from the standard contract, he knows where to look for foreign, movie, and condensation sales that form such a vital part of a book's income. It is the *selling* writer—and above all the professional writer—who needs an agent.

One final point: the author/agent relationship is a delicate one, a sexless marriage. There must be mutual trust and a give-and-take in which both are comfortable. A bad or untrustworthy or dishonest agent is a thousand times worse than no agent at all, because he can, quite literally, destroy you as a writer.

Does it help your sales to know editors?

Knowing editors helps you find out what sort of material is in current demand. And if a book or article is to be farmed out, editors will naturally turn to professionals with whose work they are familiar and who they know will produce to deadline.

But even if you've never sold anything in your life, the editor is not The Enemy. He is not some alien creature standing between you and success. Editors are skillful intermediaries between writers interested in artistic creation, and publishing houses interested in making a profit from selling books. Of course, there are lousy editors, but there are plenty of lousy writers, too.

A *good* editor is a joy forever, able to make a sick story well. I remember Lee Wright of Random House once saying to me, during a head-knocking session over a proposed novel, "Remember, Joe, the most useful word in a writer's vocabulary is 'meanwhile.' " This is a profound insight into the art of storytelling: try it sometime when you're bogged down in a plot line.

It is easy to get to know editor.. Submit salable material to them. But don't count on a first-name basis to insure sales. You're only as good as the work in hand; the fact that they buy from you this month doesn't mean they'll buy next month. Or buy a bad book or story. Or take something unsuited to their market.

Knowing editors is not the way to success as a writer. Nor is having an agent. Success does not come from slanting your material to a market, or from sitting around chanting "literature" like one of the seven names of God. Success does not even come from smoking a briar pipe and wearing a Harris tweed with leather patches on the elbows.

Success as a writer comes from writing—constantly, compulsively, in a word, professionally. Writing is communication, and writing is a craft. In any craft, practice is the only means to success. From practice comes the technical mastery which must be assumed before profound (or, indeed, light) fiction can be written. Technical mastery frees your creative intuition from worry about words, lets it create from raw sensory data and what French philosopher Jacques Maritain has called the "pre-conscious intellect," a new entity which readers will recognize as more real than reality itself.

This is what writing is all about. And this is what writing *has* been all about, ever since man first learned to tell his stories on the walls of his caves instead of just talking about them.

3

THE ESSENCE OF WRITING

By Shirley Ann Grau

ME GIVE advice about writing? Good heavens, no. That wouldn't be a good idea at all. Fiction writing (creative writing, not the made-to-order kind) is one of those intensely personal activities that are not helped by outside influences. A writer is best left alone to find his own way.

Mind you, I am not saying that writers are born rather than made. Not in the least. About the only thing a writer is born with is a certain facility with words—a talent he shares with con men, real estate agents, teachers. And so on. A friendly, relaxed attitude toward the English language is not at all uncommon in our society.

A writer is simply one who has developed this ability—and he has developed it largely by himself. This isolation, I suppose, accounts for the large number of idiosyncrasies in the group. I know one gentleman who will only write wearing a Maine hunting shirt —no matter what the weather. Another works only with the radio on—for company. Still another works in an isolated study where even the buzzing of a trapped fly must be stopped.

I myself have never been able to afford such fixed habits. I have to work when and where and how I can. After all, I have a house to run, as well as the care and feeding of a husband and four children. Though the children are grown now and life is much more predictable, during the past twenty years I have written in just about every possible situation. I have planned novels while cooking, corrected manuscript in the pediatrician's waiting room. I have written in a house filled with the babble of children, the slamming of doors, the protesting barks of dogs.

A good way to write? Of course not. But it had to be that way. Or not write at all.

Luckily for me, that mysterious personal activity called writing is infinitely adjustable.

Furthermore, I don't really think writing can be taught—in classes or anywhere else. If writing classes are helpful, it is *not* because they teach their subject but because the very existence of the class—the peer group pressure—forces a beginner to discipline himself. To put something down on paper, good or bad—that is the beginner's most difficult problem. If a writing class compels him to produce, if it makes him feel guilty about not writing—well, that's a good class.

Incidentally, most successful teachers of writing don't communicate the techniques of writing (which aren't all that complicated) but the force, the excitement of an overwhelming need to write.

After that, it's up to the individual. As it will be up to him for the rest of his creative life.

This of course is the very thing I like. I like the isolation, the mental freedom to explore the bewildering behavior of Homo sapiens. And to wonder at the unanswered puzzle of all successful works of fiction: *Why is success not really a matter of skill?* For example, why are the novels of Dostoevsky and Tolstoy, those monumental failures—so easy to parody, so easy to mock—why are they so much more alive, more stirring than their better constructed modern counterparts?

In brief, I spend half my time trying to learn the secrets of other writers—to apply them to the expression of my own thoughts.

And that is the essence of writing. I, like every other serious writer, feel that I must comment on man and his world. I want to explain, I want to systematize as much as any philosopher. I have something to say, something that I think is true and valuable. For me the goal of all fiction is simply this: to make more understandable, more bearable if you will, the muddle of human life.

That makes the writer sound like a bit of an evangelist, and that is just about what I believe. He is an evangelist whose preaching is extremely subtle and utterly disguised—quite possibly even from himself. (I know that I could not state my message abstractly.)

But then, that is not the nature of fiction. A writer's view of the world is constantly moving, shifting. Fiction at its best is a mirror of that constantly changing reality. Each serious writer with each successive book is describing another facet of his world of reality. And like his cousin the evangelist, he wants people to listen.

Now—all of this concerns writing at its highest, most abstract level. And nobody ever lives at the ideal level. Of course not.

The day-in-day-out life of a fiction writer is nothing more or less than a series of problem-solving experiments in words. A writer must think of himself as a storyteller, a mood-evoker, a delineator of character—those are all problems he faces and has to solve—for better or worse.

I prefer to think of myself as a storyteller primarily. And where do the stories come from? Everywhere. Literally.

My novel *The Keepers of the House* was taken from places and events I knew in my childhood. (Not any of them is my story. I am a secretive writer; I never write autobiography.) Another novel of mine, *The Condor Passes*, is an amalgam of the life stories of two men, neither of whom I'd ever met. I read about them in a Chicago newspaper. It was only a matter of adding details. One of my short stories, "The Last Gas Station," appeared, complete, while we were watching streams of southbound traffic on the Miami turnpike one winter day. Another, "The Patriarch," is the story of a man I really knew, a monumental old man, almost biblical in his thunderings. It is, incidentally, the basis of my new novel. I like the way the old man looks in print—I want to see more of him.

And that's the way it goes, an endless unraveling of ideas, and endless exploration of the possibilities of life.

4

ARE YOU MAKING THE MOST OF YOUR TALENT?

By Marjorie Holmes

I WONDER if teachers, particularly good English teachers, realize the profound impact they may have on developing talent? My teacher was Dewey Deal, slim, blonde, with her hair in a silken bun and a voice that was like rich velvet. I had her in eighth grade, and then by a remarkable stroke of fortune, for freshman English in college. It was there she wrote the following words on a notebook. Words that were often to keep me going during periods of discouragement; words that were to influence my writing itself:

> You must make the most of your talent—you have been endowed with so much. I can feel joy with these paragraphs, I can feel sorrow, I am moved by their imagery. I know that if you want to badly enough you can write beautiful things for people who crave beautiful things. There is a duty!

There is a duty. . . .

Talent is a gift. You had nothing to do with receiving yours, nor I with receiving mine. But each of us has everything to do with what becomes of that talent. I am firmly convinced that each of us is given his talent for a reason; and that having talent, any talent, but particularly one for writing, imposes two responsibilities.

First: It must not go to waste.

Remember that parable in the Bible? How the master distributed talents among his servants to see what they could accomplish with them. And those who put their talents to work were rewarded. But there was one guy who was skeptical or maybe just lazy; instead of investing his talent he buried it in the ground. So it was taken away and given to somebody else.

And he was miserable. The Bible doesn't say so, but he was.

I know. Because surely the most miserable people a professional writer encounters are those who speak of past glories, the promise, the prizes won; and who now are haunted by the knowledge that they have buried a precious talent. No matter how they try to escape such nagging accusations—through activity with children, in churches, coffee klatches, work, politics—they will not be still. Would-be writers send hand-wringing letters to "luckier" writers, listing excuses, begging for the kind of help no outsider can give. Because the trouble lies inside.

What is the true cause when talent is thwarted? I think it's primarily a lack of that sense of responsibility or duty. Too often talent is regarded as a mere adornment, something with which to amuse yourself and dazzle your friends. That's how it seems when one is very young. I used to write long continued stories which the kids passed around in school (ending when the tablet paper ran out). I dashed off poems dedicated to everybody in sight and read aloud on all possible occasions. I even wrote my own declamatory pieces. And it was all part of a heady show-off syndrome.

Yet deep beneath all this ran a fierce compulsion: I *had* to write. Even minus an audience, into a vast notebook, late at night, I had to write. And what clinched this compulsion for me and turned it into a profession were the words: "There is a duty."

People who fail to follow up their own bright promise seem to lack this compulsion. Or, if they have it at first, they cut it off when it begins to hurt (and it hurts, oh, how it hurts), or when it becomes hard work resulting only in a rain of rejection slips and bitter disappointments. How much easier to regard your talent not simply as essential if awesome equipment for an important calling, but as an ornament to be tossed in a drawer. You know it's there, your pretty little talent, and you can always dust if off and don it if you wish—when you're "inspired." Or to delight admiring friends. "She writes," they say of you, and you prove it by doing witty newsletters for your organizations, or composing the club show.

Yet how brief is the sweet satisfaction. You know, deep in your guts you know, you can and should be doing so much more. And the sense of guilt and failure intensifies when one day the drawer is opened to find the talent has lost its luster, or even vanished altogether.

The list of excuses for wasted talent is endless. Illness, economics, responsibilities to family, friends, the church, the community. They confront each of us every day the minute we open our eyes. The person without a sense of obligation to his own talent promptly takes his pick. The person whose talent is a serious responsibility, however, appraises this obstacle course and figures out priorities: "Which is more important, to attend that meeting or get on with my article? . . . I have to have Johnny at the doctor's by three, but that still gives me five hours at the typewriter if I get started by nine. No, subtract an hour for interruptions, that leaves four—"

When people ask how I've done it—raised four children while writing hundreds of magazine pieces and seventeen books—I tell them: "I'm disciplined and I'm organized." ("It's not lack of time but sheer waste of time that keeps people from leading interesting lives," wrote Mary Roberts Rinehart.) I learned early to forgo temptations and to budget time. Any household has a reasonable facsimile of a schedule. I schemed my writing hours to fit. When I lost a day to the school fair or the emergencies that befall a family, I made it up weekends.

Dewey Deal had said: *"If you want badly enough you can,"* and her words, framed over my desk, often goaded me on.

Neighbors and friends would sometimes deplore what seemed my "sacrifice." One morning when I appeared at my study window for a breath of air, one of them called up from the usual coterie in her yard: "Come on down. What does it get you?" " . . . ten thousand dollars, I hope," I muttered to myself—the prize in a current novel contest. And although my novel didn't win the prize, I finished it in time, and it was published.

In the end your talent does become your adornment. You make speeches, travel, appear on talk shows. But that is incidental. Its real value has grown immeasurably; because you respected your talent, were true to it, and developed it, that talent now reaches far beyond you and affects many lives.

The writer's second responsibility is this, I believe: *To use his talent for good.* Not to preach or exhort or reform necessarily, but to affirm life rather than debase it, to inspire and help and encourage. . . . *"You can write beautiful things for people who crave beautiful things. . . ."* Despite the sex and cynicism and materialism that seem to be so common, and the avalanche of products that pander to a lust for the perverse, the ugly, and the decadent, there is still a vast hunger for things of the spirit, beautiful things. And the writer who is able to nourish and fill that hunger is beginning to reap incredible and long overdue rewards.

The success of religious and inspirational books in the past few years has become the phenomenon of the publishing industry. Last year, to the amazement of practically everybody in the business, books like *Jonathan Livingston Seagull* and *The Late Great Planet Earth* outstripped the hottest sex titles, and books of prayers and meditations, conspicuous by their absence on most best-seller lists, actually sold circles around many of the titles that did appear there.

I wrote in the inspirational field from the beginning. I found that facts bored me, and research took too much time away from home and typewriter. For me it was easier and more fulfilling to write creative articles born out of my own experience or observation, personal discoveries or formulas for living. And whether torn out of the very pit of suffering, or sprung from an incessant love affair with life, all were upbeat, constructive. Like Cole Porter, I found it "Just as important to write about beautiful mornings as about dirt in the streets."

I did have one short lucrative fling at the confessions; and even these I labored to make as affirmative as possible. They were Sunday School stories compared to what is being published now, but after a while I simply could not stand any more sinning, suffering and repenting. I knew I was, quite literally, "prostituting my talent." And I was working for the wrong boss—on a dead-end street. One day a phrase from Dorothea Brande's book, *Wake Up and Live,* shook me: "Are you working at failure?" The answer was so loud and clear, I turned down an assignment to do a confession that would have meant $500 (a lot of money then) and never wrote another.

Neglect isn't the only way you can bury a talent. It can be buried under bundles of money you're not proud of earning.

Nobody, however, could be more surprised than I at turning out to be a "religious writer." I never even considered myself an especially religious person, although I recognized the Creator as the source of all creative talent, and was immensely grateful for mine. I also felt God was an unseen companion who understood me far better than I could understand myself, and to whom I could pour out everything, from the sublime to the ridiculous. Now and then, just as a change of pace in my newspaper column, I would publish one of my informal conversational prayers. ("Psalm for Scrubbing a Floor," "Prayer for Peeling a Potato.") Invariably reader response was so great, it came to the attention of Doubleday, who'd already published *Love and Laughter,* a collection of my columns. It was decided that when I'd put enough of these prayers together they might make a book.

No one expected much of it, least of all me. So all of us were astounded at the immediate success of *I've Got to Talk to Somebody, God* (which has sold nearly a million copies in hardcover counting book clubs, and is approaching its second million in paperback); its sequel, *Who Am I, God?,* and the book of prayers for girls, *Nobody Else Will Listen,* are catching up to it.

Even more amazed were the people at Bantam, who bought the paperback rights. Grace Bechtold, one of the best editors in the business, told me: "We simply did not know the audience for your kind of material was out there. Until we took a chance on *I've Got to Talk to Somebody, God,* we had never published a religious or inspirational book. But our success with it opened up an entire new branch of publishing for us."

Now that we've "let it all hang out" in literature, I doubt if we'll ever go back. Obscenity, pornography, violence and books of artistic merit filled with scenes of raw, explicit sex will continue to pour from presses as long as there is a market for them. But I find it heartening that so many people are reaching out for something else. Not pieties and preachments; not writing that simply shuts its eyes and pretends there is no evil or sorrow in the world. But rather writing that shows the basic goodness and decency of human beings despite their trials; that celebrates compassion and love and wonder and all the other things that make life worthwhile.

So long as there are people who want garbage there will be writers willing to provide it. Some of them poor writers, sure; but a tragic number of them are good, maybe even potentially great writers. And to me this abuse of talent is far worse than not using it at all.

I know, I know, the late Jimmy Walker claimed no girl was ever ruined by a book, and the libertarians quote him loud and long. Yet anyone who *reads* knows that writing has a powerful effect on behavior. And you can't have it both ways: If books can do good in the world—teach, inspire, change things for the better—then books can also damage and destroy.

Are you making the most of your talent? Only you can decide: Are you using it? And what are you using it *for?*

5

LETTER TO A SON
WHO HAS DECLARED HIS AMBITION
TO BECOME A WRITER

By Borden Deal

Dear Brett:

I was pleased to get your thoughtful letter. You have obviously done a lot of thinking since our abortive(!) discussion at Christmas about your plans for both a major and for your lifework. After all, the very best way of all into the theater is through writing—if your interest continues in the theater—because only through writing do you have the degree of control and autonomy that it seems to me is necessary for any sense of creativity. Of course all writing is of a piece, in the sense that writing a short story or a novel can teach you a lot about the writing of a play, or vice versa, just as the writing of poetry will sharpen your sense of form and precision in the use of language—skills that will stand you well in whatever else you might write. An English major background should give you the wide-ranging and general knowledge-in-depth of many areas that I think is necessary for any good writer. You simply cannot read enough, analyze enough, know enough.

I am now going to take the further risk of giving you some advice out of my own long experience of writing that might possibly make your road a little easier than mine was. You will reject it, I am quite aware—but maybe some of it will sink in eventually. At least, when you don't follow it, you will be *aware* that you are not following it!

If you have observed me and Babs,* surely you know already that the major difficulty, the primary obstacle, that a beginning writer encounters is the matter of discipline. This is a continuing

---

* Babs H. Deal is the author of ten novels and many published short stories.

factor, no matter how long or how successfully you write. After twenty years of full-time writing, I still have that moment of revulsion *every* day when I sit down at the typewriter to go to work.

I would, first and foremost, urge upon you that you establish good habits of work and discipline. This can be done only in one way. You can learn to write only in the act of writing, so I would make it my first recommendation that you establish the habit and discipline of writing something every day.

All right, you say immediately. But I'm going to college, I have classes and papers, tests and assignments; I have girls to think about. But all the time I was in college, I maintained more or less with fidelity (and more rather than less!) the habit of writing every day. The *amount* of time doesn't signify; it is the fact of knowing that *today* I'm going to write something that counts. An hour, two hours, is all that is necessary; in fact it's probably all that you can manage with your schedule of other work and other activities. But that hour, those two hours, should be absolutely sacrosanct—and you will be astonished how much writing you can get done in just a couple of hours, as long as it is every day.

Now, I am not telling you to write at random. Don't sit down and try to think desperately of something to write. Know that already —the sitting-down time is for work, not thinking. The thinking, the planning, the openness to ideas, to inspiration, to characters and scenes and dialogue, goes on all the time, twenty-four hours a day, whether you're sleeping or awake. That is how you shape your mind to receive inspiration. If your mind doesn't have the right shape to capture the idea, it will simply pass you by when it comes. The two hours a day, or one hour a day, whatever it is—that is the time to work, to turn the idea into the reality of words. Always have in your mind a backlog of things you want to work on. Right now, for example, I have my next two novels in my head and ready to go—I always know what my next two or three years' work will be. True, sometimes I'll change my mind, put one thing in front of another. But the backlog is there, working all the time, whether I'm sleeping or awake. I don't force it now, of course—it is the shape of my mind.

Do not write at random. Always have a shape, a form, an idea, in your mind. Writing is, as much as anything else, an act of character. You must know what you think about things, what you feel about things; you must find ways to embody these thoughts and feelings in character—if you're going to write fiction, at any rate.

For the beginning writer, second only to discipline is the matter of Form. Form, like shape, can be learned only by and through work. Shape and form your material into scene and structure (this is another way of saying, don't write at random). Eventually, when your mind is shaped right, the material will come to you pre-formed, but at first you will have great difficulty in this area. The beginning writer sees form as a limitation—he wants to be free! He is irked by the necessity for form. But form is *liberation*, not limitation. It is like the facets in a diamond: only through the facets can you see the true beauty of the material.

So cast your material into form. There is form inherent in all inspirational material. Later in your career it will come pre-formed. I rarely think about form at all any more. When a novel comes to me, begging to be written, the form is there in the material. Much of the inspiration you will get in these first few years will be seemingly formless, inchoate, simply a feeling, an emotion, a desire to create an emotional ambience through words. But the form is there, inherent in the material. It is your task to find it. You do not impose form on material; you find the form inherent in its nature. And in fiction that form is found and demonstrated, principally through character.

Therefore, learn to write character. Learn to write dialogue. All beginning writers love description. Why? Because description is easy to write. But beware of description. It is necessary, but it is also a heady wine for a young writer. Use it sparingly. The less description you use, the more effective it is. Remember that. Develop your fiction through character, through scene and action and dialogue. Let your people stand up and walk around; let them carry their own story. Don't impose the heavy burden of description upon them. Focus everything through character, including description, including feeling, including thought.

Now to more practical matters. Though there is little market for short stories, writing short stories is a good discipline. For one thing, there is an almost immediate realization of completion, where you can look at the whole of something you have written. So I recommend that you write short stories and send them out to the little magazines, the university quarterlies, and literary magazines like *Southwest Review, Virginia Quarterly Review, Prairie Schooner.* Get a market list of quality magazines. You will get reams of rejections, and you will deserve them. But write with the idea of being published—from the very beginning. Only in that way can you break through the stone wall of not having been published. Enter every short story contest you can find. Aim high. All they can do is turn you down. The very first short story I ever sent out, when I was twelve years old, went to *Collier's Magazine.* Strangely enough, it came back practically the day before I mailed it!

Now, at the risk of self-contradiction, I will add this advice—get to work on a novel as soon as you can. The novel is where the action is these days, and actually you stand a far better chance of getting a novel published than short stories. Since publishing is the name of the game, you should begin a novel.

That doesn't mean that tomorrow you should sit down at the typewriter and say to yourself, "Now I'm going to write a novel." A thousand times more than with the short story, you must, to write a novel, have an inspiration, a character, a *form.* Don't begin writing a novel until you know what it is going to be about; otherwise you'll start off in a great rush of inspiration—and peter out somewhere short of page fifty. You know the household joke Babs and I have had for years about all the hundreds of fifty-page novels we have in our desk drawers. Indeed, to this day, our standard remark to the other is, "Well, I've got fifty pages, so I guess I'll have to write a book now."

So—*plan* that novel—scene by scene, chapter by chapter. Now, you'll say that I don't do that. And I don't—because I plan it in my head. I carry it in my head; it develops and grows in my head. That's because I've had years of practice at it (even so, I will often outline chapter by chapter the last half of the book). But you don't have that confidence or that experience of success. So outline it on paper, scene by scene, chapter by chapter. Know what you're going to do before you do it. The inspiration will come to you—it *must,* if you're going to write a book—but as you get more experience, it will come to you with more form, more discipline, more shape built in.

As you start out, especially, write as objectively as possible. The principal failing of nearly all first novels is their autobiographical quality. You are too young, yet, to know what you think about your own experience. You are far too subjective. All writing is subjective, by its very nature—but it must also be objective. So make your first novel out of anything in the world but your own experience. You will see it much more clearly, much more in the round. My first really autobiographical novel was *The Least One* —and you know how many books I had published before I wrote *The Least One*. Until then, I didn't dare trust what I believed and felt about the events and meanings of my life—and yet every young writer sets out confidently to write his autobiographical and yet universal story.

Another thing—my strong recommendation is that you learn to rewrite, to view your work as critically as possible, as objectively as possible. This is a constant struggle. To this day I am not confident that I am objective enough, that I can see my flaws and errors clearly enough. But you must try—and try hard—from the very beginning. Consider the first draft only the beginning of work, not the end of it. Learn, if it is not already the case (and it probably isn't), to enjoy revision and rewriting as much, or more, than you do writing a first draft. You have heard me say it many and many a time: Revision separates the men from the boys.

That is enough, I think. It ought to last you, roughly, ten years, before you can say with some reasonable degree of confidence that you have overcome these beginning hazards. Because that is something else you must learn—the writer must take the long view. You must be patient, and diligent, and you must know that it is in you to write good stuff in a good way that will merit the time and attention of a reader. It isn't there now, only the potential—but you must have implicit faith in that potential. And when you have written something good at last, you must know that, too, in the face of all rejection, of all criticism, of all failure.

When you are ready to send something to me, I will be glad to read it and criticize it for you, if you want me to. I warn you—I consider criticism far too important to lie about. I won't pay much attention to the adequate, the good, or the superior, only to the bad and the weak and the inadequate. I have lost many friends because

I would not falsely praise. Nine hundred and ninety-nine times out of a thousand, when someone asks you for criticism he is seeking not criticism but praise, no matter how undiscriminating. But I would advise you to seek out criticism, truly and honestly—and believe, at least struggle to believe. But do not accept any criticism that you do not truly believe. Another contradiction, what?

But don't send me anything to criticize unless and until you are completely satisfied with it yourself, until you have taken it absolutely as far as you can go with your own sense of rightness. Then I'll tear it up for you!

I won't welcome you to the fraternity of writers, because you are not a writer until you have published. That is the name of the game, and it's the only game in town. I will welcome you when you can show me something of yours—a story, a novel, poems—in print. You may, or you may not, make it. But I think if you are diligent, and frugal with your material, if you are true to yourself and to your ideas and your feelings, that you can and will do it.

So I am pleased that you have at last come to this conclusion of ambition. Certainly, writing is all I ever wanted to do, ever since I can remember, and somewhere in the back of my mind, every day as I sit down to work on my sixteenth or seventeenth novel, or whatever it is, I am pleased and happy and grateful that I am allowed to do it. It's a rough life. It's a great life. And it's the only life that I know. It has lasted me until now—and I am sure it will last me to the end.

So, I suppose, I do welcome you, after all.

                                        Pax et Pan,
                                        Dad

6

AIM FOR THE HEART

By Paul Gallico

IF I wished to write a novel for my own edification, which really is just another way of saying for my own vanity—most of those books that writers are always telling you they are going to write someday just for themselves are indicative of narcissism—I suppose I could delve backwards into what was actually a reasonably happy childhood and find dark moments of anguish or self-induced terrors. I could manage to exploit weaknesses of my elders, sexual experiments, and produce an adequate panopticon of unpleasant subsidiary characters who frightened, harassed or disliked me at one time or another, or made me aware of my inadequacies, to be able to come up with a fair facsimile of what seems to be the modern novel and the aim of the young writer. It might even draw me one of those two-column, analytical reviews, or unwarranted praise.

But if I wanted to write a novel that would sell, I would sit down at my desk and try to think of some human and likable characters, for whose makeup I would borrow here and there from the personalities of people I had met—men, women and children—and I would then attempt to invent a situation that would try them almost beyond endurance.

I would endeavor to make you care deeply about these people, and hence I would have to care deeply about them myself first. In each one I would have to find some echoing chord of my own being: the kind of person I am, the kind of things I like, my fears, my hopes, so that these would be recognizable as genuine fears and hopes, the longings and appetites and the ambitions that might be found in any of us.

I would give these people spiritual strength coupled with near fatal flaws, good luck and bad, and a meed of cowardice, but a greater gift of courage. In the course of the trials I would prepare for

them, they would have need for all of these things and love besides—
love in the sense that it is the one emotion capable of mounting
guard over our natures. I would wish you to feel at one with someone, if not with several of the people in this book, to the point where
you entered into their adventures and lost yourself in them. And I
would try to tell my story and their story, and vicariously your story,
in such a way that once you began, once you had recognized yourself
in either the characters or the situation, you would not be able to put
it down.

I would want to tell you the story of people under adversity who
struggled and won or lost, according to their capabilities, but without too great an emphasis on victory, so that those who lost might
even be thought to have won something beyond those who seemed to
triumph.

It would be a story of man against nature, or man against man;
man the supreme being on earth, or man the infinitesimal speck. But
a story it would be, with a beginning, a middle and an end, and at
that end, after you had followed with me the travail and strivings of
these persons, I would hope that I would leave you not quite the
same as you had been before you started. That is the kind of book I
would try to write, if I wanted it to sell.

"Wanted to sell"—or just "sell" alone—has a harsh sound and
some of the stink of the market place.

Yet to sell is what the honest writer wants to do, to sell to earn a
living to feed his family, or even for the pure satisfaction of selling,
of having written something good enough to cause the largest number of people to reach into their pockets and give over money they
have earned, for the privilege of spending some hours alone with
characters and narrative that the writer has created.

The highest form of flattery comes not from the reviewer, however
erudite or complimentary he or she may be, but from the man or
woman unknown to you who enters a bookshop, finds and fingers a
copy, tests a page or, listening to the bookseller tell what it is about,
says, "I think I'll have that one," and produces his wallet.

It is possible, I know, to do this today in many other ways—by
writing the kind of obscenity one only used to see on privy walls; by
lifting the lid on human sewage pits and letting the reader look
within at the horrors; by rewriting some well-known human folly or

personal disaster into fiction form. But the great storytellers of the past never needed these, nor will the great storytellers of the future. To sell, it is only necessary to capture the human imagination and touch the human heart.

Fashions in fiction come and go, but the storyteller will never go out of date. I remember when I was a young man and sold my first stories to *The Post*, I was summoned for a visit with its great Editor, George Horace Lorimer. Several of these were sports stories, and Mr. Lorimer said that the magazine had a great need for these and hoped that I would fill it. And I remember remarking, even through my awe of the great man, that I wanted to play Hamlet. He eyed me and said, "And what form does your Hamlet take?"

I said, "Stories with a d-d-different b-background, sir, not just sports—newspapers, circuses, other things. . . ."

When I had finished stammering, he said quietly, "Young man, I'll tell you something. I don't care what background you decide to use, just don't forget to tell me a story."

Around ancient campfires, or at court, the jester with the dirty joke could make them laugh for a few moments, but it was the story-teller who had his listeners spellbound, whether he twanged his lyre in song or spoke in poetry or prose of heroes who overcame great odds, and of lovers whom not even death could part.

The anti-hero is the prototype of despair. The hero flings aloft the banner of hope. The storybook ending isn't life, but life often enough provides the storybook ending to make it worthwhile to tell about. If we thought that there was nothing but misery, degradation and dark-ness and above all perpetual defeat, what would be the use of trying to feed or clothe ourselves, raise children, and put a penny by to purchase a book to refresh one's spirit and fortify one's hopes?

It isn't easy and everyone can't do it, but everyone can try. Tell a story in which you believe, about people with whom you sympathize or admire. Tell it simply and enthrallingly, and the pile of your books on the bookstore counter will melt away like the snows in spring. Aim for the heart.

7

WHEN THE WRITER
COMES OF AGE

By B. J. Chute

THERE is no royal road to maturity for any human being, and most certainly I know of none for the writer. Coming of age is not a chronological matter; it is a lifetime process. Fortunately, there are signposts along the way, and the signposts that guide the writer are really no different from the ones that guide everyone else.

The process of writing, like the process of growing up, is one of accepting, testing and rejecting, of "holding fast that which is good." It is a process of infinite curiosity, a seesaw process of vast enthusiasms opposed by discouraging failures. For a writer, as for anyone, there are days when anything seems possible, and there are days when everything seems hopeless. Gardeners know this feeling very well. The lawn, the flower bed are full of crabgrass and a multitude of weeds, and many things done once are all to be done over again.

The first thing one learns is that this is not nearly as wasteful a pattern as it appears to be. Out of the nonsense, wildness and despair, there is always left the fine growing ground which we label experience. Experience is a dull word; another dull word is discipline. I am going to use both.

I have very strong feelings about discipline, and especially about self-discipline. I have not found life at all permissive, either in the day-to-day process of living it or in the strict professional process of being a writer. This is no contradiction to my other strong feeling, which is that life should be enjoyed. I am also a firm believer in daydreaming, wasting time, staring into space or leaning against a wall while watching the snails whizz by. There are certainly times when one's mind should be as open, empty and placid as a millpond. Who knows what attractive bugs will come to skitter on the surface,

33

or what wonderful white whales of the imagination will rise from its depths?

But self-discipline means doing one's work and doing it to the top of one's bent. I need hardly add that this often involves simple drudgery. There is no way to avoid it, whatever profession or calling you enter. There is drudgery in housework, in office work, in acting, painting, writing; it cannot be avoided, and the habit of self-discipline is the habit of doing what has to be done, even when dull. At any age, the ability to dodge disagreeable tasks comes naturally. I am not suggesting a permanent state of high-minded activity. I am merely urging you to avoid that intellectual curvature of the spine which results from lounging on the back of one's mental neck.

Mental discipline is like physical discipline. It becomes easier through practice. Any athlete knows that the first aching clumsy use of untrained muscles eventually gives way to flexibility and control. The mental muscles behave in the same way, so that knowledge, sensitivity and capacity all improve through exercise.

I need hardly say that other people's exercise will not improve *your* muscles. Here, the intellect has some advantage over the physique, since other people's knowledge can enlarge yours. But only if you use it. We are the heirs of and contemporary to worlds of experience so vast as to be limitless, but these are ours only through our own effort. Therefore, my next piece of advice has to do with what Langston Hughes meant when he said, "Listen fluently." This is an art which enlarges art; it is partly objective and partly subjective.

It is an objective art when it is derived from the world around you. In a recent book by Pamela Frankau, she writes, "There must come a time when . . . all your mirrors turn into windows." I could ask for no better definition of coming of age. When we are young, we are surrounded by mirrors, and wherever we turn we see ourselves. As we grow up, the mirrors dissolve, and the windows that replace them set our horizons free. We learn to see people as they see themselves, to understand the complexity, the shifting, the lights and shadows of other people's lives and emotions, and through understanding them to understand, in some measure, ourselves. We realize that nothing is as simple as it looked in the mirrors, but that everything is far more wonderful. And finally we learn the most marvelous truth of all: that, in the last analysis, we can never know the whole truth about anyone or anything, but that we are, like Tennyson's Ulysses, a part of all that we have met.

Now, necessarily, everything I have discussed so far applies to any kind of coming of age; but, since I am a writer, I would like to relate it to the specific problems of my own craft.

I never consciously planned to be a writer. I never pictured short stories in magazines with my name on them; I never imagined books that I would have written. I wrote because I wrote and, I suspect, also because I read omnivorously. (I will come back later to that splendid subject.) I was blessed with a grounding in grammar so solid, so stern, so basic that I have never had to think about the structure of the language at all in the purely grammatical sense. I learned it the hard way—by endless parsing, by drawing diagrams, by rote, by drill. If there is another way in which to become so firmly and surely rooted, I do not know it. I suspect there is not. Grammar is to a writer what anatomy is to a sculptor, or the scales to a musician. You may loathe it, it may bore you, but nothing will replace it, and once mastered it will support you like a rock. I have no quarrel whatever with the writer who breaks the rules of grammar intentionally, but I have a quarrel with the writer who breaks them because he has not been willing to learn them properly. The English language deserves more respect.

I learned something else from learning grammar. I learned not to mind working hard for the sake of control. I learned not to trouble myself about what appeared to be wasted pages, if through the producing of them I moved closer all the time to the thing I wanted to say in the way in which I thought it should be said. I am a confirmed re-writer. There is no especial moral virtue in re-writing; it merely happens to be my particular way of achieving an end, and if you can get your results on the first try, more power to your pen! What matters is not to be afraid of doing the same thing again, and again, and then again, if that is necessary. A writer will never be judged by his private vision, only by what shows of it on paper. It is no use sitting around admiring one's mental processes, however enchanting they may be. The reader is not sitting around in any such admiring state. His posture is "Show me!" and he is quite right to insist.

I can speak of drudgery casually, as a part of a writer's task, because I have learned there is no evading it. When I have finished a novel, taking it through as many drafts as needs be, to the point where I am almost satisfied, I expect to sit down at my typewriter and do the whole thing over once more from beginning to end, so that the words suit my ear, the effort to communicate has become the best effort of which I am capable, and the courtesy due the English language has been given to it as completely as I can. This is not a sign of nobility, but it is a matter of pride. I have no wish to encounter in print words I have written that should have been written better, and there is something very immovable about that thing called movable type, once the printer has locked it up. There is no time for reconstruction after the words lie in the bound book.

I began my writing career as a sports writer in the field of short stories for boys. I had no particular aims except to tell a story, in action and dialogue and description. I can look back now and see the growing process that took place, but I did not see it then. I could have gone on doing the same kind of writing for a professional lifetime, and I could probably have made a satisfactory living from it, but somewhere inside of me there lay a strong instinct to experiment.

The company is too noble for me, but I knew very well what John Keats meant when he described the experimentation of his new poem, *Endymion:*

I leaped headlong into the sea, and thereby have become better acquainted with the soundings, the quicksands, and the rocks, than if I had stayed upon the green shores, and piped a silly pipe, and took tea and comfortable advice.

George Bernard Shaw put it more acidly:

A man learns to skate by staggering about making a fool of himself. Indeed he progresses in all things by resolutely making a fool of himself.

I did not offer my own results in the public marketplace, because I did not need to be told what I was doing wrong. I threw them away, generally forgot them; sometimes, the effort would remain to plague me, to be taken up years afterwards when I had the skill to do what I had early wanted to do. These things will wait. The currently impossible, if one keeps on growing, becomes the possible, the probable, and at last the achieved. I urge you to be patient and to persist.

I have always loved language; I have always loved style. I had a serviceable enough style, founded on good grammar. I had an ear trained by reading, so that at least I knew when I was wrong, if not always how to make it right. I had a strong sense of respect and affection for the tools that help a writer to write well. But, above all, I think, I had the wit to know that it was no use forcing myself into writing more effectively unless that effort went hand in hand with having something to say.

So I wrote, for quite a long time, stories for young people—stories about football, track, ice hockey and almost every other sport. Later, I moved into the field of adult fiction—boy-meets-girl stories and stories about young married life, which were purchased regularly by major magazines and were very popular with their readers.

And then, one day, I wanted suddenly to write a story about a ten-year-old boy whose Air Force pilot brother had been reported missing in action. I wanted to write about how a child in a child's safe world felt when he was catapulted into a dangerous adult world of loss and misery and fear. There, for the first time, I tried something which I had not tried before, and which later became a necessary way of working for me. I consciously sought the style which would mirror and encompass the thing itself. Straight action writing was impossible; the requirements of this story were subjective, inner. The story idea, for the first time in my writing career, demanded of me an entirely new way of writing.

I remember that story as being exceedingly difficult to write, and I also remember it as being curiously exciting to write. I found I could do things I had not expected to be able to do, and I found that I knew why I did them and why they were right. It was not a particularly original idea for a short story, but, when I finished it, no one except myself could have written it in just that way. Someone else could have done it and made it his story (and perhaps a better one), but I had done it in my way, an invented way, if you like, and it was particularly my own.

It was called *Come of Age,* and I sold it to *The Saturday Evening Post.* It was not the first adult story I had sold, but it was the first time I had plunged into an entirely new way of writing, and ever since it has been my way.

By that, I do not mean that subsequent stories were written by me in that style. I mean that I had found it possible to seek out my own individual way for each story and, later, for each novel. It is just as difficult for me to do now as it was then, perhaps more so. The difference is that I have slowly acquired the skills, the techniques, and most of all the understanding that make it, if still not always possible, much more probable.

When I wrote a novel called *Greenwillow* and, later, one called *The Moon and the Thorn,* I needed everything I had learned, and then I had to learn even more than I thought I needed. Both novels depended entirely on mood and manner of telling. Both first chapters nearly defeated me, and I remember the problem of *Greenwillow* with these depressing statistics: I wrote the first chapter sixteen times; the first page, more than thirty times. *The Moon and the Thorn* was almost as exasperating, but I wrestled with it as patiently as possible, since I knew that, in each novel, the opening chapter would set the tone for the whole. If I could get this right, I would be—if not on safe ground—at least not adrift, and I used up yellow paper with a fine frenzy that must have cheered the corporate hearts of the yellow paper manufacturers. (Parenthetically, yellow paper is a boon and a blessing; it is so easy to tear up, so expendable. I recommend it to you as the most prudent extravagance in the world.)

I have not arrived as a writer; I will never arrive. No writer really does; we only travel. But I have learned that, however elusive or difficult the dominating idea of a story, there is some way to put it into a form that approaches achievement.

There is one other writing problem I would like to mention briefly: the problem of success. If you wish to write, there is only one kind of success possible. It has nothing to do with money or reputation. The only success worth having for a writer is to put on paper what you have wished to put on paper. There is a wonderful story told about a small child who watched a sculptor working on a slab of marble. Day after day, the child watched, and the sculptor worked. And then, at last, there came a day when the child drew in his breath and looked at the sculptor in amazement and said, "But how did you know there was a lion in there?"

That is success for a writer. To know there is a lion in one's mind, and finally to produce it. Compared to that, money and fame are really very negligible returns.

Now, I want to revert to that one subject I only touched on earlier: reading. Reading is only another way of "listening fluently."

My first advice to any would-be writer is that he read—creatively, passionately, chronically. I am impatient with the idea of sugar-coated reading. I do not believe in padding about timidly in the tepid waters of the merely entertaining, the placidly simple. Reading is a joint creative process between writer and listener. It is a multi-level process, more than mere ability to recognize and interpret words. It is also more than mere familiarity with contemporary fiction or a dutiful sampling of the classics. The real reader needs to have a mariner's knowledge of those myriad minor writers of past centuries who compose the vast ocean of literature.

Some writers of the past are not easy to understand. They speak in idioms not always clear to us; they reflect ways of life that are now alien. They make heavy demands on the reader to respond to their strangeness. The ear complains, "But this is old-fashioned"; the mind replies, "It was modern once." Even the classics sometimes fall heavily on the senses, and after a few chapters one's attention falters and lags, and it is tempting to say, "This is not for me," and turn to the familiar.

I think part of the trouble here rises from the theory that one is a reader because one has learned to read. One would not think of himself as a tennis player because he had mastered the elements of tennis playing, or as a skier because he was able to go downhill without collapsing in a snowbank. We willingly train our muscles to the mechanical difficulty of a powerful serve, to the controlled rhythm of stem turns, but we do not as willingly train our minds to follow the involutions of an unfamiliar way of writing. This is a pity. Batting a ball earnestly back and forth, going downhill soberly and arriving upright—this is neither tennis nor skiing. They are both exciting sports, and we work hard to become adept in them so we can know their real excitements. Yet what Baudelaire called "the heavenly mechanics of the mind" is the source of an infinity of excitement, compared to which Wimbledon and the Alps seem very small indeed.

I know readers whose whole literary world seems to be related to the so-called "modern" literary world. They are experts on the Twentieth Century of prose and poetry, widely read, subtle; but, except for the great mountain peaks of Shakespeare, Homer, Dante (the names that leap to the mind), they have none of that accumulation of reading which would illuminate, broaden, deepen every modern book they read.

I think we often fail to recognize how a wide range of reading enlarges literature. Let me take two quotations from Shakespeare, a writer with whom we all have a bowing acquaintance, to show how one kind of writing, even the greatest, can be affected by all the other kinds.

The first, from *Antony and Cleopatra*, said of the great Egyptian queen herself, beautiful in death as she was in life:

> . . . she looks like sleep,
> As she would catch another Antony
> In her strong toil of grace.

This is a marvelous bit of poetry, in and of itself. You need not be deep-rooted in literature to know that. But suppose your reading roots *do* go deep, so that the description of Cleopatra wakens within your mind a memory of other beloved women stricken by untimely frosts—Villon's "Flora, the lovely Roman," Tolstoy's achingly tragic Anna Karenina, Robert Herrick's country girls like daffodils. For the wide-ranging reader, who is not intimidated in his reading, a host of perilous and immortal women join hands. Where are the snows of yesteryear, if not imprisoned forever in the minds of the "fluent listeners"? The color from each spreads to the others, and the passage from Shakespeare, most beautiful in itself, is made more beautiful through association, through links and echoes.

The second quotation, then, from *The Winter's Tale*. A small boy is invited to tell his mother a tale "of sprites, and goblins." He is an artful storyteller, and he begins magically:

> There was a man . . .
> Dwelt by a churchyard: I will tell it softly,
> Yond crickets shall not hear it.

This is the perfect invitation to the listener, hushed, mysterious, full of shadows. The immediate echo it wakes is the childhood one of "Once upon a time." But for the skilled reader other echoes cry like bells, calling us to come, to come and listen. I think of a modern chime in that wonderful line of Scott Fitzgerald's—"Draw your chair up close to the edge of the precipice and I'll tell you a story." I think of the legends and the ballads—"There dwelt a man in fair Westmoreland," "The king sits in Dumferling town." I remember that deceptively simple opening of Dickens' which pulls us into the world of his Curiosity Shop: "Although I am an old man, night is generally my time for walking." And I am even moved to remember the harsh, dark texture of *Beowulf,* which in high school I studied so resentfully, only to know now that its granite lies in the pit of my mind forever.

Neither writer nor reader can quite talk of coming of age until these echoes and links begin to crowd into the mind. George Eliot is too alien, too Victorian? She is one of the most modern and civilized writers on earth, with a sharp wit and a broad compassion and a capacity to translate life that you will pass by at your peril. Chaucer's Middle English makes him unreadable? But his *Troilus and Criseyde,* though written in poetic form, is one of the finest psychological novels ever written, and Criseyde is as enchanting a woman as ever a great poet loved.

Stretch, I implore you, in your reading. The words are unfamiliar to your ears? The passions are foreign to your own? Reach up to them; do not wait until they reach down to you, because they will not. When Horatio said, "But this is wondrous strange," Hamlet replied, "And therefore as a stranger give it welcome." Leap to your place in reading. Bruise your mind, fracture your old ideas, stretch your muscles until they shriek in protest. I offer you no sympathy. I offer you, instead, the kind of delight that comes from effort, a delight you will never have unless you step out dangerously.

What I am saying then is, simply, that the mind grows in use. "Art was given for that," Robert Browning tells us. "God uses us to help each other so,/Lending our minds out."

Discipline and experience cannot be separated from the whole bright process of coming of age. Every writer, every reader, indeed every human being, knows in his heart that he has a capacity for growth that would astound a redwood tree. In one sense, none of us ever comes of age—not at twenty-one, not at fifty-one, not at ninety-one.

But, oh, the journey! And I wish you Godspeed.

8

THE MAGIC OF WORDS

By Richard Powell

Of course it will never come true, but I keep having this dream in which the President of the United States sends a message to Congress demanding civil rights for words. In it, he points out how badly words are abused, and calls attention to the fact that our language is a national resource that is being mistreated even more than our rivers and air. It is only a dream, however, and I do not look for the War on Poverty to be extended to the spoken and written word.

The trouble is that the poverty pockets in this case are too hard to get at, because they are not in city slums or Appalachia but inside people's heads. People are willing to use their brains on many difficult problems—avoiding income taxes, beating the horses, sneaking an extra coffee break—but apparently most of them couldn't care less about the problem of how to use words clearly and dramatically. Among these people are scientists, educators, lawyers, government officials, doctors, businessmen and housewives.

Is it possible that there are also writers among them? Yes, friends, there are writers among them.

Let us skip the problem of writers who do not know how to use words clearly. Nobody can help them, and perhaps the published writers among them do not even want to be helped, because a murky style of writing may sometimes win critical acclaim. Let us, instead, take up the problem of writers who use words clearly but with no more impact than that of a wet dishrag dropped on the floor. There are many such writers. They may do a fine job on plotting and characterization, but they handle words like a cook ladling out alphabet soup: the first collection of letters that comes out of the pot goes into the dish. Here is an example of alphabet-soup writing:

I got up this morning as happy as a lark and, as usual, ate breakfast like a horse. I sat at my desk and worked like a mule all day and ended dog-tired.

I have given you a lot of information about my day, have I not? I have also given it clearly. But how many people would be interested in hearing about my zoological day? I have used words that bored you stiff and were dull as dishwater, including the expressions I used in this sentence. I have used old worn-out groupings of words. I have used words in a lazy, thoughtless way, picking up expressions once new and shiny, but now so overworked that they have no power to hook reader attention. The sad thing about this is that there is magic in words when they are used with a touch of imagination. What I should have done, if I wanted anybody to pay attention to a very ordinary collection of facts, was to call on the magic of words. Perhaps I might have written:

When I got up this morning I felt like the bubbles in champagne, and breakfast tasted as if I were just coming off a diet. I spent the day beating a typewriter ribbon to rags, and ended as tired as the clichés I was trying not to use.

Now I have dressed my dull facts in bright clothes, and so people might pay attention. I have thrown out my collection of zoological clichés and developed some new expressions. A cliché is an expression that, when it was new, sketched a vivid picture for people. The first man who used the expression "dog-tired" no doubt impressed his audience; they would have pictured how a dog looks when he is panting and his tongue hangs out and he flops down. But, with use, the term dog-tired lost its force. Nobody who reads or hears it for the tenth or hundredth or thousandth time gets a vivid picture from it. It has become a cliché. It is now merely a crutch for lame brains; it is a mental sleeping pill. It is a way to avoid thinking. There is no word magic in a cliché.

I don't want to pretend that, when I developed some new expressions to replace the zoological clichés, I simply made a flourish and pulled them out of a hat. In the first place, I wouldn't pull them out of a hat because that's another cliché, perhaps invented soon after the first magician pulled the first rabbit out of the first hat. New expressions do not come easily to me; my brain is lazy, too, and approaches the idea of work like a teen-ager asked to do the dishes. But I have learned that if I play the harsh parent with my brain, it will go to work, even though grudgingly. It took me an hour to work out those new expressions, and if I had spent two hours on them they would undoubtedly be better. I don't advise writers to spend an hour on every sentence they write, because they might never finish a story or article. But, when you need to grab attention, you must spend time and thought on the job.

It is not difficult for a person of normal intelligence to write in a colorful and dramatic way. One summer, several years ago, I taught a writing course at Syracuse University. Included in the homework I assigned were some problems in colorful writing. I explained to my students that one method of colorful writing is to describe Item A in terms of Item B: for example, describe a mountain as if it were a living creature. (It could be an old lion crouched in the distance, or a vulture hovering over the valley.) None of my students were professional writers, and none had previously known any tricks of colorful writing. But, when given a method of doing it, they produced such examples as these:

A. (*Describe a young girl, at her first dance, in terms of another type of living thing.*) "Jane sat in the small gilt chair beside the dance floor, thin, angular, unmoving, eyes carefully blank, legs straight out before her like knobby stems. She seemed as much a fixture as the potted palms."
B. (*Describe a society matron in terms of another type of living thing.*) "Mrs. Cheyney was, he thought, like a faded rose, even to her hands with their thorns of fingernails."
C. (*And the same.*) "Mrs. Culpepper looked for her name in the society column, eager as a St. Bernard sniffing at a hydrant."

This is good writing. It is professional. Anybody who can do this on demand could have a successful career in some form of writing. The trick of describing one thing in terms of another is much used by good writers. Carl Sandburg wrote a complete poem by using this trick merely one time. The poem contains six lines and twenty-one words, and has been reprinted in many anthologies of American poetry. It is titled "The Fog," and Sandburg described the fog as if it were a cat.

Some years ago, in writing a story, I wanted to describe gulls flying, and I wrote of them in terms of ice skaters: "Gulls figure-skating against the sky." This happens to stick in my memory because *Reader's Digest* used my words on its "Picturesque Speech" page and paid me ten dollars, the first of many delightful checks from the magazine and Reader's Digest Condensed Book Club. While writing this article I wanted to see if I had exhausted the ways of describing gulls in terms of something else, and I came up with these descriptions:

The gulls went tobogganing down the snowy clouds.
The gulls did a waltz in the ballroom of the sky.
High up, a gull wheeled and curved, writing a message against the blue paper of the air.

This experiment seems to hint that there may be as many ways of describing gulls in flight as there are gulls.

When does a writer use such colorful expressions? Always? No. That might be like a steady diet of fruitcake. Colorful writing is used to create a needed effect—perhaps of mood or atmosphere or character—and when the effect has been achieved, it is a waste of time to do it over and over. Nor should colorful writing be used merely to show off. It must contribute to achieving the writer's purpose in his piece of fiction or article or poem or speech or whatever. I would not use colorful words to describe the ringing of a telephone bell, unless I needed to create a certain mood; if the mood had already been created, I would simply say that the telephone rang, and then get on to more vital things. But if the call was going to be important and I had to get the reader into the right mood for it, I might write:

I reached for the ringing telephone as if getting my first lesson in snake charming.
The telephone bell echoed in my head like a dentist's drill.
The telephone bell made a little apologetic murmur.
The telephone jingled pleasantly, like an old hurdy-gurdy.

Each of these sentences contributes to the establishment of a different mood or atmosphere. They could not be used interchangeably.

The same method, of course, can be used in describing people. In my novel, *Don Quixote, U.S.A.,* I wanted to describe my hero's physical appearance, and at the same time create a mood and tell something of his character. This called for colorful writing and for the expenditure of several hours of mental sweat to produce two sentences. As I say, these things do not come easily to me; getting them out of my head is often like trying to shake the last dime out of a piggy bank. After four hours, I had these two sentences:

Mine is not the grim strong face of the typical Goodpasture. Such a face is spare and angular, as if welded from steel plowshares, whereas my features look as if they had been hastily whittled out of balsa wood.

In those two sentences, I provided a good deal of information about my hero's physical appearance, the family from which he came, and his character. I doubt that it would have been interesting to readers if I had merely written: "All my family have strong grim faces, but mine is rather weak and nondescript."

Another way to write colorful language is to exaggerate to achieve an effect. It is not very striking merely to write that somebody is thin. If you want to create a dramatic effect, use exaggeration. Draw a word picture of how thin the person is. For example:

She was so thin she could have taken a bath in a fountain pen.

He was so thin he could have lurked behind a needle.

He was so thin he could have crawled through a pencil sharpener . . . and with a pencil in his pocket, too.

In trying to make magic with words, however, it is wise to beware of the adjective. Nouns are good words to use in sentences. They are like bones, providing the needed skeleton. Verbs are good words. They are like muscles, providing the action. But adjectives are in most cases merely the clothing or ornaments of a sentence, and it is easy to overdress a sentence. Let me quote the beginning of a famous speech, and count the adjectives in it:

> Friends, Romans, countrymen, lend me your ears;
> I come to bury Caesar, not to praise him.
> The evil that men do lives after them,
> The good is oft interred with their bones;
> So let it be with Caesar.

How many adjectives in those opening lines of Mark Antony's speech? Shakespeare didn't use any.

So, in trying to put magic into your words, don't think that a piling up of adjectives will do the job. One well-chosen adjective may be perfect, like a diamond ring on the hand of a pretty woman. Too many adjectives may be like too many diamond rings: not only does the display seem crude, but also it may hide the fact that the woman has lovely fingers.

Words should be a source of never-ending mystery and delight to any writer. All of us should be forever curious about how words were invented and evolved and what they used to mean and what they mean now. Another term for a cliché is a hackneyed expression. Think a moment about that word "hackneyed." Do you know how it originated? Well, back in the days of horses and carriages, a horse that was kept for hire was called a hackney. Such animals were overworked, and were often tired and slow and thin. Somebody started applying the term to phrases that were also tired and slow and thin: hackneyed phrases. When first used, the term was colorful, and called up a picture in the reader's mind. But how good a picture does it evoke now?

Are you the sort of writer who can look up a word in the dictionary without ever being lured into looking up others? Can you run across such words as "boycott" without digging out the sad tale of Captain Charles Cunningham Boycott? Can you hear the term "halcyon days" without discovering the pleasant old Greek myth from which it comes? If you are not fascinated by words, I feel sorry for you, because you must find the use of them a dull and tiring job. To make magic with words, a writer must know what they mean. And, if he hopes to use words in a new and colorful way, he must be able to recognize the old drab ways in which they have been used.

Words are like Cinderella: sad little drudges, wearing rags and dirtied by soot. It is in the power of writers to play Fairy Godmother, and make these drudges into shining creatures. Words can sing and dance, growl and roar, tiptoe and march. They will do all these things for any writer who is willing to wave the magic wand of his imagination over them.

9

THE CREATIVE PROCESS

By Harold Heifetz

It seems to me that every creative person hears a certain, special sound. It is that sound that makes him tick, that makes his work effort, if he is lucky, compulsive. It also seems to me that a creative person has an obligation to make a commentary upon the world in which he or she lives. I think the start of the creative process is visceral, as is the follow-through, for at least the first draft. It is pure gut feel, not cerebral feel. It is in reaching back into yourself, into the past of what is your blood and ancestry, that you find the seed, hunch or idea that makes you sit up and say, "Oh, this is it, this is one I must write."

Creating is opening up, not necessarily learning something new. It is an unraveling of something old that has been waiting to be touched, triggered. It is something you may not be able to define, but its key identification is that it satisfies you in its cry or ache or laugh. You feel instead of reason. You express your sensitivity to the pain and struggle and laughter of the whole world, the long and deep past, secret until now, waiting for you to untap it.

Intuitive feel starts you off, but it is discipline and organization that make you finish. After you have found your direction, or, rather, when the characters have found their own direction and you relate strongly to those characters, you must exercise discipline and organization, without which it is almost impossible, it seems to me, to write a well-developed and cohesive story.

I am weary of writers who just wander and make tricks and play cute, writing obscure montages and vignettes, trying to make the reader believe they have created a new kind of novel or technique. I hope there will always remain the powerful storyteller who tells the world something, who makes reality out of air, who flies with-

48

out airplanes, and who is able not only to reach back into the reader's past, but who is able to reach back into his own to find what is needed to live on today's terms and how to belong.

You should make certain you relate with your heart to the character who is going to run the show and with whom you wish the reader to find empathy, to care about. You must do this with fervor and total involvement, not from some cool and logical distance of evaluation. You have to get inside.

My involvement is total. I sweat and cry, and it sometimes breaks my heart when someone in my story has to die or get hurt. I don't do it to them; they do it to themselves. That's how alive they are. It hurts me to kill them off, but I must, and this is good. This is the involvement that makes the characters real. It is a true genesis. The writer can give birth to many, and often only from air and imagination and the silence of past generations. Everything is waiting to be released.

I make notes for months before I start, and I do lots of nonfiction reading before I start. But once I begin writing, I stop making notes, and I cut out the reading. It's time to write my own book. They have already written theirs. From that moment, my whole thinking life is dedicated to the job at hand, that one story to tell and unroll. Once I have the beginning and end (I must have those two elements), I go. It goes.

And you write moment to moment, scene by scene, each one giving rise logically to the next. You hold yourself in check with utmost discipline so that your energies are conserved and expended only on the next required objective and not on some scene you feel you want to or should write and use somewhere else later on.

If you have the maturity to discipline yourself, your story will begin to grow and write itself. If you give the story a chance, it will help you. If you reach a wall or block in the forward movement of your novel, don't try some other scene to be used in another part of the novel not yet written. Don't panic. Hold fast and keep at it. Concentrate only on the scene that refuses so far to open up for you. Keep leaning on that wall, and suddenly, somehow, it always happens—and who cares by what mysterious process it occurs? —you can open the door and walk into the next scene.

After you've finished your first draft and the heat is all out of you for the moment, you try to stand off and take a month to play with your kids, or with your wife. But that is hard. You keep walking back to the typewriter to touch the keys, and lift the manuscript, and peek inside. Then finally you say, stop wasting time; and you begin to work and snip off and cool off the ends and fragments and the overwriting and repetitions, looking dispassionately at what you did in all that passion. It is already down so it cannot be destroyed. Just know for sure that the more you cut, the better it will get, and that for everyone who hates it, there will be someone else who loves it. But most of all, you have to love it first.

It is hard work to work alone, feeling the whole world is passing you by, that a whole cluster of novels have come out that week, half touching on your theme, and you're still working helplessly on yours. Be brave and don't rush. Your story has its own life. It makes its own time. It takes stamina to work alone, to be alone, and to suffer alone. That is what writing represents, but it is all so good and beautiful and gratifying. It gives you a sense of power as well as release. You are somebody who made something. It satisfies your greed and lust and hunger and your frustration, too. What it does not satisfy is your compulsion, because you are now ready to start a new novel, having just finished the fourth draft of your last one that occupied one or two years of your life.

I'm proud to have the ability to make words come together and live, to produce substance and reality from the unreal and the long gone, and to utilize and modulate the past into some cohesive and progressive whole.

In the end, I think it is the combination of indefinable feel and definable discipline and organization that makes the successful professional—one who finishes what he starts, who makes his people real and honest with each other.

I don't give a damn if I please the reader or jar his sensibilities. But I do care if I fail to affect him. I must touch him; I must even irritate him, as long as it makes him aware of what I am trying to say through my characters. All a writer should ask for is some reaction to the people in his story and their situation. That should be enough testimony for the quality of the writing.

10

FOLLOWING ONE'S INSTINCTS

By E. B. White

STUART LITTLE, himself quite a traveler, came into being as the result of a journey I once made. In the late Twenties, I took a train to Virginia, got out, walked up and down in the Shenandoah Valley in the beautiful springtime, then returned to New York by rail. While asleep in an upper berth, I dreamed of a small character who had the features of a mouse, was nicely dressed, courageous, and questing. When I woke up, being a journalist and thankful for small favors, I made a few notes about this mouse-child—the only fictional figure ever to have honored and disturbed my sleep.

I had eighteen nephews and nieces. As a young bachelor-uncle I used to be asked now and then to tell a story. At this task I was terrible. Whole minutes would go by while I tried to think of something. In self-protection I decided to arm myself with a yarn or two, and for this I went straight to my dream-mouse. I named him Stuart and wrote a couple of episodes about his life. I kept these stories in a desk drawer and would pull them out and read them on demand. As the years went by, I added to the tale. Book publication never crossed my mind. These were the golden days before television, when children got their entertainment not by twisting a dial but by twisting an elder's arm.

In 1938, having decided to quit New York, I began tidying up what I called my "affairs." One of these was the Stuart Little adventures, now grown to perhaps a dozen episodes. At the suggestion of my wife, I carried them to a publisher (not Harper) and left them, to see whether they might be acceptable if expanded. The answer came back No, and I left for Maine, taking my rejected child along.

Seven years later, in the winter of 1944–45, I returned to New

York to spend a few months in a furnished apartment and do some work for *The New Yorker*. I was almost sure I was about to die, my head felt so queer. With death at hand, I cast about to discover what I could do to ease the lot of my poor widow, and again my thoughts strayed to Stuart Little. My editor at Harper's, Eugene Saxton, had been urging me to finish the narrative, and I determined to put it off no longer. Mornings I sat at a top-floor window looking out into West 11th Street and there I completed the story. I turned it in to Harper and then took a train for San Francisco, to join Stettinius, Molotov, Lawrence Spivak, and that crowd, for the formation of the U.N. Another springtime, another journey!

Harper accepted the book, and Stuart was off at last, after a pardonable delay of some fifteen years. Garth Williams was brought into the enterprise and began turning out the drawings that were to give shape to my diminutive hero.

A few weeks later, back home in Maine, a letter arrived for me from Anne Carroll Moore, children's librarian emeritus of the New York Public Library. Her letter was long, friendly, urgent, and thoroughly surprising. She said she had read proofs of my forthcoming book called *Stuart Little* and she strongly advised me to withdraw it. She said, as I recall the letter, that the book was non-affirmative, inconclusive, unfit for children, and would harm its author if published. These were strong words, and I was grateful to Miss Moore for having taken the trouble to write them. I thought the matter over, however, and decided that as long as the book satisfied me, I wasn't going to let an expert talk me out of it. It is unnerving to be told you're bad for children; but I detected in Miss Moore's letter an assumption that there are rules governing the writing of juvenile literature—rules as inflexible as the rules for lawn tennis. And this I was not sure of. I had followed my instincts in writing about Stuart, and following one's instincts seemed to be the way a writer should operate. I was shook up by the letter but was not deflected.

Stuart was published in October, and other surprises were in store for me. Miss Moore's successor at the Library had some misgivings of her own about the book, and Stuart met with a cool reception. He got into the shelves of the Library all right, but I think he had to gnaw his way in. The press, to my astonishment, treated the book almost as though it were adult fiction. The daily *Times* gave it a full-scale review by Charles Poore, who praised it. Malcolm Cowley, in the Sunday *Times,* said it was a good book but disappointing—should have been better. This exactly expressed my own feelings about it.

A couple of days after the book appeared, Harold Ross, my boss at *The New Yorker,* stopped in at my office. His briefcase was slung over his shoulder on a walking stick and he looked unhappy. "Saw your book, White," he growled. "You made one serious mistake."

"What was that?" I asked.

"Why the mouse," he shouted. "You said he was born. Goddamn it, White, you should have had him adopted." The word "adopted" boomed forth loud enough to be heard all down the corridor. I had great respect for Ross's ability to spot trouble in a piece of writing, and I began to feel uneasy. After he left the room I sat for a long while wondering whether Miss Moore had not been right after all. Finally I remembered that Harold Ross was not at home in the world of make-believe, he was strictly for the world of 43rd Street, and this cheered me and revived my spirits.

My next encounter was with Edmund Wilson, who stopped me in the hall. "Hello, hello," he said, in his wonderfully high and thrilling voice that sounds like a coaching horn. "I read that book of yours. I found the first page quite amusing, about the mouse, you know. But I was disappointed that you didn't develop the theme more in the manner of Kafka."

I thanked Edmund and wandered back to my room to chuckle at the infinite variety of *The New Yorker;* the editor who could spot a dubious verb at forty paces, the critic who was saddened because my innocent tale of the quest for beauty failed to carry the overtones of monstrosity. What a magazine. There's never been anything like it.

Despite the rough time the author was having, Stuart himself seemed to be doing all right. The book drew generally favorable reviews, and by October 24th Harper had sold 42,000 copies.

The next thing that happened was that three fellows turned up claiming that *their* name was Stuart Little, and what was I going to do about that? One of them told me he had begun work on a children's story; the hero was a rat, and the rat's name was E. B. White. I never learned how far he got with this splendid project, but I know he phoned Ursula Nordstrom at Harper's to alert her.

The real returns came when letters began arriving. Some were from children. Some were from teachers. They expressed pleasure, along with a fairly steady stream of abuse about the book's ending, which fails to tell whether Stuart found the bird. The letters have not stopped coming. Of the many thousands I've received, only two, I believe, questioned the odd fact of Stuart's arrival in this world and the propriety of an American family's having a boy that looked like a mouse. After twenty years, I am beginning to relax.

I learned two things from the experience of writing *Stuart Little:* that a writer's own nose is his best guide, and that children can sail easily over the fence that separates reality from make-believe. They go over it like little springboks. A fence that can throw a librarian is as nothing to a child.

11

A WRITER'S SERMON

By Storm Jameson

Two or three years ago I was asked to help a young English writer, author of one book, a volume of short stories, to get a so-called travelling fellowship offered by a generous patron of letters. I was happy when he was awarded it—that is, I was happy that he had not been disappointed. About the principle of travelling fellowships for the very young writer, and all such aids to beginners, I am far from happy. Nothing could be more delightful than a year's free travel when one is very young. And perhaps, if the chosen young man—the choice rarely falls on a young woman—is able to turn himself into a camera walking down the street (in a phrase that was more fashionable in the experimental thirties than it is now), watching people, recording gestures, looks, scenes, and listening to the familiar talk of strangers, his year will not, humanly speaking, have been wasted. Perhaps, too, it will have the additional advantage and merit of postponing for a year the moment when he sits down, with pen or typewriter, to begin writing his novel.

This sounds frivolous but is meant in dead earnest. For one genius, one writer born, who writes as naturally and inevitably as a bird sings or a tiger kills, an uncounted number of talented young writers are ruined by the haste with which they rush into authorship. Almost any device which serves to delay them is an unmitigated good.

I am almost ready to add that any device—such as a degree course in creative writing—which serves to hurry them on their way, and make it seem a pleasant respectable way, is an unmitigated evil. I was once, for one gloriously happy year, the most incompetent teacher of creative writing in the United States. I had not the haziest idea how a genuine professor teaches the subject (and never had time to find out, because my ignorance forced me to spend all day "tutoring"—that is, talking to—each of my pupils separately). My

55

total inability to train them in the acrobatics of writing had at least a negative merit—I did not do any damage.

But surely, someone cries at this point, writing is a trade *like any other?* This is one of the platitudes we all utter at least once in our lives, and assent to, happily, without reflection, when we hear it. And if it meant no more than that a writer must work at his job at least as hard as any other serious craftsman, it would be harmless. The harm, the illusion, lies in the words *like any other.* The trade of an artist is not like any other. A baker who makes superlatively good bread and brings it to the notice of the public is 99% sure of making a modest fortune. A writer's superlatively good book has no certainty, none at all—not even if he is also a superlative self-advertiser (though this helps)—of bringing him in a living. We all know this, *and we do not draw the necessary conclusion,* which is that a young man (or a young woman) must be either a hero or a madman to bet his whole life on such a risk. The folly of starting too soon is only less heroic (blind, reckless, ignorant—choose your own adjective) than the rashness of starting at all. I am not talking cynically; I am only saying (in effect) that the forces and circumstances which have turned the highly individual craft of writing into a vast industrial enterprise, heavily capitalised, employing an immense army of editors, publicity experts, professors of creative writing, and, by a strange necessity, writers (who, unlike the other labourers, are paid by results, like commercial travellers on a commission basis) are, on balance, a public and personal disaster.

If I had the moral courage, I should have said to the young man I helped to his travelling fellowship: "Take your year abroad by all means. But use it to learn a language or two, which will fit you to take a job as consul (like Stendhal), or a schoolmaster (like Mallarmé), or a foreign correspondent (like X, Y, and Z), and write your first five novels in your spare time, and God be with you. You may have the luck to make a killing with your very first book (like Norman Mailer), in which case God be even more with you, because the pressures that will be applied to you to do it again make a child's toy of the thumb screw. To resist them will demand greater will power, a cooler head, than most young writers possess."

Let us suppose that you have arranged your life so prudently that you need not hurry to finish a book by five o'clock next Wednesday, but can take your time. What, even before you sit down to write, is the first discipline you ought to teach yourself? (The word *discipline* is the correct one, since there is or should be a good deal of the monk in your make-up.) Not—believe me—not how to begin, how to end, how to use dialogue: these are skills you must dredge out of your soul for yourself, if they are to be sound. No—the first thing you should have guessed is that there is no value in the emotions, the spiritual writhings, started in you by the sight, smell and touch of your fellow human beings. You cannot avoid having emotions about them, but you can avoid boring us with them. To analyse your feelings for our attention is inexcusable clumsy egoism. When I catch sight in the novel I have just opened of a paragraph beginning, "It is difficult to say what my feelings were when I . . . ," I shudder and close the book hurriedly.

And direct analysis of the feelings of your characters is just as clumsy. Tell us what they did, what they said, and (not too often) what they thought, and from that let us infer the state of their hearts and minds. If you will take the time to read, slowly, Pasternak's *Doctor Zhivago,* you will be astonished how seldom, in this long, subtle, and subtly emotional book, he tells you anything directly about the emotions of his people. Yet their feelings are as vividly present to us as their looks and background. I am not saying—it would be evidently absurd—that no great writer ever indulges in the prolonged unravelling of an emotional web. There was, after all, Proust. I am saying that it is a weapon for the hand of a genius. If you who are reading this happen to be a genius, stop reading at once: you can look after yourself and you are a law unto yourself.

There is another good reason, apart from the probability that you will bore us, why a great deal of self-indulgent chat about your characters' emotions will be an error. The task of the serious novelist today is quite hideously difficult and complicated, demanding of him the greatest breadth of knowledge with the greatest clarity and skill in compression. His essential concern is with men and women *in their times.* He has to portray, as vividly as he can, a social landscape, a social climate, which seems to dwarf the human beings moving about in it. This is one of the moments in the history of our planet when what is personal to a man is no more important than the fears and hopes, the impulses he shares with a great many of his fellows. I do not mean that the task of the serious novelist is to write only or directly about the danger we all lie under of mass suicide, or about communism, or about the need for God. Heaven forbid! But I do mean that unless he is sharply aware of these things, unless his ears are always open to the frightened or clamorous voices coming from every corner of modern society, he cannot even write honestly a simple novel about two young people who fell in love, married and had children. Jane Austen could ignore entirely the dark impulses to murder which exist in all our hearts, because these were on the periphery of her comfortable world. We, unless we can remember their existence even while we are writing about spring and babies and calf love, had better give up writing and take to gardening or jam-making, harmless and honest occupations.

The convulsive movements going on everywhere now, wherever we turn our eyes, form the harsh country of the contemporary novel. Whether we notice it or not—but the writer *must* notice it—something which is essentially a revolution has started. In the old trite phrase, humanity has struck its tents and is on the march God knows where. In one way or another, the meaning, the energy, of this revolution must lie behind the novelist's simplest words. Or else he is not telling the truth about life in his time. This has nothing to do with putting politics in the novel, nothing to do with propaganda. Propaganda—that is, deliberate propaganda—is one use for words, but it is not the artist's use of them. And politics is only one of the activities of men and women. If it appears in a novel, it must do so not as politics but as a human impulse, expressed through passions and deeds, part of the great net in which men and women work, suffer, rejoice, and die, like fishes in water.

There never was a moment in the history of the human race so baffling to the novelist, so abominably exacting. The novelist does, or ought to do, something more than draw characters in action. Before he even begins to write, he has to form a conception of life and human nature—that is, he has to be able to answer to his own satisfaction the question: Why was I born, what does my life mean? (If he is an honest writer, the answers he finds will never satisfy him completely; he will always be asking the question afresh.) And the conception he forms for himself *is* his novel. It is the inner compulsion from which the events, the story, grow and the characters, in turn, spring from these events. These characters affect these events, or try to, and are affected by them. Before Pasternak put pen to paper, he had already decided for himself what human life meant at a given period in Russia, and his sense of its meaning colours his every word. In the same way, an English or an American novelist who is moved to write about the inhabitants of a small obscure town needs to see their story in the light of all he knows, all he can find out, about where humanity itself is going.

"Dear me," I hear at this point, "this is all very solemn and alarming. But all I want to do is to amuse and interest as many readers as possible; I want to take their minds off their dull, unromantic lives, I don't want to disturb them in any way." All right. Then forgive me if I say that although your innocent impulse to exhibit yourself in the role of entertainer bears no relation to literature, it does, in fact, bring you into the same highly competitive world in which serious writers are struggling to keep their footing. It does entangle you in the great industrial machine of modern publishing. It does compel you, if you are relying on your entertainment value for your sole living, to keep on doing your tricks before an audience which is all the less likely to be loyal to you, that is being bombarded on every side by inducements to form new tastes, to try a newer product of the machine.

And this finally is why I view with dismay all the methods, from literary prizes to three-year courses in creative writing, by which we try to stimulate the production of writers and more writers. The risk of a genius being left to die of hunger in a garret is less horrible than the glut, the ever-rising flood, of novels and novelised biographies, pouring through the mill wheels of modern publishing. This is why I feel, with guilt, that I did no kindness to a talented young man when I helped to push him out into the treacherous stream instead of saying to him: First secure to yourself a modest living, and then take all the time you really need—years, if necessary—to think through, to live through, the novel, the short stories which, for all I know now, may reveal you as the modern Dickens, the modern Faulkner, the modern Chekhov. You may write much less than you would otherwise have done, but what you write will be infinitely more satisfying.

12

THE BATTLE OF FICTION AND NON-FICTION

By Elizabeth Janeway

WHY has non-fiction become so much more popular than fiction? Why is non-fiction so much more widely read? Except for phenomena like *Love Story*, it is generally true that non-fiction sells much better than fiction. Why?

This is an interesting topic, and because it is germane to our present social situation, it is a trend you can expect to continue, rather than just a fashion of a few years. A basic reason is that fiction is much harder for people to follow than non-fiction.

Fiction, you see, is not about facts, but about relationships. In that sense, it's like algebra instead of arithmetic. Fiction isn't a straightforward statement; it's a comment on something the author believes the reader knows something about already. But today in a very heterogeneous society like ours, it's rare for people to have the sort of common background of assumption which permits fiction to speak movingly, evocatively and clearly to its audience.

As everyone knows, our society is shifting; it's much more mobile than in the nineteenth century when there was a common, bourgeois, middle-class sense of relationships—of the world being more or less the same, of standards being more or less accepted within it. This is not so today. Consequently, it is much, much, harder to write the sort of book which assumes that the reader will feel as the writer does about a given personal relationship, a given moral situation.

People are much more isolated—and that includes emotional isolation. We tend to find it harder to feel our way into other people's emotions because they are more various and less familiar. People come from other parts of the world. The reading audience now comes from many, many more different kinds of childhood than potential readers in 1850 or 1870.

For this audience non-fiction spells things out. You know how children ask you to tell them a story and want to know if it's true. And by that they don't mean is it fictionally true, is it true to a level of plausible emotion? They mean, did it really happen? Non-fiction is able to answer, yes, it did happen; or else, at least, to *pretend* that it did happen.

Of course, as we all know, history is often rewritten from generation to generation, as historical attitudes and views on life change, but historiographers and their readers still assume the facts they are discussing are the same. It takes a fairly sophisticated critic to realize how emphasis and interpretation change our map of the world—or (as I suggest in my book *Man's World, Woman's Place*) how they rework our "social mythology."

But fiction, unlike history or biography, openly and overtly requires from the reader some prior knowledge of the way life works, some sense of what's plausible and possible. Fiction—and, of course, I am talking about good fiction—demands that a society should seem to be knowable to the audience living within it. The writer and the reader have to agree that they are talking about the same facts and the same rules. We have a very bad situation for agreement today, not only because fiction writers are isolated from their possible readers, but also because social change takes place so fast. This is one place where the generation gap is wide indeed, for young people and their parents seldom read the same writers.

Fiction is about personal relationships. These relationships must seem to the readers out there to carry the same moral overtones that the author feels as being present and significant in them. But since so much of the common background of social and emotional and cultural experience has vanished, this similarity of response can't be taken for granted. Take an obvious example. One hundred years ago it was a tragedy if an unmarried girl had a baby. An author writing about such a situation could assume that this is what his readers would also feel. They might sympathize with her and they might feel that her plight was unjust, but they would feel, nonetheless, that it was a tragic situation. Today this isn't true. Our moral judgments have shifted and become much more diverse, and fluid.

An author can still set up a situation that involves the girl, her lover, the man she might have married and didn't, the child, the parents, the whole village, but his readers won't react in a predict-able way. Some people will say, "Right on," and others will say, "What about the population explosion?" Some people will say her parents are callous pigs, and the tragedy lies in their anger with the girl. In short, there will be all kinds of reactions to the situation, and not just one you can count on.

In other words, the symbols and the meanings which are the tools of fictional communication have ceased to carry a significance which will be commonly agreed upon. Fiction is becoming an archaic and special language. It is no longer a *lingua franca* that everyone can understand. I don't, myself, think that fiction will die out; but it will have to change.

Meanwhile, non-fiction reaches the readers, but, again, the writer can't take this for granted. This book of mine, *Man's World, Wo-man's Place*, is the first long work of non-fiction I have written and, in doing it, I had to learn quite new techniques. One of the things I discovered was that I had to know who my audience was. I had to think consciously about whom I was writing for. In fiction, I always assumed that I was writing for people who would understand me because we shared the same assumptions about the world.

In more stable times, when people have a better idea of what's go-ing on around them, they turn to fiction for an interpretation; whereas, in times like these, people turn to non-fiction just to find out what's going on. When people lived in tiny communities and knew each other extremely well, and could tease each other, and joke about relationships, you had communication by poetry. You didn't have to set up inter-personal relationships. You could assume that everyone knew what you meant if you wrote in lyrical form. Fiction and poetry both demand an intimate knowledge and a shared experience, based on the size and intimacy of the community, and on the rate of social change.

Fiction should be about recognizable people. That, to me, makes it very difficult to read certain writers who are enjoyed by other people. For instance, I'm not very fond of Kurt Vonnegut and Joseph Heller, writers who are difficult for me to read because their characters too often fall toward stereotypes and toward a kind of allegorical presentation of themselves in what seems to me a flat situation. A situation where right and wrong are too easily determined.

I find this unexciting and lacking in tension. I understand why writers do this: they are looking for the moral agreement that I spoke of earlier. We can no longer expect it when we're talking about an unmarried girl having a baby. But it's assumed that we will all agree that war is hell, and we shouldn't have bombed Dresden and all Air Force generals were nitwits, etc., etc.

To people my age, this is dull partly because it is hellishly oversimplified. Also, being oversimplified it seems to us false in many respects. Vonnegut and Heller and many of their followers are like Irving Berlin—they can only compose in the key of C. Berlin has had a special keyboard made that transposes his key of C tunes into B minor or F sharp for him. I wish allegorically inclined writers could do this too, and have their stereotyped situations enriched by doubt and diversity.

I suspect that another effect on fiction that we're experiencing comes out of television. McLuhan, though out of fashion today, is perfectly right about his basic premise: what is important about television is not just what it says but—much more—how it says it, how it picks up experience and processes it and passes it to the viewer.

Television speeds up the processes of life. You look at the tube long enough and you'll begin to believe that every problem can be resolved in a time span of half an hour or, at most, an hour. Leonard Woolf writes in his marvelous autobiography that when he gave up his job as editor of *The New Statesman* he found a heavenly relief. *The New Statesman* is a weekly, and he'd begun to count everything in the world, political processes, news events, human life in seven-day spans. In television everything happens, reaches a climax and is resolved in an hour at most. Of course, art and fiction compress experience, but that is not the effect that television gives.

It's difficult to know what's going to come from television. I can't be completely hopeless about it because there's a great deal of talent there. But again, I think factual documentaries are at present a good deal better than the fiction shown. When you really had some plausible and complicated fiction shown, as in *The Forsyte Saga,* you found the television audience very much moved and involved.

Now, it's certainly true that anyone my age has seen film turn into an art form in the past thirty or forty years. Perhaps television will too. As yet it hasn't achieved a depth of experience which permits art to grow, permits diversity, suspense, surprise. Art needs this richness of possibility to hold its audience. When it doesn't exist, the creator too often falls back on seeking to grab hold of the audience by a shock effect. But shock effects wear off. They can't be used too often because you begin wondering what else for an encore.

It's interesting today to see how many writers want to grab the reader via sex; and of course it works—for a while. But sex novels defeat themselves in the end, because they cease to be novels. They reach for the reader at the level of involvement which produces heavy breathing; and Janeway's law on critical appreciation declares that heavy breathing breaks down the brain cells.

In other words, personal involvement at this level wipes out critical ability. Instead of understanding the word through art, the reader experiences sensations. Now it happens to be psychologically true that the more you want something, the less you can tell how good it is until you've had it.

The remarks on this situation by a great author of former times sum it up pretty well:

> The expense of spirit in a waste of shame
> Is lust in action; and till action, lust
> Is perjur'd, murd'rous, bloody, full of blame.
> Mad in pursuit, and in possession so;
> Had, having and in quest to have, extreme;
> A bliss in proof—and prov'd, a very woe;
> Before, a joy propos'd; behind, a dream.

Which brings us directly to the question of pornography and censorship. I'd better begin by saying that I'm totally opposed to any kind of censorship from anyone: from the local police chief, from the courts—which means that I support the publication of pornography, including hard-core pornography. But I warn you not to get pornography mixed up with literature, which it isn't.

It's more like "How to Fix the TV" and "Everything You Always Wanted to Know About Air Conditioning, Hair Setting, or Septic Tank Repair." It aims at hard breathing and no thinking at all. It is a substitute for action, not a comment on it.

Pornography purports to be fiction, but it really isn't about personal relationships, and relationships are the stuff of fiction. Pornography is only about relationships within the self. It is deeply narcissistic and claustrophobic. So, though I support the publication of pornography for those who want it, I can't call it literature.

Part of the confusion about pornography arises from the fact that literature can be written and art created around pornographic situations. But this requires the introduction of human relationships into the closed world of pornography. Henry Miller is a good example. In his books, we find recognizable human beings who are caught in pornographic situations which become both comic and tragic because the characters know they are trapped, and their emotions are moving and effective. In such scenes, publication of pornography has opened the door to a wider area of consideration for fiction. To this extent literature itself may be said to have profited by it.

I have cited this example both because it is so common today and because it illustrates clearly how writing may extend its range. Humanity suffers when there are areas of experience and emotion which cannot be discussed, which are cut off by barricades of taboo. Such hidden, denied emotions are the breeding ground of neurosis, fear and compulsion. For the artist, there should be nothing human that is alien. Part of his job, his obligation, is to show his audience the reality of other people's experience. And so, the wider the range of life that can be used as material for art, the better for all of us, readers and writers alike.

13

THREE KEY QUESTIONS

By John Ball

Whenever you turn out a piece of writing—a story, an article, or a book—you create what is known in the trade as a literary property. The name is important, because the word "property" implies something of value, something which has recognizable worth and will sell in the marketplace. Unfortunately, many writers overlook this aspect of their intended profession and after a long period of effort find themselves discouraged and unpublished.

This does not necessarily mean that they lack the writing skills, the necessary talent, or the individual style. They may have all of these and still fail to create properties of commercial value. And the quick, apparently obvious answer—to put in plenty of sex and violence—doesn't work either, if the would-be author is thinking in terms of a meaningful career.

One of the major causes of disappointment lies in the choice of material about which to write. On this single rock there have possibly been more literary shipwrecks than are caused by any other one factor.

It is a sad fact to note, but it has been estimated that less than one percent of all of the literary manuscripts seriously undertaken in this country are ever eventually published. This suggests a sum total of lost work, accumulated frustrations, and disappointed hopes that is staggering. Much of this composite disaster might have been avoided if the authors concerned had been more selective about their subject matter and had avoided certain traps which seem to catch a merciless number of talented people on a continuing basis.

Before putting anything at all down on paper other than a hundred-word summary of your basic idea, it is most important to answer this question: *"Why do I want to write this particular piece?"* Here is where rationalization has to go out the window and

66

stark truth has to take its place. Often it will involve some thought. If you are capable of being fearlessly honest with yourself, you may save a great amount of wasted effort and instead channel your abilities into much more productive directions.

People sometimes undertake very long and involved writing projects for totally unrealistic reasons without ever stopping first to analyze their own motivations. They honestly believe that they have a good idea for a book, and they plot it out in their minds without ever realizing that they are being misled by one or more completely wrong reasons. When this happens, a literary success is almost an impossibility.

A classic example is the *"justification book."* At some time in the past the author had an unhappy experience which he is determined to correct, whether he consciously realizes it or not. He (or she) was jilted, otherwise rejected, or else seriously misunderstood. Whereupon the idea comes to write a book about it, a book which presumably deals with "real human problems," but which is actually a rebuttal. Usually highly autobiographical, such manuscripts frequently attempt to show how right the author was all of the time, and how badly certain other people behaved. Perhaps the creators of such works derive a great deal of satisfaction by getting all of their feelings down on paper, but their chances of seeing their efforts in print and between hard covers are obviously close to nil.

A variation of this is the book that is written primarily for one particular person to read. It may be in the personal vindication category, but it is more likely to take the form of a tribute to some particular person, especially to publicize his unrecognized achievements to the world. There are many versions of this: the career of a beloved teacher, the faithfulness of the cop on the beat, the determination of a handicapped person to succeed despite great obstacles. Once in a very great while a book of this type will be successful, but for every such success there is a painfully large number of manuscripts which never get beyond the beginning stage. The public at large simply isn't interested in how mother raised all six of us children after father died and somehow always managed to remain cheerful through it all. Most people have had too many similar experiences of their own.

Another very common pitfall is trying to write about something you do not really know. There is absolutely no point in trying to create a tender romance or a gripping suspense story laid in Venice if you don't really know the city. Poe accomplished it, but he lived at a time when Venice was little more than a name to practically everyone on this side of the Atlantic, and the intimate details of the city were all but unknown. Even if you have been to Venice on a tour and spent an exciting day and a half there, that still doesn't make you enough of an authority on the city to use it as a background without at the least a great deal of detailed research. Reading an article in the *National Geographic,* fine as most of them are, isn't sufficient.

If this seems very obvious to you, let me invite you to a wet and long drawn-out afternoon that I spent not long ago waiting for a delayed connection at the St. Louis airport. With too much time on my hands, I picked up a paperback from the newsstand in the hope of some entertainment. According to the blurb copy much of the action was laid in Bangkok and that happens to be one of my favorite cities. In a receptive frame of mind I sat down to read.

There was plenty of action in the opening pages, for the story began with an exciting car chase through the streets with the hero in a Jaguar and the man he was pursuing in a Ferrari, no less. It was at once obvious that the hero was a remarkable driver; he swung around a corner to the right, barely bouncing his tires against the curb as he used every inch of space; there was a quick flash of a horrified pedestrian just on the point of starting to cross and jumping back a split second ahead of disaster. The chase continued for several more pages, till, with burning rubber, the Ferrari turned up the main street of the city, the Jaguar in intense pursuit.

At that point I got up, walked over to the nearest trash container, and disposed of the book. For your information, if you don't happen to know already, they drive on the left, not the right, in Thailand, and the main street in Bangkok happens to be a river. True, the book was published, but I have never seen another copy of it anywhere, and I have never heard of the author before or since. It is too bad, because in the few pages that I read before he lost me completely I discovered a refreshing style and a real narrative gift.

Too often, particularly in television-writing circles, I heard the phrase, "But who will know the difference?" I cannot think of a poorer excuse for incompetent writing than that. The degree of expertise that is available is astounding; people know far more than they are usually expected to and on a vast variety of subjects. Guessing at facts that can be established is an invitation to disaster, and nothing is as completely unreliable as the insufferable, "But it stands to reason . . ."

I could name a recent motion picture that was made at a cost of about two million dollars, which is quite a bit of money. I happened to see the picture at a private screening at one of the studios and noticed that there was a scene of an aircraft taking off (a DC-8) and then, a few minutes later, a shot presumably of the same aircraft in flight, only this time it was a 727-200, a very different plane with the power plants in the rear, not under the wings. I mentioned it to the producer who came back with: "Yes, but who will know the difference?"

At the formal premiere, which I also attended, when the wrong aircraft came on the screen, the audience broke out in laughter. If you publish something like that, or try to, you will not be able to hear your reader laughing at you, but you can take it for a near certainty that he won't buy your next book—or take it home from the library. The same thing also largely applies to "writing around" something that you don't know—the evasion will be spotted by a large percentage of your readers, if your work ever gets far enough so that you have any, and your image in their minds will suffer drastically as a consequence. One blunder like that will take quite a string of well-constructed books to overcome, and the bad taste will rankle even then. To come back to the point that began this discussion, don't attempt to write about things that you don't know and haven't adequately researched. *Never* depend on the forlorn hope that your readers won't ever know the difference, or be able to detect when you are bluffing.

One more thing, if I may, to help keep your feet off the path that is paved with rejection slips. In the search for a slam-bang finale, don't assume that your reader has become so engrossed in what you are telling him that he has abandoned all reason. Not too long ago I read a story somewhere that ended with the key people escaping from the West Coast in an airplane while an atomic bomb went off and melted down the entire city of San Francisco, not to mention

Oakland and the other nearby communities. No intelligent fifth-grader would fall for that; the whole world knows that no such event took place, and there is not the remotest possibility that the reading audience would swallow that one.

Another example comes from a short-lived TV series built around the San Francisco airport. According to the story an aircraft was standing by to fly an iron lung to Salt Lake City to meet a desperate emergency. *Before* the lung was loaded, a hijacker took over the aircraft (on the ground) and held it up until he was finally chased out and shot. The next scene showed the airport manager returning to his office, still panting hard from his exertions in chasing the criminal, to be greeted by his secretary with the line, "Oh, Mr. Redblood, the iron lung got there in time, and the boy is going to live!"

There are about fifteen things wrong with this, all of them glaringly obvious. I mention this incident because two children were visiting our home at the time and saw the show. When that ridiculous line was delivered they both laughed heartily. They were eight and ten years old. Yet consider this: someone wrote that episode and, for reasons which elude me, was able to sell it to the producer. Or perhaps the producer wrote it himself. I would not be surprised to learn that that absurd finale contributed to the early demise of the show.

It is possible to go on at uncomfortable length with a protracted list of "thou shalt not's," but that isn't the purpose of this article. Let me conclude by summarizing three questions that you want to ask yourself right at the very start every time you sit down to write:

1. Why do I want to write this particular piece?
2. Am I really qualified to write about the subject I have in mind?
3. Could a rational person reasonably believe the story I have to tell?

If you can give yourself an honest, convincing answer to the first question, and a firm "yes" to the other two, then some of the worst of the writing potholes that plague so many manuscripts will lie behind you.

14

"IT'S BEEN DONE BEFORE"

By Samm Sinclair Baker

Four of the most destructive words for you as a writer, if you decide to believe them, are: "It's been done before!" During my years of teaching short story and article writing, budding writers have confronted me with such comments as, "I've been thinking of trying a magazine article on such-and-such. Would it have a chance?"

"Why not?" I'd say. "If you have a special slant on the subject, or can write it in a particularly effective way, there ought to be a market for it."

"Well-l-l," came the hesitant answer, "when I queried an editor about a proposed piece on safe driving, the answer I got was, 'It's been done before.' And I'm afraid the same thing would happen again. . . ."

If you don't learn anything else this year, you'll be way ahead if you absorb this truth: If anyone, including an editor, tells you, "Forget it—it's been done before," don't you believe it! Certainly it rules that editor out, but not the possibilities for the article.

Instead, plan and write the piece *your way*. If it's a good article or story, then sooner or later there's a good chance it will sell. My experience as well as that of other professional writers confirms that as a fact.

The reading public in general is interested in information on medical topics, and so am I as a writer. Since childhood, I'd suffered from migraine headaches, not as severely as many others—but enough to keep exploring every possible way to get rid of them. Finally, I learned how I could control and in effect be free of the oppressive headaches.

Talking to a magazine editor about several ideas I had for articles, I suggested migraines as a problem of great interest. "Oh, no," she reacted. "I've had it with proposed articles on headaches. It's been done so often that it's hackneyed. Definitely not for us."

I mailed a proposal to another big national magazine. My title: "Ten Ways to Fight Headaches." In the brief one-page summary, I emphasized that most past articles primarily told "about" headaches—interesting but not very helpful. My piece would provide in detail ten steps the headache sufferer could try for relief, control, and perhaps freedom from pain—such as I had gained.

In such outlines, I've always tried to condense the essence of the article in one sentence; in this case: "Sound, practical advice on what steps to take to help prevent and control headaches." *Woman's Day* asked to see the piece by return mail. The editor said, "Sure, the subject has been done before—but never with such specific step-by-step usable advice as you provide. That makes it *new*."

Perhaps if I'd stressed the basic difference between my proposal and past articles, the first magazine editor would have grabbed it. Perhaps. But I'd missed the boat and was very happy about it since *Woman's Day* was a bigger-circulation, better-paying market. That's another "done before" tip that can't be stressed too often: If you miss one sale, try, try again . . . and again . . . and again. . . .

How many articles or stories have you filed away—or worse, torn up—because you've been told one or more times that "It's been done before"? Nonsense! I wouldn't be a selling writer today if I'd let those four damning words turn me away.

I'd been researching diet for years in order eventually to write a book on reducing. By lucky chance, which I grabbed, I met and arranged co-authorship with an unknown physician, who, in my opinion, probably knows more about reducing than anyone else anywhere. And he proved it with a remarkable record of reducing success with over 10,000 overweight patients during his many years of medical practice.

I wrote an outline and first chapter for a book which our agent offered to a publisher. The negative response came back hard and fast: "This book hasn't a chance. In the first place, diet books have been done to death. In the second place, this is a high-protein diet —and that's been done before, zillions of times!"

With that unequivocal kiss of death from the editor-in-chief of one of the top book publishing houses, would you have accepted defeat? If so, you'll never be a pro. Our agent kept submitting the proposal to more publishers. They all turned it down just as flatly —"It's been done before." Meanwhile I kept writing until we finished the book, certainly an act of faith, since we'd had no encouragement.

A magazine editor, an old friend from my pre-selling days, accepted my luncheon invitation. My aim was to sell a condensation of the diet to her big-circulation magazine. That would be a showpiece to interest book publishers, as has happened occasionally— articles growing into books. "How about it?" I asked the editor. "Here's a proven diet backed by over 10,000 success stories in the doctor's files. . . ."

She put down her fork wearily, massaged her chin. "I'm going to be brutally frank as I rarely am with authors. Your diet hasn't a chance as a magazine article, book, anything. It's been done before—too often. Readers are fed up with such a diet—"

"Overfed with faulty diets," I countered. "That's why there are so many yearning, unhealthy overweights—"

She shook her head, "You're wasting your time on this subject. As for your book, forget it. In confidence I can tell you that two of today's top writers are completing a book summarizing every possible kind of reducing diet through the years. Readers will never need another diet book—yours included. All diet stuff will have been done before."

Other magazine editors and sixteen book publishers agreed with her in rejecting derivative articles and the book. The seventeenth publisher accepted the book because a forceful editor there said, "I don't give a damn how many high-protein diets have been done before. There has never been an all-protein diet like this. And no diet book has been written so clearly and simply before."

That book, coauthored with Dr. Irwin Maxwell Stillman, became the best-selling diet book of all time—*The Doctor's Quick Weight Loss Diet*. Four more Stillman/Baker diet books have brought total sales to over twenty million copies in all editions. National magazines compete for book excerpts and original articles. Diet books and articles by others have proliferated sensationally.

The next time anyone tells you that your article or story can't make it because "it's been done before"—remind yourself of the Stillman/Baker history. Realize that you can do it differently, better, more effectively. Authors will never lose their ability to create potent new writing, nonfiction and fiction, on any "done before" subject.

The same "done before" curse has afflicted writers of fiction as well. When I first started writing short stories too many years ago, my primary interest was in the mystery field. One of the first stories I wrote leaned heavily for suspense on the premise that the detective had to solve the case by a certain hour. I mailed the manuscript hopefully to a small magazine where I thought it might have the best chance, less competition.

I waited . . . waited . . . waited. Familiar? I'd learned that "all things come to those who wait"—especially rejection slips. After a follow-up letter, my manuscript was finally returned. At the bottom of the printed slip the editor had scrawled, "The timetable gimmick has been done ad nauseam." I went over the story carefully, changed a word or sentence here and there, tightened it up. To me it still seemed like a strong, suspenseful tale.

Well, I reasoned, I'd never seen "the timetable gimmick" done before exactly this way. So out went the retyped manuscript. Six more rejections followed. More reworking, retyping, remailing. Figuring, what could I lose, I tried one of the larger-circulation magazines buying some mystery stories, In a few days, back came a check and a request for more of my work. Their title proved further that they didn't consider the plot gimmick hackneyed—they named it, "Terror's Timetable."

Dashiell Hammett (who headed a course that I took) told me that when he first started writing mystery stories he received so many rejections that he created a working system: He made a chart listing all the mystery story markets, with the best-paying magazines on top, down to the lowliest. He'd write a story the best way he could until he was convinced that it was good. Then he'd mail it to the top magazine on the list, jotting down the submission date.

When the story was returned, he'd fill in that date, then send the manuscript to the next magazine on the list—and on and on. He was particularly proud of one story which was returned by the top publication at the time, *The Saturday Evening Post*. It came back faster than usual. Off it went to the rest of the list. Eventually it had been rejected by all during the course of a year.

Hammett said, "I believed in that story. So I started on the list all over again, mailing the manuscript once more to the *Post*. A miracle—this time it was accepted quickly."

After the check had arrived and been deposited, Hammett told the editor what had happened. "Well," the gentleman explained, "I believe that the first time we'd just run a story using the same general location and types of characters. I didn't want to repeat. But when I read the story a second time, long after, I wasn't influenced by its having been done before. It was fresh and compelling, so we bought it—and I'm very glad we did."

What price "done before"? Or dozens of other reasons why a fine manuscript may be rejected? Editors are among the brightest, best people I know. They're also human: they make mistakes as we all do. And they'll be the first to relate their whoppers.

Some readers may complain, "That's O.K. for him or her—the writer who has made it. But I'm just a struggling beginner. I can't get away with the things that the established pro can. . . ."

There's some slight validity to that attitude. But it's the wrong reaction from two viewpoints: First, it's ineffectual; it gains you nothing but the fleeting relief of self-pity. Second, it's not true— and I have over a thousand rejections to prove it. The instances related here apply to when I was a struggling beginner (ditto Hammett). Every writer, at any time, when he rolls a blank sheet into the typewriter begins, struggles.

And . . . as a best-selling author, I still get my share of turndowns, of "it's been done befores." What do I do about it? I listen. I consider carefully. Then if I'm convinced that I can do it differently, better, more effectively, I damn the editors' torpedoes, full speed ahead! At the very least, I learn from the experience. *How about you—from now on?*

PART II

HOW TO WRITE: TECHNIQUES

15

VISUALIZING FICTION ON PAPER

By Dorothy Uhnak

WRITING began so far back in childhood that I literally cannot remember a time when I was *not* writing. I spent fourteen years of my adult life as a police officer in New York City. During all that time, I wrote continually, drawing on everything around me: the unique, exciting situations, the deadly boredom, the brutality, sadness, pain, humor (often macabre), the courage, cowardice, intelligence, stupidity, greed, anger, danger, and intense loyalty which characterize the working life of a police officer.

I was a capable police officer: I was promoted three times and awarded medals twice. I worked hard, was dedicated and earnest and concerned. Yet all the time, the writer in me was compiling events, feelings, atmosphere, emotions, situations for future use. *Policewoman*, semi-autobiographical, semi-fictional, was published during my tenure as a police officer and was my first attempt to set forth some things I had observed, learned, experienced, been a part of.

My first novel, *The Bait*, was published after I resigned from police work in order to devote myself more fully to writing and to continue my education. It was awarded the Edgar for the Best First Mystery of 1968, which I felt was somewhat ironic, for I never considered myself a "mystery writer." People are my main concern as a writer, and the task I set myself is to dig into the "mystery" of human behavior in given circumstances.

I have used the police world in all my books to date in order to explore certain events occurring between people, rather than to tell a "cop story" per se.

The Bait dealt with a sex murderer. On a deeper level, it explored the tormented world of a tragically demented man and his impact on a bright, sensitive young policewoman.

The Witness, second in my trilogy set in the Manhattan District Attorney's Squad, was a straightforward story about black organized crime and corruption. It was also a story about youthful idealism, hopes and energies that were misused and betrayed. It was part of the education-in-life of young Detective Christie Opara.

The Ledger, third in the trilogy, could be described as the story of the beautiful mistress of a crime lord. It was also a character study of two apparently opposite young women: one the worldly mistress, the other the idealistic Christie Opara. It was a probing of the painful, hidden truths each girl had to face about herself.

When I undertook my latest novel, *Law and Order,* I realized it was a radical departure from anything I had previously attempted. It was to span three generations, through four decades which have seen more social, political, moral upheaval than most of the rest of our history all put together. For one solid year, I did nothing but research. I probed back more than a hundred years to gain a fuller understanding of the immigrants who came to populate New York City, to lead and dominate not only the Police Department but the political and religious structure of the city for so many years. While the main characters are Irish, I also had to study all the important ethnic groups who comprise New York, to understand their aspirations, backgrounds, influences, self-image. I immersed myself in reading and discussion not only about politics, religious and ethnic history and folklore, but in economics and the effects of the Great Depression, World War II, the post-war world, the Korean War, Vietnam, the youth movement, generation gap, emergence of the drug culture.

I spent three weeks in Ireland wandering at random through that lovely tortured country: spoke to people, listened to them, read as much Irish writing as I could absorb until I could *feel* the rhythm of Irish thought and emotion. I allowed myself to get caught up and carried by the Irish idiom.

My characters grew out of the research. Certain strong characters began to dominate the other members of their family. And it was a "family" that grew into the story. They were at the hub and center of all the changing times of their city and their world. Through the three generations of O'Malleys, my aim was to present some of the social and moral questions with which we are confronted today, in the seventies. My hero, Brian O'Malley, is first introduced as a young, inexperienced boy of eighteen, faced with the sudden responsibility of caring for his mother, grandmother, brothers and sisters at the violent death of his policeman-father. The book ends when Brian is a fifty-two-year-old Deputy Chief Inspector in the New York City Police Department, dealing as best he can with forces of corruption, coming to terms with his own policeman son, a Vietnam veteran, trying to live in a rapidly changing and always puzzling world.

One of the most exciting things about writing *Law and Order* was when the characters "took off" on their own. This hasn't happened to me as a writer very often. It is a rare, exciting, heady, exhilarating experience and occurs only when the characters are so well known, so well loved, that they can be trusted to act and react instinctively true to themselves.

The worst moment came when the manuscript was totally completed—all polished and ready to be set in galleys. I experienced the most dreadful sense of loss imaginable. All those warm, exciting, wildly active, strong and familiar people with whom I had shared my life for so long were suddenly taken from me, to be thrust out into the large and critical world.

The solution to this feeling of loss, for me at any rate, was to let a little time go by, enjoy the fruits of my labor, involve myself in other facets of the work, i.e., promotion and publicity—to relax, enjoy, take a deep breath, and begin the whole process all over again.

It must be admitted that no matter how many books I've written, how many characters created and lived with and let go, when I put the blank white paper in my machine, it is no easier for me to begin the written word than it ever has been. Publicity tours and best-seller lists, and book club and movie and TV sales are all very exciting and rewarding and lucrative. However, at the beginning of the day I am a pauper before the blank white paper. The trick is, I guess, just to keep at it from ground zero and to build on it during each session at the machine. Happily, it has started again for me; tentatively, fragilely, hopefully, I've begun a new book. Thankfully.

Since I've always been curious about other writers' work habits,

I will set down some of my own with hopes that my example will warn others to adopt other methods. Sometimes I wonder how in the world I've ever accomplished *any* body of work: I never seem to do all those things I'm positive a writer *should* do.

I've never kept notebooks filled with valuable phrases, impressions, observations. Oh, I've stacks of notebooks of all kinds— spiral ones with businesslike brown covers and spiral ones with pretty flowers on the cover. Somber little black looseleaf notebooks that fit into the palm of my hand and large ones that fill up my lap. They are all filled with empty pages, because I've never really known what to put in them. Once or twice, I've jotted down phrases which I conjured in the middle of the night, or en route somewhere on the subway, but somehow that never seemed pertinent to anything, and I spent too much time wondering what in the world I had in mind when I wrote them down in the first place. There are also pencil sketches of advertisements and some interesting doodles, not one of which is helpful.

A long time ago, I came to a strange conclusion relative to me and note-taking. Mysteriously, it has worked for me, but I do not recommend it to anyone else, merely report on it. If the thought, impression, idea, phrase, situation, or whatever is important enough for me to remember and use somewhere in my writing, I will retain it in cell x-y-or-z of my brain. If it isn't worth using, I will forget it. I don't remember how many flashing, brilliant thoughts might have been retained had they been jotted down. I do know that many conversations between characters in my stories give me a strong sense of *déjà vu*, because they were carried on in my head at some unconnected time in the past.

Another thing I don't do and feel I should: I don't have any work schedule. I mean, *I don't have any work schedule at all*. For a person who spent so many years in a structured work-situation, this leaves much room for feelings of guilt. I know I *should* sit at the machine and accomplish at least *that* much work each day, but I don't. I frankly don't know *when* I work. Sometimes, I leap out of bed at six in the morning, jump into my clothes, gulp my cup of tea and hammer out scene after scene after scene. Then, for days at a time, I avoid the top floor, which is where I work. At about three in the afternoon, the urge might hit again, and I hammer away at the next scene. I will point out that no matter how remiss I am about regulating my work schedule, at least this much is structured: I work a scene through, beginning to end, whether it runs for four pages or forty, whether it takes twenty-three minutes or six hours. Maybe it's those six-hour binges that get the job done for me.

In between actually sitting and pounding the keys, the story does go on inside my head, regardless of what else I am, physically, doing. I rake the leaves, play with the dogs, feed the cats, forget to defrost the supper, stare at daytime television (which is a horrible admission, I realize). The saving grace is that the story process continues, sometimes in some subterranean, unknown manner, because solutions to story problems sometimes take place when least expected. For example: in the shower, riding in a car at night, folding laundry, dusting the furniture, painting a wall.

When I'm well into a manuscript—in fact, during all stages of the manuscript—I rarely if ever rewrite. Probably because I wait so long before actually sitting down to the task, forming sentences in the air before I form them on paper, by the time I actually *do* sit down to work (whenever that is!), the phrases are ready and generally come out the way I want them to. Not always, but more often than not.

Generally, I am amazed at the way the pages of a manuscript pile up, given a particular period of time, because although I complain continuously about working too hard, when it's all over, I have very little remembrance of having worked *at all*.

Given one magic wish as a writer, I would want to be gifted with some kind of power to transform the scene in my head immediately into a bound, printed form without the ever-present struggle to find the words to frame and form the thought. My constant struggle as a writer is to zero in on the exact words that will enable my reader to see, feel, experience a particular scene with as much concern and intensity as I experience while visualizing and writing it.

I don't know what advice to offer young writers. I'm not even sure anyone should presume to offer any advice beyond that one tormenting, beautiful, obvious, obscure, demanding, torturous ecstasy: WRITE. Don't talk about it, whine about it, rap about it, agonize over it, dissect, analyze, study or anything else: Just do it. WRITE.

16

TOUCHING THE HEART OF YOUR READER

By Catherine Cookson

IF YOU have it in mind to enter this trade of writing there are one or two precautions you must take. You must first of all make up your mind to turn deaf ears to all those well-wishers who tell you that the markets are swamped already and that there isn't a hope in hell for newcomers; or that—take their word for it—there's no money in this game. Far better settle for a steady wage and pension.

Then, they will warn you that if you are foolhardy enough to want to suffer and you send your efforts to one of "those" agents, he'll take ten per cent of any advance royalties you are likely to receive. But, if you should ever manage to get into the paperback racket, your hardbound publisher will nab fifty per cent without blinking. And when finally they remind you with relish of what the tax man will take off the remainder, you must smile, just smile, that's all.

Oh, and I mustn't forget to tell you about the frustrated writer who'll inform you that, having received forty rejection slips in one year (and mind you, the stories were first-class; all his family and friends said so), he gave up writing . . . It was either that or suicide.

Finally, finally, steel yourself to look that other dear friend straight in the eye when he casually remarks that without a suitable education, by which he means university, your chance of landing on the literary planet is on a par with that of your being selected to orbit the moon. . . .

Early in my career, one of my manuscripts was returned without a covering letter, but written across the back page in red ink were the words: "Strongly advise author not to take up writing as a career." I cried my eyes out and stopped writing for a fortnight.

Then I said to myself, "What do they know? They have never lived in the northeast of England; they don't know that when I was a girl I was surrounded by famous characters. Why, there was a famous character in every house in our street." At that time, most of these characters would have been on the dole, and all the cupboards very often bare, but yet, for me, every household held a famous character.

Then there were the tragedies that occurred in each house, and the humor that helped to overcome them; and the neighborliness, and the spite and vindictiveness, and the narrowness, and the bigotry. But above all, there was the hope—the hope that something would turn up; the hope that, come the New Year, things would be brighter; the hope that their babies would never have to experience the same hardships they did, the hope that one in the family might even go to "college," better still, go to America and make his fortune.

I left the northeast of England when I was twenty-two. I took only one suitcase with me, but a great deal of mental luggage. Into my subconscious, I had packed all those important people. And there they stayed until I was forty years old, when my world exploded in a breakdown and out they poured, and their emergence wiped off the map all the refined, gentlemanly characters on whom I had wasted years.

In my early twenties when I was striving to educate myself, I had taken for my mentor Lord Chesterfield, through his *Letters to his Son,* and naturally he influenced my writing. This was a big mistake, for what knowledge, real knowledge, had I of 18th century ladies and gentlemen, so called? It wasn't until I realized that I had brought with me from my early environment all the material I would ever need for my stories that I wrote my first novel—and real story, and so came into my own.

There are clever people who can read a bit of history, look up a few maps, then write a knowledgeable story around the data. But there is so often something lacking in such writing. If you want to touch the heart of a reader, and I think this should be the aim of the writer, then write about the kind of people you know from the inside, whether your acquaintance with them was in the slums, in the middle class, or in a stately home, because then, and only then, will you get heart into your work. And that is what the reader wants, that is what holds the reader, that is what makes one reader say to another those beautiful words: "I couldn't put it down."

Some writers bamboozle you with highfalutin screed, as do some reviewers with their reviews on what they consider the writer intended to convey, and in the main what they both succeed in doing is to irritate the reader. It is what I call ego-writing, for both writer and reviewer have enjoyed expressing themselves.

Until you have tried it, you will not believe that the simplest language is the hardest to write.

After all, what are we writing about? Mostly two things, a male and a female, and how they react on each other in their set environment. It is my belief that it isn't the human being acting on the environment that makes the story; it is the environment acting on the human being.

Take a man and a woman into an operating room and cut them up. Whether they be black, brown, or yellow, apart from slight differences in height and breadth or because of deformities, the bone structure, the muscle pattern, the brain size of all males will be similar, and so will those of the females. Now go back in time and take two males, identical twins. Separate them, sending one to be reared in the slums of a big city, the other into the well-ordered routine and luxury of a mansion set in an estate. Jump twenty years, then look them up. One has had all the opportunities in life, the other none. All right, the very fact of his having the background of the slums might be the urge for him to strive to get out of it and to do something with his life. Here, heredity might be playing a part, telling him that he's a misfit; yet, should he achieve success, say become a millionaire, as has happened, will he be able to forget his early environment? No, never.

This early environment is the most important thing in a man's life. No matter what happens in the after years, this sticks with him. He may be able to obliterate it for a while, but as the years mount up it will return, until, in his old age, sitting in his mansion, he is back mentally in the slums.

Equally, the other twin, although brought up in luxury, might just as conceivably be ending his days in poverty; or, if we don't want to fall as low as that, in mediocre living. And with time to think. What is he thinking about? Again, mostly of his early environment.

To my mind it is the environment that is the important factor in the story. Set your environment, and the characters will fit into it.

In the course of writing each book—after some initial uneasiness —I have a feeling of deep involvement, deep excitement. And always this:

Every character in the story becomes real to me; there they all are, moving about in my head, and if I show one acting out of character in relation to his environment, he rebels. Just before I finish the book, I get worked up, tense, wondering how it is going to turn out. Will others see it as I see it?

At one time, I used to think that what I was about to produce was, if not unique, then entirely original. I imagined that nobody else could have thought up such a plot, such experiences, such characters, but in writing subsequent novels, I learned my mistake. I know now that very likely at the precise moment I get this brilliant idea for a new story, there are perhaps a dozen other writers thinking along the same lines.

This was proved to me some years ago when I thought I would write a story about a dustman, a South Shields dustman. I wrote my novel, and the week it was published so was another book about another dustman. The only difference was that my dustman was inarticulate, while the other was a man who could discourse on theories of this, that, and the other. And yet both stories grew from a similar idea.

I no longer worry that this kind of thing will happen, for I have learned that it is how one deals with the idea that counts. The beginnings may be very much alike, but the development and final form of each novel are different.

There was another thing I had to come to grips with, and that was being dubbed a regional novelist. When this term was first applied to me, I didn't like it. It was no consolation to know that Hardy, Bennett, and others had the same tag. I thought, I can write about any place I put my mind to—just give me the idea, and I'll be away. I was proved wrong, and it happened in this way.

I was coming down the High Street when I was accosted by a lady. I had never seen her before, nor have I seen her since, but she came at me, finger pointing, and in what would be called a stage duchess voice she said, "Mrs. Cookson, the regional novelist! Ha! I've read your books, but I've been made to wonder why you must always write about the northeast of England. Can't you write about any other place? You reside in Hastings—can't you write a story about this town? There are so many wonderful things that have happened here. There was the discovery of the caves, the smugglers, not forgetting 1066. Can't you write about any other place but the northeast?"

It's funny how you can come to hate somebody in two minutes dead flat.

Nevertheless, I determined to show that lady. . . . I would write a story about Hastings, and I would center it around the fishing fleet. And so I did my homework, and one day I started my story on Hastings. Six months later I stopped writing my book on Hastings because I knew, I knew that the only thing in that story that had any guts was the fish.

It was then I recognized that what they said was true: Like it or not, I was a regional writer.

I have written over fifty books and have acquired a certain technique. I have learned, and I'm still learning my craft, but I don't think I would have got as far as this had I not done a brave thing, in fact the only consciously brave thing I've done in my life.

It concerns my second novel. This book took a year to write in longhand, and the publisher accepted it, but in his letter to me he said these words: "It isn't as good as your first, but we'll do the best we can with it for you."

The best they could with it for me!

I sat down and did some hard thinking. I was forty-two years of age. I had arrived where I was under my own steam, I knew no one in the literary world—still don't; the only help I'd ever had had been from my husband. This sentence of the publishers had a touch of condescension about it: they were going to do the best they could for something of an inferior quality which I had landed them with. Well, was I going to let it go through?"

In blood I wrote to them, saying, "Send it back."

And again I cried my eyes out.

But from then on I determined that each book I wrote—and I

was going to write dozens, God sparing me—must in some way be an improvement on the one before, whether it be in construction, humor, the portrayal of reality, or, I should like to add, homespun philosophy.

I don't mind admitting now that I have eight similar rejects up in the attic; three the result of my having fallen between two stools. This can happen when you are also writing under a pseudonym, as I have done. The work I do under my own name I consider novels, as opposed to the romances I do under my pseudonym, Catherine Marchant.

I'm often asked, "How do you write? Have you set times? How do you get your plots? What sparks off the first idea?" Well, as to how I write, I now dictate my stories onto tape. This came about after I developed a frozen shoulder, caused through years of scribbling every spare minute of the day, and often far into the night. I have never had a set time for writing, and I am of the firm belief that writers, especially beginners, should make a practice of writing some part of every day, if it's only one sentence.

The germ of a story is often dug up from my subconscious. My mind is like an incubator; everything I've put into it has hatched. A small incident that happened in my youth might reveal itself, but clothed now in the slumbered growth of years; and here I will have the nucleus of another story.

One thing I am no good at, and that is doing a synopsis. If I were to show an editor a synopsis of any story of mine, I'm sure he would say there was nothing in it. And so I rarely write down anything, except names, ages, and dates. When I have gathered all the characters together, I take them to the pictures. This can happen in the middle of the night, when I see everything in film form. I play all the parts, I talk all the dialogue. By the time I get the characters onto the tape, the story line may have changed somewhat but the substance is there. My Catherine Cookson stories develop from environment and character, not from plot. Not so my Catherine Marchant romances.

I like to get down a story while it is, as I call it, hot, everything vibrating inside me. I sometimes sit for as long as six to eight hours at the tape, stopping only for coffee or a snack. As the tapes are finished, my secretary takes them down in the rough.

The telling of the story is pleasure; what follows is grind. I might go through the rough, correcting it, four times before it again goes to my secretary. When she finally brings it back to me, pure and unsullied, I let it lie for a few days, and then I start on it again. If I have to alter more than two or three words on a page, I have that page retyped. And at this stage I can return as many as a hundred pages. I know that a clean script won't help a bad story, but I've heard of untidy scripts causing editors to overlook a good one.

Have I said anything that might be of help to a new writer? I don't know. All I know is if you want to write, you'll write.

17

WRITING FROM RESEARCH

By David Westheimer

For many years, George Williams, a professor of English at Rice University, would tell his student writers, "Write about what you know."

I was one of those students thirty-seven years ago, and I still think his advice was excellent, certainly for beginning writers. A new writer has enough problems grappling with a project as large as a novel, without suffering the labor and insecurity of working with unfamiliar material. It is so much simpler to draw the material from your own background and ideas and concentrate on getting your characters developed and your story told.

But, if you have a theme so compelling to you that you simply must develop it in a novel, and that theme requires research, then research you must. If Margaret Mitchell had been put off by the amount of research necessary to do a book set in the Civil War era, we would not have *Gone with the Wind*.

Even if you are writing about what you know, it may still require a certain amount of research. My first novel, *Summer on the Water*, was set in an area I knew well, the little bayshore communities not far from Houston, Texas. But I realized I did not know enough about this setting to capture it fully in fiction. I went to some of the places I thought I knew well to refresh my memory. I looked at things through the eyes of a prospective novelist rather than of a casual visitor and discovered much that was significant in the light of fiction but which I had overlooked when I was visiting for recreation. This was research in every sense, even though this setting was one I had known since childhood. (I even looked at the area from the air, but how many fledgling writers have a brother-in-law who is a licensed private pilot and will take them up for nothing?)

You're writing something based on your own youth or childhood and set right in your own hometown, and what do you need with research? Can you really remember what was on the corner of Travis and Lamar fifteen or twenty years ago, or what an ice cream cone or a pair of Keds cost then, or what the hit song was in July of a certain year? Such little details may be useful to your story, and you'll have to look them up somewhere. That's research. If you haven't realized such little details are useful, think about it now. Ordinary facts such as those can contribute a strong sense of place and time and often react with the personal recollections of the reader to enhance the effect of your narrative.

I've mentioned two major disadvantages of writing from research —the amount of work and time involved and the insecurity of dealing with unfamiliar material. There are also advantages: You broaden your range of subject matter, you have the use of material with which to enrich your narrative, and you engage your reader's interest in what you have to say apart from, and in addition to, the story you're telling. You learn things from your research, and your reader learns them from your novel—the reader unaware and painlessly so if you use your material correctly.

Where do you find research materials? The most accessible and, unless you live in a small town, richest source is usually the public library. It has shelf after shelf of books all indexed by subject, one of which may be yours. It has encyclopedias and reference works, bound magazines and journals, often files of major newspapers. When you do research from a book, be sure to check the bibliography. It almost invariably will lead you to other works on your subject or related ones. Do not overlook the periodical files. Periodicals publish a lot of material that never finds its way into hardcovers. Periodicals, too, have subject-matter indexes.

If you live in a university town, get to know its school library. On some subjects a university library may have better research sources than the public library. If non-students are not permitted access to the stacks, it is likely you may be able to get a library card by paying a small annual fee.

Newspaper files are invaluable sources of the details of daily life and of history in the making. If the library does not have bound files of back issues, your local paper should at least have its own files. The repository of a newspaper's files was once called the morgue. Now I think it's called the library. By either name, it is usually open to the average citizen and almost certainly to a writer doing research. Just tell the librarian who you are and why you want to use the files, and you'll have no problem. Nowadays the back issues are generally on microfilm. The library will have a microfilm reader. If you don't know how to operate the machine, the librarian will show you. Never, never clip anything from a paper's bound files.

The Library of Congress and the National Archives in Washington have, of course, an immense range of books, photographs, and documents. You can get a certain amount of information by mail, including some microfilm or page copies, but really to dig into their resources, it's better to go there.

You can get information on a lot of different subjects from government agencies. Some of it is free. Some pamphlets and brochures may require a small fee. You can get long lists of available publications, including expensive hardcover books, from the Government Printing Office, Washington, D.C. 20402. Or you can write a specific department of government, say Defense, Interior or Agriculture, for information in their purview.

You can get information from industry. Want to know how an oil refinery operates? Write the public relations department of any major oil company. If you're persuasive enough and/or they're on the ball enough, you'll get an answer. This is generally true of any firm large enough to employ a public relations staff or have a company library.

There's information to be had from your local government and business firms, as well. The Chamber of Commerce is often a good place to begin a search for information. The local police department and crime lab can fill you in on crime and punishment; someone in the mayor's office can tell you how a city is run or where to find out exactly what happens after a fire alarm goes off.

People are an inexhaustible source of information. People with special knowledge, such as college professors, old-timers or your family doctor, or people in trades who can tell you how to repair or sabotage a truck, build a house or dig a well. (I made extensive use of truckers and mechanics in research for my last novel, *The Olmec Head.*) Don't be afraid to ask. They can only say no but will usually say yes when they learn you're writing a book. For *The Olmec Head,* among the many things I learned from truckers were fuel consumption, fuel capacities, load limits, cruising speeds, descriptions of equipment, truckers' jargon. A dispatcher who helped me told me that the load I was hauling would put the gross weight over the Texas limit of 78,000 pounds if transported by the usual tractor-trailer rig. But, he added, if I used a "ragtop" trailer, it would get the weight down below the maximum allowed. So I used that little detail in the novel: "That means our rig can't weigh more than thirty thousand pounds empty," Bell said. "The people renting it to you can tell you the weight. Get a ragtop trailer. That's one with a fabric cover instead of a solid top. It's lighter." (*The Olmec Head,* p. 235.)

As the above demonstrates, some informants may get involved in your project and volunteer information you did not have enough knowledge of the subject to ask about. (The mechanic who told me what could cause a diesel truck to run poorly without actually stopping it, later told me after reading the book I could have done a much better job than I did in switching a heavy load from one truck to another.)

As for researching a physical setting, the best thing to do is visit the area, study it, take pictures to use later to refresh your memory. If you can't get there, you'll have to read about it. For foreign locations, travel agencies, tourist bureaus and consulates can usually provide illustrated brochures. I used a lot of such materials for areas of Italy I did not know in writing *Von Ryan's Express.* One of the travel brochures I got from the Italian consulate mentioned the fact that a spire in Modena was visible for many miles. In the novel, the train bearing Colonel Ryan and his fellow POWs was approaching Modena at dawn. This is how I used that bit of seemingly insignificant information in the book. Ryan had to finish killing off the German guards before they reached the next town. He was not sure just when that would be. And then, "Far up ahead a slender column glistened like a white thread dangling from the rim of the sky." Ryan now knew they were getting close to Modena.

How much research do you do? For something based on your own background, probably not much. Just enough to confirm your recollections or to provide information you could not have known about. That big fire downtown was in 1953, not 1954. The President of the United States came to your town in 1948, but you didn't know that because at the time you were too young to be aware of it. Or one of your characters works in a bottling plant. You've never been in a bottling plant. Now is the time to visit one.

For work, based chiefly on research, a historical novel, for example, or a story about prospecting for gold in Brazil when you haven't even any gold in your teeth and have never been farther than the county seat, of course you must do a whole lot of research. Just remember to steep yourself in it, not drown yourself. Some writers get so involved in their subject that they research endlessly and never do get around to writing the book. Or they wear themselves out with the research and haven't the energy or will to do any writing. Either way, the book never gets written. Also, there is a tendency to continue the research beyond the point where you have enough material, simply because you feel too insecure about actually writing the book. You have to start writing, insecurities and all. If you find you don't know enough about your subject after all and were right to feel insecure, call a brief halt to your writing and do some more research. Now, however, you may find you know exactly what information you lack and can go directly to a source instead of following a lot of blind trails.

Never let research become an excuse not to sit down and write instead of a means to an end. I know "writers" who are not only unpublished but also unwritten because of that.

When you've got all this research material, how do you use it? *Sparingly.* Don't give your reader gobs of undigested information, or even crumbs of facts, merely for the sake of using something you're pleased with yourself for having learned. Your research material should enhance the narrative, or make it move, or make it more real, or reveal something about your characters and their times or life styles. Often a few significant details will suffice to establish an entire era or place or way of life.

By selecting your details carefully you can avoid bogging your story down and telling your reader more than he wants to know, and you can still create the illusion that you know everything worth knowing about your subject.

I once read an otherwise good novel about a World War II bomber pilot by a man who knew nothing of pilots or bombers except what he had learned from research. Which was a great deal—and which he found it necessary to share. He told everything he had learned about how to run through the checklist, start the engines, taxi, take off and get into formation. And it was dull, dull, dull, stopping his story in its tracks. A writer more discriminating in his use of research material would have mentioned only the most significant details of the procedures, those the reader might be expected to find interesting, and written a much shorter and far more exciting scene.

What I wish to stress is, do not use material just because you know it, or because it was so much trouble to obtain. In writing *Lighter Than a Feather,* a novel about what might have happened if the U.S. had invaded Japan instead of using the atom bomb, I sometimes spent weeks trying to obtain documents I'd heard about, and then when I had them, I realized there was nothing in them worth using in the story. When this happens, there is a tendency to force some of the material into your story just because it was hard to come by. It is a tendency that must be resisted.

Naturally, there was an enormous amount of information I could use in the many U.S. and Japanese documents I amassed in my *Feather* research. Tides and weather conditions in the invasion areas on specific dates, for example, and the location and composition of U.S. and Japanese units, descriptions of U.S. and Japanese tanks and weapons, the training of Japanese civilian "volunteer" forces, the way Japanese soldiers addressed their superiors, what Japanese soldiers ate, why Japanese soldiers did not surrender, how much Japanese soldiers of all ranks were paid. These are but a few samples chosen at random. I used literally thousands of bits of information because *Feather* depended so heavily on research. To sum up:

Try to write about what you know.

If you must write on subjects or backgrounds you don't know, do your homework thoroughly and utilize all available sources.

Don't spend so much time and energy on research that you never get around to writing your novel.

Use your material sparingly; don't smother your reader or your novel with masses of raw information.

Try for the significant detail, the one that will engage the reader's interest, add to your story and give the impression you could say a great deal more on the subject if you wished.

18

HUSH! BETH IS DYING!

By Eva Ibbotson

ONE of the disadvantages of living in England is that American periodicals are expensive and not always easy to come by. Like a good many of my friends, therefore, I chose my dentist not only for his professional skill but for the supply of *New Yorkers* in his waiting room. It was there, a few years ago, that a troublesome premolar brought me face to face with a cartoon that has always stuck in my mind. The drawing is of a typical, middle-class American living room to which a husband returns with his briefcase after the day's work, to be greeted by his wife, one finger to her lips, the other pointing to the sofa where a distraught and disheveled schoolgirl is crouched over a book. The caption is: *"Hush! Beth is dying!"*

And of course one could see it all: The meal to which their red-eyed daughter would presently be dragged, *Little Women* still tucked under her arm, the mother piling an extra helping of tart onto her bereaved offspring's plate, the father a little contemptuous of all this feminine emotion until he recalls the state *he'd* been in when the great bulldog's jaws clamped down on White Fang's throat. . . .

It has always seemed to me that this kind of total, *visceral* involvement with a book, so that at the third, or fourth, or fifth rereading one is as helplessly hooked as ever, is reading's greatest joy, just as to produce it in others is the ultimate reward for every writer.

Natasha preparing for the ball in *War and Peace* so that we know she *has* to meet a man who will love her (and she does, she does!); David Copperfield's crusty, marvelous old aunt getting the better of wicked Mr. Murdstone; D'Artagnan's first great duel in *The Three Musketeers*—all are "Hush! Beth is dying!" moments: all moments when woe betide anyone who calls us too suddenly to meals!

How is it achieved, this sandbagging of the reader for which "identification" is too weak a word? Well, as the above examples show, being a genius helps. Failing that, one can write for children, who if they read at all, read in just this visceral way. For the rest of us . . .

To begin with—and I say this with diffidence because the charges of being priggish and of being obvious can both be leveled at me—I would say that *caring* is the cornerstone. And caring in a particular way, not for your style, your storyline, your markets, but, quite simply, caring for your characters in the way that you care for old and valued friends. I'm not saying that best sellers can't be written cold-bloodedly or with the tongue in the cheek or by feeding data into a computer. There are many such "compendium" books that we read on a plane or a bus, thankful for their technical competence and expertise, and since many people spend a great deal of time on planes and buses, these books have an enormous sale. But they are not books one returns to or rereads when one is ill; they are not books which can change your thinking, as a child's relationship to animals might be changed after reading *Dr. Do-little;* or as a man's attitude to his life's task could be changed after reading Hesse's *Siddhartha* or Kipling's *Kim*. Above all, books-to-read-on-planes are books in which Beth never dies.

If I'm right, if the transmitting of emotion, the infection of the reader with the writer's own aspirations and concerns, is what writing is all about (and Tolstoy, that great and tortured soul, swore that it was so), one must now go on and consider how this is achieved. And here I'm driven to quoting the only experience one can ever reliably assess: one's own.

I took a degree in physiology and went on to Cambridge University to do some (spectacularly unsuccessful) research. It was there, as a postgraduate in my early twenties, that I first began to write—articles, short stories; quite clever, satirical stuff which absolutely no one bought.

Meanwhile, the results of my experiments had become so extraordinary that a kindly ex-serviceman decided he could serve science best by taking me away and marrying me. A year later our daughter was born, and subsequently three sons. During the next ten years I was wholly absorbed in our family life and didn't write a line.

Then we moved to an industrial town in the North of England. I was a little homesick, a little sad, and one day I went up to our attic and wrote a short story, a very simple story about a lonely spinster's longing to adopt a baby, and sent it to a British magazine, *The Lady*. It was immediately accepted. Surprised, I wrote another and sent it to *Woman's Journal*. This, too, was accepted. I never again received a rejection slip, and within a year one of London's leading literary agents had taken me on, and I was selling not only in Europe, but to *McCall's, Ladies' Home Journal, Redbook,* and other leading American magazines.

Why? In those ten years, I had not once practiced my craft, had not kept a notebook with suitable plots, hadn't even *thought* coherently about the problems involved in writing. I had done nothing that millions of women don't do every day of their lives.

And there, of course, is the answer. Marriage, motherhood, shortage of money, of leisure, of sleep had squarely aligned me with my readers, and if these were mostly women, what was wrong with that?

What's more, I was ready, now, to stand up and be counted: to say that having a baby is glorious, that fidelity in marriage is a tremendous and worthwhile ideal, that ways of loving are as exciting and diverse as ways of killing. In short, I was ready now to write *for* my readers, not *at* them.

Ready . . . but not always able. The caring had come right, but the craftsmanship had to be laboriously learned. And, of course, the more real feeling you allow into your work, the more urgent it is to discipline and shape it. For it is a sad fact that nothing is more embarrassing—and, curiously enough, more boring—to read than an unedited outburst of emotion.

If I go on now to show how my own position as a woman tied to the house by young children, living in a provincial and undistinguished town, actually *helped* me to learn my craft, it is because I have heard so many aspiring writers complain of being "only" a housewife (or "only" a plumber, a schoolteacher, a cook . . .).

Take the business of cutting one's work. Isaak Babel, that superb short story writer, describes somewhere how he cut *two hundred* pages down to seven before he got a story which satisfied him. As everyone knows, in painting, in literature, in music, and, most of all, in life, what to leave out is as important as what to put in. But to know this intellectually is one thing, and to slice out, relentlessly, one's own verbal felicities, one's unique viewpoint, is another. I learned the hard way. By telling stories on busy crossroads, in doctors' waiting rooms, at the hairdresser's—stories of which my children asked always and only one question: "What happened *then?*" "What *next?*" "What did he *do?*"

Because I believe this question is one we do not outgrow as adults, my wastepaper basket is littered with exquisitely-felt descriptions of autumn woods (but they delayed the heroine's encounter with the hero), with *bon mots* about the nature of passion (only they held up the hero's decision to cut and run).

Another thing I learned almost instinctively from my family life was how to *texture* a story. Texturing is rather a mania of mine. It's a thing we do unthinkingly whenever, say, we furnish a room with contrasting materials, with books and bowls of fruit, with silly, personal objects we've picked up on a beach, with mascots and mottoes, posters or a canary in a cage. Yet, many magazine stories are badly undertextured, underfurnished. The heroine is often just a symbol, existing only to encounter the "wrong" man and to end up —or not—by marrying the right one. Untextured, this kind of story is read as a sort of crossword puzzle. Textured, it can draw you into a rich and living world.

For texture I use anything that comes to hand: the preparation of food; the look of a garden; often, and particularly, the profession of the hero or heroine. Here, for example, from a *Redbook* story, is a description of a girl I don't much like. I could say she is a cool, pedantic person, too controlled and calculating for the warmhearted hero. But she is also a zoologist, so I make the same statement through her work:

She sat in her white lab coat, bent over the hepatic portal system of an extremely pickled dogfish, lifting with calm forceps the fragile threads of empty arteries, snipping, unruffled, among clusters of organs as delicate as Lilliputian grapes . . .

Or here, from "The Great Carp Ferdinand," a Christmas story set in old Vienna, is Tante Gerda, viewing in the bathtub in the servants' quarters, the carp, the festive meal for Holy Night, still very much alive (and destined, of course, to remain so!), strongly swimming:

> . . . Bending over the fish, Tante Gerda pondered the sauce. Here, too, was anxiety. Celeriac, yes, lemon, yes, onions, yes; peppercorns, ginger, almonds, walnuts—that went without saying. Grated honeycake, of course, thyme, bay, paprika and dark plum jam. But now her sister, writing from Linz, had suggested *mace*. The idea was new, almost revolutionary. There were the cook's feelings to be considered. And yet . . . even Sacher had not been afraid to vary a trusted recipe.

A use of food to evoke simultaneously character (that of the archetypal, caring housewife) and period (opulent, a little absurd and gone forever).

Or, in the following example, an attempt to texture a locality, in this case a camping site in Italy, which will act as a background and catalyst to the meeting between the hero and the heroine:

> . . . Transistors blared, and from the seething toilet block came sounds of dedicated nasal hygiene as a party of Greek fishmongers sniffed, rinsed, spat—and rinsed again. Rows of vastly unprovocative Flemish knickers were strung between mimosa trees; two massive Serbo-Croats were cutting their toenails into the sinks for washing up.

Quicker, and more fun than saying it was a rather squalid but basically friendly place with an international clientele, and so on.

This brings me to another point. The avoidance of *categories*. The stories I've just described were "romantic," but I also tried to make them funny, because in my life, as in most other people's, romance and humor, suspense and hilarity, fear and elation have always tumbled round together. And again we turn to the giants. What is more romantic than Mr. Darcy's courtship of Elizabeth or what is funnier than Mr. Collins' toadying to Lady Catherine de Bourgh in *Pride and Prejudice?* Is *The Cherry Orchard* a comedy, as Chekhov swore, or the tragedy that Stanislavski made of it?

Along with the avoidance of categories, I learned to spread my concern and involvement over *all* the characters. (Where would a mother be, say, who identified with only one of her children?) Of course, a story picks out a character, a hero or a heroine, and keeps his or her theme central. This theme is the melody—but even the simplest melody needs orchestrating. If Pip is the hero of *Great Expectations*, where would we be without Miss Havisham? Raskolnikov, that guilt-ridden forerunner of today's Searching Man, may be the central character of *Crime and Punishment*, but every room in every tenement house in Dostoievsky's St. Petersburg is filled with people into whose lives we can instantly enter.

To achieve this extended involvement in a short story takes skill. Not only every paragraph, but every sentence must carry meaning, texture, and emotion simultaneously—difficult but it can be done. Take my *Ladies' Home Journal* story, "The Heart That Was Tender." The heroine was a girl called Kirstie, whose mystical and life-preserving viewpoint plays havoc with the staff of the Agricultural College she has entered. Her love story with her young professor is, of course, central. But while I wrote it, I cared as much —and I hope the reader did—for the lab steward found reading *The Little Flowers of St. Theresa* in the prep room, and for the vet, unable—after she has told him that the Buddha gave up sex at thirty—to inject his failing bull. I cared for the botanist, driven demented by her assertion that his experimental turnip could feel pain. I cared for the turnip, too, respiring in its tank of CO_2. You *can* care for a respiring turnip, even in four thousand words!

And lastly, the characters themselves. Well, here once more I learned from my very ordinary life as wife, mother, and friend. I found that the people who moved me, that I loved, were never the very successful ones, the Beautiful People, the accomplished, or the rich. So my heroines are always a little flawed, a little inclined to be victims. Kate, a small, frail cellist in an opera orchestra, who suffers from unbearable migraines every time a vast soprano thumps to her "death" on the boards above her head; Maya, a defecting Russian ballet dancer, who turns out, nevertheless, not to be a very *good* ballet dancer; Flossie (the Honorable Flora Mac-Coquetdale), bankrupt and bra-less heiress to a Scottish castle which she "rents" to a rich American, only to find that she hasn't

read the small print, and he's pulling it down to ship back home.
. . . Those are the kinds of girls with which, nowadays, I involve
myself.

My heroes, too. . . . Like the men I know, like my own husband, they are obsessed by their work, by the state of the world,
by the demands of their often rather absurd hobbies: The head-
master of a slum school, tormented by longing for a new set of flush
toilets for his children; a zoologist driven to despair by the impending extinction of the Arabian oryx; a young scholar in a silent
library overcome by desire for a vinegar-flavored potato crisp. . . .

And the children—well, I didn't have very far to look there: Lin-
net, in "The Classroom of the Falling Teeth," desperate because
she of all the children in her class hasn't yet lost her first incisors;
ballet-mad Francesca, bilious with ice cream and ecstasy, as the
curtain rises on "Swan Lake"; a fat, blonde baby known as Witherspoon, in "The Gift of Tongues," who, by gurgling to himself,
solves the problems of the passersby he "speaks" to. . . . No, they
weren't my children or the children of my friends; they were themselves. But always, if they came off, they had a seed of something
that had moved me—a gesture, a sentence, some little idiosyncrasy.
You can write about nothing, said Tolstoy, unless you love it—not
even a tree.

And the rewards? Well, surely, somewhere in some unknown
room, a warning hand held up and—"Hush! Beth is dying!"

19

A STORYTELLER'S CREED

By Frank G. Slaughter

SINCE the Stone Age, storytellers have occupied a favorite niche in the affections of the people. Cave drawings in Spain show that even without a written language some men sought to portray events through pictures at least thirty thousand years ago. And one of the oldest written documents in the world, the Epic of Gilgamesh, is an exciting and revealing historical novel. If storytelling has fallen into disfavor in modern times, as the rise in nonfiction sales seems to indicate, the cause lies not in a fickle reading public, but in a deterioration of the product—a crime that can be laid to the door of television more than to any other source.

Like medicine, storytelling is both a science and an art. The techniques can be learned; the sources of ideas can be defined; the methods of their development can be set down in words; sales gimmicks have been devised by enterprising authors and publishers whereby even an inferior product can be made to catch on with the reading public. And yet, unless a storyteller possesses the same vivid imagination that made the *jongleur* of old welcome at the nobles' table—though "below the salt," it was true—sustained success is impossible.

Creative imagination is a gift that cannot, I believe, be acquired, though it can be stimulated by various psychological techniques. Being a gift, it places an obligation upon the owner to be sincere, whether he is writing a play for television, a suspense-novelette for *Cosmopolitan,* or a serious novel of the present or the past. Long ago in my own career as a weaver of tales, I formulated a personal creed which I have always followed. With the purchaser of a book that bears my name, I make an unwritten contract guaranteeing him: (1) A story that is interesting and exciting from start to finish; (2) an authentic historical and cultural background, whether the time is today, the Civil War, or 4,000 B.C.; (3) a minimum of my own personal philosophy.

I am by profession a storyteller, a literal, if not lineal, descendant of the first cave man who came home from the hunt empty-handed and had the imagination to weave a tale about the "one that got away." Luckily, this prehistoric ancestor of mine found others so enthralled by his story that they willingly contributed to his larder. His next discovery was that if his tales were exciting enough, he didn't have to go out to hunt any more but could stay home and entertain the women. Just that, in fact, is largely what those of us who are sometimes called "popular" novelists do today, since by far the greater number of our readers are on the distaff side.

But entertaining the women, pleasant and sometimes profitable though it may be, is not without its responsibilities. Women are quick to detect an implausibility. They read more and, with an intuitive instinct for getting their money's worth, demand a product that gives it to them. More important, women are essentially romantic—and thereby hangs one important key to success as an author. All romance and no plot makes pretty dull reading, after the first "heart-stopping" embrace has been described; conversely, all plot and no romance drives women readers away, and sends the author back to teaching school, writing newspaper stories or—in my case—the practice of surgery. The trick is to achieve a balance of the two ingredients, not always an easy task.

In lectures, I often describe a successful story as "exciting things happening to interesting people under colorful circumstances." Excitement implies anticipation and doubt concerning the outcome of a particular situation, in itself a definition of suspense, the essential ingredient of plot and the *sine qua non* of the storyteller's art. For unless the reader is vitally concerned with the fate of the story people, his attention wanders, and failure results. Makers of old-time movie serials carried this principle to its ultimate conclusion —absurdity; producers of daytime soap opera use a somewhat more sophisticated approach, with enormous success in terms of the looking and listening public. The successful novelist must emulate their principles but on a much higher level of quality. Nevertheless, he can also learn much from their methods.

It is a far cry from the soap opera hero and his vicissitudes to the struggles of young Oliver Twist, but the principle involved, as far as storytelling is concerned, is the same—exciting things happening to interesting people.

Moving from the ridiculous to the sublime, let us look for a moment at *To Kill A Mockingbird,* by Harper Lee. Ostensibly, this is a rambling story of a little girl, her family and friends, in the day-to-day life of a small southern town. But from the very first scene, a succession of events is set in motion, an excitement of suspense is generated, which is only resolved in the final scenes of the story. In other, less truly artistic, hands the same plot might have resulted in a polemic, one of the most difficult of all novels to write successfully because the author usually lets his personal feelings turn the story into a rostrum from which to expound them. Without the discipline of a definable plot, Miss Lee also might have wandered into fruitless byways of description and personal experience. That she did none of these is the mark of highly practical, yet nonetheless inspired, literary artistry.

It is not happenstance that many promising new writers founder and go down into obscurity after a widely-hailed first novel. Such stories are almost always autobiographical and, told with feeling and understanding, the transition from childhood to adulthood is inherently exciting. Not only is this true because the chronological pattern forms a natural plot, but because, having walked the same paths, the reader finds a natural suspense and interest in the writer's personal experience. But having once written their own stories, many young writers find themselves at sea. Not having taken the time and the trouble to learn their trade, they lack the techniques necessary to unblock imagination, to cement down the cornerstone of a plot, and build a structure upon it complete to the final shingle of the cupola. Here, I think, is the point that, to use a colloquialism, "separates the men from the boys." My personal creed, my contract with the reader, would not be binding, if I did not guarantee to him an exciting story.

Two decades ago, historical novels were all the vogue. Almost any hackneyed plot, with a sketchy historical background and an equally sketchy costume adorning the heroine on the jacket, could be sure of book club acceptance and a substantial sale. The result was predictable: a flood of inferior stories. In spite of the declining sales of most historical novels, I continue to write them because the challenge of creating a broad tapestry of an ancient era is exciting and rewarding to me. These novels take roughly twice as long to write as a story of medicine today, much of it spent in patient research, but I welcome each new expedition into the past as an adventure in learning.

After twenty years in medical practice and study, medical backgrounds pose few problems, but the task of recreating the vast panoply of the Roman Empire in the first years of the Christian Era, as seen through the eyes of a Greek physician named Luke, required six months of study before a word was written and another year of continuing research during the writing. Even more challenging was the problem of picturing faithfully the Middle East of 854 B.C., when the Assyrian invader was halted in an obscure battle at a place called Karkar in the valley of the Orontes River, and Israel was saved from destruction for nearly two centuries.

The cliché that "history is stranger than fiction" is far more truth than truism. And historical characters are often much deeper and more complex than any novelist would depict them in fiction. There was a day when a writer with an interesting fictional situation might deliberately lay it against an historical background to increase sales. But with the decline in popularity of the run-of-the-mine historical story, such a device frankly isn't worth the trouble any more. The better historical novels spring from history itself, as witness Mary Renault's fascinating picture of ancient Crete in *The King Must Die,* and many others.

All this means that a successful historical novelist today must be at least as much student as he is writer, a constant searcher through the past for colorful and exciting situations and people. What is more, in plotting his story, he is duty bound to remain as nearly as possible within the limits of historical truth, since he is dealing with what I consider to be a true art form in which sincerity and accuracy of portrayal are vitally necessary. Usually this requires an intensive use of the creative imagination, which can be exhausting and often very frustrating, yet tremendously rewarding. An equally interesting by-product is the privilege of associating in the close intimacy of a biographer with some of the most interesting people the world has ever known. All of which, of course, is part of the second clause of my contract with the reader, assuring him that the historical and cultural background of my story will be as accurate as I can make it by drawing upon my own large library, as well as the finest university and other collections in the country.

The final clause of my creed is, to my mind, the least important, since I consider myself a storyteller and not a philosophical novelist. Every novel has a theme, it is true; without it, the lack of sincerity in a story is immediately apparent. But in a professionally produced product, the theme is inherent in the actions and speeches—preferably short—of the characters, not in the sermons and fulminations of the author. As a physician with many years of experience, I could not have failed to develop some understanding of human nature; the only place where people let their hair down more often than a doctor's office is in a beauty parlor. But as a student of history and people through the ages, I can see little change in the basic facts of human nature, or human relationships and ambitions. Like the ancient Greek philosophers, I am sure most men basically desire to live decent, honorable lives. And the only sermon I ever preach to a reader, in as few words as possible, is one preached long ago: *"A new commandment I give unto you, That ye love one another, as I have loved you."*

20

THE FINE ART OF
EAVESDROPPING

By The Gordons

For many years now, we've been eavesdropping. It's a part of our work, a very profitable part, to hear what people around us are saying. We've trained our ears so that unconsciously they scan with radar swiftness the surrounding area at a party. If anything interesting turns up, the built-in recorder in our brain takes over.

Our best dialogue has come from our eavesdropping. There was that time at the Hollywood Bowl when a row of teen-agers sat behind us. Now, we have no teen-agers of our own. We wish we did, a whole pack of them. Our friends who do tell us we would commit suicide. But we wouldn't because they would be making us so much money. We'd have tape recorders going all over the house.

This night they were chattering away like mad. Not rock-and-roll dialogue but spontaneous talk that crackled like a string of firecrackers going off. We don't know what the attraction was in the Bowl that night. We were too busy jotting down snatches of conversation that eventually found their way into the talk of the Hayley Mills character in *Undercover Cat*, the novel that became the Disney movie, *That Darn Cat*.

"*. . . I'm going in and tell Mr. Hopkins he's simply, absolutely got to give me another home room teacher, and if he doesn't I'm going to try tears. I'm going to cry my heart out. . . . You're learning, Babs, you're learning fast. . . . That school does everything except put numbers on our backs. . . . Isn't she the most? Don't you like her an awful lot? . . . Did you see that movie with John Davidson? I think he's a living doll. My pulse was going 150 a minute. I get these crushes on people I don't know and never will. . . .*"

These are the bits of conversation that we used. But in getting them we discarded pages of dialogue that we wrote down that night.

Much of it was repetitious. Virtually all talk is. Much of it was inane, and only amusing because the person talking made it so.

Shortly after we took up eavesdropping, we discovered how boring a conversation can be when set down verbatim—and how exciting it can be after having been edited. So we turned city editor, searching for those words and phrases that would characterize someone, that would bring him alive. Soon we realized that no dialogue we manufactured could compare with edited, condensed, highlighted conversation, both heard and overheard.

"I was so mad. The next morning I told him, why didn't you tell me? I pulled him in, that's what he needs. It was terrible but damn it, he doesn't have to fix her tire. He's got plenty to do here at home. She could've called the auto club but she talks him soft and he does what she wants."

We overheard that one-way conversation while waiting for a phone at a market. There were five minutes more of the same. We kept only the first paragraph. Funny, but people usually say all they have to say in a few sentences and then can't turn the record off.

Occasionally, of course, we want to give the impression of a garrulous character without letting her actually ramble on paper, which for us would be devastating. William Faulkner could get by with it but few writers can.

In *Undercover Cat Prowls Again,* the sequel to *Undercover Cat,* a young couple catch a snoopy old woman next door spying on them from behind a hedge. She says, "What a turn you gave me, you did. Didn't know a soul was about. Thought I was all by my lonesome. Oh, Mr. Kelso, good evening. Didn't see you there. My eyesight's failing me. Was to the doctor twice last week and he told me I was no spring chicken, and I'd have to—but I'm glad to see you, Mr. Kelso. Always does my heart good when I see you. . . ."

This is an actual conversation, but when we heard it, the party kept repeating, "What a turn you gave me," and told in detail about her failing eyesight and going to the doctor. If we had put it all down, we would have lost some impatient readers.

Aside from unedited rambling, we resist another hazard in this business of eavesdropping, the temptation to use new slang. Six months from now it may sound as dated as "the cat's meow." This is especially true of high school and college slang. Such expressions as "dig" and "cool it" have become fairly well established, but every year there is a plethora of new words that won't last until fall.

While we scan for unusual words and phrases, we are more interested in how people put them together. Most of us use at best a few hundred basic words, but we have endless ways of stringing them together. In the above conversation, where the woman doesn't want her husband to fix the neighbor's tire, it's the way she shuffles ordinary words around that characterizes her, that makes for interesting dialogue. She could have said, and most of us would, "I told him I didn't think he had any business fixing her tire when there were so many things he had to do at home."

In this tricky matter of dialogue writing, we went through several phases. First, our characters all talked the same—exactly like us. So, of course, the dialogue sounded wonderful—to us. It had such a natural ring! Without question, this is the easiest way of writing conversation, and we're not saying it will ruin your fiction. One very famous novelist writes this kind of talk. Everyone speaks the same: old men, children, suburban housewives. And people buy her books by the millions.

Nevertheless, when a kindly editor eventually tapped us on the shoulder to tell us what we were doing, we decided to reform. We then took to writing dialogue the way we *thought* people talked. Most of it we picked up unconsciously from the movies. And this wasn't always bad. Most of Hollywood's film and television writers work diligently at coming up with good conversation. The only trouble was that it was secondhand by the time we used it. And it sounded like it.

Next we turned to manufacturing the kind of talk that we thought would characterize our people. By this time we were on a characterization kick. Sometimes we were devastatingly clever. You know the kind of dialogue. Now and then you'll hear it on the stage and say, "How'd anybody ever think up all that brilliant conversation?", not realizing, of course, that the playwright has cribbed from George Bernard Shaw and Abe Burrows. This type of chatter may be entertaining, but people just don't talk that way.

Eventually, we discovered there was more conversation floating in the air around us than we could ever use. All we had to do was to jot it down and *edit* it. In our files, which look like magpie nests, and where our two cats love to sleep while we are working, we have pages headed, TEEN-AGE TALK, 80-YEAR-OLD CONVERSATION, BOY-TWELVE, PLUMBER, MURDERER, MEXICAN-AMERICAN, etc. We should hasten to add that the file listed MURDERER was accumulated while covering a trial. We regret that we have no killers among our friends. This necessitates our making long, weary journeys to courtrooms where we sit bored for hours on end waiting for that electrifying moment when a witness or attorney comes alive. Nowhere do you need to edit more than in a courtroom, but the little that is left after the blue-penciling may make the trip worthwhile.

We have found better spots: cafés where we eavesdrop on the people in the next booth, sports events where there's always one character close by giving vent to his feelings, movies during intermission, and neighborhood gatherings in the summer when everyone is more relaxed than at formal parties.

As writers, we owe a great deal to the teen-age and college crowd. They do inject new words into our speech—they and the sports writers and a few others in occupations that seem to call for expressive vocabularies. They keep English a living, vibrant tongue. For the most part these are words that accurately peg a feeling or thought. If it weren't for the teenagers and sports writers and truck drivers and such, English might become a pretty staid, dull language. We get a terrific boot when we hear some youngster come up with a word that hits an emotion or thought right on target, what we call a real *wallop* word.

We find it great sport to eavesdrop. We'll come home from a party and one of us will say to the other, "Did you hear anything?", and the other will say, "Yeah, were you around when So-and-so was telling about getting the parking ticket?" And then one of us will say, "We ought to invite her to dinner some night. She's got a terrific way of putting things."

And then months later, when a book or piece of ours comes out in print, we chortle, "Old Sam said that." Strangely enough, none of our friends has ever recognized any of his own dialogue. And grateful as we are, we don't dare thank them. They might clam up—and put us out of business!

21

BUILDING TENSION IN
THE SHORT STORY

By Joyce Carol Oates

THE most important aspect of writing is characterization—does a character come alive, is he memorable in some way? But the means of disclosing character is also important, for if a story lacks a strong narrative line, an editor or reader might not be patient enough to discover even the most stunning of fictional characters.

Novels are complex matters; the density of interest has to go up and down. Short stories, however, are generally based on one gradual upward swing toward a climax or "epiphany"—moment of recognition. A good chapter in a novel should probably be based on the same rhythmic structure as a short story. The novel, of course, can be leisurely while the average short story must be economical. Certain modern stories are so economical that single words or phrases are used to reveal the story's meaning—for instance, John Collier's "The Chaser," which ends with the words "au revoir" and not "goodbye."

While I think the best kind of contemporary story is much more rich and complex and daring than the Chekhovian-type stories so fashionable a few decades ago, still the writer must be careful to limit the range of his "secondary" material—descriptions, background. If he succeeds in winning the reader's attention by dramatic means, then the more important aspects of his story will be appreciated. We have all written wonderful little stories that are "hidden" somewhere in overlong, awkward, unsatisfactory masses of words.

Here are two examples of short story beginnings, each leading into a different kind of story:

1) "Let me tell you something about the Busbys," the old gentleman said to me. "The Busbys don't wash themselves—not adequately. And especially not as they grow older."

2) Just around the turn, the road was alive. First to assault the eye was a profusion of heads, black-haired, bobbing, and a number of straw hats that looked oddly professional—

The stories following these beginnings are to be found in *Prize Stories 1965: The O. Henry Awards,* edited by Richard Poirier and William Abrahams. The first story, "There," by Peter Taylor, invites the reader to listen in on a confidential, gossipy conversation: the words "Let me tell you" are intriguing enough, but the surprise comes in the second line. And we are introduced to a strange little town, "There," where each family seems to have a peculiar trait all its own—not washing properly, eating too much, narrow-minded complacency—and dying. Peter Taylor, the author of many excellent short stories of a rich, complex type, builds tension in a highly refined manner. We listen in on this old man's monologue, amused by his portraits of people back "there," and gradually we become emotionally involved in the pathos of his love for a girl who belonged to a family with a secret common trait—and then we find out, along with the narrator, that this common trait is dying. The girl has died young; the lover, now an aged man, has married someone else; there is no tragedy here, everything is muted and understated. But the story is unforgettable because Taylor has built so very gradually and unobtrusively the tension that arises out of the girl's impending death. Everything is past tense, but vitally alive.

The second beginning is from a story of mine, "First Views of the Enemy." Beginning with a near-accident, this story relies on tension building up within the main character's mind. A bus carrying migrant fruit pickers has broken down at the roadside, and when a young mother with her child drives by, one of the Mexican children darts in front of the car to frighten her. The tension between the young, American, rather materialistic woman and the socially-marginal people is the theme of this story. The woman arrives home safely, but she carries the image of this "enemy" with her into her expensive home, which now seems to her vulnerable. Her realization that she could lose everything she owns drives her to an orgy of selfishness as she locks things up, closes her drapes, even picks her most beautiful flowers and forces food upon her child. The tension is psychological, not active; the "enemy" does not appear after the first encounter. We see that the true "enemy" is the woman's hysterical selfishness, which she is forcing upon her child also.

Franz Kafka's classic, "The Metamorphosis," begins like this:

As Gregor Samsa awoke one morning from uneasy dreams he found himself transformed in his bed into a gigantic insect.

Incredible, of course. Unbelievable. But Kafka's mild-mannered prose proceeds on as if an event of no great dimensions has taken place. You, the reader, find out about Gregor's metamorphosis at the same time he does. You are surprised, yes, but so is Gregor—a quite ordinary young man, devoted to his family and his work. This surrealistic story is much more "realistic" in its ability to convince emotionally involve than most slick fiction with its easily-reci able people. But Kafka thrives on tension. He builds it from his first sentence on. Kafka is always asking, "What happens next?" and then he asks, "After that, what happens?" Like Simenon, he drives his characters to extremes and tests them. "The Metamorphosis" is beautifully constructed in three sections, each dealing with the tense relationship between the stricken Gregor and his family, until Gregor dies in order to release his loved ones. Tension is achieved on the literal level—what is going to happen to the insect-man?—and on the symbolic level—what will be the outcome of the "love" between members of a family when one of them is mysteriously stricken and is no longer "human"?

These three stories, widely differing in technique, build up tension through an accumulation of detail. If violence erupts in fiction, it should be the outcome of tension; it should not come first, nor should it be accidental. Action stories are of interest to certain audiences, but quality stories usually refine action onto a psychological level. There is "action"—movement—but it takes place in a person's mind or in a conversation. If someone finally kills someone else, it is simply the climax of a rhythmic building of tension that lasts long enough to be convincing but is short enough to be interesting.

Remember that tension created for its own sake is cheap; no one will read your story more than once. The tension is part of your technique but technique is only a means to an end; it is never the end itself. That is why the French "new novel" is so boring—it has no capacity to move us—while older, stormy works like *Wuthering*

Heights (which could only be "camp" to today's *avant-garde*) will be interesting to all imaginable future generations. I think the stress placed today on technique is misleading. A writer should imagine his scenes dramatically, as if they were to take place on the stage. There, empty, wordy passages are found out at once. It isn't "words" or "style" that make a scene, but the content behind the words, and the increase of tension as characters come into conflict with one another. "Words" themselves are relatively unimportant, since there are countless ways of saying the same thing.

A final suggestion: be daring, take on anything. Don't labor over little cameo works in which every word is to be perfect. Technique holds a reader from sentence to sentence, but only content will stay in his mind.

22

THE ONLY WAY TO FLY

By Cecilia Bartholomew

LIFE today is real and earnest, we are told.

Fiction can no longer compete with it, we are told.

But that's not where the trouble lies. Fiction is the only way to treat the real and earnest. Fiction is the only way to fly.

The trouble lies not with fiction, but with the writers of fiction. They are giving us the dull for "the real." They are giving us the boring for "the earnest." The result is fiction that is pompous. Fiction can withstand anything but the pompous.

We *are* living in serious times, in violence, in continuing war, in total destruction, including the destruction of space. All the more reason to create something else. I don't mean escape. I mean the very opposite.

Man has been described (perhaps erroneously) as an animal who has been successful in carrying over from infancy and childhood the ability to play. Play is man's unique contribution. Play is the essence of life. And we have stopped playing. For true play is creative. We have even stopped playing love. What has become of flirting? First, in the fifties there was going steady, which was deadly serious. Then in the sixties came sexual freedom, which ought to be play if anything is, but somehow we have managed to turn it into solemn posture. Play is not something you do to impress. Call that by some other name. Play is indulged in for your own enjoyment. What has become of enjoyment? Total earnestness is death. We have killed joy in work, and we are now working at killing joy in play.

Flirting is dead. Unnoticed, unmourned, it is gone. I am not being frivolous. If one thing more than any other has been responsible for its death, that thing is nudity. It is impossible to flirt in

the nude. The only thing you can in any decency do when nude
is copulate. Everything else is indecent. There is, when all is said
and done, a limit to the number of ways to copulate, as there are
limitations to the body. Copulation is for real and earnest; it produces babies. But there is an endless number of ways to flirt. Flirting is an art. There are no limitations to art. I say, let's restore
art to our lives, and expand our minds. But art requires work.

Today we reject work. We reject the world bequeathed to us,
we have retired from the Establishment, and we turn our backs
to it, in cynicism or in contemplation—take your pick. We wrap
ourselves in the philosophic cloak of aphorism, superbly unaware
that it is as invisible on us as aphorisms generally are, as the
emperor's new clothes. And when we are able to see our nudity, we
flaunt it. We congratulate ourselves that we are, indeed, naked—
saggy-breasted, pot-bellied, varicose-veined, hairy, freckled. As if
to be naked were an accomplishment. As if we created the naked
body. The only thing we can create is the decoration that we put
upon the body. And the bruises.

Appearances count. It is the puritan in our ancestry who denies
appearance, and preaches doom. Doom is death, and of course the
puritan sets his course by death. But appearances count more than
anything else. What doesn't show can be denied. Perhaps it doesn't
even exist. Life *is* serious; anybody who tries to live it knows that.
But we can put any face on it that we choose. "Any face that we
choose." That's the power of fiction! And that's its role. What
makes life livable is suspense. "Anything can happen" is more than
a phrase. Read on and find out.

It is no accident that nudity is given such a large part of the
"scene" today. And it is no accident that the word "scene" has
replaced the other words for here and now, for life. People are
being pushed back into the woodwork. Life is being made as static
as a stage setting. We need less nudity, and more striptease.

"Take it off, take it off" was crude, but it was art. Striptease
partakes of the "and then . . . and then . . ." of story. Striptease
is a becoming, like life. A becoming undressed is no great aim, but
there is effort, and elaboration; and there is play. Even poorly
done, there is movement, there is suspense. At the moment of com-

plete revelation, the lights flash on, and then there is the blackout.
The blackout is very important.

For some, there may be shock in nudity. But shock is short-lived.
Nothing is more fickle than the senses. Whereas true suspense is
as endless and retreating as space, as versatile as the mind of man,
which can provide an endless supply of food for the senses. Familiarity need not breed contempt, but total round-the-clock familiarity will breed boredom. Man needs challenge. He needs the
mysterious, the unknown. He needs the closed door, the veil. Questions are the beginning of creativity. Man does not live by knowledge alone. He needs suspense. "What if?" is a magic key.

In the days of the pulps, the writer was paid by the word. The
longer the story, the bigger the check. Sometimes, at its worst, that
resulted in a thinly spun-out story. At its best, the effort to lengthen
the story by valid complication and motivation developed the writer's craft. There is no substitute for craft. On the television screen
when the camera dawdles over a skyline, or travels slowly from wall
to wall of a room, you can bet that there isn't enough story; but
there could be if the writer knew his craft. I recall a successful
western writer who created a continuing hero who stuttered, and
every time he got stuck on a word (but-but-but-but) the author got
paid four times, not once. This is not to be recommended generally,
but too many stories today leave out the stuttering, and some even
leave out the stutterer.

Curiosity is what separates the members of the animal kingdom
from vegetables. It is an instinct, as basic as survival. Rebecca West
has suggested in one of her books that it is a reflex, built in, as
predictable as the one that makes the foot jump when the knee is
tapped by the doctor's little hammer. When that knee reflex doesn't
work, the man is in a bad way. When the curiosity reflex doesn't
respond, mankind is in a bad way. We are so in earnest today that
we have anesthetized the curiosity instinct. Curiosity is not operating any more in space: science is. What can be known, must be
known, Oppenheimer said in the fifties. And the mind thrills to that.
But let's keep a few unknowns to be curious about. We know more
about the moon now, but where has the wonder gone?

Laurence van der Post, writing about the bushman in the interior
of Africa, relates that this nomadic prehistoric people, depending

upon the rains for survival, will share even water with the en-countered stranger; but what they will not share until the stranger becomes the friend, are their stories. They know the value of the "and then . . . and then . . ."

This is a basic rhythm of life. We have discovered (prodded by Marshall McLuhan) that life is simultaneous as well as consecutive, and like children we have seized the new and want to throw away the old. If we throw away the consecutive, we throw away the baby with the bath water.

In stressing the simultaneous to the exclusion of the consecutive, we have made life static. We have turned stories into photographic shots. I would not be surprised to see us go back to the stereopticon. It is no accident that this is a time that has seen the revival of the one-act play. We are reducing art, and we are naïvely delighted with what we have done. Life isn't static. The only thing in life that is static is death. Fiction isn't dying: we are killing it.

Pompous, I said above. We are preachers, mouthing platitudes, clichés, moralities, aphorisms. Every generation has to find its morality for itself, but let's not be self-congratulatory. Let's not reduce art to a proclamation.

Preachers have their role. Cassandras have their role. But neither preachers nor Cassandras are curious. They are sure. The writer's role is a different one: it is to be curious, and to be hopeful.

To prove that today's Establishment relegates old people to the trash can, the play *Endgame* by Samuel Beckett literally upends the old people into a trash can right on stage. And that is called subtlety.

To prove that life is a metaphor for waiting, the same playwright in *Waiting for Godot* asks us to watch his characters on stage wait. Life *is* a metaphor. And there is something noble and ennobling about man's endurance. But not when he stands and waits. Only when he lives as fully as he can. Someone has said that man cannot change his fate, but he can change how he reacts to his fate.

We are all acquainted with the man who yearns to be a writer and never gets around to it, who has a notebook full of good titles, but never writes the stories. That man has bided his time, and now he has us at his mercy. He has found a use for all those titles. He is pawning them off on us, in lieu of the stories themselves.

Are we lazy? Is that all it is? Well, inertia is the last tie between man and the rock from which he came. But man's history has been his efforts to overcome laziness. Inertia is to be overcome. "I think I can. I think I can. IthinkIcan. IthinkIcanIthinkIcan," said the little red engine as it pulled its long load over the mountain.

Disaffection is convenient. It allows you to be self-indulgent, and a Demonstrator at the same time. You can be distinguished, even a martyr, and your lazy inert self. You can get paid, as Hildegarde once sang, for doing what you like best to do. But the non-hero is a contradiction in terms. We have to go back to the hero. And a hero is a man who acts for himself. In life, fate may happen to your advantage, but fate may not happen to the advantage of your hero. What fate has in store for him is bruises.

He must also speak for himself. We are growing so lazy that we cannot even stir ourselves to speak in words. Slogans suffice. The shorter the better. "Love!" "Peace!" You've said it, man, when you've said that. Breathe in on "om," breathe out on "pah." Obscenity, man, that says it. Yeah, right on. But if we are not careful, we are like going to like ruin those four-letter words. They are going, going, gone. They have already become trite, the clichés of today, not tomorrow. The reader is always from Missouri. The man sitting there cross-legged and nude may be wise, but we are not going to believe it until we hear him speak.

We are growing so lazy as writers that we are substituting happenings for art. It began with the development of movie cameras light enough in weight to be hand-carried. You could walk with them; you could even run with them. The faster you run, the lower the cost of the movie. All you have to do is run around with a movie camera in your hand, and you've got a work of art. At first it seemed that we were moving into a marvelous new dimension in moviemaking. But to pretend that anything and everything that the camera picks up is art, or even good enough to show to one's friends, is really giving in to inertia. Someone should have nerve enough to say that the emperor is naked. Beautiful things come out of happenings; boring, meaningless things do also. We are being given self-conscious, self-congratulatory happenings instead of story; we are being given platitudes instead of insight, aphorisms for originality, shock for suspense.

Some congratulations are in order. It is not surprising that the accidental (that is what a happening is) results in the mediocre and the boring. What is surprising is that anything at all results. It proves how instinctive, how basic, is man's urge to form. Prehistoric man drew paintings on his cave walls before he even bothered to make a bowl to eat out of. He had two tools—rocks and flints—and at that point in his development, he had a very sophisticated art.

By its very definition, art is not life. It is a lie, a magnificent lie, that can be truer to our hopes and our destiny than life. A man's eye can learn something from a camera, but it can see deeper than a camera, it can go far beyond the range of the camera's eye. Let's stop trying to be a lens. And let's start the train moving, ourselves, with our own efforts. And with a hero. Under the guise of involving the audience, under the novelty of the new, we are being self-indulgent. Call it something else, if you want it; but don't call it art.

The writer's job is not to quote universal truths, but to flesh them out with individuality. The art is in the clothes, in the elaboration of character. What is happening in fiction is the melting down of individuality into types; and worse, into archetypes. Yes, we are an earnest, humorless, moral generation. There is no paradox in the juxtaposition of morality and nakedness. These times breed men who do not see themselves in the variety of their clothes, but naked. These times breed bigots.

A good play about old age would say not a word about trash cans, and certainly there would be no trash cans on stage. But the audience leaving the theater would be compelled to say, in horror, or in amusement, if they could speak at all under the impact, "Why, they might as well dump all the old people into the trash can." That is truly involving the audience. All you can say coming out after a morality play is smothered in a yawn.

A good play about the meaning of life would not forget that life is to be lived. We must make life (and art) a way, not a wait.

Leave the moral, the aphorisms, yes and the profanity to the reader. A reader has no responsibility to be creative. He can be dull. He doesn't have to find the right word. We will accept swearing from him. Even the essayist may preach. But not the storyteller. The fiction method is by implication.

It is time for writers to shift back to entertainment. Entertainment is not solely frivolity, though, God help us, there is nothing wrong with frivolity either. But entertainment is a worthy aim. It will help us get through our lives. Growing pompous on the one hand, or retreating into inertia on the other hand, will only make the waiting long.

Put the story back into fiction. Put the conventions back into art, or new conventions, but there must be conventions, there must be something for the artist to work against. There must be opposition before there can be growth. Before there can be a work of art.

Put the hero back. I trust him. If he is given the slightest chance, I am confident that he will prove himself interesting, worth reading about. He will prove himself a man who can play, who can think, who can act, who can create. Anyway, he will try. Bruised and shaken, he will get on his feet. Laughable, weak, scared, ridiculous, he will be in there fighting, living.

Fiction is the only way to fly.

23

THE NEW MYSTERY

By Joseph Hansen

THE way to write a mystery novel is to have a dead character and an assortment of living characters who might have killed him. That's all there is to it. No form is simpler. Nothing is easier to write. But from the evidence nothing is harder to write well. For every good mystery there are twenty bad ones.

What is usually wrong with the bad ones is that they aren't life-like. Even those not wholly bad are likely to be lifelike only up to the solution of the crime. Then the writer betrays his book by asking the reader to accept an impossible killer. Why does this happen? Why do writers, some of them professionals with long lists of titles to their credit, so often wind their books up lamely?

Because you can't give the reader the strongest suspect and not disappoint him. You have to give him a suspect he didn't suspect. It's a basic rule, the heartbeat of the classic mystery form. But failure to do so is also what wrecks so many mysteries.

There's no reason this should be so. Every suspect ought to be strong. Naturally, motive one or two may be more urgent than motive three. But if each motive is legitimate and is ingrained in the character whom it drives, then there can't be any letdown for the reader when the killer with motive three turns out to be the guilty one. So why is it that this is where most mysteries fall down?

Because the writer has put plot before people. Yes, the plot of a mystery has to be strong. But this means only that the characters must be even stronger. Both must be true to life. But any plot is likely to be tidier than life. If it weren't, we wouldn't read it. Characters, on the other hand, needn't be tidy; if they are to seem real, they won't be tidy.

With real people in a strong plot, a detective story can become more than that—it can become a real novel. The need for story is as basic to humans as the need for love. Most straight novelists these days forget this. But most detective story writers make as bad a mistake—they forget that story isn't everything.

My most nagging fear as a writer is that my readers will be bored. That's the best reason I can give for writing mysteries. Like every writer of fiction, I'm interested in people and the way they interact, the way they cope with life and with each other, with birth and death, hunger and fear, love and lust, rage and cowardice and courage, logic and impulse, money and the lack of money. And the thousand ills that flesh is heir to.

And in the novel with the strongest story line—the detective novel—I see the chance to deal with these things and still keep the reader turning the pages to find out what's going to happen next, how it's all going to turn out. Whodunit is a device I use to keep the reader's eyes fixed on the words and what I mean by the words.

In the case of my novel, *Death Claims,* I wanted to say some things about how in our society a catastrophic illness can take away everything a man possesses, about how the collapse of an industry can set a craftsman adrift without any way to make a living, about how the needs of an ailing wife can turn a scrupulous scholar to forgery, and how drug addiction can drive a formerly decent man to blackmail and theft. And in that book, as in the one that proceded it, *Fadeout,* I wanted to talk about the homosexual, how he manages or fails to manage in a society that treats his existence as, at best, a sick joke.

To look without flinching at real problems, hard problems, is as much the right of the mystery writer as of the writer of books without killings and clues. Readers of mysteries are for the most part brainy people. They like puzzles with substance. Poor mysteries fail them because in poor mysteries the characters are mere functions. The writer's purpose isn't large enough or near enough to life. The mystery that is also a good novel is peopled by men and women, not functions.

And men and women are restless, dissatisfied with themselves and others, are lonely sometimes and sometimes wish for loneliness. They lose and regret their losses. They hope and as they age know their hopes to be futile. They spend themselves unwisely, make mistakes, drink too much, waste time, speak too soon, judge too harshly; they grieve and suffer pain. Put such people in a mystery and it will transcend its plot, however crafty.

Such people have weight and shape and meaning. The writer using them will avoid the weakness of which the detective novel in general is rightly accused—of having nothing to say, of being trivial, a waste of time. When the reader of a mystery filled with people who seem real to him closes the book, he ought to say and feel, "That's sad." Because murder among real people is sad.

It involves—not just police officers and pathologists, judges, lawyers and juries, but mothers and fathers, husbands and wives, lovers, sisters, brothers, friends, children, business associates. It involves the end not just of a life but of the part the dead one played in countless lives.

If the mystery is to be a real novel, then the end has to be as much question as answer. Because this is the function of real literature—to ask questions. A novel is usually bad and unreal to the extent that it offers solutions. Life is never so simple as in slick fiction. Life is much more apt to be a hopeless tangle as in *The Brothers Karamazov*—which is not only one of the best novels ever written but is a mystery novel.

That the mystery novel has to climax with a solution to the murder is true. But that this solves anything in the larger human sense for the characters involved, if those characters are written faithful to life, is untrue. A sudden death by violence and the sudden end of the road for the killer—these alike will breed more problems than they solve. And the reader will come away from the book with a sharpened awareness of human frailty and vulnerability.

He's less apt to do this if the characters are from a world too remote from his own. If the writer picks characters out of the familiar life most of us are trying and failing to live from day to day —those "lives of quiet desperation" of which Thoreau spoke—then I think his book has a chance. Yes, the beautiful people suffer. The rich, as Hemingway said to Fitzgerald, are different from the rest of us only in that they have more money. And, I suppose, the poor in that they have less. But extremes are shaky ground for realistic fiction. The danger is of writing—to paraphrase Rust Hills' definition of the difference between bad and good fiction—daydreams instead of nightmares.

In *Death Claims,* my insurance investigator protagonist comments to a friend, "Repeated encounters with nice, normal, everyday people who kill each other for money can wear a man down after a couple of decades." And I think that's central—a man or woman dead, who could have been a man or woman we know, and killed by someone who turns out to be not only true to his own character in that last desperate gesture, but also could be someone we know. So that the tragedy is not only the dead's and his executioner's but ours, in that we shared their lives.

If as much truth, clear-eyed, steadfast and loving, can be brought to the characters in the mystery as in the novel without crime, then maybe the mystery can move out of its literary ghetto. There was a time when all novels were popular novels—the time of Dickens, Thackeray, George Eliot, best sellers, all of them. Then, at the turn of the century came the concept of the literary novel, lifting away from the common reader. It's a false and pernicious distinction. There are only two kinds of novel—the good and the bad.

But there is no reason except failure of nerve and imagination why the detective novel, the mystery novel, can't join, in far larger numbers than those already there, the ranks of the good. There is every reason, I think, for the young writer today who wants a future outside university libraries and reviews in literary quarterlies to try writing mysteries. It's a chance to say what you honestly feel about the human predicament and still hold your reader with a compelling plot.

There are added advantages. Out of twenty-odd-thousand new hardcover titles published in the U.S. every year, only a scant three hundred are whodunits—and the bulk of these are written overseas, mostly in Britain. There is room on publishers' lists for more mysteries. There is a steady, year-in-and-year-out public for this kind of book. The pay is not fantastic but it is decent if what you write is above average. And beyond the hardcover, which may sell only three or four thousand copies, is the paperback sale that generally follows a first-rate hardcover, and sales overseas where they are hungry for good thrillers, *romans policiers, Detektivgeschichten.*

But your greatest satisfaction will, of course, come from reaching readers with your vision of the world, your insights into what human beings and the life they live are all about.

24

REALISM IN MODERN GOTHICS

By Susan Howatch

WHEN my first novel, *The Dark Shore,* was classified as a Gothic I was surprised, not only because at that time, 1965, I had no idea what a modern Gothic novel was, but also because even when I found out, it was at first difficult for me to think of my story from that angle.

In my view, *The Dark Shore* was a whodunit featuring a troubled man drawn back into a past he thought he had buried at his former home in Cornwall. However, in the view of the editor who bought the manuscript, it was also a romantic mystery story about a girl in distress at a sinister house by the sea—instant gothic, as I can see over ten years later! I mention these different views both to prove that there can be two ways of looking at the same story and to illustrate my personal approach to this type of novel: When considering plotting, I aim for the mystery of the whodunit; when considering characterization, I aim for credibility, which in Gothics means paying special attention to the hero; and when considering setting, I want more than just scenic glamor; I need a location which is integral to the story from the point of view of plot as well as atmosphere.

This personal approach of mine can be summed up very simply: I want realism. A contradiction in terms for a Gothic? Not at all. I'm telling a story—a tall story, I admit—and in order to tempt the reader to turn the pages, I have to produce a semblance of reality so that the reader can identify with the characters, live their story vicariously and so willingly suspend his disbelief.

This makes characterization the most important ingredient in the story. Unless the characters interest me, I have no desire to plot a story for them; if they do interest me, I find plotting the story easier, because I soon know them well enough to realize what they can, can't, will, or won't do. Plausible characters may not guarantee a plausible plot, but they certainly make its achievement more likely. But what makes a plausible character? It's easy to talk of creating three-dimensional flesh-and-blood characters who are psychologically valid, but what exactly does this mean?

This is where I follow my approach by paying special attention to the hero. By now we must all have met those Gothic heroines who are so maddeningly stupid and foolhardy; but any Gothic aficionado will tell you that a good heroine should be sensible and spunky, although capable in adverse circumstances of being vulnerable and scared—just like the rest of us.

This is reality, someone "the rest of us" can identify with. But what about the leading man of the story? What about our tall, dark, handsome, brooding, mysterious hero? Well, all too often he's exactly that—a cardboard figure without a third dimension to hook him up to reality. Now there's no reason why he can't be tall, dark, and handsome, but what goes on behind that splendid facade? Could he conceivably be a little selfish and egocentric? This possibility may not be consistent with the image of a knight in shining armor, but it is consistent with the facts of the everyday world where beautiful people become accustomed to too much admiration. Does he think about sex? You bet he does, if he's at all normal. Sexiness in the hero is often glossed over in Gothics, and this coy omission may be the one hangover from the classic nineteenth-century Gothic which isn't yet obsolete. But come on! It's not a crime in the 1970s to be sexy, least of all if you're a tall, dark, handsome hero.

For example, in my book *April's Grave*, this is the heroine's first impression of the hero:

"Darling," the friend had screeched to her above the roar of the cocktails, "a wonderful man . . . must meet him . . . English professor—botanical science, darling—devoted to trees . . . so sweet . . ." And Karen had turned, expecting to see a white-haired, stooping scholar, and had come face to face with all six foot of the charm and grace and frank sexual interest which emanated from Neville Bennett.

In other words, he's gorgeous, but he's accustomed to getting his own way with women, and his way isn't all moonlight and roses. Go ahead, Karen, but watch out.

Similarly, there's no reason why the hero can't be brooding and mysterious, but if you want to keep him plausible, you'd better provide an explanation for his withdrawn behavior. In *The Dark Shore*, the hero starts with the burden of loneliness. My opening sentence reads: "Jon was alone," and I emphasize his isolation even though he's in the middle of a vast city. But soon loneliness is the least of his troubles. He receives an anonymous phone call about his dead wife; he wants desperately to see a woman he had been determined not to meet again; his new fiancée chooses the wrong moment to arrive from Canada to see him. He has problems, problems, problems! No wonder he's reserved and enigmatic—or, in standard Gothic terms, brooding and mysterious.

One word of warning: don't be so swept away that you make the hero a complete heel. In an early draft of *April's Grave*, Neville was so self-centered that he became too much of an antihero to be acceptable. To bring him back to life, real life, where no one is either all good or all bad, I had to face up to the fact that it was permissible for him to be racy to a fault only if he had some counterbalancing redeeming feature, and eventually I solved the problem by showing he was capable of loving other people besides himself—particularly his small son.

In addition to the hero and heroine, the minor characters need attention, too. In a mystery story where the characters must form a tight circle, it's important that they contrast with, as well as complement, each other. For example, they should have some variations in age, social type, even nationality. This will make it easier for the reader to distinguish quickly among the characters and turn his attention to the plot.

Plotting is very difficult for me, and this is why I like to write mysteries. So much intricate plotting keeps me in good mental training! Because it's so hard, I never attempt to hatch the whole plot at a single sitting. I do a little, leave it, then return in the hope of achieving a fresh outlook. This process goes on for several days and involves writing several drafts before I produce anything resembling a working outline. However, I always do make an outline for mysteries because I'm no good at carrying all the pieces of the puzzle in my head. I have to see them set down on paper.

The main problem of plotting is how to sustain suspense. You can have your twists and cliff-hangers, of course. That goes without saying. But there can't be too many, or the plot will be overcomplicated. My early drafts of *April's Grave* contained so many twists that I lost sight of the plot, and it was only with the help of several kind people that I finally learned that clarity must come first.

I also learned that one needn't rely on twists in order to sustain suspense. Almost more important are the nuances which accompany the clues, the little innuendoes which make the reader stop and wonder. For example, a solid, dependable character can suddenly be caught for a second in a very different light. In *April's Grave*, Marney, Neville's loyal, reliable but "square" best friend, is glimpsed during a moment of tension as follows:

Marney was drinking steadily, the glass of whiskey never leaving his hand except to be refilled.

But Marney's not a hard drinker. Something's bothering him very badly. Perhaps there's more on his mind than he's admitted . . . and so on. These innuendoes keep the reader's nerves jangling, pave the way for the big twists, and contribute to the gathering momentum of the story.

Meanwhile, the story needs that mystical extra dimension, the setting that will enhance the atmosphere and dovetail with the plot. For me, the setting is like an extra character—real, three-dimensional and with a special part to play in the story. In *April's Grave*, it was crucial that the house in which the action took place couldn't be reached by road. So, changing the names, I used a real location in Scotland where I had once stayed, a crofter's cottage separated from the road by a loch which one had to cross by boat whenever communication was necessary with the outside world. The scenery was magnificent, but the remoteness was unnerving, and I drew on my ambivalent feelings towards the place when I was trying to create a beautiful yet chilling setting for *April's Grave*.

This brings me to the age-old debate: Can one write about places which one has never visited? All I can say is I know it can be done—but not by me. In fact, I don't think I would even want to write about a place before I'd seen it, because I like to make my own translation, as it were, of the scenery and atmosphere and not to have to rely on the impressions of other people. I felt especially strongly about this while I was writing my long novels, *Penmarric* and *Cashelmara,* although as these two are sagas and not Gothic mysteries, they fall outside the scope of this article.

Or do they? I think it was the experience and discipline of writing my mysteries that enabled me to tackle a big project like *Penmarric.* The same principles apply when mixing the ingredients— the meticulous plotting, the three-dimensional people, the meaningful setting, the striving for realism. Perhaps Gothics aren't so different from "straight" novels after all, or perhaps the real truth is that a good story is a good story, no matter whether you call it a Gothic, a saga, or a western. The old phrase which says you can't judge a book by its cover should now be updated to read: "You shouldn't pre-judge a book by its category label." Write on, Gothic writers!

25

MULTIPLY BY TWO

By Doris Betts

IN MY story-writing classes, I can almost predict the content of a first student story. Paragraph one will describe the morning sky, and establish the weather through ten adjectives and adverbs about the condition of that firmament. In paragraph two, we will see the exterior of some building, then pan like a slow camera through an upstairs window and focus on a ringing alarm clock. A hand will reach from under the covers and turn off the jangle. Note that a *hand* will do this. In amateur stories whole human beings rarely function, but disembodied hands, feet, and eyes swarm in midair like insects.

Now a man will get slowly out of bed, and for several long sentences his left foot and then his right foot will carry him into the bathroom where we will have some mention of the "cool tile." As he examines himself in the mirror, the reader will receive his physical appearance plus his full narrated biography, and while *hands* shave his *face*, will be introduced also to his sad memories and sensitive thoughts. By page four, shaven, he will walk to his bedroom window, examine that familiar sky, and will think one profound page, gradually getting around to some dilemma, which will then be explored by flashback. If he happens to own a dog, things get worse. He will explain that dilemma to Fido in lengthy speeches. Fido will wag his tail sympathetically, and so forth.

When I complain to students that nothing is really happening, they are artistically outraged. "Aha! You want me to write pulp plot stories!" To the contrary, my interest is in the literary story which has descended from Chekhov, Joyce, Mansfield, Hemingway, and Katherine Anne Porter. Here, as in *True Confessions*, a story is about meaningful events. Distinctions of "good" and "bad" applied to literary or slick stories are not very useful. It works better to talk about simple or complex stories, in the same way one describes simple or complex biological organisms. The mockingbird, for example, is simply doing more things with life than the amoeba is able to do.

Once that old bugaboo is out of the way, we can direct attention to the material in this typical amateur beginning for a short story. What is taking place? If the reader closes his eyes to visualize events, he will be able to see no more than a turned-off alarm clock and some short whiskers. The writer's clue may lie in the verbs he has chosen to use. In a static, nothing-happening story, these are usually forms of *to be* (he *was*) or weak verbs in which action is either minimal or boring. (He looked, walked, glanced, put, smiled, frowned, thought, remembered, saw, turned, etc.) A character alone, thinking, is not a visualized event, but only a snapshot of a still-featured man lost in thought, raising his eyebrows occasionally. And unless the character is as complex as Hamlet, the writer had better avoid soliloquies.

This is what led us to the dictum for beginning fiction writers: Multiply by two. Start the story with two people on the scene, or bring in a second character before more than five sentences have elapsed. Yes, this produces at first a great many "There-was-a-knock-on-the-door" stories, but at least we are into the area of conflict and interaction, and subtlety will come.

Anyone interested in writing fiction will benefit by reading a book published in the late twenties but still appropriate, *Aspects of the Novel*, by E. M. Forster. Here, Forster points out that there are only five universal human experiences. All men are born, but this is hearsay experience. We do not remember it ourselves, and doctors and mothers must tell us about it secondhand. All men must die, but we have not experienced this yet and can only anticipate its mystery. The corpse has left us no direct testimony. All men sleep about eight hours a day, but although Freud has given us insight into dreaming, there is a limited amount of fiction spent on the act of sleep itself. All men eat about two more hours a day, but how much time in a novel or story is spent on this activity? It is used for social events, for busy scenes, for revelations about families or small communities. This leaves the writer, Forster said, with the fifth universal activity to which men devote the remaining fourteen hours of every day—relationships with other people. So no wonder the writer is tirelessly preoccupied with relations between human beings, through which he may also portray conflicts with self, society, and perhaps God.

Whether students aspire to writing slick, pulp, or literary fiction, we ask them to write dramatic scenes in which two characters will participate. We ask to know where we are—rapidly—and to have some tension exist between these characters. Perhaps one is angry at the other, or wants something, or is trying to get the better of the other. Their dialogue and activity will carry the story forward through an event and an interaction. If a flashback occurs through the viewpoint of one of these characters, it will be "triggered" by something legitimate in the scene—something done or said. None of this gazing at the stormy sky and remembering a sweet day in May twenty years before.

The word "drama" comes from a Greek root which means "doing." Once two people are in a scene, the verbs will begin to "do" something and we can move to the second dictum of short story writing, "Show me, don't tell me." In fiction, interpretation and mood must be sunk below the surface of events, where they will permeate action like a visible stain. A sentence like "Mary was happy," which explains a state of mind, will be revised to "Mary ran laughing up the stairs." The happiness has become implicit in something Mary did, and we have—as our grandfathers used to say—killed two birds with one stone.

The focus on event, as it sinks meaning inside activity, will inevitably shorten stories and make them more dense and compact. Chekhov said in a letter to his brother, "I can speak briefly on long subjects." Never has there been a better definition of what a short story can do. The well-chosen event is, itself, a comment on life. Someone once said the short story writer would do well to adopt as his motto the one used by the Bank of England: *Never explain, never apologize.*

Having two people in a scene brings up automatically other writing techniques such as point of view. So long as the story is rambling along in the author's tone of voice, the author will assume it is focused and unified. After all, this is the way we are accustomed to hearing stories. Somebody relates what happened and nudges us in the ribs to make certain we get the point.

But questions of choice and perspective appear when two characters exist on the same page. Whose story is it? Which of the two is the more important? On whom will the full effect of these events fall? Through which character should the story be told? If Character A is chosen, Character B may not ramble off into his flashback; was the flashback really essential to the story? Is there a third character? What is his relationship to the first two? Like painters, we must decide on a background and foreground, where we will make our picture more vivid and where we will let the less significant recede. As the story is revised and begins to have shape and direction, the writer has a better basis for asking himself the two chief questions used in revising: Do I need it? Does it work? Even if he has written three pages in which his character is taking a long and thoughtful walk in the woods and remembering his old love affair, he may find that the story does not really begin until the character returns to town again and meets his old love with a baby on her hip.

The main value of insisting that a beginning writer "multiply by two," however, is that this alone will help him define for himself what a short story is. It is not the mental experience of a character. It does not take place within a human skull, and attempts to make it do so will only give the reader claustrophobia. One may not begin with a plot and then manufacture characters to act it out; one may create two characters who—by their own natures—will exude disagreements and plots.

Look back at some of the stories in your drawer which were turned down by magazines. How many of them start with a description of the sky? How many make use of dramatic scenes? (The average published short story has five dramatic scenes, in which something takes place *between* characters.) How many of them contain long passages where your main character is all alone, recalling an event which took place before the story actually began?

Multiply by two. Try rewriting the story so the meaningful event takes place—not in the past—but in the story's "now" time, before the reader's eye, with more than one human being on the scene. Often a good idea can be rescued when two characters act it out, and one character stops thinking-it-out.

26

YOU CAN GET THERE FROM HERE

By Eileen Jensen

Writing, like making love, is more fun when you know what you're doing. Editors keep telling me, a working writer, that my short story transitions are good. In looking through my story files to find transitions from my published work to illustrate this article, I was surprised to discover that I was using good transitions ten years ago. I can't brag about it, however, because in the beginning I honestly didn't know what I was doing. What came naturally to the young writer has become conscious craftsmanship. It's a lot more fun now.

What makes a good transition?

A good transition has thrust. It shoves your story forward like a booster rocket tilting a spaceship. Well-timed and carefully triggered, it will put your story into orbit.

Every story has its own pace. Some glide. Others race. A few seem to hop along, grinning. The best transitions are smooth. They do not jar the reader. Transitions, like cosmetics, are most successful when you are unaware of their presence. I believe any intelligent writer can learn to write good, quick, viable transitions. Two things are required: you must pay attention, and you must practice.

For the most part, I use three kinds of transitions in my short stories. I think of them as TIME transitions, ECHO transitions and LEAPFROG transitions.

TIME transitions are the easiest. They also are the most obvious, and you must be careful not to make them dull.

ECHO transitions are more interesting. They link one part of a story to the next part by repeating a certain word or activity or thought on the far side of the transition.

LEAPFROG transitions set up a scene, and skip over it, landing on the next lilypad. This is a tricky transition, but it is lively and interesting and forces your reader to participate in the action.

The TIME transition keeps your reader chronologically oriented. He knows where he is because he has been there before. The story is moving in intervals of time which he understands and relates to. Saturday night means something to everyone. Sunday morning is a different day, indeed. Monday morning? Ouch!

The Time transition becomes art when it is used in a story where time itself (meaning time-passing) is important. Time passes at two levels in such a story. A good example from my own published short stories is "The Loveliest Grapevines in Cleveland" (*Woman's Day*).

This is a story about children growing up in today's migrant culture. I related it through the planting, cultivation, harvest and distillation of one crop of grapes. Time was vital to the story in every way. The family was always moving. It was important to keep track of the ages of the growing children, the number of times the family moved, the length of time it takes a young grapevine to grow and bear fruit, and how long it takes to make wine. Even the passing seasons were important to this particular little story. The children, the grapevines, and the story matured together, going from one transition to the next through time within the story. I planned it that way. The mother in the grapevine story is the star. She's a loving gardener. Susie, the nine-year-old younger daughter, is the narrator. Early on I set the reader to thinking about time:

Last year for Mother's Day, Daddy gave her a riding mower . . .

This mother holds the family together in spite of constant relocation. She does it by cultivating a loving relationship as carefully as she husbands the grapevines. I don't say this in so many words (it's fatal to preach), but I plant the idea in almost every Time transition throughout the story:

When we move to a new house, my mother makes us feel it's home. The first thing she does is plant flowers . . .

I take the time to show the mother doing that. Then—

We've lived in Cleveland for three whole years now. I know Mother cringes at the thought of ever leaving our big old white house on this half-acre . . .

And then I flash back, moving the story backwards with a Time transition.

The week we moved in, an old man in the neighborhood brought us a wooden churn as a housewarming gift . . .

And forward—

She planted a willow whip that first year. It's taller than my sister Lissa now. It casts a shade. Buddha could sit under that tree . . .

The mother plants the grapevines.

The next year they didn't look a whole lot better . . .

The mother teaches her girls about life through the example of the vines.

Suddenly, our willow was taller. Buddha could stand under that tree. Our grapevines, three years old now, began to look great . . .

The harvest is near, and the pace quickens. The skilled writer will go to shorter sentences now. Transitions will speed up.

In June we knew we were going to have a crop . . .
In July robins perched on the trellises and eyed the green fruit . . .
In August, the grapes turned from green to bronze to velvety blue . . .
It was the first Wednesday in September, and school started the next week . . .

They make the wine. They wait two months. They bottle it. Eight bottles.

Mother said we would open it for Christmas. Let's see, if we open one bottle a year at Christmas, it will last until I'm eighteen. That's not bad.

Even at the end, you see, I am pushing the reader ahead of time, pointing him into the future.

That may be the most time-oriented story I ever have written. And yet, my files reveal that as far back as October 1959 *McCall's* published my story, "Some Day He'll Come Along," an equally time-conscious tale. In those days I wrote stories in the way some people play the piano—by ear. I knew when it sounded right. Now, so many years later, I can read music—and even compose a bit.

In "Some Day He'll Come Along," I took a romantic girl from the age of twelve through marriage and childbirth at age twenty-seven. She was searching for the one man she would love. The transitions are similar, if somewhat less skilled, than those in the grapevines story.

During her senior year . . .
It began to look as if she'd have to find him in college . . .
The next day he told her he was going into the army after college . . .
After college, her parents sent her abroad . . .
She was twenty-four when she married Howard . . .
Amy worked hard at being Mrs. Howard Garvin . . .
She began to wear maternity clothes . . .
She was twenty-seven when their child was born . . .

Surely any beginning writer can do as much. Or more.

ECHO transitions are the swift ones, extremely valuable in the short-short story. Take "Seasons of the Heart" (*Good Housekeeping*). It is a time-oriented story—but a short one—and transitions must be lightning quick. The narrative is related through gardening metaphors again. (I'm a gardener, and I am sensitive to the parallels between plant life and human existence.) I chose Echo transitions for sheer speed.

This is a story about Meg, a pretty young widow trying to adjust to the untimely death of her husband. When the story opens, Meg is pregnant. She and her husband Tony buy a small apple tree to plant in the backyard of their new house. They plant it while Diana, the disillusioned divorcée next door, watches cynically. Tony boasts—

"My son will play in the shade of this tree."
"If it lives," Diana says.
The tree lived, but Tony died—killed in a speedboat accident.

The echoing word "live" is the trigger to the quick transition. There is life here—going, coming, snuffed out. The transition is accomplished within the space of six words.

Later in the story as Meg struggles to adjust, Diana ridicules the young widow.

Meg burst into tears.
It was the last time she cried. In January, she brushed up on her shorthand and took a part-time job.

The Echo in the transition is the word "tears" as related to "cried." I doubled the effect in that same paragraph when Meg reveals that she is taking

". . . temporary office work. A Skelly girl. It isn't much money, but you meet such interesting typewriters." She also met men, but they were either married or bachelors with dependent mothers, or ex-wives to whom they owed alimony and child support.

The Echo word is "meet." I take her from her first job through a series of men, and do it with one transitional echoing word.

And note that it's also a LEAPFROG transition as well. Meg meets and passes several men within that one transition.

I leapfrog again in the transition in which she accepts a glamorous date with her sophisticated boss who wines and dines her and invites her up to his apartment to see his stamp collection:

"He didn't even have a stamp!" Meg reported indignantly to Diana the next morning.

The transition is both Echo (stamp) and Leapfrog, because we jump over the seduction scene in the man's apartment. The reader knows exactly how that encounter went. We don't need to document it.

Warning: you must not leapfrog any scene which is out of the ordinary and different from the usual encounter. If it's vital, write it! If it's valuable only in passing, leapfrog it.

You can take giant leaps. Imagine this one:

Debbie lay awake all night, thinking of Jim.
Jim lay awake, too—in another woman's arms.

I recall one of my early stories in which I described a lovers' quarrel which broke up an engaged couple. It took place before a dancing party.

They didn't make it to the altar.
They didn't even make it to the dance.

By now you should recognize and identify the transitional technique in the quarrel. It's both Echo (didn't make it) and Leapfrog (skip the dance scene).

When you are reading, watch for transitions. Learn to identify them. Be conscious of the writer's craftsmanship. When you begin to notice and recognize what is going on, you will begin to use good transitions in your own writing.

27

THE NOVELIST AS VILLAGE IDIOT

By Ursula Zilinsky

Almost as often as they are instructed to double-space their manuscripts on plain white paper, keep their typewriter keys clean, and use a fresh ribbon, beginning writers are told to Write About What You Know. It is good advice, and like all good advice it works better for some people than for others. Since I am one of the others, I would like to give what is generally considered to be very bad advice. Why not write about what you don't know?

It's a walk through a jungle, admittedly. You may get lost. It is even possible you will get eaten alive. But it's a lot more exciting than a walk to the supermarket. And if you get a book out of it, that may be exciting, too.

There are various ways of knowing and not knowing. When a blurb tells me that the author has spent three years working in a Chinese laundry to get the background for his novel, I find that I approach it with great wariness. It will probably be full of fascinating information about detergents and bleach, and just as probably, the characters will be cut from the same cardboard that stiffens the folded shirts.

It is of course possible that the novelist became obsessed with the character of a Chinese laundryman, who gave him no peace until he was put into a book. In that case, there will be very little cardboard, but a live story and live characters, and he could have written it without ever going near a laundry. The people in his head would have told him what he needed to know.

Which is not to say that research is never necessary and accuracy can be sacrificed to fine poetic frenzy. It is, after all, the storyteller's aim to be believed. And if your hero lives in Chicago, where he meets the heroine in Central Park, your credibility is bound to suffer, no matter how convincing your story is otherwise.

(Don't think such obvious mistakes can't happen. When I wrote *Before the Glory Ended* I gave, in a fit of generosity, Munich's prettiest park to Vienna. The mistake survived the copy-editing and galley-correcting both here and in England, and was not noticed until two years later when my Austrian publisher caught it, fortunately before publication in Vienna. It hadn't occurred to me to double-check. After all, Munich is my hometown.)

Gremlins are inordinately fond of writers. So beware!

But the kind of research that calls up dismaying visions of dusty libraries and unappetizing books with crumbling covers and bad print need not bedevil most novelists. Getting together one's background materials can and should be a lot of fun. You are, after all, passionately interested in your characters, and, therefore, in their time, place, and weather. If you're not, why are you writing a novel about them? There are easier ways to drive yourself crazy.

Interest channels the attention; you find what you need, often without consciously looking. For *Before the Glory Ended* I had to know what Budapest had been like before World War I. In a junk shop, where I had gone to try to match the broken lid of a teapot, I came upon a *Harper's Magazine* from the year 1892 with the description of an American tourist's visit to Hungry. I doubt that I would normally have noticed this under its layers of dust, but the word Budapest, at that moment, leaped through the dust into my line of vision. I bought the magazine for five cents. It told me all I needed to know, and it even had a useful street map. The teapot is lidless to this day.

Anyone who is intensely involved with a novel will experience these small gifts of fate with great frequency. It seems hardly fair to call them by the depressing name of research.

Accuracy is necessary, but it cannot substitute for three-dimensional characters and a live story. The flattest, most unconvincing stories are invariably defended by their authors with the claim, "But it happened exactly that way." No doubt it did. But truthfulness of this sort is not a virtue in the fiction writer. Indeed, he may lie like Ananias, so long as he can make me believe him.

A fact is not the same as the truth. Journalists are supposed to ask: Who? What? When? Where? A newspaper will tell you that on March 7, 1848, Delphine Delamare committed suicide at Ry,

France. The novelist must add two more questions to the journalist's four. How? And why? Flaubert will tell you why Emma Bovary swallowed arsenic and how she came to the act. The how and why is the truth of a fact.

And how did Flaubert know what it is like to be Emma Bovary, or indeed any woman? By reading a medical book? By asking his girl friend? He did it by *becoming* Emma Bovary. That too is a way of knowing. Sometimes it is the only way.

How is it done? Easy. It requires one thing only—imagination, which Vladimir Nabokov calls "the muscle of the soul." The village idiot in the old joke found the lost horse by putting himself into the horse's mind and going where a horse would go to get lost.

Like the village idiot and the lost horse, the novelist cannot remain outside his characters and be satisfied merely to ask what it would be like to be such and such a person. The horse will never get found that way. The characters will remain cardboard until the writer is ready to become them.

This can be a frightening, near-schizophrenic experience. Flaubert wrote in a letter to Hyppolite Taine: "When I described the death by poison of Emma Bovary, I had a strong taste of arsenic in my mouth. I was so poisoned myself that I gave myself two attacks of indigestion . . . and vomited my dinner."

Any writer who has ever been that deeply involved with one of his characters will recognize the truth of Flaubert's statement and sympathize. But every reader of *Madame Bovary* will callously feel that she was well worth a bellyache and a lost dinner.

All of this may sound complicated, but much of it will happen—given the initial leap into another place and person (the village idiot's transformation into the lost horse)—without the writer's effort and often without his volition. He becomes the stenographer for his characters. They act, he records. If they don't act, if they have to be forced, stage-managed, put in their place, the writer is being warned that something is wrong. A live character is stubborn, opinionated and exasperating. He will go, but he will not be sent. He will insist on choosing his name and his background; with any luck at all, he will even choose his own story. He will not be commanded.

When I began to write my second novel, *Middle Ground,* both my narrator and my hero dismayed me by electing to be Prussians. For a Bavarian like myself, this was a serious blow. All Bavarian children were taught to regard Prussians as both dangerous and comical—a deadly combination. Would I have to spend however many years it took me to write my novel in the company of two childhood bogies?

Push them as I might, they declined to come South. They agreed to live in Austria for the purposes of my plot, but they resolutely refused to relinquish their accents, their manners, and their blond hair. Once I gave in to them, however, they behaved beautifully. The novel practically wrote itself; I could hardly take dictation fast enough.

I was, incidentally, writing about what I did *not* know with a vengeance, since my hero was a homosexual. What this suburban housewife, mother of two, did not know about the intimate emotions of a crippled, drunk, homosexual Prussian general was considerable. There isn't all that much research one can do, so I had to rely on the village-idiot-lost-horse to help me. It was the only way.

There is a common assumption that the events in a novel must originally have happened in "real" life, and that fictional characters have their "real" counterparts. Many writers do, of course, use real-life events and characters in their novels. For them the advice, "Write about what you know," is so good as to be superfluous. They are the writers psychoanalyst Otto Rank called "classical," the dashing, glamorous adventurers who go off in search of war and sex, and then spend as brief a time as possible at their desks, transforming their experiences into a novel. Not being of their kind, I have always felt that they are the ones who have all the fun.

The second category, called "romantic" (a peculiar designation) by Otto Rank, are the spider-writers, who just sit home and spin it all out of themselves.

To the writer who uses his adventures and companions in his novels, the assumption that they must have real counterparts is no doubt a compliment, showing that he has been able to transfer events and people alive to the page, a difficult feat. But to the spider-novelist the same assumption is peculiarly irritating, indicating that to his readers he appears as an unimaginative clod who couldn't invent a convincing excuse to weasel out of a traffic summons.

Flaubert could say: "There is nothing true in *Madame Bovary*," and yet claim that he was Emma. For though he based the story and characters on the fact of Delphine Delamare's death, he had made them completely his own and had invented a new truth. Not by reporting and copying, not by relating facts, but by becoming, and the transformation of the imagination was the most real (*not* realistic) of modern novels written.

Whether he creates *Madame Bovary* or a story only his long-suffering family will ever read, the symbiotic involvement with his characters is ultimately the stay-at-home writer's greatest reward. It is the one way he has of knowing what cannot otherwise be known, of living other lives. Whether he writes a masterpiece, a best seller or a manuscript for the back of the drawer matters less than this: He has been allowed to experience feelings outside his usual range, has loved and hated people he would never meet, has stayed at home and yet experienced travel and adventure. And that, given the mundane limitations of most people's lives and the unavoidable fact that three-score and ten, give or take a few decades, is all we can count on, is no mean gift.

The village idiot becomes a lost horse. The writer becomes—what? Within the limits of his imagination and daring he can be anyone and own the world.

28

THAT ALL-IMPORTANT REWRITE

By Lois Duncan

A FEW years ago, to my great surprise, I was invited to teach a course in Magazine Writing at the University of New Mexico. I say "surprise"; actually, a better word is "amazement." Not only had I no teaching experience, but I was not a college graduate.

"There's only one way I can approach this," I finally decided. "It must be on the basis of practical experience." Although I was education-poor, I had been writing for magazines since the age of thirteen. I would provide a course that would resemble as closely as possible the situation my students would encounter in the outside world.

When the first set of assignments was turned in, I wrote critical comments on them and handed them back for the first rewrite.

"Rewrite!" a wide-eyed coed gasped in bewilderment. "But you haven't even graded them!"

"How can I grade them," I asked, "when you haven't even finished writing them?"

"*Mine* is finished," she snorted, glancing about at her classmates for support. "A paper doesn't have to be perfect to get a B or a C."

I drew myself up into what I hoped was a professional stance and delivered my first lecture:

"There is no such thing as a B or a C in Magazine Writing. Your article is either salable or it isn't. A halfway good manuscript is as much a failure as one that is completely awful. Neither of them is going to make it in the market."

Well, I've mellowed a bit since that first traumatic semester. I've accepted the fact that there *are* B and C students whose major interest is in some field other than writing, and I grade for effort and attitude as well as production. I now accept papers that come in past deadlines (if a good excuse is offered), I'll take a handwritten first draft from a non-typist, and I've adjusted to the inevitability that no matter with what dignity I begin the term as "Ms. Duncan," I'm going to finish it as "Lois."

The issue I have not given in on is the rewrite. That is too important. My students write their articles—and write them a second time—and a third—and a sixth—and a tenth, if necessary, until both they and I consider them truly salable. Then, like releasing birds for flight, we send them into the market.

And in many cases, they fly! That's the thing that has so far kept me from being tarred and feathered. Class sales, over the past couple of years, have been made to such varied publications as *True, Holiday, Saga, Home Life, Junior Scholastic, The Denver Free Press, Catholic Digest, American Girl, New Mexico Magazine* and *St. Anthony Messenger.* In one semester alone—seventeen students, some of whom had never written before—made over two thousand dollars.

What exactly is a rewrite, and why is it so important?

To begin with, I think it is necessary to rewrite in order to allow the first draft to be spontaneous. Writing habits vary from person to person, but my own technique is to follow a general outline and pound out the first draft of my story at top speed without giving a thought to detail. I compare it to the way an athlete approaches a high jump. There's no time for him to think about being beautiful; the thing he is trying to accomplish is to pick up enough speed to sail over the bar. If he stops to worry about whether his position is graceful and who may be watching from the stands and whether his hair is staying in place, he never gets his feet off the ground.

My first drafts are a mess, and I wouldn't ever want anybody to see one. If, when I die, there should be a first draft lying on my desk (and there probably will be, because there always is), I want it burned unread. All I hope to do with a first draft is to give my story shape and movement. I find this especially necessary when writing at length. With a novel, for instance, it's easy to find yourself with a string of compartment-like chapters, each an entity in itself, instead of one great sweeping whole. By keeping a fast pace without pausing to search for the perfect way of saying things, I find I am better able to achieve a sense of continuity.

There are, of course, successful writers who do not work this way. There are some, I've heard—I can't say that I've ever actually met one—who write with such precision that their original wording cannot be improved upon. Their first copies are their final ones; no rewrites are necessary. Such writers do exist, but I cannot believe that there are many.

In one of my recent classes, there was one particular student who was the bane of my existence. He was also a delight. He was bright, funny, talented and so prolific that stories of all types—mysteries, juveniles, romances, psychological thrillers—came reeling out of his typewriter at the rate of several per week. Then he put them into envelopes and sent them away.

"Here's a copy of my new story," he would say, handing me a carbon. "I wrote it yesterday."

"Where," I would ask him, already sure of the answer, "is the original?"

"On its way to *Playboy*." Then, seeing my expression, he would smile ingratiatingly. "I know you want us to rewrite, but I just don't like to work that way. When I've finished something, I'm through with it. I want to get started on something else."

Which is understandable. But, did it work? Did his stories sell? No, they didn't, and they *should* have. For he had talent and sensitivity and drive, all the elements necessary for a successful professional. But he was releasing his birds with their wings still imperfect, with their tails trailing in long drooping arches behind them and their feathers of uneven lengths. He would not admit that this was the reason they didn't reach the treetops.

"It's the editors," he'd mutter. "They don't even look at the work of newcomers. They have their stable of regulars, and they won't buy from anyone else."

But these regulars were once newcomers. There are people breaking into the top magazines every day. I'd be willing to bet that they're not breaking in with their first drafts.

When my rough draft is finished, I usually stick it away in a drawer for a couple of days until I can read it over objectively. Then I ask myself a list of questions:

Is this story shaped right? Does it build to make its point? Is the hook interesting enough to intrigue the reader? Is there a smooth transition between this hook and the body of the article? Am I making all the points I want to make in the right order? Have I put in excess material that does not contribute? Does my climax come too abruptly so that I need more buildup? Do I wait too long so that my reader is worn out before he reaches it? Do I hit my climax hard enough to make it worth the reader's effort to get there? Do I wind things up neatly so that the reader is left with a feeling of satisfaction?

You may have noticed that I have been using the words "story" and "article" interchangeably. This is because these same questions apply to both fiction and articles. The basics of construction in writing are as constant as the basics in any other kind of creative building. Whether you're making a stabile or a coffee table, you have to get it in balance, or it's going to fall over.

When this rewrite is done, I again give it a rest period. The next time round is the one in which I try to make it beautiful. Now the questions I ask myself concern smoothness and polish:

Are the anecdotes appropriate and well-handled? Is the dialogue natural? Does my story read easily with neither choppy paragraphs nor long unbroken ones? Have I used the best words possible to express my meanings? Have I used a favorite word too often? Am I overworking my adjectives and adverbs? Are there spots where I have been too wordy? Are my sentences grammatically correct and in a style in keeping with the sort of piece I am writing? How is my spelling?

All in all—is this the best, most polished job I am capable of doing? Am I proud of the result? Is there any way that I can improve upon it?

These same questions are the ones I force upon my students. I have a pile of their manuscripts here on my desk now. As I write, I can glance over and see some of the notes I have attached to them:

"Andre—Exciting story, but I feel you've rushed your climax. You work for fifteen pages to get us into the big scene in the ballroom, and then you zip us through it in a page and a half. Can you make it longer and stronger—hit it harder—make it go 'bam!' instead of 'poof'?"

"Stephani—Lovely writing. Almost like poetry. But the girl's dialogue seems stilted to me. Would she really speak that way? Read it aloud to yourself and see what you think."

"Kevin—Incredible! You're the last person in the world I thought would come through with a confession story. You've caught the style well, but I think you need to do something to make your heroine more sympathetic. Can you enlarge your flashback to show more of her last marriage? If your readers understand her better, they'll be able to forgive her sins more easily."

"Jean—You'll have to do some heavy cutting if you're thinking of trying this on *Good Housekeeping*. Their short-shorts run closer to 1200 words than 2500. And do you realize that you've used the word 'very' three times in one paragraph?"

I wish I could say that Magazine Writing is the most popular course the University of New Mexico offers. It isn't, and I know it. There are students who drop it, and I cannot blame them; there are certainly easier ways to pick up three credits. There are some who suffer through it, moaning and grumbling with impatience and frustration.

But there are others, too, people like Tony, a young married veteran, whose twenty hours of classes were supplemented by his job in a supermarket. He turned up in the morning with circles under his eyes, but he never missed a class or a deadline.

At the end of the semester there was a note attached to his final manuscript:

"I want to thank you for forcing me into something I never believed I could achieve—self-discipline. This article is now the best I am able to write."

Two months later he phoned me. I was not at home at the time, but he left a message with my daughter. On its first time out his article had been accepted by *Argosy*.

29

THE WILLING SUSPENSION OF DISBELIEF

By Elizabeth Peters

ALTHOUGH Coleridge coined the useful phrase, "the willing suspension of disbelief," it has been the goal of storytellers since the pre-literate dawn of time and of writers since fiction began. Writers of suspense fiction particularly depend upon this gesture of good will on the part of the reader, but successful achievement of that goal depends upon the writer as well as the reader. Presumably, the reader of thrillers or novels of suspense starts each book in the proper mood of suspended disbelief, but he ·cannot sustain this mood if the author taxes his intelligence too much. How, then, does the writer of suspense fiction create an aura of plausibility which will allow readers to accept his creation, "for the moment," as Coleridge adds?

The so-called Gothic novel is a sub-category of the novel of suspense. In most cases, the term "Gothic" is a misnomer, for the romantic, "damsel-in-distress" thrillers which publishers label "modern Gothics" are not Gothics at all. Their ancestors are not Mrs. Ann Radcliffe's *The Mysteries of Udolpho* or Horace Walpole's *The Castle of Otranto,* but Wilkie Collins' *The Moonstone* and Charlotte Brontë's *Jane Eyre.* The true Gothic novel requires an atmosphere of brooding supernatural horror and a setting that includes ruined castles and desolate moors. I don't consider my books to be true Gothics, but it would be pedantic of me to object to the term, which is certainly more succinct than more accurate designations. I may then be forgiven if I refer henceforth to this form of fiction as "Gothic."

The most important thing for a writer of Gothics to recognize is that the genre is inherently incredible, almost as unlikely as a fantasy novel. Personally, I find it as easy to believe in the green Martians of Barsoom as I do in the adventures of Gothic heroines. Some writers of Gothics seem to feel that because their plots are fantastic, they need not be logical. The converse is true. The more fantastic the plot, the more important are those factors that invite belief, or, at least, the suspension of disbelief.

What are these factors? Some may be seen in the three elements of plot, character and setting.

The pot of a Gothic novel must be tight, consistent, and logical —within the given framework. Like the fantasy novel, which starts with a single fantastic premise, the Gothic begins with what I like to call an "initiating coincidence." The heroine happens to over-hear a conversation between two people who are planning a mur-der; or she happens to accept a job as governess in an isolated household whose inhabitants all suffer from severe neuroses. None of these situations is very likely, but we can admit one such for-tuitous occurrence in order to get our plot moving. From that point on, however—no coincidences, no lucky accidents. If the hero is walking down Main Street at the moment when the heroine, cor-nered by the villain, screams for help, the hero must have a reason for being on Main Street at that vital moment. It will not suffice to explain that he keeps in shape by jogging down Main Street every fine afternoon. If the heroine is to be rescued—and Gothic heroines always are—the rescuer must be brought to the spot by hard work and/or logical deductions.

Plausibility of character is as important as consistency of plot. The two are related, of course. A stupid heroine's foolish behavior can lead to plot complications. Indeed, the plots of the poorer Gothics seem to depend wholly on the heroine's incredible naïveté, as she falls into one pitfall after another. But it is difficult for the reader to identify, or even sympathize, with heroines of such consummate imbecility. Admittedly, Gothic heroines have a pro-pensity for getting into trouble. It is one of the important elements of the Gothic plot, but it can also be one of the great weaknesses of the genre. Critics justifiably jeer at the dim-witted girls who take nocturnal strolls around grim old mansions. If you must get your heroine out of her nice, safe, locked room in the middle of the night, after two murders have already been committed, do give her a good reason for leaving that security. (I cannot think of anything that would induce me to leave my room under those circumstances, except perhaps the voices of my children screaming for help.) Your heroine must have an equally pressing motive. Better yet, have her stay in her room and get into trouble in some less conventional manner. And no mysterious notes asking for a midnight rendezvous in the castle crypt, please. Critics sneer at that one, too. A heroine ought to have sufficient intelligence to check with the hero to make sure he actually sent the note before she ventures into a crypt.

The characters of Gothic novels are not profound or complex; in two-hundred-odd pages we do not have space for such luxuries, since we must spend a good deal of verbiage on plot and atmosphere. But if our characters are cardboard, they need not be absurd. They must not exhibit flagrant personality aberrations, or behave so idiotically that the reader begins to hope they will be murdered in the crypt, as they deserve to be.

Of course, the more fully developed and realistic your characters, the more plausible their actions will seem. One of the classics in the field, Daphne du Maurier's *Rebecca*, has a heroine who has always exasperated me by her timidity and docility; but she is believable, because she behaves in a way that is consistent with her background and her personality.

Atmosphere and setting are particularly important to thrillers of this type, and the same rule applies: the more unusual or exotic the setting, the harder you must work to give it an appearance of authenticity. In these days of jets and travel books, Samarkand is no more exotic than Paris or Rome. But you must make sure that your descriptions of these cities are accurate, and that you include enough details to convince the reader of the reality of the setting in which your heroine's wild adventures are to take place. I do not subscribe to the theory that a writer can write only about things he or she has personally experienced. I have personally visited all the cities and countries I have used in my books; but I could not have written about them without the aid of maps, photographs, and detailed notes taken on the spot. Perhaps a conscientious writer can do this with a city he or she has never seen—but it will require a great deal of work.

The rule holds even when you are inventing a setting. In one of my books, the action takes place in Rothenburg, a small German town I know fairly well, but for various reasons I decided to add an imaginary castle to that city instead of using an existing structure. I did almost as much research on the castle as I did on the city, reading about medieval castles and Franconian architecture, so that the description of my imaginary castle would agree with details of real structures of that period. If your characters do a lot of running around, draw floor plans. Readers love to spot discrepancies, and will write irritated letters if you have your heroine descend a staircase where no staircase can conceivably exist.

One useful trick to make sure that the reader will accept your devices of plot or of setting is to prepare him for them well in advance. A strategically located doorway, through which the hero gains entrance to the conference room—a secret passage whereby your characters can escape when danger threatens—these, and other devices, will seem more plausible if they are mentioned before you actually need them. Again, the more unusual the prop, the more carefully you must explain its presence. A secret passage in a medieval castle needs only a sentence or two of description, since the reader knows that medieval castles abound in such conveniences. A secret passage in a modern split-level house requires considerable explanation—and perhaps a brief character sketch of the eccentric individual who had it built.

Plot props require the same advance preparation. If the heroine's knowledge of Urdu is going to save her from a fate worse than death, or expose the master criminal, you must tell the reader early in the book that she is an expert in this abstruse language. If you do not, she will resemble Superwoman when she comes up with the information. And for pity's sake, if she or the hero is to be an expert in ichthyology or Egyptology, learn something about those subjects before you talk about them. I was once put off an otherwise readable Gothic because it involved a reincarnated Egyptian princess named Cha-cha-boom, or something equally absurd. No reincarnated Egyptian, fake or genuine, would have such a name, and the repetition of the inane syllables grated on me so strongly that I never finished the book. The author could easily have found an authentic ancient Egyptian name in the encyclopedia. I remember another book I never finished reading because the villain, a German sea captain, kept shouting "Grüss Gott!" in frenzied moments. If you do not know that "Grüss Gott" is a friendly greeting in southern Germany, have your villain stick to English.

You may think that few readers have much knowledge of Egyptology or other abstruse subjects. This would be a dangerous assumption. Archaeology is a popular field, and for some odd reason, which I mean to investigate one day, archaeology buffs seem to be especially addicted to thrillers. But that is not the important thing. The important thing is that plausibility depends upon the accumulation of consistent, accurate details. They really do add verisimilitude to an otherwise bald and unconvincing narrative. The reader may not consciously note all your errors; but a series of careless inconsistencies will tax the reader's willingness to accept your imaginary world, and a single glaring error may be enough to snap that fragile thread on which the suspension of disbelief depends.

Of course, you are bound to slip up occasionally, no matter how conscientiously you research your book. As I work through revision after revision, I come across howlers I can't believe I missed the first and second times. To my chagrin, a few of them escape me even in the third and fourth revisions and get into print, despite the additional efforts of my intelligent editors. In one of my books, written under another name, an integral plot prop was an old family Bible. Long after the book was published, a reader wrote to me inquiring how the Bible happened to survive the conflagration that had destroyed the equally ancient family mansion and most of its contents. "I can imagine several possible solutions," she added charitably, "but I do think you ought to have *told* us."

She was absolutely correct. I should have told her. And I would have done so, if I had noticed the discrepancy. However, errors of this sort are not in the same category as careless mistakes or poorly developed characters. An occasional gap in the plot or an error of fact will not be serious if the rest of the plot is as tight as you can make it, and if the other facts have been checked and rechecked.

I could go on, giving examples of the basic rule, but if you read many Gothics, you will spot plenty of other cases, of success and of failure. Of course there are some writers who seem to be able to break all the rules and get away with it. Don't bother writing to tell me about them. I know about them. I only wish I knew how they do it.

30

THE PEOPLE ON YOUR PAGES

By Peggy Simson Curry

PEOPLE! Every editor seeks the pleasure of their company. He wants to know them in the flesh, fully rounded out in dialogue, action, thought, and emotion. On the printed page, as in life itself, people are the most important element. It has always been so. And the task of creating lifelike characters has always been the greatest challenge facing the writer.

Where does one begin to meet this challenge? First, by trusting one's own emotional responses. When characters do not come alive, it is because the writer has not allowed himself to establish emotional identification with them. Trying to crawl inside the skins of his characters, the writer too often takes with him his own sense of restraint, his fear of revealing honest emotions. Emotional impact is the measure of good fiction, and the writer can achieve this only by giving his characters believable emotional responses, filling them with his own feelings.

The second basic thing that the writer must know is that he can't identify with people who do not seem alive to him. He can't transfer his emotions to dummies. The surest way to find believable characters is to take patterns from life. Look at the people you know best—family, friends, acquaintances. Think about people you meet in books, magazines, newspapers. Listen when people talk about an individual who interests them. These real people should suggest fictional people.

If you are hesitant about using real people as patterns, remember that distinguished writers have deliberately used people they have known. Somerset Maugham, James Joyce and Flaubert had no qualms about lifting their characters from life. Louis Bromfield, in a charming book, *Dogs and Other People,* confessed that he used many times a middle-aged woman he knew and liked.

A character can't become real in the writer's mind until that character has a name, the right name, for a name is an intimate identification tag. Carry the names of your main characters in your mind *before* you begin writing, until those names seem to fit real people. Then, try to relate these people to your story idea. Visualize them physically; know them emotionally. What motives drive them? What are their backgrounds? What are their dominant traits, abilities, peculiarities?

Keep your story idea—or plan—loose. This allows your characters to dominate the working out of the plot. The resulting story will grow out of the characters rather than being imposed upon them.

To illustrate these initial steps in creating believable characters *before* you write, let me refer to a story of mine, "Gooseberry Run," published in *Boys' Life*.

Several years ago, the fiction editor of *Boys' Life* asked me to try a Christmas story. I started looking for an idea or angle about Christmas that hadn't been done to death. After some mental sweating, I remembered a small Wyoming town where the school buses had been driven for years by carefully trained high school boys who had achieved a remarkable safety record. The longest bus route was known as Gooseberry Run and covered a vast stretch of prairie to reach the remote ranches.

I had my idea—a bus run. Now I needed my people. Obviously, my main character had to be a boy, around seventeen or eighteen years old. Where did I find him? Thinking about a few teen-age boys I knew, I came up with a composite character based on them, and promptly named him Denny O'Keefe, a slender, sensitive, cautious, responsible teenager, proud to be driving Gooseberry Run.

I then began to think of him in relation to the story idea. What if Denny O'Keefe ran into a blizzard while driving the kids home for Christmas? He would be scared but courageous. I had faith in Denny O'Keefe. However, was the blizzard sufficient obstacle to allow me to realize Denny as a dynamic person? Wouldn't the story be stronger if there were more conflict—perhaps someone on the bus who was against Denny? I would then have two basic struggles to test the strength and ingenuity of characters—man against nature, and man against man.

I searched for a second major character, one who would provide a contrast to Denny O'Keefe. I thought of a devil-may-care, irresponsible but likeable boy I had once known. I transported my long-ago acquaintance into the present, changed the color of his hair and eyes, and named him Billy Martin. The name seemed just right. It sounded bold and breezy and tough.

I began to live intimately with the two teen-age boys, Denny O'Keefe and Billy Martin, thinking of both of them in relation to Gooseberry Run. I liked Billy Martin, ornery though I knew he was, and I wanted the readers to like him. Let him be a thorn in Denny's side; let him complicate that bus trip; let him make a serious mistake. And give him *reasons—motivation—*for his behavior. This would make him more real and understandable. Why didn't Billy like Denny? Because Billy wanted to drive Gooseberry Run, but refused to take the rigid training course. He knew the country by heart. He was no smarty dude who had moved in from California—like Denny O'Keefe.

I didn't know then what serious mistake Billy Martin would make. At this point in my thinking there was a lot I didn't know— and *didn't want to know.* If you decide too much before you write, imagination is fenced in, and your characterization is stale.

For the next two weeks, in my imagination I moved Billy Martin and Denny O'Keefe around in relation to my story idea, and did some research on survival in a blizzard. I also came up with my title, the obvious one: "Gooseberry Run." And in my mind I composed the opening paragraphs, visualizing them as though they were already in print.

When you have composed your opening paragraph or two, either in your mind or on paper, ask yourself the following questions: Is your main character presented in such a way that the reader meets him *alive?* Is he rooted in setting, circumstances and emotion? Is there a hint of trouble, obstacles?

Here are the opening paragraphs of "Gooseberry Run":

Denny O'Keefe waited impatiently in the driver's seat of the small yellow school bus. The sky was low and gray. The air had a strange, damp stillness to it.

Denny worried about driving his bus route . . . a 70-mile road through lonely Wyoming prairie. . . .

In these few words the reader knows what Denny does, the kind of country he must drive over, the condition of the weather, and how Denny feels. The reader also senses something is going to happen—the weather and Denny's state of mind convey this. Action is forecast.

When you have started writing your story, remember that characterization cannot happen in a void. The reader must meet your characters supported by informative detail.

As "Gooseberry Run" goes on, Denny frets about the time it will take him to get the kids home. He has mail sacks, newspapers, and Christmas groceries as well as his passengers to deliver.

Now, with Denny firmly established in the reader's mind, we have reached paragraph four. It is time to bring on the minor characters. I haven't lived with these minor characters or tried to visualize them. If this seems a contradiction to the way I have handled my major characters, I can only share with you the fact that—for me—there is a peculiar and wonderful cumulative effect related to characterization: If you are able to bring alive your major characters, and trust in what they do and feel, the minor characters will literally spring forth in all their splendor when you need them. I have complete faith in this cumulative process of creativity.

Paragraph four:

Now the Three Wise Men came jostling out the front door of the grade-school building. Their purple and yellow and red robes fell from under their heavy coats, trailing color on the snow. They were followed by Mary, splendid in voluminous white, her coat hooked to her shoulders like a cape. She carried a cradle in which the baby-doll Jesus was tucked under a blue blanket. Behind these leading characters of the grade-school pageant came other passengers for Gooseberry Run— a pushing, squealing, laughing group laden with popcorn balls in plastic sacks and Christmas gifts with wrappings carelessly folded around them.

Again note the use of *familiar* as well as *specific* detail to support characterization. I decided, after writing this paragraph, that the four minor characters should be named the Three Wise Men and Mary throughout the story. This blends them into the Christmas background. Whenever character and background can be blended a story is strengthened.

I have now come to paragraph five. I have to introduce Billy Martin, giving him emphasis, for he is my second major character:

Denny's attention shifted to the high-school building. *Where was Billy Martin?* Several times in the last month Billy Martin had deliberately lingered, making Denny late in starting. And there were other methods Billy used to annoy him. Twice he had brought mice on the bus, loosing them as Denny drove along the lonely prairie road, sending the little girls into hysterics. Another time Billy had carried a rattlesnake in his hat. It had taken Denny a while to convince the smallest passenger that the snake was really dead.

To have Denny recall only that Billy heckled him is not enough. Billy has to be shown in specific actions rather than in generality. This makes him real.

A paragraph later, Billy Martin comes on the scene:

. . . Billy Martin sauntered from the high school and moved at a leisurely pace toward the bus. Tall, dark-haired and thick-shouldered, he swung a bright red stocking cap in his hand. . . .

The story develops with mounting tensions. Although the weather forecast has been "mild snow flurries," a storm approaches. Billy informs Denny that Old Shifty, a drifting ranch hand, has predicted a terrible blizzard. Denny grows more uneasy. He knows that people in Gooseberry Run country believe that Old Shifty has strange powers of looking into the future. (Old Shifty came into the story on his own. I didn't expect him, but he served to back up Billy's heckling.)

The blizzard strikes. By then only the Three Wise Men, Mary, Denny and Billy are left on the bus. Denny can't see the road; he stops driving. At this point in the story, I suddenly knew the mistake Billy Martin is going to make. He is going to take the bus away from Denny and drive it.

Billy argues with Denny and knocks him down. The bus starts moving. Billy Martin is at the wheel when moments later the bus plunges off the road and down a steep ravine. No one is seriously hurt but Denny is bitter. He holds Billy responsible for the first accident on Gooseberry Run.

From this time on the boys must work together to save their own lives and the lives of the children. My interview with a veteran country bus driver helped me make the terrifying night on the bus as vivid as possible. We had discussed what items on the bus might help save lives—wrapping paper, Christmas packages, newspapers, a few groceries, Mary's cradle and the spare tire.

The front of the bus, near the heater, could be curtained off, using the robes of the Three Wise Men and items found in the Christmas packages: an electric blanket, a tablecloth and three large bath towels. Lettuce would freeze quickly, but the children could eat apples and oranges during the night.

Why mention all these items of survival? I want to drive home the point that in every story there is a climactic scene where significant detail may enrich characterization, create greater reader identification, and make the scene more vivid. All three add to the climate of reality. Don't trust to guesswork. Take time for research, library or interview, when you need it.

To go back to Billy Martin—his ingenuity and courage supplemented Denny's. It was Billy who entertained Mary and the Three Wise Men with songs and stories, making them forget their fear. And while it was Denny who suggested ripping up bus seats for insulation, it was Billy who forced Denny to run up and down the aisle of the bus to keep from freezing. Allowing Billy to have positive traits as well as negative ones keeps the characterization human, interesting, and believable.

The blizzard stops at daylight. The boys burn the spare tire some distance from the bus, and a search plane locates them by the tall column of black smoke. A rescue party arrives in snowmobiles.

The final paragraphs in their way are as important as the opening ones, and should have some kind of emotional impact, leaving the reader satisfied with this last brief sharing of the lives of the characters.

Denny struggled to speak, to find words to tell everybody how great Billy Martin had been, to say Billy Martin had kept him from freezing to death. He tried to talk about the small brave people, Mary and the Three Wise Men. But he could find no words; it was all too big for words.

Then he looked at Billy Martin. Billy Martin was looking at him, the bold black eyes warm with respect and admiration. "Merry Christmas, Denny," Billy Martin said.

Did a theme emerge from this little story? I think so: *In time of crisis people put aside personal animosities and work together.* It also reveals the great courage and resourcefulness of young people.

Billy Martin and Denny O'Keefe are still very real to me. Occasionally I think fondly of Mary and the Three Wise Men. I endowed them with the emotions I knew best—my own. I designed them from living models and gave them the names that suited them. I lived with them long enough to relate them to my story, believing in them as real people. I introduced them to the reader in specific settings and vivid circumstances. I gave them obstacles to face, to show that their characters would develop. All through the story I supported them with the most specific and carefully selected details I could find.

But always I set them free to live their own story in their own way, within the loose, never-confining idea of what I thought their story might be.

31

BIRTH OF A SAGA

By R. F. Delderfield

Let me make my position clear at the outset. Nobody, in my belief, has ever taught anyone how to write a novel, and nobody ever will. It was therefore with some hesitation that I accepted the Editor's invitation to offer beginners technical advice on the craft, and I might have declined the invitation had he not used a certain noun and prefaced it with a certain adjective, both commonplace words in themselves but somehow inducing second thoughts. The noun was "guidelines." The adjective was "certain" . . . *"Certain guidelines* on the subject of storytelling and story planning. . . . to help beginning writers create a convincing story." The terms of reference were broad. I decided to do an honest, earnest best.

For the benefit of those (almost surely a majority) who have never set eyes on a work of fiction written by me, I admit to dealing mainly in sagas, or three-deckers, as our grandfathers called them. I also admit (very cheerfully) to something else. Weaned on the novels of a century ago, I am cast in an old-fashioned mould—which even American critics who are very kind to me always say in their reviews—and about this I am unrepentant. Hence, I am qualified to give only old-fashioned advice: For what it is worth, here it is.

I do not see the professional writer as a prophet, a sage or a missionary. A majority of novels published since World War Two have little to offer me. The best of them, as I see it, are brilliant fireworks displays. The worst of them are pretentious and boring, shot through with a gloom and defeatism that override any storytelling virtue they might conceivably have possessed had the author sat down and learned his craft before lifting the cover from the typewriter. Some, and these include the dreariest, are deliberate attempts to shock. Others, even those that are plotted, are so larded with misery, suffering, degradation, and self-pity that the unsuspecting reader who picks them up in the hope of being entertained is a man seeking relaxation on a bed of nails.

I like to think that I regard the fiction writer's function more modestly. He is, after all, the lineal descendant of the man who once sang for his supper in a baron's hall, and his main concern should be to interest and entertain. If he also succeeds in making his customers think, then that is a bonus.

Forty years ago, when I was eighteen, a London playwright gave me a laconic piece of advice that I heeded—possibly the only literary advice I ever did heed. He said, glumly, "For God's sake, don't try to please the public! Write what you like and at least you'll please yourself. There is a hundred to one chance you will also please others. By accident." Only now, after getting on for half a century at the game, do I see the wisdom of that remark, and this gives me guideline No. 1: *Unless you feel delirious with excitement over the prospect of telling a story, don't tell it!*

For secondary guidelines I draw on my own experience. Every writer, even every saga writer, approaches his task in an individual way and perhaps mine is slightly more individual than the majority. I invariably begin a three-decker with a map of the kind Stevenson used in *Treasure Island,* for it is essential to me to know not only where I am going but where my characters are going. By this I do not mean north or south but something far more precise.

When I began the three-year stint that resulted in *A Horseman Riding By,* I drew a corner of the English West-country where every river, hill, wood and farm was marked. I then named the farms. It was only when the topography of the Sorrel Valley was starkly clear in my head that I invented characters to live in those farms, and sometime after that when I fixed the span of years the story was to cover, 1902–40.

I went to work in precisely the same way with *The Avenue,* the story of a suburban road outside London, but here I numbered the houses and marked out a dozen as rallying points for the narrative. The story, in this case, covered the period 1919–1947, and I was able, well in advance, to use those rallying points for social aspects of the decades. Thus, No. 22 harboured a militant Socialist, and No. 17 a small-time Fascist. Further along the street, I had other houses I intended to people with jazz musicians, a cinema pianist, a suburban adventuress and a slick tradesman to be earmarked for easy money in the black market period between 1940–45.

And this leads me to another important guideline. In the name of God and Charlie Dickens, *never make a firm plan for your storyline*. In a book of this type, it is absolutely essential to keep the narrative fluid and to let the characters behave as they want to behave and not as you hoped they would behave when you started out.

I can give a good example of the advantage of flexibility. In *Horseman*, I had every intention of allowing the hero, Paul Craddock, to spend his life, and raise a large family, in partnership with Grace, an attractive and very intelligent woman he met the first night he set foot in the Valley. Alas, it was not to be. Grace's temperament made it quite intolerable that she should bury herself alive in a remote rural backwater, and I was obliged, like it or not, to enlist her in the suffragette movement and offer Paul a divorce. In this way, he married Claire, a far more suitable partner for him, and Claire (a walk-on part in the first section of the book) ultimately became its most important female character.

I can give another example. In *The Avenue*, I invented twin brothers, Berni and Boxer, and grew very fond of them, as one does when one spends years in the company of fictitious characters. It was my intention, however, to let Boxer, the lumbering twin, learn to stand on his own feet at the age of about twenty-eight after Berni had been killed at Dieppe in 1942. Five times I tried to bring a mortar shell down on Berni, and five times the page went into the wastepaper basket. In the end, I came to terms with the strength of the bond. I was physically incapable of destroying Berni Carver and compromised by depriving him of an arm. He lived on, a repatriated prisoner-of-war, and played a useful part in the final third of the book.

The reading public are incurably inquisitive about an author's source materials. I rarely give a talk on the subject without being asked, "Do you create characters or do you lift them from life?", so that I have pondered this innocent-seeming question for years.

Now I think I can give an honest answer. Every character I have ever created has not *one* living prototype but any number up to a dozen. In writing the R. A. F. comedy, *Worm's Eye View,* I went so far as to compose a list of the airmen who had contributed to the five major characters. When I toted up, there were nineteen names on the slip.

I ramble on. How are we doing for guidelines? We have so far three vital ones: *enthusiasm, familiarity with background,* and *flexibility.* To sum up, write only of places, themes, and people *capable* of generating excitement in you; get to know the background well in advance; and, above all, let the characters, once created, follow their own inclinations, even if they lead you straight up the gum tree. Suppose we poke about for other guidelines, not so vital, perhaps, but each contributing something material to the strength and structure of the story. Period research, for instance, and a word of warning about that.

Do not imagine that however well researched your saga is you will not be caught by some triumphant smart aleck at least once a chapter. Every day, from all over the world, letters arrive on my desk beginning, "I enjoyed your book immensely, but. . . ." There is always a "but," and many of them make my ears burn. In the first chapter of *Horseman,* for instance, I awarded a C. B. E. to a doctor fifteen years before the honour was initiated here in Britain.

You cannot research every line of a saga. If you did, you would never get it started, let alone finished. Every now and again you have to take chances and make inspired guesses, particularly if you are writing of a period in which you have not lived, but do not let this depress you. You are giving someone somewhere immense satisfaction. *He* knew, and *you* didn't, and if he took the trouble to write, at least he read the book and read it carefully. Research a period, of course, but never let it frighten you. It is far more important to get the *feel* of a period than note down its trivia, and perhaps the best way to do this (and get away with it) is to learn to love your characters as you go along, even those you project as unsympathetic characters. Galsworthy began his *Forsyte Saga* loathing Soames. He ended up by making him the true hero of the series. I found this hard to believe until I worked on Archie Carver and Elaine Frith in *The Avenue,* both greedy, heart-

less people. After 400 pages I found myself warming towards them
in a way I could not begin to do as respects far worthier characters,
so I eventually married them to one another and was cock-a-hoop
one morning when a reader wrote, "I found all the honest people
in that *Avenue* prigs! The book was saved by Archie and Elaine!"

And now discipline as it concerns the writer. How can I throw
out a guideline on this without sounding outrageously priggish myself? For of all the guidelines this, surely, is the mainstay of any
literary creation, especially one running to several hundred pages.
As a professional writer, I think it is essential to work regular
hours, no matter how uninspired you feel when you roll the first
sheet into the typewriter. The reading public have a fixed idea
that most writers sit about waiting for inspiration. Poets may, for
all I know, but saga writers don't. They slog away, six to eight
hours a day, seven days a week and sometimes 365 days a year.
More reflective work comes with revision, and it is a good idea not
to begin revision until you have a pile of manuscript at least
twenty pages thick. There is a great deal of truth in that assertion
that ninety-nine per cent of any creative job is the result of per-
spiration rather than inspiration, and this is not simply a figure
of speech. On the coldest days, after a stint resulting in some
5,000 words, I have been drenched in sweat.

Writing a book, I sometimes think, is rather like preparing a
good, substantial meal, and writing a saga is like cooking a ten-
course banquet. To do it at all, you must, of necessity have a well-
stocked larder, and let me hasten to add that I do not mean to imply
you have to be particularly well-informed or generously endowed
with brains. What you need far more is a retentive memory that
enables you to distill material from the attics of the brain to the
blank page. The professional writer should train himself never to
forget anything but to file it away for future use. Conversations
overheard in a bus or train, an unfamiliar scent, a cloud pattern, a
physical sensation, a trick of expression on the face of a stranger,
the sound of distant thunder—all these things must be hoarded, for
there is not one of them that will not prove useful, and the odd thing
here is that they tend to pop out of the attic filing cabinet the moment they are needed.

The rewards for this back-breaking toil? They are many and

often unlooked for. Financially, if you succeed, it can provide a reasonably good living and, what is more important to the artist, personal independence. Then again, once a book is in print, readers will seek you out by mail from every corner of the globe, and the letters almost always give you a queer satisfaction, for you feel, somehow, that you have contributed something to their lives and have not wasted your time in a back-alley occupation. But the real reward is in the job itself, in the exhilaration of plucking something out of nothing, fashioning it, perfecting it—at least to your own satisfaction—and sending it out into the world to earn its living. In this instance a comment of the British novelist Ernest Raymond comes to mind: he once wrote regarding the craft of fiction, ". . . some of its ways are plenteousness and all its ways are joy." Which returns me to what is, I suppose, the central theme of this piece. *Enjoy your work. For if you don't nobody else will.*

32

STORYTELLING, OLD AND NEW

By Elizabeth Spencer

Being a Southerner, a Mississippian, had a good deal to do, I now believe, with my ever having started to write at all, though I did not have any notion about this at the time it all began. Having had stories read to me and having listened to them being told aloud since I could understand speech, I began quite naturally as soon as I could write to fashion stories of my own. I now can see that my kind of part-country, part-small-town Southerners *believed* in stories and still remain, in my own experience, unique in this regard. They believed, that is, in events and the people concerned in them, both from the near and distant past, and paid attention to getting things straight, a habit which alone can give true dignity to character, for it defeats the snap judgment, the easy answer, the label and the smear. Bible stories, thus, which were heard at home and in church, were taken literally, and though the Greek and Roman myths which were read aloud to me, along with Arthurian legends and many others, were described as "just" stories, the distinction was one I found easy to escape; maybe I did not want to make it. And we heard oral stories, too—Civil War accounts and tragic things, some relating to people we could actually see uptown, almost any day. All ran together in my head at that magic time—I trace any good books I have written, or stories, right back to then.

Starting at the other end of things, however, is what the writer who daily faces the blank sheet must do: that is to say, O.K. about childhood, what about now?

The work of fiction begins for the writer and reader alike, I feel, when the confusing outer show of things can be swept aside, when something happens which gives access to the dangerous secret pulse of life. What is really going on? This is the question that continually tantalizes and excites. For the fiction writer, the way of getting the answer is by telling the story.

Right back to stories. You see how quick it was.

A story is a thing in itself. It has a right to *be* without making any apology about what it means, or how its politics and religion and pedigree and nationality may be labeled. The writer can be guessed at by the stories he puts down, but the writer is not the story any more than an architect is a building. The events in a true—that is to say a real, or honest-to-God—story are a complex of many things, inexhaustibly rich, able to be circled around like a statue or made at a touch to create new patterns like a kaleidoscope. Such a story may be absorbed sensually or pondered about reasonably; it may be talked about by friends or strangers in the presence or the absence of the writer. The story should be allowed to take in all its basic wants. It may want discipline, but it may not get it, depending upon how greedy it is or how obsessed the writer is about it. A story has the curious, twofold quality of seeming all in motion and at times even in upheaval while it is being told, but when finished, of having reached its natural confines and attained repose. Many times characters seem to have life outside the story in which they engage. So much the better; the story will not question this.

Each story I have written commenced in a moment, usually unforeseen, when out of some puzzlement, bewilderment, or wonder, some response to actual happening, my total imagination was drawn up out of itself; a silent magnetism, without my willing it, had taken charge. What was it all about? It is just as well for the writer to pause here and consider. Not that the writer will take the imprint, literally, of people and event—though for some writers the main worry falls here. To me, it is rather the power of the story that one should be warned about: Don't enter that lion's cage without knowing about lions. For the writer enters alone. He may be eaten up, or mauled, or decide to get the hell out of there, but even if all goes splendidly and ends in fine form, the person who comes out is not the same as the one who went in.

Anyone who takes stories as an essential part of life is only recognizing the obvious. Religion, love, psychiatry, families, nations, wars and history have all become deeply mixed up with stories and so find no way to shed them without violating or even destroying their own natures. Every human being is deeply involved with at least one story—his own. (The Southern tendency to get involved with family stories has accounted for the larger part of Southern fiction—if we add to this hunting stories and war stories, then we have just about accounted for all of it.) The present faint-hearted tone which some critics now adopt when discussing the future of fiction is surprising, for stories, being part of the primal nature of human expression, are in one way or another going to continue to be told. What disturbs us all, I believe, is the debasement of the story into something mass-made, machine-tooled, slick and false. (The lion was stuffed or drugged or doctored some way.) At its highest level, a story is a free art form, daring to explore and risk, to claim that it recognizes truth and that even when inventive, what it imagines is, in terms it can splendidly determine, true.

At a level short of this highest fiction, but shared by it, many group stories exist, the bulk of which never get written down. They are told every day, repeated, embellished, continued, or allowed to die, and some are better than others; inventive and factual at once, both commonplace and myth-like, they grow among humanity like mistletoe in oaks. They are much better than average TV fare, and anyone who wants to write should start collecting everyday accounts that are passed about offices, campuses, neighborhoods, or within family situations, noticing whatever there is to be found of humor and terror, character, achievement, failure, triumph, tragedy, irony and delight. The modern theme of self-exploration with heavy emphasis on the private sexual nature and fantasy has been done to the point of weariness. Can we think of ourselves again in communion with others, in communities either small, medium or large, which may be torn apart disasterously or find a common note, an accord? One word for it, maybe, is love.

33

PLOT, PLOT—WHO'S GOT A PLOT?

By Robert L. Fish

It seems to me there are enough occupational hazards to being a professional mystery writer—starvation not being the least—so that some form of protection should be provided against the more non-essential fortuities. Among others, I refer to the interrogations one is forced to face at social gatherings, and which—no matter how they start—inevitably end up taking the form of the query: "Where on *earth* do you *manage* to get your *plots?*"

My main objection to the question, however, is not that it is fatuous, or even that it is invariably a lead-in to a very boring discussion. My objection is that it is a very difficult question to answer, or at least to answer honestly, and cocktail parties are no place for this sort of thing. Where does one get one's plots? Well, about the only positive answer is that one very seldom gets them from questioners at cocktail parties.

A friend of mine gets most of his plot ideas from newspaper stories, usually involving some macabre or outlandish event in some far-off place, preferably with an exotic name. A mine disaster in Chiang Mai, a mass suicide in Cachinal de la Sierra, a ship burning off the coast of Tamantave—one of these is all he needs to begin working out all sorts of dishonorable motives for all sorts of unprincipled people to have brought about the macabre or outlandish event. The major problem he faces is that he sweats blood during the writing of the book in fear that someone else will beat him to press with a book based on the same news event. Actually, this has never happened, since other writers face the same fear. His novels, therefore, are safe, but his constant worry has left him with an ulcer and a tendency to leap at unexpected noises, scarcely recommendations for his method.

We are forced to conclude, therefore, that writers get their ideas from various sources, and that it is impossible to set down any rigid rules for unearthing plots. My own favorite method—and I merely mention it in passing, since it is not the point I wish to make in this article—is to dream up some inexplicable occurrence. For example: A man is murdered for a package which contains nothing but a dead coral snake. A man legally sells diamonds at a price far below what he legally paid for them, and manages a very nice profit as a result. A man absconds from the United States with a briefcase chained to his wrist, supposedly filled with money but actually containing worthless blocks of newsprint. At great expense in time, money and trouble, a man goes into a jungle to destroy a bridge that leads nowhere. Now, having established the illogical nature of the situation, the idea is to proceed to explain it in a manner that not only defends the logic of the seemingly illogical situation, but proves it to be inevitable. Out of the explanation, a book evolves.

But, as I said before, this is not the point I wish to make. The most important thing for beginning writers to recognize is that plot in itself is probably the least important element making up a fictional work. More important by far is characterization—and *most* important, of course, is the ability to write the English language in a manner that makes other people want to read what you've written. Plot alone will never induce anyone to turn a page, and getting people to turn pages is the true definition of successful writing.

There was a time—and I speak now of the mystery field, with which I am most familiar—when the discovery of a new method of slaughter, supposedly undetectable, was considered by many writers to be sufficient in itself to carry a book. The injection of air bubbles in the bloodstream, the icicle dagger, etc., etc. For anyone who still holds to this theory, I would recommend John Dickson Carr's deservedly famous essay on the subject. I honestly believe the only murder method not used to date is boring people to death at cocktail parties, and I'm exposing that one right now.

There was also a time when involved plotting was the be-all and end-all of mystery stories; when the phrase "Who-Dun-It?" meant exactly that, and the reader was being challenged directly by the author to match wits. (I have always considered this contest basically unfair. After all, the author had months and months to solve the problem, and the reader is given only minutes to arrive at the same conclusion.) In any event, today such mysteries are few and far between, and the authors who continue to write them are all old professionals of excellent skill who can depend for their success more on their ability to write convincingly and interestingly, and to characterize superbly, than on the eventual unmasking of the butler.

Today the old "Who-Dun-It?" has largely been replaced by what might be called the "Where-Did-He-Go-And-More-Important-How-Did-He-Get-There?" (I have a feeling the title will never catch on, but the idea remains.) These are the adventure-suspense novels and concern themselves to a very large degree with the chase, the oldest—and possibly still the best—suspense device in the fictional bag of tricks. Yet these books really have no plot at all, and certainly not in terms of those convolutions once considered essential. It is extremely simple: our Hero must get from place A to place B—usually a good distance apart—in a very limited time and for any one of a number of good reasons: to warn the settlers, to deliver a vital message to headquarters, to bring the last fragile vial of antidelirium tremens serum to the plague-stricken village, to lead the natives to safety before the volcano erupts, to get the mortgage payment to the bank before the moment of foreclosure, etc., etc. In addition to the stormy weather and the treacherous terrain across which he must travel, there are also bad men who are being paid to prevent the success of his mission. This they attempt to do: by crippling his horse, by dynamiting the rope bridge over the chasm, by changing road-markers, by drugging his sarsaparilla, by decoying him with sensuous sirens, by sniping at him from ambush, and—if all else fails—by physically molesting him.

Ludicrous? Corny? Only if the author makes it so. The most successful suspense novels of the past few years have had no more plot than those mentioned above. But the writing was good and exciting, and the people in them were human beings with human reactions, whose motivations were understandable, both hero and villain, and were not wooden puppets being put through the motions. When we read a series suspense novel, for example—meaning one in which the same hero appears in book after book—we know even before he climbs out onto that crumbling two-inch ledge skirting the eighteenth floor of the murderer's hideout that he isn't going to fall. But if the situation is presented to us properly, our hands will still sweat as we fearfully peak at the next page.

There are many other examples of non-plot writing; the entire so-called "slice-of-life" school prefers to take a section from everyday living and describe it with skill which translates itself into an emotional response on the part of the reader. This type of writing continues to produce quite successful and often great, blockbusting novels, as well as to find a market at some of the higher-paying magazines. Actually, how much plot is there in great symphonic music? Still, it manages to communicate, which is the important thing. It gets us, in effect, to turn the page.

I suppose my advice to the beginning writer, in the matter of plot, is to put it into its proper perspective and not allow it to become an insurmountable obstacle to a successful writing career. Someone once said there was only one basic plot: Boy Meets Girl, Boy Loses Girl, Boy Finds Girl. In general it's a correct concept, and what makes one book different from another is the quality of the characterization and the writing.

And think how lovely it would be if this obsession with plot were eliminated and replaced with more important concerns. I dream of the day when someone comes up to me at a cocktail party and asks, "Where on *earth* do you *manage* to get those weird *characters?*" Think how simple it would be to look them right in the eye and tell them where I got one of them, at least. . . .

34

SIX WAYS TO SUCCESSFUL CONFESSIONS

By Florence K. Palmer

"To my surprise—" an English professor at a large university said of the magazines I'd sent her, "the confession is just a good story that makes use of every basic principle of short story writing, but with stronger emotional overtones."

It's also a capsule of life, relived vicariously by millions of housewives, schoolgirls, working women—and yes, some men—who read the thirty-odd confession magazines currently published for information and guidance, as well as entertainment.

For serious freelancers both of these facts are important, particularly for those writers struggling to get into a sadly shrunken fiction market, at the same time condemning unread today's liveliest short story medium.

Actually, although the confessional tone has been preserved, titles and blurbs are all that remain of the once shoddy confession. Inside the flamboyant covers now there is a concerned searching into, and compassionate understanding of *human behavior*. The modern confession writer analyzes motivating factors, and relates them to the effect on, or problem of a story narrator.

Besides a genuine love of people, however, three things are absolute—*first-person viewpoint*, *reader identification*, and a *hold-nothing-back discussion* of the narrator's mistaken course of action in resolving her problem. This calls for strong characterization, and as the writer, you must feel every doubt and fear exactly as if you were that person—your typewriter keys are the bridge between a heart that listens, and a heart that reveals. If there's any secret to writing confessions, this is it!

Perhaps you've never suffered the agony of a child's death, nor known the heartbreak and disillusion of marital discord. How then can you write convincingly of emotions outside your personal experience?

The surest way is to go back in your mind and heart to your childhood. Relive the moment a favorite doll was broken, feel again the utter hopelessness of cradling those bits of shattered china, knowing full well that no other doll will ever be quite so precious. Put that same feeling into the heart of a bereaved mother, and you'll find it possible to express her deeper, more elemental grief with verisimilitude.

And remember the time a flip little newcomer to junior high walked off with your steady boyfriend? The outrage, the bitterness, and frustrating inability to do anything about such piracy isn't too different from a rejected wife's reaction!

Yes, by all means write about what you know, but don't underestimate the depth of your own knowledge either. Somewhere in your life there is a counterpart of almost every human emotion, but you must have the insight and imagination to recognize the analogy.

But—and watch this—all people are different, and no two persons will react in quite the same way to the same problem. So, in creating a confession character, work with universal traits and emotions. Let the individual reader apply your solution in her own fashion to the similar problem she herself faces, for these first-person problem stories aren't intended as add-water-and-mix advice, but rather to help others help themselves.

Keep in mind, too, that good fiction begins and ends with people, not plot. Whatever the story germ, it can be told only through the words, actions, and emotions of real people in conflict with real problems. You must, therefore, climb inside your narrator. For the space of twenty to thirty typed pages, you see, hear, taste, and feel only through her senses. You must, or the confessional tone is lost, and with it, that all-important reader identification.

So, how are those basic short story principles applied to confession writing?

1) *You must confront your narrator with a problem.*

Is her husband unfaithful? Do her parents refuse to believe a teen-ager is capable of mature, lasting love? Has she gone into debt for the material possessions her more secure neighbors take as a matter of course? Is she afraid to bear a child because her own mother died in childbirth? Has she allowed a mistaken concept of religion to channel her life?

Your choice is limitless. It can be swift and dramatic, or seemingly trivial, but in general, the problem is a common one that could trouble you, or a family down the street. Once the problem is selected, however, something must happen to set the action in motion—something that leads inevitably, incident by complicating incident, to a resolution which will have a marked influence on the narrator's whole future.

This brings us to the kind of character defect most likely to trigger things. Perhaps your narrator is bedeviled by envy, or maybe only discontented with the monotony of dishes and diapers seven days a week. To make her sympathetic to readers, though, you go into the whys and wherefores of her particular flaw, or mistaken attitude. A woman doesn't hate her children, or make the drug scene, or suffer an emotional collapse overnight—and that convenient phrase, "I don't know what made me do it!" won't satisfy anybody. You must know and transmit the underlying reasons, which is merely another way of saying that there must be sound motivation or your story will fall flat on its tear-stained face!

And what about the incident or situation that pinpoints the problem and creates a necessity for the narrator to take decisive action? This is the *narrative hook*, and can be in the form of dialogue, action, or a bit of philosophy—all are good confession openings, so long as they stress the problem's immediacy. For example:

The mother with teen-age youngsters and an after-forty baby on the way has the problem of family adjustments. She begins her story like this:

Honestly, I could practically hear Betsy already. "Oh, Mom, what's everybody going to say—how'll I tell the kids at school?"

She may go on to say that her son won't act as if she were a freak, or doing something downright indecent. But she'd "see the flush of scarlet creep into his ears, catch the way his eyes avoided mine."

At least her husband would feel differently about a belated addition to their family:

Joe's a darling, and loves children as much as I do, only the trouble is, he'll start working twice as hard to earn more money. Probably keep on wearing his shabby old topcoat, and cutting down on cigarettes, or lunch. . . .

And here's the immature wife, who becomes involved in what she thinks is an innocent affair:

If it hadn't wound up another scorcher that day, a lot of things might've been different. I don't know, I really don't, because maybe it wasn't the weather at all, maybe I was just spoiling for trouble.

Anyhow, with the temperature nosing 80 before noon, I was dripping wet even thinking of the ironing left to do, and that bucket of soft, purple salal berries still to jell. And if that wasn't plenty, Timmy picked the hottest day of the year to get active enough for twins, let alone one small three-year-old!

All the same, I should've known when I married Kale what it'd be like—living in a logging camp, I mean. So what was I kicking about? He was a lumberjack, wasn't he? And loggers have to live where they work—in the woods!

In both of these, the problem is presented, a hint of the narrator's background, the other characters involved, and in one, you also learn the locale. This is done, you'll note, in less than a page, or about 150 words.

2) *The format of your story is the next consideration.*

Will it be told by flashback, or chronologically? The full flashback, or opening at the so-called "dark moment," is no longer very popular, although some stories demand this method to get background material and motivation in at the outset.

The following is an example of the full flashback:

They started coming while we were still elbow-deep in scrubbing out the house, curiosity plain on their faces, and paper-thin excuses at the tip of every tongue.

"Knew you'd need a chair or two until you're settled," that was Mrs. Grunwald, the old crow! "We got an attic full of Ma's stuff; no reason you shouldn't have it."

"That's how they are!" I stormed to Shep when he protested my curt refusal of the furniture we really did need badly. "Shoving their charity at me the same as they did after Mom died, and Dad—"

The narrator is now back to the time when her father went completely to pieces, "not giving a hoot for anything except the rot-gut he began to drink morning, noon, and night." That was bad enough by itself, but then the "do-gooders" pitched in to make them a sort of neighborhood project:

Little kids aren't particularly touchy that way, only I was older, a string-bean twelve, and rawly aware of a humiliating undertone to their generosity.

Oh, sure, we needed the things all right . . . but with nothing to give in return it amounted to outright charity, and that's one thing I wasn't taking from anybody if I could help it. . . .

Here is the *cause* of the narrator's character flaw, which motivates everything that comes later. But its warping *effect* should be lived, not just told. By using this "happening right now" treatment of the flashback, you show your reader the opening scene again without his feeling that he has been taken on a round trip into the past, and the story can then move forward without any interest-losing break.

But since confession editors prefer the chronological form, fragmentary flashbacks are an effective means of speeding the pace of a story. Such flashbacks are woven into dialogue and narration as the story is happening, without slowing the forward movement: "I hadn't even thought of Rick Bradley in years, not since his folks moved to Denver our junior year of high," tells in one sentence what would otherwise take a paragraph or two. Then, you can bridge the time between like this:

I stared up at the tall, laughing-eyed man incredulously, remembering how red he'd gotten, and the way he had stammered asking me for a dance at our class stomp. "My gosh, are you the Richard Bradley that's headlining that big show at the Palace?" I exclaimed.

Each of these transitions from past to present, however, should be preceded by a sentence (as I've done above) to justify a situation that might seem illogical, and indicate the upcoming incident's purpose.

3) *With your story now underway, write in scenes—live the action and conflict, don't just tell it.* And, since the confession is intended to be informative as well as entertaining, use specific locales whenever possible. The Puget Sound area, for instance, provides a colorful setting, by which the reader learns something about the rugged Cascade Mountains, or Seattle's busy seaport where vessels from all over the world take on cargo.

Your own part of the country may be equally interesting, or draw on memories of that trip out west, or weekend at the beach.

Regional backgrounds are always a plus, but they must never dominate the story. It must be capable of standing alone, without the aid of any crutch.

The same applies to the narrator's occupation. Weave in the information about particular types of work through dialogue and action, but don't make your story a textbook on how to repair TV sets, or the daily routine of a dance instructor!

Incidentally, there is no confession vocabulary per se. Just sit over coffee with an intimate friend, and talk your problem out, breathlessly, urgently. Use action verbs—race for hurry; whirl rather than turn—and the contractions—I'm, he's, would've—to create this illusion.

But avoid purple writing or breast-beating—they're only an emotional veneer, and slapdash writing doesn't get by in today's confession. Which reminds me, let's not hoard lovely bits of imagery for "something better"—they can make your story sing, and be the difference between a standard three-cents-a-word sale, and the five-cent rate paid by top confession magazines.

4) *How does your narrator go about solving her problem?* As in real life, because of that motivating character flaw, she'll see only one way out of her predicament—and, of course, her warped judgment will prompt the wrong decision, which plunges the narrator into the *dark moment*.

5) *The climax.* This is a tricky point in the confession story, and its challenge can't be wrapped up with a flimsy, "Suddenly I realized—!" Instead, the narrator, faced by an apparently hopeless situation, begins to understand the *why* of it. She examines her mistaken attitude, delves into the past for its basic causes, and is determined somehow to overcome that troublemaking character flaw. In other words, your narrator has actually been in analysis all along, and her story is "the couch in print."

6) *The theme.* Up to this point, confessions follow the general pattern of every other short story, but their endings are peculiarly confessional. They go one step beyond the climax, because here the problem's resolution is also an exemplification of your theme—*and the theme is always the lesson to be learned.*

The true purpose of this tagged-on ending isn't to preach, but to offer the reader reassurance that she is not alone, and that God is still in His heaven. "Here is my life," the narrator, in effect, says, "I was just as mixed up, too . . ."

Speaking of themes, did you know that scores can be found in Aesop's Fables? *Happiness cannot be bought, Pride goeth before a fall, Greed can cost your all*—confession themes, and yours for the writing.

Then for a real treasure trove of story ideas, what about the Bible? With no irreverence meant, "The Prodigal Son" is one of the greatest confessions ever written. "The Story of Ruth" parallels the attitude of many a wife today, and "Jephthah's Daughter" underscores the tragic consequence of a promise rashly given.

Daily newspapers are another excellent source, as are your friends and own family. Wherever you find the idea originally, however, it is wise for you to keep some sort of memo. The date of a news item, or what sparked your story is enough, and may save a lot of bother if there's ever any question of its being public property.

There is one drawback to writing for the confession market—you are bound to get rather harsh comments from less informed freelancers, those who haven't looked inside the cover of a *True Story*, or *True Confessions*, or *Modern Romances* since they were knee-high to a cricket.

"You'll never be able to write anything worthwhile," they sniff. "Confessions are a literary limbo—trash!"

Yet, some of the finest documentaries on medical achievements and sociological advances have used the pages of a confession magazine to reach the widest possible audience. Some of the most moving stories presented on movie or TV screens were first printed in a confession magazine. And some of today's most honored by-lines have been made by writers who learned to create flesh-and-blood characters for the confession market.

Will confessions harm your other writing? Not if you write sincerely, and with perception. Then, the facility gained through this person-to-person handling of human problems and emotions is far more likely to enrich whatever you may write, fiction or nonfiction.

35

INSIDE URIAH HEEP

By Nina Bawden

THERE are two kinds of fictional characters, the flat and the round. "Flat"—that is, seen objectively, with no intrusion by the novelist into his character's skin—is not a dismissive adjective. Most of the memorable characters in literature are "flat." We don't know what it would be like to be inside Uriah Heep, or Mr. Micawber, or Mr. Collins, and they would be less "real," perhaps, less effective, if we did. Detail would blur the sharpness of the picture.

Flat characters are, of course, the supporting cast in most novels, the backdrop against which the heroes and heroines, the "round" characters, act out their bigger parts. And "act" is the word, because the novelist is inside them, impersonating another human being who may be quite unlike himself: handsome where he is ugly, or a different age, a different sex.

Success depends on the skill and imagination employed. But sometimes one gets the impression, however great the writer's skill, that the impersonation is a kind of gymnastic exercise, a contortion that has been forced on the writer simply because it is no longer possible to write straightforwardly—that is, in the tradition of the old novels when the novelist was omnipotent and could speak with his own voice. He could be inside his characters but outside them, too—writing about, as well as through them.

This is a freedom we have lost. Without it, a writer can do one of two things. He can, like Françoise Sagan, whose heroines grow older as she grows older, write only about himself, under one or another thin disguise. Or he can perform what amounts to one virtuoso ventriloquist act after another.

This "internal" method of characterization may be bewildering for the reader who opens a book by a young man in his twenties and finds himself inside the consciousness of a middle-aged woman going through the menopause, but it is almost always fun for the writer. Learning to see through someone else's eyes, to speak with his voice, is a fascinating and challenging experience. But it has its dangers, too.

The only person you can really know is yourself. You can observe how other people look and behave, listen to what they say, guess how they think and feel—but you can only guess. The young man cannot know how it feels to be a middle-aged woman: he can only impersonate her.

It might seem to follow from this that the most successful characters in fiction must be those the writer has been closest to, the ones whose ideas and feelings match best with his own. It would explain, certainly, why so many modern novels seem to be a voyage of self-discovery, a sort of private joke, or game. As an illustration of what I mean, my last novel was about two women, one a timid ninny, a fanatasist; the other cheerful and extroverted, a kind of female buccaneer. Both these women were me—or rather, aspects of them were in me—and often, as I wrote about them alternately, slipping slyly from one personality to the other, I found myself shaking with silent laughter at some contradiction, or absurdity, that no one but myself would ever see.

Writing this novel, and the one before it, I became aware of the difficulties (for me) of writing through someone too much like myself. Although her situation was different from mine, Elizabeth, the heroine of *A Woman of My Age,* was my own sex, my own age, and came from the same educational and social background. As I wrote about her, I found we intruded on each other—not just I on her, but she on me. She was a frustrated woman with an overbearing husband; I became so involved with her, so indignant on her behalf, that I lectured my husband one suppertime on how badly he was treating me, how constricting my life was. My family listened, putting down their forks and watching me with mild, astonished faces. When I had finished—worked up, by this point, into a fine, righteous rage—my son said gently, "But you're not talking about *yourself,* are you?"

Elizabeth and I had grown too close. I had to remove myself from her, stand back to see her clearly. I managed to do this—at least, I hope I did—by making her physically different from myself: large-framed instead of small, long-haired instead of short—a simple, idiosyncratic trick, but one that worked in this case and prevented confusion of identity.

It is important, if you do not want to gaze Narcissus-like into the mirror, to distance yourself from your characters, who might, otherwise, become no more than vehicles for your thoughts, your perceptions. Your "round" characters will be bound to have a bit of you in them—and since we are all many-sided, infinitely complex, this is not as limiting as it sounds—but they must have their independence as well, their own life. I have found that one way to achieve this is to write as a man: it seems, in some ways, less inhibiting, and gives a broader focus. Or to write as a child or young adolescent. There is an additional freedom in this method because the child is naturally distanced from us in years, and yet, if our memory is good, we know him well.

To be at a distance from, and yet to know. That is the ideal, I think. To be far enough away to see objectively and still be able, without too much trickiness, too much contortion, to get inside the skin of someone who is quite different from you.

Which brings me to what is—paradoxically, perhaps—another danger for the novelist who is writing not just for and about himself, but for and about other people. Again I can best explain it through an example from my own work. Twelve years ago I wrote a book, *Devil by the Sea,* about a nine-year-old girl who became obsessively involved with a child murderer. She was a perverse child with what school teachers call an "unfortunate manner." She had a pretty younger brother, and somewhat insensitive parents, but she was not, in any objective sense, neglected: she simply wanted more love and attention than came her way, and, not getting it, felt it must be her own wickedness that deprived and isolated her. As a result of this fairly common, childish belief, she identified herself with the murderer whom she thought of, for reasons too complicated to go into here, as the Devil.

I have recently written a script of this novel in collaboration with a film director who was worried about the psychological exactness of the child's behavior. Would this type of child have reacted quite like this to this situation, or, if she did, shouldn't she be a different sort of child? There were one or two textbooks which contained accounts of the child who is "accident-prone," likely to be a victim in this kind of crime. Wouldn't it be a good idea to read them? I did read them. The result, to my gratification, was confirmation, not confusion: *my* child, established both in my mind and on paper, was more real than any number of case histories. And why shouldn't she be? Nothing that happened to her had ever happened to me, but I knew what it was like to *be* her: an awkward, difficult, greedy child, not worth loving. But if I had read those case histories (and taken them into account) before I wrote my novel, would she have been more convincing, more "real"? At the risk of sticking my neck out, I'd like to say I don't think so. I might easily have been overawed by the opinions of people who seemed to know more than I did, and constructed a sterile, composite character. An Identikit Child. . . .

We know so much now: psychiatrists and sociologists have taught us to take people apart like clocks. And to put them in categories: The Graduate Wife, The Organization Man, The Status Seeker. As if, fitting ourselves into slots, we could understand ourselves better.

But do we? There are no individuals in a statistical sample. If there is anything in the complaint that the modern novelist no longer writes about "real" people—and how many characters from recent fiction can you remember as clearly as you remember Anna Karenina, or Fagin, or Huck Finn?—it may stem from the fact that we have lost, not only the old, sure sense of our place in society, but also our belief that the individual is important within it. Or if we have not lost this belief, we are half-afraid to assert it. We do not wish to appear trivial. And so we write "important" novels about this Problem or that; put in a lot of sex (because in bed we are all alike, the sense of character is lost); try to expand the narrow world of the particular into some grander, more diffuse design.

It is no good, of course. The novelist's business is with the particular. You cannot inject universal significance into a novel about the old man next door who is dying of cancer by writing about The Problem of Terminal Illness in Old People in Suburban Communities. If you tried, your book would be stillborn, because you would be writing from the outside in, letting the tail wag the dog. There are no Old Men for you, just one old man. He is a retired merchant sailor, let's say, who keeps a collection of wood and ivory elephants in the front room of his bungalow and grows roses and vegetable marrows in his garden. His wife has been dead ten years, and he doesn't miss her as he misses his mother who now seems younger, in his thoughts, than his wife. He has a daughter who is married to a truck driver and a son who is a professor of mathematics. He is jealous of his son but pretends to be proud of him. He has tufts of hair growing out of his ears and a wart on his right index finger which bothers him when he ties his shoelaces. He doesn't know about the cancer, which he thinks of as "his old stomach trouble," but he is frightened sometimes when he wakes in the night.

Of course, you cannot know exactly what it is like to be that old man, but you will know *something:* who hasn't been jealous, who hasn't, at four in the morning, been afraid of death? Stick with your old man. Look and listen, both for the exterior and the interior truth about him, and you may, if you have paid attention and are honored with talent, end up by finding that the universal has been there all the time, looking out from the particular.

36

THE USES AND ABUSES OF DIALOGUE

By Bill Pronzini

Perhaps the most important technique a fiction writer must master in order to achieve any degree of lasting success in today's highly competitive magazine and book markets is the art of writing believable and appropriate dialogue. Without that mastery, he is foundering in heavy seas, and, like as not, he'll go down and fail to come up again.

Many beginning writers tend to de-emphasize the importance of dialogue. They believe that narrative is the key to salability, and hence, to success. But, in my opinion, the argument that characterization, mood, and plot line should be set forth primarily in expository passages in which the author alone does the talking is not valid. The characters themselves *must* have a voice—a strong voice. They have to corroborate the author's statements about them, about their qualities, temperament, eccentricities, etc.; they have to reflect and intensify the established mood in their spoken words as well as by their actions; they have to advance and re-affirm and assist in clearly establishing the plot line by what they say and how and why they say it. In short, and in a very literal sense, if the characters aren't able to speak for themselves—if the reader can't believe them simply on the basis of what they *say* —then the author has failed to do his job properly.

The best-selling novelists in all fields—for example, mystery-suspense, science fiction, westerns, mainstream—are to a man (or woman) highly capable practitioners of the art of dialogue. Prime examples are found in the mystery-suspense genre, into which perhaps 75% of my own writing output is channeled. Evan Hunter, whom most everyone knows is also Ed McBain of 87th Precinct fame, is perhaps the best writer of realistic dialogue. You can learn almost everything that needs to be learned about composing believable, moving, suitable colloquy from reading and studying his work. Chandler and Hammett and Erle Stanley Gardner became giants because all were able to write superb fictional conversation. Other contemporary craftsmen who come to mind are Donald Westlake, John D. MacDonald, Thomas B. Dewey, and Ross Macdonald.

The following ideas have for some time governed my own writing of dialogue. They certainly aren't intended to be hard-and-fast rules, for they are what works best for one *individual* author, but I hope that in some small way they might prove helpful to beginning writers.

There are, basically speaking, two schools in the writing of dialogue. One is the "short dialogue" school; the other is the "exposition dialogue" school (some writers, though I'm sure not many, believe in a composite of both—and all writers, of necessity, are members of both schools at times—but as a general rule you can place any author into one or the other category merely by examining his work). Both schools are perfectly tenable, and have their distinct advantages, but I belong—heart and soul—to the "short dialogue" school.

This is to say that I believe conversation in a fictional endeavor should be short and crisp between speakers whenever possible. When you consider it, this is normally the way you and I converse with friends, relatives, business associates every day of our lives. When an individual asks a question, it is most often a single, brief question; and having asked his single, brief question, he will usually wait for an answer before asking another question or continuing on to something else. And the answer, more often than not, will be as succinct as the question—a single, concise sentence, or perhaps two concise sentences. For example:

"Where were you?"
"At the park."
"Which one?"
"Oak Hill."
"What were you doing there?"
"I went to find Jack."
"Did you find him?"
"No. He'd already gone home."

A brief answer follows a brief question, a simple corroboration or negation follows a simple statement. This kind of dialogue flows quite nicely, for both the reader and the writer. And the reader is not overloaded with ideas, questions, or factual material presented in blocks. There is time for him to assimilate each detail before going on to the next.

Unless a writer is accomplished technically, expository dialogue (in which each speaker is given several sentences, some of which may take on the characteristics of straight narrative, before he relinquishes the floor to the next speaker) can be very difficult to write. The progression has to be planned *ahead* of time, rather than allowing questions, answers, statements to flow naturally from one speaker to the next and back again. Of course, there are times when I'm forced to write expository dialogue—these are unavoidable, especially when unraveling a complicated plot—but I've found that people simply do not, on the average, speak in intricate, verbose sentences and paragraphs. Most individuals run out of ideas (if not inclination) after three successive statements and wait to be led on by someone else's comments.

People generally speak idiomatically. All of us utter clichés, overwork certain words, use double negatives, preface ten sentences in a row with the word *well*, swear, and pretend that we've forgotten every grammatical axiom we ever knew. We seem to have an affinity for words and phrases like *sure, uh-huh, right, well, O.K., listen, look, why not?, all right, yeah, huh, oh, ah, um-m, hm-m,* etc. Should fiction be any different?

I am not advocating that every character's dialogue should be idiomatic or exhibit all of these features, or that these speech traits should be used indiscriminately. But a sprinkling of them will make any piece of dialogue seem more real, less stilted and contrived. The following example, while perhaps *too* idiomatic, will serve to illustrate my point:

> "Listen, let's go to a movie."
> "Why not?"
> "Which one you want to see?"
> "Oh, I don't care."
> "How about John Wayne?"
> "Yeah, he's good, all right."

"Or maybe Rod Steiger."

"Sure."

"Well, which one?"

"It makes no difference to me."

You *can* go overboard with this kind of thing, especially if you follow the methods of some writers to reveal lack of intelligence and/or education, and of other writers hung up on backwoods dialect. These are the authors who write phonetically, combine words and phrases, drop g's, and so on—perpetrators of the *gonna, wanna, c'mon, whyain'tcha, yer, ya, lessee, whazzat, whozzit, dunno, comin', goin',* etc., school.

While fictional characters should be made to speak as realistically as possible, there are limits. A reader can grow very weary of page after page of lousy English, and if he is forced continually to decipher elided words and phonetic spellings, he can very easily lose the flow of the story. And, ironically, this kind of writing does not establish lack of intelligence or lack of education—nor is it particularly representative of the backwoods. I've known educated men who went around saying "gonna" and "wanna" and dropped their g's; and I've known some "down-home" types who spoke clear, grammatical English.

Writers who persist blithely in this sort of thing are largely responsible for fictional stereotypes: a back-country sheriff saying ponderously, "Wal, Sam, them there fellas ain't goin' ta get away, I'm tellin' ya that"; a criminal raised in a slum district saying out of the side of his mouth, "Less'n ya want dat dere cement overcoat, bud, ya'll keep yer yap buttoned up, see?"

Careful, sparse usage of such devices is permissible, of course, but there are simply better ways of accomplishing the same purpose. To show that a character is uneducated or unintelligent, for example, the author can give him a limited vocabulary, have him repeat favorite words or phrases, or stumble over words of more than one or two syllables and seem not to understand words and phrases whose meanings should be apparent—and so on. In this way, stereotyping is eliminated and, at the same time, character is effectively revealed.

Slang and dialect should be employed by the fiction writer to achieve realism as long as he keeps three things in mind: 1) Don't use slang that is out of character (i.e., having a sheltered spinster say, "He's groovy" or "She's up tight" or "They're really cool"). 2) Don't overuse dialect or slang; there's nothing more irritating to a reader than to be confronted by one slang expression after another, especially unfamiliar ones. 3) Don't use slang expressions or jargon that is likely to go out of date. What is an "in" phrase today may become passé tomorrow. If a supposedly hip character uses slang which is obsolete and the reader is more hip than the author, the author is in trouble.

Dialogue, as I mentioned earlier, must be an integral part of a story. Dialogue which does not move the story along, or add to the mood of the story, or have an easily definable reason for being there at all (such as to establish important characterization), should be considered superfluous and therefore cut.

As a means of telling the story itself—moving it from Point A to Point B to Point C—dialogue is invaluable. In many instances, when the author has a choice of writing a scene in narrative or in dialogue, he would do well to choose the latter. Conversation is a superb way to build tension and suspense between two or more characters—and, at the same time, to build tension and suspense for the reader. Character A speaks, and the effect of his words on Character B is reflected in B's response as well as in B's actions. The effect of B's response on A is then reflected in A's subsequent response as well as in A's subsequent actions. The impact is therefore *doubled*. That is why scenes with more than one individual can be (if the conversation is skillfully handled) much more exciting, can move much more swiftly, than scenes involving only a single character and his actions, or two or more characters who do not exchange words and their actions. And that is why stories and novels using well-written dialogue can be more exciting, more rapidly paced, than stories and novels written primarily in narration.

Without conversation that flows smoothly, a story can noticeably drag; it can lose some or all of its impact on the reader; it can be divested of mood, characterization, even plausibility. If the dialogue is stilted, illogical, overwritten, patronizing, condescending or consistently inappropriate or unsuited to setting and situation, it does not matter how well the plot or the narrative is constructed;

chances are that the story or the novel will not sell "as is" in today's market.

There is nothing wrong with the word "said." Some writers, especially beginners, seem to spend more time thinking up synonyms for that perfectly good word than they do in plotting their stories or novels. There is no good reason for this. Words are *spoken;* they are not *ejaculated, flung, rasped, gurgled, expostulated, hissed, grated, sneered, predicated, heaved, gulped, vociferated, wheezed, blatted, pontificated, croaked, bubbled, fumed, proclaimed,* or *asserted.* Indiscriminate use of such substitutes can weaken otherwise acceptable dialogue, and make a scene less than effective—perhaps even ludicrous.

Certain *said*-substitutes may be used now and then to avoid constant repetition. Such words as: *agreed, admitted, replied, answered, asked, muttered, whispered, shouted, told* (him, her or it), etc., are all excellent synonyms. But in two out of three instances, a simple "said" is sufficient.

Some writers seem to feel the need to use *said*-substitutes to convey manner or emotion. All a writer needs to do to show that a character does more than simply "say" something is to add an appropriate adverb after the word *said* (or *asked* or *answered,* etc.); *slowly, warily, evenly, happily, cheerfully, argumentatively, solicitously,* and so on.

One thing to keep in mind, however, is that no one makes a statement or asks a question with particular inflection or emotion or purpose *every time.* Most often, we simply make statements and ask questions. Adverbs are fine as long as they're used sparingly, and when genuinely necessary.

To illustrate the foregoing, I offer the following two passages of dialogue. Which would you consider the most effective?

"Where's the money, Harry?" Jack asked.
"I don't know," Harry said.
"You stole it, didn't you?"
"No."
"Don't lie to me," Jack said.
"I'm not lying!"
"I can always tell when a man is lying," Jack said coldly.

Or

"Where's the money, Harry?" Jack hissed.
"I don't know," Harry ejaculated.
"You stole it, didn't you?"
"No."
"Don't lie to me," Jack blatted.
"I'm not lying!"
"I can always tell when a man is lying," Jack iced out.

Almost any kind of fiction can be effectively written if the dialogue is properly constructed and used. The best sex scene and the best tender love scene I have ever read were both done entirely through dialogue. There were no graphic bits of narrative in the former, and no "shining eyes of love, and palpitating heartbeats" in the latter. Both were memorable—real—because all the elements of humanism and emotion were inherent in the words which were spoken by the characters.

Mastery of the art of dialogue truly *can* make the difference between sales and rejection slips.

37

TICKET TO TIMBUKTU

By Norah Lofts

This article is not directed at the well-to-do, or the footloose, or written for anyone whose imagination can only be sparked off by something that his physical eyes have seen. I am writing it specifically for people who are bound to a job, or to a family, or even to a wheelchair and have an impulse to tell a tale set against a background with which they are unfamiliar. Such people are often inhibited because they have been overexposed to the theory that one can only write about what one knows at firsthand, and are a little too ready to believe that only Mr. X, who has spent a lot of time and a lot of money in Timbuktu, can possibly use it as a setting. This simply isn't true. Given the story, enough curiosity and determination, enough time and enough exercise of what Wordsworth called "that inward eye", you can, without losing a day at the office, without being unfaithful to the kitchen sink, write your book about Timbuktu; and presently people will write to you and say, "When were you there? I lived there for twenty years and, believe me, your book made me positively homesick."

So far as I know, nobody has yet come up with any real evidence that Shakespeare was ever in Denmark or Venice or Padua. There is a strong likelihood that he was hobbled in London, earning his bread, saving his money for his old age, and keeping his eyes and ears open. In the Thames-side taverns, he probably talked to sailors who had visited far places; and it is true that his audience was less critical and less well-informed than ours. To balance this, we have wider resources: all those books by Mr. X, accurate maps, pictures, films, television documentaries.

The thing is not to be timid. Maugham once said—I can't give the actual words, but this is the gist—you don't go out and find stories, stories come and find you. A story about Timbuktu may have found *you,* seemingly the least likely person to write it, tethered as you are by all these Lilliputian strings, some so frail as the question, "But what will happen to my dog?" The thing is that this story has found *you.* You are the one to do it. Stories are wiser in their generation.

Another thing is not to think for a moment that to write about a far place without seeing it is easy. The material has to be found, studied and checked with more care than is required when you write of what you know. Two accounts of the same place may vary wildly; then you must find two more, find, if possible, someone who has been there and is willing to talk. Quite recently I met, on a train journey, a woman who had spent twenty-six years behind the Iron Curtain; she was talkative and fair-minded, and told me many things, both good and bad, about the regime. I was all ears, though at the time I had no intention of using anything she told me; but later on, two stories found me and I wrote them; both have been published and so far I have had no complaints. And if you are by this time thinking that nobody would bother to correct a blatantly ignorant writer, think again. The world is full of frustrated schoolteachers who are, like God, "extreme to mark what is done amiss." Ironically enough, the harshest reprimand I ever invited, and a well-deserved one, came after I had written something that I really did know about—or thought I did. Born and reared a Methodist, I thought I was safe with a Methodist hymn, quoted it without checking, and presently was slapped down in a letter from Malaya.

I know that the method I advocate and practice is often denigrated by the term "armchair traveling." I contend that the armchair traveler is a far more cerebral creature than the man on the spot whose mind is subject to physical concerns: will his money last out, has the last train gone, what was in that queer-looking dish that now lies so uneasily in his stomach, could that really be a bedbug? It is all too possible to look upon the Bridge of Sighs or the Leaning Tower and to be preoccupied with the site of the nearest lavatory. The books of genuine travelers often reflect this physical preoccupation which the reader can afford to skip or minimize. I remember one travel book through which the sentences, "We harnessed the yak," and "We unharnessed the yak," ran as recurrent themes. I had no responsibility for the animal and, after noting that in this particular place the yak is a form of transport, could afford to concentrate upon the scenery.

There is this, also, to be considered: If armchair traveling were not a pretty adequate substitute for firsthand experience, how would historical writers fare? So little of the physical past remains, and most of what remains has changed so much, that an effort of imagination is required to give even a glimpse of what it formerly was.

Once, in the company of a member of the you-must-go-and-see school, I traveled all the way to Spain to see a certain palace. There were bits of ruined wall, shoulder high in places, but the site was a pleasure garden, full of people, noisy with children, bright with kiosks selling ice cream. True, we stood on the spot where something had actually taken place, there was that satisfaction; but there was little to be learned, the atmosphere was wrong. For me, at least, a contemporary description, a picture, even the words "a castle in Spain," would have been much more productive.

I sorely disappointed—and this I regret—the kind person who took me to Rome and said, as proudly as though he had just built it, "There is the Colosseum!" I said, "I know. It is exactly as I imagined it." That was true, in a way, yet profoundly untrue in another, because in my imagination the marble facing had still been in place, and the seats had been filled with avid spectators, the gladiators' quarters occupied, the lions complaining of hunger.

I have to confess that when the time came for me to abandon armchair traveling for the other kind, my immediate reaction to any place was—I have been here before, and it was better then.

And to clinch this argument, let us think for a moment about my own home town. It grew up around a great Benedictine Abbey, the second largest north of the Rhine. St. Edmund, King and Martyr, was enshrined here, kings patronized and endowed it, it was a place of pilgrimage. Somewhere, sometime a story concerning its two most famous Abbots, Baldwin and Sampson, or its best known scribe, Jocelyn de Brakelond, may find somebody behind a desk or a counter or a cooking stove in Oklahoma. This chosen person may be one of the go-take-a-look practitioners. He will come to Bury St. Edmund's, which is well worth a visit, and he will receive a warm welcome. With his own eyes he will see the Abbey Gate, a Norman tower, two splendid churches which were once chapels to the Abbey and survived the Dissolution as parish churches and have been practically rebuilt in the intervening years; and he will find a public pleasure ground with lumps of grey ruin here and there. He will see only one thing which conveys the size and magnificence of the Abbey in its prime and that is a picture which hangs inside the Abbey Gate. This picture is a reconstruction, based upon actual measurements and upon contemporary or near-contemporary documents. From that picture the traveler will learn something that his own eye, however imaginative, could hardly have told him as he stared at the flowerbeds, the tennis courts and bowling green—that the buildings still standing are, compared to the Great Abbey Church, as a matchbox is to a two-floored house. In fact, with this picture and a few books, this would-be writer has a far more certain entry to the Abbey as Brakelond knew it than his actual visit could confer.

This is an age of realism; there may be some danger that the imagination, underexercised, will take the way of the appendix and end with nothing but a nuisance value. Publishers delight in announcing on a book's jacket that Mr. X spent four years in Timbuktu and that the book was ten years in preparation; they feel that this adds to its worth. If Mr. X has done a sound job, his book has worth, not least to those of us who need the information he imparts. But this kind of approach, used often enough, tends to make the writer who is unable to travel feel inferior, incapable of writing about anything but his own backyard. And this may mean a loss to the reading public, for a book's most real and lasting value is the pleasure that it affords to the reader. Remember this and be bold.

As a postscript this may sound frivolous, which is a pity, for everything I have so far written has been sincere and borne out by my own experience. But if, having studied books and maps and pictures, talked to people and done all that you can to provide your story with an authentic background, you still feel hesitant about launching it upon a critical world, call your place Gimbuktu; the story will not suffer; the initiate will know what you mean, and you are insured against any small slip or omission. Trollope did it: there is no English county called Barsetshire.

38

USE THREEFOLD MAGIC

By Jean Z. Owen

A number of years ago I wrote a multiple-plot novelette that dealt with the problems of four women who, for one hour, were caught between floors in a department-store elevator. When I had it finished I took it to my friend.

She frowned as she read it.

"There's something not quite right about it," she told me. "The plot and characterization are sound enough, but there seems to be a lack of balance in the story that I find irritating. Perhaps you are trying to juggle too many major characters. Do you suppose you could eliminate one of them?"

I was aghast. Couldn't she see that the story needed all four of the problems if it were to say all I meant it to convey? I was positive that the deletion she suggested would ruin the story; I felt my opinion was vindicated when the story—just as it was—promptly sold to a top slick magazine, and then to television and to a number of foreign markets.

Several years went by, and I thought no more about it until the story finally appeared as an hour-long television drama. I had no part in the adaptation, and as I watched the play, I was astonished to observe that although the cast had been cut from four to three major characters, the play seemed complete and well-rounded. I went to my files and dug out the yellowing carbon of the story and read it with fresh perspective. Now—belatedly—I could perceive the lack of balance that had disturbed my critic. I recalled, too, that the magazine novelette, *A Letter to Five Wives,* had appeared on the screen as *A Letter to Three Wives,* and that *Four Secrets* had been changed to *Three Secrets.* Other motion picture titles came to mind—*The Three Faces of Eve, Three Smart Girls, Three Coins in a Fountain,* and many more.

It dawned on me, too, that I had begun to sell nonfiction pieces only after I learned that the most effective means of presenting factual material is via the classic threefold method—1) tell them what you're *going* to tell them, 2) *tell* them, 3) tell them what you *told* them.

The more I thought about it, the more convinced I became that a writer must pay attention to the Number Three. I don't know *why* this should be so. Some persons think it has a religious basis, while others point to mythology and to the Greek triads. Numerologists have their own explanation. I am inclined to suspect it may be a carry-over from our nursery-rhyme days when we learned to react emotionally to the vicissitudes of the three bears, the three little kittens, the three blind mice, the three little pigs, the three Billy Goats Gruff, the three little fishies, and Wynken, Blynken, and Nod.

I do not wish to imply, of course, that all stories can be forced into a three-sided mold. But I have found that in my own stories and in manuscripts other writers have asked me to evaluate the use of tricornered characterization frequently provides the solution to a stubborn problem of roughness or imbalance.

Once I became aware of the Number Three, I discovered that it can help a writer in many ways. Take the matter of *plants,* for instance. Just as language experts assure you that you can make any new word a permanent part of your vocabulary merely by using it three times, a triple repetition will firmly convey any information you wish your reader to retain.

Suppose, for example, that the climax of your story is going to involve the collapse of a bridge. Even a beginning writer knows that if you toss this at the reader "cold," with no preliminary build-up, you will have the word "coincidental" tossed right back at you. So you painstakingly plant the fact, early in the story, that the bridge may go down. And the best way to do it to make it seem a logical, inevitable part of the story (and a suspense-building factor, as well!) is to mention it three times, from three different viewpoints:

1) Your hero drives across the bridge and notices that it creaks and sways *dangerously* in the wind.

2) An old-timer remembers a storm of 1890 when the old bridge—sturdier, by cracky, than this newfangled flimsy one—washed away as if it had been made of matchsticks.

3) A fortuneteller warns of approaching peril; her crystal ball has revealed a glimpse of people falling into water from a collapsing structure.

This is an oversimplified example, of course. Most of the stories for today's market require less obvious repetition. A plant must be handled so subtly, so artfully, that the reader is not consciously aware of the fact that important information is being accented. The best way to find out how skillfully it can be accomplished is to read again some of the recent stories you have enjoyed. Look for the triple plants—they will be there!

The same principle holds true of characterization. If you describe Ellen, your heroine, as having *shy* brown eyes—if you have some other character mention the fact that it's a shame Ellen *can't seem to mix with people* as easily as her sister Kate—if you show Ellen *flushing with embarrassment as she makes a casual remark*—your reader will thereafter see Ellen as a quiet, retiring, indrawn young woman. If you belabor the point by excessive use of such phrases as "she said timidly" and "she glanced up shyly," the story will seem overdrawn and amateurish. Merely make certain that everything Ellen *says* and *does* and *feels* lies within the framework of a timid personality; your reader will automatically supply most of the stage directions far more effectively than you could possibly depict them.

Another area in which Number Three can help you is in smoothing out jarring sentences and rough paragraphs. There is a natural, euphonic cadence to three modifying words or three descriptive phrases that makes for a smooth, even flow. See what happens if you try adding to, or taking away from these examples: *Blood, sweat, and tears. Of the people, by the people, for the people. Three cheers for the red, white, and blue. Bell, book, and candle. Tom, Dick, and Harry. Morning, noon, and night. Tall, dark, and handsome. Love, honor, and cherish. Healthy, wealthy, and wise. We're having fun-fun-fun! See no evil, hear no evil, speak no evil. Faith, hope, and charity. Gold, frankincense, and myrrh.*

Very likely you have been utilizing three-word or three-phrase descriptions without realizing it. Just for fun sometime, hunt up the rough copy of one of your old stories—or, for that matter, take a look at the story or article you are working on right now. Find one of the paragraphs that sounded uneven, harsh, and amateurish as you first wrote it. So you wrote it again . . . and again and again. And finally, after switching sentences around, putting a phrase in here, pulling a word out there, you could get on with the story, secure in the knowledge that the difficult portion now has a polished "feel" to it. Look at it again; I'll give you odds that you'll discover much of the smoothness resulted primarily from using sequences of three words or three phrases.

(Notice the above paragraph. *Uneven, harsh, and amateurish. Again . . . and again and again. Switching . . . putting . . . pulling.*)

Perhaps the greatest asset Number Three gives a story is a natural, built-in suspense mechanism, free for the writer's taking, simply because in our culture we are geared to react with an automatic "This is *it*" feeling when we reach number three. Three strikes and you're out. One-two-three-*go!* The third time's the charm. Three on a match and evil will befall. Trouble comes in threes. A *three*-time loser is sentenced to life imprisonment.

When we wanted to prove to the world that our space program was something to be reckoned with, we sent John Glenn around for three orbits. Playgoers sit contentedly through Acts I and II, knowing that Act III will give them the same kind of emotional payoff that kindergarten children expect from the *third* wish the fairy queen has granted the poor woodcutter. And next time someone says to you, "Have you heard the one about—?" I'll give you odds that the punch line of the joke will directly follow two build-up lines.

For a writer, the awareness of the fact that the reader's *feeling of expectation* will automatically reach its highest pitch at the third climax of the story is like knowing that one's house is electrically wired. When the occasion calls for it, all you need to do is to plug in your story and the vitalizing current goes to work for you.

Again—an oversimplified example: Your hero wants to get the girl; he tries—and fails. He tries another approach—and fails again, more abjectly than before. So, from the depths, he rises to make a third attempt and *this* time . . . ! If he were successful on the second attempt, it would give the reader the same thudding sensation you get when you lift your foot to step up, only to find you've already reached the top of the stairs. Success on the *fourth* effort is very likely to make the reader bored and impatient. Three—and *only* three—climaxes give the reader his expected quota of emotional impact.

To those of you who protest, "But that's *formula* and I thought formula stories were *out!*", I can only refer you to the best of the non-formula stories that are being printed. For although *story formula* may be discarded, *story form* remains constant, and any fiction, whatever its type, is only as good as the emotional response it draws from the reader. If you will study the markets you will observe that the one-two-three-*payoff* principle works just as strongly in the artistic as it does in the strictly commercial story. The difference lies only in the subtlety of its presentation.

Why is Number Three so important? I haven't the faintest idea. I don't understand the principle of electrical refrigeration, either, but a few moments ago, as the California sun beat down on our house, I pushed the button that turns on our air conditioner—and I strongly suspect that the breezes now wafting through my study are just as cool as they would be if I had a degree in electrical engineering.

Think about Number Three. Note how often it appears in our culture—how frequently it is reflected in the work of writers you would like to emulate. It's only a minor bit of technique, perhaps—but for the writer who seriously seeks to perfect his craftsmanship it can be another tool that can help him create effectively.

39

POINT OF VIEW: EXPERIMENT IN LIVING

By Marjorie Franco

A few years ago I walked into a New York office, gave my name to the receptionist and sat down. The receptionist, a young girl, turned to me and inquired, "Are you an actress?" "No," I said, disappointing her, "I'm a fiction writer." I had the feeling she wanted me to be an actress—it's more glamorous, I suppose—and to make amends I said, "Inside many a writer lives an actor." Nodding agreeably, but clearly dissatisfied, the girl returned to her work. Had she been interested I could have explained that writing, like acting, is an experiment in living, and that the writer (and the actor), by lifting himself out of his own particular life, looks at life from another point of view.

What is point of view, and what does it have to do with writing, or acting, or the persons behind either of these creative arts? The dictionary says point of view is a "position from which something is considered or evaluated." All right; that seems clear. The writer takes up a position from which to tell a story. What position? A reader might say, "That's simple; he tells a story in either the first or third person." It might seem simple, but for the writer it is not.

There are at least six third-person viewpoints and five first-person viewpoints, some rarely used. To discuss all of these or to discuss technique without a story to hang it on can be confusing. Even though the writer has an intellectual mastery of viewpoint techniques, he may not create a good viewpoint character. Writers learn by doing. Did Chekhov sit down and ask himself, "Should I adopt the position of concealed narrator and third-person protagonist narrator restricted, or what?" Or did he simply write "The Kiss"?

This is not to say that it is unimportant to learn technique, for a writer needs to learn as much as he can about the tools of his craft. But tools are only a means to something more, and a preoccupation with them can lead to mechanical writing. Viewpoint, then, is not a matter of manipulation, of attaching oneself, willy-nilly, to a position, to a character, and then telling the story through that character's mind and feelings. Viewpoint is organic, and writers have in common with the actor the method to make it work.

An actor trained in the Stanislavski method knows the psychology of his character; he knows *how* he does things because first he knows *why*. The actor tries to put himself in his character's place, to enter his world, live his life, master his actions, his thoughts and feelings. His truth. It is not enough merely to think of an emotion. Abstract emotions don't come across, or they fall into clichés. It is better to imagine what a character might think or do in a *certain situation*. Then the emotion comes of itself.

A writer uses a similar method of organic viewpoint. He puts himself in his character's place, enters his world, indeed creates his world, suffers his pains and celebrates his joys. If a writer has never laughed or cried at his typewriter, then I doubt if he has ever been deeply inside a character.

Before a writer takes up a viewpoint position he might do well to consider his own temperament and personality and the limitations these impose on his choices. Fiction is personal, as personal as the writer's imagination and emotional experience. New writers are often told, "Write what you know." I would broaden that by saying, "Write what you know emotionally." Love, hate, anger, joy, fear—these are universal. They become unique when they are connected to experience. Our emotional experiences are stored within us. Filtered through memory and a well-developed imagination, they can be called up, made fresh and organized into the work at hand. Creative imagination is the writer's valuable gift, and even though it is somewhat limited by his experience, within that sphere of experience it is unlimited in variety and combination. Hopefully the writer is always enlarging his sphere, adding to his storehouse with outward experience in reality.

Out of the sphere of my emotional experience I wrote "The Poet of Evolution Avenue" (*Redbook*), the story of a young wife and mother who was, also, a bad poet. She believed her creative gift was being hampered by the intrusion of her family. She had neither the time nor the privacy to write a real poem. Time and privacy are practically forced on her in the form of a vacation alone in her father's California apartment, but it isn't until she is ready to go home that she is able to write a real poem, and then only because she doesn't want to go home empty-handed.

This story is based on the old Ivory Tower idea: a poet is more productive when isolated from the world. My poet discovered that she had been making excuses for herself, that her world was her stimulus, and that she had trouble producing poetry without it.

The idea for that story came out of my own emotional experience. Some years earlier I had gone to California to be near my father while he was in the hospital undergoing surgery. For three weeks I lived alone in his apartment, a large, tight-security building in which I rarely saw the other residents. I had brought my typewriter, thinking I would turn out a volume or two between hospital visits. It didn't work. I was accustomed to working with people around. Interruptions. Interruptions can be marvelous. They take the place of pacing, a necessary activity of some writers. I learned that I am not an Ivory Tower writer, ideal as that may seem; I need the stimulus of family and friends.

Every writer has his own voice, and it is up to him to find it and use it with authority. That voice comes through as male or female, child or adult, humorous or serious, but behind it, within it, is the author's brooding presence, his vision of life. He describes the world from his point of view. He is on intimate terms with his viewpoint characters. Henry James could imagine what his focal character (he is never named) in *The Aspern Papers* might think and do when he is forced to admit to the woman who loves him that he has been using her for his personal gain. But I doubt if James could have lived inside Bigger, as Richard Wright did in *Native Son*, and chased and killed the huge rat in a Chicago tenement. Who is to say one view is better or worse than another? Each is different, unique.

Recognizing his limitations, an author adopts a viewpoint position he can understand emotionally as well as intellectually. My story, "Miss Dillon's Secret" (*Redbook*), is about a teacher. I have never been a teacher, but teaching is within the sphere of my emotional experience. I have been a student, of course, and my husband, now a principal, was once a teacher. His experiences have rubbed off on me. I believe that a natural teacher is born, not made, that the qualities in such a person work together to make learning exciting. The title character in my story, Miss Dillon, is drawn from a real person, an experienced teacher whose students come back to visit her with their husbands and wives and children and grandchildren.

I adopted the viewpoint position of a young teacher who had worked with Miss Dillon. There were more decisions for me to make. Will I place myself inside or outside the viewpoint character? And how far inside or outside? This can be a difficult choice, for each character has its own limitations, and the author, to keep his voice appropriate to the viewpoint, puts limits on his "knowledge" accordingly. He seems to know less than he does. Consider, for example, Hemingway's camera-eye view which limits his "knowledge" to what can be seen from the outside. Or, at the other extreme, Joyce's deep internalizing, which limits him in the other direction.

For my viewpoint character I adopted a position somewhere in between. With the story told in the third person, my character's problems are external, but her discovery of Miss Dillon's secret is internal, brought about by an emotional experience with one of her former students.

We might ask ourselves certain questions concerning viewpoint: 1) Who will be the narrator? author, in first or third person? character, in first person? or nobody (omniscient narrator)? 2) From what angle does the narrator tell the story? Above, center, front, periphery, shifting? 3) Where does the author place the reader? Near, far, shifting?

Sometimes an author adopts a viewpoint position instinctively, and all goes well. The voice flows from a stable position. At other times an author finds himself tangled in clumsy sentences and tedious explanations, surrendering his surprises too early, battling predictability, placing his best scenes offstage. When this happens, the problem could very well be the viewpoint he chose. He may be looking from the wrong angle. Usually I can tell by the way it "feels" if I'm in a good or poor viewpoint. But not always. Four years ago I wrote a short story called "The Boy Who Cooked." The title character, Benny, was the antagonist, and the viewpoint character was a woman protagonist whose name changed with each of the many versions I wrote. I couldn't sell the story. But I continued writing it, on and off, for four years, always keeping the boy, but frequently changing the characters around him, including the viewpoint character. The total number of pages devoted to that story runs into several hundred, which is some indication of my devotion to a character. But finally I gave up and put the story away.

Meanwhile, I had written and sold a story called, "No Such Thing as a Happy Marriage" (*Redbook*), in which the viewpoint character was a wife and mother named Jenny. Six months after that story was published, my editor, in a letter to me, mentioned Benny, the boy who cooked. Even before I had finished reading the letter, Benny, like Lazarus, rose from the dead. Why couldn't I write a new story for Benny? And why couldn't I surround him with the same cast of characters I had used in "No Such Thing as a Happy Marriage," with Jenny as the viewpoint character? I could, and I did. This time the viewpoint felt right; the voice flowed clearly from a stable position, and I wrote the story in a matter of hours. After four years of roaming through my typewriter, Benny had found his place, and his story, "The Boy Who Cooked," was published in *Redbook*.

The author's attitude toward a character (and his desire to create a similar attitude in the reader) can help determine the angle from which he views him. If the character is obviously sympathetic, the reader will identify. With some characters, however, the reader may feel only a tentative sympathy, until he is shocked into understanding by some revelation which allows him to feel complete sympathy. Sometimes, reader and character start out with a great distance between them. Perhaps their worlds are totally different. The author gradually pulls the reader into the character's world, and the reader ends by feeling sympathy. (I have this experience, as a reader, when I read Jean Genêt, for example.) A difficult relationship for an author to achieve is one in which the reader is forced to identify, perhaps unconsciously, with a character he dislikes. He is left wondering what there was about the story that fascinated him. What he may not realize is that, being human, we all

have our share of unattractive qualities, and seeing them in someone else stirs our recognition. Playwright Harold Pinter frequently
achieves this kind of relationship.

In my story, "An Uncompromising Girl" (*Redbook*), my aim
was for tentative sympathy and eventual complete sympathy. As
the author (concealed narrator), I speak in the third person
through the focal character. The channels of information between
author and reader are a combination of the author's words,
thoughts, and perceptions, and the character's words, actions,
thoughts, perceptions and feelings. I used the angle of the character attempting to see herself from the outside, but erring in her
vision—a position which placed limits on my "knowledge" of the
character.

Earlier I spoke of the writer's voice, which I related to his vision
of life and which includes his entire personality. Now, to that voice
I would add two more voices: the story voice, which is the pace,
the music, the tone of the story; and the voice of the viewpoint
character, since it is through his eyes that we see everything that
happens. Actually, it is impossible to separate all these voices, fused
as they are into a creation that has passed through a maturing
process in the author's mind and found its way to the page, either in
harmony or dissonance. But for the sake of clarity, let us for a
moment consider the voice of the viewpoint character.

If a story is told in the first person through a character (and not
the author), then that character's voice is ever-present, and the
writer, like the method actor, must know the character's every
thought, act, feeling and desire. He must know his truth, his conscious and unconscious life, what he wants, or thinks he wants, and
the difference between the two. My story "Don't Call Me Darling"
(*Redbook*), was written from such a viewpoint. I had to know my
character's attitude toward herself as a woman pursuing a career.
I had to know how she felt about women's rights in general. And
how she felt about friendship and human communication. I had to
understand her intellect, her ambitions, her habits, and her insights. When she spoke, she revealed herself as a careful individual, and this voice had to remain consistent throughout the story,
even though some of her attitudes were undergoing a change.

When an author knows the details of action and speech in a

character, he is in control of his material. He can become more familiar with his character by spending time with him, engaging him in conversation or argument, as if he were a living entity. He may even want to get up from his typewriter to act out a detail, a gesture, or an entire scene, in order to visualize it more clearly in his mind. Creating characters, seeing them come to life, is an exciting experience.

The entire experience of a story, from start to finish—and it may cover a period of several years—is an exciting one, in spite of the hard work, frustration and failures. Not a small portion of that excitement lies in the discoveries that are made, for in any work of creative imagination one looks for insights. What does the story have to say? Does it reinforce a shallow view of life? Or does it open up new insights for the viewpoint character? When I write a story about a character who seems very real to me, am I not at the same time making a discovery about myself? Writing, like acting, is an experiment in living. It is looking at life from another viewpoint. And life can be exciting wherever it is lived, or re-created—on the stage, or on the page.

40

WRITING THE MYSTERY SHORT STORY

By Edward D. Hoch

When I was first beginning to write, a well-known mystery novelist advised me to forget about short stories and concentrate on novels. "Why waste a good plot idea on a short story?" he argued.

I've now been publishing short stories for eighteen years, with a total of close to 400 in all, and I don't feel that I've ever wasted a plot. In fact, I sometimes think that the plot devices used in my occasional novels might have been put to more effective use in a shorter length.

But the difference between novels and short stories is much greater than mere length or payment alone. Graham Greene, a writer I greatly admire, wrote recently that in spending some years writing a novel, "the author is not the same man at the end of the book as he was at the beginning." For this reason, he views short stories as a form of escape for him, "escape from having to live with another character for years on end, picking up his jealousies, his meanness, his dishonest tricks of thought, his betrayals."

The economics of modern mystery novel writing generally preclude an author's spending more than a few months on its composition, and yet he can still suffer from the sort of problem Greene mentions. If a story is to have any sort of unity, there should be a unity to the author's mood while he is about the business of writing it. This unity, obviously, is more easily achieved in a short story.

Basically, that is why I prefer writing short stories to writing novels, and here is how I go about it. If my remarks are directed mainly toward the mystery short story, it is because this genre has been the most successful for me. But they're just as applicable to science fiction, adventure, or any short story where the emphasis is on plot.

I suppose the ideal short story should be written, as John O'Hara wrote many of his, in one sitting. I have achieved this ideal occasionally with short-shorts, but never with anything longer. The technique I use most often is to plot out the story in great detail in my mind before starting to write it. I do not use written outlines for my short stories, though an outline of sorts exists in my mind before the first words go down on paper.

I begin sometimes with a character, or an unusual setting, or a plot twist that has occurred to me. Often I have started with nothing more than an unusual, provocative title—only to have an editor change the title after the story was sold. At times, when a new plot does not come full-bodied to mind, I will often try to combine two or three separate elements from my notes. Thus, I combined a newspaper article on a shooting at a wedding reception with a magazine article on a new Hollywood technique for faking bullet wounds. By the time I'd worked out a way of combining the two, I had my plot for "The Leopold Locked Room," a story published in *Ellery Queen's Mystery Magazine,* and later dramatized on television's *McMillan and Wife* (NBC-TV).

A personal experience of mine—a trip to a hospital emergency ward for treatment of a gashed forehead—afforded a plot which virtually wrote itself in my mind while the doctor was stitching up my wound. The story, "Emergency," was published by *Alfred Hitchcock's Mystery Magazine.*

By its very nature, a detective story—and to some extent, a crime story—must have a beginning and an ending. While a mainstream short story might well be started without its author's knowing quite where he's headed, this is virtually impossible in the detective short story. On the few occasions when I've started with only the beginning of a plot in mind, I've generally had to rewrite that beginning completely by the time I reached the end. For me, at least, it's much easier to have the story plotted out in my mind before the writing starts.

Certainly, this does not mean that every detail, every clue, every encounter, must be thought out in advance. Much of the fun of writing (and it *is* fun most of the time) comes from creating little plot twists as you go along—extra pluses that help make each story something special.

I'm often asked by beginning writers if they should concentrate on short stories as I have done through much of my career till now. Frankly, the markets are few, and the pay in most instances is not especially high. But once an author has published a number of stories, there are many secondary sources of income: anthology appearances, foreign sales, television adaptations, movie options. With luck you might even find a publisher willing to gamble on a collection of your stories.

The key to all this, of course, is to be prolific. I now publish about thirty stories a year in a variety of magazines and original anthologies. Almost all are mysteries, or science fiction stories with a strong mystery element. For those who wonder how it's possible to come up with thirty separate plot ideas in a year's time, I can give a fairly simple answer: *create series characters.*

These characters can be detectives or criminals, but it's important that they grow and develop with each story, that they become familiar to the magazine's regular readers. The first story I ever published concerned a mystic detective named Simon Ark who went on to appear in twenty-seven stories during the years that followed. At the present writing, six of my series characters appear regularly in the pages of *Ellery Queen's Mystery Magazine,* a publication especially amenable to the series format.

There are two prime reasons why a short story author (or any author) should try to develop series characters. The first is the obvious economic one. An editor who has already purchased a story about a given character is a ready market for a second or third story about the same character. But perhaps more important, a series character gives the writer a starting place, a familiar viewpoint that can be a big part of the story.

Sometimes, a plot will come to mind simply if you put your familiar series character in an unfamiliar setting or have him meet a strong or unusual protagonist. Especially effective in adding depth to your continuing character is the gimmick of having the crime he's investigating somehow involve his personal life. In this way, my series detective, Captain Leopold, uncovered a forgotten murder when he was invited to a reunion of his old high school class. This story, "Reunion," grew out of my own class reunion and has been widely reprinted since its original publication in *The Saint Mystery Magazine* back in December 1964.

The best detective stories naturally depend upon a surprise solution or unexpected twist at the end. Ideally, this should be saved for the last possible moment—even the last sentence of the story. This last sentence can be used effectively to reveal the murderer's identity or to deliver a shock of the sort the reader will remember, as in my story, "The Oblong Room" (which won an Edgar from the Mystery Writers of America).

In some cases where post-revelation explanations are in order, the story must continue for a page or so after the killer is revealed. It is important in such instances to avoid dullness in your explanations. Break up the paragraphs with questions from other characters, and if possible, still save some especially clever clue or twist for the last line. It will send the reader away satisfied.

In a series detective story, it is usually best to use some secondary character to serve as a "Watson" of sorts. If you use a series criminal, where no formal detection is called for, it is possible for him to be more of a loner. But we've come a long way from those days when the Watson was typed as a bumbling friend or stupid policeman. Today, he can be almost as smart as the protagonist. He may be the detective's friend or co-worker, or even a superior to whom our hero must report periodically. (This last is especially effective in spy stories.) With an eye on possible television sales, you might even want a pretty girl cast in this secondary role, with or without romantic interest in the detective.

Much of what I've said about series detectives applies equally to the short story or the novel, of course. The major difference is that character development in a series of short stories can come over a period of several episodes. Interest is built as readers learn a little bit more each time about the detective, his past life and personal quirks.

Occasionally, if one story in a series proves especially successful because of plot or setting, the author can return to something similar in a later episode using some of the same characters. Thus, my series spy Rand in "The Spy and the Nile Mermaid" (*Ellery Queen's Mystery Magazine*) journeyed to Egypt, where he shared

an adventure with a girl named Leila Gaad. The encounter proved
so successful that Rand has returned to Egypt for two further adventures, creating a series within a series.

But one important thing to remember with a series character
is that the reader must not be cheated. Each story must stand on
its own feet as a story. Such a caution is even more important
when writing a non-series story. You must give the reader some
reason for an emotion at the finish—whether that emotion be pleasure or sorrow or even anger at having been tricked.

I'm often asked how much rewriting is necessary, and my reply
is that it depends upon the individual story. I've sold good stories
without changing a word, and I've sold equally good stories after
laboring over them for weeks, writing three or four drafts. In most
cases I rewrite only portions of the story, to insert some extra clue
or description or bit of characterization. On the whole, a mystery
short story usually requires far less rewriting and revision than
would a novel, and not simply because it's shorter. The story is
short, yes, but the creative time span is also short. There is a unit
of time and purpose.

To paraphrase Graham Greene, if you write short stories, you're
usually the same person at the end of a short story as you were at
the beginning.

41

THE INNOCENCE OF EDEN—ALMOST

By Linda Jacobs

REMEMBER first love, when you held his hand, wore his ring, and trembled from a single kiss? The two of you were Adam and Eve, returned to the innocence of Eden.

If you can capture that memory without becoming maudlin and update it for today's young readers, you have the makings of a light romance writer.

Light romance doesn't pretend to present life as it is, but sets itself the task of presenting it as we'd like it to be. It's an almost-Eden world of innocent love, uncomplicated by deep psychological problems, and untinged by sex. Its heroines are all pure and virginal; its heroes, noble. Its endings are always happy. The theme is always some variation of the old "love conquers all"—or, more specifically, unselfishness and hard work will win love and triumph over hardship.

You may ask, in this era of sex and gore and depressive reactions, who reads such wholesome stories?

Thousands of female readers, that's who. The target audience is teen-age girls, but the actual audience is any female between twelve and ninety. This large readership devours huge numbers of romance novels in both hardcover and paperback. You can share this enthusiastic audience by mastering the simple, basic formula:

A young woman (of say, twenty-one to twenty-seven) finds herself in a new and exciting environment. Perhaps she has taken a new job or entered some kind of athletic or artistic competition.

She faces both a career problem and a choice between two young men. In the career area, she may need to win some prize, or accomplish a particularly difficult task or prove herself in some way. In the area of romance, she must choose between two attractive young men, both of whom are interested in her.

One of these men is usually somewhat older and has a broken romance or other hurt (perhaps even a scandal) in his past. He rattles the heroine's composure every time she sees him.

The other young man is not so mysterious and far more friendly. The heroine feels comfortable with him.

Other complications, in the form of a woman interested in one of the men—or even two women, each interested in one of the men —can get in the heroine's way.

Whatever happens by the end of the book the heroine has achieved her career objective and chosen the right man. (He's usually the mysterious one.)

The left-over man is paired off with one of the other women, or he is revealed to be something of a rat.

To turn a cold formula into a warm and exciting story, begin with your heroine. Make her a spunky, courageous girl. Give her a temper. Or an iron will. Or a sense of humor. Or all three. The "Fragile Flower of Femininity" is out in modern light romance.

Preferably, your heroine should have one or more characteristics that make her vulnerable in spite of her spunk. In my novel, *Rainbow for Clari*, the heroine Clarissa Roberts had ". . . a figure that insisted on being plump, a face with too many freckles, and strawberry blonde hair that looked as if somebody had spun carrots into silk." She also had a voice that squeaked whenever she was excited or upset.

Once you've created an appealingly vulnerable and spunky heroine, give her a career interest. A dictionary of occupational titles will yield numerous vocations with dramatic possibilities. I've used a drama student, a teacher, an artist. What about a social worker, a dancer, a singer, a lawyer, or a dress designer? What about a lady pilot? Occupations such as these lend themselves to exciting situations. Which brings us to the next thing your heroine needs: a new environment, fraught with career challenges and peopled with interesting characters. I put my drama student into a make-or-break scholarship competition. In *Rainbow for Clari*, the heroine was an artist who won a fellowship to paint at a famous resort.

You can create many exciting scenes as your heroine struggles to achieve her ambitions. Many more interesting scenes come from her involvement with other characters in the story. Most impor-

tant of these characters are two young men, both of whom are interested in the heroine. Make them as different as possible from one
another, but both attractive to the heroine. Then watch your plot
boil!

Clari Roberts was already semi-engaged to Mike Stokes and
found her life complicated by Bart Channing. Mike was carefree
and irresponsible. He "looked like a sun-tanned Viking prince,
noble but only half-civilized." Bart was a serious-minded man with
an injury that caused him to limp. He "was built like a football
lineman, with a craggy face that would fit perfectly carved into the
stone of Mount Rushmore."

As the creator (writer), you will, of course, know which man will
be your heroine's choice. For maximum suspense, start the reader
rooting for Mr. Right early in the story, but make Mr. Wrong into
a viable opponent until the last possible moment. You'll worry your
reader to enthralled distraction!

One good way to start reader sympathy in the right direction is
to make the first meeting with Mr. Right into a genuine Momentous Occasion. To achieve this effect, I like to use an embarrassing
situation. In one book, I had my heroine doing a pratfall in spilled
currant jelly at the moment the hero came on the scene. Even in
the final love scene, he was still teasing her about girls who swim
in currant jelly.

In *Rainbow for Clari,* I decided to forgo the embarrassing meeting because I used Bart's limp to lend drama. I didn't want Clari's
interest in him (or the reader's) to center entirely on his handicap,
so before she realized that he limped, I had "something" make her
nervous. Then Bart asks her a blunt question about her work:

> The question was so sudden, so direct that Clari was stunned. She wasn't too
> stunned to realize, though, that the something making her a bundle of nerves was
> Bart Channing. . . . He chuckled, a mellow sound deep in his throat. "I don't
> bite, Miss Roberts."

Bart is already established as an interesting and compelling man
before he gets up from his desk and reveals his handicap. Clari respects him too much to be either curious or patronizing. Bart obviously appreciates her tact:

"Thanks for not saying, 'Oh, did something happen to your leg?' I hear that too much for comfort." . . .

"I thought you might," Clari said softly.

No use being hypocritical and telling him she hadn't noticed (she thought). Bart chuckled softly under his breath and . . . guided her to the door as if she were his date at a fancy party instead of just an applicant for the artists' program.

To find a Momentous Occasion for your first meeting, remember that you want to arouse the immediate interest of the heroine and the reader in the hero. Think of ways for the hero and heroine to meet that are dramatic or funny, silly or sad.

Once they've met, get them immediately involved with one another. Throw them together constantly. Let the hero rescue the heroine from some uncomfortable or dangerous situation. Complicate their relationship with Mr. Wrong, with personality differences and suspicions. Perhaps the hero has a tragic past romance with a beautiful and mysterious woman. This woman could be only a memory. Better yet, she could return to his life at just the wrong moment. If she is cruel and calculating, the heroine can oppose her from the start.

Clari's rival was an exotic, green-eyed woman named Renée, who had broken her engagement to Bart because she didn't want to marry someone with a handicap. After two years, she returned during the story and made cutting remarks about Bart's limp. Because of this cruelty, Renée became Clari's enemy long before Clari realized her love for Bart.

All of your characters move through a steadily building series of incidents, until the heroine has achieved her career objective, discarded Mr. Wrong, and realized her love for Mr. Right. At the time she realizes this love, she should be wholly convinced that the hero could never love her.

Two chapters before Clari realized her love for Bart, she accidentally saw him kissing Renée. A device such as this sets the stage for you to extract maximum drama from the moment when the heroine admits (to herself) that she is hopelessly in love with the hero.

That moment should be heart-tugging and dramatic. I used a fight between Bart and Mike to let Clari realize her love for Bart and finally repudiate the irresponsible Mike:

[Mike] grabbed Bart's arm, whirling him around. Bart's bad leg threw him off balance, and Mike's fist rammed into his stomach . . . "Oh, Bart," Clari whispered, kneeling beside him . . . "Let's get out of here, Clari," Mike snapped. "No," Clari shot back . . . and her heart supplied the reason that the memory of an exotic green-eyed woman forbade her to speak; I love you, Bart Channing.

With this private realization on the part of your heroine, you can delay the actual love scene and play that final agony for all it's worth. When the moment looks blackest and the heroine is ready to leave without confessing her love, don't ease up on her! If possible, have a final, quick incident that seems to confirm her fears. It can be an erroneous remark by a minor character or something she sees and misinterprets.

Clari saw Bart ask to talk to Renée—alone. She ran back to her room to cry and look at a painting she'd done of him. She had told him earlier that the painting was sold, but—believing it was all she could ever have of him—she had secretly kept it. That set the stage for Bart's arrival, and the love scene.

The minute he stepped inside, he spotted the painting . . . [Clari's] tears wouldn't stay back. Her love for him poured out . . . "Oh, Clari," he breathed, "you do love me. . . . I knew last night that you were over [Mike] Stokes, but that didn't mean you were ready"—he broke off, pain and tenderness mingling in his eyes. "I love you, darling."

Clari vowed her love, and the remainder of the final scene cleaned up loose ends, with an explanation for Bart's kissing Renée and for his asking to see her alone.

Your love scene should be emotional but sexless, sweet without being sticky. It should also be brief. Don't pour a ton of adjectives into that climactic love scene where hero and heroine fall into each other's arms. When the hero and the heroine pledge their love, answer dangling questions, and bring the book to a close with a summation that sings like the triumphant chord of a symphony. I ended *Rainbow for Clari* simply:

The old love—the unpredictable, youthful recklessness of it—was gone. This was deeper, sweeter. This was the rainbow that would last forever.

You can achieve this "final chord" effect by echoing a symbol that you've used several times throughout the book. The "rainbow" appears in the title, in a scene where Clari paints a rainbow, and in her thoughts about the unsteady nature of her relationship with Mike. Its appearance in the final sentence ties the whole book together. Elementary symbolism of this type is effective in light romance. It enhances meaning and—not incidentally—intrigues and pleases the reader.

In writing light romance for modern readers, guard against being overly sweet or coy. Go through your finished manuscript on a purple prose hunt. Cut adjectives. Cut handwringing and excessive tears. Cut any hint of cowardice or self-pity on the part of your heroine. Excessive sweetness isn't the only thing that can kill a light romance. Slang or self-conscious attempts to be "with it" are just as bad. Write your dialogue straight. Create a world of your own where "now" can be anytime.

To understand this almost-Eden, any time world of light romance, read examples of the genre. Get a feel for the tone and style and permissible variations in the formula.

If all that reading leaves you eager to plot your first light romance, then go to it. If it leaves you cold, then try some other kind of writing. Don't try to write light romance if you think it's "stupid." Only if you believe—as I do—that innocent heroines and noble heroes ought to have a place in this world. Even if it is only in fiction.

42

FROM WOULD-BE TO HAS-BEEN

By Susanne Jaffe

WHAT a terribly negative and down-beat word: "has-been." It brings to mind the image of a once bright and brilliant light who has burned out his power, or worse even, a light who burned bright and brilliant but once.

Don't let the word fool you. There's a wide-open and potentially lucrative field available to the writer who is willing to be patient and take the necessary precautions to go from would-be hopeful writer to has-been hopeful. Not has-been writer, mind you; just has-been hopeful.

That field is the original paperback book market. In recent years, hardcover publishers have suffered from the profits of their step-child. While hardcover houses still turn out new literary endeavors, they stay in business primarily from the sales of a handful of established "name" writers and the sale of rights to a paperback house. Most hardcover houses suffer too much prestige and too little profit. They cannot afford to take too many risks; they cannot afford to publish unknowns. Many paperback houses not only survive but thrive on the risks they take with unknown, previously unpublished writers.

As an editor for several years with the commonplace burning desire to "be a writer," I watched my would-be dreams roll on, while my typewriter stayed silent. Until vanity became the better part of laziness.

I grew tired of reading and accepting other unknowns' work. I felt it was high time I stopped procrastinating and got down to business. The worst that could happen was that I would get one of those deadly, ego-shattering, confidence-destroying rejection notes—but hadn't I read somewhere that Hemingway had received a "trunkload" before he sold his first piece? I, too, would survive.

But where to begin? It is no secret that editors of major hard-cover publishing firms usually prefer reading agented manuscripts. Those that come in over the transom or as part of the "slush" pile invariably take longer to make their way to the top for editorial consideration. Original paperback publishers, especially the smaller houses, are not so unfeeling. Their editors will read unsolicited manuscripts, and eagerly. They know that the possibility exists that somewhere in that heap is a potential best seller, and they gladly ferret through the pages to find him. Lesson number one, then, in going from would-be hopeful to has-been is, *Do not be afraid of submitting your manuscript on your own.*

There are several outstanding guides on the market for the un-agented writer which tell him about the various publishers. Start with a small house, if possible, where you can almost be guaranteed that your manuscript will be read. Your payment, if your work is bought, will not be outstanding, but that should not be the point. The idea is to get published, and to see your name on a book cover in your local bookstore. The feeling is unequalled! Many writers go for years, go throughout their writing career without an agent; it is better, however, to have one working for you, and this can be done after you've made that first sale. You no longer are an un-known quantity—you've published; somebody paid you for the words you put out. That means that an agent can probably get someone to pay you more the next time. But right now the impor-tant thing to remember is that you *can* do it on your own.

Lesson number two now comes into existence, and it is a vitally important one. *Study your potential market.* There is nothing an overworked, underpaid editor detests more than reading inappro-priate material. Most publishing houses have general fiction and nonfiction divisions, and categories such as westerns, Gothics, sci-ence fiction, romance, mysteries, how-tos, and so on. Some houses are based only on categories and do not have a general fiction or nonfiction department. It is particularly distressing for a Gothics editor, for instance, who knows he *cannot* purchase any other kind of book, to come across a well-written adult novel and have to reject it, suggesting to the author that he send his manuscript to a competitor.

Those same market guides for writers tell you the kinds of books in which a particular house specializes. Study these guides; read some of the books a specific publisher has brought out. Don't make the mistake of storing your historical romance in your attic because it was turned down by a science fiction editor somewhere. You can avoid this by knowing what paperback houses handle your kind of story.

At this point you have your manuscript, you have a list of potential publishers for it, and you're already counting your royalty checks because you've shown the book to some of your friends, and they think it's excellent. It very well might be the best book on Jewish mothers since *Portnoy's Complaint*, but don't tell an editor that in your covering letter. That's what he's paid for—to judge what's good, what's publishable, what's most salable. So lesson number three to remember is basically the *technique of submitting a manuscript*. Send in a simply query and keep a record of the date you sent it; if you have not received an answer in three weeks, move on to the next house on your list. A query may save you the whole problem of wrong submissions. And *don't hedge in your query*. If your manuscript is primarily a romance with a hint of mystery, don't claim it as a Gothic or a mystery because you think that is what the publisher would like. If you get a positive answer on your query, send in your *completed* manuscript with return postage and envelope. As an unpublished and unagented writer, you need to send in the complete work rather than a partial or an outline. The editor is willing to take risks but not foolhardy ones. Too often, an editor will come across seventy-five or one hundred outstanding pages and a powerful outline, ask for the completed work, and find it a deadly dud. There is no arguing the point that this leaves the writer somewhere out in the wilderness. His manuscript may be sitting for months on an editor's desk only to be rejected, but this is the risk he must take.

There are certain other areas, dealing more with actual writing style, that many original paperback editors stand firm on. They concern: characterization, dialogue and narrative, sex and author intervention. These four points, when mishandled, can do as little for an editor as receiving the wrong type of manuscript.

Though you have probably read and heard many times that you should write about what and whom you know, this is often carried to an extreme by the writer trying to break into print. *Do not be overly truthful*. A writer's gift is not only his way with words but how his imagination lets him create a believable story out of his observations and conclusions. Whether you are writing a mystery, a romance, or whatever, an editor does not want to feel it is a biography or autobiography. Characters should be based on people you may know, but they should be developed through your imagination. This fusion breathes life into them, makes them more real—which they should be in words. This does not mean your characters should be caricatures. The idea is to use what you know to create what others will find interesting and original.

Do not carry dialogue into narrative, and *do not forget that dialogue is the spoken word*. These are pitfalls of many neophyte writers, and they make the editor take out his blue pencil and work. Dialogue should be supremely realistic, appropriate to the people, environment and era you are writing about. Two bearded hippies arranging to make a drug connection would not say, "I will be there tomorrow at seven o'clock. I will see you then." Yet this is often the kind of writing an editor reads, because the writer has not discovered the knack of letting the words flow *naturally* when spoken, of fitting the dialogue to the thrust of the book. The same thing occurs with narrative, but in reverse. Narrative should appeal to all readers; there should not be regionality about it, nor idiom. Narrative furthers the story simply, cleanly, without ado. Yet again, editors often find themselves rewriting entire paragraphs because the author used quick, breezy, idiomatic, dialogue-style writing where straightforward narrative was called for.

Unless you're writing specifically for a pornographic publisher, *don't go overboard with your sexual descriptions*. True, today sex books are selling better than almost any other kind, but even they are not truly pornographic. An editor is quite human and enjoys reading a good healthy sex description in his normal work day, but cute euphemisms that you may have thought up for parts of the anatomy, and strange contortions that make the editor stop to wonder if they are physically possible—this the editor does not enjoy reading in his normal work day. Again, study the publisher(s) you plan to send your manuscript to and see just how far they go.

Do not preach. Undoubtedly, you are writing your novel in some small measure because you have something to say; you have feelings about certain things that you would like to share with others. Share them, but through your characters and their actions and motivations. Do not place yourself on a podium and give your opinions as you would say them. Let the story do it for you.

As I said at the outset, the original paperback book field is a wide-open and lucrative one, especially for the beginning writer. You know what editors of these publishing houses consistently avoid, and what they wish you, the writer, would avoid. There is no guarantee that if you avoid these pitfalls, your manuscript will be read and accepted, but your chances are improved. Remember: original paperback publishers not only survive but thrive on new material—good, salable material—and you have just as much chance of breaking into the market as anyone else, if you meet the publisher halfway. From there you're only a contract away from would-be to has-been.

43

PLANNING A MYSTERY

By Stanley Ellin

It took me ten long years of apprenticeship at my trade to learn that the closing lines of a mystery story are more important than the opening lines, which is why I was a haggard thirty when writing became my vocation, and not a fresh and bouncing twenty.

This hiatus between the time I first sat down, forefingers poised over an old Underwood, and the time I became what writers' magazines fondly call a "Selling Writer" was not altogether my fault. When I was twenty, we were still in the golden age of detective pulps (observe that they were "detective" magazines, not "mystery" magazines) and one was distinctly given to understand that the formula for cranking out a proper story in the genre was as rigid as that for a No play. The big thing was a Narrative Hook calculated to grip the reader's attention instantly and get the story's hero off to a running start, after which he was kept running through and around various plotted obstacles until, within five thousand words, he finally disposed of the villain.

If the hero's strong point was deduction, the deduction was frequently given a vital assist by the villain himself, who, when cornered at the story's climax, would immediately blubber out a full confession of his crime, including motive and method. Most professional criminals, as I have since learned, are inclined to be tight-lipped fellows, glad to have their lawyers do all their talking for them, but the detective magazine villains in the golden age rarely fell back on that kind of shoddy device. Lucky for the writers they didn't, or it would have ruined many an epic tale.

The fact is—and anyone who has plowed through enough back issues of the old pulps will verify it—the golden age of pulps was really much more brass than gold, which, if I may be forgiven a digression, sometimes has me wondering about the golden ages of

Greece, opera, and television. As far as pulp writing went, it had gone its limit very quickly after writers like Dashiell Hammett, Raymond Chandler, and James M. Cain turned away from it. What remained was a host of their admirers filling the pulps with imitations of them, and while imitation may be the sincerest form of flattery, it also means sure death to a literary form when it hardens into tired formula. Even without the entrance of paperback books and television on the scene to sweep the pulps out of existence, pulp detective story writing had already doomed itself to death anyhow, just the way slick magazine fiction doomed itself to death soon afterward by petrifying into formula.

But this is hindsight, of course, and does not change the fact that there I was in the mid-1930's, solemnly striving to master the art of the Narrative Hook, cooking up heroes and villains, and gory episodes for them to plunge through, making sure my stories ran to exactly five thousand words, often in the way of a tailor snipping off pieces of customer to fit the suit, and, for all of it, collecting rejection slips by the carload. Between times, I devoted myself to reading articles in the writers' magazines where authors who were successfully belting them out at the rate of a million words a year cheered me on by explaining that very often they started a story going without the least idea of its plot or complications. "Once I get going, the yarn just seems to tell itself," they would remark, snapping the rubber bands on their fat bankrolls. Obviously they had a point. If a story was merely a string of episodes linked by a thread of plot, there was no reason why it couldn't go in practically any direction at all with fine effect, providing you had that Narrative Hook just right to start with. Apparently, I never did have it just right.

It was ten years, as I have remarked, before I saw the light and started to consider the writing of a mystery story from the correct angle, which is back to front. The change was forced on me. There were no more detective pulps left. What was left was a constant reprinting of de Maupassant and Saki and stories like Hemingway's "The Killers" and Maugham's "The Letter" and Faulkner's "A Rose for Emily" and Anatole France's "The Procurator of Judaea", which remains just about the finest short story ever written. And, as time went on, there appeared among the fiction studies of exurbanite *Weltschmerz* in *The New Yorker* some stuff by somebody named

Roald Dahl and, great day, a story called "The Lottery" by a lady named Shirley Jackson. The Dahl and Jackson stories were as out of place in *The New Yorker* as a leopard would be in granny's parlor, especially since that magazine dislikes arrant shockers in fiction and regards the name of O. Henry as anathema; but these two writers, using the O. Henry shock-ending technique, were in *The New Yorker* simply because they were too good to be left out.

From the vantage point of my old age, I can say that O. Henry's technique can be studied with profit by any mystery writer. The trouble with O. Henry was never his technique, which is so frequently brilliant, but his tendency to use types instead of people, to depend too often on surprise for the sake of surprise, no matter how logically he built to it, and, above all, to lean toward open sentimentality. Even his occasional cynicism seems weak and hollow. Now, if it had been the healthy, believable cynicism of a Hammett or Chandler—!

In a world denuded of detective pulps, it was writers like Jackson and Dahl who suggested the direction to take if one still had an interest in writing stories about murder or robbery or swindle. And part of the lesson to be learned was that dealing with a story idea from back to front didn't mean adherence to just another kind of formula, but, in fact, meant freedom from formula. It meant that the climax of the story, its point and purpose, must dictate everything that goes into the narrative along the way. It meant that it's better to know where you want to go before you start. The scenery along the way will be just as interesting, and added to it will be a sense of direction which is far more effective, in intriguing the reader than the most violent, but purposeless, episode can ever be.

This process of working out a story idea from back to front is not as easy as it may seem at a glance. It usually demands a period of gestation—it can be weeks or months—where the writer goes around with the story idea developing in his brain until he can see just how it should move to its climax. That climax is the thing. The outlines of the narrative leading to it may remain nebulous in the mind, they may take on a different form every time the writer turns his attention to them, but once he knows in precise words what the final lines of the story will be, everything else starts to fall quickly into position.

When those final lines are set, it's good policy to write them down. Now, when the narrative—the whole body of the story—is reappraised, it must be strictly in terms of what has been written down. The infinite decisions on what must go into the story, what characters will play it out, what length it will be, what point it will start from in its opening line—all this is to be determined solely by the need to build logically to that pre-written finale. The objective is to use only the material and treatment which will establish the climax logically, at the same time providing the reader with a *frisson,* an impact, the shock of recognition one experiences when he finds that a logical sequence of events has led to a logical—but unpredictable—conclusion.

In this process, the story one has been carrying around in his mind as a sort of smoky substance will undergo its vital transformation into hard-knit, tightly structured drama. This does not mean the reduction of it to telegraphic form. A tightly woven story can be ten thousand words long and present twenty characters. What it does mean is that every line of narrative must contribute to the final effect. Digressions are out of order. Lingering descriptions are usually out of order. Dialogue should stick to the point while enlightening us as to the nature of the speakers. Revision of the completed manuscript must be ruthless under these conditions. A character, an episode, a single phrase which doesn't contribute to the progress toward the story's pre-written climax must be penciled out.

So it was that I finally won my first bout with the editors by treating a story idea from back to front. The idea concerned a restaurant where the customers themselves, when properly fattened like Hansel and Gretel by the solicitous restaurateur, were literally fed to each other, although without knowing it. The story treatment, I decided, would not make any great effort to conceal this shocking fact from the reader; the climax would simply be a sentence or two which would assure him that his macabre supposition about what was going on in that restaurant was gruesomely correct.

I got off to a dozen futile starts on the story, and then at last it dawned on me that I was in trouble because I didn't know exactly what my final climactic and revelatory lines were going to be. The solution, I decided, was to write those final lines before anything else, and it took a couple of weeks before I even understood exactly what

they had to set forth. It was the picture of a customer, a key character in the story, being happily led into that fatal kitchen by my restaurateur, and, without specifically stating it, I had to make it plain
that this customer was a lamb for the slaughter. The lines I decided
on read:

> The restaurateur held his kitchen door invitingly wide with one hand, while
> the other rested, almost tenderly, on his customer's meaty shoulder.

It was that word "meaty" which took the longest time to hit on
and which, I knew intuitively, locked up the story. From that instant, the restaurant owner, his doomed patron, the restaurant itself,
and the whole structure of the story started to take on form by themselves; an outline of episodes leading to the finale seemed to spring
magically to mind. It took much revision to get everything trimmed
down to its essence, but now that I knew exactly what I wanted to
say, the revisions, like the story's episodes, almost imposed themselves on the material.

The final draft was sent to *Ellery Queen's Mystery Magazine*, and
a few days later the editor let me know that the story's title was
henceforth to be "The Specialty of the House," and that I was now a
Selling Writer. And, since it seemed sound policy to stick with a winning system, I've followed the same principle of writing down the
closing lines of every story I've tackled since then, before even considering the opening lines, and I have had no cause to regret this
back to front approach.

Admittedly, this method of preparing a final polished draft of a
short story adds up to a slow and laborious time of it, especially
when one has a complicated story to tell. But time is no longer relevant in writing stories for mystery magazines. On that barren plain
filled with the bleached bones of the defunct detective pulps now
stands an impressive beacon, *Ellery Queen's Mystery Magazine*,
surrounded by a few lesser lights, perhaps a half-dozen in all. Once
upon a time, a capable and prolific story writer could make a living
from the detective pulps by flooding these magazines with acceptable
material. Today, he would simply flood himself right out of any market in a short time. So writing for the present market is best done
with tender, loving care as an avocation, not a vocation.

Ironically, despite the limited market, the demand for stories is greater now than it was during the palmiest days of the detective pulp. The scant dimensions of the market plus the editorial demand for quality instead of quantity seem to keep writers at bay and the result is a *shortage* of good stories.

From my experience, it is possible that planning and writing your mystery story from back to front will do much to alleviate the shortage.

44

THE BIOGRAPHICAL NOVEL

By Irving Stone

THE biographical novel is a true and documented story of one human being's journey across the face of the years, transmuted from the raw material of life into the purity of an authentic art form.

The biographical novel is based on the conviction that the best of all plots lie in human character; and that human character is endlessly colorful and revealing. It starts with the assumption that those stories which have actually happened can be at least as interesting and true as those which have been imagined. Alexander Pope said that the proper study of mankind is man; the biographical novel accepts that challenge and sets out to document its truth, for character is plot; character development is action; and character fulfillment is resolution.

The biographical novel attempts to fuse not only its parent sources of biography and the novel, but that of its grandparent, history, as well. It must tell the story of its main character, not in the bulk of millionfold detail, but in essence; it must recreate the individual against the background of his times, with all of its authentic historical flavor; and it must live up to the exacting demands of the novel structure.

Let me joyfully proclaim that basically the biographical novelist is a yarn-spinner, and the biographical novel a vigorous medium that has been created in order to tell the fine stories that have been lived. The form is fortunate in its opportunity to utilize the single greatest virtue of the novel: growth of character. This growth may be into good or evil, into creativity or destruction; it cannot be static. There are few joys for the reader to surpass that of watching an interesting story unfold through growth of character; and in this field no form surpasses the biographical novel, which by the very definition of its nature is always about people rather than impersonal forces.

The biographical novelist has a greater freedom to interpret than has the biographer, and the reader has a greater chance of coming away with a more personal understanding of human motivation. If there is a tendency to oversimplify, it is in the same fashion that man's memory does as he looks back on his span of time, forgetting nine-tenths of the bulk, remembering only the distillation which has meaning. For the biographical novel is based not merely on fact, but on feeling, the legitimate emotion arising from indigenous drama. Facts can get lost with almost too great a facility, but an emotional experience, once lived, can never be forgotten. Nor can this emotion be artificially induced for the sake of raising the reader's temperature. While a biography can be written purely out of a life's worthiness, with details of important names, places and dates, the biographical novel must emerge naturally and organically from the conflicts of man against himself, man against man, or man against fate.

Now that the biographical novel has come of age, a few ground rules can perhaps be laid down for its practitioners.

The first of these must surely be that history is not the servant of the biographical novelist, but his master. No biographical novel can be better than its research. If the research is deep and honest, the novel will be deep and honest; if the research is sleazy, shallow, evasive or sensation-seeking, the novel will be sleazy, shallow, evasive, sensation-mongering.

Not every life will fit into the form of the biographical novel. There are specific dramatic elements that must be present, recurrent themes of conflict and accomplishment woven through its entirety, an overall, perceivable pattern into which the parts can be fitted to make an organic whole. There are many lives, important and significant in their end results, which are nonetheless diffuse, their content and design antithetical to the nature of the novel; others seem to have been lived as though the subject himself were constantly aware that he was creating a dramatic structure.

While the biographical novelist is assuredly licensed to search out and select those lives which make good copy, the basic demonstrable truth cannot be pushed around to serve a plot purpose. The writer who must twist or pervert the historic truth to come out with what he thinks is an acceptable or salable story is a tragically misplaced person in his field. The biographical novelist, on the other hand, who becomes moralistic or political, turns into a pamphleteer. An integrated, successful, first-rate biographical novel can emerge only from a union of the material chosen and the author of the choice.

The author has a right to ask, as he looks at the outline of a human life, "Can this story serve my purposes?"—but only after he has demanded of himself, "Can I serve the purposes of this story?"

How is a reader unacquainted with the field to distinguish between the honest and dishonest biographical novel, the complete and the fractional? How can the question, "How much of this is true?" be answered? Only by insisting that the biographical novel must be as complete in its documentation as the most scholarly history and biography, and as honest in its interpretation.

If it takes four years to train a schoolteacher or engineer, five years to train a pharmacist, six a dentist, seven a lawyer, and eight a doctor, is there any reason to believe that it can take less time to develop a qualified and professional biographical novelist?

He must become experienced in the writing of imaginative novels, wrestling with this form in order that he may come up against the challenging complexities of structure, mood, master scenes, dialogue, with its accompanying lyricism of language, the mounting involvement and suspense of the fictional tale. He would be well advised to write a half-dozen plays to absorb the superb economy of the form, and learn how to stage his tale under a proscenium instead of in the wings: for what the reader does not see with his eyes he never really knows.

He must be trained as a biographer, working at the assembling of materials about one man or group of men, mastering the technique of close-knit organization of these materials, the perceiving and the weaving back and forth of the life theme, evolving a style, personality, and manner of writing by means of which one man's story can be brought to life all over again by black hieroglyphs on white paper: the eternal miracle of literature: for each life has a distinctive face and figure; and this must be captured in order to differentiate this one special story from the hundreds of millions that have been lived.

Though research is as fascinating as the resolution of a crossword puzzle or a murder mystery, it is also hard work, thoroughly exhausting and unending in its demands. The researcher sometimes gets lost in his forest of facts. To change the metaphor, the biographical novel must be built like an iceberg, about one ninth of solid substance showing above the literary water line, and the other eight-ninths submerged, but giving a solid base to that which is permitted to appear. If the biographical novelist does not know nine times as much as he reveals, the substance of the print he spreads over the page will be painfully thin: for the eight-ninths which he does not reveal permeates the whole, giving to the pages a discernible bouquet, a subtle emanation which enables the reader to feel comfortable and secure.

I would like to outline some specifics.

Having determined that he is going to write a biographical novel about the life of Leonardo da Vinci or Alexander Hamilton, the biographical novelist must put out of his mind for six months or a year any illusion that he is a writer, and become a library mole. He must read all the books and articles written by his subject, study the works created by him, be they art or engineering, read every findable word that has been written about the man or work. He must read all the letters that have passed between the hero and his contemporaries, as well as his private notes, journals and memoirs; or, in the case of a heroine, those wonderfully confiding diaries that are kept locked in the middle drawer of a desk. If the subject is of recent times, there will be a need to interview or correspond with everyone who has been involved in the drama, no matter how slightly.

Having grasped more fully the outlines of his story, the biographical novelist then takes to the road, seeing with his own eyes the places his hero has lived, the quality of the sunlight, the native earth beneath his feet, the personality of the cities and the feel of the countryside: for only then can he write with the intimacy and knowledgability of tactile experience.

This is the first and direct line of attack. The second is equally important: the biographical novelist must now begin the study of his hero's times, its fads and fancies, its majority and minority ideas as well as the prevailing conflicts in religion, philosophy, science, politics, economics and the arts; in short, the overall social, mental, spiritual, esthetic, scientific and international climate in which his characters lived and evolved their codes of conduct. He must read the source books of the period in order to absorb its background, the old newspapers, pamphlets, magazines, the novels, plays and poetry of the times, in order to learn the uncountable thousands of illuminating details which he must have at his fingertips in order to recreate the period: what people wear, the architecture of their houses as well as the fabric on their furniture, how they heat their homes, cook the foods they eat at the various hours of the day; what they are buying in the shops and why, how much it costs as well as how it tastes and smells and feels; what ailments they are suffering and how they are treating them; what colloquialisms they are using to enrich their conversation; what their preachers are preaching on Sunday morning and their teachers teaching on Monday morning.

If the biographical novelist has any feeling for his job he will eventually find emerging out of this seemingly vast and inchoate mass of material certain recurrent patterns, strains of character and action that provide a dominant motif and rhythm for the story he will tell, even as the dominant strains of a symphony are enunciated early. Above all, the biographical novelist is looking for those interwoven designs which are perceivable in every human life: for nearly every life works out its own tightly woven plot structure. Any action forced upon the participants which does not arise indigenously, which arises instead from the author confusing motion with direction, tears the fabric of the story.

Yet by the same token the biographical novelist must be the master of his material; the craftsman who is not in control of his tools will have his story run away with him. For after his research labors, the biographical novelist must then expend as much time and energy as the writer of fiction to create a novel structure which will best project his material, and be unique to the particular story to be told.

And all this new knowledge must never come between the reader and the narration. In the biographical novel a basic tenet is that the author must stage his story as though it were happening right now; he may not emerge at intervals to inform the reader of what will happen two or twenty or two hundred years later. The reader may never be in possession of information which is not available to those who are acting out the day-by-day passion of their lives. The story must unfold for the reader even as the pageant of events unfolds for the participants. There are few soothsayers; the biographical novelist may not turn himself into an *a posteriori* prophet. Whatever the reader may divine about what lies ahead must arise from his own perception, and not from the biographical novelist fudging on time sequence. If there be wisdom in the author (and God grant that there may sometimes be!) it will emerge from the nature of the story he wants to tell, from his selection of materials within the framework of that particular story, from his understanding of what motivates his people, and from the skill with which he shapes the unassimilated raw action of human life.

Since I did not know how much I did not know about the writing of a biographical novel, I sat down to my first morning's work with a little calling card in front of me on which I scribbled four strictures: 1. Dramatize. 2. Plenty of dialogue. 3. Bring all characters to life. 4. Use anecdotes and humor.

Beyond the specifications for any one particular book, I found the following *obiter dicta* to be essential to all biographical novels:

No use of names because they later become important elsewhere. No asides, or smart whisperings. No fixations, no prejudices carried over from past feelings or readings. No harpings, or preconceived "theories, into which all history and happenings must fit." No name-calling; let the reader call the proper names. No fiery passions, for or against; they cloud judgment. No assumptions as to the reader's tastes, opinions, ideas, education. No writing for any one class, age or geographic group. No condemnations of people or events; give them their rightful place in the story, and let God judge them. No seeking the sensational for its own sake; and no philosophizing. No concealing of important evidence, no lies, cheating or defrauding the reader. No dullness; throw out the slow, meaningless passages. No striving for effects, no manifest anger or hatred, no browbeating. Watch comparative materials and balance them; no disproportions about materials where I happen to know more. No inheriting of other people's prejudices, hatreds, blindness. No details that illuminate little but themselves. No posturing, no exhibitionism: "See what I know!" No striving for novelty for its own sake. No doctrinairism, or fitting material into one school or pattern. No destructivism, nor defeatism. No pugilism or blind spots. No lethargy. No weasel phrases; all space is needed for direct lines. No meandering down pleasant paths. No use of material that does not tie into focal core of book.

Because of the tender youth of the biographical novel there has as yet been little discussion of its particular character, of its strengths as well as its limitations. Is it a history, a biography, or a novel? Is it none of these? Or perhaps all three? If here I presume to provide a beginning critique, standards of judgment against which the biographical novel may be viewed, it is done with the happy reassurance that all such strictures will be altered, expanded and materially improved by later practitioners of the craft.

The biographical novel has suffered from an excess of good taste and respectability, perhaps because the biographical novelist has been awed by the fact that his characters once actually lived, and hence were endowed with certain inalienable rights, not of concealment, but of privacy and decorum. Bedroom scenes of which critics complain in the lurid, so-called historical novels are not to be found in the biographical novel, a sometime limitation to the sale of the genre, but one which calls forth the subtlety of the biographical novelist if he is to convey to the reader the all-important love and sex life of his subject.

The biographical novelist is a bondsman to the factual truth; yet he will succeed very little if he remains a mere reporter. As Robert Graves said to me, "The biographical novelist who does not have strong intuitions about his subject, and later finds from the documents that his intuition has been substantiated, is not likely to get far in understanding his subject."

Inside the skeletal outline imposed on him, the biographical novelist is free to soar to any heights which his own inner poetry and perception will allow him. There are few if any differences of structure between the two types of novel; with the biographical novel the reader asks, "Did this happen?" and with the fictional novel, "Could this happen?" Therein lies the major distinction between them. Credibility lies at the base of both. A chance reader, unacquainted with the material, setting and character of the two stories, should not be able to tell them apart; he should be able to think that the fictional novel actually happened somewhere, or that the biographical novel was invented by the author. I remember with considerable satisfaction the day in September 1934 when Mrs. Stone asked the telephone operator in her office how she had liked *Lust for Life,* and the girl replied, "Fine, but why did Irving have to kill off the poor man?"

The historical novel is the closest to the biographical novel in its nature and scope; again the difference is not of form but of approach. In the biographical novel all of the characters have lived; in the best historical novels, such as *War and Peace,* only the history has actually happened, while the characters are invented, or built up by accretion, and then set in the authentic framework of the period and the action being written about. The main characters of the historical novel become the apotheoses of their times; they are true in that such characters did live in this particular period, and this dramatic series of events did take place, but to other people, perhaps half a hundred of them, in modified form and sequence. Sometimes the historical novel will be close to the biographical novel.

The differences between the straight biography and the biographical novel are considerable, not in substance, since both draw their nourishment from the same source, but in structure, manner, attitude, and relationship between the author and the reader.

The biography has traditionally been in indirect discourse, a chronicle told by a second party, the writer, to a third party, the reader. The biographer, for example, relates what his principals have said; the biographical novelist enables the reader to listen to the conversations as they develop. The biographical novelist, in order to recreate a character, must not only understand his every motivation, but must write of it from behind the eyes of his protagonist. Only then can the reader feel everything that he feels, know everything that he knows, suffer his defeats and enjoy his victories. The biography has been expected to be objective; too often it has been written in cool blood. The biographical novel must be written in hot blood.

What are the criticisms that have been and still are, in some unconvinced corners, levied against the biographical novel? It is said to debase the biography and the novel, discrediting both and adding to the stature of neither. Allegedly it mines biography without regard for the verities, strains history through the author's personality, reshapes that history to fit the novel form, oversimplifies, prevents the reader from separating fact from fiction, chooses only those subjects which allow for a lively sale, violates the privacy of people long dead, and makes character the victim of plot.

All of these criticisms have sometimes been true, and probably a good many more of which the critics happily have not yet thought. But to decide that any art form is untenable because of its weakest example or its potential for error is similar to saying that the human race should be obliterated because of the shortcomings of its least admirable percentage.

One of the assets of the human race is said to be that it can learn from experience; history and biography constitute the greatest mine of lived experience; and it is the fond dream of the biographical novelist to bring the wisdom of that experience to the problems and complexities of the modern world.

My own biographical novels have had two motivations: I have hoped to feel deeply about simple things; and I have wanted to tell the story of man, against obstacles, for man.

45

STORY PLOTS AND THEMES

By Marlene Fanta Shyer

In my "Hopeless" file, I've accumulated at least a dozen clinkers, stories that have flopped here and abroad and represent more than a year's work which will never see print. I keep them for sentimental reasons; these are the efforts that carried me from the Bridge of Sighs to the Bridge of Sales; they've taught me how to sell, if not how to write.

Before I unburden myself with one more word of self-pity about how long it took and how difficult it was to get there, let me stress that there would have been no transition without persistence. In the years preceding my first sale, I gave up writing a half dozen times, the result of overdoses of failure, but each time I crept back. Persistence is to selling what will power is to diets; only one writer I've ever heard of sold a first story to the slicks, and she admitted that the next twenty were rejected! So endure the rebuffs, tolerate the rejections and faithfully read the stories that the slick magazines have chosen instead of yours. Like dieting, it becomes easier with time.

Watch a pattern emerge. Some things are *in* at the slicks and some are *out*. To mitigate the frustration of your apprenticeship I've capsuled some bylaws that distinguish the commercial from the *non*, and include as case studies some of my hopeless cases, hopeless characters and hopeless themes to illustrate where I went wrong—as well as a few that made the grade.

Next to giving up smoking and learning to address your mother-in-law as "Mom", it seems to me the hardest hurdle in a writer's life is learning what makes a good plot.

I've written enough stories to know how to put together a hero and heroine and make it all come out all right in the end, but after all these years I still get the shudders when I sit down in front of a naked piece of paper with not an idea in my head. Where, I ask myself, are all these other authors coming up with the sort of clever and complicated story convolutions that add up to a check? I stare at the paper, secure in the knowledge that I'm a published writer with a strong will and a dandy style. So why haven't I got anything to say?

One reason is that every plot has to go steady with a theme. It took me a mountain of rejections to make this discovery. Nobody thought to warn me. Actually, I don't think I ever really knew what a theme was. Now, after a lot of wasted postage and a few years of crushed hopes, I know. A theme is the answer to the question that is raised when your story is finished: What does it all prove?

Pull your story together and let it *say* something, and you're in. For example, if, in your story, your daredevil hero gets hit by a street-cleaning truck, he must learn something in the end. If he learns to beware of street-cleaning trucks, that's no theme. If, on the other hand, he learns that he must temper his incaution because his life is valuable not only to himself but to others (like a good little wife and apple-cheeked children you've introduced earlier), *that* could be a theme.

Themes must be positive or forget the whole thing. If you take a jaundiced-eye view of humanity in real life, reform fast or go unsold. The slicks are not convinced that life is a drag; they want to hear about generosity, love and the bluebird of happiness—preferably subtly.

Don't spell it out in black and white, if grey and white will do nicely. The reader is getting wiser and likes to use a little imagination, like putting his own egg in the cake mix. Go easy on the "I suddenly realized" department. Dialogue can be more effective than narrative.

When I began I wrote delightful stories with beginnings, middle, and ends, full of wit and sprightly characters. I have these stories and enjoy a laugh over them now and then. They are themeless orphans and might have sold to the *Woman's Home Companion* in the forties, when fiction was not so serious. For now, they score minus ten with every editor. One of these, "Daddy's Girl," concerned a lively girl who disobeyed her father and ultimately fell in love with the man she rebelled against because he was her father's choice. Theme? Obey your father. But no one has to be told that!

A story in *Good Housekeeping*, "Life and Love Upstairs," probably less witty than "Daddy's Girl," brought me a large check. The plot is simple: A young family is badgered by the lady downstairs, who vociferously objects to the noise of their lives being lived above. The simple theme: The young must come to understand and to tolerate the forms of loneliness of those who are old and alone.

The theme is the stuff of which the story is made and is as important nowadays as the paper on which it appears. It must have a basic truth, perhaps even a message. It does not have to be spelled out at the end like an essay on ethics, but even a witty story should be sewed together with one serious thread.

"First Smile," quite a funny story I wrote and sold to a Canadian magazine, concerned the disastrous results when a brand-new mother is faced with her overly helpful mother and mother-in-law, who come to assist with the new arrival. The story was light from beginning to end, but the new baby's first smile brought in the happy ending, complete with theme: becoming a grandmother is every bit as difficult as becoming a mother.

So now you know you've got to have a theme as well as a plot and here you are, face-to-face with your Smith-Corona, without a thought in your head. In answer to the question, "Which came first —the plot or the theme?" I start with the chicken, the meat, the plot, usually. When I've worked out some characters and action, I ask myself what it all means. Often I sit shrugging my shoulders over this problem for days. It often doesn't mean a thing.

For example: I thought up the beginnings of a very tidy plot about a girl in a country hospital (*Good Housekeeping*, "Rx: One Mended Heart") and a boy in the next room. The rollicking possibilities seemed fine: an escalating romance in an offbeat setting peppered with bumbling doctors and erratic plumbing.

But what about the egg, the theme? In other words, so what? I wasn't going to touch the typewriter until I'd nailed the answer. Finally, little by little I began to build. Suppose this girl hated the country, had just come up to visit, had broken her leg and was now stuck in this rustic wasteland? I elaborated on this; I gave her a solid city past, a job, and an urban beau. Here she was, lying in the hospital and feeling desolate.

The boy in the next room also had a past, and a fiancée who coincidentally wanted him to move to the city.

Now I brought the boy and the girl together through the machinations of a country hospital telephone operator, and they fell in love. In the end, the girl is convinced that country life is exciting and wonderful. Note the formation of theme with plot. The theme: Happiness is where the heart is.

Where did I get my idea for a country hospital in the first place? I don't have a little notebook full of spontaneous jottings. I carry my ideas in my head and wait for them to pop up at propitious moments. Sometimes they do and sometimes they don't; one needs patience.

Not the kind of patience that means you go out on the town instead of sitting at the typewriter. I mean the kind required for sitting somewhere quiet and really trying to build a story from scratch.

I don't mean a whole story. It doesn't have to jell from A to Z before you begin, unless you're the fastidious outline type. It seems to me that some of my best stories begin with a vague outline, a theme, and a firm idea of the end. As I work, new ideas pop unexpectedly into my head. Suddenly, the story begins to zip along in its own clever way, independent as a ouija board. The outcome often surprises me. Occasionally even the theme is changed. Often the firm ending is not the one I originally had in mind. This writer's serendipity is one of the great pleasures of writing.

The country hospital idea came, as it happens, from nowhere. I've never been in one, I've never seen one. I made it up. That's really my job, as a writer. Often I have help; I get an idea from something real, something that's actually happened. Slick fiction should mirror ordinary life, so I try to garner everyday things from people's conversations, the very things they wouldn't report to a writer.

For example, my last few published stories dealt with 1) a pair of neighbors, grown very close, who are now to be separated; 2) a husband who is promoted and can't seem to cope with success; 3) a mother, laid low by a brief illness, who finds no one can substitute mother-love; 4) a gloomy, rainy Sunday that helps a young wife to realize how lucky she is to have a family.

All these plots are based on the most mundane, day-to-day experiences, easy for the reader to recognize as real, incorporating pleasant characters with which the reader can identify.

I listen, I observe and I think. Then I stick a few things together, change the end, revise, cut, and I'm all set. Easy, isn't it?

That part of a plot which is pivotal in a story, I have dubbed the "hinge": the point toward which the characters must move all along, the point in a plot once known as the climax. Climax, nowadays, is too strong a word for this pivot; it can consist of a word or a look, instead of a war or a first kiss, but it changes the direction of the story and the writer must have established this point before his fingers first touch the typewriter. He must have planned it with utmost strategy, sneaking in forecasts of it almost from the beginning.

My clinker, "Christmas Incident," ran as follows: Joe's daughter had alienated him by a forced marriage to a man of whom Daddy doesn't approve. Joe is lonely and bitter, but on Christmas Day, he decides he must accept his daughter's invitation to visit her and her new baby. On the way to his daughter's house, Joe drives past a frozen lake and notices some children trying out their Christmas ice-skates. The hinge: Just as he passes, a young girl ventures too far and falls through thin ice. The water is not deep, and she is quickly hauled out, but the moment of fear has shifted Joe's sentiments. He is reminded of his own daughter in childhood, the fragility of their present relationship and immediately realizes how precious she actually still is to him. With this fresh viewpoint, he continues to his daughter's, determined now to accept his son-in-law and make peace with his daughter.

This hinge is marred with the anathema of coincidence and is therefore unacceptable. It strains the reader's credibility to believe that Joe just happened by as someone was about to be drowned; it does not stem logically, in A-B-C order, from the structure of the plot. It is a trick, and sounds as if it had been stuck in as an afterthought.

An example of a thoroughbred hinge appeared in *Redbook,* in my story, "The Difficult Part." The story concerned a mother who was told that her young son had musical talent. Without consulting him, she forced piano lessons on the boy, and despite his lack of interest, she made arrangements with his teacher to have him appear at a students' recital. The hinge follows naturally: The boy, frightened and a poor beginner, plays some wrong notes and runs off stage in a panic. His humiliation changes the focus. His mother realizes that "children do not always fit into the tuxedos their parents weave for them in their imaginations."

Here is the natural outcome of a logical hinge that does not depend on chance or coincidence. The reader, finishing the story, might say, "I could have guessed that would have happened," without actually having more than a clue and certainly without making the story predictable.

Whitewash the heroine—and that goes for the hero as well. The editors of the women's magazines are unified in demanding a protagonist with whom the reader can identify. This does not mean Pollyanna and Little Orphan Annie rolled into one, but it does mean, *no big vices!* She never embezzles, gossips or has dirty fingernails, and if she has a questionable past, it wasn't her fault. She's allowed little shortcomings and may be given to shyness or absent-mindedness or disorderly ways, but she is Virtue Personified, like you. That goes for her husband, too, and all those people near and dear to her with whom she's going to mingle in her plot. Not too much unpleasantness anywhere, please, as there was in my ill-fated story, "New Boy."

Strictly speaking, the protagonist of this story, one I considered excellent before it came back and back and back, was a sensitive boy. He adored his dear and loving parents who were, unfortunately, jewel thieves. If the readership of *Good Housekeeping* were composed of gun molls, this would have gone over big; unfortunately in this case, the readers of women's slicks are ladies between the ages of eighteen and forty, and for all practical purposes, they do not steal. They prefer to identify with paragons rather than felons.

And "New Boy" taught me something even more important: aim for non-fiction fiction. Avoid, like rejection slips, the incredible. The response that the writer must aim for is, "This is real. It's just like what happened to me last year!" or perhaps, could happen tomorrow. Jewel thieves don't happen to anyone, but car mishaps do, as in my *Good Housekeeping* story, "All My Own":

A young wife wants a second car for her own use. Husband says no but finally relents long enough to buy, reluctantly, an old heap from a used car dealer. These things happen every day. The hinge: the car, containing our *pleasant* heroine and three children, stalls and dies in the middle of a traffic tie-up leading to a huge department store parking lot. Please note: The car does not explode or hiss fire or lose a couple of wheels. These things *could* happen, but the slicks are not interested in improbable catastrophes. They want everyday occurrences. Whose battery, after all, hasn't gone dead at some time or other? In short, the trick is to be original—in an *ordinary* way!

Of all the mistakes my clinkers made, lack of action is the most deadly. Narrative, like aspirin, is only effective in small doses, except, perhaps, in *The New Yorker*. If you aim for the slicks, make the story move—no—jump from scene to scene. Jump into the dialogue at the beginning, if possible; if not, keep your introduction short because it will amuse only you and those who love you enough to be bored by overdoses of your descriptions of the mountain flowers that grew on the west side of your heroine's house. A successful writer I know once told me that she plans her stories like scenes in a play. Put your reader into a time and place immediately and avoid heavy details that can flower through dialogue. In a story I wrote recently, for example:

> Cass fumbled with the wrapping paper; I saw Dickie strain forward.
> "A muff! A muff! Cass cried, stuffing both hands into the white fur. "Thank you, Grandma!"

This is the rewrite of the original:

> Cass fumbled with the wrapping paper; I saw Dickie strain forward. She peered into the box, then pulled out a white fur muff. "Thank you, Grandma."

A slight difference, perhaps just a shade. But the rewritten paragraph jumps!

Unlike the slice-of-life fragments that are characteristic of small quarterlies, unlike the offbeat pieces that are occasionally seen now in such magazines as *Playboy,* the current high-paying slick market is oriented toward the sort of story which can best be described as optimistic. The jaundiced eye does not go over well here, and defeatist themes are generally unpopular. (There are exceptions.) This does not mean that you must tack a happy ending on everything; still, if things don't work out for the heroine at the finish, try for a ray of hope, at least. The experience you have put her through must have taught her a lesson or given her some insight, and at the end, things should be looking up.

Another criterion high on the editor's list is the predictability of the plot. If he can guess how it's going to end much before it does, you'll get the story back; the days of boy-meets-girl, loses girl, gets girl are over. And fantasy, slapstick, and farce went out with the mustache. The it-could-really-happen is very much *in*.

That goes for dialogue, double. No rhetoric, please. Characters must talk, not give Gettysburg Addresses. And, the briefer the better; it is amazing how many redundancies crop up in monologues, my own in particular. In real life, people tend to be repetitive; they don't dare to in fiction; still, they must sound real. "No!" is as effective as "No! No! No!" so learn to cut, even if it brings tears to your creative eyes.

And learn to stay on the track. Beware of those tempting extraneous details that derail your theme. Those beautifully written paragraphs about the heroine's life at the Sorbonne will have to go, unless they have a direct bearing on her situation right now. This is both the challenge and the limitation of writing for the slicks; plot first, style second. Don't let your own talent carry you away.

While you're cutting, be suspicious of double and triple adjectives. Sometimes they can't be helped, but consider trimming "She looked into a cold, flat, grey sky" to "She looked into a slate sky," and congratulate yourself on your economy.

Never, however, strain for an analogy or overdo a metaphor. This kind of overwriting is the mark of the neophyte.

Ready to begin? Of course you are. It's the middle of the story that sends the writer running, defeated, from the typewriter. The I-can't-go-on plateau is as common as a cold. Remember persistence? It's the only remedy.

46

STORYTELLERS' STREET

By Sanora Babb

ONCE in a faraway place in an evening of summer, I was wandering through an ancient narrow street, aware of its people in their odd mixture of Eastern and Western clothes, the unknown language, the sounds and smells and heat, and all around me an atmosphere that was the sum of these parts and yet something more, something intangible and powerful. It convinced me of the reality of my own experience, and remains in my memory to evoke the wonder of that evening.

Walking on, I came to a quieter street and turned in. Still under the spell of the atmosphere, I did not at first feel curious at this variation, but soon I became aware of a distinct difference, especially in the sounds: fewer voices, and islands of intense listening quiet surrounded by little seas of emotion. I was in Storytellers' Street.

This was not its official name but its *real* name, used by everyone for centuries.

The old men, for most of them were old, were telling their tales, and around them squatted boys and girls, men and women, who had worked all day and come into this street at evening to be entertained, or to expand their lives in the experiences of imagined tales freshly spun, or the old, known loved ones they had heard many times. They contributed their small coins, these "readers", and lost themselves to their living books.

Each storyteller had his following. There were omnivorous "readers" who sampled them all. Here and there, a young or a new "author" told his stories to a few adventuresome listeners. He was most likely starving and struggling like his fellow beginners everywhere in the world. But he had his own style, and perhaps he was telling the old themes in a fresh way, or adopting the formulas of popular-old tellers.

255

Some told stories that began and ended in one sitting, while others related episodes or chapters that charmed their audience back for more. By watching the faces of the listeners, I observed how expertly the storyteller aroused their desire to hear "what happened next"; how well he expressed himself, how lightly or how seriously he spoke; how deeply he involved their emotions. Their eyes shone with delight or sympathy or tragedy or nobility. And sometimes they were glazed with boredom or cool doubt, in which case the listener moved to another teller. Mostly, the audience showed respect, esteem, even affection for the storytellers.

The best storytellers evidently possessed a sense of character and story structure and evocation of emotion that caused their listeners to suspend their disbelief. When they rose to leave, many of them walked still in the world of the story.

That evening, I learned a great deal about writing, in spite of the fact that I could not understand the language. I, too, went along the street dreaming, overwhelmed and extended by my experience, and filled with first-hand knowledge and respect for the timeless role of the storyteller in the world.

Those men, all so unalike, and several of them obviously trusting their intuitive powers to create as they went along, skilled by practice in their form, gave me the assurance to continue to follow my own way, write my own stories, which, in the end, were the only stories I *could* write. In my ignorance I had rejected technique, confusing it with formula. There, I saw emotional tension achieved by imagination disciplined and released through technical skill. I emphasize discipline and rich release as opposed to the debris-filled flood of careless expression.

Storytellers' Street was an unforgettable experience, but I realized that only the experience of writing and writing and writing could develop my own talents. It seems to me that one writes first and learns after to estimate and comprehend the various inherent elements of a good story. To begin too soon to appraise one's intangible emotion-idea or the sudden effulgence that often announces creative work, is to hamper its true growth. Writing requires infinite patience, and to hurry to apply the tools may be to mechanize or even destroy the pattern originating in another area of our minds to which we should give the utmost acceptance.

To take pride in a know-nothing attitude is to deny that writing has its craft. Every art is the more clearly and fully expressed by the excellence of its technique. Technique is a *way* of doing, and only when method dominates meaning (thought and feeling), does it fail its role, its subtle, integral role of bringing the whole to its best possible realization.

Every word should have a purpose. If it has none, it should be cut without regret. The purpose is not mere action, but story action, and this includes every value that contributes to the whole effect. The purpose of the story itself is to arrive at its destination. The journey may be one of soaring, or probing deeply, or traveling on the surface, but it must be a *journey*—within or without—of implied or dramatized conflict. Characters must live and change within a structured time. Change is the result of an encounter with an idea, emotion, person, animal, nature, circumstance, or any of these in combination; and it is the writer's artistic responsibility to show, to reveal, to dramatize, not tell about, this encounter.

A single point of view is far more than a formality. It is the difference between knowing one person well, sharing an experience, and wandering about among acquaintances or even strangers. It is true that it helps the reader to identify with the character, while acrobatic viewpoints scatter his attention and the story's unity, but very importantly, and first, the single point of view helps the author to identify with and more effectively give life to the character.

A pleasure in, a respect for, a love of language, though not always traits of the writer, would seem to be vital, since after all, language is the means for conveying the reality of the created experience. Few writers attain a distinctive style, as style is as much an expression of the writer's unique creative personality as it is his experience-trained language; or, perhaps it *is* the language of the writer's personality. Nevertheless, the exact word, the fresh phrase, the attempt *to say truly* what one means, lead toward coveted simplicity. Simplicity is not bony writing any more than a skeleton is a human being. And, "to say truly" gives individual scope.

But the story itself will excite or involve no one if it does not move. Life moves, everything is changing every moment. *Creative* is the opposite of *static*. And yet, movement alone does not insure life. Movement must *grow* out of the characters and not mechanically from the author's head, and these characters must be allowed to speak and act for themselves, which they will do if they are not fitted into arbitrary molds, the story ending in a lifeless concoction.

Evocation of emotion, that vital, living authority, may exist because the author has achieved all these things, but more likely because he has an indefinable ability to produce it, perhaps through intense feeling and heightened affinity for all that he creates.

If he is fortunate, his quantitative substance has metamorphosed into the qualitative state of form. Not by accident. Outwardly, form is shape, design, pattern, but totally, form is a coalescence of all the elements of internal reality projected into external reality. It is the climax of art, the aura of life of which one is deeply aware but cannot "see" and must not confuse with structure, its composed and inseparable associate.

In this subtle matter of art into life, it may be reassuring to remember that there can be no form without craft, and the writer does better to go respectfully about the business of writing his stories. By respectfully, I mean that the familiar techniques of the short story should not be imposed upon the material, but rather, that each story be permitted to make its particular claims upon its craft, to grow up an individual within its generic laws. Whether the story achieves the rare state of art or mortal excellence, or mere and often admirable competence, its organization and structure are vital. Organization may take place as a part of the mysterious creative process, or it may be consciously built, but it is not the proper fitting together of parts for the simple reason that there is no proper or correct story.

This is no contradiction of the story's integrity, no license for careless writing but an attempt to emphasize an imaginative approach to the *whole* story, to use technique, not be used by it. The exciting challenge of writing the short story is its demanding symmetry and the variety of possibilities within that symmetry, that balance.

My method may seem vague to the writer who functions best with a plan or outline or a thought-out story. But every writer writes as he can. My stories "arrive" when they are ready to be written. I have never been able to finish satisfactorily a story that arrived too soon. Of course, they do not appear from nowhere; they grow from experiences, some direct, others from a suggestion, both created through imagination. Once I write the first sentence, the story begins to unfold as I write, swiftly or slowly, being "worked out" within, as I go or long before. Who knows? I have a sense of destination, only a sense, without knowledge of events in between, and as I work, I am aware of the destination (event or meaning or both) as a reason for what I am writing down. It is as if, were more revealed to me, I should lose the sense and feel of the moment.

I write the whole story first, and later, go over and over it, checking its structure, cutting, revising, rewriting, polishing. Parts remain intact. Principles become, it seems, a part of the intuitive approach, as if my imagination uses techniques I have learned by practice. Revising, to me, is as creative as original writing, because once again into the mood of the story, I am creating, experiencing, being the characters.

All this may sound as if in some esoteric way my stories have been written for me and present themselves to be typed, which is far from the whole truth, and every writer knows this. E. M. Forster gave this valuable advice: "The act of writing is inspiring." True. The total act of writing is hard work, also. This is frequently said as a drawback, a threat, a warning. But, why not hard work? Why are we hesitant to admit what we all (or almost all) feel when working: the joy of work?

One part of this joy for me is the creation of atmosphere. While I recognize that it is only one element, and perhaps not a vitally important one at that, writing begins for me with a strong, almost overwhelming sense of the atmosphere of my story, whether it is weather or place or emotional climate. Characterization, dialogue, tension and the rest develop more easily within their felt state.

Excerpts from dramatic texture inevitably lose values of emotion and meaning, but the following may partially illustrate:

That evening the canyon was strangely quiet. Lights blazed from every window of the house on El Ramo Way. No shadows passed the bright panes. The city below was jeweled in faraway, deceptive elegance. One tall, white flowering yucca glowed on the dim hillside like the ghost of reality fled. At times a little wind came up Viento Road carrying a brief reminder of the sea. The night air was tropic-sweet with jasmine. A woman's crying drifted faintly through the evening under the cricket's song. ("Woman On A Balcony," *New Mexico Quarterly Review*.)

When the Santa Ana comes, blowing off the Mojave Desert two hundred miles away, people walking along the city streets are suddenly embraced by a lasso of warm soft wind. The air has a radiant clarity. The atmosphere becomes strange, subtly exciting. People begin to unwind, to gentle, to feel young, to delight in breathing, to be aware of being alive, and sad that they've been dully taking it for granted. The wind enfolds them and kisses them like petals, and they begin to feel in love—in love with being alive; and this is so rare, like a primeval sensation coming up through all the centuries, that they are a little frightened, but the wind soothes them, and a tender wily restlessness sets in. They aren't what they call *themselves* until the wind ceases and they can get back into their protective masquerades. The wind sometimes blows a day and a night. The time is enchanted with an alien beauty. It is as if love had come without a lover. ("The Santa Ana," *Saturday Evening Post* and *Best American Short Stories 1960.*)

. . . fascinated to see a woman's hat of another era hanging on the supporting frame of a dresser mirror. She knew at once that the the hat had been placed there years ago and never removed; it had deteriorated with dust. A breath would scatter it! Under the bed were two high-heeled slippers whitened and warped with the time they had rested there. Old finery and cans of talcum lay on the chairs, and over everything was a coat of ancient dust. Holly imagined Mrs. Polk young and willowy, wearing the dress she had on today, entering the bedroom, kicking off her slippers, and with a wide lamenting gesture, placing the hat, looking at herself in the mirror; and in that moment, closing a door, a massive knobless door. Why? ("The Tea Party," *Seventeen.*)

For each writer, one element or another may act as a key. Atmosphere helps me to live in the world of my story. If the author lives there, perhaps the reader will live there, too. This is rather like the teller of tales and the listener to tales who live for a time on Storytellers' Street.

47

SHORT STORY OR NOVEL?

BY JEAN RIKHOFF

A SHORT story ceases to interest me almost the moment I conceive of it. Already the people I have first envisioned have begun to grow; soon their proportions and problems are far more complicated than those which could be encompassed in the few pages of a short story. I begin dreamily to think in terms of something bigger, something that will give my people time to develop—in other words, a novel. This inability to keep a small set of characters in a localized setting in the center of one elaborated or elongated incident—which I more or less take as a definition of the short story—has been, in the end, my saving. No matter how many times it has been said before, it must be said again:

It is much easier to sell a novel than a short story.

Let's take an example I know well, my own. For years I hopefully sent out short stories and as near as I came to selling one was a nice, encouraging letter now and then cheering me on to try harder. Far more representative was the wastepaper basketful of printed rejection slips I set afire at the end of each week. It was tiresome, repetitious, unencouraging, certainly uneconomical, and—let's face it—self-defeating. What I wanted to do was break into print and I certainly had no evidence to show I had done so or was ever going to do so. And even if I had had a story or two a year accepted, the acceptance would probably have come from one of the little magazines, which, if they do pay, can hardly be accused of making a writer wealthy (they may, however, make him eventually famous, so think twice before turning up your nose at the little magazines).

If you want something done, do it yourself, the old maxim goes. Speedily, a group of us were organizing our own magazine and putting out announcements that we were interested in publishing fiction and poetry—let the academic reviews concentrate on criticism. Running *Quixote* for six years taught me a good deal more than I care to know about the impossible plight of the short story writer. We were a small literary quarterly, coming out of England first (later Spain), with a woefully small subscription list (we never had over five hundred *paid* subscriptions, but we still managed to make our influence felt, as is evidenced by the fact that a number of the stories were reprinted in the *Best Short Stories* of the year in which they were published and that Grosset and Dunlap still publishes an anthology of the best stories the magazine printed *), yet we were inundated by manuscripts. Sometimes it seemed to me everyone in the world was pouring out his heart on paper. From the letters that came into *Quixote* from writers whose material we did accept, we received a fairly accurate and dismaying picture of past discouragements, disappointments, utter disinterest from the publishing world at large. One would imagine that somewhere along the line the punishment-pleasure principle would have begun to operate, and these writers would have faced up to the fact that no matter how dedicated they were, the odds were against their publishing anything at all *ever* and that they would do better expending their energies in chicken raising.

I know of writers whose stories we accepted and with whom we entered into long, revelatory correspondence who had been sending out stories week after week, month in and out, year after year, *up to twenty years,* who had never come near seeing anything of theirs in print.

To be practical (just for a moment): Say a writer writes one story every two weeks (on the average). That's twenty-six stories a year, and over twenty years that would be upward of five hundred stories, equal in length to a considerable number of books if the effort had been put into the longer instead of the shorter form.

But books are too hard to write, they take too long: one hears that again and again. Very well. That means that those who do attempt a novel and manage to keep at it until the last word is set down have a nice mathematical advantage over their fellow short story writers. The majority of writers who even begin a novel don't have the stamina to carry through—and that is precisely the point. The writer who does finish a book has immediately been set apart from the vast ma-

---

* *The Quixote Anthology,* Grosset's Universal Library.

jority of writers—by more than half, I'd guess, though an awful lot of people write books, too, and a surprising amount of these are published. If you look at the number of bad books published as compared to the number of bad short stories, the inevitable conclusion seems to be that it is easier to publish a bad book than a bad short story, though I wouldn't want to defend this thesis in, say, *Publishers' Weekly*.

Granted, then, that the novel has it all over the short story as far as possibility of publication is concerned (provided, of course, that the writer has a modicum of ability), how do you finish a novel? Anyone, obviously, can begin one; the trick is to get through it and get into the publishers' offices.

I know only one rule for writing novels and it suffers no exception. How do you write a novel? Day by day. You must place yourself at a desk with the sole purpose of working on the novel and *nothing else* for at least two to three hours a day. No letter writing, no paying bills (if you can), no dabbling in your diary, no making project notes in your journal (you can do that later), no exceptions whatsoever, just you and the work in progress, and this means the *novel* in progress—not a new idea for a short story that has just popped into your mind, not a note to remind you to pick up some coffee and drop off the dry cleaning that afternoon, not a quick dip in the morning paper before you settle down to real work. It doesn't make any difference if, for a time, you don't write a word, if, in Simone de Beauvoir's felicitous phrase, "sentences wither at the tip of the pen." Don't give up. Sheer desperation will force you to make up something, and once begun, momentum will carry you along. After a few weeks you will sit down and begin to write out of a sense of preservation. Nothing is quite so nerve-racking as fifty minutes of staring at a blank sheet of paper, listening to noises sifting in from that outside world that tell you what you already too well know, that non-writers are a lucky breed who have escaped the crucible of composition.

And speaking about composition—how do you compose a novel? Some people use outlines. I loathe them, I think they are confining and take up too much time, and I have the suspicion that people who labor long over them are using their creative energies wastefully. I know there are some writers who do draw up elaborate outlines and specify for themselves every scene that will take place in a novel before they write down one word. I have never found this a workable plan. In the first place, characters have a tendency to insist upon lives of their own at certain points in a book and the outline must either be rigidly adhered to or thrown away, something that produces panic in either case. Secondly, there is something to be said for a freedom of feeling in attacking anything, and most particularly a book. The spontaneity and excitement of stumbling on a "great scene" gives energy and impetus to a writer; once outlined, the material is pretty much *déjà vu*.

I usually start with people in conflict. It's as simple as that. Plot is always conflict of one kind or another, a character at odds with his society, his fellowmen or himself. This is perhaps a simplified way of stating that people, of whom all books, even those of the new wave of anti-novels, are composed, have come a cropper with the values which hitherto they have acted on unconditionally, unconsciously, automatically. Character in the true sense of the word—that which makes up the beliefs of a man—is suddenly in a dilemma because the inner supports are threatening to give way or have given way. The things by which a man has always got along no longer serve; conflict means he must make some kind of fight to keep his life going or it will collapse under him. Therefore, plot—to use a somewhat old-fashioned word—is really people in situations which tax them beyond their resources so that they are called upon for new insights, new energy, greater understanding and undertakings in their lives. If they fail to make these, they are defeated—not always irrevocably, however. Tragedy shows us the voice of conscience able to verbalize its understanding of the overwhelming obstacles that are in the process of destroying the central protagonist of a story. By being able to put that understanding into powerful expression, the defeated triumphs, for he has, in his determination to assert values against inevitable defeat, once more pointed up the indestructibility of man and his beliefs. Thus, the defeated man fails in the name of something better; he is not defeated; he has reaffirmed (to use the old word) a better vision of the universe, has refined for us aspects of a better tomorrow. Rigidly speaking, plot is of no great importance, if we mean by plot the *events* of a book. What is of concern is the individual struggle. Or, to put it succinctly, people matter, not plot.

Thus, we begin with character in the deepest sense of the word, and in conflict. Often the unfolding idea for a novel is vague—why *did* these people who gave me so much pain act like that? Why did *I* act as I did? For most first novelists (and quite rightly) usually begin to go into old wounds. In this way, writing has been called therapy—or revenge. As the great psychiatrist Theodor Reik remarked on Ibsen's observation that writing means to sit in judgment on oneself, "It also means to acquit oneself."

I must say that I myself feel that writing is an act toward understanding. It is an attempt through tearing down, to rebuild, this time properly; to take apart and remove the pieces bit by bit so that the whole structure can be understood, from its smallest component. But we are most apt to understand the familiar house in which we have lived; hence the old and workable adage, Write about what you know. Most of us, if the truth were confessed, know little about anything, most especially the workings of the human heart; yet that is the novelist's territory, the contradictory, complex human heart. Without people of depth and concern, there is no book.

Certain limitations have already been imposed, then, before the writer even begins. Most obviously, shallow people are hardly of much universal concern. (A good case can be made for the fact there are no shallow people, only shallow see-ers. I would grant this, but the act of imagination and the gift of understanding are limited in all of us, and given these limitations, we are apt to get on better with some kinds of characters than with other kinds, generally those drawn from the people who have influenced our lives strongly.) For good or evil, the strongest characters in a novel are generally those which exert the most pull on the novelist. The writer, who comes finally to feel he has understood the whole love-hate relationship between his parents and himself, his mate and himself, his life and himself, is the one who draws a deeply moving portrait of these. It is only after the individual example has been explored that any universal connotation can be made. In these terms, then, the writer who concentrates deeply on—say—one love affair and all its aspects has a better chance of saying something universal about all love than the writer who starts out to write about Love with a capital L.

So far the formula for putting together a novel sounds deceptively simple. "Deceptively" is certainly the word. It is not "simple" to understand your characters' true motives for their acts (perhaps—

no, often—even unknown to them), nor is it easy to present human beings in their most prevalent attitudes, many of which are paradoxical and contradictory. The trouble arises from the fact few of us act on one instinct alone, nor do we live by a set of ethics that do not in themselves come into conflict; our lives are constant questionings and inner warfares. Often our actions appear absolutely inexplicable.

Think through your characters—your plot—your ideas, your theme—and then argue with yourself about what you think. Is this character only surface-explored? Is this *really* the way this character would act? Have I taken the easy, obvious way out in ending this episode? Is what I am writing as much of the truth as I am capable of seeing or is it only as much as, lazily, I've been willing to glance over? Am I *really* exploring a theme, or am I only using plot to pull me through? Do I really know my material? Have I dug down far enough to make discoveries? "It has been said," writes Koestler in *The Act of Creation,* "that discovery consists in seeing an analogy nobody had seen before"; he goes on to say that "this leads to the paradox that the more original a discovery, the more obvious it seems afterwards." In connection with this, there is a triumvirate of words that serves a writer well in testing every phase of his work:

Imagine
Argue
Act

The great pitfall in all this is that the writer begins to take himself too seriously. "Total absence of humor renders life impossible," says Colette; she might just as well have added it renders literature impossible, too. Instead of putting a character in a situation and letting him demonstrate the opposing sides of his nature, the novelist lets the action grind to a halt, the character fades into the background, the conflict is forgotten or hastily pushed aside, and the author jumps center stage and begins to talk. Unfortunately, the fatal flaw in most of this talk shows up at once. It is a lecture we must listen to, *the writer has something to say* (after all, haven't all of us heard ad infinitum that we must be instructive as well as entertaining?), and the promising scene is lost in a harangue about the good or moral or corrupt life. Humor, objectivity, action—all these desert the page in deference to high seriousness, and virtue, observes Bellow's Herzog, bores mankind. (Was it one of the Mauriacs who said there were few histories of happy loves, which means, I suppose, that where conflict does not exist, where placidity reigns, so does disinterest.) Therefore, perhaps the golden rule that ought to be embossed above all writers' desks is

SHOW, DO NOT SAY

But if you *must* say, at least say *some*thing. Nothing can be so paralyzing as the forum seized only to cover old arguments. Few of us need to be told (and certainly not at length), for instance, that war is hell, that children are more often ungrateful than not, that the loss of youth is some kind of tragedy we still do not understand.

To recapitulate for a moment: The novelist begins with a protagonist or a group of protagonists at odds and in conflict; brooding over the intricacies of these, he tries to understand. In the act of understanding, other ideas—often in the form of concrete scenes—suggest themselves; the novelist finds he is interested in writing a book about some human situation, which by its very nature participates in all human behavior. Tentatively, gropingly, he sits and begins to write (type, tape record, dictate). He has now embarked, and the only way the voyage will be made is day by day, bit by bit—what we are taught is "one step at a time"—the end does not come by the writer's telling himself that he *must* have a rest, that he will get a better perspective on the material if he goes off on a little vacation, that really the lawn must be attended to today and the book can wait one day while the grass is taken care of; or that it is such a perfect day that the only thing to do is throw everything up and rush out to hit a few around the links.

From the beginning it is best to be prepared for moments of insurrection and rebellion. The working writer cannot be blamed if he begins to feel he is skimping on his life, that he is denying himself the ordinary everyday pleasures most people take for granted, that he is nothing but a drudge for a lot of people—not even real—he has come to hate because they are robbing him of all the things he likes to do—skiing, seeing an old friend, reading, even going about the necessary business of life which must be attended to. A deep guilt springs up even when he is doing chores that simply must be done during the hours he knows he should be at his desk. Nothing can be worse than tidying up the daily dirt of our lives—which ordinarily we hate and credit with robbing us of so much valuable time we might be using toward "worthwhile" things—and then, instead of feeling righteous, being overcome by awful anxiety. That awful anxiety is the sign of the conscientious workman who has put away his tools before the job is done. There will be other beautiful days, other years in which to ski; the world will not crack if the lint collects a few hours longer under the bed; the friend will wait, but the book will never be done unless it is done day by day, and it can never be done day by day without an organized and determined discipline.

In other contexts, this might be called self-sacrifice.

48

SUSPENSE: RULES AND NON-RULES

By Patricia Highsmith

"Too much thought is bad for the soul, for art, and for crime. It is also a sign of middle age. . . ."

Patrick Hamilton wrote this in one of his novels about Gorse, a real-life criminal who started early and successfully, but later began to plan a bit. It was his doom.

I wrote Hamilton's words down in the back of my notebook, where I keep other people's remarks that I wish I had made myself. I do not set much store by logic, no doubt because nature did not give me much. Novels are products of emotion, and to my illogical mind Hamilton's statement seems doubly true, because a suspense writer must be at the same time an artist and a criminal. It is probably better to be young for this. Middle age does bring thought, alas, and looking before leaping. Not much can be done about middle age, but thinking and logic should be discouraged, except in minutiae of the plot: e.g., would X really have had time to wipe up the blood, make a telephone call, and get all the way from Hoboken to Grand Central in seven minutes?

People who don't write often ask writers where they get their ideas from, not knowing that writers get them out of thin air a good part of the time, and at other times from incidents so trivial and fleeting that the incident, or face, or phrase can hardly be recaptured and repeated as an answer as to where their novel came from. Is this logical? Of course not. The unconscious mind takes the germ of an idea and develops it, but usually this happens only when a writer has tried hard, and logically, to develop it himself. After he has given it up for a few hours, getting nowhere, a great advancement of the plot will pop into his head. I have been waked up in the night sometimes by a plot advancement or a solution of a problem that I had not even been dreaming about. Everyone functions like this to some extent, and it is what people mean when they say, "I don't want to make up my mind today, I'd better sleep on it."

I like a wild coincidence in a plot—as in *The Blunderer,* in which I had Walter guess the murderer (Kimmel) and his method of killing his wife, then attempt the same kind of attack upon his own wife, or rather contemplate it, because to give the plot a further twist, I had him not carry it out. His wife committed suicide. It looked like murder. And the similarity of the circumstances to Kimmel's tragedy exposed the guilt of Kimmel. *The Blunderer* has been made into a French film, *The Murderer.*

Wild implausibilities I highly recommend, too. My most celebrated —thanks to Alfred Hitchcock—is *Strangers on a Train,* which might be described as a series of almost incredible events. They were a little too incredible for the scriptwriters of the film (they cut out the second murder), just as the story, when presented as half the written novel and a synopsis of the remainder, was too incredible for six publishing houses which turned me down. They thought it could not be made convincing. The novel when finished was accepted by the next publisher I showed it to, Harper's, which shows the power of persuasion of illogical prose.

And I like harebrained schemes that must forever waver on the brink of discovery, as in *The Talented Mr. Ripley* (later the film *Purple Noon*), in which Ripley impersonates the man he has killed, though he does not look enough like him to pass for him among even his casual acquaintances. By an act of even greater audacity at the end of the book, Ripley allays any suspicion of himself, acquires his victim's income for life, and gets away with it all. Of course they couldn't have him get away with it either on television or on the screen, but the novel won a prize from the Mystery Writers of America in 1956 and in 1957 the Grand Prix de Littérature Policière in France.

Young writers often worry about pace and atmosphere. Pace is no problem if one has a story. If I find my pace slowing, it is because the story is vague in my mind and I am muddling about, getting stuck on details and overdescribing. A writer should be quite sure of his story for at least thirty pages to come, and as for myself, I like to rush ahead—in a way, as if I were narrating a story to someone and talking a little too fast. Some writers, I know, like to plan very carefully, make outlines before they begin, and I do not mean to say here how writers should write, I am only saying the way I prefer to write and probably the only way I can write. My headlong method often necessitates heavy revision and major changes and then a new plunge. But often it comes off, too, as it did in *The Talented Mr. Ripley*, certainly the fastest book I ever wrote (five months) and consequently the fastest of all my books to read. When I begin a book, I have no more than sixty pages clearly in mind, often much less, but I have an idea of the effect I want to create—tragedy, success, a sense of being hopelessly trapped, as in *This Sweet Sickness*, a plodding gloom, as in *The Blunderer*. And I do know what the end will be, therefore. After a few pages (it ought to be before the first line) the characters are alive and move, they have directions in which they move, or they have directions that circumstances prevent them from taking. Anyway, one has a dynamic situation, and from then on—certainly by page sixty—the book seems to write itself. When writers look through one of their printed books, see all the twists and turns, the speculations of harassed characters and their possible lines of action (all brilliantly set forth, of course, like spokes radiating from a wheel hub), surely many must say to themselves, "I don't remember thinking all that out in such detail. My goodness, I don't even remember writing it." This has already happened to me on looking through my book, *The Two Faces of January*, which I wrote only a few years ago.

Atmosphere? I am grateful to reviewers for saying that my books have it, but it is another thing I have never given any thought to until now. And it seems to me that laboring it, like laboring anything in a creative work, is fatal. If I have any suggestion as to the building of atmosphere, it is to let the characters react to whatever environment they are in. Thus one presents a setting through the senses (how does it smell, what color is it, how does the color strike the person looking at it?) and also reveals a great deal, effortlessly, about the character perceiving it. A formal garden in Italy may delight a spinster schoolteacher; she may want to sit for hours on a cold stone bench reading her favorite poems in it; it may make a young American football player want to scream, tear out the hedges with his bare hands, or at any rate get out of it as fast as possible. Either reaction gives "atmosphere." A melancholic scene, mist on a deserted beach at night, may please another character who (for some reason) has certain associations with such a place. Characters' reactions produce atmosphere more vividly than solid paragraphs of prose about places—though even solid paragraphs can be relieved and made more alive by one small "he felt . . ." in regard to colors, sounds and smells.

I disapprove of the word "discipline" in regard to writing—that is, in the grim way in which it is generally used. A young writer looks, I imagine (I once did), with wide-eyed and respectful bewilderment at the well-meaning teacher who advises him to get it and keep it, for without it he can do nothing. No wonder the young person does not understand—not completely, because he probably already has the makings of this severe and abstract thing called discipline. Writing is a way of life, and what teachers mean by discipline is the habit and necessity of writing. Discipline never made a writer. Discipline is for the armed forces. And I think distractions and non-writing never unmade a writer, because a real writer will chuck his obligations, shed them somehow, and get away by himself and write. Writing is a way of organizing experience, or of organizing something imagined, of making something perfect and beautiful—even something as small as one sentence—in a world that can be at times chaotic, wretched, ugly and upsetting.

The habit of writing often begins in adolescence, sometimes even earlier. In adolescence, when emotion is intense, when many emotions bring tears, and the teen-ager picks up a pencil or a pen and writes a poem or a paragraph about it, and feels better—that's the beginning of writing. And all art comes from the prolongation of this childlike intensity, which many people lose even at puberty. When writing becomes a habit and a necessity, the writer need never give a thought to discipline, because writing is a pleasure. Then friends and relatives will say, "Ah, what discipline!" on seeing the writer at work, not realizing that it would take more discipline than they dream of for him to spend the next few hours in their company. After a good day's work, when one is feeling rather godlike, it is a different matter, a writer looks on the human race with a new joy, and feels like saying even to the Fuller Brush man, "Come in! Got time to sit down for a few minutes?" Discipline may be needed later when a writer has to cut forty pages from a manuscript he already considers cut, for instance, or his editor tells him to get rid of his favorite minor character because he doesn't advance the plot.

Life can also be chaotic at forty, of course, and a writer can feel he is written out, that he has nothing to say—at least not at the moment. I have just had a letter from a writer friend saying this, that he's written out, and so forth. He hasn't been writing very long at fiction (he was formerly a newspaperman), and he has also rather recently been married, and his wife has had a baby. He writes that he is getting tired of little marital tiffs—among other things—but mostly he writes about not being able to get settled in the book he is trying to start. I suggested to him that his problem might be the sense of loss-of-importance of what he wants to write—a ghastly condition that can easily come when one is faced with marital tiffs, household bills, a sick child, a weekend shattered by a visit from the in-laws, or, above all, by lack of privacy. It is astounding how after days of being with people—sometimes out of necessity, social or economic—a good and exciting idea becomes pale and wan, vague, and not worth writing. It is just as outstanding and thrilling when, after a day or so of solitude, silence, daydreaming and loafing, the same idea comes alive again, beautiful and bright like a wilted plant that has been given a good soaking in the rain.

It takes a few years to learn this. It takes a lot of skill and scheming, make-believe and trickery, to preserve one's enthusiasm through the hideous periods of reality, of people, of obligations, of non-privacy. It is sometimes necessary to avoid thinking about one's story in the midst of people, because it can be crushed like a violet— a violet tossed on a subway platform in the rush hour. I so often think of young writers everywhere who are not able to have, yet, that most expensive commodity in the world—aloneness. I think of young writers who get married thinking that their wives will be so cooperative about their weekend stints at the typewriter, of writers whose wives are cooperative and who themselves are jangled by obligations that will not let their minds be at peace, or by interruptions their wives are not militant enough to prevent. The greatest service a wife can render her writer husband is not typing his manuscripts for him, but keeping people away from him. Of course, a husband might do the same, if his wife is the writer.

How to make psychopathic types attractive? I would suggest making them young, perhaps even rather handsome, tidy in their dress (heavens, what a picture of impropriety we could conjure up by remarking quietly that our psychopathic hero was wont to be untidy in his dress), or give them a nice trait or two, like being generous, or kind to old ladies and animals. A sense of humor is also of tremendous help. This, perhaps, does not always work. Tom Ripley was nice looking, though his face was thoroughly forgettable; he was tidy; he had a sense of humor, and many readers liked him; yet others said they disliked him, with an "Ugh-h!" and a shudder. But the likers and dislikers kept turning the pages, the dislikers with an attitude of "Good Lord, what's he going to do *next?*" What writer could ask for more? And I also feel sure it would be possible to write a book with an untidy, fat, sloppy psychopath as hero, if one only gave him enough fascinating and audacious things to do. His more repellent qualities might have to be introduced gradually, but if you introduce him in some kind of action, the reader will be drawn along. Good action and a good story are irresistible.

Of all my published books, two, I think, are decidedly dull. They are *A Game for the Living* and *The Cry of the Owl*. In the first, a psychopathic murderer-hero is missing; in fact the murderer is off-scene, unknown, so it becomes a mystery whodunit in a way—definitely not my forte. In *Owl*, the hero is too square, becoming a sitting duck for the more evil characters, a passive bore. In both, I tried to do something different from what I had been doing, but left out some elements vital for me: surprise, speed of action, coincidence, and the stretching of the reader's credulity—which I ordinarily do to excess and without scruple. The result was mediocrity. It would be easy for me to keep on writing stories with heroes like Bruno of *Strangers on a Train* and Ripley, but it would also be cowardly and unenterprising. My conclusion is that it is well for a writer to realize what he can do best: a frightened heroine, a mad hero, a chase; and what emotional elements he does best: anxiety, the destructiveness that is associated with the criminal mind, the playing off of good against evil —and use them as the strong points of his story. I believe that any story, about anything, in the suspense category, can be told using some of the writer's stronger points, if he takes the trouble to find out first what his strong points are. I did not in these two dull books, and it was unforgivable of me.

49

WRITING THE GOTHIC NOVEL

By Phyllis A. Whitney

EVER since the name "Gothic" came to be used for a certain type of story, people have been asking, "What *is* a Gothic?" During their period of runaway popularity in the softcover field, the questions were often raised, "Who reads them, and why?" Since the genre continues to sell steadily, writers want to know what makes a good novel of this kind.

First, why the label, "Gothic"? I would like to make a switch in terms. "Gothic," for all its usefulness as a catchy term, is too limiting, with its gloomy-old-house atmosphere. Already the boundaries are being pushed out from the "true" Gothic. The writer need not feel restricted. I prefer a label which gives me more room in which to perform. I have always called my own books "romantic novels of suspense," and I ask that this descriptive phrase be used on the jackets by way of identification for the reader. The Gothic can easily be included in this larger category. The same readers like the broader horizon just as well, and the basic ingredients are similar.

The word Gothic has always carried darkly romantic medieval connotations, but it was an editor of paperbacks who first used the term in our time as a marketing label. Considering the long reprint life of Daphne du Maurier's *Rebecca,* he wondered if there were books of a similar type which had been published in hardcover and could be reprinted in a softcover series. He came upon my own hardcover *Thunder Heights* and decided to start his softcover venture with that title. The name he gave the series derived from the gloomy, arched and towered architecture so often described in these stories. The name caught on with the success of the series and has now come to stand for the romantic novel stamped by a brooding sense of mystery and terror.

Of course, stories of this type have been with us for a long time.

Even before the Victorian years the true Gothic novel was originated with romantic hair-raisers like the melodramatic *Castle of Otranto* (1764) by Horace Walpole, Mrs. Radcliffe's *Mysteries of Udolpho* (1794), and others. The Brontë sisters added psychological problems, depth of characterization, and greater credibility for the eerie doings. Since then, a great many writers, mainly women, have written romantic mystery novels in this tradition. They seem to be read by women of all ages, from teens to grandmothers—by schoolgirls, housewives and businesswomen. Men, too, read the more adventurous books of this type, such as those written by Mary Stewart. But it took the "Gothic" label and the selling excitement that followed in the softcover field to put them on the market as a distinct genre.

As to the *why* of the Gothic's popularity, one can only speculate. The women readers of these books appear to like stories with strong human problems and an avoidance of the police procedure that marks the more orthodox murder mystery. They find psychological action more interesting than the physical action of books aimed primarily at a masculine reader, though of course there must be a mixture of both. They enjoy the woman's viewpoint, and they like heroines who solve their problems. The anti-heroine who is destroyed by her problems has no place here! Women enjoy the sort of suspense that keeps them eagerly turning pages, and they want a love story as well. There is about these stories—and now I'm speaking as a reader —a certain wonderment. One steps into what Monica Dickens has called "a dear familiar landscape," in which anything at all may happen, romantically speaking. There is an entrancing promise, sure to be fulfilled by the skilled writer.

Gothic novels are not, as a rule, serious novels. They are entertainment—which does not bar you in the least from putting the best writing possible into them, or from bringing to them your own feelings and understanding about human beings and life. You must realize, however, that there is a performance involved. You are a magician standing on a stage. If your illusions are skillful, so that you both hold and fool your audience, you succeed. If you fumble and are caught, you fail. This skill takes a good deal of effort and practice to learn, but it is a lot of fun along the way. It takes a very real understanding and mastery of technique. In the course of writing some thirteen books in this field, I have had to learn something of my craft. There are definite ingredients involved in this type of story, and I would like to share what I have learned about these ingredients—learned both as a reader and a writer. Let's consider them:

BACKGROUND

There must be color and romance in the story setting. In the traditional Gothic this usually means a spooky old mansion set in a brooding landscape, whether up the Hudson River, on the coast of Cornwall, or wherever. Yet I have used the sunny island of Rhodes, with my characters living in a hotel, and the background still had romantic suspense. Background is basically used to create atmosphere and the writer can concoct this out of all sorts of things. The very period of the story can provide atmosphere. Victorian times lend themselves nicely to mood, and of course credibility is more easily achieved if the events take place in a distant time. But be careful not to sound exactly like a Victorian writer if you use that period. A blending with the modern is necessary, with an avoidance of strictly modern terms.

If you use the modern scene, you'd better remove your characters to some isolated spot where you won't have as much trouble with believability. Such isolation can even be achieved in an old brownstone in today's New York, if you can shut out the outside world to a sufficient extent. These books seldom concern themselves with the wider problems of the world. There are plenty of problems, but they are of a personal variety.

When I use a foreign background, I always make the story modern. I can do my research of the modern scene more easily than I can probe back into foreign history. It would be much too difficult to find out everything I would need to know about life in, say, Istanbul a hundred years ago.

ROMANCE, EMOTION

No feeling, no story—and that's a rule! Of course there must be a strong love story, though the ingredient of emotion may come in on several levels. In my *Window on the Square*, emotion arises from the presence in the story of a small boy who is supposed to have murdered his father. The heroine champions him against his mother and stepfather—while falling in love with the latter. This makes for complications, conflict and tension. A big, dramatic, hard-to-solve problem will contain plenty of emotion in itself, and has never hurt any kind of story.

There must be obstacles to true love, naturally, and the obstacles must be real and hard to surmount. The more difficult the corner you paint your characters into, the more interesting the story. And if you find a way out the reader never expects, you have successfully passed one of the principal tests.

One footnote on the matter of this obstacle: I have sometimes used an obnoxious wife or husband of the hero or heroine—who must, therefore, be disposed of by the end of the story. This is not supposed to be cricket, for some reason, though it provides a strong story situation. Of course the reader will realize—if he thinks about it—that if hero and heroine are to get together, the obstruction must go. But for someone caught up in the spell which a magician has cast, this doesn't seem to matter. You know that card didn't really vanish —but you believe it at the time. All sorts of variations can be played. In *Columbella* the wife dies two-thirds of the way through the book, but her evil influence continues after her death, so that the obstacle remains. The only rule is that the removal of the obstacle—whatever it is—must be credible; even better if in retrospect it seems inevitable.

SEX

Although there are never explicit details about sex in these books, and your hero and heroine may indulge (onstage) in no more than a warm embrace, don't think sex isn't there. Charlotte and Emily Brontë both knew about sex. It smolders in *Wuthering Heights,* and it is present in *Jane Eyre* as well. If you'll go back and look, you'll find that Jane possessed a strongly passionate nature, for all that she has been a much maligned heroine.

This is a tricky thing to handle. It is a good deal more difficult than to detail the act of lovemaking clinically. Yet it's worth the effort. A scene that is underplayed, suggested, rather than stated, can often have greater emotional effect because of the way the reader's imagination will work for you.

So physical and emotional attraction between hero and heroine must certainly be present, even when they are fighting each other. Perhaps especially then. In the true love scenes, there is always an underlying tenderness that, for a woman, can be an exciting factor in sex—James Bond to the contrary.

Sometimes men writers who are quite aware of this factor have gone to the extreme of handling the love story element in too delicate and supposedly ladylike a fashion. Catherine and Heathcliff would turn in their graves! Look to the masters for the genuine physical feeling that should be present, even though its consummation is postponed (as a rule) until after the last chapter.

DAMSEL-IN-DISTRESS

Although a damsel-in-distress is necessary, you can get into trouble here. We want a heroine with real spirit. She should be intelligent, too (as all Mary Stewart's heroines are). She may or may not be pretty, and quite often she regards herself as plain. A wholly self-confident beauty can lose the reader's sympathy fast. A beautiful heroine will serve your purpose only if she is engaging enough to overcome this dire handicap. The best of these heroines have a touching vulnerability about them. They are brave, and sometimes reckless, they meet adversity with courage, but they are fearfully open to hurt, and the reader must feel this, believe in it. Perhaps this is why the put-upon little governess in all her variations has done so well. Max de Winter's young wife was vulnerable in *Rebecca*. So was Mary Stewart's charming heroine in *Nine Coaches Waiting*. Victoria Holt is a master at evoking this sort of openness to hurt. Our heroine must be vulnerable because of her love, because of her involvement with other characters, and because her initial position is one of helpless unimportance. All this she overcomes in the end. She is in trouble, but it must not be trouble brought on because she is a total idiot.

Above all, make sure that your heroine is faced with a problem— probably continuing problems—which she can *do* something about. The problem must be largely hers, and she must not just sit and look at it without taking any action until the end of the story. In every chapter she must *act*, whether in a large or small way. Or she must be planning action, so that the reader will know she isn't sitting still. Just worrying is never enough.

A STRONG HERO

Here we play all the variations possible, since this is the character most likely to be typed. In fact, I've never found a sure way to avoid this kind of typing entirely. Your hero is descended from some pretty distinguished ancestors, and the mark of his heritage is likely to show: Heathcliff, Mr. Rochester, Max de Winter—all driven, bedeviled, stern, dark men (dark in the sense of the dark brooding quality usually associated with this sort of man). He is generally older than your heroine by a number of years and has experienced a good deal of living. He is the sort of hero who seems to fascinate women readers, and of course he has a real need which the *right* woman can fill—and what satisfaction for any woman to find herself needed by such a man!

I've tried to get away from the type by giving all these qualities to the villain, and making my hero blond and cheerful, as well as strong, with the result that the villain became the more interesting character. Sometimes, of course, the hero may even appear to be the villain for a good part of the way through the story—which leads to even more desperation on the distraught heroine's part. Mary Stewart did this with as thrilling a chase scene as I've ever read in *Nine Coaches Waiting,* and Du Maurier frightened us badly about Max de Winter toward the end of *Rebecca.*

Play your own interesting variations, if possible, but don't wander too far afield. After all, this is the type of hero who will give you (and the reader) the best run for the money. His admiration and love are both worth the winning, but not to be easily won. He will never readily succumb to feminine wiles, and he will remain strong and perverse to the end—always the master.

Don't let your hero remain offstage for too long at a time. If he can't be actively present, we must at least think about him, and deal with him through the heroine's developing problems. An offstage hero who pops in at the beginning and then at the end of the story will do you no good at all. He must participate actively at the very center of your plot. He can't stand around on the outskirts trying to help without being himself caught up in the central involvement. He must *do* something. He may or may not come to the heroine's rescue at the end. It's rather nice if he does, but not absolutely essential, provided there is a wind-up to a romantic clinch at the end.

Your other characters should be "interesting," but don't make them all eccentrics or your story will lose believability. Some of your actors will be mainly good, others mainly evil, but all should be in-esting. What makes them the sort of people they are is important. When I am planning a story, I spend more time writing up dossiers about each character than I do on all the other preparation. You can't develop an interesting character in depth quickly and easily. You must give him time to grow. In this growth, you will discover useful events in his past—even back into his childhood—and you will know what his secrets are. You will work out the relationship between each character and every other character in the story, and know exactly how each thinks and feels about all the others. If you don't do your homework here, you'll come up with the shallow, the superficial, and your motivation may be too thin to carry real story interest.

Don't forget the importance of characterizing some of the people who are dead before your story starts. Rebecca was dead long before Max brought his nameless (what a trick for a writer to play!) young wife to Manderley, yet she is one of the strongest, most important characters in the book. So if you have a character who is no longer alive, but whose actions have set into motion all the trouble that is happening in the present, be sure you spend time getting to know that character as well as you know those who are performing on-stage.

A child can be enormously useful. So can an animal, if well charac-terized and important to the plot. Don't overlook either, but don't let either one take the story away from your main character. Both are notorious scene-stealers.

SUSPENSE, MYSTERY

Gothic novels are not simple romances. The mystery element, the building of suspense, is all important. How well this element is han-dled is the test of a good Gothic novel.

From the first, there must be a sense of urgency, of growing threat, of fear that mounts to terror. And there must be something *real* for the heroine to fear. This element can't be faked, or be "all a mistake." The sense of sustained terror that comes in certain scenes and builds to a climax at the end will make or break your story.

This sense of urgency must not come from outside forces alone. It should grow from the heroine's interrelationship with other characters. Equally important is the genuine feeling of evil, existing in some unknown form. In all good mystery stories, there must be the vital clash of good and evil. Before the end of the story, your heroine should feel thoroughly trapped, so that escape from her predicament, a solution to her problems, seems impossible both to her and to the reader. Out of such trappings will grow high suspense.

There must be mystery *right now*. From scene to scene, you make the reader ask questions, but you don't answer the last question until the final scene. Urgency—always urgency! Time is running out, the plight is desperate, all is about to be lost. In the beginning, curiosity will carry you for a while, but soon it must be the real character conflict that builds story interest.

Beware of the problem that gets stuck in one groove. Things that go bump in the night, and continue to do so with monotonous regularity, lead only to boredom. The problem must shift, grow, develop, or we lose interest.

There may or may not be a murder. I usually avoid an onstage murder because that brings in the police, and I don't want them cluttering my scene. I am not writing a detective story. If the reader can't add up the clues for himself, I'm not going to waste pages "deducting." I am playing a different sort of game. So, the death, if there is one, is often thought to be accident or suicide, and the police get out of the picture as fast as possible. Only the heroine, or some other character, begins to see past the easy answer to what may really have happened. Or it is possible that a real murder took place before the story started, and the murderer may be lingering around uncaught. Or evidence may come up to reopen an unsolved crime— reopen it by one of the story characters, if not by the police.

But there is danger in that past murder. One of my favorite ways of bogging myself down in a story is to have the past action so exciting and so interesting that it begins to take over, with very little present action resulting. A fatal disease for a story to develop is "past-itis." Your story is *now;* whatever effect past events may have, things must happen in the present.

Use your background, weather, season; use moonlight or glaring sunlight unhesitatingly to build suspense. Sometimes the gloomy atmosphere of a storm goes along with what is happening; sometimes it is equally effective if you use contrast.

When I was in the Virgin Islands doing research for *Columbella,* we had a hurricane scare. Of course I made notes all through it, and then used a near-hurricane in the climax of the story. In reviewing the book, one critic said I should never have used the device of a storm to help along the climax. Why not? I will use anything that enhances the feeling of terror, of mounting suspense, that seems to fit in properly with my scene. Don't cheat your reader of the drama he craves because you are afraid of being called corny.

Make surprises your stock in trade. Don't let a chapter, or even a scene, go by in which the unexpected doesn't happen. Once a reader knows exactly where you are taking him, he doesn't need to finish the book. Because you know your characters so well, you will know that they can take unexpected turns which the reader will never guess are coming.

Things, objects, will prove useful to you in this respect: a mirror that gives your heroine an eerie sense of the past, a seashell used in a strange way, an animal killed in a way that strikes terror into the heroine. Physical objects can often be used as symbols as well. The Columbella shell was a symbol for the evil Catherine. Almost everything has been done, of course, by other writers, which is all the more reason for you to try for unexpected variations to make your way different.

SOURCE OF EVIL

Of course there must be a villain, either male or female. There must be someone to provide the source of evil that sets everything in motion. Hiding the identity of this person is one of your main illusionary effects as a magician. As you trick and fool, while playing as fair as you dare, so will the reader be pleased. This is not a game which your opponent wants to win. All sorts of methods can be worked out for the role of the villain. Sometimes he's not a real villain, having caused trouble inadvertently or mistakenly. Sometimes his face is revealed ahead of time and the suspense lies in how the heroine is to escape the trap in which she is caught. I reveal the identity of the villain long before the end in *Seven Tears for Apollo*, but the suspense continues.

MEANING

Call it what you like—theme, moral, significance—it must be there. Not preached, but underlying. I've heard this element dismissed as being of no importance because readers of these books want only to be entertained. Of course no reader will tell you that he picks up such a book for anything but entertainment. But you, as a craftsman, had better understand why a reader is disappointed when the story doesn't add up to anything at the end.

All good fiction—being a reflection of the basic course of life—is an account of growth or deterioration. Because so much fiction these days deals with deterioration, a good many readers are turning in relief to the story which builds toward its main character's growth. If your heroine learns nothing at all in the course of the story, if she is the same at the end as she was in the beginning, the reader will have a sense of letdown, of disappointment.

A good story of this sort is about somebody who *grows*. Your heroine is human—she makes mistakes, she stumbles, she learns—and in the course of her maturing you cannot help but say something to the reader. Something worth saying about life, about living, about maturing. This is an element which leaves an intangible sense of satisfaction in the reader when the book is closed. Even your dark-browed, sardonic hero might be able to learn a few things by the end of the story. It wouldn't hurt him at all!

HAPPY ENDING

No other kind of ending will do. We read a story of suspense so that everything will stop hurting at the end. The final clinch should take care of that. But don't think you can tack on a whole chapter given to romance when the mysteries are all solved and the story is over.

There is always plenty of explaining to be done. The expert writer starts feeding in his explanations long before the end, holding out two or three items the reader really wants an answer to until the very end. Only then can the author hold his audience.

Make sure your heroine deserves her happy fate at the end. If she hasn't earned it, there will be no reader satisfaction.

A final word. I doubt that you can write Gothic novels unless you like reading them. You must be able to throw yourself genuinely into your performance as you write. While I am in the process of writing, I am submerged in my heroine and her problems—and having a wonderful time. Me and all those dark-browed heroes! I'm sure this is the first necessary ingredient, though I'm mentioning it last.

Not long ago at a meeting of the Authors' Guild, I heard a bookseller of many years' experience say something which is worth remembering. In a really good book, she said, "the juices must flow." But such juices cannot be produced synthetically. It is the writer's own feeling that must flow through his characters to bring his story to life and vitality.

50

BACKGROUND—THE MOST IMPORTANT CHARACTER

By Elisabeth Ogilvie

NOVELISTS have always been intrigued and inspired by the power of environment to influence human lives. Since we're all readers, I don't have to list even a half dozen classic examples; you can name ten in as many minutes. And they all observe the rule for the background novel; whatever the situation may be, the cause, the working out, and the final effect are influenced by the milieu in which the characters experience their jealousy, hatred, love, adultery, greed, or sacrifice.

The word "background," in itself as flat as a backdrop on a stage, is a misnomer for the environment in which we live our lives. We are what we are because of it; if we are completely at home in it, we are shaped to it, but if we fight it, it becomes an impersonal yet hostile force that shapes us in another way. Or we have a love-hate relationship with it: we can't live with it and we can't live away from it, and that turns us into ambivalent creatures, never at home anywhere, always eaten with homesickness for we don't know what.

You have *your* background, which you know in every detail because you've been born to it, or else you've come to it with fresh and excited eyes, seeing things which the native doesn't even notice anymore. It can be a corrupt and fascinating old city in Europe, or a suburb full of status-seekers; or you may have a useful knowledge of steel mills, ranch empires, ocean liners, or research laboratories. Whatever and wherever the territory, as a writer you contemplate its citizens and its effect upon their personal lives. If there is an impressive physical setting to be described, so much the better. You are rich beyond the dreams of avarice, and you are going to spill these riches out on paper.

Now, where to begin, and how to get it all down on paper? You're not only spendthrift, you're like the enthusiastic new painter who wants to get every last twig of that enchanting scene onto canvas, not knowing that to leave out some of it is to strengthen the rest.

Or, you have people and their fundamental problems in human relations, and you want to use a rich and unique setting which you know well, but your problem isn't that of disciplining a mass of material, but of how to use it at all.

The rule in both cases is as essential and simple for you as it was for Emily Brontë, Thomas Hardy, and Mark Twain. In the novel of background, events must happen *because* of the background. Ask yourself this: Are these people acting the way they are because they live in a certain place, under certain conditions? Or could they be found anywhere? Could the whole action be picked up and set down somewhere else? If you say *yes* to these questions, you are not using your background correctly.

I write about fishing and lobstering people along the coast of Maine, more specifically about two islands. I live on one, which I used in my novels, *The Witch Door* and *There May Be Heaven*. The other is Bennett's Island which I used in my *Tide* trilogy, and in *The Dawning of the Day*, *The Seasons Hereafter*, and several juvenile novels. This island, twenty-five miles out in the Gulf of Maine, rugged and magnificent, turned me into a writer at the age of fifteen because I had to express my passionate emotions about it in some way. I still haven't finished exploring all the aspects of its disturbing influence on human beings.

Here is a world of stunning beauty and often of stunning brutality. Here are men making their living in an intensely physical way, on terms of truce with the elements. The women live accordingly. (Ask yourself, in what ways are the people in my setting different from other people? To what unique situations must they react in their daily lives?) The suburban woman whose husband is late getting home knows he has probably been caught in traffic on the freeway. The fisherman's wife, who may read the same magazines and whose children may be watching the same thing on TV as the children two hundred miles away in Newton, Massachusetts, knows that when *her* husband is overdue, his engine could be broken down and he may be drifting out there in the dusk, or he has lost his course in a surprise snow squall and piled his boat on a ledge. He may already be dead. She says nothing to the children, but lets out a long breath when she looks out at the harbor for the twentieth time and sees a moving light at his mooring.

In *The Seasons Hereafter,* as in the *Tide* books, I kept the strong rhythms of life beating like a counterpoint to a woman's private experience by the use of a few simple devices. To say that description and local color are combined with action may sound too simple:

> She got frantically out of bed and saw Western Harbor Point and the break-water washed bronze and rose with the sunrise. A boat was going out by the breakwater, and the man was putting on his oilclothes, now and then touching the wheel.

Vanessa is frantic with her own confusion, yet life goes on, there is a clear sunrise and the boats are going out. The harbor is the heart of the place, it dominates her. She keeps coming back to it:

> The changeable harbor seemed curiously empty and lifeless this morning in spite of the skiffs at the moorings and the gulls picking through the fresh wet weed on the ledges. It was as if an invisible tide had gone out with the men and wouldn't return until they did.

In a quick sketch you get the look and feel of a fisherman's harbor when the boats are out.

They go out, they come in, no matter what happens to her. She has been waiting all day for her lover, "watching *White Lady* ride into the harbor on towering seas; Steve Bennett's *Philippa* rolled deep on one side, and Nils Sorensen came in behind, easing his boat when she slid downhill on the smoking green slopes. Charles rounded the breakwater after him, sinking out of sight in the trough. . . . When the family came in, it was an armada." This is the family whom she resents and tries to despise.

Walking to the store, what does Vanessa see that the farm or city woman doesn't see? "Seine dories newly painted buff and blue at the edge of the coarse grass, a graveyard of old hulls rotting beside a little pond." She smells a whiff of bait and wet lobster traps brought in to dry out. She recognizes the sound of trapnails being driven into a lath, oarlocks, an engine being tried out. And there are always the gulls that haunt the place like its familiar spirits. Vanessa is concentrating intensely on herself, yet you and she are forever conscious of messages from the outside.

"When she came into the house, Barry had been in and gone out again. His dinner box was on the table, and his rubber boots stood against the wall. He had cooked some lobsters and eaten a couple; the shells were in a sink." She takes two lobsters for herself, "breaking them open with quick professional twists of her hands and getting the meat out in big pink and white chunks."

The dinner box, the rubber boots, the fresh lobster bring Barry's work into the room; implicit are the long hours on the water in the rolling boat. The way Van handles the lobsters shows another of the small but significant differences that give validity to her and her background.

A child's accident can be of any kind, anywhere. Make the bad fall or burn something that could only have happened *here*. Don't miss any chance to strengthen the sense of apartness. A child in *Seasons* sees a starfish from a wharf, goes down over the ledges to get it, slips on wet rockweed, and falls in. Vanessa goes down a steep ladder to get him. Just as she casually handles lobsters live or dead, and can stuff salt herring into a baitbag, she is used to ladders at low tide. The suburban wife doesn't quiver at the thought of city traffic or the farmer's wife at helping a cow to calve.

In *The Seasons Hereafter*, the love affair begins and is carried on in secrecy only because it happens where it does. In the first confrontation, the man appears suddenly at Van's door looking for her husband to help him seine herring. In five minutes, simply because Owen Bennett heard herring "puddling" in the harbor, his and Vanessa's lives are changed, and they will never be the same again.

Because he is a lobsterman, it is perfectly legitimate for him to hire her to knit trapheads for him. This is a tiresome job many men don't want to do or have the time to do. It is a dying skill, and the person who can knit (actually *net*) can always be sure of work. When he brings her the twine and meshboards, the businesslike meeting is as intimate an encounter as exchanged glances over cocktails or dancing together at a party:

As he started to give her instructions for the heads, she said, "Wait a minute, I'd better write everything down." But she could find neither pencil nor paper, and she got very hot and her eyes stung. "Oh, damn it," she wailed softly, pawing without sense at magazines, and he called to her, "Never mind, I've got something in my pocket." . . . He was sitting at the table writing on the back of an envelope. She stood looking at the bulk of his shoulders and the back of his neck, at the way the wiry black hair grew down on it and at a small puckered scar, a white seam against the burnt-dark skin. She lit a cigarette after several futile attempts to scratch a match because her hand was unsteady.

They discuss technical details. Then, when he is about to leave, he tells her, apparently off-hand, that he'll be going around the shore in a dory looking for traps of his washed ashore:

"This morning I saw three down in Ship Cove."
"I'll bet your youngsters will enjoy going with you."
"I'm not taking them. They'll still be in school."
"Oh." The syllable floated between them, a leaf or a feather. . . .

As simply as this, the appointment is made; they can meet in a lonely cove because the island has so many such coves, and because he has a legitimate excuse to be out there at midday. She of course can take long walks without question. On an island with no automobiles, people still walk for recreation.

The nylon trapheads become a sexual symbol.

Soon they would be handled with careless expertise by those brown hands with the long thumbs which she could see so clearly as they wrote, gestured, lit a cigarette, and held out the meshboards.

The trapheads represent the way of life which has thrown these two together, and something more subtle. This is something his wife can't do. What other need can't she fill for him?

The familiar situation in which secret lovers are crowded in with other people and must hide their feelings can also contribute to authenticity. In this case, it's a severe gale when the men stay up all night to watch the boats. Van is upset at being in close quarters with Owen, her husband, and another couple. What makes it more agonizing is that Owen ignores her:

The scene around the table lacerated her nerves, yet she could not bear to go away from that oblivious black head. He could at least look in my direction once, it's his trapheads ruining my hands. . . . I wish all their damn boats would

come ashore at once. Then you'd see some hopping and swearing. And I'd sit
here and laugh. I'd laugh myself sick and never stop. She drove the needle hard
through the loop and gave a vicious pull.

Just when she thinks she can stand no more, a boat is driven
ashore, and the men fly out in a grand scramble of oilskins and rubber boots. She is saved by one of this salt-water world's particular
disasters.

Another appointment is made, this time almost within earshot of
his children, the girl knitting baitbags for pocket money, the boy
gathering ballast rocks to help his father: a tiny design to help bring
out the whole pattern of the fabric.

This date is for a weekend. The island makes such occasions for
lovers, because there are twenty-five miles of water between it and
the nearest dentist, doctor, lawyer, or income tax official. A couple of
errands that could be done in one morning by a mainlander take up
two or three days for the islander.

These lovers, each with a different errand (Van's is false), travel
across the bay at the same time, speaking to each other only casually. On the mainland they meet again, they go away, and because
they are what they are, they seek another island. The stolen time is
spent in a place of great beauty, no sordid hideout, and they are
bemused and betrayed into believing for the first time that they can
have a life together. In this spot between sun and sea, where he could
go on being the fisherman and the islander that he was born, everything seems possible.

At home, waiting for the time to make a move, she rows across the
harbor to relieve tension, as a mainland woman might get in her car
and go somewhere. She thinks, "Anyone could row all around Jes-
sup's Island in a few hours. I would like a little dory like the one we
went out there in." She sees herself watching for Owen's boat to
come up the thoroughfare on that far coast; she sees herself painting buoys while he builds traps. She is always true to her background, even in her dreams.

And at the end, who is to say whether his wife holds Owen or
Bennett's Island does? Vanessa doesn't know.

When you are planning your story, take into account the hazards,
the rewards, the triumphs and terrors of the world you are trying to

create. What in his professional life makes a rancher, a doctor, or a schoolteacher happy? What depresses him or, worse, terrifies him? The fire in *The Seasons Hereafter* doesn't ruin everyone, as it could have done with the right wind blowing, and the fire department twenty-five miles across the bay, but it is a catalyst for Vanessa and a disaster for squalid little Gina, whose struggles run parallel with Van's. The two of them are, each in her own way, victims of the most important character in the novel—the island.

The island has made its people what they are. It imposes a peculiar discipline on them, and they must obey if they are to survive and prosper. It exercises a Lorelei charm on men like Barry, stronger than his rage at Van's betrayal.

Here's a final sympathetic word if you're afraid of swamping hardboiled editors with masses of descriptive matter, but can't hold back. *Don't*. Put it all in that first draft; go madly poetical with description, or splash it on like thick paint. Don't refine as you go. Don't try to understate. Be free-swinging and uninhibited. But come back to it sternly a month later with a handful of sharp pencils, and *cut*. The essence will be there.

Without false emphasis but with a sure knowledge of your background and a meticulous attention to detail—from the games of children to the adults' tragedies, whether on a city block or a Maine island—you can make your reader *see, smell, hear,* and *feel* its presence below, above, and behind everything else.

51

YOUR PLOT IS CONTRIVED

By Charlotte Armstrong

"The plot is contrived," says your reviewer. You, who always pay attention to criticism, of course, in order to learn, may confidently conclude that he finds something wrong with your story. But you should realize that he isn't saying what he means.

I could argue that all fiction is, and must be, contrived. When the story writer sits to his desk, opens his notes and begins to ponder, I'd like to ask what in the world *else* he is doing! Even the reporter, the historian, the biographer must select, omit, and arrange. It is his art to do this to some facts. The story writer must do all of this and, furthermore, do it to facts he was never given. To invent the "facts" and arrange them, at the same time, is his *art*.

Or, to get away from that word with its hovering capital A (since I am about to discuss the suspense story), let's call it his craft. Which *is* to contrive. And what your critic meant to say, you see, was that you didn't contrive very well.

Of all kinds of fiction, perhaps suspense fiction must have the most plot, plenty of happenings, confrontations, actions and reactions. It cannot be a mood piece that moons along, being ever so sensitive and all that, but almost exclusively the dialogue of one brooding mind with itself. It had better not be written in a style so obscure that the reader has to guess what happens, either. The suspense story must *be* a tale and it must be *told*.

This being so, the first thing the writer of these yarns does is to settle his wits to the cooking up of his plot. How is this done?

The germ of a suspense story may come to you in several ways. You may have taken notice of a certain kind of person, of an interesting complexity, and you would like to "create" him on paper. Or you may find yourself excited by a theme. There is a point you'd like to make, if you can only figure out how to embody it in fiction. Or you may be intrigued by a certain setting.

But most often, the event comes first (or soon, in any case). You must say to yourself, "O.K., now what happens?" And immediately you must add, "to whom?" Even when the germ has come to you in the first place in the guise of an event, you must at once consider the kind of person to whom you will make it happen, because upon his character depends his reaction, and upon that reaction depends what happens next.

Here is a crude example. Suppose a car breaks down at night on a lonely road. What will the occupants do? It depends on who they are, surely. If they are a couple of elderly widows, ignorant of machinery and afraid of the dark, that's one thing. If they are a frolicsome pair of courting young people, that's another.

When the event is an act by a person, first he must be the kind of person who *would* act so, and then the consequence of what he does will depend upon the characters to whom, or before whom, he does it.

So the whole problem of contriving well lies in the matching of events with characters.

It seems to me that the very definition of character is what a given individual will or will not do. Some people wouldn't tell a lie. Some people *will* snoop at your mail. Some people wouldn't think of such a thing!

Why will or won't a person do what? Well, he has his share of the culture, his training, his degree of sophistication, his ignorance or knowledge, his status, values, prejudices, maybe even principles. He also has a state of health, physical or mental, peculiar to him, and his private relationships with, and attitudes toward, all the other characters.

I don't know whether it is better to say that he is what he does, or that he does what he is. But you, his creator, had better be sure what this character *would* naturally do, according to the lights you've given him. Or vice versa.

I say vice versa because, during the part of the work that is the contriving (the composition of the text comes much later) you should hold both characters and events in a fluid suspension, until you succeed in adjusting them to each other.

For instance, you may, and often do, come to a place in your ten-

tative chain of happenings and discover one of your characters simply digging in his heels and refusing to do what you wanted him to
do. You have your reasons for pushing him around, but he'll have
none of it. He just wouldn't *do* that! He's not that kind of person.
It's absurd to pretend that he *ever* would, and worse, impossible to
make anybody believe it. Why, you can't believe it, yourself!

When you hit this impasse, there are two ways around it. You can
give up that particular plot element, and sometimes you must, even
when doing so really messes up the sequence. Or, you can change the
character and make him over into the kind who *would* act as you
need him to act. This means going all the way back to his roots, not
only to the point where you plan to introduce him to the reader, but
as far as you yourself have needed to go back into his life, which is
always farther than the text goes.

Now, I am by no means saying that a character must be static.
Not at all. The most fascinating characters are those who change
under the pressures of happenings. But in order to create one of
these "growing" characters, you must know *from* what he is changing, *to* what, and also *why*.

Therefore, if you are going to have the miser give the beggar a
thousand dollars, or the coward jump the chasm, or the meek rise
and fiercely dominate the meeting, you must take care to work this
up, as slyly as you like, but nevertheless clearly and soundly, so that
the "surprise" turns out to be "Well, of course!" or even "Hooray!"
Otherwise, some critic will say that your plot is contrived. But the
truth will be that you just didn't work long enough, or hard enough,
or well enough at your contriving.

Nobody sits down and spins an excellent plot for a suspense yarn
(or any other, I suspect) right off the bat. He works at it. And the
work does grow under his hand.

Sometimes, when you are imagining-in-detail, or trying to put a bit
of flesh on the next projected happening to check it out and see that
it will work, suddenly there comes to you a truth, something that one
of your characters *would* do here. But of course he would! It's not
what you had been planning for him, but it's better. It gives the
story a bonus of excitement. Many of your best so-called "devices,"
marvelous "twists," the kind that carry both surprise and recognition (the best kind) are found in just this way. You couldn't have

dreamed that up in a million years—not from scratch. It comes out of work already done. It appears. And who says this kind of work can't be fun?

Into the weaving of a plot come many other threads, of course. Some may have to do not only with this story, but with stories in general. Let us say that you are in possession of a promising "what-if," an event. What if a housewife, walking down her own residential block, finds a note on the sidewalk that purports to be from somebody who is imprisoned, nearby? Sounds pretty fair, for a thriller. O.K., what does she do? Well, what kind of housewife is she? If she is timidly respectable and doesn't want to get involved, end of story as far as she's concerned. (That won't do.) Yet if she is a conscience-ridden, brother's-keeper, you may have the dickens of a time making anybody *like* her, and you'd better remember that. If she goes overboard in involvement for a stranger's sake, the reader is going to begin to say to himself, "Aw, come on." If you are expecting to get her into any wild trouble, you'll just about have to make her stupid. If she's sensible and turns the note over to the cops, *she* falls out of the story. But if she turns out to be related in any way to the prisoner, ah, ah . . . coincidence. Mustn't touch!

So, unless you can change either the event (there was no prisoner) or the character (she isn't a housewife)—or both, you had better put this one deep into the drawer.

Many things, you see, must be considered and all at once, and they modify each other.

There is, besides, the over-all tone. You do not take the same tone with every story. If, for instance, you are working within some stern realistic mode, your characters had better not react with light-hearted pranks, out of tune with the prevailing effect, *unless* you are using this very incongruity to make a stern realistic point. By the same token, if you are working on a yarn that you intend to make a romp, an entertainment, in semi-frothy or even semi-satirical style, you must be content to let any profound observations of the human scene clothe themselves in the same style. You cannot, for instance, have your gay young protagonist preached at by some grim moralist and *therefore* change his spots. Not out of left field, you can't.

Not only every thread, you see, but the sheen of the finished cloth must be carefully contrived, and, preferably, before you put down a single sentence.

It's possible that only he who sits down and does this sort of thing knows how it's done, and then, perhaps, he knows only how *he* does it. But it is not as simple as some may think, to do it well, and not the least challenging task in the world, and *definitely* not the dullest.

Your plot is contrived, eh? Well, I should hope so!

52

THE CATEGORY NOVEL

By Isabel Moore

With the demise of the pulps in the thirties and early forties, the young writer had a hard time finding a training ground, especially for fiction. Now, however, all young writers should be encouraged to know that the pendulum has swung all the way back, and a brand-new—and very hungry—market has emerged. This market is known in the trade as "the category novel," and it provides a solid stepping-stone to good novel writing just as the pulps were a proving ground for the future writer of slick fiction.

First, let me tell you what the category novel is: It is formula writing, by which I mean it has fairly stock characters, a beginning, a middle, a black moment, and a happy ending—*plus* a special category. For instance, we do not sit down just to write a "nurse novel," but to write a novel about a certain kind, or category, of nurse. Thus, you will see among the paperbacks on the newsstand, "Resort Nurse," "Psychiatric Nurse," "Surgical Nurse," "Student Nurse," and so on.

I am going to use the nurse-category novel as my chief example of the category novel because, first of all, it is among the easiest for an unknown writer to sell; secondly, I actually sat down with an unpublished author and helped her work out the writing of one of these, having my greatest reward when she looked up from her typewriter toward the end of our story and said triumphantly, *"I* see how it's done—"

I hope, by the time you have finished reading this article, you, too, will see how it is done. Before we finish, I will offer three possible themes of the "category" novel for the young, inexperienced writer and show, briefly, how each novel would be begun, developed and ended. First, however, let me digress for just a minute to show you the scope of the category novel and point out how, by deepening the characterization and polishing the writing—after you've had a little success with the simpler forms—you can carry your experience into the better paperback and even hardcover novel.

Three novels which, during the past few years, have achieved hardcover publication and have earned a great deal of money are "category" novels: *The Best of Everything,* by Rona Jaffe; *The Group,* by a fine writer named Mary McCarthy; and *Everything But A Husband,* by Jeannette Kamins. They are "category" novels because, had they been written by lesser talents, a paperback editor, sending a résumé to his superior, would have slugged them like this:

The Group—Four Vassar graduates go to the Big City in search of fame, love, husbands.

The Best of Everything—Four young girls in a big New York publishing company invade the Big City in search of fame, careers, love and husbands.

Everything But A Husband—Four girls at a summer resort in search of a husband.

The whole idea of the "category" novel grew out of the need of the paperback publishers—swamped with manuscripts as well as ready outlets for their merchandise—to establish certain categories, and then to determine how many of each category they would publish each month. But, as you can see, if the writer streamlines his thinking by placing his novel in a "category," he need not limit himself to the simple kind of "category novel" I am going to describe in detail here. Many, many young writers, now under contract to hardcover publishers, won their literary spurs by laboring long and hard in the vineyard of the simpler, pulp-paper, category novel. It is well to bear in mind that nothing limits a writer but his own ability, but, faced with a story to tell and a blank sheet of paper in the machine, the novice will be able to get off dead center and get started if he confines himself, first, to a category novel.

I find, for instance, that most beginners have trouble bringing more than two people on stage at the same time. But if you start with your four girls in a typing pool, or at a summer resort, or at the wedding of a classmate, why, lo and behold, there they are, all on stage at once with practically ready-made dialogue as they explain to one another how they got there, and why.

The category novel is also of enormous help in getting a story started. For example: Take the paperback novel with which I helped my young friend, a professional writer of nonfiction, who, when she tackled a novel, did what so many young writers do—put in enough plot for five novels. Her time sequence was all off, moving first forward and then back. Her story sat down and wagged its tail, while she gave the reader a mass of detail unrelated to the story in hand. And, finally, she got trapped, as what beginner does not, in that familiar swampland—the flashback.

The first thing to do when you embark on a category novel is to choose a background with which you are familiar. I know there is a whole school of thought—and I respect it for its beliefs—that says you can find plenty of novel material in the morning newspaper. Maybe you can. I never have, nor have I known many successful examples of this technique. For one thing, you automatically limit yourself and make your writing job doubly difficult, if you write about something you know little or nothing about. Even the simplest story must be embroidered with detail about how your characters earn a living, the kind of home to which they return at night, whether they eat a meager stand-up lunch or a lavish, charge-account, sit-down lunch. Job conflicts, family conflicts, and love conflicts must be felt by the writer to be believed by the reader. The talented professional, or the genius, can just take off into outer space, perhaps, but the beginner is wise, I think, to stick to things he knows about.

FIRST STEP: Choosing the category. My young writer friend had worked for two years as a "lab assistant" in a small-town hospital. She understood the career, love and loyalty problems of doctors and nurses, as well as their conflicts with patients, rich and poor. So we chose as our category, "Small Town Nurse."

SECOND STEP: Theme. Since this novel was slanted at a primarily teen-age audience, we chose that timeworn theme—*love-versus-duty*. Our heroine, Melanie Woods, was a dedicated student nurse who was to become a problem to the man who loved her, her superiors in the hospital and the other student nurses, all of whom saw nursing as primarily a means of earning a living until the right man came along.

THIRD STEP: Conflict. It is to be Edith Rogers, superintendent of nurses—whom Melanie worships because Miss Rogers saved the life of Melanie's father long ago—who becomes Melanie's remorseless foe. This comes about when Melanie realizes that Miss Rogers, in her own cold dedication to duty, puts rules and regulations above patient welfare. As the two lock horns, conflict deepens: Melanie will either be Miss Roger's kind of "by the book" nurse or no nurse at all.

FOURTH STEP: Background—a small hospital in upper New York State.

FIFTH STEP: Draw up a list of additional characters on a sheet of paper. *Decide the part each character will play in helping resolve your protagonist's basic conflict.* No matter how tempted you may be to dally along the way by indulging yourself in whimsey, you must be ruthless about cutting out every character who does not advance your plot! And don't tell me—as many young student writers in my courses have told me—about all the great writers who allowed their story to roam all over the lot. Of course they did. But you're not a great writer yet, or you wouldn't be reading this article. Master your technique first, then embellish your story!

SIXTH STEP: From your own background, I assume you have now decided on the category you wish to choose. In place of a student nurse, you have mentally substituted your own protagonist. You have chosen a theme, set up the basic conflict. (I will give you a few possible examples of these in a minute.) On a piece of paper you have drawn up a list of characters who will play a part in the working out of your protagonist's problem. So, now, let's get started with that terrifying, "Page One, Chapter One."

Its terrors will diminish if you will stick to this category novel, I promise you. You have already, mercifully, limited yourself as to time and background. Now, I will ask that you limit yourself once more; the more limitations you put on yourself at this stage, the simpler your job will be. Take another sheet of paper, and make subheads for each chapter. When you start to write, you will, of course, ignore these subheads, but they are wonderful guidelines. I told my young friend to make every other chapter take place in the hospital—with career-patient conflicts—and every other chapter out of the hospital, with love-family conflicts. You see how smoothly a mass of material begins to be codified? And since people are more interested in people than in jobs, we start Page One, Chapter One by showing Melanie on her way to the hospital with a friend, another young student nurse. (Always open a chapter with two people in conversation. Their dialogue is the simplest way to explain to the reader who the main character is and what problem is facing her.)

Since we know our theme is *love* versus *duty*, our dialogue is, again, as in the case of the more complicated category novels I mentioned earlier, practically ready-made. Melanie's friend asks her when she and her beau are going to be married; Melanie answers, not until she receives her cap, and her friend says, "Suppose he won't wait?"—and we learn why Melanie is such a dedicated nurse when she explains to her friend (thereby to the reader) why she feels she must repay the profession that saved her father's life by becoming one of nursing's most shining lights.

On their way to the hospital, the girls see the town drunk, Jerry Oakes, lying in the gutter outside a cheap saloon. Melanie's friend is all for hurrying on, but Melanie's sharp eye perceives that the man who seems to be dead drunk is, actually, turning blue because he is suffocating. Melanie, forgetting that "nurses nurse and doctors doctor," realizing there isn't a moment to spare, has the man brought inside the beery tavern and laid on an oilcloth-covered table, where, using a kitchen knife, she swiftly performs a tracheotomy which saves the man's life.

We have set our dual conflict in motion at the end of the first chapter (ten pages) when Melanie's friend, Cookie, says, "It was wonderful and brave of you to do it, Melanie, but you broke the rules, and Miss Rogers might even throw you out of nursing school." This career conflict, plus the love conflict revealed in the girls' early dialogue, sets the stage. Will Melanie lose her career? Can compassion finally triumph over duty? Will Melanie lose her beau as well?

Chapter Two takes place in the hospital in Miss Roger's office. And here I am going to let you in on another secret in trying to simplify the writing of your first novel. Open every chapter with a different character. For example, at the end of the first chapter just summarized, as the girls head back up the hill to the hospital, their last exchange of dialogue is about Miss Rogers. Open Chapter Two, therefore, with Miss Rogers. She has heard about the incident and has dispatched an ambulance. She reviews her own duty-dedicated life that included losing the man she loved (now head of the hospital), and unless she upholds that dedication to duty, she will, in a sense, make her own sacrifice meaningless. So we know Melanie is in for trouble. She gets a bawling-out, a warning that if a rule is broken again she will be dismissed from the nursing school. In tears, Melanie, feeling let down by the woman she has worshiped all these years, runs blindly out into the corridor where she collides with the young doctor who is going to be the man she finally marries—but not until she's practically saved the whole town by once more refusing to follow rules blindly.

Chapter Three, then, swings back to Melanie's personal life, her encounter with the small-town boy whose family feels that what Melanie did was shocking, and he indicates they'd better break the engagement.

Chapter Four—We're back in the hospital for further love-duty complications among the patients. And so on. As you can see, it is as regular as a Shakespearean sonnet—and a lot easier to compose! One by one, those characters you listed on a slip of paper are dropped into the hopper of your story, broadening the base of conflict. All this while, of course, tension mounts as Melanie gets closer and closer to her black moment: She loses the small-town beau; the young doctor she's come to love leaves to marry a rich New York debutante; the older doctor who was once her friend sides with Miss Rogers in deciding Melanie has to leave nursing school, and so on. The black moment comes when Melanie allows a dying man to have the sip of bourbon which, with morphine, helps lessen his pain. The bottle is discovered, Melanie is dismissed in disgrace. The small-town beau is off with a beautiful young artist from New York. Then a fire breaks out in the ancient hospital and that ex-drunk, Jerry Oakes, now a worker in the hospital laundry (and cold sober) is, along with Melanie, the hero of the day. Among the patients they save is the richest man in town, who promptly orders that a new hospital be built, and that Melanie be put back in uniform.

So, begin with personal-plus-hint-of-career conflict.

Plan that every other chapter will take place within the office, school, hospital where your career conflict will be developed and, finally, resolved.

Save your emotional resolution till last—girl never gets boy until almost the last page.

Save yourself a lot of heartache and hard work by making a list of chapters, giving each a subhead: a) Melanie; b) Miss Rogers; c) Melanie's wild sister who wants Melanie to help her not to have a baby; d) the young doctor torn between marrying the rich girl in New York and Melanie, whom he has learned to love. You will see that just by giving each chapter a name, you are checking on whether your story is moving forward toward the moment of decision, followed by the black moment, and finally by the ending.

Now, I said I'd mention three possible categories that might fit into the life of any young writer who is toiling at work he may hate during the day, in order to write at night. In other words, I'll mention three possible plots that engage your protagonist in a business-career as well as in a love-duty conflict.

Category A: Ambitious young man, rich older woman, with *ideals* versus *economic pressure* at stake. An ambitious young man, weary of working at menial labor to buy time to write his big novel, paint his picture, is tempted to marry a rich older woman. No sooner has he married her than he a) sells the novel that's been rejected by ten publishers; b) meets a beautiful young girl with whom he falls in love. He is ready to ask the older woman to free him, when her doctor tells him the older woman is dying of an incurable disease. Does he, out of loyalty, stay with the older woman or does he, feeling that he has a right to his own life, that he has given this older woman two years of marvelous companionship, leave her? It is easy to see the other characters who come into play: the woman's grown children; the young girl's fiancé; a greedy lawyer; perhaps another young man this older woman married years ago and who has since debauched himself, convincing our young hero that the older woman is basically cruel, selfish and greedy.

Category B: Nurse-Doctor. Young girl receptionist in office of a doctor she has fallen in love with, finds he has become a drug addict. Does she expose him for the sake of the patients who might die at his unsteady surgeon's hands, or does she try to save him by devoting her own life to at least temporary exile with him? Complications: Patients who have come to mean a lot to her, especially one young man due for serious surgery. She saves the young man, exposes the doctor, marries the young man, receives grateful thanks of patients.

Category C: Young girl has devoted most of her life caring for invalid mother. Story opens six months after mother's death. At dinner with the young man whom her meager savings have put through law school, she expects him to say, "Now we can be married." Instead, he says, "I'm married—I never thought you'd be free." She turns to an older man, marries him. The young man's marriage breaks up. We have that hardy perennial, *love* versus *loyalty* again. To whom do we owe a duty? Ourselves or the people who love us? Complications: The young man's deserted wife who is pregnant; an older woman who loved our heroine's successful husband before he married her; the business itself (does it fail, making it more urgent than ever that our heroine not leave him now?).

A few brief words of advice to the overly ambitious beginner: Don't scorn the category novel. It's a great teacher, just as the pulps were. Don't put roadblocks in your path by introducing characters or situations so unique they have to be explained (and probably won't be believed). Whenever possible, add interesting details of the business in which your characters are involved. This is known in the trade as a "plus-value" and also helps round out your novel by giving your characters a place to go to in the morning; a luncheon dialogue; an office (or factory) conflict; a train to catch at night (more dialogue and neighbor-conflict). My own way of working this out is always to think, "morning, noon and night; morning, noon and night." Get your characters out of bed, have them welcome or dread the day ahead; take them to luncheon with a boss, wife, rival; send them home to a pleasant or unpleasant meeting with wife, children, friends and tuck them into bed again.

The category novel can be science fiction; life on a college campus; athletic director at a resort—there's no end to the ramifications of this simple, formula-type novel. It requires no skill in handling flashback. The story moves steadily forward. Use stock characters and warm them with your own interpretation of their conflict—let your background be unique, keep your characters familiar, placed in unfamiliar situations but always struggling for things any reader can understand and sympathize with: love, honor, success, companionship.

And now I hope that you, like my young friend, will look up from your typewriter halfway through *your* category novel and cry, triumphantly, "*I* see how you do it!"

53

"YOU-ARE-THERENESS" IN FICTION

By Joan Williams

It is my inclination to write as if the reader were standing beside me. I want the reader to feel drawn into my setting and to receive a mood from it. It is my hope that he will see and feel and taste and smell as the character does. But I had not thought much about this being my method until recently when I was asked how to go about trying to achieve a feeling of "you-are-thereness" in fiction. And I had not realized exactly what influenced me toward this way of writing until last summer when I visited in Memphis the professor who had taught me freshman English in college. We had not seen each other in the twenty years since. He had been ill and after a pleasant conversation I was about to leave, thinking he must be tired. Instead he drew from a table beside him an old Manila folder and said, "Wait, I've been saving something to show you." He had followed my career with interest, he said, because from the beginning of his class I had expressed interest in being a writer. But the whole first semester I had showed no promise. However, in the second half of the year a turning point had come. He smiled and asked if I recalled all the paragraphs we had had to write on topics he assigned. And he asked if I remembered that he had stressed vividness, one element of writing he believed could be taught. Until he reminded me of the paragraphs, I had remembered freshman English mainly as the time I first struggled over writing an autobiography. He went on to say that for twenty years he had been saving paragraphs he thought were good examples to show incoming classes. Did I remember a particular assignment called, "How Joe Studies"? I had to admit that I did not. Well, he said, opening the folder, he thought that paragraph had been my breakthrough. After almost a year of reading unimpressive papers from me, he read this one and felt that at last I had understood what he had meant about vivid writing. Then with an odd feeling, I was holding in my hands the paragraph I had written when I was eighteen years old:

Joe slumped down on his spine, sprawled his feet on another chair, and turned the radio a little louder. He took another bite of chocolate cake, afterwards carefully wiping his fingers on the margin of the book he was holding. With a pencil he added a moustache and more eyebrows to the stately gentleman adorning page 781 and then turned to the next page and adorned that margin with B–29's and grinning cats in bow ties. He stuck a piece of bubble gum into his mouth, got up, went to the phone, and held a lengthy conversation, then returned to his chair and radio program. He looked at a few more pages in the book, ate the rest of his cake, sighed deeply, closed his book, turned off the radio and went to bed. Joe had studied.

I think for the first time I must have said to myself that the professor doesn't mean he merely wants to know how Joe studies, he wants to *see* Joe studying. It would not be enough to say that Joe sat in a chair and studied. He had to study in some particular way that was different and that would impress him on the professor's mind. The word "particular" is important. I believe that to write vividly the author has to deal in particulars. It would be easy to write a vivid sentence saying that while studying Joe stood on one foot and balanced a glass of water on his head. But, to me, this is cheating because it is not logically what a person would do. It is much harder to think of logical particulars to bring Joe alive; and that is the aim: to make the reader feel he sees and knows places and people which exist really only in the writer's mind. My own old schoolbooks have margins adorned with drawings and so now do those my children bring home, though their airplanes are a long way from B-29's. It gives a reader a pleasant shock of recognition if a character does something the reader knows he would do in the same situation. And who has not scribbled in his schoolbooks? It is a characteristic almost universally true of students. Even so, the reader does not see anything if the writer says only that Joe drew in his schoolbooks. But the reader will have a visual image if the writer mentions particulars like coats, bow ties, grins and airplanes. Again, Joe did not merely eat cake but a particular kind of cake—chocolate. Do you see, as I did, his mouth closing over a piece of dark brown cake with a shiny fudge icing?

If I were writing the paragraph today, I would give a description of Joe himself, though what is called for is only how he studies. I wonder if I avoided a description back in freshman English because I did not know how to make him memorable when he was also ordinary. This is still a difficult thing for me to do. It is easy to assign to a character a wart on his nose or to make him six feet eight inches tall; but it is difficult to impress on a reader a character he would not ordinarily notice in a crowd. In a book I am writing now, I want to make the reader well acquainted with a pretty girl. But to say she is pretty gives no picture to the reader's mind. A writer has to go to every length to avoid using clichés; I cannot say she has curly hair, blue eyes and rosy cheeks and let the description go at that. My girl so far has long blonde hair but that is by no means a description that is good enough. I wrote a scene in which the fact that she owns a beige cashmere coat with a mink collar becomes important. Now, at least, the reader sees her as a girl with long blonde hair in a beige coat with a mink collar. Throughout the book, more identifying characteristics will have to be added. Hopefully, the pretty girl will become a distinct personality.

If the setting is given in vivid detail, the reader is more apt to feel that he is there. A character can't be set down only in a room or house or in the country or the city. Even if a character is put into a well-described room, the reader will feel more that he is present if he is told about the room in particulars and not in generalities. Beneath a beautiful blue sofa against one wall there is a dog's bone; there is dust on the grand piano in the corner. These settings, with these particulars, can be clues also to a character's personality. He is a kindly person who loves his dog or a lazy housekeeper who never runs a broom under his sofa. To convey a sense of agitation the writer might describe a room minutely and say that the character in the room saw none of it. But how much more vivid for the reader to have seen it and to know just how agitated the character must have been to have missed all the details. Is agitation the reason a character has not seen dust on the piano? Perhaps the character does not notice jonquils poking up in a flower bed outside the room. Now the reader knows also that it is spring; but he has learned it through his own senses, which is more effective than if the writer had merely put down the words, "It is spring." The words could be digested without giving the reader any visual image. Instead, he has stood in a room where a dog's bone is under a blue sofa and dust is on the piano and

looking out the window he has seen that spring is coming; in a flow-
erbed the earth is erupting; the green tips of leaves are appearing, as
he has seen them every spring in real life.

Beginning writers are troubled sometimes by wanting to write
about places they have never been. But it is easy to borrow particulars from around you and transfer them to other settings. Perhaps
you are writing about New York and have said everything you
know. There are tall buildings and crowded sidewalks and busy
streets. Then go outdoors in your own town and see how the sunlight
falls across a building or your own house at five o'clock in the afternoon. Why can't it slant across a New York building in the same
way? Looking up from a busy street, your character sees late afternoon sunlight glancing off the Empire State Building. What does it
matter if the reflection on the windows is really the way sunlight
looks against your own bedroom windows some place else? Go to
your local bar or restaurant. Particulars you see there can be transferred to a sidewalk café in Paris.

Repetition is valuable in impressing a mood, a place, a character
on the reader's mind. In my second novel, I wanted to convey a
man's long struggle to succeed. He is a dynamite salesman traveling
the rural South, and over and over I touched on how tired he was
when he came home, and many times I described the hot Southern
summers and the dusty, inadequate roads and the difficulties he had
getting his car into and out of places where there were no roads at all.
By these repetitions I wanted not only to impress on the reader's
mind the sense of struggle but also the sense of time. It was at the
end of each week that he struggled home tired, and it was summer
after summer that he fought dusty roads. Eventually he traveled
modern superhighways, and this, I hope, conveyed a sense of how
many years had passed. I hoped that the reader would think back to
the beginning of the book when the roads were tire tracks through
weeds and have the feeling that he had experienced many years of
the character's life.

In a scene in *To the Lighthouse*, Virginia Woolf lingers over what
was eaten for dinner. Very particularly her characters ate Boeuf en
Daube, served in a huge brown pot. The meat in the dish is described
as being yellow and brown and the reader is told that the stew contains bay leaves and wine. The servant girl removes the lid "with a

flourish" and we learn that the pot gave off an "exquisite scent of olives and oil and juice." These particulars give a sense of reality to a book where the main focus is on what the characters are thinking. We identify with sitting at the table because we do it often. We, too, have waited for a lid to be whipped off a pot to see what we are going to have for dinner. If it smells good, we are glad. In any kind of novel, then, particulars can be used to make the reader feel he is present wherever the writer wants him to be and that he has grasped what the writer wants to convey.

54

WHAT MAKES A SALABLE CONFESSION?

By Jean Jackson

ONE of the least discouraging and best-paying places for a writer to begin to sell is the confession field. The confession market is tremendous, and confession editors seem to need capable writers today more than ever before. New confession magazines are always appearing on the stands, and the old ones continue on and on. There are currently, I believe, more than twenty-five confession magazines. Each one uses six to ten regular-length stories and one or two double-length stories. This means that around two million words go into print every thirty days. At three to five cents a word, approximately $720,000 to $1,200,000 is paid into the bank accounts of confession writers every year. Some of it might as well go into yours.

But before you are going to get your share of that enticing sum, you're going to have to learn what makes a salable confession.

I like to think of the writer as a sort of middleman between *Life,* the manufacturer, and *Editors,* the retailers. The editor in turn sells to the individual customer, the reading public—and what the public demands and buys are solutions to its problems. The difference between the writer and the wholesaler in ordinary business is that the writer must also act as a kind of purifier or filter. A manufacturer offers a nice, clean-cut, shapely product to his distributor. Life doesn't. The problems Life gives you glimpses of, very often remain unsolved, or at least get whisked away out of sight before you can see how they work out. The writer, therefore, must supply, from his imagination, the solution to Life's problems. It is, when you stop to consider it, a tremendous and somewhat alarming responsibility to be expected to be all-knowing and all-wise. But, in the confession field particularly, the answers are very simple. The reader must be firmly guided along the paths of righteousness.

Now let's see if we can find out what makes a salable confession. You must find out first what the confession reader needs. Your best clue to this is in the advertisements. If you have never studied the confession magazines, you may be surprised to find that the same products are ballyhooed in them as in the slick women's magazines. The higher-paying confessions, such as *True Story, Modern Romances,* and *True Confessions,* contain ads not only about the same products, but, month by month, exact duplicates in layout and copy of the ads in *McCall's, Good Housekeeping,* and *Redbook.* Toothpaste, hand lotion, soap, shampoo, baby powder, clothes, deodorants and antiseptics, silverware, cosmetics, rugs, furniture, medicine— all products dealing with phases of the average woman's main interests—love and romance, marriage, a happy home, and healthy, well-adjusted children.

What, then, is the difference between the confession reader and the slick reader?

The first difference is in the amount of education she has. Graduation from high school is about as far as the confession reader ever gets, and many of them don't get that far, though one of the policies of the magazines is to urge them to finish school and not marry too young. Once in a while you will find a story with a college background, but that is the exception rather than the rule, and some editors will not even read such stories, much less print them.

The second difference is a matter of income. The confession reader is a typist, dressmaker, salesgirl or housewife, in love with or married to a hotel clerk, factory worker, or small-pay white collar worker or someone of this sort. She wants to read about people she knows and understands, not about those who move on the society pages of her local paper. She simply cannot visualize fifteen-room mansions, diamond bracelets, and half a dozen cars in the garage. One of her major problems in life is making both ends meet from payday to payday, and she has a hard time understanding why anyone who doesn't have to worry about money should have any problems at all. You and I know this isn't true—that just because you have money in the bank, it doesn't follow that you get into no emotional tangles. But the confession reader, stretching dollars from day to day, is an inveterate bargain hunter, because she has to be. She shops where she'll get the most for her money, even among the magazines. That's why she buys the confession magazines, which offer her eight or ten longer-than-average stories in each issue, instead of the three or four per issue of the slick magazines.

A point I want to bring out here—and I cannot emphasize it too strongly—is that you cannot write down to a confession reader. Not and get away with it. All of you who are reading this are probably better educated than the average confession reader. If you weren't, you wouldn't be writing. You probably are much better off financially than she is. But if you feel a cut above the confession reader; if you believe, even without saying it aloud, that you're "better" than she is, you won't write a passable confession. You will not be able to get inside a confession heroine, reason as she would reason, muddle your way through problems as she would, and I would strongly advise you to forget the confession market and concentrate on the slicks.

The age level of the confession audience is from about thirteen to thirty-five years. Older women do read them, but when they do, they're generally reliving the problems they encountered during those twenty-two years. Confession readers consider eighteen, the age of consent and the approximate age of graduation from high school, as mature enough for marriage. Before that time, the confession heroine is emotionally a child. At eighteen, she suddenly springs, full-blown, into womanly wisdom. Frankly, this reasoning of confession editors has always baffled me, but that's the way it is, and you might as well keep it in mind. I think you'll find the marrying age of slick story heroines is somewhat higher.

Let's get away from generalities and down to particulars. For example, do you really know what a "formula" is?

A formula is a simple, basic pattern upon which a story is built. It has nothing to do with plot or conflict or flashback or complication or any other of those confusing terms you may have had thrown at you. It can be expressed in one or two sentences at the most, and it never varies. There are, in all, only about twenty-five story formulas in existence. One is the confession formula; three or four, I believe, are Western formulas; the rest can be classified as belonging to the slick field. I'm not going into formulas in general here, but will try to explain the confession formula to you.

The confession formula is very hard to find by reading confession stories in print, because it is so overlaid by unbridled emotions, by weeping and wailing, tearing of the hair and beating of the breast that it gets buried beneath all the lamentation. Then, too, unlike a slick story, the action of a confession can be stretched out over weeks or months or even years. I found the confession formula right in my own manuscripts. I wrote dozens of confessions without having any idea what I was doing. Suddenly, they began to sell with some regularity, but I didn't have the faintest idea why. I looked over all my carbon copies and found that, in the scripts that had sold, the story had invariably followed a pattern that was clear enough to see on the typewritten pages. It was then that the Great Light dawned!

You may have heard that the confession story formula is "Sin, Suffer and Repent." That is not exactly true. The protagonist does sin, she does suffer, and she does repent—but not necessarily in that order. Sometimes she sins and suffers anyway, in spite of repenting for pages in between.

There is, I think, a clearer way of expressing the confession formula: "The protagonist persists in making a mistake, and by so doing brings down tragedy either on herself or on those she loves. She realizes she has been wrong and sets about rectifying the mistake as far as possible."

I want you to notice that word "persists." I used it with a purpose which I'll take up with you in a minute. Right now I know what is going through your heads. You're saying, "Why, that's nothing but sin, suffer, and repent, and she said they didn't have to come in that order." They don't. You'll have a better story *if they don't!* If you can arrange your plot so that the heroine sees the light first, but has already, by her actions, set the wheels of tragedy in motion and cannot stop them, your story will probably be bought at a higher rate, or, at least, be featured on the front of the magazine that buys it.

Let me try to illustrate what I mean from a story of my own, which I called "The Middle One" because the heroine, Nora, is the middle child in a family of three. (*Intimate Story* subsequently changed the title to "I Accused Him for Thrills," which is, I admit, a title with much more come-on.) This is a story of a high school girl who has never had much attention. After being overlooked, one way or another, in desperation she blurts out what she thinks is just a mild exaggeration of a meaningless pass made at her by a moronic dishwasher in the high school hangout across the street. Things move along. She brushes off a "wild" boy, accepts a date with a nice one, justifies herself by believing that the nice boy has noticed her because of the fib she's told, and that the talk will die down of its own accord. What she doesn't know is that she has already started the wheels of tragedy moving, and no matter what she does, they are not going to stop. The story runs twenty-six pages. On page 16 she finds out—well, let me quote a bit:

> The uneasiness I'd been feeling rushed over me in a great, engulfing wave, setting the blood to pounding in my ears, as I realized what must have happened. Somehow, the story had got twisted as it ran like wildfire through the school! People thought Uncle Willie—dear, sweet old Uncle Willie—had tried to— Even in my mind, I couldn't quite say the ugly words! [Uncle Willie is a sweet old man who owns a confectionery and all the students love him.]

So you see, she realizes long before the story ends that she's made a mistake, and is terribly sorry about it. The rest of the story deals with the tragedy over which she has no control—in this case a mob scene in which the students, believing Uncle Willie is an old lecher, descend on his shop and wreck it and send him to the hospital with a bashed-in skull. I managed to work out a reasonably happy ending for this one, too, though you can't always do it.

There is one major difference between a slick story and a confession story besides that of formula. In both, the protagonist is faced with a problem he must solve. You know how a slick story is put together. I like to visualize it as a flight of steps going up, with a short and steep slide at the end. The slick heroine keeps going along the wrong way almost to the end; then, when she simply can't get in any deeper and has to decide between right and wrong, she chooses right—with a capital R—and in one or two paragraphs slides down to the solution and splashes into a pool of happiness. The turning point of a slick story, in other words, is almost at the end.

The confession heroine doesn't have such an easy time. The turning point in the confession story comes just halfway through the action—and at the high point, the protagonist *always* makes, not the right, but the *wrong* decision. Because of this decision, tragedy inevitably follows. She then bumbles her way back through more complications to a logical conclusion, with at least a "glimmer of hope" for the future.

Now let's get back to that word "persists" which I used in stating the confession formula. I used it because, all the time that the confession heroine is heading the wrong way, she has a sneaking suspicion of exactly what she's doing. She knows the difference between right and wrong, yet she "persists" in going the wrong way toward an inevitable wrong decision. Here is where you begin to get into difficulties in writing—that delicate matter of reader sympathy for the heroine. Even you, the writer, are going to have trouble sympathizing with your own character when you know she is heading the wrong way, for the wrong reasons. How, then, can you make the far more critical reader like her?

You turn the screws! You make the pressure on her so great that she is pushed, almost against her will, along the path of "sin," to the wrong turning, into the woods where she is lost. Disheartening incidents, people's reactions to her—everything piles up on her, and at the decision point, when she stands hesitating, the signs pointing in the wrong direction are so much bigger and easier to read than the others that she *apparently* has no choice. If you can do this successfully, the reader, while he may not *like* the heroine, can understand why she goes astray. That is what reader sympathy in a confession story is—not necessarily liking for a character, but understanding of her reasoning processes. In a slick story, your central character is almost always a lovable critter underneath. In a confession story, she may not be. She just has to be motivated by circumstances strong enough for the reader to think, "I'd probably do the same thing myself."

Yet, you can't let your heroine gallop gaily down the wrong road, without any thought at all for others or for what is the right thing to do. You have to give her little twinges of conscience now and then, followed by an event that seems to outweigh, by far, what her conscience is telling her. She teeters back and forth in her thoughts, as people do in real life. Confession stories are much closer to real life than slick stories, as you'll realize when you start being "I" in one of them.

This matter of reader sympathy may sound hazy and difficult, but it isn't hard to do once you get into the swing of it. Let's go back to my story, "The Middle One," to show you with specific examples how I handled reader sympathy. Nora is an average girl, not brilliant like her younger brother or beautiful like her older sister, and as a result she's always been sort of taken for granted, though, like everyone else, she'd just love to be important. Not much of a situation, is it? Nothing very novel or out of the way. She's dissatisfied and wants things to be different. Now let's begin turning the screws.

I started the action on the morning of her sixteenth birthday. She wakes up with that beautiful feeling that things are going to be better now. The problem, as it stands, comes in the first three paragraphs:

I woke very early the morning of my birthday, smiling to myself even before I was fully awake. On the ceiling overhead, the naked branches of the maple tree outside made flickering shadows. The autumn air from my window was cold and crisp and clean, and from the kitchen downstairs came the appetizing smell of bacon frying.

I yawned and stretched, savoring the day and all the days ahead. Life is wonderful when you've reached sixteen at last, and can catch glimpses of all the enchanting vistas that being an adult will open up. The Junior Prom next month —surely someone would ask me to go. Maybe even Tim Hartford! A little thrill shot through me at the thought.

I saw in my mirror that I had changed in the last few months, rounded out and matured even while I grew tall and slender. My blonde hair had taken on a new sheen from constant brushing, and now that Mom allowed me to use lipstick, anyone who looked could see my lips were full and soft and tantalizing. Oh, I'd never be beautiful enough to be a model like Angie, my older sister, or too smart for my own good like Dink, my ten-year-old brother. But maybe now someone would notice me.

You know at once that she wants attention from her world in general and from a certain boy in particular. At the bottom of page 2, the pressure begins. Her folks have forgotten it's her birthday and hustle off about their various businesses without even a birthday greeting:

I just stood there, listening to the clatter of her heels on the porch and the snap of grease sputtering in the skillet. They were gone, all of them! I was sixteen today, and nobody'd even said Happy Birthday!

There's the first incident.

She goes to school feeling pretty let down. Tim, the boy she likes, can't even remember her name:

I sat the whole hour staring at the back of Tim's head, willing him to turn around and look at me. He didn't, of course. Later, I met him in the hall between classes. He looked toward me and smiled, as you would do at a familiar face you'd seen someplace. "Hi, Tim!" I sang out with bright, forced gaiety.

He looked vaguely puzzled. "Oh, hello there—uh—Nora," he answered after a minute, walking on. What was the use? I thought dejectedly. All the old hurt of this morning came back with a rush. Great stuff, wasn't I? My family forgot all about my birthday, and the fellow I was crazy about could hardly remember my name!

There's incident number two.

She keeps hoping against hope that a birthday celebration is in store, but her busy family has actually forgotten. They remember at the last minute and try to make it up to her:

The kitchen door came open slowly, and they all sang "Happy birthday to you!" Dink headed the parade, carrying the pound cake. He'd stuck sixteen toothpicks in the cake and lighted them like candles. I didn't know whether to laugh or cry.

Dink set the cake down in front of me. "Blow, quick!" he cried. Automatically, I did, and the blackened toothpicks scattered all over the tablecloth. "Happy Birthday, Nora!" Angie said, thrusting her best blue formal in my arms. "I know you've been wanting this for a long time. Now it's yours!" Mom leaned over and kissed me gently on the cheek. "Oh, honey, we're all so sorry! Such a terrible thing, to forget all about your birthday! It's just that we've been so busy—" She stopped, then went on, her voice breaking a little. "You're such a good, steady, thoughtful girl— Oh, I'm sorrier than I can ever say!"

"It's all right," I said shakily. But it wasn't. Deep inside, I ached with unhappiness.

Well, you see how it goes—right up to page 13, *the exact middle of the story,* where she's given a final chance to retract her lie, which has brought her the attention she desires. What does she do? The formula says she must make the wrong decisions, so:

And yet wasn't it because of that very hubbub that Tim was here beside me, his jaw square and firm, looking as if he'd willingly tangle with anybody who bothered me? I knew it was. If Tim hadn't got wind of what I'd told Jane, he never would have noticed me. It was too late now to deny the story. If I wanted to keep Tim's interest, I'd have to play along now and hope the story would die out of its own accord.

And then tragedy follows.

On the surface, it may seem that confession stories begin anywhere, but if you will study them carefully you'll find that they really begin at the beginning of the problem. Sometimes the problem actually starts way back in the heroine's childhood. If it does, begin your story there, and tell it straight. Confession editors don't like cumbersome flashbacks. In this story, for instance, the only real flashback is worked into these two sentences, which are hidden in the presentation of the problem:

I saw in my mirror that I had changed in the last few months, rounded out and matured even while I grew tall and slender. My blonde hair had taken on a new sheen from constant brushing, and now that Mom allowed me to use lipstick, anyone who looked could see my lips were full and soft and tantalizing.

There are only a few other minor points that I think may help you in writing your confession story. It will be, of course, written in the first person, although a few editors are now experimenting with third-person stories. The central character will preferably be a female. Confession editors run about one out of ten or twelve stories with a male protagonist, so your chances of selling are much greater if you stick to the feminine viewpoint.

Emotion in a slick story goes deep, but it flows beneath the surface, like an underground stream. In the confession story, on the other hand, emotion is visible, audible and tangible, as exciting to the eye and ear as a turbulent stream rushing noisily along its rocky bed. The reason for this takes us back again to that matter of education, which leads us to suppress our emotions, to keep them under control. It also teaches us to look beneath the surface in other people for subtleties and innuendoes. Many confession readers, lacking the refinements of education, give vent to their emotions in real life and want the characters they read about to do so, too.

At first, you may feel very silly when you try to write in this highly emotional style. You'll feel that if anyone should happen to read what you are writing, you'd blush and shrivel with shame. After a while, however, you'll realize that being allowed to write this way is fun. You can be as primitive as you like, say the things you don't dare say aloud in real life, scream at the neighbors you hate, kick the dog, snarl at your husband for not hanging up his clothes, rise to ecstatic heights when your dream prince kisses you, plummet to the depths of despair and wallow gloriously in misery. Really, confession story writing is a wonderful way to express, via the typewriter, all those instinctive emotions that civilization forces you to control.

Remember to work in, somewhere in your story, a physical description of your characters, not forgetting that of the protagonist "I." Just as the confession reader wants emotion laid out where she can see it clearly, she wants to be able to visualize the people in her story without being forced to exercise her imagination.

The most salable length for a confession story is between five thousand and six thousand words, about a thousand words longer than a slick short story. This does not, however, mean that you can write sloppily just because you are allowed more leeway in wordage. A confession story must be as tightly knit as a slick story. Actually, when you start setting down all those thoughts that flit through your heroine's head, as well as the action, you'll find you don't have as many words as you thought you had, and every one has to count.

There are no abrupt transitions in a confession, no definite breaks where you pull your heroine out of one scene and plunk her down in the middle of another. The action flows along smoothly, and even if there is a gap of years between incidents, you have to build a bridge of words upon which the reader can cross without jumping and skipping around. The action in my story about Nora begins Monday and Tuesday. Nothing more happens until Friday, but I have to get Nora through the week somehow:

That night I went to sleep smiling happily, and for two days I walked around with my head wrapped in rosy clouds. Maybe it was the clouds that kept me from seeing what was going on at school. Maybe if I hadn't been so excited about dating Tim, I wouldn't have pushed aside the remembrance of the awful lies I had told. As far as I could see, it hadn't made any difference anyway, though. Wednesday and Thursday the kids flocked across the street into Uncle Willie's store after school as usual, though I went straight home. I'd been right, I thought. A story like that is like a headline in a newspaper, causing a lot of uproar today, and tomorrow completely forgotten. . . . Friday afternoon I was the first one home.

To sell, you must watch the trends in confession magazines as closely as in any group of magazines. Sometimes the confessions lean heavily on youth, specifically delinquency and sex problems. They like drama and excitement, leading up to sex scenes, treated naturally, not clinically but emotionally; or they may want stories dealing with teen-age problems caused by dating, dropping out of school, or too-early marriage, which they discourage. For a time, they were all going light on sex, but then the trend shifted, and sex reared its ugly head on page after page.

If, bearing all these minor points in mind, you can dream up a confused teen-age heroine torn by an emotional problem, have her solve it the wrong way, thereby bringing about some kind of tragedy, go through emotional hell, and see at least a faint light of hope for the future—I can practically guarantee you a letter beginning, "I am happy to inform you . . ." and a beautiful, beautiful check enclosed therein.

55

WRITING THE POLICE-ROUTINE NOVEL

By Dell Shannon

THE police-routine novel, which we are seeing more of these days than formerly, makes an emotional connection between the reader and the police, those overworked and much-hampered and harassed guardians of our public and private safety. When the evil forces of conspiracy, encouragement of lawlessness, are today making the police officer's job a thousand percent more difficult, it is salutary that somewhere, in some fashion, the upright forces of law and order should be shown as "the good guys"—which they largely are. I do not mean to say that we writers in this field should show police officers as winged and haloed, but as they really are—and these days the vast majority of police forces have quite high standards and requirements, and attract most excellent men and women.

The detective novel is the morality play of the twentieth century, and a really good detective novel is possibly the most difficult form of fiction to write. It is also the most challenging form. Most detective novels are somewhat shorter than the average "straight" novel, and it is always more difficult (and challenging) to compress adequate characterization, description, and plot-themes into, say, 65,000 words or so, whereas a novel of another kind may run to 100,000 words with no editorial demur. Moreover, of course, the average detective novel has a much more intricate plot than the average novel.

I say the detective novel is our new morality play because about 99% of them (all of them by implication) are on the side of the angels: the good guys, the law officers, always come out on top. In this amoral century, the detective novel fills a great need and serves a great purpose, humble though its form may be, looked down on often by our so-called Great Writers; detective novelists may regard themselves as the plebes among the genus scribblers, but they may turn out to have been the most influential spokesmen. For, while these days the detective novel is no longer crude black versus white, or content to deal in intricate plots minus any attempt at characterization—indeed, some of the most polished and stylistic writing is being done today by detective novelists—still, it deals primarily with basics: with truth versus lie, law and order versus anarchy, a moral code versus amorality.

I don't remember who first said that "everything has the defects of its advantages," but that is particularly applicable to the police-routine novel. But if the writer is handicapped in some ways—e.g., most of the time he must stay with his police officers, writing from their point of view—he also has a great many advantages of much practical help to him in working out the "mystery" part of the story. In the natural course of events, lab reports take time in arriving; witnesses may be difficult to locate or hostile to questioning (this kind of thing is often of great help in marking time, or skipping passages of time plausibly). In most police stations there is always apt to be something going on, so that in the process of constructing the story, perhaps creating interest even in a very simple plot, the writer has a choice of all sorts of "reader distractions"—other police cases besides the major one around which your book takes place; the brief intrusion of some amusing or eccentric or tragic character whom you come across on routine police business; incidents in the detectives' personal lives. These are among such reader distractions, and all offer the writer a useful amount of leeway in constructing a police-routine novel.

Obviously, the detective's personal life—which is not really a "distraction" at all, of course—is the most important. Even in such a relatively narrow field as the police-routine novel, there are many different kinds of novels—all the way from Ed McBain's *The Con Man,* for example, to Hillary Waugh's *Born Victim;* from the Gideon series by J. J. Marric, and Josephine Tey's *The Man in the Queue,* to Ngaio Marsh's urbane tales and Richard Lockridge's Captain Heimrich series. All of these writers have many devoted fans, and I doubt very much whether any of them eagerly reaches for the new McBain or the new Lockridge solely from interest in the plot. They're interested in what new is happening to their favorite sleuth —in seeing him in action once again. Here, of course, we find an overlapping of the "series" field and "police-routine"—but the latter is usually also the former.

Perhaps the greatest amount of reader interest is always in the detectives, not the plots (although the most fascinating police sleuth imaginable will not survive dull plots!). Thus the writer who uses the same detective for several novels has some solid part of the book already created (or sketched out in his mind), ready to be set down. Because of the carry-over reader interest in the detective as a person and the consequent necessity of introducing a certain amount of new material about him in each succeeding book, the writer automatically allots a certain amount of manuscript space to the detective—his foibles and interests and family and his life outside his professional job.

I am lucky that the particular police force I am writing about really happens to be the top force anywhere—the Los Angeles Police Department. I am always being asked, Is there a real counterpart of Lieutenant Mendoza down there at Central H.Q., or Sgt. Hackett, or any of the rest of the boys? I'm afraid I don't know. And I really don't know how these books get written, either. All I did, back there some while ago, was start to write a little suspense novel, and Lieutenant Mendoza rose up off the page, captured me alive, and refused to let me stop writing about him—egoist that he is. I try (always with the exception of the extraordinary Mendoza!) to show these men *as* ordinary men—with all the problems and domestic backgrounds of ordinary men. But also—writing these modern morality plays—I try to involve the reader *from the police viewpoint*. For I believe that this is no more than the duty of those of us who have taken sides, as it were, in the never-ending struggle between good and evil.

I cannot speak for other writers, but in getting involved as I am with four "sets" of series detectives, I have found that the series characters, once evolved and set in motion, tend to develop themselves in logical and sometimes surprising directions.

If it is no longer a convention in detective fiction that the detective must be a good deal larger than life—an eccentric and nearly-omniscient Holmes, or as full of personal foibles as Lord Peter Wimsey—still, he or they must be *enough* larger than life, enough distinctive as persons of definite and interesting individuality, to capture and retain the reader's continuing interest.

Perhaps the popular police sleuth of fiction can never be a *completely* accurate portrait of the police officer, for if the real police detective is—as in most cases he is—an honest, intelligent, trained, and hard-working officer, we are still not apt to find a real Lieutenant Mendoza or Roderick Alleyn or Charles Luke or Stephen Carella sitting at a desk at our local precinct house. It is the job of the writer in this field to convince the reader that he *might*.

Obviously, of course, the writer of police-routine novels must know a good deal about police routine. If he is writing about a real police force, or even a compositely-imagined one based upon real police forces in his county or city, he should know something about how the real forces work: police terms and locally used radio call-numbers for various offenses, criminal slang (which is commonly used also by police officers, of course), and something about police laboratory work. Almost any good library will offer various texts on these subjects. Offhand I might recommend *Crime Lab* by David Loth (Messner), *The Investigator's Handbook* by Arthur Liebers and Capt. Carl Vollmer of the New York City Police Department (Arco), *The Art of Detection* by Jacob Fisher (Sterling), and *Modern Criminal Investigation* by Harry Söderman and John J. O'Connell (Funk & Wagnalls).

Ogden Nash tells us, "If it's trite, it's right"—and up to a point that's so (why else do we call them clichés?). But there are a few rather tired old gimmicks in the field which the tyro should be warned about, as somewhat too hackneyed for warming over. The detective's-wife-who-wants-him-to-quit-the-cops-because-it's-dangerous has been met a bit too often; likewise the bright young modern sleuth resented by the less efficient superior; and (despite my own inadvertent possession of one, or vice versa) the independently wealthy officer dedicated to the job. And in thinking up plots for the boys in blue to grapple with, the ambitious writer need not, in fact *must* not, attempt to outdo John Dickson Carr. Few police cases in real life are very complex, and the aim in writing a police novel is (or should be) plausibility, above all else. There are many ways to inject some element of mystery into the fictional police case without either reaching into outer space or devising interesting but unlikely complexities. Ed McBain has set a good example here, as I like to think I may have done too, in a few books (perhaps notably *The Ace of Spades* and *Detective's Due*).

One of my own (admittedly this is a personal foible and maybe quibbling) objections to some police-routine novels set in large cities, is that the fictional action seems to imply that the sleuths are happily handed only one case at a time to solve. A husband is shot, a wife is strangled, a teen-ager is stabbed, and for the next two hundred pages the plainclothes sleuths concentrate on that alone—just as if, in a city of any size, all the drunk drivers, holdup experts, juvenile delinquents, belligerent brawlers, suicides and other murderers considerately postponed their own moments of truth until the central case of the story is wound up. This is scarcely plausible, if we are trying to give a reasonably accurate picture of real-life police routine. It is perfectly permissible and plausible, on the other hand, when the setting in question (as for instance in Waugh's *Born Victim*) is a small town where the "big case" is very rare; but it is a factor to keep in mind. The locale has a good deal to do with how a police-routine story unfolds.

Much of the creating I do—the sometimes agonized search for plots, for characters, for clue-gimmicks, and the like—is done while I sit staring vaguely into space thinking: "Suppose the corpse looked like one type of person and turned out to be another. . . ." Or, "If you had that kind of witness, then it would follow. . . ." And, "Of course that clue would mislead the cop to think. . . . But what about the wife? Surely she'd realize. . . ." Painfully, some vague notion of a central plot takes shape. I find that I must know just enough about a plot—*and not too much*—when I start to write the book, in order to leave plenty of room for the surprises. The surprises occur when quite unexpectedly some character comes alive—asserts himself, demanding a page or two more space than I had thought would be needed—and when sudden inspirations descend out of the blue, sometimes changing a major part of the story.

If the story is there, get to it and write it! For one thing, I feel that in completing a manuscript in the shortest possible time, the writer necessarily stays closer to the material. I have no quarrel with being methodical; once I have finally committed myself to a plot (however vague), I'm methodical, all right. I start each chapter, writing in longhand, at a quarter to ten each succeeding night, finish the chapter by about half-past twelve, and then type it out with a carbon next morning; so when I finish the thing I have a nice top copy. I evolved this method because typing is the hardest work I do. And from long experience, I have to get the thing written right the first time around; I seldom go back to change anything.

This is a very personal, individual sort of job, and every writer has his own peculiar way of going about it (some of them can be *very* peculiar). If the root of the matter is in you, you will find out how to write in your own way.

As with the writing of any other kind of fiction—or anything at all—only practice and experience will enable the writer to produce top manuscripts in the police-novel field. But suppose you do—you learn all the rules (some of which can conveniently be broken), you write a lot of unpublishable stuff, begin to find your own style, begin to sell, and suddenly one day, lo, you're in business with a beginning-to-be-popular series of police-routine novels. There's another important rule to keep in mind—and to practice, if you can.

One day after that you'll likely find yourself saying, "Oh, dear Lord, it's time I wrote another one to make that deadline. . . ." And the prospect is infinitely boring, you are sick and tired of this preposterous sleuth's mannerisms and attitudes, and try as you will, no vestige of an idea for a plot comes to you.

Right there you had better consciously recover enthusiasm! For if *you* are not interested in your sleuths, no one else will be. But if you are caught up in the fascinating police world as it exists today and really want to please your reader, once you've laboriously worked out a plot and have actually started writing (with many groans), all of a sudden the urgency and excitement flood back and the old fire blazes up again: "This is going to be fun, seeing how it works out in black and white. . . ."

Sergeant Lake thrust his head in the door and said tersely, "It's an APB, Lieutenant!"

—And you're off on another adventure.

Come to think, I'd better start thinking about the next Mendoza, and that's not too bad a beginning, just off the top of my mind. Only what's the All-Points-Bulletin *about?* And what kind of corpse will turn up? And where in the city jungle is it going to happen? And what kind of clues are we going to find? And—I'll have to start thinking about it!

56

THE ARTICLE: A NONFICTION STORY

By Mary T. Dillon

WHAT, exactly, is an article in today's popular magazine field? Let us consider first what it is *not*.

An article is not a term paper, with bibliography and footnotes, although like the term paper it may be based on careful research. It is not the sort of detailed informational report a businessman might prepare for circulation to his associates or a legislator for his fellow committee members. Nor is it a news report either, although newspaper reporters persist in thinking that it is. And finally, an article is not an essay—neither the formal essay of the nineteenth-century English prose writers, nor the once-popular personal or familiar essay, now unfortunately in decline.

Well, then, what *is* an article? The successful magazine article writer will answer, if he thinks objectively about it at all, that it comes closest to being a nonfiction story—characterized by the same meticulous attention to detail, the same concern for unity ("a story must have a beginning, a middle and an end") that is found in the good short story. His aim must always be to engage the reader's attention at the start and hold it to the end.

I can think of no better training for this than to study the works of such masters of their craft as Ernest Hemingway, Flannery O'Connor, Frank O'Connor, and others who have, in their various ways, made the short story perhaps America's outstanding literary genre—and this at a time when the popular market for fiction (for magazine publication, at any rate) has been on the wane. Significantly, one of the best article editors I know has three shelves of short stories by assorted writers, classic and contemporary.

Of what use are short story techniques in an article on liver disease or space exploration, for example? Short story writers tend to use their material evocatively, while the magazine article writer, working on a more mundane level, presents the facts straightforwardly. But he will not succeed in gaining and holding the reader's attention unless his account contains essentially the same elements the fiction writer uses—the color and sound and scent of the happenings, the recorded reactions of the writer or of his protagonist, as picked up and synthesized through the senses. Nancy Hale in her excellent book, *The Realities of Fiction,* points out that "reading a short story is purely volunteer work." The same holds true for the general-interest article. Miss Hale notes: "It is hard to listen for very long, whether you are being read to or are reading to yourself. It is much easier and more vivid to see. The author who can make us see his story as it happened . . . is the author into whose arms we fall with cries of joy and relief after we have been reading stories, of whatever integrity, written with no gift of seeing."

To my mind this applies perfectly to the writing of articles as well. In both fiction and nonfiction, the writer must help his reader see the scene against which his story is set, hear the sounds of what is taking place, smell the sea—or the spruce woods or the scent of honeysuckle on the warm evening air. Until he does this, the reader stands apart, uninvolved, and unconcerned; the article fails to "grab" him. Magazine editors work constantly to wrest from their writers the small detail, the quick telling quote, the additional tidbit of information that will give immediacy, conviction, empathy to the text.

It is unfortunate that the framers of college curricula so rigorously separate journalism courses, in which magazine article writing is included, from English courses, where the short story is studied and efforts to produce it encouraged under the heading of Creative Writing. For many of the fiction writer's techniques are readily adaptable to the effective presentation of factual material in article form.

First and foremost, the storyteller must grasp and hold his reader's attention. So, too, must the article writer, if he is to sell his work to an editor or find a reading audience for it when it is published. To do this the skilled fiction writer has learned to involve the reader in his story's happenings and make him feel, along with the hero and heroine, the emotions prompted by those happenings.

This can't be done without setting the scene for the reader, then making the characters in the story real through careful description and painstaking care in the reproduction of their speech.

Granted, the magazine article writer works within strict limitations of space. He must be prepared to present in language at least as economical as is required of the fiction writer the characters in his story, the essential background of events, the kinds of people and places he writes about. No word can be wasted; every detail should contribute to the whole. The reader, with no background of information, needs help in order to visualize what he is reading. It was just the ability to bring abstruse material home to the reader that made J. D. Ratcliff the tremendously successful nonfiction writer he was. Graphically exemplified in his long series of *Reader's Digest* articles on the human body ("I Am Joe's Pancreas," Liver, Ear, Foot, etc.) was Ratcliff's skill in involving the reader, in dramatizing the factual details of his story, the major component establishing him as the most successful free-lancer in recent magazine history.

Take "I Am Joe's Brain," for example, published in *The Reader's Digest* some months after Ratcliff's death in October 1973. (The magazine published eight of his "Joe" articles that year and sponsored the television dramatization of an earlier piece on Joe's heart.) The lead is dramatic: "Compared to me, other wonders of the universe pale into insignificance." Immediately following, Ratcliff tells us what the brain looks like: "a three-pound mushroom of gray and white tissue of gelatinous consistency." No need for diagrams or illustrations. From the start we have a mental picture that will stay with us as we read the paragraphs that follow. Into them are fitted a score or more statistical and other facts about Joe's brain, which is later likened to a telephone exchange and again to "a vast unexplored continent." The skull, "a well-protected fortress" for the brain, encloses it; a blood-brain barrier serves as gatekeeper, letting some things in, denying entrance to others.

And so it goes. The figures are visual, the facts astounding. In conclusion: "My [the brain's] resources have barely been tapped." There is hope ahead for greater accomplishment. On this note of inspiration the article ends.

Factual though it is, the article is in effect and in structure a story.

Fortunately, several of our best short story writers have set down their thoughts about their craft. Sean O'Faolain defines the short story writer's problem of language as "the need for a speech which combines suggestion with compression" and goes on to analyze the opening sentences of various stories in which the writer succeeds in making "an immediate and intimate contact with his story." So, too, must the article writer labor over his lead, the few lines of type with which he reaches the reader and holds him. No part of an article receives greater attention in the editorial office.

A slim volume of Flannery O'Connor's lectures and incidental writings, titled *Mystery and Manners,* includes "On Her Own Work" in which she remarked, "A story really isn't any good unless it successfully resists paraphrase, unless it hangs on and expands the mind." This is a high ideal to aim at, but one would like to think that even a modest magazine article could "hang on" for a little while in the reader's mind. ("Is it quotable?" *Reader's Digest* editor DeWitt Wallace used to ask routinely when an article was proposed to him. "Is it memorable?") If, at the same time, it seems to expand in the mind, so much the better. Miss O'Connor used extreme situations to reveal her characters; in a magazine article the writer may be presenting almost any sort of material, but he will want to highlight its drama, whatever it may be, and show its impact on people in every way he can. Only so can he get the reader to empathize, to share what is going on in the story he is writing.

Even in a straight factual piece he must remember to help the reader by providing quick answers to the questions that will occur to him, perhaps unconsciously, as he reads. (The margins of a promising article returned to the writer for revision are likely to be crammed with questions—How much? How many? Just when? Who he? What does he look like? etc., etc.) An article on exercise may lead off with statistics on overweight, number of deaths caused by heart disease, and so on. It will tell where efforts are being made to combat these problems, how industrial exercise programs are fitted into the working day at certain plants, what the provable results have been. It could hardly conclude without offering the reader specific advice on exercises he can do, when he might do them, what he can expect from them.

In working with new writers, the most common weakness I have found is the lack of specifics, the failure to pin down each and every generalization with a statement of fact or a concrete illustration. Anecdotal examples are often the most effective method, although admittedly they do not always provide scientific proof. Direct quotes from authorities lend substance, but should not be overused. Language that evokes visual images can be immensely useful. *The New Yorker's* "Talk of the Town" took off a while ago: "An old, old gentleman we had known years ago turned up recently, tapping his way along the street." There is a concreteness, a visual clarity here that merits attention. In fiction or nonfiction, this kind of image-evoking lead can't be beaten.

Obviously, our analogy shouldn't be carried too far. There are clear differences between short stories and articles, and especially between some short stories, which may succeed simply by evoking a mood, and some articles which may quite effectively grab the reader with a startling collection of facts about a newsworthy subject. But to succeed both must have a shape that in itself provides a reason for telling the story or relating the facts. Without the beginning, the middle, and the end that form that shape, neither will succeed. And without the kind of writing that brings the story home, involves the reader in what goes on, makes it important for him to continue to the end, article or short story might as well not be written.

57

WRITING THE QUERY LETTER

By Ben Pesta

THE query letter is the first impression that editors receive of most writers. It's not a completely indelible impression, but it's very important nonetheless. Almost all of us would be mortified to come home from a formal banquet, remove our black ties, studs, and waistcoats, look into the mirror and find that we'd just spent three hours being witty and charming—with an enormous green glob of spinach between our front teeth. *That,* unfortunately, is the sort of first impression many (if not most) queries leave.

I know. As an editor of a major magazine, I've read lots of them.

Why do writers write poor queries? Most often, because they harbor some very vital misconceptions about editors. Your queries will be much more effective if they are informed by accurate knowledge about what editors do and what they are looking for when they read query letters.

Here are a few points to remember about writer-editor relations. From here on, what I'm about to say holds true, I think, for most of the editors of the nation's major slick magazines. But to a lesser extent, I believe that this is probably true for *all* editors, even those of small publications.

1. An editor is always looking for good writers in general. But he or she isn't looking for *you* in particular. What this declaration means is that a query letter should give some indication that you fall into the general category of "good writers."

2. Editors have a very limited amount of time. They are expected to spend the available time and their publishers' money in creative ways, that is, in buying topical, arresting articles of wide public import. So they are obliged to allocate most of that time to writers of proven ability or those who can "sell" with their queries.

3. Your query sells your idea more strongly than it sells you. (This point is more true of the major slicks than it is for smaller or local publications.) The reason is simple: When an editor reads a query letter, he or she still doesn't know if the writer can organize, can write with a clear and readable style, and can do all the other things that writers are supposed to do. But the subject matter of the query may be so intriguing that the editor will want to find out. *Caveat:* A query letter *can* make it instantly and painfully clear that the letter-writer is no writer. Someone who can't write a query almost certainly can't write a well-organized piece.

Most of the more commonly made mistakes in query-writing stem from misconceptions about these three points. Many of them will seem so obvious that they shouldn't need discussion; but they aren't, since aspiring writers still make them. If *you* don't, please don't feel insulted. Instead, give yourself a mental pat on the back for your professionalism.

1. *Poor spelling.* Nothing makes a writer resemble an illiterate quite so much as a query letter with a lot of misspelled words. Unfortunately, learning to spell is a bore, especially when compared to the exuberant rush of expressing your feelings creatively. And fewer schools seem to be teaching spelling skills these days. I've perceived a vague feeling on the part of writers that spelling is a tacky detail not worth the notice of a true, creative writer, and that a preoccupation with it is more appropriate to the mind of a clerk than that of an artist. *Don't believe it!* I know, I know Scott Fitzgerald could barely spell his name. But Max Perkins, his editor at Scribner's, was a saintly and patient man who must have had more time to correct spelling errors than most of us have nowadays.

2. *The biographical query.* Editors do *not* want to know your life story. So, please don't start your query with a *curriculum vitae.*

The fact that you have three children, that you "have always wanted to write," that you are "an insurance broker and an observer of the human comedy," that you were "editor of my college newspaper"—all irrelevant. (*Every* writer edited the college paper.)

There are two exceptions. If you have been a staff writer or reporter for a newspaper or magazine, it doesn't hurt to say so. But say it briefly: "For six years I was sports editor of the Denver

Post." And it's helpful to present a *brief* credential if you're proposing a piece on a technical subject, or one that presupposes special knowledge on the part of the writer. Any editor who is queried about an article on "Selected Aberrant Reactions of Sodium-Salt Compounds at High Temperatures" is reassured to look at the writer's signature and see below it the words, "Chairman, Department of Chemistry, California Institute of Technology."

3. *Deficient knowledge of markets.* If you want to sell a piece to a magazine, you should know what kinds of articles that magazine publishes. The best way to learn is to read some recent issues of the magazine itself (but *not* by asking the editor to send you three or four back numbers). What could be more logical? Yet every editor receives a constant stream of queries from writers who obviously last read the magazine in question in 1943, if at all. You may indeed have been granted an exclusive, personal interview with Linda Lovelace, in the course of which you asked her many incisive questions; but a general family magazine probably doesn't want to know the answers.

4. *Form queries.* Editors regularly receive queries on yellow, printed forms. The forms explain that the writer is doing the editor a favor by sending me this handy memo, with four lines of explanation about the story and a lot of little boxes that can be checked off, depending on how the editor reacts to the query. Each box has its own little name: "Yes," "Tell Me More," "We'll Pay You ————," and "No, Thanks." Can you guess which box most editors usually check?

Form queries confine the writer's explanation to a short space, which means that they probably can't tell the editor all he should know about the writer's ideas. In addition, they make it too easy for the editor to react negatively. This is not to say that editors never turn writers down if they write query letters. It's just that you, as a writer, are under no obligation to do the editor's job.

5. *Handwritten queries.* This sin is almost as cardinal as poor spelling. You may have your Palmer Method certificate framed on the wall, your bank teller may be awestruck by the artistic way you sign your checks—but editors just don't have the time to bother with this sort of thing. No one's handwriting is as easy to read as a

typed letter. And you want to make it as easy as possible for an editor to be impressed with your ideas.

6. *Personal asides to the editor.* This is a catch-all category for such time-waster sentences as the following.

"Because of the extreme timeliness of this story, I would appreciate a very quick response." Very few editors at major magazines read and act on queries the day they receive them. Most of them read and answer queries once or twice weekly, and answer them *immediately.* So don't bother to enjoin an editor to respond quickly. He probably won't even *see* the message for a couple of days, and when he does, he'll respond quickly anyway.

"I have offered this story to several other magazines, so a prompt answer is essential." Editors can't be pushed, especially not as unsubtly as this. Simultaneous submissions usually work only for big agents who are selling hot articles by famous writers.

"This story has been rejected by *Ms., Esquire* and *Cosmopolitan,* but . . ." The implication here is that those other editors didn't have the wit to recognize this gem for the rough Star of India that it is, but the writer is sure that *you,* dear sir, are smarter. Rot. No editor is influenced by the decisions of other magazines. Worse, in 99.8 percent of such cases, the message is a tipoff that the editors at *Ms., Esquire* and *Cosmo* were absolutely right.

"I'll bet you won't dare to print this!" Some version of this sentence appears in an astonishing percentage of query letters. The writer is almost correct, too, not because an editor is afraid to have a Bernstein-and-Woodward-sized controversy on his hands as a result of the article, but because such pieces are invariably so libelous, obscene, untrue or just plain dumb that if an editor ran one, he or she would be reading the "Help Wanted" ads in the *Editor and Publisher* the next day.

"You are free to edit this story to your specifications." The editor is free to do so whether you give him your permission or not. If you can't live with the necessary changes, the alternative is to try to sell the piece elsewhere.

7. *The brash approach.* This mistake is most often made by younger writers. Don't write, "I am the best writer under twenty-five on the East Coast," "I'd like to do this piece for you in my

own, unique style," and "I'm what you've been looking for!" Give editors a little credit. Most of them are reasonably bright, articulate people, and they're *very* unlikely to be snowed by a writer's self-estimate. In general, avoid *all* adjectives about the quality of your own work. If you *are* the new Hemingway, an editor will recognize you. If he can't, your telling him so won't help.

What *will* help is to send tearsheets of one or two pieces that you've written that are fairly close in scope and style to the article you're proposing. If you have *nothing* similar, just send your best and hope for the best. (But *don't* cite a few pieces you've written and invite the editor to go to the library and look them up himself. Believe it or not, many people do this. You can imagine how ineffective an approach it is.)

8. *The big story query.* Don't write to the slicks asking to cover Evel Knievel's Snake River jump, Bob Dylan's comeback tour, or the Super Bowl. The editors *all* know that these things are going to happen, and if they want them covered they'll assign someone whose style and reportorial ability they know and trust.

So much for the Editorial Penal Code of Query-Writing Felonies and Misdemeanors. You now know what makes a bad query bad. The question that remains is, of course, how do you write a good one?

In my experience, the best queries always seem to be written very much like news stories. They're *never* written in that terrible press-agent style, with lots of exclamation points and one-word sentences. The important facts, the grabbers, are up in the first paragraph. Before an editor has spent much time on these queries, he has a pretty good idea of what it is the writers want to say.

The writers themselves are confident that the subjects they've chosen will make the editor want to read further to learn the details. The details they give are always significant. They focus on the importance, eccentricity or humor of the article, and they convince the editor he or she would like to know more about it—which usually means that the editor thinks the *readers* would like to know more about it. And that's the difference between a successful query and the other sort.

Editors of slick magazines don't often make assignments from queries. But when they give an affirmative response to a query, they're telling the writer that his idea has possibilities, that if the piece is well written, there's a possibility that he can make a sale. They usually send a short note to the writer about length and format, and mention that if he has further questions they'll try to answer them. (But not by telephone!) There's nothing worse than having someone working on a piece on speculation, calling an editor several times a week to ask how he should handle each paragraph. And, yes, as an editor I *have* bought manuscripts "over the transom"—not many, because the numerical odds are all against it, but enough to make me aware that the slush pile and the query pile aren't a complete waste of time. And some day, perhaps, you'll write that completely irresistible, well-organized, clearly written query that will result in the article of the century.

58

INTERVIEWING FOR ARTICLE WRITING

By Omer Henry

PERHAPS the greatest asset the magazine article writer can have is learning how to obtain pertinent information. He gets that information, by and large, from personal interviews. Therefore, it is imperative that he become an expert in conducting such interviews.

How does one conduct a personal interview efficiently and effectively? What are the ground rules? Are there dangers, techniques, and principles which one must learn?

Indeed there are! And the sooner one learns them, the better. A major danger is the surface question. If the writer asks only elementary questions, he hurts himself. He should know that before an editor will buy an article it must contain data which readers will find of real value. Such an article is the result of an in-depth interview.

Another danger arises from using generalities rather than specifics. No professional magazine article writer will quote an interviewee simply as saying, "I owe my success to service," without a specific example.

If the interviewee makes such a statement during the interview, the alert writer will ask, "Exactly what services do you offer?" He may want to follow up with, "How do your services differ from those of your competitors?" The writer must insist on concrete facts which, when included in an article, will show readers how they may emulate the interviewee and thereby improve their own businesses.

An even greater danger is the "shotgun" interview. In conducting it, the writer tries to cover everything the firm does. The result is an out-of-focus piece that isn't much good for anything. The trouble is that the writer has not selected his theme carefully enough. Before he undertakes an interview, he must decide exactly what information he needs from the interviewee.

How does the writer know what information he needs? His theme tells him. It limits his field of inquiry, tells him to explore his particular subject in detail and to avoid all other angles. This will result in an in-depth interview.

An editor will often supply the writer's theme by telling him precisely what phases of the subject he is interested in for his magazine. One editor recently did this for me. He had heard of a firm that was using a new wage-incentive plan for its mechanics, and he wanted to know how the plan worked. Knowing exactly what this editor wanted, I was able to draft a set of questions, the answers to which gave me the facts I needed to write and sell the article.

Here, then, is the first fundamental principle: The writer's first step in planning a personal interview is to establish the theme of his article. Until he does that, he is in no-man's-land without a compass.

Once the writer has established his theme, he can prepare questions that will proceed in a logical manner toward the desired objective. The interview will move. Interviews prepared in this manner are likely to produce articles which will bring the writer additional sales.

This happened to me when I was doing an article for *Ford Truck Times*. The article concerned Guardian Tree Experts and was to point up the methods which had made that firm successful. Before I called on the president for an interview, I considered the possibilities of using different aspects of this material for various markets. It seemed to me that *New,* for one, might buy an article which showed how Guardian Tree Experts use Christian principles. Also, I knew a boy who, upon graduating from high school, had gone to work for Guardian Tree Experts and in the course of a few years had become vice-president of the firm. Therefore, it seemed reasonable that *Event*, a publication for teen-agers, might be interested in an article giving high school boys some insight into this business.

As a result, from the interview with the president of Guardian Tree Experts, I obtained all the information I needed for three articles—each one tailored carefully to the editorial requirements of a particular publication.

I was able to do this only because I knew quite clearly just what data I needed for each article. Also, by following this procedure, I greatly increased the efficiency of my operation, thereby increasing my income.

Here, then, is another basic principle: Before the writer plans an interview, he should consider the possibility of multiple sales. If he can see the probability of additional sales as a result of a single interview, certainly he should plan his interview accordingly.

Now that the writer knows what information he will require, he must consider the best source for it. For the new writer this is sometimes quite a problem, but it need not be. He must find out who can supply him with authoritative, valid information. The key word is *valid*. He can determine this by selecting a high official in the firm which is to be the subject of his proposed article. It is reasonable to suppose that such an official can give accurate data about his own company.

If the article deals with a small business, the writer should approach the owner, manager, or president of the firm for the needed facts. Should the subject of the article be a large business, the writer may find it advantageous to call on the firm's public relations office. There he may obtain the facts and figures which he will need for his article, and be directed to the proper official.

This, then, gives us principle number three: The writer must select a valid source for his information and must identify that source by name and official title. That official's statements give the article validity. The selection of a source is, of course, only the beginning. There remains the all-important task of obtaining the cooperation of that official. A writer may approach this individual by letter, telephone, or by a personal call. I find that a splendid approach to an owner or manager is knowing a notable feature of his business and complimenting the man on his astuteness. Such an approach must be entirely honest, and, if the writer can suggest in this way that he is something of an authority in the field, so much the better. Some businessmen are not at all eager to cooperate with writers. Therefore, one should be prepared to point out certain positive results which may accrue to the company from the publication of the article.

"Your company's reputation," the writer may say truthfully, "is your firm's most valuable asset. My article would help you to build an even greater reputation."

How?

"By showing your firm's management achievements, innovations, personalities, and services, the article will present your firm favorably." This is true because no editor will publish an article unless it presents *helpful* information, thus reflecting favorably on the company.

Perhaps the prospect remains unconvinced. If so, the writer may point out the following:

• A magazine article may demonstrate the firm's management expertise and help cement relations with other companies.

• The company may distribute reprints of the article to its customers, stockholders, and potential customers. This would help to improve its image—and business.

• The article may be used as a basis for news releases in the local press to help business.

• In a consumer publication, an article can create a demand for the firm's products.

Principle number 4, then, is clear: The writer must get the complete cooperation of his subject before attempting the interview. And further, unless the subject is entirely willing to cooperate, the writer should pass up the story. It is foolhardy to attempt to do an article unless the necessary information is available.

When the subject has agreed to the interview, the writer must prepare for it. Again, homework is involved and the more painstakingly one attends to this chore, the more successful he is likely to be.

Now is the time to consider the theme in depth. For instance: Recently, Suit & Wells Equipment Company of Marlboro, Maryland, agreed to cooperate with me in producing an article for *Farm & Power,* a publication which goes to farm implement dealers. This company is notable from many points of view: It sells a high volume of machinery, it has an outstanding salesman, and it handles displays in a spectacular manner. Any one of these angles would make a good piece for *Farm & Power,* if reported in depth.

Which should I choose?

I decided that my story would feature the star salesman. I would show how he managed to win outstanding honors and to make plenty of money for his firm and for himself. That, I felt, would have the strongest possible appeal for *Farm & Power* readers.

This slant told me what information I needed. I must learn how the salesman did the job. Such statements as, "I work early and late," "I see to it that my customers are happy," and the like would not be enough. The article had to be a "nuts-and-bolts" piece—one which would give readers really helpful information.

In my article I would point out any unusual techniques, tricks, gimmicks—anything that had helped this man to distinguish himself as a salesman.

On the human-interest side, I wanted to know why this salesman worked so hard. Certainly he did not find this necessary. Why, then, did he do it? What was the force that drove him?

I wanted to know how he learned to sell, what he had learned, and—of course—I wanted several good quotations from him. Obviously, the salesman himself was my best source of information. Therefore, I made a list of questions which I proposed to ask him. To make the interview as easy as possible, I arranged the questions in a logical order. Here are a few of them:

1. You have been selling J. I. Case equipment for 20 years. Why did you take this kind of job?

2. Have you sold any other line of equipment? If so, why did you come back to Case?

3. How do you get prospects?

4. When a man comes through the door of your office and announces that he is looking for a given piece of machinery, what do you do? Why?

5. Have you had some near-sales that didn't come through? Do you analyze them to see where you failed? What have you learned as a result of this action?

6. What are some of the pitfalls an industrial equipment salesman must face? How do you avoid these pitfalls?

7. What was the most difficult sale you ever made? Why was it difficult? How would you handle that customer today?

8. How important is the human element in selling industrial equipment?

9. What drives you to work so hard?

10. Do you ever go out to check a machine which you've sold? Why? Does this help you to sell more machines? How?

11. What are the human qualities that would help one to become a good industrial equipment salesman?

12. What suggestions do you have to offer to individuals who are in the industrial equipment field?

I typed all of these questions—and many more—in my notebook so that when the time of the interview arrived, I could proceed rapidly and still get all of the information I needed. When this was done, I was ready for the interview.

Principle 5 emerges from all of this. It is: The writer must do his homework in detail before he begins the interview.

It is necessary to make an appointment for the interview. I like to do this by telephone. It is convenient for both parties, can be done quickly, and is a bit more personal than a letter.

During the phone conversation, the interviewee may request a list of the questions he will be called upon to answer. If he does, grant it. Sometimes, I have offered the questions to an interviewee prior to the interview. In this way, he could prepare his answers and give me the best possible replies.

No rule can be made for the length of an interview. It should be as short as possible, yet long enough to provide the necessary information. My own interviews are seldom an hour long, unless they are highly technical. I make a strenuous effort to avoid a re-interview.

The writer must be prepared to report the interviewee's comments accurately. Although one may do this by making notes in pencil, undoubtedly the best way to handle this detail is by using a tape recorder.

Do interviewees object to having their comments taped? In my experience, almost no one objects. Most businessmen appreciate the fact that the writer is working in such a professional manner.

As the interview progresses, it well may be that the writer will wish to intersperse a few additional questions. This is often quite helpful, but such questions must be pertinent, clearly stated, and few in number. No writer should attempt to ad lib an interview.

Sometimes a writer finds it difficult to get a number of anecdotes suitable for use in his story, because few individuals, when asked for illustrative incidents, can produce them.

A far better way to obtain such anecdotes is by stimulating the interviewee's memory. Using this device with the Suit & Wells salesman, I told him about a dealer who had consummated a $47,-000 sale. When I finished the story, my interviewee recounted a comparable experience of his own, thus giving me an excellent anecdote for my article.

Another point: The interview must produce several usable quotations which convey the flavor of the man speaking. My tape recorder solves this problem by recording every word the interviewee speaks. Thus, I can quote him accurately and—if I like—at length. And the quotes sound like him! This adds considerable interest to the article, makes it far more readable, and helps me to sell the piece. They are a plus value for any article.

Here, then, is a most important guideline for an interview: The writer must make sure that he records all that the interviewee has to say at the interview. Some of this may not appear to be important at the time, but the writer should get it down. That's how a professional writer operates.

Does this end the interview? Is the writer now ready to say, "Thank you, sir, for a fine story," and take his leave? Not quite. He has yet to think of the pictures he will need for illustrations. It is true that taking pictures is not a part of the interview *per se,* but to save time, the writer should get the pictures while he's there. Consequently, when I plan an interview, I also outline in my mind —and often on paper—the pictures I'll need. I take with me to the interview the necessary photographic equipment. At the conclusion of the interview, I discuss the pictures with the interviewee and take a few action pictures of him. As I go about the plant taking pictures for the article, I observe the displays. Are they really attractive? Is there something new and helpful about them? Is the place clean? Does the showroom have any striking features? I make note of anything I find that appears to be of interest to the industry. And when, later, I sit down to write the article, all of this information helps me.

All in all, it should be clear that planning and conducting an interview requires time, thought, and skill. And what is the result of handling an interview in this manner? Is it worth all of the time and effort? Does it actually pay off? Did it pay off, say, in the Suit & Wells story?

When I returned to my study after the interview, I had all of the facts I needed for the article. This made the writing quite easy. I knew what I wanted to say, and I had the material for the piece. Thus, I did the writing in a couple of hours.

I mailed the manuscript and pictures on February 21; on March first I had *Farm & Power*'s check for the article. That's proof enough for me. But, if there are doubters among my readers, let me add that this is a regular pattern for me.

Yes, the ability to handle a personal interview well is the magazine article writer's best insurance. Without it, he cannot hope to succeed, but with it, he can hardly fail. The shrewd writer will take immediate steps to master the personal interview, because this skill will pay him daily dividends in direct proportion to his expertise.

59

ARTICLES FROM EXPERIENCE

By Rollie Hochstein

When I began writing magazine humor—it cannot be more than eight years ago!—I had a miniature ax that wanted grinding. I was, at the time, the mother of two very young children and had recently taken up residence in the suburbs. I think I was having an Identity Crisis. In those days it was not enough to live impromptu: I felt somehow that I needed to know exactly who and what I was. Experience in both areas has taught me that labeling is utterly irrelevant; but at that raw, unsettled time of my life, it seemed crucial for me to decide whether I was a housewife who wrote or a writer who kept house.

The chief antagonists in my battle for identity were The Sociologists, who continually showed up in mass media authoritatively lumping The American Housewife into one great, sticky glob. The glob was oppressed by a male-dominated culture. The glob emasculated its husbands. The glob was spoiled, child-centered, over-educated, under-emancipated. There I was, having an Identity Crisis, and there they were—those snide Sociologists—trying to agglutinate my Identity!

My method of protest was to burn them with a searingly satirical article, which was to begin: "The sociologists make me feel about as individual as a stick of spaghetti." I really liked that phrase. I clearly remember the demonic relish with which I typed it. And I also remember the reluctance with which I crossed it out when, after many rereadings of the first draft, I had to admit that it didn't go. It was a "pre-peat" of the second sentence, and the second sentence was more germane to the rest of the piece. The final version—called "I'm a Method Wife"—was published in the old *Coronet*. It began: "Whenever I pick up a magazine or tune in a panel discussion, some sociologist is lecturing me about my role in life."

Publication made me feel much better: with one shot, I'd got something off my chest and something into my bank account. It was a fine feeling, but the spaghetti lead was still a-dangle and I was avid to use it.

About four subsequent articles originated with the spaghetti simile and all four, by the final draft, started some other way. My grouch about the sociologists developed into other more general, less didactic, more amusing, less irritable subjects, and that first lead—for unity's sake—had to go. The spaghetti sentence, until now, never made print. It stopped mattering after a while: having authored several personal essays and other kinds of magazine articles, I no longer felt threatened by sociological de-personification. Nobody could make me feel like a stick of spaghetti, and I was far too busy with writing and housekeeping to ponder over pigeon-holes.

That's a personal essay. I wrote it (a) for fun, (b) because the editor asked me for an article about technique, and (c) to use as an example and a basis for discussion.

The personal essay is a most satisfactory way to get published. It requires no research, no interviews, no scholarship, no legwork. All you need is an interesting (marketable) idea and the ability to present it pungently.

Editors like to buy personal essays and, I am told, they have a hard time finding usable ones. Mine fall into the category of "domestic humor," and about twenty of them have been published in half a dozen women's magazines and newspaper supplements. Last time I looked, *Good Housekeeping, McCall's* and *Redbook* were running regular reader-written first-person features. *The Reader's Digest* uses several such features under different names. *Playboy* and *Esquire* use satirical essays. *The Atlantic* and *Harper's* run first-person humor on occasion. Though they are often written by VIP's, personal essays often appear in *Vogue, Harper's Bazaar, Holiday* and *Mademoiselle.*

I've gone through some grand markets here, but I should tell you that my earliest anecdotal articles were published in diaper service giveaways, such as *Baby Talk* and *Baby Time*. I was delighted then, too, to get paid for saying something that I wanted to say. I think it's accurate to say that, while the category is special, the market for personal essays is broad.

What I'm writing here is a *how-to* article in the tone and shape of a personal essay. I'm using certain principles that I practice in my domestic humor pieces. The first two of the following principles are probably most applicable to the women's and family field; the last three, I believe, are compulsory in all personal essays.

1. *Reader identification.* When a reader says, "It sounds just like me," or he writes, "That's exactly the way it happens in my house," the writer has done a good job. In women's magazines, I deal with fairly typical domestic situations—the problems of party-giving, a slant on sibling rivalry—written from the viewpoint of a fairly typical housewife. In the first sentence or two, I set myself up for quick and easy identification. A lead might go something like this:

"When a woman has a six-room house to clean, three choosy children to feed and a hearty husband to keep in step with, she finds it hard to understand that the phrase 'Working Mother' means somebody else."

In all my domestic humor pieces, not one line has ever suggested that I do anything other than keep house, raise children, buy clothes, give parties, attend P.T.A. meetings and whatever else is common to all us housewives. Any clowning must be done gently and always with the implication that, though sometimes harassed, I manage to come out ahead, doing a good job at all these things. "Never make a jackass out of yourself," an editor warned me. That's reader identification.

Now notice, in the first paragraph of this article, how quickly I introduce myself as a writer. Right off it gives you and me something in common. The clause, "it cannot be more than eight years ago!" not only tells you that I'm experienced, but it also humanizes me. Time goes too quickly for me, too. You're interested because I'm a professional writer; perhaps you'll learn something from me. You're interested because I've confessed a human weakness and am less likely, after such a confession, to bore you with a lecture from a posture of distant superiority. I tell you that my ax was miniature: it's an indication that I am laughing at myself and that what I will say might be amusing as well as informative. The next sentence may have cost me some male readers, but I'm pretty sure that all writing mothers kept with it. In that opening, I achieved reader identification.

2. *Intimacy.* If you're going to sit down and share your opinions, observations and/or experiences in a humorous or poignant manner, you need a warm relationship with your reader. Back to my opening anecdote: we are introduced; we find we have something in common. I proceed to talk to you in a frank and friendly way. I even take you into my confidence: "I think I was having an Identity Crisis." I capitalize the fashionable phrase to make it humorous; I append "I think" to make it whimsical; but I am still opening myself up to you when I make that statement. It makes us friends and I continue, as a friend, to tell my story. I can talk about things that interest me on the assumption that they will interest you, too.

Here, we must stop to make a distinction. The *I* of the personal essay is not necessarily the author. The unity required in such an essay makes it almost impossible for the *I* to be completely the author; most of us are multifaceted, far too complex to be single-minded about very much. But once the *I* has set up a relationship with the reader, the author must not interfere with it. At no time should he double-cross his reader by contradicting or questioning himself. To keep his rapport, he should make his points directly. The *I* should say what he means and mean what he says. He should never slip out of his role by turning sarcastic, hostile or obscure to his reader. This is not schizophrenia; it's professionalism.

3. *Unity.* One theme is announced, developed, varied and concluded. One idea is proclaimed, clarified, illustrated, modulated and summed up. The personal essay requires disciplined thought and tight writing: no rambling, no diversions. The truth is that you and I are not really friends. You may have to listen to a friend's boring stories, but you can easily turn me off with a flick of the page. Therefore, every sentence that I write should compel you to read the next one. Every sentence must belong to the total structure; that's why my spaghetti line had to be eliminated.

Writers are not paid for expressing themselves. The personal essay, like all other professional writing, is meant to entertain, inform or influence—any one, two or three of these aims—and it must be interesting. What you want to say is your business. How you say it is the writing business. Where there are neither important facts nor famous figures to hold your reader's interest, your stated ideas have to do all the work. They have to be tightly organized; only in unity will they have the strength to hold readers.

4. *Style*. Style, like personal charm, is an elusive quality, highly individual. Writing style is a combination of language, tone and pace. More than any other kind of writing, except poetry, the personal essay needs to be meticulously worded and phrased, cut and polished. The words are selected by weight and color, as well as meaning. I fool around a lot with my essays, substituting bright words for drab words, trimming flabby sentences, lightening heavy ones, compressing, relaxing. I take pains to find the precisely right word; hardly a piece gets written without consultation of both dictionary and thesaurus.

The tone—droll, irate, bewildered, harassed, nostalgic—should be set in the lead and, with minor variations, sustained throughout the essay. If you are ear-minded, it is not difficult to set and maintain a tone. You hear it as you read over what you have written. If not, I suppose reading aloud will help. The tone of my early paragraphs here is, at least to my ears, one of sophisticated amusement. After the first five paragraphs, it turned earnest.

Pacing is almost impossible to pin down. If it's right, nobody except a professional notices it. Wrong, it's something like cold chicken soup: the fastidious are distressed and reject it; the apathetic suffer through with vague discomfort. Many writers get by without it. Non-paced novelists, I've noticed, are the ones called storytellers. In most nonfiction, pace counts as nothing more than an extra added attraction. I'm not even sure that it's compulsory in all essays, though it is a necessary component of the humorous essay. All this leads up to the fact that I can't tell you how to do it. Me, I've always listened a lot to such stand-up comedians as Alan King and Myron Cohen. While I haven't analyzed their timing, I think I've absorbed some of it. Also, I like to read metrical poetry: sonnets, ballades, rondos and villanelles; the footed works of everybody from Chaucer to Ciardi; the crisp couplets of Pope and the iambic pentameter of Shakespeare.

My own style, in fiction as in articles, is always under the influence of other writers. I'm particularly impressed by elegant English novelists: Jane Austen, Evelyn Waugh, Nancy Mitford; and American black humorists: Joseph Heller, Shirley Jackson, Bruce Jay Friedman. I would suggest that anybody who wants to develop a style should do a lot of selective reading and listening, always open to the tones and timings and words that please him.

5. *Arrogance*. The personal essayist has to be assuming. He has to assume that what he's saying is interesting enough to attract and hold a great many people he's never even met. Modesty and self-doubt have to be set aside as he develops, without reservation or qualification, the theme he arbitrarily chooses to present. Even if, like Leacock in "My Financial Career," you are posing as a bumbler, you can't take a clause to apologize or explain yourself; you must be the complete bumbler, arrogant in your ineptitude. You have to take on an authority that—at least in the beginning of your career—you are hardly likely to feel. What else is there to do? You're the author of the piece, and it's all you—or a projection of you. You have to be authoritative.

It takes a certain amount of arrogance plus ardor to get a first personal essay written and off to the editors. A middle-class, public school-educated American is not ordinarily brought up to believe that he is anything special. On the contrary, he (and particularly if he is a woman) is usually led to believe in the virtues of inconspicuousness, humility and keeping his mouth shut. Writing in the first person is not a humble thing to do. It's rather brash, is it not?, to expect to publish a piece of writing based on nothing more than your opinions, experiences and observations. "Why me?" is the question you may ask yourself.

The answer is: "Why not?" Actually, none of us is a stick of spaghetti, and nobody else in the world sees things, feels things and can express things exactly as you do. Nobody else can write the personal essay that you can write.

60

PLOTTING THE BIOGRAPHY

By Catherine Drinker Bowen

A NOVELIST informed me, with magisterial assurance, that compared to fiction writers, biographers have an easy time. Their plot is ready to hand before they even begin to write. When I asked, what plot, exactly?—the novelist said it was self-evident: "Birth, education, marriage, career, death."

Surely the novelist was mistaken, and his five neat sequential nouns indicated a chronology rather than a plot? Consider Monday, for instance, which has its beginning and ending; the sun rises and sets. One breakfasts, works, lunches, takes a walk, goes out to dinner perhaps, comes home, goes to bed. Yet if a writer wishes to engage a reader's attention concerning Monday, his hero must that day meet with trouble, face an obstacle, a danger, a grief, and conquer it. Or if the writer prefers tragedy, then Monday's obstacle can be conqueror, and draw a reader's tears.

The book trade calls it conflict, suspense. By whatever name, it is a quality vital to biography as to fiction. The difference is that the novelist invents his plot, whereas the biographer finds it in history, in actual fact as indicated by the given material, by events as they unfold, and more particularly by the character of the biographical subject, the hero. Maurois has something to say about this. The biographer, he believes, "has greater difficulty than the novelist in composition. But he has one compensation: to be compelled to take over the form of a work ready-made is almost always a source of power to the artist. It is painful, it makes his task more difficult; but at the same time it is from this struggle between the mind and the matter that resists it that a masterpiece is born."

Graduate students of history, having labored for years on a thesis, often feel ambitious to see their work in print. Approaching some available professional writer they inquire how their production can be fixed up for trade publication. "Popular presentation," they have learned to call it.

The professional writer is wary of such assignments. A biography must be planned *before* it is written, not afterward. Yet as an example, the graduate student's problem can be worth careful inspection because it is actually the same problem the seasoned biographer confronts in the early stages of his books. The material is gathered, now what is to be done with it? These pages—this thesis—dry, correct, with serried footnotes, can be extremely useful as reference on a library shelf. And it covers the ground, certainly. But it moves on mechanized wooden legs, without head or guts, humor or humanity. Yet humor and humanity cannot be stuffed into a book at later convenience but must grow from the narrative as it progresses, springing hot and hearty from the writer's own bias and involvement as he sits and thinks about his subject.

Ask such a graduate student what his thesis, his book, is about. Not merely the name and life schedule of the hero, but what the book is *about,* what is its plot, what carries it along? For answer you will be given a chronology, a train of events. Let us say the biographical subject is an agent for Indian affairs on the American frontier, *circa* 1775. Captain B—— has fought the French, he knows Indians; he is prospering and minding his business, when along comes the Revolution—and he chooses the Tory side!

Divided loyalty! Here is a theme, here is plot enough to carry to the end. For what is biography but the story of a man or woman in conflict with himself? Moreover the subject is fresh; the Tory in our Revolution has not been explored in depth, as the professors say. Yet—take the manuscript in hand and what is presented on the page? Battles, boundary lines, Indian raids, with actual tallies of the scalped and the dead. Footnotes, chapter notes, bibliography. Everything neat, verified—and bloodless even though the scene itself is soaked in blood.

But the man who wrote the thesis is not dry. When he talks about his hero-captain he is entertaining, he is funny; what he says concerning his characters is quick and sharp. One knows of course that such qualities, transferred to the page, are of no help toward graduate honors. Yet this young man has not come to discuss academic degrees. Ask him then, if his hero suffered, if the captain doubted his position and his choice, felt sadness at the loss of old friends among the Americans.

For answer the young man begins to explain what it meant to be a loyalist in the Revolution, and what his captain's soul will lose or gain thereby. Suddenly his very word is gold. Write it down! the professional says. Write it on the back of an envelope, quick before it vanishes. . . .

There is, one assumes, proof of the captain's struggle, quotations available in letters, diaries, if not from the captain's hand then from someone in a like position. Did the captain have a family and did they share his views and loyalties? More legwork, as the reporters call it, was desirable, but legwork with a different end in view. Canadian libraries might yield a harvest. It would be worthwhile to visit repositories in Ottawa, Detroit. . . . The thesis is filled moreover with names of Indian tribes, Indian chiefs with whom the hero had close dealings. Is there some indirect way of repeating what they said? We must not have fictional conversation around the council fire. But treaties were made with the French, the English. The language is available, it is written down.

The young man had been excellently trained in evaluating evidence. He could spot a bad source, a dubious statement across a library room. In short, he had completed one phase of a biographer's training. But if he aimed beyond the classroom, if he wished the world to read about his hero, his Tory captain, he would find the next phase of training equally rigorous. He must move into the realm of feeling, of men and women and their emotions. Through historical evidence, fortified and animated by his own experience of living, he must pick these people up bodily from his dry pages, turn them over in his hand, stare at them long and searchingly.

And there is a further task, a pleasant one to my way of thinking. It concerns scene. What about terrain, one asks the writer—the rivers, the hills? This is an outdoor story. We must see the hero's country; a Tory captain does not float in air. In the thesis as it stands there is no field or forest or blockhouse or cellar that one can remember or describe after reading—let alone a face, a voice the figure of a man. The words on the page should be evocative, call up colors, sounds, sights, smells.

This of course is reckless counsel. Not everybody can write a scene or describe a man's face. Not everyone has eyes to see a field, a tree in life, let alone set it down in writing. There is no sense pretending that technique will take the place of talent. Yet here again, practice counts, in perception as in writing. Moreover, at certain stages heroic measures are called for, strong medicine to clear the writer's vision, turn him about to face another direction. He must free himself from his strict specific training, which for its purpose was excellent. Like the student who has mastered the fundamentals of grammar he is prepared, he is ready. Of what he has learned nothing will be forgotten, neglected or distorted. But the time has come to make the material his own, transform it into words that live, that pulse, communicate.

Once the beginner has his plot in mind—his central animating theme—he will do well to think over the chronology of the hero's life, the big things that happened. These he can note down in scenes, as for a stage play but with the dates, keeping always in mind the direction his work is heading, the climax which by now must surely have declared itself. This exercise might fill three or four pages of $8\frac{1}{2}''$ x $11''$ paper. Then he can begin to write his book, working from scene to scene, as the composer of a symphony heads for the next theme, whether a secondary subject or a development.

So simplified a program will not of course make a book. But it is a step taken, a map, a way out of the wilderness of research into a final choice of incident. It leads from the library into life, narration, drama, plot. An outline need not, however, be a rigid plan that must be followed letter for letter. Indeed, I have seen biographical outlines so complete, so detailed and heavy they bade fair to crush the story, deceiving the author into thinking he had written his book. What one advocates is a loose chronology which reads vividly simply because the incidents, the characters or occasional quotations from hero or heroine are themselves vivid. For example, Queen Elizabeth, as a young woman, "told the French Ambassador de Foix that whenever she thought about marriage, she felt as if someone were tearing the heart out of her bosom." Again, to her ladies, on hearing that Mary Stuart had borne a child: "The Queen of Scots is lighter of a fair son, and I am but a barren stock."

When Elizabeth Jenkins [author of *Elizabeth the Great*] came across those words in the records, surely her mind leaped forward, imagining the time and place where she could set them in her book.

It is easier to tell someone how than to do it oneself. E. M. Forster is a master of his material, a master of narrative. Yet even he confesses that "people will not realize how one flounders about."

Floundering about is endemic to writers, a phase we all go through at the outset of a work. Psychiatrists say this initial block is intrinsic to the creative process, a forcing of the writer deeper into himself. The procedure can be called by other names: thinking, brooding, dreaming. I have heard it said that most authors sit down at their typewriters too soon. Before words go on paper the biographer must put his notes away, out of sight, while he sits and thinks, or walks about and thinks—a painful exercise which may consume days or weeks while the paper remains blank in the typewriter.

This thinking may well turn upon the business of what the biography is about: its theme, the axis upon which its wheels may turn. Does the plot concern a happy man, a life fulfilled? It has been said that happiness has no story—which in itself is a challenge and a half. The biographer must write very well indeed to make his happy hero come alive; he has an extra dimension to reach, an eighth hurdle to surmount. Happiness has many definitions. Grief is part of living: *Sturm und Drang* does not necessarily mean unhappiness or unfulfillment.

But how variously lives are arranged! The biographer may choose a hero who began in poverty and climbed, or one born into luxury and place, thence falling or maintaining his position as circumstance and his spirit dictate. And how much objective history will these projected chapters include? It is a vital question. Every biography is of course a "life and times." Yet there are degrees and proportions. The life of a statesman is three-quarters "times"; the life of a painter or composer of music may show a very different mixture and balance. A biographer of Justice Holmes told me solemnly that his ambition was to "show Holmes's influence on the stream of American intellectual consciousness." But how could one aim at such an effort or be sure this intellectual stream existed? Will such a plot carry, is it feasible? A biographer can be too high-toned for his own good.

In the biographies I most admire, the story moves forward implacably, inevitably. The reader *believes* in Mary Tudor, Elizabeth the Great, Lord Melbourne, George Sand (*Lélia*), Balzac (*Prometheus*). The reader cannot but believe. There are no awkward hurdles, no holes to fall through. Nothing is stretched too far or condensed to the point of collapse. The narrative—the plot—contains us, we know where we are going.

61

THE MAGIC SENTENCE

By Barbara Lang

CREATIVE writing is not simple. It never was, and there is no reason to expect it to become so in an increasingly complex world with increasingly complex ideas to convey. Perspectives are widening, outlooks are more sophisticated. In the face of all this, the challenge to gain and hold the reader's attention increases to seemingly forbidding proportions. Yet there is a helpful element in writing technique that is so simple it may be overlooked. For me, this is "the magic sentence."

The whole point of the magic sentence is to lead the reader onward. In practice, this may take the form of a tantalizing suggestion that useful information is forthcoming or that a provocative insight will be revealed; or that, through the writer's individuality of approach and style, a truly new reading adventure lies ahead. These magic sentences are *promises*, and the good writer keeps them.

In a short, straightforward article, there may be only one such sentence. It usually appears near the beginning of the manuscript and frequently relates to the focus or "hook" of the article. Take for example a piece I wrote for the *Ladies' Home Journal* on theater tickets. Title: "Tickets, Tickets—Who's Got the Tickets?" Opening paragraph:

A hit show, by definition, is something you can't get tickets for. Or can you?

Then followed a description of how theater tickets are distributed, how some are sold before they are even printed, of the roles played by owners of house seats, theater parties, theater clubs and agents, and of the box-office and mail-order procedures. My goal was to arrive at sound advice for the guidance of the individual playgoer. But at the start, the reader kept going, led onward (I trust) by the promise of those three magic words, "Or can you?"

Another guise in which the magic sentence appears is that of one or more deliberately provocative questions, again with the implied promise of—and the writer's sacred obligation to provide—answers.

An article I wrote on tipping, also for the *Ladies' Home Journal*, held some automatic albeit far from joyful interest for most women facing Christmas tipping decisions. The problem was to make the reader aware that there was human interest in the subject and to dramatize the point that this article wasn't merely a dry listing of "to whom and how much at Christmas." Since tipping is not the best-loved of our social customs, I felt the article would gain if it opened in a sympathetic and hopefully entertaining manner. Here are the first two paragraphs of "Jingle All the Way," with the key magic questions asked at the end of the second paragraph:

The greeting card is signed, *With Love and Kisses from your Newsboys Louis, Tony, Petey, Benny, Sammy and Mike.* It is a small card, the missive from these mystery children who materialize annually in early December; but it commands your attention because it clearly signifies the start of the Season—the Tipping Season.

While most people dislike tipping, they recognize it as part of "the system." And whether they give out of social pressure, holiday cheer, to reward good service or because they are aware that many of the people who serve them count on Christmas tips as part of their income, tip they do. And while tipping is a highly personal matter, one often ponders this twilight zone of payment with curious thoughts of what is really expected. What are other people tipping? When, if ever, are presents more appropriate than cash? And is there, anywhere, the individual with courage to deny a tip to someone who has roundly not earned it?

I have always been especially interested in that last question and felt that it in particular might excite the reader's curiosity.

In longer, more complex articles, every time there is a change of direction or a change of pace, every time a new subject is introduced, the writer may profitably invoke another magic sentence to lead the reader still farther onward. These sentences are an integral part of the structure of a piece. As the writer builds his article with major blocks of material, these sentences cement the blocks together. Each one is virtually saying: "Go on; there's more to come and it's fascinating and/or important."

In an article I did some time ago for the *Ladies' Home Journal's* "How America Lives" series (the subject was teen-age marriage), one can find those interlocking sentences, often at the beginning of paragraphs and sections. Here are three:

And yet Dee Dee Floyd . . . was not the type whose friends thought she would marry young.

All the time, without realizing it, the couple was working to break the ties that still bound them to their parents.

What if Dee Dee had to live the last two years over again?

Each carries the reader and the article onward for a bit; thus when impetus threatens to wane, fresh energy is added.

This type of magic sentence involves the matter of pace, which is, I think, knowing when to change the subject. After the change, interest must be renewed. These are, in that sense, *subordinate* magic sentences.

Let us return to the *primary* magic sentence. Even—and possibly especially—in a lengthy, complex article, there is a need to compel, then direct the reader's interest. This demands the writer's best efforts to produce a beautifully turned, provocative magic sentence. It must say something about the *whole* subject and make the reader take the first firm step into the article. It is wider in scope than the ones quoted immediately above; it arises from the writer's being absolutely sure of (and articulate about) his focus and granting his reader a glimpse of its fascination; it creates suspense and it promises revelations; and above all, it beckons invitingly near the beginning of the manuscript. Needless to say, it therefore benefits directly from a strong, dramatic opening that will capture the reader's attention and hold it until this sentence (or two) wings him on his way.

For an example, I'll go back to the beginning of the article mentioned above. The title was "The Teen-Age Marriage: Love Finds a Way." A kind of romance-fraught-with-problems feeling, plus a dash of happy-ending promise. All in all, a subject of potential interest to *Journal* readers, although hardly unique or necessarily dramatic. Here are the first two paragraphs:

Dee Dee Floyd, a vivacious, petite brunette, was 17 and a senior at Headland High School in an Atlanta suburb. John Kortes, tall, blond and reserved, was 19 and a sophomore at the University of Georgia. Both looked even younger, and they had been dating for only two months. But they were in love, and on January 3, 1964, they eloped. Their friends were surprised. Their parents were shocked. Dee Dee and John were ecstatic. They still are.

"We just couldn't wait," says Dee Dee with the excitement of a small girl.

The Korteses' best friends, the Greens, agree that Dee Dee and John did the right thing. Randy Green, who is also a teen-age husband, puts it like this: "You always think when someone quits school to get married it must be because of pregnancy. But sometimes it's just because they really want to be together, the way it was with Dee Dee and John."

Now the first part of the title tells the reader that this article will have relevance to the general subject of teen-age marriage. The first paragraph develops an immediate focus on Dee Dee and John in a compact, almost fictional narrative style. The second paragraph expands on their excitement and hopes; it also reassures the reader (consider the market) that this was not a "marriage of necessity."

And now it's high time to tell the reader just what it is that's going to keep him (or, in that magazine, her) interested in those two particular young people. Here it comes:

And John is, perhaps, the most pleased of all. "From our first date we knew we were going to get married," he says. It is one of many beliefs that John finds hard to explain and adults will find hard to understand. And yet it is no mystery. *Like most teen-age couples, John and Dee Dee decided, in effect, to do much of their growing up while they are married, not before. And so it is really not surprising that their thoughts and actions keep ranging from the remarkably innocent to the model of maturity.*

The last two sentences (italics added), promising the surprises and contrasts that were already written into the article, are the pivotal ones—and they were my editor's addition. I only had the good sense to recognize what they did and the good fortune to mumble something about their being magic sentences, thereby giving a name to an element of technique I had sometimes employed instinctively and have since benefited from using consciously in the articles I write.

I have, of course, used the magic-sentence approach in writing this piece. You might be interested to seek it out. You might even want to borrow it. You're more than welcome!

62

THE HISTORIAN AS ARTIST

By Barbara W. Tuchman

I would like to share some good news with you. I recently came back from skiing at Aspen in a party of three, which means that one was always odd man when riding in the double-chair ski lift. On one such occasion I rode with an advertising man from Chicago, who told me he was in charge of all copy for his firm in all media: TV, radio, *and* the printed word. On the strength of this he assured me—and I quote—that "Writing is coming back. *Books* are coming back." I cannot tell you how pleased I was, and I knew you would be too.

Now that we know the future is safe for writing, I want to talk about a particular kind of writer—the Historian—not just as historian but as artist, that is, as a creative writer on the same level as the poet or novelist. What follows will sound less immodest if you will take the word "artist" in the way I think of it, not as a form of praise but as a category, like clerk or laborer or actor.

Why is it generally assumed that in writing, the creative process is the exclusive property of poets and novelists? I would like to suggest that the thought applied by the historian to his subject matter can be no less creative than the imagination applied by the novelist to his. And when it comes to writing as an art, is Gibbon necessarily less of an artist in words than, let us say, Dickens? Or Winston Churchill less so than William Faulkner or Sinclair Lewis?

George Macaulay Trevelyan, the late professor of modern history at Cambridge and the great champion of literary as opposed to scientific history, said in a famous essay on his muse that ideally history should be the exposition of facts about the past, "in their full emotional and intellectual value to a wide public by the difficult art of literature." Notice "wide public." Trevelyan always stressed writing for the general reader as opposed to writing just for fellow scholars because he knew that when you write for the public you have to be *clear* and you have to be *interesting* and these are the two criteria which make for good writing. He had no patience with the idea that only imaginative writing is literature. Novels, he pointed out, if they are bad enough, are *not* literature, while even pamphlets, if they are good enough, and he cites those of Milton, Swift and Burke, are.

"The difficult art of literature" is well said. Trevelyan was a dirt farmer in that field and he knew. I may as well admit now that I have always *felt* like an artist when I work on a book but I did not think I ought to say so until someone else said it first (it's like waiting to be proposed to). Now that an occasional reviewer here and there has made the observation, I feel I can talk about it. I see no reason why the word should always be confined to writers of fiction and poetry while the rest of us are lumped together under that despicable term, Non-Fiction—as if we were some sort of remainder. I do not feel like a Non-something; I feel quite specific. I wish I could think of a name in place of Non-Fiction. In the hope of finding an antonym I looked up "Fiction" in Webster and found it defined as opposed to "Fact, Truth and Reality." I thought for a while of adopting FTR, standing for Fact, Truth and Reality, as my new term but it is awkward to use. "Writers of Reality" is the nearest I can come to what I want, but I cannot very well call us Realtors because that has been pre-empted—although as a matter of fact I would like to. "Real Estate," when you come to think of it, is a very fine phrase and it is exactly the sphere that writers of Non-Fiction deal in: the real estate of man, of human conduct. I wish we could get it back from the dealers in land. Then the categories could be poets, novelists and realtors.

I should add that I do not entirely go along with Webster's statement that fiction is what is distinct from Fact, Truth, and Reality because good fiction (as opposed to junk), even if it has nothing to do with fact, is usually *founded* on reality and *perceives* truth—often more truly than some historians. It is exactly this quality of perceiving truth, extracting it from irrelevant surroundings and conveying it to the reader or the viewer of a picture, which distinguishes the artist. What the artist has is an *extra* vision and an *inner* vision plus the ability to express it. He supplies a view or an understanding that the viewer or reader would not have gained without the aid of the artist's creative vision. This is what Monet does in one of those shimmering rivers reflecting poplars or El Greco in the stormy sky over Toledo or Jane Austen compressing a whole society into Mr. and Mrs. Bennet, Lady Catherine and Mr. Darcy. We realtors, at least those of us who aspire to write literature, do the same thing. Lytton Strachey perceived a truth about Queen Victoria and the Eminent Victorians and the style and form which he created to portray what he saw have changed the whole approach to biography since his time. Rachel Carson perceived truth about the seashore or the silent spring, Thoreau about Walden Pond, De Tocqueville and James Bryce about America, Gibbon about Rome, Karl Marx about Capital, Carlyle about the French Revolution. Their work is based on study, observation and accumulation of fact, but does anyone suppose that these realtors did not make use of their imagination? Certainly they did; that is what gave them their extra vision.

Art Buchwald, by the way who started out as a comedian but now frequently produces genuinely creative political satire, is a realtor who has made himself a creative writer by exercising his imagination upon observed fact. It may not be satire in the grand manner on the human condition like *Candide* or *Gulliver's Travels,* but it has that quality of being both perceptive and suggestive which seems to me the mark of the artist.

Trevelyan wrote that the best historian was he who combined knowledge of the evidence with "the largest intellect, the warmest human sympathy and the highest imaginative powers." The last two qualities are no different from those necessary to a great novelist. They are a necessary part of the historian's equipment because they are what enable him to *understand* the evidence he has accumulated. Imagination stretches the available facts—extrapolates from them, so to speak, thus often supplying an otherwise missing answer to the "Why" of what happened. Sympathy is essential to the understanding of motive. Without sympathy and imagination the historian can copy figures from a tax roll forever—or count them by computer as they do nowadays—but he will never know or be able to portray the people who paid the taxes.

When I say that I felt like an artist, I mean that I constantly found myself perceiving a historical truth (at least, what *I* believe to be truth) by seizing upon a suggestion; then, after careful gathering of the evidence, conveying it in turn to the reader, not by piling up a list of all the facts I have collected, which is the way of the Ph.D., but by exercising the artist's privilege of selection.

Actually the idea for my book *The Proud Tower* evolved in that way from a number of such perceptions. The initial impulse was a line I quoted in *The Guns of August* from Belgian Socialist poet Émile Verhaeren. After a lifetime as a pacifist dedicated to the social and humanitarian ideals which were then believed to erase national lines, he found himself filled with hatred of the German invader and disillusioned in all he had formerly believed in. And yet, as he wrote, "Since it seems to me that in this state of hatred my conscience becomes diminished, I dedicate these pages, with emotion, to the man I used to be."

I was deeply moved by this. His confession seemed to me so poignant, so evocative of a time and mood that it decided me to try to retrieve that vanished era. It led to the last chapter in *The Proud Tower* on the Socialists, to Jaures as the authentic Socialist, to his prophetic lines, "I summon the living, I mourn the dead," and to his assassination as the perfect and dramatically right ending for the book, both chronologically and symbolically.

Then there was Lord Ribblesdale. I owe this to *American Heritage* which, back in October, 1961, published a piece on Sargent and Whistler with a handsome reproduction of the Ribblesdale portrait. In Sargent's painting Ribblesdale stared out upon the world, as I later wrote in *The Proud Tower*, "in an attitude of such natural arrogance, elegance and self-confidence as no man of a later day would ever achieve." Here too was a vanished era which came together in my mind with Verhaeren's line, "the man I used to be"—like two globules of mercury making a single mass. From that came the idea for the book. Ribblesdale, of course, was the suggestion that ultimately became the opening chapter on The Patricians. This is the reward of the artist's eye: it always leads you to the right thing.

There are, I think, three parts to the artist's creative process: the extra vision with which he perceives a truth and conveys it by suggestion. Second, medium of expression: language for writers, paint for painters, clay or stone for sculptors, sound expressed in musical notes for composers. Third, design or structure.

When it comes to language, nothing is more satisfying than to write a good sentence. It is no fun to write lumpishly, dully, in prose the reader must plod through like wet sand. But it is a pleasure to achieve, if one can, a clear running prose that is simple yet full of surprises. This does not just happen. It requires skill, hard work, a good ear and continued practice, as much as it takes Heifetz to play the violin. The goals, as I have said, are clarity, interest and aesthetic pleasure. On the first of these I would like to quote Macaulay, a great historian and great writer, who once wrote to a friend, "How little the all-important art of making meaning pellucid is studied now! Hardly any popular writer except myself thinks of it."

As to structure, my own form is narrative, which is not every historian's, I may say—indeed it is rather looked down on now by the advanced academics, but I don't mind because no one could possibly persuade me that telling a story is not the most desirable thing a writer can do. Narrative history is neither as simple nor as straightforward as it might seem. It requires arrangement, composition, planning just like a painting—Rembrandt's "Night Watch," for example. He did not fit in all those figures with certain ones in the foreground and others in back and the light falling on them just so, without much trial and error and innumerable preliminary sketches. It is the same with writing history. Although the finished result may look to the reader natural and inevitable, as if the author had only to follow the sequence of events, it is not that easy. Sometimes events at different places are simultaneous in time—as in the case of the battles on the Eastern and Western fronts and at sea in *The Guns of August*. This presents a problem in sequence.

In *The Proud Tower,* for instance, the two English chapters were originally conceived as one. I divided them and placed them well apart in order to give a feeling of progression, of forward chronological movement to the book. The story of the Anarchists with their ideas and deeds set in counterpoint to each other was a problem in arrangement. The middle section of The Hague chapter on the Paris Exposition of 1900 was originally planned as a separate short centerpiece, marking the turn of the century, until I saw it as a bridge linking the two Hague Conferences, where it now seems to belong.

Structure is chiefly a problem of selection, an agonizing business because there is always more material than one can use or fit into a story. The problem is how and what to select out of all that happened without, by the very process of selection, giving an over- or under-emphasis which violates truth. One cannot put in everything: the result would be a shapeless mass. The job is to achieve a narrative line without straying from the essential facts or leaving out any essential facts and without twisting the material to suit one's convenience. To do so is a temptation but if you do it with history you invariably get tripped up by later events. I have been tempted once or twice and I know.

The most difficult task of selection I had was in the Dreyfus chapter. To try to skip over the facts about the *bordereau* and the handwriting and the forgeries—all the elements of the Case as distinct from the Affair—in order to focus instead on what happened to France and yet at the same time give the reader enough background information to enable him to understand what was going on, nearly drove me to despair. My writing slowed down to a trickle until one dreadful day when I went to my study at 9 and stayed there all day in a blank coma until 5 when I emerged without having written a single word. Anyone who is a writer will know how frightening that was. You feel you have come to the end of your powers; you will not finish the book; you may never write again.

There are other problems of structure peculiar to writing history: how to explain background and yet keep the story moving; how to create suspense and sustain interest in a narrative of which the outcome (like who won the war) is, to put it mildly, known. If anyone thinks this does not take creative writing, I can only say, try it.

63

TITLES THAT TANTALIZE

By Kathryn M. Wilson

Having title trouble, especially with articles? Best you can do is "Schools Face Trouble," or "Snakes Are Interesting," or "Honesty Is the Best Policy"? Don't turn the page! Here are some available sources for titles that tantalize.

Look through the Bible. You'll find many expressions, warnings, proverbs, and phrases that will dress up your article instantly. Some can be changed effectively to blend with the subject matter. The familiar "Am I my brother's keeper?" changed to "Am I My Mother's Keeper?" would make an ideal title for an article on the problem of care for aged parents, so much in demand now. Also, either the first half or the last half of "Many are called but few are chosen" would aptly fit a career preparation article. Other possibilities to consider: "Heed your own heart's counsel," "A time of calamity," or "Train a boy in the way he would go."

Keep on hand a copy of the complete works of Shakespeare. Almost every page contains at least one phrase which would make a good title for an article. From Portia's "quality of mercy" speech alone, in *The Merchant of Venice,* have come many inspirations for titles. Titles have come from the "Tomorrow, and tomorrow, and tomorrow" speech in *Macbeth,* and "To be, or not to be," in *Hamlet.* You can find hundreds of less well-known phrases for titles in other Shakespearean plays: "mortal instruments" (*Julius Caesar*); "the worst of words" (*Othello*); "mechanic slaves" (*Antony and Cleopatra*); "bounds of modesty" (*Romeo and Juliet*).

Of course you have a copy of Bartlett's *Familiar Quotations.* It is a gold mine for the non-fiction writer, not only for quotes but also for title ideas. You can search the index under subject matter or key words and find excellent quotations which can be cut in half, turned around, or changed to fit the article. As you go through the book, you'll come across many familiar phrases that have already been used as titles of articles; therefore, try to choose an original arrangement for your own use.

More sources? Nursery rhymes and fairy tales are studded with good titles. Examples: "Ten O'Clock Scholar" (I used that one myself for a school article); "Sleeping Beauty," "Little Boys in Blue," "Pocketful of Rye" (this has been used frequently, as in, "Pocketful of Money," "Pocketful of Herbs," etc.).

Alliteration, which means the repeating of the same sounds or letters in several words, is an excellent way to form a title. For example: "Barbie's Baubles" (about Barbara Hutton's famous jewels); "Kids, Kisses, and Kindergarten" (my own, covering a get-ready-for-school article). And "Tears, Teens, and Trouble," or "A Whiz at Wisdom," etc. Try your own!

Still stumped? Song titles are full of suggestions, too. Change a word or two, and come up with a catchy title. "My Old Unlucky Home" (nostalgia piece). "Hello, Trolley!" (history of trolley cars). "Tiptoe Through Your Own Tulips" (simple article on raising lovely tulips). "Whittle While You Work" (exercising while doing housework).

Now for some quickies: Proverbs and axioms have been done to death, but you still can come up with some good ones. "Make Sure Your Policy Is an Honest One" (insurance racket warnings), or "Taste Makes Waist" (dieting advice). See how it works?

Also to consider: slogans, colors, school phrases like "ABC's of . . ."; plays, speeches, advertisements, science, and history. The Declaration of Independence, the Constitution, and Lincoln's Gettysburg Address are full of good ideas for titles. Lately, too, many articles have titles related to outer space, containing words like "countdown," "rockets," etc. Some good titles have been devised from the latest teen-age expressions—"cloud 9," "dig it," "get with it," etc.

Everyday exclamations can be turned into titles. For instance, "sakes alive" turns into "Snakes Alive"; "gosh darn it" can be "It's easy: darn it!" (advice on easy mending); "for Pete's sake" slides into "For Heat's Sake" (proper furnace maintenance). Get the drift?

There you are. If you try these methods, you may sometimes feel it's easier to find a title than to write the article itself. And sometimes the methods will actually trigger ideas for new articles—that is, you'll find a good title and write an article to fit it!

64

THE CRAFT OF POETRY

By Arthur Gregor

As AN editor responsible for the poetry list of a major New York publishing house, and as a frequent leader of poetry workshops, I have had to concern myself, to grapple with, the one consideration that precedes all others in evaluating and studying poems—a manuscript of them or individual ones. There are of course many considerations that go into the creation of a successful poem or book of poems, but to me none is as telling, none as critical as *clarity*.

One may well ask, just what is meant by clarity in connection with poetry? There are many celebrated poems—such as Eliot's *The Waste Land* or Wallace Stevens' *Le Monocle de Mon Oncle* —whose literal meanings do not immediately reveal themselves; and there are many examples of bad poems whose literal meanings are apparent at once but whose poetic qualities of any distinction are totally wanting. Clarity in poetry, then, is not merely the clear articulation of literal meanings; rather it is the poet's clarity of *intention*—his ability to articulate this intention verbally.

In trying to understand the process by which a poem comes into being, it is safe to assume that the process starts with the desire to create, to embody into a poem a perception, a feeling, a state of being, an experience. Whatever that original impulse is, it should be allowed to emerge and assert itself forcefully, and the writer should identify with it totally during the emergence of the poem.

There is, then, first this clarity—reality might be a better term —of intention, reality of intention, of first impulse, and next the clarity of articulation. The two, reality of intention and clarity of articulation, combine to make up the major overall consideration in both the writing and the evaluating of a poem: clarity of intention.

This clarity of intention—since it represents the overall means by which a poem conveys itself, comes across—depends not only upon precise, literal meanings by which the literal component of the poem is expressed, but relies as well on another element in a good poem, namely *tone*.

Precise language may convey accurate literal meanings, but for a poem, the language must be chosen not only to convey the literal intentions but the tone as well.

Any good poem has its own musical fabric. This comes about by selecting words in such a way that the aural demands for the poem are met as well as the literal ones. Like a musical composition or a painting, a poem is cast in a certain key. The good poet makes sure that the key, the tone, the entire intention of the poem is indicated right off, in the first words, in the first line, if possible. Once that is established, then the tone and the meaning are further developed, allowing the poem to emerge.

The literal meaning of the poem as such is perhaps the least significant aspect of the total poem. What is most significant is the poem's total meaning, of which the literal one is only a part. In the best poem, the literal meaning is merely suggested. In the best poem, the meaning of the poem is the recognition of a human experience. Sharp visual clarity, a good ear, conciseness—all of these combine in a good poem to allow its meaning to reverberate from start to finish, and to leave a deep impression. That meaning is by no means merely literal—no more, no less than the sight of a flower in sunshine, of a leaf on water; the heart beating at the sudden sight of these can be said to have only literal meaning. A poem is a totality, a creation, a self-contained reality.

Therefore, it must have its own organic life—its spine, its structure, its tonal fabric. That all of this can be achieved by an arrangement of words makes poetry the awesome and difficult art that it is.

With sounds the composer creates a feeling, a state of being; with color the painter conveys an impression; with words the poet transforms nature and the world into a human statement.

There is another element without which clarity can never be achieved. What the poem aims to convey is, in a good poem, never merely thought up, never merely imagined; the good poem is the embodiment of that which *is*. The more deeply felt the poem, the closer the poet is to the reality of his intention, the more shared the experience generated will be, the more universal.

The good poem aims to articulate the poetic reality inherent in human consciousness shared by all, one and the same in all. Only the poem can speak for the poetic strain inherent in that common consciousness—and that is its ultimate function, its meaning.

Since poetry revolves around an inherent poetic reality, creating a poem cannot—strictly speaking—be taught any more than seeing or hearing can. However, although the poetic reality is a universal one—as is that of light and sound—once expressed, once formed, it differs as individual personalities differ.

It is the basic poetic reality that impels an individual to attempt the creation of a poem. It is his own unique personality that will give his poems their own unique quality. Therefore, in the process of creating his work, he is giving *voice* to his own poetic personality. While this cannot be taught as such, the proper teacher will help to stimulate the individual's poetic personality and can suggest the paths an emerging poet can take in allowing his poetic personality, his own voice, to come forth.

Perhaps *style* is nothing but that voice. But style does involve *technique,* and technique is something that the experienced teacher —presumably an experienced poet—can help the emerging poet to discover.

It is all a process of discovery: the poetry that is there like water in the earth, and the craft by which that water can be brought to the surface. The truly engaged young poet is as much in love with the craft as with the basic element, the poetry itself. The two are obviously totally interdependent: the individual's poetic personality, and his craft. One cannot be achieved without the other. The poetic personality cannot be taught, and its emergence by means of craft can only be suggested.

Everything that is said about poetics—poetry and its craft—is bound to be general and abstract unless applied to a specific poem, a book, or a poet's body of work. Like life itself, poetry cannot be defined. There are of course many definitions and each may be correct in itself, but no one single definition can suffice. Yet, it is possible to take a poem that succeeds and to point out why that is so; and similarly why that is not so.

Ultimately the good poem is like an object. It has its own reality, stands on its own, is fixed within its own laws, solid as rock protrusions in a stream, yet yielding, flowing like the stream itself.

In a session of emerging poets conducted by an experienced poet, much excitement can be generated by looking at their poems, studying them as objects that are made, delighting in them as in a work of jade, shaping or discarding those whose clay is not quite right, or hopelessly misformed. But this has value only if it contributes to the process of the emerging poet's self-discovery. What is this discovery but the ever clearer recognition of the poetic component in the life experience?

During some workshop sessions I conducted this past year, the discussion of a poem by one of the workshop members frequently faded out into silence. A point of understanding—assent, silence— had been reached in the analysis of the process that had brought forth the poem. During these moments, I would frequently find myself turning to the large windows that looked out on the hills of the campus, gentle green slopes over which the late afternoon sun had cast bright, yet deep and darkening shades. I would then see some students crossing one of the roads that divided the campus, other young men and women lying on the lawns, some sitting there heads bent over a book, or sometimes a guitar. Without saying a word about it, everyone in the room surely understood, surely felt that what we had been concerning ourselves with for weeks inside that room was deeply connected with the world we turned to just then, with what we saw looking out—the sunny hills, the quiet life of the campus late in the afternoon.

65

HOW TO WRITE GOOD POETRY
AND GET IT PUBLISHED

By L. E. Sissman

CAN you write good poetry? I don't know; not everybody can. But there are ways to test the verse you've written to find out if it's good or not. First, there's the freshness test. Read over a poem you've written. Is there any phrase or image in it that is completely fresh and apt—that doesn't resemble anything else you've read before? Be objective; if you can still answer yes, you may have something as a poet. Second, there's the compression test. Write one of your poems out as a single prose paragraph. Does it read like prose? If it does, it's not a poem in the first place. But if, on the other hand, it's too terse and compact and energetic for prose, perhaps you're really a poet. Third, there's the influence test. Write down the names of the ten poets whose work means the most to you—not just important names, but people whose work holds deep meaning for you and influences what you write and how you think about poetry. O. K. Now get hold of a copy of Mark Strand's recent book, *The Contemporary American Poets,* and see how many of your favorites are included. If it's fewer than four or five, your influences are not contemporary—and your verse is probably not close enough to the mainstream of what's being written now to be good, at least by contemporary standards. There may be a few poets who are exceptions to this rule; there aren't many.

But suppose you've passed these tests. Suppose you feel very deeply that you do have a talent for poetry, and that you want to pursue it. Then, obviously, your object should be to produce a body of poems—and to get them published. I'll deal with these two points in turn, using my own (admittedly very subjective) experience as a rough guide to what you might expect.

377

Some years ago, I found myself with a suspected poetic talent and, at the age of thirty-five, not much to show for it. I had won a poetry prize in college; I'd published a few poems in little magazines; I had a thin sheaf of verse written ten to fifteen years before. I decided it was then or never; that if I did have talent, I would have to prove it in my thirties or forget it. So I sat down with the very cold-blooded, hard-headed objective of writing as well as I could and as much as I could, beginning right then and there. It wasn't very easy, as you might expect. But I had three invaluable assets to help me get started again. First, time. I could spare two evenings a week to concentrate on writing; every Tuesday and Thursday from eight to ten, I wrote. Second, a helpful wife. She understood what I was doing and made a time and place for me to do it in. Third, a friend. One who had a good knowledge of poetry and was willing to spend a lot of time and effort to read what I had written, to criticize and encourage me.

These three assets got me over the first hurdle: I found myself actually writing poems and slowly building up a file of them. I learned that it was absolutely necessary for me to begin with a firm idea of what the poem was about and what I wanted it to say; in addition, I learned never to set the first line down on paper until I had worked it out to my complete satisfaction in my mind. Having avoided a false start, I found it easier to go on to the next lines with confidence. And as I worked on these lines, I often found a kind of exhilaration coming over me—a feeling of excitement that the poem was beginning to shape itself, to dictate its own form, so to speak, and to carry me along with it until the end, when my own judgment would reassert itself to provide an apt ending.

At first, because the material seemed simpler to work with, I concentrated on nature poems—short quatrains about things I'd observed in the small town where I live. These soon grew into sonnets, then into sequences of sonnets. Then I began writing longer poems in four-line rhyming stanzas—and my subject matter began to expand. I found myself writing poems about my own experiences in school and college and afterward. I found myself developing that very important (and elusive) thing, a tone and style. In my case, this tone was dry, amused, analytical, a little above, in a mocking way, the experiences it described. The style made use of impacted bits of diction—sharp and smooth edges of language thrown together in such a way as to create a fresh impression of sound unlike, I hoped, anything the reader had heard before. To this I added dialogue, mimicry of sounds, parody of and allusion to other poets of every period. And the whole mix began to develop an individuality, a personality, of its own.

At this point I badly needed the outside encouragement of publishing something—somewhere, anywhere. Fortunately, it materialized. An old friend called and asked if a poem I had written years before could be printed in an English magazine of which he was an American editor. I said yes, of course; and this tiny encouragement was enough to keep me going for a while. But eventually, I knew, I would have to publish one or more of my new poems in order to establish the validity of what I was trying to do. This wasn't easy. I had to decide on my markets and besiege them with poems, in the hope that one would eventually yield and publish something. Rather than scatter my poems broadcast over dozens of literary magazines, I determined to aim high and to send them only to a few publications I particularly respected—*The New Yorker, The Atlantic, Harper's, The Kenyon Review, The Hudson Review,* and a couple of others. It was my plan to send each poem to each magazine on this list until the editors would at least become familiar with my name and style. This I did. For six months or more, I sent each new poem off to these magazines—and garnered a desk full of the usual printed rejection slips. But then a subtle change began to happen: one of the editors sent me a scrawled note of rejection instead of a printed slip; another sent me a typewritten letter of regret, with a request to see more poems. Apparently I was beginning to make some sort of impression. Four more months went by. Then, suddenly, *The New Yorker,* a magazine known for its careful reading of manuscripts submitted by unpublished writers, wrote to say that they were taking a short group of three poems; soon after, *The Atlantic* accepted a sequence of four sonnets. Next, an idea for a light, topical poem occurred to me; I wrote it in one afternoon and rushed it off to *The New Yorker.* They took it, too.

All this was more than enough to make me really serious about my writing. I began to turn out verse in quantity; in the year following my first acceptances, I must have written over 2,500 lines of poetry, much of which was, in turn, accepted by the magazines I had set my sights on. At this point, I became increasingly indebted to the poetry editors of these magazines, not only for accepting my work in the first place, but also for their skilled and excellent criticism and editorial comment, which often rescued a poem from failure. In the years since, I have come to value their judgment and to welcome their suggestions on everything I write.

Today, I still write verse (along with articles and book reviews) at a pretty consistent rate. I try to make every poem strong enough and different enough to warrant publication; then I try to get it published in one of the magazines where most of my work appears. So far, I've been most fortunate; about 75% of the poems I've written since 1964 have seen publication, and I still have hopes for some of the others. I have published three books of verse.

That, in a few hundred words, is my story. Now, let's get back to yours. At the beginning of this article, I suggested a few objective tests to determine whether you're capable of writing poetry that can be published in this day and age. Assuming that you're still reading this article because you have passed these tests, I have some more advice for you.

Though no two people, and certainly no two poets, are alike, the experience I've just outlined suggests that I've run across some basic rules that any aspiring poet can profitably follow. Let me list these and comment briefly on them.

1. *Make writing a habit.* Fortunately for all of us, good habits are as easy to get into as bad ones, and just as hard to break. If you make it an ironclad rule to spend a certain number of hours writing on one or two specific days a week—if you treat it as a hard-and-fast schedule—you'll soon find yourself with a good habit on your hands. Even if you don't have a specific writing project in mind each time you sit down, you'll discover that the leisure to think and concentrate will generate new ideas for you—ideas that will soon turn into words on the page. I don't have a lot of advice about time of day; you should just pick a time that will let you work, free of outside distractions, for a minimum of two hours at a sitting. If that's early morning or late at night, so be it. As far as writing materials are concerned, I'd recommend against a typewriter, on the grounds that typewritten copy seems so final and

unchangeable; it's better, I think, to use an ordinary #2 pencil with a good eraser.

2. *Write about what you know.* This is an ancient rule for writers of all kinds. It's still a good one. The material of poetry is not far-flung, exotic, romantic. It's your own life, what's under your nose.

3. *Think it through before you write it down.* Even with a nice, erasable #2 pencil, words have a way of crystallizing on the page once you've put them down. So don't put them down in the first place until you're reasonably sure of the form they're going to take —and the effect they're going to make. Oh, sure, detail changes and revisions are fine. But make sure that the basic structure is sound before you commit it to paper. This will save you many a false start and a dead end, especially as it applies to the beginning of a poem —and the ending. But even in the middle, when everything is (or seems to be) plain sailing, think before you write.

4. *Concentrate on those beginnings and endings.* As I've said before, those are really the parts of the poem where you're on your own; the middle tends to write itself. So labor hard and long to make every opening a model of power, grace, and impact, and to make every close a model of finality and rightness—the only possible ending for that particular poem.

5. *Use form to help you get started.* You may be absolutely dedicated to the idea of yourself as a stunning free-verse poet, but you'll find it a lot easier to start your career if you begin by working in traditional forms—the pentameter line, the couplet, the rhymed quatrain, the sonnet. Why? Because, paradoxically, following these forms makes less work for you, leaves less for you to think about, frees you to concentrate on the content rather than the form. Most free-verse poems are fiendishly difficult to write, precisely because you have to make up both form and content as you go along; conversely, a formal poem does part of the job for you by presenting you with a ready-made jig, so to speak, to assemble the words in. Also, there's this to consider: you wouldn't attempt to be a great abstract artist without first studying the rudiments of perspective, composition, and anatomy; by the same token, you shouldn't attempt to become a free-verse poet without first studying the traditional forms in which nearly all of the great

English poets have written. It's part of your basic training, no matter what kind of poet you may eventually become.

6. *Get expert criticism.* Unless you're far more objective than most of us, you can't hope to evaluate your progress all by yourself. You need some guidance from an expert. If you're lucky, as I was, you'll have a friend who can supply the needed—and continuing —criticism of your developing verse. If not, seek out such a person: perhaps the instructor in a poetry course at a local evening college or school of adult education. Secure his interest; show him your work over a period of time; take his advice and act on it.

7. *Pick your markets and bombard them.* I'll repeat for emphasis: select the places you'd like to be published; send each of them in turn every new poem you write, once you think you've reached a publishable level. Keep bombarding these chosen markets with your work; sooner or later, if you have an individual voice to offer, somebody will start to listen—and start to encourage you. Read *The Writer* to keep up on poetry markets; go to the library and familiarize yourself with the actual magazines, so you'll know whom you're submitting to and what they expect of their contributors.

8. *Keep at it.* Few poets burst into prominence overnight. Nearly all labor in obscurity for years before they find a market and an audience. You will have to do this, too. And it's not easy. But the right combination of hope, self-confidence, doggedness, and humility can keep you going until the day you get your first acceptance. And that time isn't wasted: in those long weeks and months when your work is unknown except to yourself and perhaps one mentor, you're actually dedicating yourself to the task of perfecting your outlook, your viewpoint, your style and technique, the individual voice you're striving for. In the time of obscurity, the real poet is made. It is, as the adage says, always darkest just before the dawn.

66

A POET'S LETTER
TO A BEGINNER

By May Sarton

You have given me a sheaf of your first poems to read. Are they real poems, you would like to know? And if so, where shall you send them, and how does a young poet get published?

You have just discovered the excitement of seeing before you on a page, separated from yourself, and ready to be given to the world as a gift, a piece of your mind and heart. These first poems seem altogether wonderful to you. You are still astonished, perhaps, at how easy it was to write them, once you got started. You have read them aloud to some of your friends, and they have been most encouraging. You have a strong suspicion that you are a genius, and in your heart of hearts what you hope from me is an accolade. You do not really want criticism any more than someone bringing me a bunch of flowers, and saying, "I grew these myself" wants it. You want to be welcomed into the company of poets, *now,* without further ado. And you hope I shall say, "Let me send these wonderful poems to *The Atlantic Monthly.* They will surely be eager to print them."

If I did not take you seriously I might just brush you off with a few words of easy praise. I might not feel that I had either time or energy to put my mind on your work, as if it were my own. Perhaps you have no idea (I did not at your age) how many such requests an established writer gets, and how hard we have to fight for time to do our own work. It would be easy to spend one's life answering letters, alas! I am taking the time to tell you honestly what I think because although these are not poems yet, in my judgment, they are perhaps the seeds of true poems. I hope that you will come to respect them as seeds, yourself, and give them the care such vital life should command.

Let us take a cold hard look at these pages, at what has actually been put down there in black and white. I am struck at once by the fact that you do *think* in *images,* that your instinctive tendency is to move from the abstract to the concrete. If there is one single quality that tells me you may become a poet, it is this. For before words enter in, concepts exist. The philosopher's kind of mind desires the general and the abstract; the poet's mind desires the specific and the concrete: "to see the world in a grain of sand." You say, for instance, "fire engine color" about an autumn leaf. About love you say, "Bells pealed in my head when I saw you walk down the street." (I shall' come back to these images later.)

It looks to me as if a few rhymes came rather easily to you, and you have used these, scattered them around among lines that otherwise have no form, at random as it were. When you tried to follow through on a rhyme or to create a stanza, you had the sense that your precious feeling was being distorted, that to use a formal metrical pattern would be to force it to submit to a Procrustean bed. And this seemed to you not only a kind of dishonesty toward your "inspiration," but actually to do it violence.

First, let me say that rhyming is the least important element in English poetry, although the mastery of it is a challenge and a fruitful one, as one proceeds. (Keats has written a superb unrhymed sonnet, for instance.) What is important is the shape and weight of the poem as a whole, to sense this; the rhythm of the idea is important. The tone is important. I do not get the feeling from your poems that you have given much thought or attention to these matters.

You have, I fear, mistaken the signposts for the destination. It is quite true that when we are in a "writing state," lines and phrases float up and demand to be put down. Some of this is flotsam and jetsam; some of it may turn out to be pure gold. And I would go so far as to say that if nothing is "given" in this way, at the beginning, there will be no poem. But these "given" lines and images that come pouring out without your will are signposts. They help you to find the direction of the poem. Sometimes a single "given" line may suggest a metre; it may even groove the movement of the whole poem. But in themselves, these "gifts" are only communications from your subconscious to you, the maker, the fashioner. They are not communications to a reader.

If I have confidence in your talent, it is because as *first drafts,* these poems have real potential. It seems to me that you see the way a poet sees, and feel the way a poet feels. But you have not yet come to grips with the *fashioning* of your vision. At present you are a poet with no, or very little, *craft*.

How does one learn craft? You will perhaps think it a compliment if I tell you that I see no influences on your work; I do not sense its roots from a craft point of view. We learn our craft by studying other poets. The rebel must know very well what he is rebelling against for the rebellion to be meaningful; sometimes our best masters are those with whom we violently disagree, and against whom we sharpen our wits. Influence is not imitation. It is more fertile and subtle than that, and less conscious. It comes about when we are driven to possess another poet, to absorb him or her as if he were a necessary food.

Have you ever gone really deeply into a single poet, living or dead? By "deeply," I mean beyond just reading for pleasure, or even learning by heart . . . I mean studying the way a young baseball pitcher studies the great pitchers. I can't help wondering. My guess is that you have felt an affinity for a few of your immediate contemporaries, poets who have chosen to break away from form. They appear to you to be more "honest" than their immediate elders, such as Richard Wilbur, whom you call, no doubt, "academic." You want, instead, the naked raw stuff of experience itself. But what you forget is that no work of art *is* experience in that sense; it is something else, something that gives us the illusion of "reality." Craft is the means by which we create the illusion of "the naked raw stuff." If you choose to deny yourself all the magic and charms that severe forms release for a reader, you have got to find a substitute for them. At present, the substitute seems to be shock, shouting, violence of language—and the danger is that shock cannot be *renewed*. A poem may shock once at first reading, but it will not shock a second time: we have "had" it. One of the great values of poetry is that it provides an *indefinitely renewable experience*.

The renewal of craft often occurs when a poet reaches back in time to the generation before—or several generations before—his immediate ancestors. So T. S. Eliot, for instance, revitalized English poetry when he rediscovered, as usable for his purposes, the metaphysical poets, and especially John Donne. There is a huge rich past for you to discover for yourself. My advice is, study both poets whom you instinctively like, and also those whom you instinctively hate. Those you dislike will help you to define and recognize what you yourself wish to aim for.

Each poet has to discover his own true *voice*. And he does this not by instinct, as a bird sings, for bird songs are monotonous and repetitive, but by discovering the past that is usable for him, given his nature and his own relation to his times, and by allowing himself to be fertilized by it. If what you are after is a sort of naked honesty, a thrust, a shock, it might be worth looking Wyatt up again. If you are tired of the long iambic line and feel that it sounds musty, it might be worth looking into Skelton—and, at the opposite pole, Gerard Manley Hopkins. You will pour your own "shocking" language into these old bottles, and the mixture, I think, might be rather potent.

What I hope to suggest to you is that analysis precedes synthesis. The time to exercise your powers of analysis is when you are *not* writing poems, not in a state of inspiration. It is no use, for instance, to decide suddenly to write a sonnet, look up the form in a dictionary, and set to work. But if you have at your command the sonnets of Milton, Shakespeare, Donne, Hopkins, you will perhaps recognize a sonnet idea when you *are* in a state of inspiration, and there will be no need to look anything up. The sonnet form will be there in your subconscious ready to be used. Just as a tennis player does not wait to learn the backhand drive when he is in the midst of a tournament. He has practiced it for hours so when he is actually playing he can forget all about "technique."

More than most of us willingly recognize, the art of writing poetry demands thought. If you will look into Gerard Manley Hopkins' letters, or Dylan Thomas' to Vernon Watkins, or John Keats's or T. S. Eliot's essays you will see this kind of thinking at work. In fact, I would go so far as to say that the process of writing a poem is a process by which we think our feelings out, just as it is also a process by which we feel our thoughts out.

But let us get back now to your own work. I would like to see you learn to test these poems. Against what? Against your own feeling, first of all. There is something wrong for me about naming the color of an autumn leaf, "fire engine color." Why? Because "fire engine" is such a powerful image that what I see is not "bright red," as you intended, but a large red *machine*. The luminosity of leaves is not that of a hard reflecting surface like painted metal, but comes from their transparence. So your image, instead of making us see autumn leaves, does not do its "work"; it makes us see a fire engine instead! What looks strong at first sight turns out to be weak.

A good metaphor surprises us into recognition by bringing together two apparently dissimilar things which are exactly alike *in one respect*. Its explosive power has to do with the distance and exactness. Carl Sandburg's "Fish crier, dangling herring before prospective customers, evincing a joy identical with that of Pavlova dancing" is an example of what I mean. Your image of the "peal of bells" comes closer to this explosiveness than the "fire engine" did. The shock of seeing someone you love might be described in terms of a quick loud *sound*. What troubles me is the "peal," which suggests something that goes on for an interval; what you need is a sound that "shocks," on the instant.

You see, the process of revision is exciting because by means of it, we come to understand more and more about the experience itself. It is a process of self-discovery. And we know only when we come to the end of the poem—after perhaps thirty revisions—what it is really about.

Very well, you may say, but how then does one know when a poem is finished? Is there not a danger of killing it, of over-manipulating? The answer is, yes, there is a risk. There is always a risk. But in time you come to recognize when there is nothing more to "discover," when the poem survives all tests you can think up, and stands there, a complex singing *whole*. Far more poems go dead because the writer of them did not know how to push the limits, than because the writer lost his impetus and became a mere manipulator. Technique is never, once and for all, "learned." For as we ourselves grow and change, our craft also changes and grows. It is possible sometimes to master all that is needed for a specific poem, but the next one will require a whole new set of trials and triumphs.

By now, perhaps I have answered your second question. "Where shall I send these poems?" Send them home to yourself. Keep them. Think and feel them through. They are not ready to send out. They are seeds.

But the time will come, in a few years, when you will surely have a sheaf of true poems ready. Then what? You need the sense of achievement and the recognition that only publication can bring. And you are bound to suffer. For you will find that people like me who have been kind to you while you were still an amateur, will suddenly, if they are editors, become quite ruthless. For it is not you in relation to your own poems that is at stake, but your poems in relation to those of every established poet. You have never stopped to ask yourself, I presume, how many poems a day pour into the *Atlantic* offices, and how very few can be published—two or three in each monthly issue. You are preparing to crash into a world beside which the business world is child's play, from a competitive point of view. For every village and town in the country contains consumers of almost every product *except* poetry. In Finland, a literate country compared with ours, a book of poems by a young poet may sell 6,000 copies; here, only the top five, those who have already won major prizes, can hope to sell even half that many.

But fortunately there is a saving grace: the "little" magazines. *Beloit Poetry Journal, The Lyric, Poetry Northwest* and dozens of others—are always on the lookout for new poets. Try to remember that rejection will not mean that your poems are no good, any more than a few acceptances will mean that you are an authentic genius! As a young poet, you will oscillate between arrogance and despair. Both are expensive emotions. But in the end—this I think can be said with assurance—if you are a true poet, you will be published.

What is beautiful about the life of a poet is that it is still gratuitous. No one, not even Robert Frost, is able to earn a living only through publishing poetry. The only reason for writing poetry is because you *have* to, because it is what gives you joy. At best even glory is a by-product. Write because you need to find out what you really mean; write because you want to define your experience and because you want to communicate it to your friends. If they turn out someday to be counted in thousands, then you are lucky. But you are lucky *now* to have the wish, and to begin to learn about the skill, to do what in any age, in any country, very, very few people ever achieve. So let me welcome you, dear young poet, not into the company of the angels, but into the great company of those who work for joy alone, the poets. . . .

67

THE EXPERIENCE OF THE POEM

BY ANN STANFORD

ONE may think of the ingredients of a good poem as an experience and a fresh perception of that experience. The experience need not be original or new, but the perception should be. Think of Gerard Manley Hopkins' delight in spring, a feeling old as humanity, couched in the freshest of images:

> Nothing is so beautiful as spring—
> When weeds, in wheels, shoot long and lovely and lush;
> Thrush's eggs look little low heavens, and thrush
> Through the echoing timber does so rinse and wring
> The ear, it strikes like lightnings to hear him sing;
> The glassy peartree leaves and blooms, they brush
> The descending blue; that blue is all in a rush
> With richness; the racing lambs too have fair their fling.

Hopkins' language is vital because his feeling about spring is intense and his own. He has taken the familiar ingredients of a poem about spring and made them into a new vision.

A contemporary example of a poem drawn from everyday experience is May Swenson's "Water Picture,"* which describes the reflection of objects in a pond; it begins:

> In the pond in the park
> all things are doubled:
> Long buildings hang and
> wriggle gently. Chimneys
> are bent legs bouncing
> on clouds below. A flag
> wags like a fishhook
> down there in the sky.

---

* From *To Mix with Time*. Charles Scribner's Sons. Copyright © 1963, by May Swenson.

The arched stone bridge
is an eye, with underlid
in the water. In its lens
dip crinkled heads with hats
that don't fall off. Dogs go by,
barking on their backs.
A baby, taken to feed the
ducks, dangles upside-down
a pink balloon for a buoy.

Seen in detail from a new angle, an ordinary experience becomes extraordinary and the substance of poetry. The fresh perception makes the old experience unique.

And the perception is conveyed through language. The words and combinations we choose must be carefully screened to see that they are not the old stereotypes through which we blind ourselves to the world. In his poems, e. e. cummings tore words apart and put the parts back into new combinations so that his language might reveal a new view of the world. Most of us will not follow his way, but we need to be sure we see what we see as it is, not as we think it is. There is a tree before you. What kind of leaves does it have? Are they alternating on the stem? Do they resemble plumes? Are they flat on the air like lily-pads in the water? Hopkins' journal frequently takes account of such phenomena:

Elm leaves:—they shine much in the sun—bright green when near from underneath but higher up they look olive: their shapelessness in the flat is from their being made . . . to be dimpled and dog's eared: their leaf-growth is in this point more rudimentary than that of oak, ash, beech, etc that the leaves lie in long rows and do not subdivide or have central knots but tooth or cog their woody twigs.

Such careful looking, such precision in visual perception, is a first step in writing poetry. If you cannot see what a tree looks like, it will be hard to tell anyone what a feeling feels like. Because in poetry we are dependent on the concrete manifestations of the world to use as symbols of our feelings and our experiences. This is especially true in lyric poetry. But apt suggestive details give credibility to narrative poems and character sketches as well. A good exercise in poetry is to record exactly what you see before you with no large statements about what is there. Simply describe it as if you are seeing it for the first time. An artist practices by carrying a sketch pad and drawing wherever he may be. In the same way, the result of the poet's sketch may not be a poem, but the practice will help develop a technique for handling a more complex subject when it does appear. Here is an example, a description of a shell done as an exercise:

> Being which is the size of my palm
> almost and fits the upcurled fingers
> flat-cupped the thirty-four fingers
> end in points set close together
> like the prongs of a comb
> sea-combing straining the waters
> they are printed on your back
> brown waves cutting light sand
> waves—merging inward
> lighter and lighter and closer
> whirling
> into the self-turned center
> of yourself.

Just as there are two kinds of perception—what is seen and what is experienced—there are two kinds of possibilities for exact or innovative language. And there are chances also for trite or easy observation on both levels.

A poem will not always die of a single cliché; indeed, a common observation can even be used for a deliberate artistic purpose. Only someone who has really mastered his craft, however, should dare to use a phrase which borders on the trite. Dylan Thomas sometimes uses old phrases but remakes them by small changes, so that they emerge as live word combinations like "once below a time." But I can think of no poetic situation in which a "rippling stream" or "glassy pond" can add anything but tedium. Worse than the cliché at the literal or visual level, is the cliché at the experiential level, the large abstract concept such as:

> Life, like time, moves onward.

The large concept gives the reader a stereotyped experience. Perhaps this is why some very bad poetry appeals to a number of undiscriminating readers: it repeats the stereotype of experience they have in their own minds and gives them nothing new to test it by. A good poem should jolt the reader into a new awareness of his feeling or his sensual apprehension of the world. One of the great mistakes is to make a poem too large and simple.

Poetry is an art which proceeds in a roundabout fashion. Its language is not chosen for directness of communication, for the passing on of facts, like "the plane arrives at five," or "today it is raining," although either of these facts could be a part of a poem. The truth that poetry attempts to communicate is reached by more devious means. Many of the devices thought of as being in the special province of poetry are devices of indirection: the metaphor or symbol, which involves saying one thing and meaning another; paradox, the welding of opposites into a single concept; connotations beyond the direct meaning of a word or phrase, and so on. When we think of the way things are in the world, we find that poetry is not the only area in which the immediate fact is disguised, distorted, or concealed. Poetry does this in order to reach a more complex truth. Other situations involve indirection for other reasons. Purpose determines the directness of statement. Take the guest telling his hostess he enjoyed the party. Did he really? But in saying this he is expressing some other feeling beyond the immediate situation. He may be expressing sympathy or long affection or any number of emotions rather than measuring the quality of his enjoyment of the moment. Take advertising, which often tries to pass along not so much a fact as a feeling about something. Take the art of the magician—the better the more deceiving. For the poet to speak too glibly may be to oversimplify his experience. The poet must constantly ask himself: "Is this the way it really felt? Is this the whole experience? Am I overlooking or suppressing part of it?"

As I write this, a living example has appeared before my eyes. I am looking at the tree just outside the window. If I should give you my visual experience at this moment, I should have to include a lizard that has climbed twenty feet up the trunk and is now looking at me. In my stereotyped picture of trees, birds sometimes come to rest, but not lizards. In my stereotype of the loss of a friend through death, there is sorrow, not anger. But I have felt anger at the death of a friend, and there is a lizard in this tree. The real includes these disparate elements. The poet must think of what he has really experienced. He gives certain real details, certain suggestions. The reader combines these into the experience intended by the poet, the real message of the poem, and so participates in its creation.

The poet uses three types of ingredients in his poem: at the first level is what can be immediately caught by the senses—by sight, by hearing, tasting, feeling, smelling. I call this the literal level: the poet describes what is literally there. This poem of my own is written almost entirely at this level:

THE BLACKBERRY THICKET *

I stand here in the ditch, my feet on a rock in the water,
Head-deep in a coppice of thorns,
Picking wild blackberries,
Watching the juice-dark rivulet run
Over my fingers, marking the lines and the whorls,
Remembering stains—
The blue of mulberry on the tongue
Brown fingers after walnut husking,
And the green smudge of grass—
The earnest part
Of heat and orchards and sweet springing places.
Here I am printed with the earth
Always and always the earth ground into the fingers,
And the arm scratched in thickets of spiders.
Over the marshy water the cicada rustles,
A runner snaps sharp into place.
The dry leaves are a presence,
A companion that follows up under the trees of the orchard
Repeating my footsteps. I stop to listen.
Surely not alone
I stand in this quiet in the shadow
Under a roof of bees.

The sights and sounds caught by immediate sensation are described; the memories are of the same immediate quality. Even the ending of the poem is a literal description, although the reader may find there, if he likes, connotations that go beyond the literal.

Much of modern American poetry is written at this level. If not total poems as here, at least sections of poems. Most readers of modern poetry, many editors, look for this literal quality. Here, as I said earlier, the poet must look carefully and sensitively and report exactly. Notice, next time you read a poem, how much of it contains this literal looking and what details the poet has chosen to give the appearance of reality. Even an imagined experience should have some of this literal quality.

---

* From *The Weathercock*, by Ann Stanford. Copyright © 1955, by Ann Stanford. Reprinted by permission of The Viking Press, Inc.

The next level of poetry is the metaphoric, in which one thing is compared with another. The conventional poetic devices of simile, metaphor, symbol are part of this level. Comparison often mingles with the literal. In Elizabeth Bishop's well-known poem "The Fish," * exact description is aided by comparison:

> I looked into his eyes
> which were far larger than mine
> but shallower, and yellowed,
> the irises backed and packed
> with tarnished tinfoil
> seen through the lenses
> of old scratched isinglass.

The juxtaposing of two things that are not wholly alike but that are alike in some way is one of the ways that poetry creates a new view of the world. Comparisons or analogies can be used thus as part of description, or they can make a total poem. They can be either one-way or two-way comparisons. For example, the fish's eye can be said to resemble isinglass, but isinglass does not remind one of a fish's eye. It is not always necessary or desirable that the comparisons work both ways. Another example, Shakespeare's comparison of true love to a "star to every wandering bark," is effective even though within the poem he is not also comparing a star that guides to love. He is defining love in terms of a star, but not a star in terms of love.

However, often the poet uses a two-way analogy. The doubleness of the analogy is especially effective where the whole poem is in the form of comparison. Here is a poem of mine which satirizes the work of committees.

THE COMMITTEE †
by Ann Stanford

Black and serious, they are dropping down one by one to the top of the walnut
    tree.
It is spring and the bare branches are right for a conversation.
The sap has not risen yet, but those branches will always be bare
Up there, crooked with ebbed life lost now, like a legal argument.
They shift a bit as they settle into place.

---

* From *Poems: North and South*. Houghton Mifflin Company. Copyright © 1955, by Elizabeth Bishop.
† © 1967 The New Yorker Magazine, Inc.

Once in a while one says something, but the answer is always the same;
The question is, too—it is all *caw* and *caw.*
Do they think they are hidden by the green leaves partway up the branches?
Do they like it up there cocking their heads in the fresh morning?
One by one, they fly off as if to other appointments.
Whatever they did, it must be done all over again.

Here, what is said about the crows can be applied to a committee, but it is also true of crows, at least the ones I have observed in my neighborhood. This, then, is a two-way analogy.

There is another level at which poets sometimes work: the level of statement. Much of Wordsworth's poetry is statement, as:

> This spiritual Love acts not nor can exist
> Without Imagination, which, in truth,
> Is but another name for absolute power
> And clearest insight, amplitude of mind,
> And Reason in her most exalted mood.

This is a hard and dangerous level for most poets. Much poetry, especially amateur poetry, constantly attempts statement without backing it up with the literal or analogic or comparative level. The poem which merely states, except in the hands of a master, falls flat because it does not prove anything to the reader. He is not drawn into the background of the statement. He is merely told. If his own experience backs up the statement, he may like the poem, but he likes it only because of his experience, not because of what the poem has done for him.

Masters of poetry, on the other hand, sometimes make o. ɔ large statement and spend the rest of the poem illustrating or proving it. Hopkins does this with the statement "Nothing is so beautiful as spring—"; May Swenson does it in a more specific way in "Water Picture." William Carlos Williams in "To Waken an Old Lady" defines old age by describing a flock of birds in winter. His only reference to age at all is the first line, "Old age is." Without the first line to suggest the definition, the poem could be simply a nature description. Emily Dickinson often makes an abstract idea come to life by defining it in visual terms:

> Presentiment is that long shadow on the lawn
> Indicative that suns go down;

The notice to the startled grass
That darkness is about to pass.

It would be a rare poem which could exist on one of these levels—
that of literal description, that of metaphor, or that of statement—
alone. Poems usually combine these in varying proportions. There
are dangers to the poetry, besides triteness, at all levels. Flatness,
dullness, and poor selection of details menace literal description.
Metaphor is endangered by irrelevance; a metaphor which does not
contribute in tone or feeling may turn the reader away from the
poem as a whole. Statement is most dangerous, for it must be proved.

A poem which succeeds may also have a fourth level—the transcendental level, where the connotations of the poem extend on beyond the limits of the poem. But the transcendental may hardly be
striven for. We only recognize it when it shimmers in the exceptional
poem.

Meanwhile the poet works at what he can. He looks for the whole
significance of the experience. He renders it—even more, he understands it—through language built around his own view. His new seeing is what will make the experience of the poem worth telling once
more.

68

VISION AND REVISION

By Doris Holmes

LET's see, what are my views on writing poetry? Are special traits, training, insights needed? Can one cultivate imagination? Do you grind out a poem and see it through, or does it come to you in a flash?

The questions you have just read are fake. I concocted them to demonstrate how profoundly our most casual speech reflects certain notions about creativity. The notions I refer to all assume an alliance or a resemblance between creative power and vision or seeing.

How many "visual" phrases do you find above? There are six in those four questions. A very little reflection or research would uncover many more words whose roots suggest that imagery is the work of the visionary, the man who sees the light. Imagination, that magical power of the artist, is the ability to see that which is not, which does not exist (yet), to see it in the mind's eye. The reader, listener, viewer, must also have imagination, to enjoy what the artist sees. However, there are usually two differences between the appreciator and the artist: the artist sees it before other people do; he then "makes" it. This second difference is the significant one.

Before considering the making, the practical matters of technique, let us review (!) some traditional concepts about the vision of the poet.

In the first place, poets are supposed to be good at simply seeing physically. They are always observing, noticing concrete details, or over-all atmosphere. They see eternity in a grain of sand, and they also describe the mica, or is it silica? If they don't know, they look it up, and become fascinated with the words of the definition. They see the violet hidden by a mossy stone, but in addition, insist on the violet in the lady's complexion. Outside the window, the tree is a fountain. The tulip has stripes; one brick is missing from the wall. A

397

skate case is lying among the seaweed and beach debris. It's true, they may be less likely to notice that the gasoline gauge is down, the liquor bill up. They may, though, be alert to the similarity in atomic and stellar arrangements. At any rate, *vision as observation* is certainly an essential poetic power as well as practice, trait as well as training, the poet's gift, in both senses, from life and to life.

Perhaps it is a modern symptom to treat physical vision first. Surely the most central kind of vision associated with the poet over the centuries was what we may call *prophecy*. The poets of the Old Testament were seers (!) who sang forth. As we were taught, the prophets were not foretellers, or fortunetellers, but forth-tellers. Sometimes they predicted—doom if their listeners didn't reform, paradise if they did—but the prognosticating was done with rhetoric rather than sorcery. They saw the handwriting on the wall and told their people to "behold." Sometimes their zealous conjurings were fulfilled in actual later events, and that, combined with their effective verbal performance, brought awe and admiration for ancient bards. Isaiah's prophecy and the coming of Christ need no comment, but it is still eerie to think of Tennyson in the 1840's writing (in "Locksley Hall"):

> For I dipt into the future, far as human
> > eye could see,
> Saw the Vision of the world, and all the
> > wonder that would be;
>
> Saw the heavens fill with commerce, argosies
> > of magic sails,
> Pilots of the purple twilight, dropping down
> > with costly bales;
>
> Heard the heavens fill with shouting, and
> > there rain'd a ghastly dew
> From the nations' airy navies grappling in
> > the central blue;
>
> Far along the world-wide whisper of the
> > south-wind rushing warm,
> With the standards of the people plunging
> > through the thunder-storm;
>
> Till the war-drum throbbed no longer, and
> > the battle-flags were furled

In the Parliament of man, the Federation
of the world.

We who live somewhere between the "ghastly dew" of Hiroshima
and the last unrealized international union may pause over the place
of prophecy.

Inspiration is what we all want, and the non-writer often assumes
that it is some magic that descends from above. It is totally capricious and beyond our manipulation according to this theory. The
muses hit some of us and not others. The poet may go into a kind of
trance or frenzy. He is in some abnormal state, excited and heightened above the mundane or even the real. His vision, then, approaches *hallucination*. The madman, the fool and the artist have
always had something in common. It is not necessarily easy to dis-
criminate between the flights of fancy that indicate talent, and the
flight to phantasy that may mean the mental aberration that is illness. In the richest of writing, though, the author is diving, perhaps,
but not drowning. He sees a phantom of delight, is nearly carried
away, but not quite. He celebrates it, the phantom or his experiencing the phantom. Maybe he seems to play with the materials of his
art. The divine inspiration may look like the divine discontent, but
the true artist has a rage for order. He may be big enough to incorpo-
rate a lot of chaos but that's what he does: incorporates it, gives it a
body, with shape or form. His hallucination, then, may issue in some
lucidity after all.

Vision also connotes a kind of *intelligence*. In business or government we say "he is a man of vision" if he has foresight, imagination
and faith. That last element of confidence is, in some subtle manner,
part of the poet's vision, too. He may not be a confident person in
other ways, but he believes, maybe even obsessively, that the thing
may be done, the picture painted, the novel written, the music composed. The poet's vision is sharp, smart. Perhaps he has an angle
view of society and reality, but it's a kind of 20/20 look at life. All of
this vision traditionally "flashes upon the inward eye which is the
bliss of solitude" when his vistas are "recollected in tranquillity."

Psychology teaches us how our subconscious mind relates seeing
with sexual potency, and blindness with loss of that power, or castra-
tion. These deep symbolic processes are beyond our fathoming, of

course, but there is something very basic in our assumptions about vision as a primary part of any human power.

"Writing makes it seem clearer," said Strindberg somewhere in his journal. Many writers feel this way. Writing is a way of pulling things together, of seeing your own experience more clearly, of *revising your vision of life*. This re-viewing and re-ordering gives the writer esthetic pleasure whether his creativity is involved in arranging the facts of reality (as in non-fiction) or in making, or making up, the artifacts, the "fictions" of his craft.

So having submitted that poetry is a kind of revision to begin with, let us look at the more conventional meaning of revision. Of course that holy fire of inspiration that we mentioned must be transmitted through the words of the poem. Whether the poet began with an idea, an experience, the sight of something in the natural world, a grief, an ironic understanding, a lyrical phrase that seems to haunt him, a desire to imitate or translate, a fascination with rhyme, or a free passion, he has to put it down. Even the most beatnik primitive has probably been unconsciously and swiftly revising as he translates, transcribes, transmits his initial impulse into words. Responsible poets have always revised. Of course the Homers of the oral tradition chanted out without benefit of eraser, but they repeated lines, changed them slightly if necessary, and kept in composing trim by constant practice. They had various devices to keep the epic going while they revised in their heads. Have you ever told a story three or four times, polished it till it was a well-rounded anecdote? You've probably pruned the unnecessary parts the second time around, changed key words, highlighted the climax, and so on.

Some poets retain their work sheets. It can be intriguing to follow the patterns of such a poet's thought as you read through his additions, subtractions, enlargements, associations. The hunt for a single word, the perfect word, is still the crucial job. He may need something more specific than his first draft produced. The new word may suggest a whole cluster of new, related auxiliary ideas. The poem may take a different turn then. Or he may be hunting for a rhyme. The margin of his manuscript may have a couple of dozen words that will rhyme, from which he must choose one. His original may have been too obtrusive or too flat. The substitution will change a lot more than the sound, hooking him into a new stream of thought. Scratch-ings in the margin may be a column of synonyms or near-synonyms, or words that he hopes will lead him to something just beyond his consciousness or memory.

Other poets do this associating in their heads, so their work sheets don't reveal the intervening steps. Some compose on the typewriter, retyping and rewriting or revising, at the same time. They thus re-manage the whole with each revision.

When a writer is very "dry," has no idea, no song, and is miserable because he wants to write, one ploy is to scribble out anything, any foolish random thought, phrase, comment, word, that comes to mind. "But suppose nothing comes to mind?" Sit and look at the room and describe it; record your irritation, blankness, frustration. Write down how stupid you are. You may turn up something that's been escaping you. Tune in on your daydream, even if it's cloudy brood-ing. Allow strands to ooze up from the great marsh where your rea-son hasn't organized everything. You may be surprised at the flora and fauna of what you called "blank." Don't underrate straight de-scription either. Precision of expression, the fineness, the accuracy if not the beauty of the words may hook you, or re-hook you. And *looking*—that may do miracles.

I do not usually keep work sheets. Some seem to survive—they may have a gem up in the corner, a provocative word or two for future use. But once in a while a poem simply resists conclusion. I believe it was Robert Penn Warren who said you don't finish a poem; you abandon it in despair. I have one here that has been ex-tant in my life and papers for years. I select it because it is small, as well as in the process of revision, and it may illustrate the preceding commentary. I need hardly say that this selection is offered not as an example of the first word in the title of my article, but as a case of the third:

When I die the telephone

Autobiographical details would help but also delay the presentation here, so I'll be brief. The telephone is part of my life. The poem began with the first line. That's all. I was about to dial a number. Smiling, I heard the first line in my head, which is another way of saying I was talking to myself. I imagined the cleaning out of my house after my demise. Early on, the poem was "Doris' Dirge," half comic. (I have always loved "Fidele's Dirge" in *Cymbeline*, which you remember begins "Fear no more the heat o' the sun.") Here is an early version of my "dirge":

TELL AND TELL

When I die the telephone
Will hang still till
The men rip off my black sin,

The wall rest from the dirt,
My love to the round hole in
Its listening heart.

The coiled cord to my ear
Twisted you all
In my hair,

Dear wordy ones
Who rang me and ring me;
Thanks, from my quiet bones.

The New England Telephone and Telegraph Company became New England Telephone, diminishing my pun in the title. Norma Farber thought "black sin" sounded terrible, like bad Anne Sexton. Margoret Smith said "bones" were absolutely out; too hackneyed. A bright young woman in the Boston Winterfest audience where I read the poem asked why I used so much sexual imagery. I pretended it had been intentional and spouted something about oral compulsion. She also questioned my grammatical structure and I immediately realized that "rest" had to be either "rests" or "will rest" paralleling "rip" or "will hang." Maybe the "will" could be understood, but I never felt comfortable about it again.

I thought "sin" was funny, because true. I thought of "dirt" as the chatter, as well as the actual mark on the wall where the phone had been. "Ring" meant the circle of mourners around my grave at the end, as well as telephone ring. And so on.

Then the pattern bothered me. The dirge was so nearly a tight little artifice of half rhymes going aba cac dbd, etc. But criticism had centered around avoiding clichés and making images sharper. I tried not to be rigid, and attempted variations:

When I die the telephone
    Will hang still till
    The men jerk out the black vine

    The wall rests from the dirt,
    My love to the round hole in
    Its listening heart.

    The coiled cord to my ear
    Twisted you all
    In my hair,

    Dear wordy lovers
            merchants
            wielders
            mothers
            lovers
            sellers
            pedlars
            singers

    Dear wordy lovers of harangue
    Wordy mothers of harangue
    Who ring me and rang;
    Thanks, from my settling tongue.

My children knew this piece in its original form, and made bleating noises when I forced them to listen to the new version. Children are conservative anyway, but the truth was, the early lines rang with an inevitability for me, too. Years passed. I left "Dear wordy ones" and a pencil list of phrases after "from" in the last line including "What remains, that dead tongue, the monotones, quiet bones, the silent tone, my quiet tongue, graver tones and my settled tongue." This year I faced "Tell and Tell" again and set about a more formal arrangement, so that the half rhymes came out aba cac dcd ede. My witchlike insistence that I would haunt my friends forever would, I hoped, carry, if not passion, at least eeriness, the spookiness of machines as well as ghosts:

    When I die the telephone
    Will hang still till
    The men jerk out the black line [not vine]

    While the wall rests from the dirt,
    My love to the round hole in
    Its listening heart.

The coiled cord to my hair
Curled your report
Into my ear.

Dear wordy ones
When you ring me no more
I will still sing, in your dial tones.

I cannot rid myself of "Tell and Tell." Perhaps it is only an exercise in revision. I must say, though, that it meant, means more than that to me. I *saw* myself, by composing it, and I laughed. For such vision, microscopic though it may be *sub specie aeternitatis,* I am humbly grateful. Perhaps some day a revision will satisfy me enough to want to see it published.

69

LIGHT VERSE: QUESTIONS
AND ANSWERS

By Richard Armour

Light verse is a minor art or craft, but there is a good deal of art and craft to it. In fact there is often more technique involved in light verse than in serious poetry. Phyllis McGinley once said that light verse is (or should be) less emotional and more rational than poetry, though I think she won the Pulitzer Prize not so much for light verse as for what I would call light poetry. At any rate I agree with her that light verse is not to be taken too lightly by the writer. Quite aside from talent, and a special way with words and ideas, one must know the fundamentals, and more than the fundamentals, of versification: meter, rhyme, and all the rest.

 The best modern light verse writers, such as Phyllis McGinley, Ogden Nash, David McCord, Morris Bishop, Arthur Guiterman, Samuel Hoffenstein, Dorothy Parker, Margaret Fishback, and Ethel Jacobson, have also been poets or mock poets. Having read and absorbed the writings of poets and light verse writers who went before them (and light verse is as old as Chaucer), they sharpened their skills and eventually developed styles of their own.

Some of these poets are still with us and still writing, but not quite so much and not quite so lightly. It is about time for a whole new generation. Magazine markets are fewer and book publishers more wary, but there is still a substantial readership for light verse if it is original and skillful and has something to say. I thought it might be helpful to give some basic pointers and to put them in question and answer form. These, at any rate, are the questions I am most often asked and the answers I most often give:

Q. *What is the difference between light verse and poetry?*

A. Light verse is a kind of poetry. It is poetry written in the spirit of play. Since it may not have the high thoughts or the imagery of poetry, it makes up for lack of these by emphasis on technique. The first requirement of a light verse writer is sure command of meter and rhyme. But along with technique, as in any writing, there must be something new to say, or a new way of saying something old.

Q. *What are the best subjects for light verse?*

A. Since you are writing for people, you should write about what people are most interested in. And people are most interested in people. In other words, the best subjects are those that have to do with the foibles of the human race, such as the relations of man to wife and of parents to children; the effort to get along with one's neighbors and one's colleagues and one's boss (unless one *is* the boss); the struggle with waistline and hairline; bank accounts, charge accounts, and no accounts; hosts and guests; passing fads in food and clothing and cars and sports; buying a house or building a house or running a house or being run by a house; vacations and travel and luggage and tips; pets; youth and age and the in-between adolescent; illness and doctors and remedies and recuperation and exercise; automation and the computerized society in relation to the bewildered individual; people who are meddlesome or pompous or stupid or inconsistent— in short, all aspects of the human comedy. Here is an example of a piece of light verse on a subject of universal interest:

> MONEY
> Workers earn it,
> Spendthrifts burn it,
> Bankers lend it,
> Women spend it,
> Forgers fake it,
> Taxes take it,
> Dying leave it,
> Heirs receive it,
> Thrifty save it,
> Misers crave it,
> Robbers seize it,
> Rich increase it,
> Gamblers lose it . . .
> I could use it.

Q. *Where does one look for ideas?*

A. You not only look but listen. You keep your ears open as well as your eyes. Sometimes a chance phrase or a cliché will trigger a piece of verse. In addition to looking at and listening to people, you read, read, read. You read books and magazines and newspapers. Now and then, if you are on the alert, an idea will pop up. Newspapers, especially, are mirrors reflecting the absurdities of mankind—and womankind. Light verse should concern subjects that concern people. It should strike common chords, be human, be universal.

Q. *What is the best length for a piece of light verse?*

A. Brevity is a requisite of all forms of humor. Recently a critic writing in *Esquire* made the wise observation: "Humor is like guerrilla warfare. Success depends on traveling light . . . striking unexpectedly . . . and getting away fast." This applies especially to light verse, which is a condensed, almost telegraphic, form of humor —verse being more compressed than prose anyhow. Light verse is briefer today than it was in the more leisurely nineteenth century, and less intricate than in those days of the ballade and the villanelle. Usually it runs from two lines to eight or ten or twelve. Only rarely to sixteen or more. That is, if you want to sell it. By the way, this is the shortest piece I ever sold (to the *Saturday Review*):

MAID'S DAY OUT
Thurs.
Hers.

Q. *What are the best verse forms to use?*

A. Simple iambic and anapestic meter, rather short lines (trimeter or tetrameter), couplets and quatrains. If you don't know what these are, go to your local library and get Clement Wood's *Poets' Handbook* or look at the back part of Clement Wood's *The Complete Rhyming Dictionary*. You can't expect to enter a highly competitive field, in which technique plays such a large part, without knowing the fundamentals of versification.

Light verse should be technically correct in rhymes and meters, and, if possible, not only correct but fresh and original. I have mentioned short lines. You may also use the longer pentameter (five stress) line, which has been the most popular form in English poetry ever since Chaucer, but it usually leads to somewhat more serious treatment, and the rhymes (much more important in light verse than in serious poetry) are a bit far apart.

Q. *Are there any other suggestions for writing salable light verse?*

A. It should, usually, have an element of surprise or some sort of clincher at the end. (See "Money" quoted above.) But it should not rely too much on the last line, in that case spoken of slightingly as "terminal humor." Good light verse should be amusing all the way through, with maybe something a little special at the close. And it should be given the additional help of a good title—one that is original and appropriate.

Q. *How do you find markets for light verse?*

A. You can look at the market lists that appear from time to time in issues of *The Writer* (or write in for the back issue containing light verse markets). But you should also examine the magazines themselves, to see whether they are using light verse and, if so, what type. I take a good many magazines, but in addition I spend many hours on my haunches at newsstands, checking the magazines I don't take. (Forgive me, managers of drug stores and supermarkets. I still buy enough from you.)

As for knowing markets—submitting light verse to the right place at the right time—this is as important today as ever. It is perhaps more important now than it was thirty years ago, because the markets are fewer and the competition is keener. But, again, when I started out I knew my markets, *The Saturday Evening Post* and *The New Yorker,* as a long-time reader of both.

Markets change and you have to keep up with them. *The Saturday Evening Post* still uses light verse on the "Post Scripts" page, but there are few poems scattered through the back pages of the magazine. And *The New Yorker* uses less verse, and such verse as it uses is less light than in what I think of as the Good Old Days, when Harold Ross was editor.

Today, in addition to the "Post Scripts" page, there is "Light Housekeeping" in *Good Housekeeping*, and "Parting Shots" in *The American Legion Magazine*. In addition to these well-edited pages, where you have to fight off a multitude of free-lancers, there are other more specialized magazines like *Gourmet* and *Golf* that occasionally use light verse. You will find more of these in market lists or discover them for yourself by reading the magazines.

Q. *How do you submit light verse?*

A. Type it, double-spaced, one poem to a page, with your name and return address in the upper corner (it makes no difference whether left or right) of the page. Submit one to three poems at a time. You may be able to get in four, along with a stamped self-addressed envelope, for the same postage, if the paper is not heavier than sixteen-pound weight, a good weight for all manuscripts. No letter is necessary or desirable. What could you say? Editors have enough to read anyhow. Another thing—there is no need to say anything about protecting your manuscript. Editors are honest and the U.S. mails are safe. If something is bought, what is usually bought is first North American serial rights, which means the first run in a North American newspaper or magazine.

Q. *Do you need an agent?*

A. An agent might be helpful, but most agents won't bother with light verse. And most don't know the markets as well as you will know them if you study the magazines as I have suggested. It's a do-it-yourself field.

Q. *When do you do your writing?*

A. Whenever I get a chance, which isn't often enough. I long ago gave up "waiting for an inspiration"—else I would still be waiting. I also gave up trying to set aside regular hours for writing, though I would do this if I could. Since I have several other time-consuming activities, I write when I can. But my conscience or compulsion or whatever it is weighs so heavily on me that I feel frustrated and remorseful if I do not write a little something—prose or verse—each day, seven days a week. (I am writing this on a Sunday morning—

after having gone to church.) Some days I write for ten minutes; some days I write for ten hours. One advantage of light verse is that it can be written during short periods. With a schedule such as mine, I am glad I am not a novelist.

Q. *Do you still get things back?*

A. Yes, indeed. I use returned verses as scratch paper on which to write new verses. My method with editors is erosion. After a while, I wear them down. But it takes patience and postage. The difference between the professional and the amateur, in this business, is that the professional becomes discouraged less easily.

Q. *Do you get printed rejection slips or letters?*

A. Both. And sometimes I get neither—just the poem back, in the return envelope, which is really very sensible. I think rejection slips are a waste of paper. If I get a poem back, I know, without any printed explanation, that it has been rejected. Of course I am grateful for a letter, or even a brief note. One editor with whom I dealt for many years used to grade my poems, as if I were a student in Freshman Composition. Though he might buy a poem that he graded "B minus" or even "C plus," only once did he ever give me an "A." It was for this piece, which is included in my collection, *Nights With Armour:*

THE LOVE LIFE (AND DEATH) OF A MOOSE

Up in Newfoundland some 20 moose, mistaking Diesel train horns for mating calls, have been lured to death on the tracks.—*News item.*

> Imagine this beast of the frozen Northeast
> With its annual amorous craze on,
> Seduced by the toot of a choo-choo en route
> Into making a fatal liaison.
>
> Conceive of its sighs as it straddles the ties,
> Unaware of the killer it's dating.
> The honk of the train has gone straight to its brain,
> And its mind is completely on mating.
>
> Appalling? Of course, but just think how much worse
> It would be, and no words shall we weasel,

Should an engine tear loose from its tracks when a moose
Makes what sounds like the call of a Diesel.

This, by the way, is a pretty good example of playfulness, zany point of view, exaggeration, out-of-the-ordinary rhyming, and fancy footwork (with metrical feet)—some of the ingredients of light verse.

Q. *Of the light verse you have written, what is your own personal favorite?*

A. This is almost impossible to answer. Sometimes, in a depressed mood (that is, daily), I like nothing I have ever written. Other times I run onto something I wrote years ago, and had forgotten, and wonder that I had ever written anything so good. This, instead of making me happy, depresses me further, because it convinces me that I am on the downgrade and shall never do so well again. But usually I like best whatever I have written most recently. This goes not only for my light verse but for my books. Perhaps I can dodge the question by quoting a piece of light verse that seems to be a favorite of others and is fairly typical.

MY MATTRESS AND I
Night after night, for years on end,
My mattress has been my closest friend.

My mattress and I are cozy and pally;
There are hills on the sides—I sleep in the valley.

It clearly reveals the shape I'm in:
Where I'm thin it's thick, where it's thick I'm thin.

Its contours reflect the first and the last of me.
It's very nearly a plaster cast of me.

I miss my mattress when I am gone;
It's one thing I've made an impression on.

This is about all there is to it. Everything depends on your sense of humor, your original way of looking at things (including yourself), your handling of rhyme and meter and words, and your ability to be critical of what you write and to compare it honestly with what is being published.

Now I have to get back to work, because light verse, no matter how easy it looks (and it should be made to look easy) is work, hard work. And when a piece of light verse comes off right—when it is original in concept, and funny, and nicely turned—the light verse writer gets, in his way, as much of a feeling of accomplishment, even creativeness, as a serious poet.

70

WRITING CHILDREN'S VERSE

By Aileen Fisher

You like children—the frankness of their reactions, the nonsense of their humor, the verve of their imagination. You remember your own childhood and recall in flashes of detail how you felt about this or that, and what you thought and wondered about. And you have always liked rhymes—from the time your mother read Mother Goose aloud until you started to jot down some verses of your own. You have, in fact, quite a collection of "poems" hidden away in your desk drawer. Now, looking at the booming market for children's books, you wonder how it would be to try your hand at writing children's verse as a free lance. What are your chances?

One writing friend advises you: "Don't waste your energy on verses. So many of the good children's magazines have fallen by the wayside. And those that are left are flooded with manuscripts. *Everyone* thinks he can write children's verse."

Another friend, who works in the adult field, says, "I'll ask my agent."

The agent's reply is anything but encouraging. "There's so little money in children's verse, most agents can't afford to handle it. And many publishers won't even look at a book of verse. It takes years for a writer in the field to build up a name. I should think your friend would be wiser to stick to fiction or non-fiction or plays."

Are they right?

Yes and no.

I should say the first question you should answer in your own mind is: What is my aim in writing? Is it to make money? Is it to be published? Is it for the satisfaction and fun of putting ideas down on paper on the chance that someone else may sometime get pleasure or inspiration from them?

If you want to make money (and for some reason people have an

idea that a great deal of money is to be made at any kind of writing),
the children's verse field offers few lures. Only the exceptional writer
makes a living at it, whereas a number of writers of children's fiction
and non-fiction are able to support themselves year after year.

Of course, there are exceptions to the rule of small financial returns. But I don't believe that the handful of writers who have done
well in the children's verse field ever expected to. Certainly it was
not with a bank account in mind that A. A. Milne wrote his Christopher Robin poems, and probably no one was more surprised than he
that they became so famous. He wrote because, as he watched his
son grow up, his own recollections of childhood were rekindled and
illumined, and whimsy and humor bubbled forth. I think it is safe to
say that Milne had as much fun writing *When We Were Very Young*
as anyone ever had reading it.

But it is one thing to try to make a living at writing children's
verse and quite another to supplement income from other writing or
from a job. The incidental income becomes more and more substantial as one's name becomes better known. After you have been in the
field for twenty or twenty-five years, your earnings from verse may
really amount to something.

There is the original (usually small) check for first publication in
a magazine or newspaper. Then, after a lag of time, perhaps a reprint
fee or two for republication in an anthology or textbook. Besides, if
you are careful about reserving book rights, you can use published
verses in a collection of your own, and royalties will start coming in.
After book publication, more requests may come along for permission to reprint. And these fees add up over the years. Recently, for
instance, I received a check for $25 for the use of a poem that sold to
Story Parade years before for $9. And a firm putting out a combina-
tion "picture-board" and recording recently offered $30 each for the
use of five verses for which I had received a total of $27.50 (for the
five) for first serial rights. A reprint fee of $10 or $15 for a verse of
twelve lines or so is common enough.

Now, what about the market?

Your best bet as a beginner is to try to get verses published first in
one of the juvenile magazines or school papers, or even in your
hometown newspaper. Dorothy Aldis caught attention and applause
years ago by having some of her verses appear in the column "A

Line o' Type or Two" in the *Chicago Tribune*. I tried it, too, somewhat later. The first verse I sent to "The Line" was published; then
my luck stopped. Obviously I was no Dorothy Aldis!

Although it is true, and regrettably so, that some of the outstanding children's magazines have gone out of business, there are still
plenty left. Just turn to the annual market list of *The Writer* covering the juvenile and teen-age field, and you will find dozens of publications that print verse. Many of them pay very little, it is true, but
just getting published when you are starting out is more important
than making money. Keep verses going in the mails, four or five in a
group, and don't be discouraged by rejection slips.

We all get those slips that are guaranteed to keep a writer humble!
It's part of the free-lance picture. Always remember, though, that
the editor feels no personal malice toward you or your work. She has
problems of her own, plenty of them. I remember reading an article
in *The Writer* some years ago by the editor of *Child Life*. She
pointed out that at least 18,000 manuscripts a year were submitted
to *Child Life*, and only about fifty stories and one hundred poems
could be published. That's less than one acceptance in a hundred
submissions. Somebody, a lot of somebodies, are bound to be
rejected. That's the way the free-lance market operates. For every
need there are dozens of writers offering their wares. But success
waits at the top of the hill for the persevering climbers who have
something worthwhile to offer.

After serving an apprenticeship by having verses published in the
"first serial" market, you come face-to-face with the flourishing business of children's books. Your goal will be book publication, of
course. And what are your chances here?

The field is a big one, and the children's book business is booming.
Each year several thousand new children's books are published. A
score or more of these will be books of verse, new collections of individual poems, or anthologies of both old and new material. Add to
that several hundred other books of children's verse in print, and
you have an impressive total. And that is not all. More and more
picture books are being written in verse, and, as everyone knows,
picture books are perennially popular.

What this adds up to is that the writer of children's verse today
has a wider market than he had a generation ago. Of course, he prob-

ably also has more competition. But openings are there! And a writer's investment in trying to attain publication is negligible. You can write verses anywhere, with little equipment—no months of painstaking research, no doctor's degrees, no electric typewriters. You automatically have the background you need, since you were once a child yourself. And it costs little to keep verse manuscripts in the mail.

Some people have an idea that verses are written only in an ivory tower. "If," they say, "I had a set-up like yours, with such a view from my study window and such peace and quiet all around, I could write, too." But surroundings really aren't the important thing. It's having something to say that counts, and taking joy in saying it—something to open a child's eyes, to make him laugh, or wonder, or venture through a door ajar.

The most reprinted lines I have ever written were jotted down in the most "un-ivory-tower" imaginable. I was working in Chicago at the time, saving every cent I could "to escape to the country." One of my economies was to live in a cheap, dark, first-floor room in a third-rate hotel on Chicago's South Side. The one window opened onto a cement areaway leading to an alley, and there were bars across the panes to keep out prowlers! The room had a steel cot, a wardrobe badly in need of varnish, two straight-backed chairs, and a kitchen table I used for a desk.

I remember coming home from work one winter evening and jotting down some lines I had thought of on the brisk walk from the station. Then I went out for dinner at a little restaurant around the corner where I could get a meal for sixty cents. When I got back to my room, I was amused by the nine lines I had hurriedly written, and I sent them off, with several verses, to the editor of *Child Life*. I have lost track of how many times "Otherwise," written in those stark surroundings, has been reprinted. Here are the nine lines:

> There must be magic,
> otherwise,
> how could day turn to night,
>
> And how could sailboats,
> otherwise,
> go sailing out of sight,

And how could peanuts,
otherwise,
be covered up so tight?

Another verse I wrote during that hectic Chicago interlude has been reprinted time and time again. I was on an elevated train, on my way home from Evanston after a busy day as reporter on a neighborhood newspaper. The train was noisy and crowded, clattering along past rickety back porches and grime-stained apartment buildings. Grayness hung heavy over the city. I yearned for the clean openness of the countryside in northern Michigan where I had spent my childhood. The country! In a flash I was there. Eight short and simple lines wrote themselves on the back of an envelope:

DOWN IN THE HOLLOW

Down in the hollow,
not so far away,
I saw a little ladybug
when I went to play,

Swinging on a clover
high in the air . . .
I wonder if the ladybug
knew that I was there.

If you are interested in writing children's verse, it is a good idea to keep looking, listening, and wondering about things. How can an apple tree hang all those apples around? What's inside of me making me grow? Where do woodchucks get enough dreams to last them all winter? How is an egg made . . .

You'd think the yolk
and white would run
before the shell
was ever done . . .

But hens don't lay
a scrambled one!

But to get back to the ivory tower—it is, of course, far easier as a steady routine to write in pleasant surroundings. After five years in Chicago, I "escaped" to Colorado, and my production curve went up. But even so, few of my later verses have been reprinted as often as some of those early Chicago ones.

Here are a few bits of advice I can give you, gleaned from experience. Write. Keep on writing. But don't "write down." An adult should be able to read children's verse with pleasure. Keep accurate records of submissions and sales. Put down all the flashes about your childhood that come to you. If a poem doesn't work out, or doesn't sell, don't throw it away with a gesture of impatience. Keep it on file. You never know when lines written years before may generate a spark that will light more than one fire. Many times I have gone back over old verses, filed away alphabetically by title, and have come up with something unexpected.

A few years ago I was caught up short on rereading an old verse of mine about birds: How clever they were to balance themselves on wires, to jerk themselves up trees like a woodpecker, to grow webbed feet and swim like a duck. The last four lines struck the spark:

> Oh, birds are clever,
> but where would they be
> if they ever, ever, ever
> wore shoes like me?

"Wore shoes like me." That set me to thinking about going barefoot. How eagerly my brother and I used to wait for warm weather so we could throw off our shoes and stockings and be like the rabbits and birds—barefot! I began to think of all the ones who went barefoot the year 'round—raccoons with their footprints looking like the tracks of a child, deer with their patent-leather hoofs making sharp marks, mice embroidering the snow with dainty stitches. Before I knew it, I was writing stanza after stanza about going barefoot. Some days later, I had nine or ten pages, more or less unified. I sent the manuscript to Thomas Y. Crowell Company, where I was not entirely unknown, since they had published a number of my verses in an anthology the year before. In eighteen months, for the wheels of publishing often turn slowly, *Going Barefoot,* with illustrations by Adrienne Adams, came out as a picture book.

That was only the first fire lit by the spark of a forgotten verse. The editor suggested that I do a series of nature picture books in verse. So I wrote a piece on hibernation (*Where Does Everyone*

Go?), without featuring the perennial woodchuck. Then, remembering how often I had been surprised in the woods and fields by a creature so well camouflaged that I had almost stepped on him, I wrote a little book on protective coloring—*Like Nothing at All*. Leonard Weisgard illustrated it.

Then followed *I Like Weather*. I wrote it from the heart because I do decidedly like weather . . .

> days and days and days
> with different kinds
> of smells and sounds
> and looks and feels
> and ways.

A boy yearning to have a wild rabbit for a pet (*Listen, Rabbit*), a girl taking a birthday-present walk with her father (*In the Middle of the Night*), a lonely child finding all kinds of unexpected "houses" near his own (*Best Little House*)—the subject-matter for children's verse is endless because children's interests and enthusiasm are endless. They rise to the quiet and familiar as well as to the exciting and strange.

Like most writers in the field, I started from scratch and served a long apprenticeship. I knew no editors, had no contacts, and never went to New York to see publishers. Because I loved to do it, I just kept writing children's verse as one string to my fiddle. You can, too. And remember, there are more children than ever these days who are reading, in school and out. There are more books being published. And editors are always on the lookout for something refreshing and original.

71

ADVENTURES IN PLOTTING

By Elizabeth Honness

Where does a writer of mystery stories get her ideas? What starts teasing the author's imagination until she is finally impelled to start thinking up a plot? Having written eleven mysteries for children in the eight-to-twelve age group (all still in print), I am frequently asked these questions by young readers.

Sometimes an empty old house, mute about its own past but crying silently for a past or present to be invented, will set me off. Other times, it will be an item in a newspaper or perhaps an anecdote told me by a friend, or something that has happened during travels to distant lands, and once even a dream triggered a plot.

Needless to say, plot is of prime importance in a mystery or suspense story, but the writer should know the solution to the puzzle she is constructing before she begins writing. (I did not realize this when I started writing mysteries and had to find out the hard way.)

Once the idea for the story has revealed itself, there are five questions that must be answered: where? who? when? what? and how? As soon as the where or setting has been determined, the characters—the who—begin to take shape. They tell me their names, and before I start writing the story, I type pages of descriptions of how they look, their likes and dislikes, their personal quirks.

Sometimes I have to invent family trees for them, going back several generations because something that happened in their ancestral past may have a lot to do with what takes place in the present. This was true of my book, *Mystery of the Hidden Face,* which was suggested by the portrait of my own great-great-grandmother, who was born before the American Revolution and died at ninety-four at the end of the Civil War.

Then I steep myself in where my story people live, drawing

floor plans of the house in the story, so I can visualize their movements through the rooms which I always have fun furnishing. I
invent the local geography if I have not chosen an actual place or
landscape. A time chart for the WHEN is a necessity, so I can have
clearly in mind just when each action of the plot occurs. The
WHAT (the mystery) and the HOW (its solution) require a tentative outline of each chapter with clues leading to the denouement.
I say "tentative" because often in the course of writing the characters take things into their own hands and do not behave the way I
had planned. This leads to usually beneficial changes in the action.
When I am writing dialogue, the characters often take over, too,
and surprise me with words I am not aware of putting into their
mouths!

My first mystery did not start out to be one at all. It was intended to be a story about a happy summer in the Catskill Mountains when I was young, and my father was the department engineer in charge of building the Ashokan Reservoir for New York
City. We rented from the City for the meager sum of ten dollars a
queer old Victorian house that looked like a birdcage or birdhouse
with porches on two sides, upstairs and down. The dining room
floor was on such a slope the soup slanted in the soup plates; there
was no indoor plumbing or running water except for a pump in the
kitchen. As soon as the reservoir was completed, the house was to
be destroyed, hence the token rental. The birdcage house, as we
called it, provided two wonderfully happy summers for my brother
and me and our two white rabbits, which accompanied us—along
with bicycles, two maids, and the necessary cots, beds, chairs,
tables, cooking utensils, and china. The setting seemed ready-made
for a children's book. My characters, except for one boy, were
ready-made, too, since I used my own family and friends. There
were many funny and interesting real happenings to draw upon.
There was also a built-in conflict to suggest the plot which became
the mystery. This conflict arose from the forced removal of the
families who had always lived in the houses to be flooded by the
reservoir and their natural resentment toward the City and its engineers.

The mystery which developed out of this situation concerned
the efforts of the Waring boy to find the gold pieces that his dead

grandfather, who mistrusted banks, had hidden in their abandoned home, keeping the secret of the hiding place from all of his relatives. Sally and Bob, the engineer's children, encounter the grandson unexpectedly when they are exploring his empty house. They manage to win his trust, help him decipher the only clue his grandfather left and thereby discover the gold. This book was fun to write, for it helped me to recreate many happy memories from my own childhood at a time when it was pleasanter for me to live in the past than in the present.

Mystery of the Diamond Necklace caused me the most trouble, because when I began it I did not know the solution, much less what the mystery was about. An empty French chateau in the Catskills, which had been a sort of spooky play place for me and my friends, provided the setting. I invented a college professor's family spending the summer in their cottage across the road and the dismay the children felt the morning after their arrival when they found the chateau being refurbished and made ready for occupancy. At the end of two chapters, I was firmly stuck. The first idea for the plot had to do with the theft of ration coupons and their concealment in a stable behind the chateau. Today's child, I realized, would have little knowledge of ration coupons, so I abandoned that idea. The first two chapters traveled back and forth to the Jersey shore with me for two summers before I began to work out the plot I finally used.

My first New Hampshire auction led to another mystery. I bid on and acquired a small, handmade wooden trunk with dovetailed corners, hoping to find inside some dress-up clothes for my small daughter. Instead, the trunk was filled with rolled-up pieces of dreary looking material: coat linings, percale remnants, and the like. At the auction I had taken notes of the amusing lingo of the auctioneer which I later used in the book. The plot was suggested by an article I had clipped from the old *New York Herald-Tribune* about a primitive Marblehead artist, John Orne Johnson Frost, whose work did not receive recognition until years after he had died and many of his paintings had disappeared. A seaman, cook, and restaurant owner, he was seventy before he began to paint. His neighbors refused to take him seriously and poked fun at his quaint, crudely-drawn scenes of Marblehead from colonial times to this century. Discouraged, he stopped painting, and when he died in 1929, only a few pictures could be found. Twenty years later critics hailed Frost as an outstanding primitive painter, and collectors of Americana began to offer high prices for his pictures.

Then, to the amazement of Frost's admirers, thirty more of his paintings were discovered by the new owners of his house when they tore down a partition between rooms and found it was made of the wooden panels he had painted on instead of canvas.

In *Mystery of the Auction Trunk,* the Marblehead painter becomes a New Hampshire carpenter who was also an unappreciated artist during his lifetime. The Holland children bid on a small wooden trunk at an auction, are as disappointed as I was at its contents, but resist the efforts of a stranger to buy it from them at a higher price. They learn that the trunk was made by the old carpenter whose house they have just acquired for a summer home. Later, they find in a pocket of an apron in the trunk a letter written by the old man to his sister expressing his discouragement over his efforts at art but saying that he has thought of a use for his work, even though no one appreciated it. With this hint that some paintings may still exist and the depredations of a squirrel who steals the younger brother's socks for a nest in the attic, they find the paintings, but not before the stranger, an art dealer from Boston, has tried to get their home away from them through a faked flaw in its title.

One of my mystery plots was started by a dream. I was spending the day on the island of Capri with members of the University of Pennsylvania Museum. We had been traveling on a Greek ship, visiting Greek ruins in southern Italy, and anchored at dawn in the harbor of Capri. A friend and I, seeking the Villa San Michele where the famous Dr. Axel Munthe once lived, mistook a street sign for the villa sign, climbed a marble staircase between lush vegetation, and entered the open door of a handsome dwelling. We encountered no one as we wandered through its rooms seeking a loggia from which there should have been a splendid view of the Bay of Naples. But when, on an upper floor, we came upon beds stripped for airing and with dust covers removed from furniture, the horrid suspicion dawned on us that we were trespassing in a private house, and we beat a hasty retreat, thankful not to meet anyone. That night after the ship sailed, I dreamed that two girls entered such a villa, mistaking it, as we had done, for the Villa San Michele. They were startled to hear the sound of water running in a bathroom, but before they could retreat, the door opened, and an impressive looking woman appeared. She was as startled to see them as they were to see her there. While explanations were being given, they suddenly heard a pounding on a wall and a faint cry for help. At that inconvenient moment I awoke, but I knew at once that I had the beginnings of a mystery plot. I switched on the cabin light and jotted my dream down in a notebook for future reference. The result was *Mystery at the Villa Caprice*.

I had to do considerable research on the early history of that lovely island and the Emperor Tiberius's connection with it. The plot concerned opium smuggling and a secret cave where the opium was converted into heroin and shipped in false bottoms of Greek vases to the United States.

Perhaps I should mention here that children's mysteries, at least mine, are *not* murder mysteries, though there was an attempted killing in this one, and in another, *Mystery of the Secret Message,* the head of a spy ring commits suicide as he is being taken away for questioning.

Another archaeological expedition to the Maya ruins of Tikal in the jungles of Guatemala led to my writing *Mystery of the Maya Jade*. While we were staying in the Jungle Inn at Tikal, the Museum filled with rarities found during the excavations was broken into, but nothing was taken. This provided the idea for the plot. In my story a rare jade figurine of a kneeling Maya Indian is stolen from the Museum. Pamela Bacon, a young American girl traveling with her botanist aunt, and Toby Burns, son of the resident archaeologist in charge of the Tikal dig, become involved in tracking down the jade and uncovering the activities of an American importer of Guatemalan handicrafts whose business is a cover for spiriting out of the country pre-Columbian artifacts.

On travels I always keep a journal in a ruled notebook in which I record local color and considerable information about the sights, sounds, people and places I see. Then if a plot rears its welcome head, I have ready at hand the necessary details of the setting. Much additional research and reading were required for the *Maya*

Jade mystery, for I tried to weave into the story details of Guatemalan life today, as well as some of the lore of Mayan culture of yesterday and of the archaeological discoveries at Tikal.

In the days when I was writing a mystery a year and running a house, I discovered the value of always carrying a notebook. I could then make use of scraps of time (waiting in doctors' or dentists' offices, riding on trains, eating lunches alone in restaurants) to record dialogue and put down whatever was happening next in my story. I transcribed these scribbles into typescript as soon as I got home, and the story would begin to take shape.

72

EVERYTHING CAN BE TOO MUCH

By Elizabeth Allen

Several years ago when we were remodeling our kitchen, our daughter came in from the backyard and with some distaste said, "There's everything out there but the kitchen sink!" And indeed there was: old chairs, tables, broken dishes, *junk*. The she added, "In fact, the kitchen sink is out there, too." The whole unlovely scene reminded me of a letter I had received from an editor which said, "You have everything but the kitchen sink in this story."

I always think that I am keeping things in focus, but I often fail, forgetting just what I am trying to do, which is to *tell a story*. I put everything in but the kitchen sink, and *everything* is too much. Whether you choose to tell your tale with one all-revealing "moment of truth," in what Frank O'Connor calls the *conte*, or in a string of episodes, which he refers to as the *nouvelle*, you have still to keep the reader turning pages. You must cast a spell.

Probably the first thing to keep in mind is that you cannot have a large cast of characters in your story. We all know (or should know) that a character cannot appear on the scene as mere window dressing or as a walk-on. There isn't room. There isn't time. But what about the minor character who makes a real point in your narrative, or who you think really adds to the mood of the story? He seems necessary. But is he?

I had many difficulties with several minor characters in a story I wrote about a lonely young mother living in an isolated subdivision. Louise has almost no family except her husband and four-year-old Pam, no neighbors, and is expecting a second child. She misses her friends in a crowded apartment complex, and the story starts with her visit to Barb, who is stimulating and fun but rather scatterbrained. Barb is also a very casual mother. Louise enjoys talking about books with Barb, but something about her freewheeling friend worries and depresses her. In fact, because of her isolation and the difficulties she is having in getting a reliable person to stay with Pam while she is in the hospital, Louise begins to become anxious. The mood of the story darkens. But Louise hates to admit that she is being weak and silly. Cal, her husband, has said to her, "We are all weak when we should be strong; fragile, and easily hurt, and we have to protect ourselves in ludicrous ways. . . ." Louise tries to realize that if Cal, who seems such a tower of strength to her, can occasionally feel "weak," then everyone must, and that her feelings mean nothing. She shakes off her depression and happily goes on planning for the new baby.

So far so good. But this is where, in early drafts of the story, I went wrong. I used a spooky, witch-like neighbor who moves in and frightens Louise. I had a relative of hers call and tell Louise she had no right to have another child "in this day and age." All these things added, I told myself, to the story. Then I thought, *what story?* I was throwing in too much. I needed Barb, who horrifies Louise by deserting her family, but I did not need the witchy neighbor or the nasty relative.

I had to decide what to keep and what to discard, and finally went on to tell of a frightened woman who goes to the hospital wondering if she really ought to have a baby, but who finds in the unexpected strength of her newborn fresh hope for herself. "To Be Weak, To Be Strong" appeared in *Good Housekeeping,* also sold to England's *Woman.*

My next two attempts at fiction were failures. Part of the failure was the length of the stories, and I resolved to try to be more concise.

I started a story about a college-age girl called Cecelia, who is in a state of near shock because of the death of her fiancé. I had purposely limited my cast of characters, and redundant "walk-ons" were not a problem. But in order to show Ceci's home atmosphere, I needed some description of her physical surroundings. The story originally started with this paragraph:

I sat on the sunwarmed brick wall above the sunken garden and stared at a single rose just below me as I brushed my hair dry. Maybe if I stared at one rose long enough I would be able to forget everything that had happened. I kept on staring until I heard cars start to arrive, and remembering that Mom was giving some sort of party that morning and might need help, I got up and started walking under the trees toward the side door of our house. Before I went inside I stopped to stare at the huge oak which almost blocks our circular drive. We really should cut it down, but it's supposed to be a Council Oak, and no one in the family can bear to have it destroyed.

Although I kept this paragraph until I had finished the story, I was dubious about it. It told something of Ceci's home and family, and hinted that she was trying to get over a sad happening, but there was too much detail. And what was worse, there wasn't *enough* detail about Ceci herself, and Mark had not even been mentioned. I finally changed the paragraph to the following:

I sat on the brick wall above the sunken garden, brushing my hair dry. "It's like brown silk," Mark had said once. Maybe it was. I brushed my hair and tried to think of absolutely nothing. Mark and I had planned to try meditation, I remembered, but we hadn't. At least I hadn't. Perhaps he had; Mark had tried about everything. When my hair was dry, I got up and went into the house.

This paragraph gets the story off to a better start and gives us a glimpse of a troubled girl thinking about a boy. The narrative goes on to show Ceci talking to her brother, who is obviously concerned about her, and to her mother, also concerned. The mother is giving a large party, and Ceci offers to help, telling the reader, "I plan little chores for myself." It is necessary for Ceci to plan little chores; the searing memory of a senseless motorcycle accident has made her life almost unendurable.

What was important in this story was Ceci's meeting with Mark's mother, and so I got to it as soon as I could. Mrs. Wallingford has been cruel to Ceci, blaming her for the death of her son. "If you had been with him, you could have saved him," Mrs. Wallingford had once told her, and Ceci now avoids her. They share a mutual grief, but hostility crackles between them. Besides, Ceci has always considered Mrs. Wallingford silly and superficial. Then, in an unexpected encounter, she realizes the genuine anguish of the older woman:

"I plan a job for each day," Mrs. Wallingford tells Ceci. "It'll be harder this summer, because so many activities stop. . . . I signed up for this humanities course at the college, but I don't know. I feel kind of funny going over there; I'm not all that smart, and I won't know where to park or anything. But if I don't do that, I'll do *something*. I plan a job for each day."

Ceci realizes that this is what she herself is doing: planning something for each day, getting through the hours one at a time, going on somehow despite her despair. The story ends with Ceci's turning toward Mrs. Wallingford. They can do nothing for a boy who is gone, but perhaps they can help each other. "The Encounter" was published in *Seventeen*.

Detail is, of course, necessary to a story. We need descriptive bits; we must delineate character; there is no way to cut out dialogue (we are, after all, writing fiction!), and if a story is intense enough to engage the reader, there should be a leavening touch of humor. But repetitious and extraneous material has no place in a short story. Sometimes it is a good idea to finish the job, putting in everything that occurs to you. Perhaps, for some reason I cannot explain, you *need* to put all this down, you *need* those walk-on characters and long descriptive bits to fully realize the narrative. But then, a careful look at the finished story is essential. What can you discard, and what can you keep? Have you made your descriptive detail work?

For example, in "The Encounter," I mentioned a "tall old clock" near the stairs which strikes, making Ceci jump. This detail serves two purposes: it gives us a hint of what the house is like, and, more important, it reveals the state of Ceci's nerves. She hears a telephone ringing in the distance but has no interest in answering it. Again, the telephone ringing "in the distance" shows us the spaciousness of the house and, even more important, Ceci's apathy. Dual purposes are served.

It is often a good idea to leave your too-long manuscript and work on something entirely different for awhile. When you return to your story, those unnecessary sentences will really jump out at you, and you'll know what to keep and what is *too much*.

73

WRITING JUVENILE MYSTERIES

By Arnold Madison

As I scanned a recent *New York Times* Children's Books Section, I noticed an abundance of mysteries by British authors. Although there is an accepted belief that the British are the best mystery writers, I firmly believe American authors can be equally successful in the juvenile mystery field. Mystery writers the world over have the same five ingredients at their disposal: PLOT, CHARACTERS, SETTING, STYLE, TITLE. The results depend on the quality of each element and how well they are mixed, prepared, and served. Let us take a closer look at each of these ingredients.

Plot is often the downfall of many juvenile mysteries. Writers may work so hard creating suspenseful plot turns that illogical events and faceless pawns moved by an author's hand are the result. True, many children's mysteries fizzle out because they have only one strange thing happening in chapter one, and the remainder of the book is given over to solving that single puzzle. A mystery should keep developing with new twists, unexpected turns. But watch the believability.

One finds it difficult to accept eight- or ten-year-olds capturing criminals. They may be *involved* in the capture, however. Here is a potential story idea which actually happened on Long Island last year. Two children who had received drug education lectures in their elementary school spotted a suspicious-looking plant on a neighbor's apartment terrace. One afternoon, the large plant was blown off the terrace by a violent thunderstorm. The children rushed out and broke off a branch which they brought to the police. The tenant was arrested for the possession of marijuana. In story form, this plot would seem possible and yet there would be suspense. Does the man know they are watching his apartment day after day? Where is he when the plant falls? Will he catch them snatching the branch?

In addition to believability, the theme of the story is important and just as necessary to a mystery as to a straight novel. In choosing your characters and setting, you make a statement. Many juvenile mysteries are thin, mere fluff, because their only purpose is pure entertainment. My theme for *Danger Beats the Drum* was how hate can destroy you if you let it. In *The Secret of the Carved Whale Bone*, I wanted to tell the reader that we should open ourselves to progress and be prepared to capitalize on the positive aspects of change and combat its negative results. Not earthshaking philosophies, I admit, but ones I hold to strongly. Although they are cloaked as mysteries, I think they are stated as validly as they would have been in an ordinary novel.

Every writer has beliefs and ideas he wants to tell the world. Put the *you* into your mystery story. That's where satisfaction lies.

The second ingredient—characters—is vital to the success of your mystery. And for that reason it raises some questions. Do you want a boy or girl main character? How old should your hero or heroine be? Should a single or multiple viewpoint be employed? Fortunately, there are general rules-of-thumb for your guidance.

For instance, when selecting a boy or girl main character, remember something known by every children's librarian: Girls read anything and everything. Boys read only fiction in which a boy is the main character. There are exceptions, of course. But few.

The question of your main character's age should not be dismissed lightly. Publishers generally group children's books into three categories: for children ages 6–8, 9–12, or for teen-agers. Your main character should be as old as the person at the upper end of the age bracket. Children do not want to read about people younger than themselves. They have been through that. Only adults are nostalgic about times gone by. Young people expect tomorrow to be even better than today.

Recently, some publishers have started to designate their books for children ages 10–13. The reasons are twofold. They hope to capture both the elementary school and the junior high school library markets. Also, editors have observed that readers older than thirteen usually select adult fiction and mysteries for their plea-sure reading.

A rather firm rule exists concerning the use of single viewpoint, but books for older children are often published with more than one viewpoint character. I believe, however, that younger chil-dren are confused by changing viewpoints. They prefer to stay with one character all the way through a story.

There is another consideration about characters which makes it difficult to understand the popularity of British books with Ameri-can editors. I learned an important fact from twelve years of teach-ing—twelve years of forty-five minutes a week in a library with twenty-five elementary school children. *American youngsters are more interested in reading about other American children than about youngsters from foreign countries.* They get enough fictional-ized accounts of "Mustapha: Goat Herder of Turkey" in their text-books and nonfiction trade books. Stories dealing only with young people of other nationalities always have a slight aura of "school" about them. Also, the dialogue of American children is easier for them to read and understand. Our children *do* like to read about American youths in foreign places and enjoy meeting minor char-acters of different nationalities.

The depth of your characterizations will depend on how well you know and *like* children. If you are always complaining about the children and teen-agers of today, I would hesitate to suggest that you attempt a book about them. Naturally, no one condones everything that is done under the name of youth. But can you ap-preciate the qualities peculiar to the young? A boy who hasn't the patience to paint a wall carefully will spend long, sweaty hours on a greasy garage floor meticulously adapting a power mower engine into a motor bicycle. A painfully shy girl will stand on a curb beseeching passersby to sign a petition for a politician she truly believes is an idealist. Young people are hard to pigeonhole.

Yet the characters in so many juvenile mysteries seem stereo-types. Perhaps the author did not delve deeply enough into his peo-ple to develop them fully. Recently, in discussing Nina Bawden, an English writer of juvenile mysteries, an editor commented, "I do not attribute Nina Bawden's success to any British characteristics, but rather to the fact that she is a consistently good writer, and her characters are drawn with depth and easily come alive to the reader."

For characterization-in-depth also read *Mystery of the Fat Cat* by Frank Bonham, a story about young blacks living in an urban ghetto. Here are children so real that the reader feels as if he has met and talked with them. And those are the kinds of characters all children's mysteries deserve.

Another aspect of mystery writing in which Americans sometimes suffer by comparison to British writers is the story setting. The tired clichés in the American books often become painfully evident if a selection of mysteries is read. Attics have been done to death. I used one in *The Secret of the Carved Whale Bone* and have had pangs of guilt ever since. I know I took the easy way out. If I had forced myself to search for an original idea, I might have found something more exciting. And, to be frank, how many houses have you visited where there was a secret panel or hidden staircase? Or restaurants where jewel thieves at a nearby table were planning their next caper?

But worse than employing worn-out devices is the misuse of background. Publishers do like a foreign setting because it increases the chance for good sales by offering a curriculum tie-in to school libraries. But authors do not have to choose exotic backgrounds. Mysteries can take place anywhere. The important point is that the author know his setting very well—not just the flora and fauna, but the mood of the people, the underlying economic stresses, the effect of the past on the present. All these affect plot, characters, and dialogue.

Phyllis A. Whitney's *The Secret of the Samurai Sword* is an example of good setting-plot relationship. The heroine, an American girl, visits Kyoto, Japan. The story Miss Whitney tells could only happen on that street, to those particular people, and because the girl arrived from the United States. The city, the past, even the weather play an important role in determining the plot. Although the author zeroed in on a tiny section of a large city, the theme has universal implications about East-West and young-old conflicts.

Now we come to a quality of mystery writing which may explain the success of British mysteries with our publishers. Personally, I feel that many editors, being literate people, are attracted to the British juvenile mystery by the style of writing. I believe, however, that American writers have more to offer our young mystery fans.

This is an important point. I noticed, too, in my elementary classes that the slower readers would hunt for mysteries. These children want fast-moving stories, not long blocks of descriptive writing or pages of introspection. Exciting scenes need fast, staccato sentences with punchy dialogue that can be easily understood. Phrases like "Don't be daft" or "Would you mind awfully?" or "Oh, rot!" spoken by ten- and eleven-year-old boys in intense situations in British mysteries jump out and give American children the feeling that these characters are sissies.

Of course we American writers want to be sure not to go too far the other way with dialogue. Topical terms and current slang will often date before your book is in print. Writers should be careful whom they label as a hippie, for instance, since the term is no longer widely used. And who knows how long phrases like "spaced-out" and "right on" will be in vogue? A year at the most?

As long as we watch out for the pitfalls, our style is likely to interest and hold our younger readers.

The last of the five points to consider in juvenile mystery writing is the title. Publishers engage artists to design colorful and eye-catching jackets to snare readers. Yet book covers are the *second* magnet to attract an audience. Children stroll down library aisles, scanning the hundreds of narrow spines for a promise of excitement, puzzling clues, danger. *The Phantom of Walkaway Hill* crooks a skeletal finger, as does *The Secret of the Dark Tower*. These titles conjure up a mental picture, and the image is a sinister one.

The search for an appropriate title should stretch throughout the entire planning and writing period. Pick a working title at the beginning, then set aside a page where you will list all possible permanent titles.

Some editors prefer the words "mystery" or "secret" to appear in the title. For ages 8–12, the use of these words seems wise, but they may carry a too-young image for grades seven and up. My first book started out as *The Secret of Shadow Lake* and twelve titles later ended up as *Danger Beats the Drum,* a title more appropriate for the teen-age reader.

The juvenile mystery is fun to write. Careful attention to the five components discussed here should produce a substantial story that is exciting to read. And that is what all editors want!

74

WRITING FOR CHILDREN

By Irene Hunt

Any writer, whether he writes for children or adults, must face and answer the questions posed by Goethe to would-be writers:

> Do I have something to say?
> Is what I have to say worth saying?
> How best can I go about saying this thing
>   which I consider to be worth the saying?

Any fictional writing if it lays claim to being literature must leave the reader with a clearer picture, a deeper understanding of some aspect of human behavior, of human needs, a more profound knowledge of the human heart, if you will.

Thus the writer must find his answer to the question "Do I have something worthwhile to say?" by discovering what aspects of human behavior he wishes to explore.

Will it be the courage of a child in overcoming his inner fears, in overcoming a hostile environment, in overcoming physical or emotional handicaps? Will it be a child's perceptions of the adult world around him? Will it be the insights of a young person into his own behavior? Will it be the interplay between environment and human needs?

There are an infinite number of problems which beset the family of man, and they lie waiting for us to present them in a new light —to clarify and illuminate them through our own originality.

When the question of what one is going to say has been resolved, the writer must decide how best he can say it—what characters, what situations he can create which will provide the best setting for the ideas which are the core of his writing.

Armstrong Sperry, in writing of courage which overcame a terrible fear, chose the terrors of the sea, of storms, of primitive savages to illuminate his theme in *Call it Courage*.

Scott O'Dell pointed up another kind of courage, the courage to live, to survive, in his Robinson Crusoe-like story, *Island of the Blue Dolphins*.

E. B. White and Kenneth Grahame chose fantasy—a fantasy accurately reflecting human values—and where is the child who can miss the dignity and compassion of some of their characters, the bumbling foolishness of others?

Now, a look at the qualifications of the writer himself—the man or woman who aspires to write for that vast crowd of young readers and who aspires to write wisely and well for the audience he has chosen. First, his ability to write for children involves a close affinity with his own childhood, and if he has this, it follows that he will have that same affinity for childhood in general. He must remember! He must remember the anxieties and uncertainties, he must remember the loneliness of being teased or misunderstood. He must remember the dreams, the perplexities, the sudden flashes of joy over something that seemed trivial to adults. He must remember his reaction to tastes, to smells, to colors; his love of a kind hand, his fear of a harsh mouth. He must remember the imaginary companions, the wonderful secret places where he could be alone, the hoarding of nondescript material in an old box—guarding it, rearranging it, caring greatly for it without quite knowing why.

This affinity for our own childhood and for that of others is something that not all of us possess; it is, I sometimes think, as final an attribute as the color of our eyes or the shape of our ears. If we don't have blue eyes or brown, we don't, and there isn't much we can do about it. If we don't understand childhood, we don't, and I doubt if we can ever develop that understanding. This quality is not correlated with either age or intelligence; some great scholars have it, some don't. Some people of twenty have it, some have already lost it at that early age. Some people of sixty or eighty have it; others of the same age do not.

Writers of adult literature are sometimes dismayed when they have turned from their own field to that of children's literature. They often find that they do not know how to speak to children, that they are unable to establish the bond of sympathy which they had believed would be so easy to do. They have found they long since have left their childhood behind them and that they are aliens in a community of readers who sense their kinship with one writer without ever quite realizing that it is present, and who sense equally well the lack of kinship with another writer.

People who have forgotten their own youth tend to carry with them a picture of rosy childhood, protected from all evil, bathed in love and security and winsome innocence. Those of us who remember the anxieties, the anger, the fear—sometimes the cruelties which we perpetrated and have never been able to forget—we are the ones who know that childhood is not always a period suffused in a rosy glow. And those of us who remember the delight at a word of praise, or the sound of a birdsong; the sweet comfort of being understood, the heady excitement of running against the wind, the sense of security in hearing a mother singing at her work —we are the ones who know that childhood delight is not all a matter of camping trips or toys, parties or the approval of peer groups.

Another point which the writer for children must keep in mind is that he must have respect for his audience. Can he lend dignity to a child of seven or nine—or is he one who would say, "No child of such an age can possibly have felt grief or fear or anxiety with such intensity?"

And again, is the writer in tune with that bittersweet period of life which we call adolescence, or does he believe that adolescents are concerned with nothing more than getting a date or getting on the football team or romping around camp for the summer? Worse still, is he one of those writers who have great fun in depicting adolescents as callow, silly, uproariously funny to the "sophisticated" adult? How naïve can such writers be? Have they completely forgotten the sensitivity, the bewilderment, the groping for beauty and truth that are so often characteristic of these years —the years which, I often think, may be described by the words which Dickens used to describe the closing years of the eighteenth century—"It was the best of times and the worst of times; it was an age of foolishness, an age of wisdom."

Children have dignity—they appreciate respect for that dignity.

Children perceive and evaluate, they feel intensely and they look for answers to the many questions with which a capricious society often baffles them. If the writer for children does not remember this, he will soon need to turn to another field.

Closely associated with respect for childhood is the ability to write without preaching. This is difficult. As parents, we are inclined to preach. As teachers, we are very much inclined to preach. And as writers, we still feel the urge. We want to spell the idea out. We're afraid the immature mind may not be aware of the pearls we are offering it. We want to say, "And so you see, boys and girls, if children do this or that, then these or those results are going to ensue." Paul Hazard in his great book, *Books, Children and Men,* has this to say on the subject: "A glance of the eyes, a thrust of the thumb is all they need. They sense the coming of a sermon and they skip it with dexterity."

Preaching is not the only cardinal sin either. There is the matter of the author feeling that he must be instructive. We like to say— implicitly, of course—"I know that you selected this book because you thought it was fiction, but you're going to get a little lesson in science or history or anthropology on the side."

There is nothing wrong with children learning something of science or history or anthropology in a book of fiction. BUT—and this is a very important BUT—it is up to the author to make this kind of information so much a part of the story, to endow it with so much of human interest, that it is an integral part of the story. When a child picks up a book from the shelves devoted to fiction, he has a right to expect a story. He heartily resents the intrusion of what he perceives as a "classroom bit" interfering with that story. He doesn't mind if it's a part of the story; *Johnny Tremain,* for example, contains a wealth of history concerning the American Revolution, but that history *is* the story of Johnny Tremain—it *is* the story, and not a fringe benefit.

Again I quote Paul Hazard when he writes of some of the early works of what was whimsically called children's literature: "To admire an oak for its beauty was considered time wasted; children needed to be able to calculate what the oak might yield in board feet when it was cut into planks."

Next, an author must be true to himself. If he has a story to tell, he must tell it without worrying whether it will appeal to children of seven or ten or sixteen. Incidentally, if it is a good story for a child of seven, it is in all probability a good story for any age. Take Rebecca Caudill's *A Certain Small Shepherd,* for example—take *Winnie, the Pooh,* take *Charlotte's Web*—what age group will like these stories? Any age from seven to ninety, provided the reader has learned to love excellent literature.

I feel that the writer who has a story lurking around in his mind and heart should present it as *he* sees fit. He should be allowed to forget vocabulary and taboo subjects, he should close his ears to the chorus of "children are no longer interested in this or that." One educator told me with a finality that left little room for doubt that children would never read a story of the Civil War: "They are fed up with it," she said firmly. Of course, what she meant was that *she* was fed up with it. I have more than a hundred letters from children all over the country who have read and have told me that they loved my book, *Across Five Aprils.*

Other members of this free-advice chorus have told me, "If your book is written in the first person, you had just as well throw it away right now. Children simply *won't* read books written in the first person." Oh, won't they? Have a look at *Huckleberry Finn,* at *Treasure Island,* at *Island of the Blue Dolphins,* at *Onion John,* at *It's Like This, Cat.* And my own *Up a Road Slowly* is doing pretty well. My advice to writers is: Ignore the chorus, and write as you please. Children are interested in almost any subject, written in either first or third person, if it is presented in an interesting context, if it is written honestly and well.

There is no need to be upset if we feel that we are dealing with a subject that has often been dealt with before. Some authors strain very hard to be original, confusing novelty with originality, forgetting that it is what you as an author bring to the subject which constitutes originality. Flaubert, Tolstoy and Thackeray used the same, time-worn theme: woman's self-destruction. And yet, Emma Bovary, Anna Karenina and Becky Sharp stand out as different, as unique, as sharply drawn as if each had participated in a situation never described before—products of their specific creator's originality.

I feel that originality is that special blend of color and contrast, that quality of vigor or poetic mood, that depth of characterization with which the writer presents his story. Novelty is only an arresting factor; originality is the quality which gives a book endurance. In children's literature, *Alice in Wonderland* is a shining example of novelty. But it is not novelty that makes this book great. It is not Alice's unusual acquaintances or her experiences with changing size or her encounters with frightening incidents which make the book a great one. It is the satire, the wry wisdom, the impish lashing out at certain stupidities of society which give the book greatness—it is the quality which only Lewis Carroll could give that situation—that very personal and private attribute of a writer which is his originality.

Young writers are often concerned with style—they wonder how they can develop that concept which is so elusive, which does not easily lend itself to definition. Style, it seems to me, is an outpouring of the writer's self—his perceptions of life, his grace or lack of grace, his courage or his whining self-pity, his humility and compassion or his cynicism and arrogance.

Think of the delicacy of Katherine Mansfield, the robust humor of Mark Twain, the gentle wistfulness of Kenneth Grahame, the sweet, prim morality and great warmth of Louisa M. Alcott. Each one has a style all his own because each one has poured out a part of himself, the kind of person he was or is, into his writing.

The young or beginning writer cannot copy a style authentically any more than he can *be* the person whose style he admires. He may be influenced by another's style in that he has read and admired the writings of an author until he has come to accept that person's viewpoint. But if he is wise, he will not seek to emulate another writer's work; he will set himself to the task of telling his own story as clearly, as honestly, as gracefully as he possibly can. When he has worked for a while, he may suddenly discover that he, too, has expressed some inner feelings in a way that people will speak of as a particular style.

In conclusion, I would say that our concern over children's books is justifiable and understandable. There is a great need for excellence in children's literature just as there is a need for excellence in all other aspects of education. To train a nation of readers, of people who have at an early age commenced to deal with ideas, who have come to recognize a system of values which includes such concepts as insight, compassion and understanding of human behavior—to do this carries a responsibility which is of towering importance.· For whether a child becomes a scientist or a housewife, a mathematician or a mechanic, a teacher, a business-man, a statesman, a factory worker, a farmer, these values are basic to his fulfillment as a human being.

We must remember that children are not born with these values. Their understanding and appreciation of literature and of life do not suddenly appear full-blown like Athene from the forehead of Zeus. It comes from reading and discussing and learning to love good books; it comes from guidance in discovering wisdom and beauty, it comes because authors and teachers, librarians and parents are providing the books of wisdom, of beauty and joy, for these young learners. The good books, the gay, the sad, the wise ones are providing a basis for a nation of readers, a nation of people who understand themselves and those around them a little better. We do not learn courage, humility, compassion, honor or human decency from penny lectures or from a special unit in the classroom. We learn these things through the people around us—we learn them largely from the behavior of those characters who march through the pages of our books.

75

WRITING BIOGRAPHIES FOR YOUNG READERS

By Olive W. Burt

One of the most popular, and for many writers most rewarding, types of writing for young people is the biography. This seems to be a field in which there are never too many books for the eager youngster, or (what is more important to the writer) never too many for the publishers.

There are several things to be decided before one pitches into such a project. First, of course, is the choice of subject. If by chance you are one of those fortunate people who have publishers sending you frantic telegrams for a book, you may not be free to choose your subject. The publisher may have told you what he needs—subject, age level, and treatment. But let's suppose you are on your own and can decide for yourself what you want to do.

About whom shall you write? Hasn't everyone important been covered in a biography? A glance through several publishers' lists will almost convince you that there is no one left for you to write about. Messner's "High School Shelf of Biographies" now numbers more than two hundred subjects, chiefly Americans. Bobbs-Merrill's "Childhood of Famous Americans" series has over one hundred and fifty titles. Franklin Watts' "Immortals of Science" lists more than thirty books. Watts also publishes other series of "Immortals" in literature, science, engineering, etc.

All this needn't scare you. Your book about any individual will be different from any other book that has been written. If you have something new, some hitherto little-known facts, or just a different approach to your subject, you can write—and sell—biographies even about such perennial favorites as Lincoln and Washington. The spate of books about John F. Kennedy—many

443

just rehashes of newspaper articles—shows that publishers bring out books on subjects that have appeared on competitors' lists.

There are, however, plenty of less well-known persons who are worthy of treatment. It gives an author a peculiar sense of achievement to produce a book about some person children should know, but have, so far, had no opportunity to meet in a biography. A few years ago, *Publishers' Weekly* printed a list of twenty new biographies for young readers and asked how many adults could identify the subjects and their accomplishments. On the list were Anne Neville, Bartholome de las Casas, Francisco de Orellana, William Dampier, Fridtjof Nansen and Kateri Tekakwitha. Some astute writers had performed a real service in presenting these people to children.

Writing for children, you will not want to do an exposé of the sins and foibles of some person, however fascinating these may be. Your purpose should be to present a character whom the young reader may wish to emulate. To do this successfully, you must honestly admire the person you choose to write about. Insincerity is quickly detected by the sharp perception of youngsters. If they once mark you as a hypocrite, your value in this field is lost.

You will, of course, choose a subject you already know something about. Your knowledge may, however, be vague and inaccurate. So you begin to read, swiftly—and without much note-taking —the best biography on your subject that you can find. This will help you to decide whether you have made a wise choice, what age group will be interested, and how you wish to handle the material.

Biographies written for young people fall into the same age-level classifications as do other books. The pre-school child will probably have little interest in biography, but the 9-12-year-olds, the teens and the young adults love it. For the younger readers, the preferred length is around 20,000 to 25,000 words, and it's growing shorter every year. Teen-agers can handle a book of 40,000 or even 50,000 words. Books for young adults may be any length, though many publishers prefer to keep them under 60,000 words.

Biographies for young readers, as, indeed, for adults, may be written either factually or fictionally. The factual treatment is a straightforward account of an individual's life and the events which shaped it. It is completely accurate as to dates and events, but should not have footnotes. It is generally permissible for the writer to invent some dialogue of which there is no record, provided there is evidence that such conversations took place. In using the *factual* treatment, the author is all-knowing. He can present facts and incidents of which the hero is unaware, provided these facts are important in shaping the individual's actions. In writing a factual biography of John Charles Frémont, for example, the author might tell of the cabinet meeting in Washington and of the debates that led up to Frémont's court-martial—events which Frémont, out in California, could not have known.

Fictional treatment is a bit more complicated. Here the author disappears entirely—he tries to get "right into the skin" of his main character, to think and feel as this person must have thought and felt. Nothing can be told that the subject does not know for himself. If events occur beyond the hero's ken, the reader may know of them only when, as and how the subject, himself, learns of them. This point of view must be maintained throughout the book. The author has an advantage, however, in that he may introduce characters and events that are entirely imaginary. But these imagined events and characters must be true to the time and place of the story and *must* be necessary to the development of the character.

Personally, I prefer to write the fictional type of biography. I used it in doing a biography of Frémont for Messner, and in that book, Frémont knew nothing of what was going on in Washington until a messenger brought the news.

Sometimes a combination of the factual and the fictional treatment is attempted, but in such cases the result generally falls short of the ideal. Either history or fiction suffers.

By now you will have read enough about your chosen subject and thought enough about it to be able to write an intelligent letter to a publisher. It is wise to find a publisher before you spend months in research and writing. You are not likely to find one who will say right off, "Yes! I'll take that!" But you may find one who will agree to look at a chapter or two "on speculation." Then it is up to you to produce something the publisher can accept. But how to find a publisher? Visit the library and examine books brought out by various publishers. Or consult the special seasonal issues of *Publishers' Weekly* at your library, and study publishers' lists there.

It is often easier, especially for a person breaking into the field, to get a start via one of the series. The field is large. In addition to those already mentioned, Nelson has "Picture Biographies" for the 9-to-12-year-olds; Putnam publishes "Lives to Remember" and "Westerners." Sheed and Ward's "Patron Saints" deals with the lives of Catholic saints, and Bruce's "Catholic Treasure Books" present the lives of noteworthy Catholics.

Select the publisher you think, from your investigation, will be most receptive to your idea, and write a query letter to the editor of books for young people. It is more effective if you address this editor by name, which you can find in *Literary Market Place* at the library. In your letter, you state clearly, simply, and briefly the name of your subject, a little about him or her, and how you would like to handle the biography. Also, ask the editor if he is interested in seeing two or three chapters and an outline of the whole book. If the answer is yes, get right to work and do those chapters before the editor forgets about you—or takes another book on your subject from an author who is more prompt.

If you write to several editors and do not find one who is interested in your project, you may drop the idea as unfeasible; you may put it aside for the time being and go to work on something else; or you may go ahead and write it anyway, trusting that your fine work will sell the book, once it is written.

The selling of a finished book is difficult, and grows more so every year. Today, the publisher likes to decide on his forthcoming list and then approach writers he knows can fill his requirements. Also, at the risk of ruffling the feathers of some fine editors, it seems that a few feel that to take a book as sent in by an unknown author indicates that the editor has been outguessed. If consulted before the book is written, he can be not only the "chooser," but also the director of the project.

Let's assume that whether you have a go-ahead from a publisher or not, you decide to go on with writing your book. Now you begin *intensive* research, which is far different from the preliminary work you have done. First, you will read all the published biographies you can find about your subject, especially scholarly, accurate works. Read also magazine articles, biographies of your subject's contemporaries, and the history of the period. If possible, study original documents, letters, newspapers, journals—anything written during the period in which your subject lived. These will give you an intimate glimpse of life and language, dress and foods, which you will find nowhere else. Try to visit the locale where your subject lived. If you can see his home, handle his books, touch the doorknobs he turned, you'll find yourself better able to think and feel as he did.

All this time take careful and accurate notes. And always, without fail, make a record of the source of every note, listing the title of the book, author, publisher, date and place of publication, and the page on which your material was found. This may sound like needless work, but I can assure you that if you fail even once to make a complete record, that very item will be one you later wish to check, and you will never, never be able to find it again. Moreover, if the publisher wants a bibliography, as some do, you will have the information handy and will not have to redo your work.

When your research is completed and you feel you are ready to begin writing, you will need an outline of some kind. An effective chart-outline can be drawn on a large sheet of paper. Rule it into columns. In the first, put the dates of your subject's life, chronologically from birth to death. In the second, write the names of family members and their ages at particular years. In the third column, list the names of friends and relations, especially any special or close friend. In the fourth, note where the subject was living in that particular year. In the fifth column set down local events; and in the sixth, national affairs. You may want to add other columns for other information.

A glance at such a chart will show you some years that were especially significant to your subject—highlight years. These will make dramatic chapters. Insignificant years can be passed over with a few phrases of transition. Select the highlight years and arrange them as chapters. Set the scene, as if you were writing a one-act play: set the stage, bring on the characters, give the dialogue, making sure that every word, every action advances the story. Make the whole chapter a unit in itself. Think of it as a one-act play.

These scenes can be linked together by links of transitional material which should be just long enough and detailed enough to bridge the gaps—but they must do that, to bring the characters smoothly into the next act.

Now you can begin writing. The first page is important. Select one of the highlights you have marked as your first scene. This should come from early enough in the character's life to make a good starting point, but it needn't be his birth nor his fifth birthday party. It can be the first significant event—the one that started his career. In *Frémont,* I began with the boy's first job, in a lawyer's office. I started *Jedediah Smith* with Jed's joining Ashley's party of trappers. For my Brigham Young biography, I chose the boy's first camp meeting. Each of these events started a chain that led inevitably to the accomplishments of later years.

Write as fast as you can. Guided by your outline, let your mind and feelings race ahead. If you come to a word, or a date, or a name you can't recall immediately, just draw a line there and go on. Don't stop your flow of thought to look up details. This speed will give your book the accelerated pace young people like.

When you have finished it, put it aside for a while—a week or more. Then read it over carefully. Supply the facts you missed. Correct grammar and punctuation. But more important than these technical jobs is the task of improving your style. Have you used the same word too often? Almost everyone has a favorite word that pops up everywhere. Do you begin several sentences the same way—with a participle, an infinitive phrase, a question? Have you kept the point of view consistent? If your treatment is factual, have you editorialized too much? If fictional, have you slipped up at some point and let the hero know something he could not have known?

Maintaining the viewpoint is sometimes really tricky. It might seem all right for the author to say of his hero, "His eyes blazed." But this immediately puts the author *outside* his subject through whose eyes he is supposed to be viewing the world. The character himself would not know that his eyes "blazed." When in doubt, put the sentence in the first person, and you'll see how ridiculous this is: "My eyes blazed."

Be alert for anachronisms. Clothing, food, furniture, language— all are traps for the unwary. Slang is treacherous. If your subject is a lively child—as are many in the "Childhood of Famous Americans" series—he will probably use some innocent slang expression. But if you do not know what expression children actually used at that time and place, it is safer to make up a word that sounds true to the character, the time and the place.

Watch for spots where you can use senses other than sight and hearing; appealing also to the sense of smell, taste, and touch will help make your book more vivid. In reading the manuscript of my book, *I Challenge the Dark Sea* (John Day), an editor observed that my description of Tangiers was "peculiarly non-smelling for the odoriferous tropics." I corrected that lack with some noisome dogs, horse manure, and rotting fish.

After you have done everything you can think of, and have a clean copy from which to type your final version, set this aside for a week or two and then go over it as carefully as you did before, still correcting, smoothing, polishing. Then, at last, make a final copy for the editor, with at least one carbon, preferably two in case one is needed for the illustrator.

One thing that will help sell your book is humor. It is a help if the subject, himself, is bright and cheerful. But all too often, alas, a great person has little sense of humor. Jed Smith is an example. In his journals, in all contemporary accounts, there is no indication that he ever cracked a smile, let alone a joke. But his biographer is saved by Jed's companions, among whom were the biggest liars in the mountains. Their tall tales, their antics offer the happy element that children delight in.

Needless to say, don't write down to children. Writers for young people who break this rule should not—probably will not—see their books in print. Straightforward, simple, direct language, with vivid phrasing, is needed to give distinction to a writer's style.

Writing biographies for young people is work, but it has its own rewards. Of course, there is the money: A good biography for children may sell far more copies than an adult best seller. Augusta Stevenson, who wrote *Abraham Lincoln,* the first of the "Childhood of Famous Americans" series, in 1935, is said to have sold more than 150,000 copies of that one book alone. After more than thirty-five years, it is still a big seller, and Mrs. Stevenson has produced twenty-five more books for this series, with total sales of more than a million and a half copies.

But money is not the only reward—nor even the most attractive. A person writes because he wishes to communicate with others, and there is no one more ready for communication than a child. A writer feels well repaid when he gets an enthusiastic letter from a young reader, even though it may be as terse as one I received from a little girl: "Madam, next time you write a book, notify me." Such things make the time and effort worthwhile.

76

LET'S BUILD A SKYSCRAPER, BUT LET'S FIND A GOOD BOOK FIRST

By Roald Dahl

Approximately five out of seven of all children's books being produced today are a cheat. They have glossy King-Size cardboard covers, and if you tear off the covers of one of them and hold only the paper pages between your fingers, you will find that you are holding something that is slightly thinner than a slice of modern, mass-produced, vitamin-enriched, steam-baked bread—and just about as worthless.

If you count the words in this "King-Size" book (the thing is usually too tall to fit into a bookshelf), you will discover that they add up to anywhere between 150 and 1,500, averaging perhaps midway between the two. You can read the whole text to your child in about fifteen minutes, which includes looking at the pictures, and that, almost invariably, is the end of that. When you have done, you lay the book aside with a distinct feeling that somebody has made a fool out of you and that you have been robbed; so you apologize to your child and turn out the light and slink downstairs to wash away the memory with a glass of whisky and water.

For this masterpiece of bookmaking, you have paid perhaps as much as $3.95, which is another way of saying $4, and the profits, if any, from that dismal transaction have been split, albeit unequally, among the bookseller, the publisher and the writer. For them, it is strictly a business, the business of conning parents into buying junk for their children—although I must say that one out of the three profiteers, the poor bookseller, can hardly be blamed for the quality of the product, or indeed for selling it.

I have been buying these books for my children for a number of years now, and I suppose I shall go on buying them for several years to come. Don't ask me why, although I imagine it is for the love of betting on a long shot and for the thrill I experience when I happen to pick a winner. But the winners are very few and very far between. I am sure I have paid $1.95, $2.95 and $3.95 many hundreds of times for a book that takes ten minutes to read, is read only once, and is then, quite probably, never looked at again.

Perhaps it is my own fault. I should examine them more closely in the bookshops, and should spend four or five minutes skimming through the text before buying. But somehow I cannot bring myself to do that. Instead, I foolishly keep insisting that every book that a publisher has taken the trouble to publish must surely possess a modicum of merit. The publisher, with his experienced and discerning Juvenile Department, has accepted the text and commissioned the illustrations and put the thing together, and therefore he, and he alone, must take the blame.

And up to a point, so he should. Unfortunately though, the children do not see it that way. They blame me because I was the one who bought it. At least, they *used* to blame me, but I have recently started to instruct them—all parents should do this—to point their criticism in the proper direction, and now, whenever we read a real stinker, the first thing they say is, "Good heavens, who published *that?*" To which I reply loud and clear, "The house of so and so published it, my darlings. Let us try to remember that name, shall we, when we go to the bookshop next time?"

I know very well that this evil propaganda is only partly deserved, and that the writer is the original culprit; but the notion that writers can be fools is a very dangerous one to instill in the minds of a writer's children, and I refuse to do it. The publisher, though, with all his wealth and power, is fair game, and nothing but good can come of teaching the young that this man, if not always a fool, is anyway a sly and rapacious fellow. All of them are—all except my own.

My own publisher is neither sly nor especially rapacious. Instead, he is a terrible wrathful man with a slow fuse burning in one end of his belly and a stick of dynamite in the other. This is nice, because explosions are exciting. Lovely explosions can be set off inside him by any of one of the following: bureaucracy, circumlocution, bad prose, Irving Wallace, indifferent wine, other publishers, *The New Yorker* magazine and children's books with restricted vocabularies.

The last item will always cause an extra large explosion, and it is only a pity that it isn't big enough to blow all those restricted vocabulary books to smithereens. They are a device of morons and they do a grave disservice to children. More and more, modern scholars are finding that the child who does best in school is the one who has acquired a large vocabulary in the home, both from his parents and from the books that are put in his way. So what in heaven's name do these people think can be gained by depriving the child of the opportunity of learning new words? Nothing. Beatrix Potter could have told them that years ago. (I wrote a restricted-word story once, and I am very sorry that I did so.)

The heads of great publishing houses do not themselves write the books that are published by their Juvenile Departments (there is one notable exception to this rule), and therefore, to be perfectly fair, practically all the blame for the scarcity of good new children's books in these days must obviously fall upon the writers. It seems to me that most writers in this field have become thoroughly lazy. If they can persuade their publishers to accept a manuscript of 750 words of absolute rubbish about a pony or a rabbit or a day at the zoo, they will happily do so. The more threadbare the text, the more illustrations the publisher will have to put in as padding.

The writers know this, and it pleases them very much. It pleases them firstly because it means that the hard work will have to be done by the illustrator, and secondly because they believe that a book containing lots of pictures and few words sells better than its opposite. Well, maybe it does, but for children of six and over, there is no doubt that too many pictures in a book is a bad thing. It teaches *them* to be lazy also. It makes it unnecessary for them to use their imaginations and to visualize a scene in detail in their own minds. Television, in a more vicious way, has the same effect.

How many writers of children's books will take the trouble to sit down and construct a story or a fantasy of twenty-five or thirty thousand words? Precious few. That sort of thing is hard work and it takes a long time. But it is in this category that the good ones come up, books like *The Lion, the Witch and the Wardrobe,* by C. S.

Lewis; *Charlotte's Web*, by E. B. White; *Pippi Longstocking*, by Astrid Lindgren; *The Secret Garden*, by F. Hodgson Burnett; *The Railway Children*, by E. Nesbit; *My Naughty Little Sister*, by Dorothy Edwards; and *Mary Poppins*, by P. L. Travers.

These are all long, wonderful books, written with care and skill and patience, and were you to take these seven, and only these, and were you to read from them one after the other to your 6- or 7- or 8-year-old child for ten or fifteen minutes every single night, they would still last you for half a year. Each of them possesses that rare quality—the mark of a first-class children's book—which makes it just as acceptable to the adult who reads it aloud as to the child who listens. What is more, the books mentioned are nearly all available in paperback (in England, anyway), and one is therefore getting an astonishing quantity of good reading for very little money.

To me it is incomprehensible that anyone should go out and buy a single copy of one of those ten-minute, one-night, coy "King-Size," copiously illustrated, almost textless, completely pointless, $2.95 or $3.95 books *until* they have bought and read all the lovely long ones that have real stories in them and that last for a month on the first reading, a month on the second, and a month on the third. It makes no sense at all. All it makes is money for the three profiteers. The reason I buy the silly ones myself is simply that we have read and reread all the good long ones we can think of, and we can find no more.

It is more difficult, I think, to write a long book for children than it is to write an adult novel of comparable quality. I have written only two long children's books myself, and for all I know, they may be completely worthless. But I did make the effort. Each of them took somewhere between eight and nine months to complete, with no time off for other work, and eight or nine months is a big slice out of the life of any writer, and a big drain on his batteries. For one who is used to writing for adults only, it is also an uneconomic diversion.

These days, original works of fantasy and imagination are becoming scarcer and scarcer. Forty years ago, we had almost nothing else, and it was wonderful. Today they hardly ever appear. Instead, we are being showered with those horrible things that are called educational books—*The Life of the Guppy, Your Wonderful Body and How It Works,* and *Let's Build a Skyscraper.* The emphasis, right from the start, in this increasingly practical and materialistic world we live in, is upon practical things and upon cramming the head of the child with facts. Ten years from now, there will probably be a spate of children's books with titles such as *How to Sell Insurance, The Thrills of Being an Advertising Man* and *The Stock Exchange Is Fun.*

There is nothing wrong with facts, and there is nothing wrong with learning about the body or the guppy or the stockbroker, but don't forget that the poor child is going to have to concentrate upon almost nothing but the assimilation of facts all the way through from the age of ten to twenty-three, and it would seem not only wise, therefore, but also kind, to give him a break during his early years. The nicest small children, without the slightest doubt, are those who have been fed upon fantasy, and the nastiest are the ones who know all the facts.

77

WRITING FOR YOUNG CHILDREN

By Charlotte Zolotow

CHILDREN's book writing includes fiction for children from picture books on up to the young adults, non-fiction—biography, autobiography and factual books—and of course poetry. In short, it includes every category of adult writing that exists, and everything that is true of distinctive writing for adults is also true of fine literature for children.

But there is in writing for children an additional skill required. It is easier to address our peers than those who are different from ourselves. And children are different from adults because they live on a more intense level. Whatever is true of adults is true of children, only more so. They laugh, they cry, they love, they hate, they give, they take as adults do—only more so. And this is what makes writing for children different from writing for adults.

One must first of all, over and above everything, take children seriously and take writing children's books seriously. Over and over I have met people who feel that writing for children is a first step to doing "something really good." A fairly successful, but undistinguished author of many children's books said to me one night, "Some day I'm going to do something really good. I'm going to write a novel or a play."

What this gentleman's abilities as an adult writer will be, I don't know. His children's books, however, lack something. There is nothing in them that would make a child put one down and say, "What else has this person written?" (A question children have asked many times after first reading a book by Ruth Krauss, Maurice Sendak, Else H. Minarik, Laura Ingalls Wilder, Margaret Wise Brown, E. B. White, Marie Hall Ets, E. Nesbit, P. L. Travers, Beatrix Potter—the great writers of children's literature.)

This remark of his made me understand why. *He doesn't respect what he is doing.* If he ever gets to his serious play or novel, it won't be that he came via children's books, but that he finally did take seriously what he was doing. I don't think writers of this sort should be writing for children at all. Children's books are an art in themselves and must be taken seriously. Anyone who regards them simply as a step along the way to "real" writing is in the wrong field.

I should make clear here that when I use the word *seriously* I don't mean *pompously.* I don't mean that every word is holy or that it should be heavy-handed. Some of the most delightful humor in books today is in the books for children. Some of the wildest kind of nonsense is there, too. But the writers are saying something seriously in their humor and in their nonsense—something that is real to them and meaningful to them—and they are saying it the best way they can without writing down to an audience whose keenness and perception they must completely respect.

There is a popular misconception about children's books that exists even among literate people. And it exists most particularly in the area of the picture book. A television writer once told me, "I never read my children what's in a picture book. I make up my own story to go with the pictures." He was quite pleased with himself—had no idea of the absurdity his smug assumption "that anyone can write a children's book" contained. He didn't realize that though his stories might amuse his own kids, delighted with the sound of his voice, the expression of his face, and the feeling of well-being his spending time with them gave them, a *published* story must be a finished, well-rounded work of art. In cold print, a story has to be good. The wandering, sketchy bedtime stories we tell our children have to be formed and shaped and sharpened before they can be printed, illustrated, bound in a book to be read over and over again to thousands of children who are strangers to the author's face and voice.

Some of my own books have indeed come out of stories I originally told my children, but years later, and after much thought, much reforming, reshaping, pruning, and in a voice or style that was a writer's, not a mother's. There is an immense difference.

In some picture books there are just a few words on a page. Certain immortal lyrics are four lines long. A sonnet has only fourteen lines. But the brevity doesn't mean they are "easy" to write. There is a special gift to making something good with a few words. The ability to conjure up a great deal just from the sound of a word and its relation to the other words in the sentence, the gift of evocation and denotation, is not only special to the poet but to children themselves. To say that he has had a good time at school that morning, a child may simply tell you, "The teacher wore a purple skirt." The recipient of this confidence would have to be close enough to the particular child to know that purple is her favorite color; that summing up a whole morning's events by that color is equivalent to having an adult say, "excellent wine"; that, in fact, in this child's vocabulary "purple" is a value judgment and the sign of a happy morning. And since children themselves so often use this oblique, connotative language, the writer who is fortunate enough to have retained his own childlike vision can speak to them in this special poetic shorthand that evokes worlds in a word.

A picture book writer must have this gift of using words carefully, of identifying with, understanding, projecting himself into the child's world. He must know and feel what they know and feel with some of the freshness of their senses, not his experienced adult ones. He must know what children care about a given situation. This is usually quite different from what an adult in a similar situation is thinking, wanting, seeing, tasting, feeling; and sympathy and empathy (and memory) are necessary, not condescension, not smugness, not superiority, not serious observation from an adult point of view.

And while the brevity of a picture book makes the author's use of words particularly selective, the rest of what I've said applies not only to picture books but to books going up in age group to the young adults. It is a question of experiencing at that particular level how the small or "middle-aged" child feels.

The best children's book writers are those who look at the world around them with a childlike vision—not childish, which is an adult acting like a child—but with that innocent, open vision of the world that belongs to the various stages of growing up, a clearer, more immediate, more specific, more honest, less judging vision than the adult one.

Children come fresher, with less cant, less hypocrisy, less guilt, to the world around them than even the most honest adults are apt to. Children smell good and bad things without inhibition. They taste, they hear, they see, they feel with all their senses and not so much

interfering intellect as the adult, who will label things by applied
standards, preconceived standards of good or bad—a good smell or a
bad smell, a good taste or a bad taste. Children are realists of the
first order. They have fewer preconceived ideas than adults. To
them, flowers may smell bad. Manure may smell good. They have no
fixed judgments yet. Most things are still happening to them for the
first time. The first time water comes from a faucet, heat from a
radiator, snow falls, the *real* itself is *magic*.

Because of this, children are open to belief in fantasy—fairies can
exist if snow can fall, magic can happen if there are cold and heat,
moon and stars and sun. Nothing is routine yet. They live more immediate lives than adults, not so much of yesterday or tomorrow.
They are open to the moment completely. They respond to every
detail around them completely. (That is why they are so often tiring
to be with.)

I remember once the poet, Edwin Honig, came to visit us. He had
never met our daughter Ellen, who was then four. They liked each
other immediately. And when she offered to show him the house, he
left his drink on the front porch and went off into the house with her.
When I came in a few minutes later, he was holding her in his arms,
and she was pointing into the living room.

"That is the fireplace where we have fires in winter.

That is the rubber plant where one leaf died.

That is the radio where we had the tube fixed.

That is the best chair but our dog sits in it." She might have invited him to see if he could smell the dog in the chair if I hadn't
come in.

"You know," Honig said to me, "she's living everything here for
me."

A poet could understand this. And in this sense that is what everyone who writes for children must be.

Always remember that the field of children's books is exciting and
specialized. It is full of pitfalls that adult writing is free from, not
the least of which is that a child's point of view is so different from
that of an adult—more different at three than at six, and more so at
six than at nine. And even when the child and adult reaction is identical—at any age level—in being hurt, in wanting, in hating, in loving, it is more intense. Adults are like a body of water that has been

dammed up, or channeled. Children haven't these constrictions yet on their emotions. They abandon themselves to emotion, and therefore everything from a cake crumb to an oak tree means more to them.

If you are to write for children, you must be absolutely honest with yourself and with them. Willa Cather once advised a young writer never to hold back on any idea or phrase when it fitted something he was writing, in the hope of using it later in something better. Never hold back on what fits the book you are writing for children either. Remember how you felt about things when you were a child; remember, remember that adults might laugh and say, "tomorrow he'll forget," but right then, at the moment, the child feels and believes in his pain or his joy with his whole being.

Ursula Nordstrom, director of children's books at Harper and Row, has, I think, discovered more wonderful children's writers than anyone. "Young people can and will accept the very best truly creative people will give them," she says. And in a recent *New Yorker* article about Maurice Sendak, one of the finest children's book artists and writers today, she said, "Too many of us . . . keep forgetting that children are new and we are not. But somehow Maurice has retained a direct line to his own childhood."

This is what anyone who wants to write for children must do.

78

WRITING THE PICTURE BOOK STORY

By Mary Calhoun

You want to write for children. Picture books. You tell stories to your children or the neighbor's children, and they just love your stories. *And this is good.* If you're telling stories, you already have the first qualification for writing picture books: You are a storyteller. The person who can spin a yarn is the golden one who will fascinate the four-to-eight-year-olds.

Then why aren't the publishers snapping up your stories and publishing them in beautiful four-color editions? Just what I wanted to know when I first started writing down the stories I'd told my boys. Rejection notes from editors commented:

"Too slight."

"Not original."

"We've used this theme several times."

"Too old for the age group."

I can't tell you all the reasons editors reject picture book scripts—such as "might encourage kids to make mess in the kitchen," "might encourage kids to try this and kill themselves." You'll just have to experience some of the rejections yourself. However, these are the general heart of why picture books are rejected:

"Not enough body and plot."

"Idea not big enough."

"Not ready to be a book."

"Things happen to the hero rather than he making things happen."

"Action too passive."

"Basic situation not convincing."

And over and over, "Too slight."

Sound familiar? Use the rejection list to check your stories—my compliments. The thing is, there's a lot more to writing for children than reeling off a story.

461

Now about picture books.

First, definitions: A picture book is one with pictures and a story to be read to or by a child between the ages of three and eight. (Publishers usually say four-eight, but many a "mature" three-year-old can enjoy having a picture book read aloud to him.)

Of course, there are other picture books for young children. For the two- and three-year-old there are the counting books, the ABC books, the "see-the-cat" books. There are picture books with a very slim text line, books conceived by the artists mainly for the sake of the art work. (No, you don't have to supply the artist for your story; the editor will do that.) There are the "idea" books: non-fiction— exploring "what is night?", "what is time?"—and such books as *A Hole Is to Dig* and *Mud Pies and Other Recipes*, charming ramblings on an idea, but not stories.

Here let's concern ourselves with the traditional picture book, one with a story from which the artist gains his inspiration for the pictures.

What goes into a picture book story?

As I see it, the elements are four: idea, story movement, style and awareness of audience.

First of all, the *idea*. Without a good idea, the writer is dead. Most often, I'd guess, a picture book script is rejected because the idea isn't good enough. What's a good idea? Make your own definition; I suppose each writer and editor does. I'd say, though, that basically the hero is vivid, the basic situation and the things that happen in the story are fascinating to a child. And generally there is a theme, some truth you believe, such as "you can master fear." Not a moral tacked onto the story, but the essence of the story, the hero and events acting out the theme.

How do you come by good ideas? Perhaps in the long run only heaven can help you, but it seems to me that primary is rapport with children—and a strong memory of your own childhood feelings and reactions.

"Tell me a story" many times a day keeps the old idea-mill grinding. Many of my picture book and magazine stories grew directly from contact with my children.

One day I hugged Greg, saying, "You're an old sweet patootie doll." "What's a patootie doll?" asked Greg, so I launched on a spur-of-the-moment tale. The theme was (I discovered after I'd written down the story) "know who you are and be glad for it." *The Sweet Patootie Doll* was first published in *Humpty Dumpty's Magazine* and later became my first published picture book.

A magazine story, "Cat's Whiskers", came into being because Greg was always climbing into things and getting stuck—in buckets, under the porch, even in the washing machine. I coupled this with the idea that cats use their whiskers to measure whether they can get through openings; in the story the boy sticks broomstraws on his face for whiskers, and the story goes on.

However, here was a story idea too slight for a picture book. Not enough happened, really, and there was no real theme in the sense of a universal truth.

This brings us to a point valuable to beginning writers: If your story is rejected by book editors, try it on the children's magazines. The magazines have high standards, too, of course, but they can be your training ground and means of being published while you learn. It was my lucky day when a book editor said, "Not ready to be a book. Have you thought of sending it to a magazine?" My story, "Lone Elizabeth," went through many rewritings, but finally was published in *Humpty Dumpty's Magazine*. "Bumbershoot Wind" was termed "too slight" by a book editor but appeared in *Child Life*.

Actually, all of the elements of a story are tied into the idea, but let's go on to consider them in detail.

Story movement. I choose to call it this, rather than plot, for this suggests just what a story for children must do: move. Children like a story that trots right along, with no prolonged station-stops for cute conversation or description. Keep asking yourself (as the child does), "What happened next?"

In picture books there needs to be enough change of action or scenery to afford the artist a chance to make different pictures. Some stories are very good for telling aloud, but when you look at them on paper, you see that the scene hasn't changed much.

A book editor pointed this out for me on my "Sammy and the Something Machine." In this fantasy, Sammy makes a machine out of which come in turn mice, monkeys, mudpies, pirates and hot dogs. (It grew from my Mike's chant at play, "I'm making, I'm making!") This story went down on paper perfectly well in *Humpty*

Dumpty's Magazine, where there are fewer illustrations than in a picture book. But the scene doesn't change; there's that machine, over and over, turning out different things.

When your story is moving along vigorously, the scene changes will follow naturally—*if* the idea is storybook material. If the story moves but there's not much possibility for picture change (better let the book editors decide this), it may still be a fine story for some magazine.

Style. Of course, your style will be your own, and only you can develop it through writing and trying out and thinking about it and forgetting about it as you plunge ahead in the heat of telling a story.

The story content to some extent will indicate the style, that is, choice of words, length and rhythm of sentences. The story may hop joyously, laugh along, move dreamily, or march matter-of-factly. For study, you might read aloud folk tales and attune your ears to varieties in cadence: the robust, boisterous swing of a western folk tale; the rolling, measured mysticism of an Indian folk tale; the straightforward modern "shaggy dog" story; the drawling wry humor of the southern Negro folk tale.

If you already are telling stories to children, you're on your way to developing your style. However, "telling" on paper is slightly different from telling aloud, where the *effect* is achieved by a few judiciously chosen words and the swing of sentences.

I've had some success with one approach to the written story, and I've seen examples of it in other picture books. I call it "vividry." To me it's more vivid and succinct to say that than "vivid effect," and this explains what "vividry" is: words chosen with economy for their punch. For example, in a certain book I choose to say "little mummy mice." "Mummified mice" might be more proper, but to me it sounds textbookish. "Mummy mice" rolls off the tongue and seems a more direct idea-tickler for the child.

In college journalism courses, our bible was Rudolf Flesch's *The Art of Plain Talk.* From it we learned the value, in newspaper writing, of using sentences of short or varied length; strong verbs; short, strong nouns and many personal pronouns. Flesch might have been writing a style book for children's picture books.

We all know the delight in finding "the exact word" for a spot in a story. Never is this more effective than in children's books. Magazines for children generally have word-length requirements. Try putting a full-bodied story into 800 to 1,000 words. Every word counts. Writing for the magazines can be excellent training in choosing words and cutting out the lifeless ones.

I'm not saying, however, that big words have no place in a picture book script. Writing "controlled vocabulary" books for the young is a specialized art, and those books are used mostly by teachers and parents to stimulate a child's desire to read. Several book publishers now put out series of "easy-to-read" books. If you are interested in this field, read some of the books and query the editors on requirements. In the general picture book, though, I think children like to come upon an occasional delightfully new and big word. Haven't you seen a four-year-old trotting around, happily rolling out "unconditionally" or some other mouthful he's just heard? It's the *idea* of the story that the writer suits to the age group, not every given word in the story.

And this brings us to *awareness of audience*. I've mentioned rapport with children. If you're around them you know what they're thinking and wishing, what their problems are. And you'll know if a story idea is too old for the three-to-eight-year-olds or just plain wouldn't interest them.

With a small child underfoot or in tow, you see the details of the world that fascinate him: how a spot of sunlight moves on the floor; a cat's relationship with his tail (I used this one in "Tabbycat's Telltale Tail"); or the child's own shadow. (I haven't been able to make a good story of this; maybe you can.)

A child will watch a hummingbird moth at work in a petunia bed and report wisely, "He only goes to the red ones. White petunia must not taste good."

All of this, *plus awareness of the child's emotions, plus turning your mind back to remember how it was with you as a child*, tells you what to put into a picture book.

And then there's the other way to be aware of your audience: reading, reading all the good books and stories written for that age. Then you begin to see what has pleased children. You get the feel of what is suitable for that age group. You also see what has already been done, so that your own ideas can be fresh, not trite. You read "The Three Pigs," and the books about the Melops and you say to yourself, "Very well, but a story about a pig has never been told just in *this* way," and you start off on your own particular pig story. As you read (perhaps to a child to catch his reactions, too), you may begin to draw your conclusions of what is good in children's literature, what is slightly sickening, how the stories are put together, what has worked.

It has interested me, for instance, to notice how many of the traditional stories are built on what I call a "core of three." Three brothers, three mistakes, three attempts at a solution. "The Three Pigs" makes me wonder if the composer weren't slyly trying to see just how many times he could use three. Three pigs, three encounters with men carrying building materials, three houses visited by the wolf, "chinny-chin-chin," etc. In so many of the stories, the use of three attempts to solve the problem is effective in building intensity to the climax.

So there you have it: idea, story movement, style and awareness of audience. Study them, use them in your rewrites, let them sink into your subconscious.

And then don't worry about techniques as you tell the story. For the first, last and most important thing is: you must *like* the story! You're having a ball telling it. Right at this moment, it's the most wonderful story ever told to man or child.

That, finally, is what gives the story sparkle and makes editors say, "This will make a wonderful picture book!"

79

WRITING FOR THE INSPIRATIONAL AND RELIGIOUS MARKET

By Dina Donohue

Not long ago, a manuscript submitted to me at *Guideposts* was accompanied by a letter reading, "Dear Editor: This article was turned down by the *Reader's Digest,* so I thought I'd send it to you." Too many writers regard the religious or inspirational magazine as an easy mark, and if a piece can't sell elsewhere, they think a church publication will want it. Perhaps this was once true, but the religious and inspirational market is different these days.

Although religious publications still offer a good open market for articles, fiction, and poetry, a great change has taken place in this market possibly because there has been a change—or more accurately, a revival—taking place in the church, combining some of the enthusiasm and devotion of the past with today's needs and tomorrow's hopes.

"Inspirational" does not necessarily serve as a synonym for "religious," although very often the two are combined in one article or story. It does not mean a sermon or theological treatise.

What then is the inspirational article? I might start with a very obvious definition—the inspirational piece is meant to inspire the reader. It can do this by depicting goodness, unselfishness, love in action, with the ultimate aim of challenging the reader to try to apply the same good qualities of strength, hope and charity to his own life and problems.

Now, as before, religious and inspirational magazines are concerned with the problems facing the world today, and the scope of the subjects discussed in their magazines bear this out. Magazines for young people are especially aware of the problems youth face and try to present articles to help solve these problems. Here are some titles recently published in the religious press:

St. Anthony Messenger (Catholic)—"Should a Mother Work?"
A.D. (United Presbyterian edition)—"Miracles Do Happen"
Reform Judaism (Jewish)—"Mixed (Up) Marriage"
Christian Century (Protestant)—"Will There Be Another Holocaust?"
Christian Life (Protestant)—"Does Your Child Listen to Garbage?"
The Church Herald (Protestant)—"The Sex Education We Often Forget"
Campus Life (Protestant)—"City Summer—Anything Good in the Ghetto?"

A word of warning: don't be frightened off by the word "religious." Sometimes a manuscript will have no mention of organized religion or any spiritual emphasis, and yet it will be well received by a religious magazine. Whether true experience or fiction, however, it should have an inherent moral point.

But you can write for more than one religious denomination or faith. My material has appeared in *Jewish Digest, Catholic Digest,* Baptist *Secret Place, Christian Herald,* and Unity publications, as well as interfaith *Guideposts.*

The *story* or narrative approach is the important ingredient. Even when writing a factual piece or an organizational article, if you use an anecdote in your lead, you have immediately aroused your readers' interest. Devotional articles also are enlivened by anecdotes. One of the major reasons an article may be rejected (aside from sloppy presentation or triteness) is that it contains a sermon-essay on the author's spiritual beliefs. Editors and readers want anecdotes to tell the story. In the religious magazine field, as in writing for the secular press, you have to use good but brief descriptions of your setting, reality in your characterizations, dialogue that moves the story along, and struggle and conflict in resolving your plot.

Some magazines which list their editorial needs as religiously oriented actually use the inspirational piece, merely giving it a different "label." *Sunshine* Magazine, on the other hand, says they do not use the religious, but only the inspirational. Hence, studying the market is particularly important if you wish to write for this relatively open field.

At *Guideposts,* we do look for a spiritual emphasis in our articles, but the inspirational quality is inherent in the line which appears each month above the name on the cover: A PRACTICAL GUIDE TO SUCCESSFUL LIVING.

We honestly believe that to be inspirational, an article or feature needs to do more than set forth an interesting idea. There should be a definite challenge or help for the reader. Take the cover feature in a recent issue. Sgt. Lysle Newberry, a state park police officer, told how he almost lost his life trying to rescue a group of people swept to the edge of Niagara Falls. They were saved by the combined concern of many. Some were involved in heroic rescue efforts, others prayed. Inspirational? Yes, because it showed us how, in time of danger, we can avert disaster by perseverance, prayer and calmness. Of course, all articles do not need to be as dramatic. Other so-called secular publications also print what can be termed the inspirational or religious piece. "Garden's Up!" by Marjorie Holmes, which appeared in *Reader's Digest,* was an inspirational piece on a different level. This was also a first-person account, a re-living of a childhood memory and the part gardens played in the author's life. The inspirational quality comes from the nostalgia that helps us relive our own early years and from the author's wish that her children could also know the joys of growing things. This perhaps will spark a similar interest in readers of the article.

Before getting involved with the specifics of style, type of article, or marketing, the first question usually asked by the writer is, "Where do I find such article ideas?"

For the dramatic rescue piece, the lost child account, or the individual achiever, your local paper can be a gold mine. (Whenever I travel, I always buy local newspapers.) The newspaper items may not always be spectacular, but the writer must read with an open eye for the story behind the article. Try to find out the motivation for an act of heroism, the scope of a difficult project, the outcome of an act of kindness. Consider the slant: One article could be told by a number of different people. The Sgt. Newberry piece was told in *Guideposts* by him. It appeared elsewhere as a third-person reporter's account. It could have been written by one of those rescued.

Another source for article material is in what you hear and see. I'm writing this on a Saturday afternoon, a day in which nothing much has happened. During the day—eating breakfast with my husband in a diner we frequent weekly, visiting the beauty salon, talking with neighbors—I have met interesting people who can serve as characters in feature articles. I have heard about situations which could provide dramatic anecdotes or leads. In one short day (it is now four P.M.), a neighbor and I discussed the importance of raising children so that they will be independent enough to leave home at an early age. We spoke of young people we knew who had made a success of this—and some who had not. I met a man who has had a real problem with alcohol and now faces a turning-point in his life and another who was disregarding doctor's orders in order to live a fuller, if shorter life. There is a good possibility here for an article.

I also spoke today to a newly-married teacher who has taken a gravely-ill friend into her home (with her husband's permission) to make sure the sick woman receives the care and treatment not available in her own town. And there were still other article possibilities in the day's conversations and meetings. Of course the writer does not use any material with real names, etc., without permission.

One of the best tools for the writer—after learning the rudiments of style and craftsmanship—is CURIOSITY. Be alert to people you know or meet. Perhaps someone in your family, neighborhood or church has a special hobby of helping people in a creative way. If the idea is different enough, something that others would wish to emulate, then you have the makings of an inspirational piece. Its success depends on how you handle your material and the market for which you intend to write it.

Listen to conversations in restaurants, elevators, subways, at conferences and conventions. In this way, you get not only anecdotes and ideas for stories but an understanding of human nature, good characterization, and, if you listen with a truly open ear, patterns of dialogue. I keep a notebook in which I record the more interesting items or ideas which may come to me—not to use verbatim but as background material for some future manuscript. After a time, I reread the notebook items, which are really in rough form, and discard those that are not worthwhile. The others I type on 3 x 5 cards and file for later use.

The important thing for the beginner as well as the established writer is to write about interesting people doing interesting things. Stress their spiritual motivation and be sure you give *facts*.

In writing the true inspirational piece, you have to have the same regard for facts as you would for a regular article. The difference is that for the inspirational you have to delve a bit deeper to make certain you leave the reader with the challenge to try to put the good actions or thoughts into his own life or, at the least, to arouse the reader from complacency to an appreciation of the finer attributes of his fellow beings.

The unselfishness of the teacher mentioned above aroused my interest, and I did try to find out from the young lady why the special attention, the sacrifice of time and effort. The answer might well be an article some day . . . or a character or situation in a fiction piece. Because we can also take true stories and characters and change them somewhat to fit the needs of a fiction piece. There would still be an inspirational quality in the young wife's desire to help her friend. For a fiction piece, I'd simply have the husband against the idea and thus develop conflict, etc.

Another source of article material can be your own life. This is where Marjorie Holmes found her idea for "Garden's Up!" Go back in memory some time and ask yourself some questions. The answers might provide an inspirational piece. For example:

What was the most memorable experience in my life?
What was the saddest day? The happiest? Funniest?
I remembered how frightened I was when . . .
I remember how much I wanted . . .
My most meaningful Christmas . . . Easter . . . Hannukah.
The day I discovered death . . . joy . . . love . . .

These are just samples to spark creative thoughts. I've used this technique in my writing classes at conferences and it's interesting to see the totally different articles which evolve.

One of the easiest ways to begin writing for the religious magazines is to do a personal-experience story. All of us, no matter how limited we might think our lives, have had scores of personal experiences which may be of interest to others. And, very often, of inspiration and help to others.

All too often we look for the truly dramatic story when the quiet one may be just waiting to be written.

All of us can benefit from a little dreaming and remembering. Try it sometime—in fact, make a habit of daily daydreaming. You might be surprised at the story material that comes to mind. You may recall interesting personalities, an incident that illustrates how to handle difficult situations, a time when your faith helped you meet a special problem. Or you may even come up with a recipe.

For church-oriented inspirational or religious stories and articles, it is necessary to give the reader something more than just an interesting piece of writing, story value, amusement or knowledge. At *Guideposts* we try to give our readers three extra ingredients which are applicable to other religious magazines as well:

Reader Identification: Make readers *feel* for the author's problem or story, even if it is not one they have been involved with themselves.

A true adventure story about an old man lost in the mountains might not appear to be within the experience of many readers. True, being lost might not; but the focal point is that an elderly man faces a seemingly insurmountable problem and has to solve it by himself. Readers can identify with his initial fear and distress and the realization that he is in danger.

Takeaway: Regardless of the problem—hating a neighbor, loss of a job, an alcoholic husband, fear of the dark, gossip—we look for a practical "how to meet and overcome the problem." The man lost in the mountains might have found it by calling to mind the Bible promise: *Fear not, I am with you always,* and, in the resultant quiet and peace of mind, his panic subsides. He is then able to think and act clearly and prudently and to save himself.

Special Emphasis: At *Guideposts* we are especially concerned with giving our readers some spiritual truth or message that they can carry away with them. Bible quotes are an easy way out, and there are other solutions. One reason for rejections is that the author will write five pages about the problem and then only one page of solution: Very often a Bible verse is remembered by the protagonist, and all is well. This doesn't mean that an appropriate quotation that really helped is not acceptable—it just mustn't be obviously brought in to provide the "religious" angle. The author has a responsibility to his readers. Showing how the main character in a story or article overcame a difficulty, not in a preachy way but with specific anecdotes and examples, can often provide readers with help.

The desperately ill person who has found a faith in God and is able to bear her pain and who shares this fortitude can help many readers who might be unhappy and disturbed in their own illness.

There might be a daughter-in-law who resented her mother-in-law's interfering. When the younger woman recognized the older one's feeling of frustration and asked her to help with cooking and caring for the children, there was a healed relationship. Practical? Yes, because it worked. Religious or spiritual? Yes, because first the daughter-in-law had to love the older lady and had to forgive what she called interference and worse. The daughter-in-law had to recognize her own fault of impatience. And in most stories there comes a time of almost complete despair when there seems no way out—usually, prayer becomes the last source of help.

Here the writer needs to be specific regarding prayer—there are so many kinds of praying. It usually isn't enough to say "I prayed for help and immediately felt better." Give details—how, why, when, where. Skimming the surface is unfair; it leaves a hole in the reader's understanding. Tell how prayer worked, or, if it didn't, tell how the characters became reconciled.

Most articles in the religious and inspirational magazines do have happy endings—readers want it and editors do look for it. But be careful you are not too much the Pollyanna, overcheerful author.

On the other hand, I have what I call my "tear duct test." If any manuscript makes me feel weepy, I give it a second reading, perhaps a third. Not that we are looking for the very sad story, but there is nothing wrong with emotion. By the same token, a little humor is also appreciated. That is why light verse can often be placed.

There is a good market for the inspirational and religious article. More and more writers are recognizing this. I am aware of it from the growing pile of manuscripts which comes across my desk each week.

To sum up, there are many varied types of magazines which use what is roughly termed inspirational material.

First, there are the denominational magazines published by the church presses. Some of them are very modern in concept and unlike what we have come to consider a "church paper." The serious writer should become familiar with these publications. Some are religiously-oriented with special denominational taboos or slants which the writer must honor. Others are quite liberal. The youth magazines vary—some are particularly creative in both art and copy.

Inspirational pieces and short items appear in many of what we term secular magazines. A good project would be to check through *Reader's Digest, McCall's, Woman's Day* and other popular magazines to see how many items could be termed "inspirational." You might find one telling how a worker or founder of a group reaches out to help others. Or an account of a terminally ill man—how he faced death with courage—might be another. Usually the presentation is the deciding factor. Take the account of a mother's thoughts on a child's first day at school. If written with tongue in cheek or irony, it might fit into a slick magazine. But if the mother has insight into what this means in the child's life, and her own, despite worries, it fits the inspirational pattern.

The writer of the inspirational piece needs a few things to help him: one, a special desire to write this type of material, perhaps a spiritual motivation; two, a grasp of good writing techniques and style; three, a knowledge of the market; and four, persistence, so that rejections are not unduly discouraging. The wealth of material coming to magazines each month means that many of the pieces are rejected not because they lack merit but because they are similar to others on hand. So "try elsewhere" can be good advice.

80

BOOK REVIEWING

By L. E. Sissman

AFTER years of stumping and (I hoped) dazzling other people with anything I cared to try in verse, at the hoary age of forty I became a book reviewer. Now it was my sworn and bounden duty to penetrate and unravel the obscurities of other writers' methods and messages, to dissipate the wet and inky smokescreen in which the wily squid conceals himself, and to set the delicate skeleton of the author's true design in so many words before my readers. Besides being hard, grueling detective work, this was both scary and risky; armed only with a shaky analytic gift and my spotty, idiosyncratic store of reading, I was laying my sacred honor on the line each time I tried to pick another literary lock in public.

For the first couple of years, I drove myself to write reviews like an aristocrat driving himself to the gallows, with superficial sang-froid as thin as onionskin and a real clutch of fear each time I sat down at the typewriter.

Then, mercifully, I began to learn the ropes and look a little more objectively around me. I discovered that reviewing was not simply something that a *soi-disant* literary man did to fill time, amplify his tiny reputation, and (of course) earn a little money. *Au contraire.* Reviewing, it was slowly and astoundingly revealed to me, was a vocation, a craft, a difficult discipline, with its own rules and customs, with a set of commandments and a rigid protocol. Mostly by making painful mistakes and leaping brashly into pitfalls, I began to amass some notion of the shape of a reviewer's obligations to himself, to the author he reviews, to his editor, to his readers.

In short, I became aware of the moral imperatives of book reviewing. Funny as that may sound in a literary world raddled by cliques and claques and politics, by back-scratching and back-stabbing, by overpraise and undernotice, I now believe that the would-be conscientious reviewer must be guided by a long list of stern prohibitions if he is to keep faith with himself and his various consumers. In the interests of controversy (and, I hope, of air-clearing), I set these down herewith.

1. Never review the work of a friend. All sorts of disasters are implicit here; a man and his work should be separate in the reviewer's mind, and the work should be his only subject. If you know the man at all well, you become confused and diffident; your praise becomes fulsome, and you fail to convey the real merits and demerits of the book to the poor reader. The hardest review I ever wrote was of the (quite good) novel of a friend four years ago. Never again.

2. Never review the work of an enemy. Unless you fancy yourself as a public assassin, a sort of licensed literary hit man, you will instinctively avoid this poisonous practice like the plague it is. Corollary: never consent to be a hatchet man. If Editor X knows you are an old enemy of Novelist Y, he may (and shame on him, but it happens all the time) call on you to review Y's latest book. Beware, on pain of losing your credibility.

3. Never review a book in a field you don't know or care about. Once or twice I've been touted onto titles far from my beaten track. The resulting reviews were teeth-grindingly difficult to write and rotten in the bargain. Unless you're a regular polymath, stick to your own last.

4. Never climb on bandwagons. You are not being paid to subscribe to a consensus, nor will your reader thank you for it. If a book has been generally praised (or damned), you add nothing to anybody's understanding by praising (or damning) it in the same terms. Only if you have read the book with care and found something fresh to comment on should you attempt a review. Otherwise, find something else (how about the work of an unknown?) to write about. Or skip it; you'll earn that money you need for a new 500mm mirror lens somewhere else.

5. Never read other reviews before you write your own. This is a tough rule to follow, because all reviewers are naturally curious

about the reception of Z's latest book. Nonetheless, you can't help being subtly influenced by what *The New York Times* reviewer (or whoever) has to say. Eschew!

6. Never read the jacket copy or the publisher's handout before reading and reviewing a book. Jacket copy (I know; I used to write it) is almost invariably misleading and inaccurate. The poor (literally: these downtrodden souls are, along with retail copywriters, the most underpaid people in advertising) writer is probably working from a summary compiled by the sales department, not from a firsthand reading of the book. The handouts are more of the same, only flackier.

7. Never review a book you haven't read at least once. Believe it or not, some reviewers merely skim a book (or even depend on, horrors, the jacket copy) before reviewing it. Not only is this a flagrant abdication of responsibility; there is always the lurking danger of missing a vital clue in the text and making a public spectacle of yourself. It should happen frequently to all such lazy reviewers.

8. Never review a book you haven't understood. If *you* haven't figured out what the author is up to, there's simply no way you can convey it to your reader. Reread the book; if necessary, read some of the author's other books; if you still don't know, forget it. The cardinal sin here is to go right ahead and condemn a half-understood book on the covert grounds that you haven't found its combination.

9. Never review your own ideas instead of the author's. Unless you're the ranking pundit in the field and you have a scholarly bone to pick with the author, you have no right to use the book under inspection as a springboard for a trumpet voluntary of your own.

10. Never fail to give the reader a judgment and a recommendation on the book. And tell why. A reviewer is really a humble consumer adviser; his main job is to tell the public what to read and what to skip. It's an important job because nobody can possibly keep up with all the books being published today.

11. Never neglect new writers. First novelists, in particular, get passed over too frequently for several reasons. The obvious reason is that Norman Mailer's new novel is better copy than Hannah Furlong's maiden effort. The less obvious reason is that it's much

harder for a reviewer to get an intelligent fix on an unknown. In short, it's harder work to review a debutant.

12. Never assume that a writer is predictable. This is, in a way, the converse of the previous proposition. Part of the pleasure of picking up a new book by a writer you've read before is *knowing* what you're about to read—the themes, the style, the old, familiar tricks. But what if the novelist has *grown;* what if he does something daring and unexpected? That's when a lot of reviewers, myself included, are tempted to put him down for not rewriting himself. The only answer is to approach the book with great caution and read it on its own merits, forgetting what has gone before.

13. Never forget to summarize the story or the argument. What's more maddening than a review that rhapsodizes (or bitches) for two thousand words about the author's style, his technique, his place in letters without ever giving us a clue to the nature of the story, beyond the mention of an incident or two?

14. Never, on the other hand, write a review that is merely a plot summary and nothing more. This happens surprisingly often, especially in newspaper reviews. The reader of the review deserves a judgment, a rating, not simply a recapitulation.

15. Never impale a serious writer on his minor errors. Nobody's perfect, as the old gag line says, and, given the susceptibility of even the most powerful piece of work to ridicule, it is frighteningly easy for the reviewer to have his fun at the author's expense and end up distorting the value and import of the book. (Example: I recently read a good novel in which the author consistently misused the word "fulsome" and mixed up "she" and "her." It would have been an act of willful irresponsibility to take the author to task for these small miscues, which were also his editor's fault.)

16. Never write critical jargon. The day of the New Criticism, for all its good, is mercifully past, and so, I'd hope, is the compulsion of some reviewers to pose and posture as anointed gospelers of the true and beautiful. The reviewer who writes for a general-circulation newspaper or magazine should have his typewriter unplugged if he persists in pedagogeries.

17. Never fail to take chances in judgment. Because it forces you

to enter the mind of another on his own terms, reviewing is literally mind-expanding. Often the reviewer is astonished at his new conclusions and afraid to put them down on paper. This is a mistake; one of the highest critical acts is to arrive at a new understanding and communicate it to the reader.

18. Never pick a barn-door target to jeer at. Not long ago, one of the daily reviewers in *The New York Times* wasted an entire column on the new novel by one of the Irving Wallaces. Irving Stone? Jacqueline Susann? Or whoever. Anyway, it was painfully easy—shooting fish in a barrel—and painfully unworthy of the reviewer's taste and talent. He might far better have reviewed a good first novel.

19. Never play the shark among little fishes. Being a reviewer does not entitle you to savage the beginner, the fumbler, the less-than-accomplished writer. A sincere and decent effort demands a sincere and decent response. If you've ever struggled to write a book yourself, you know the vast amounts of pain and love it takes. To put down an honest attempt in gloating arrogance is to deal a crippling blow to a nascent career of possible promise.

20. Never compete with your subject. A reviewer is not, at least during his hours as a reviewer, a rival of the person he's reviewing. If he sees flaws in the work under inspection, he should report them, but he should not give vent to a long harangue on how *he* would have written the book. (If his hubris is that keen, perhaps he should take time off and write a book himself.)

In a word, then, the sins and temptations of reviewers are legion. As an incumbent sinner, I have more often than I like to think about been brought up short by the realization of my own weaknesses. Thus the list above. While I know I don't have the constancy and fortitude to follow it to the letter, I try to bear it in mind, like a catechism, when I sit down to write about another person's work. It is the least I can do for another poor sufferer who has taken the supreme risk of letting his dreams and talents go forth between covers, and for all those poor sufferers who simply like to read, and who rely, for better or worse, on the dim and uncertain skills of reviewers for a guide through the maze of new titles in their bright, unrevealing jackets on the shelves.

81

THOUGHTS ON PLAYWRITING

By Robert Anderson

I AM AT a period in my life (52) when I would much rather be getting wisdom from someone else than trying to give it to others. I have just finished a new play, which means that I have spent over a year wrestling with what I know, what I don't know, shapes, forms, the new modes, the old modes. I have ended up with an imperfect piece of work, as we all do. Every writer knows better than he can manage to do. (I am reminded of the story of the government agriculture advisor who watched a farmer for a week and then sat him down to give him some advice. The farmer cut him short by saying, "Hell, I'm not farming as well as I know how to farm right now.") In the same way, no writer ever writes as well as he knows how to write because material just never presents itself to us that neatly. Someone said that the act of writing is the act of undoing a dream. We never end up with the near-perfect piece of work we dreamed of writing. I never read over anything I have written on a play until I have finished the whole play. If I knew day by day how far short of my "dream" I was falling, I probably wouldn't go on.

These, then, will be some rather tentative, disorganized thoughts on playwriting. They may inform and encourage the right people and inform and discourage others.

This is a really fine time for the young playwright. Never before has there been so much opportunity for him to see his work done: colleges, cafés, Off-Off-Broadway, barns, parking lots, lofts, street corners, churches. This is all to the good. But I keep worrying about these young playwrights ten years from now. Things were never worse for the "established" playwright with a family who must make his living from his work. By and large there is very little money for the young playwright in the colleges, churches, Off-Off-Broadway, etc. This is all right. He is learning, enjoying himself and entertaining others. But this can go on only so long, especially if he is a family man. I have been quoted a number of times as saying, "You can make a killing in the theatre, but not a living." (Incidentally, the killing usually goes for taxes.)

The playwright generally has to be a moonlighter in one way or another. Before *Tea and Sympathy*, I worked on my plays in the morning, wrote for radio and TV in the afternoons, and four nights a week taught from eight to eleven. My second play was an artistic success but earned me almost zero, and I started writing movies to supply me with the money for the two to three years it takes to write a play and get it produced. Very few playwrights I know make their living solely from the theatre.

Very often young playwrights say to me, "Oh, but you're established. You have it easy." This is not true. My first successful play, *Tea and Sympathy*, was turned down by almost every producer, and my agent, Audrey Wood, told me that it was still being read by one producer, but it would probably be returned and I should get on to my next play. It was not returned, and my career was started. Thirteen years later my plays, *You Know I Can't Hear You When the Water's Running*, were turned down by almost everyone, and they were on their way into my files when two young producers rescued them. The same was true of my next play, *I Never Sang for My Father*, which waited five years to be produced. In short, it never gets easier. It would be unthinkable if novelists like William Styron, Philip Roth, or John Updike couldn't get their novels published. But there are many established and successful playwrights who cannot find producers for their new plays. The cost of production is enormous now, and few people have a continuing interest in a playwright and his work. (I will pass along a terrible story. I attended a preview of Tennessee Williams' play, *The Seven Descents of Myrtle*. I was alone, as my wife was acting in one of my plays. Before the curtain went up, Tennessee appeared in one of the boxes, and some people recognized him and started to applaud. Most of the audience joined in. The lady next to me said, "Why are they applauding?" I said, "That's Tennessee Williams." She said, "Why are they applauding when they don't know whether or not they will like the play?" My blood ran cold. But I know this is the prevailing attitude. The years of great plays Williams had given us meant nothing. The lady would applaud only if *this* one pleased her.)

It is generally conceded that playwriting is the most difficult form of writing. Add to this the difficulty of getting a play produced (depending on availability of the actors, director, theatre, *and* money). Add to this the deplorable situation now prevailing in New York where a bad review from the critic on *The New York Times* can finish off your play, and one wonders why anyone wants to be a playwright.

For a playwright there is the "What?" and the "How?" *What* he feels, thinks, believes, loves, fears, hopes, and *how* to express these in terms of theatre. Very often a young playwright is first attracted by the *how's* of the theatre, the theatricality, just as a girl might be drawn to being an actress because of a striking entrance she saw some great actress make one evening. To be thus stagestruck is a good thing. Infatuation of this sort often will see a person through the inevitable doldrums to follow. But the playwright soon learns that the theatricality must convey drama, and the aspiring actress learns that there was more to the entrance than show.

Right now the theatre seems to be very much concerned with the *how,* the manner, the outward show. The Emperor's clothes. I am often inclined to think that the clothes have no Emperor, that the matter with the theatre is that the manner is the matter. But in the end this is probably healthy, fun and stimulating, to call attention to the stage as stage, the theatre as theatre. A friend of mine who teaches in a college theatre department tells me that the students come to work in the theatre full of ideas of how they want to do something on the stage—projections, soundover, turntables, lights—but they rarely have any idea of *what* they want to do, what they want to convey by all these devices.

And the *what,* of course, is what finally makes the writer. Perhaps I am old-fashioned, but I finally tire of an endless barrage of stage effects signifying little or nothing. The playwright, of course, must learn to communicate in terms of any and all techniques available to him or congenial to him, but there must be something there to communicate, a strong feeling expressed as drama or comedy. (Comedy is just as serious as drama.)

Granted that a writer knows how to write, the most important asset for him is strong feelings. I once was encouraging a young writer of short stories. I sent him to Edward Weeks, then Editor of *The Atlantic Monthly*. Mr. Weeks read his story and then said to him, "You want to be a writer, but you didn't really want to write *this* story." There is great wisdom for all writers in this sentence.

Someone has said that art gives form to feeling. There must be the feeling first. Like all writers, I am offered a number of stories or ideas by friends, acquaintances and passers-by. I hardly ever listen to such stories, first, because of a certain pride in dreaming things up for myself, but secondly because they rarely make a connection with any reservoir of feeling inside me. I think it was Tennessee Williams who said in an interview that he writes about what's bugging him at the moment. Centuries ago, Sir Philip Sidney said, "Look in thy heart and write."

One word of warning and contradiction. Often the thing that is bugging the writer most is his life as a writer. This is of little interest to anyone except another writer. I think an audience asks of a writer, "Were you there, Charlie?" This does not mean that they want a writer to write nothing but autobiography, but they want to sense the author's involvement with his story, his knowledge of the truth of whatever he is writing about. With television documentaries and movies, we are able to know so much more about the factual truth of everything that faking on this level is hardly possible any longer. But faking on the psychological level is hardly possible either. I do not want to read someone who knows no more about a situation than I know or than I could pick up from the papers and magazines and television. I want to know what it's really like. I want a letter from the front. I do not want to seem to imply by this that I just want something strange and bizarre beyond my ken. As a matter of fact, while this is sometimes fascinating, the great works usually deal with areas of life known to us all, but I want to know that the author knows that area, has suffered or laughed in that area, that he is, in short, authentic.

When I taught playwriting, I used to have a great deal to say about technique, concepts which were dramatic or not dramatic, shape and form. The more I see, the more I read, I think a great deal of the problem comes down to one word, PROGRESSION. It is the nature of an audience, any audience, to bore quickly. People in groups become restless much more quickly than they do when alone. The majority of plays I read or see which do not "work" are static. They are mood pieces, brilliant in their observation of human nature, but they start nowhere and get nowhere. Much has been said about the vanishing need for plot. It's presumably a dirty word. But whenever I start getting bored in the theatre, a voice keeps murmuring inside me, "Get on with it! Move!" And plot, no matter how slight, is what moves a play forward and holds our interest. I hate it. I fight it. It is Hell sometimes to try to wrestle with your "marvelous material" so that you can get some movement into it. I have written plays without progression and suffered the consequences. Forward-moving action is the most difficult thing to come by. But it is what holds our interest while we are absorbing the richer texture of the characters and the relationships. The developing action sometimes is relatively unimportant, but it keeps us in a frame of mind to enjoy the rest.

For example, in *Life with Father*, what we remember are the charming family scenes and the characters truly and humorously drawn, but what holds our attention though we may not know it at the time, is the simple plot of Mother trying to get Father baptized. In *Mister Roberts*, the texture is the characterizations, the humor, but the story is hung on a simple progression, Mr. Roberts' efforts to get transferred. In *The Glass Menagerie*, the story moves forward with the efforts of the family to find a gentleman caller for Laura. I have seen more beautifully written, deeply felt plays bog down after thirty minutes simply because they were going nowhere. I have often thought it would be good training for us all to write farce and melodrama, which are all forward-moving action, progression.

To give you some idea of the principle of progression . . . I was once involved in a summer theatre production of *The Emperor Jones*. You will remember that a feature of this play is the drum which starts early in the play and keeps going to the end. I remember at one rehearsal the director stopped the actors late in the play and called back to the drummer, "I can't hear you. I can't hear the drum." The drummer came forward, haggard and frazzled, and said, "I'm hitting it so hard I'm almost breaking it." The point is that we had been listening to the drum for twenty minutes or so, and in order for us still to be conscious of it, the drummer had to beat it almost beyond the point of possibility. Progression. Lines which get laughs in the First Act will not get laughs in the Second Act. A situation which will alert an audience in the First Act will leave them nodding in the Second Act. The demand for progression is basic in human nature. Think of the sex act.

For the rest, my words of wisdom are the same as always. Work. Write, act, direct. See and read as many plays as possible. It's a long haul, depending as much on your rate of personal growth as on your acquisition of dramatic technique. And at the end of the haul, there is one man who determines whether it was worth it or in vain . . . whoever may be the critic on *The New York Times*. Madness, right? . . . I must end this now so that I can start on my next play.

82

SCIENCE FICTION: SHORT STORY AND NOVEL

BY HARRY HARRISON

THE western novel is about the west, the historical novel is about history, the crime novel is about crime. The science fiction novel is *not* about science.

There are people who like to list all of the inventions that were written about first in science fiction, but this is thinking after the act. There is so much gadgetry proposed in science fiction by writers who know their technology, that it would be strange if some of it did not prove workable at some time. This is completely incidental. Science fiction is about the impact of science upon people, and upon our environment and society.

It is very hard to give a single definition that will adequately describe *all* science fiction, so I shall not attempt it. It is enough if we realize what science fiction does. First, and most important, science fiction deals with today and tomorrow. All other fiction is about yesterday. Take almost any mainstream short story or novel. With a simple change of props, horses instead of autos, it could have taken place at any time during the last hundred years— because these writers are most interested in the eternal verities of interpersonal relationships. Even if "today" is mentioned in the book, or if this concept is in the author's mind, it is "yesterday" by the time the book is published.

Science fiction holds the opposite view. If the story takes place "today," it is the real today, even by the time it sees print, because it is about the existing world that has been changed in every way by the arrival of science on the world scene. If the story is about tomorrow, it is about the continued alterations and results of these changes. Science is the inescapable bedrock of science fiction.

In the paleolithic science fiction days, the hard sciences dominated the field: chemistry, physics, biology, and the like. The wonders of the new things that could be invented and discovered were of the utmost importance. The rocket story was about how the ship was put together in the cellar, and the story ended when ("with a licking tongue of lambent flame . . .") it blasted off. If you read about a rocket today, it will probably be treated as just another vehicle, as prosaic as the Boeing 707 is now, and the story will concern itself with the passengers aboard it. The softer sciences are being admitted to science fiction, and you will find stories based upon sociology, psychology, anthropology, political science —anything and everything.

The basic attitude of the science fiction author must be humanistic. He must feel that man is perfectible, that human nature can be changed, that this will not come about through wishing or praying, but by the application of intelligence, using the tools that the scientific method has given us. Once this is thoroughly understood, there will be no question about how science *fact* blends into science *fiction*.

The facts of science are there, all around us, inescapable. The science fiction author buys all of the scientific magazines and books that he can afford because he is fascinated by the ceaseless discoveries and the endless permutations of nature. There is even material galore in the daily press. I have a clipping on my wall with the headline "DIRTY AIR MAY CAUSE ICE AGE": EXPERT. Isn't that a plot for a story? A few months ago, there was an article about how the Marines in Vietnam use dowsing rods to locate mines. This story plots itself: the contrast between the old soldier who doesn't believe this and the rookie who does.

Or take the announcement that flatworms fed on their intelligent and chopped up brothers became smarter themselves. Curt Siodmak read that and wrote *Hauser's Memory*.

And how about the frightening overpopulation and overconsumption figures? I read them and applied them to New York City in the year 2000, and wrote "Make Room! Make Room!"

The list of extrapolations from new knowledge could be extended. (Science fiction has borrowed the term *extrapolation* from mathematics and made it its own: using present knowledge to extend a trend or possibility into the future.) Of equal importance is the "what if" type of plotting that can be traced right back to H. G. Wells and his, "What if pigs had wings?" Brian Aldiss said, "What if no more children were born into the world?" then he wrote *Greybeard*. Robert Heinlein said, "What if we used the moon as a penal colony?" then he wrote *The Moon Is a Harsh Mistress*. Daniel Keyes said, "What if we could raise a moron's I.Q. by chemical methods?" then he wrote *Flowers for Algernon* (*Charly* in the movie version).

In order to write science fiction, one must not only like science fiction but must like science as well—some one science, any science, all science; the science fiction author must be a *fan* of science. He must realize that there are no monster brains lurking in computers, ready to destroy us all, just as there are no secrets that mankind "should not know." The scientific method is mankind's crowning achievement. It is the only really new thing in the entire universe. With it our race of hairless apes can talk around the world in the fraction of a second—or can refine a few pounds of a particularly heavy kind of rock and blow up that world. If you don't think this is the most fascinating thing to ever come down the pike—then you should not consider writing science fiction.

Science fiction is idea-oriented. The idea comes first—and is many times the hero—and the story follows. The complexity of the idea is what determines the length of the story. A single concept produces a short story. It might be argued that most science fiction short stories are back-plotted, *i.e.*, the ending is known in advance, then the story is filled in to reach the desired ending. Or the sequence is reversed and they are front-plotted, with a "what-if" statement, then a solution. There is little or no character development, because the characters are there to illuminate the concept. The basic story is not about the characters as people. The story is *concept*-oriented, not person-oriented. One, or at most two, of the characters will be fleshed out with personalities. The rest will be cardboard props with labels (laboratory assistant, soldier, second pilot) who do their bit and vanish.

Only in the science fiction novel, and in the longer intermediate lengths, can character be developed to any degree. Even then, rounded and real as the people may be, the concept is king. John Wyndham had real people in *The Day of the Triffids*, yet their names are forgotten while his strange plants lurk in memory. Can you remember the name of a character in any science fiction story or novel you have read recently? Now try this with *Gone with the Wind,* or *Crime and Punishment,* or any other general novel that you recall with warmth.

There are exceptions, of course, to all these rules and statements, as well as an entire school of science fiction writers, often referred to as the "New Wave," who would deny everything I have said. But these new writers would all admit that they write science fiction because they first read and enjoyed the basic stuff. You have to learn the rules before you can break them.

As an editor, I can truthfully say that there is very little good science fiction around in any length, old or new wave. As a writer, I can say that good science fiction is not easy to write. Of course the bad stuff is just about as simple to do as hack westerns—and is just about as important.

Where the science fiction short story is a vehicle for a single idea or concept, the novel, when it is not just a short story written long, can not only explore more complex concepts, but can show interrelationships. Ecology has far more interconnections than are possible between all of the characters in *War and Peace.* An ecological concept would have to be handled in the form of a novel. All of the "earth destroyed" novels are ecological, as are the multi-generation starship novels.

The "world created" is also a novel-length concept. This is rarely found outside of science fiction—*Islandia* and the Tolkien books are the only examples that come to mind—yet this label could be applied to at least 9 out of 10 novels inside the field. (Or more. I just went to my unsorted-science fiction-novels shelf, and the first twenty out of twenty books are "world created" novels.) In the science fiction field, this concept is as old as H. G. Wells, the man who invented modern science fiction books such as *The Sleeper Awakes* and *The Shape of Things to Come.* A first-class science fiction writer can invent a world, down to the smallest detail—or generate the illusion that the smallest detail has been revealed—then populate it and set a story in it that could take place in no other possible world. This, I believe, is one of the reasons for the continuing, and expanding, interest in science fiction. The western is in the west, and the murder mystery has a corpse, and we have been there many times before. But, from time to time, in the best science fiction novels, the reader will have a chance to enter a wholly new and logical world and to watch an interesting story take place there. No other form of fiction can make this statement!

I wish there were an easy formula that I could give to tell just how to write the science fiction novel, or the short story. There is none. As a first step, the prospective science fiction writer must seriously *like* the stuff. Then he must accept the idea that we live in a changing world, not a repetitive, generation-unto-generation feudalistic one. Change in itself—like science—is neither good nor bad. It is just there. Then he must accept the concept that we can change change, that all things are possible. (Whether probable or not is another matter.) Then he must read a great deal of science fiction, both old and new, to see what has been done and what is being done. Then he must read a lot of *non*-science fiction to understand what good writing is, because so much of science fiction is so terribly written. Then he must apply seat to chair and fingers to typewriter and create something that never existed before.

Then, and only then, he may have written a salable piece of science fiction. Maybe.

Still, there is very little competition at the top. Or at the bottom either, for that matter. It is certainly worth the try.

83

A LITTLE LIGHT ON LIGHTHEARTED WRITING

By Richard Armour

Most people who write want to be read. I know that is true of me. If I suddenly lost all of my magazine markets and if no publisher would take my books, I am sure I would quit writing. And if I quit writing I would also probably quit living. At any rate, I would quit making a living.

After a good many years in the business of writing to be read (i.e., published), I have learned some basic principles which I should like to pass along before I pass on. I wish someone had told *me* these things thirty or forty years ago. Some apply to almost all kinds of writing, but for the most part they apply to the kinds of writing I have chiefly done: humor and satire in prose and verse, personal-experience articles, and playful-factual books for adults and for children. I leave it to others to explain how to write and sell short stories and novels. As for playwriting, my one venture was disastrous: a play that had a brilliant run of one night.

I am going to divide the essentials of writing, and then selling what you have written, into three parts: (1) subject matter, (2) writing techniques, and (3) marketing. This is all very personal. I am giving you a chance to learn from experience without having to do all that experiencing.

It is not necessary, in fact it may not be best, to write about a large, earthshaking subject (unless you are an authority on earthquakes). A small subject, or some aspect of a small subject, written about with thoroughness, originality, and loving care, has the virtue of getting you away from the obvious and down deep under the superficial. But this small subject should ideally be universal, something of which virtually everyone is aware but had not thought much about—or had not thought as much about as you have.

In the course of one year, for example, I have written *and sold* articles on the thumb (to "The Phoenix Nest," syndicated by the Associated Press), on TV commercials having to do with stopped-up nasal passages and the like (to *Family Health*), on seating ladies at the dinner table and thus scoring points with my wife (to *The Saturday Evening Post*), and on the etiquette of travel (to *Western's Way,* the magazine of Western Airlines), etc. If you think I got away with small subjects because these were light, humorous articles, I should tell you that I also wrote seriously, for a variety of publications, on such topics as President Garfield's ambidexterity, the return of the bow tie, a woman who tells fortunes by reading the soles of the feet, what might have happened had Napoleon been a tall man, garage sales, and my forecast of fads of the future. These articles were not serious in the sense of being profound, but I hope they were also not dull. It is a nice change of pace to write sometimes lightly about the serious and sometimes seriously about the light.

The above are only a few of my two hundred pieces, some prose and some verse, published in this one year. During the same year, two books of mine were published: one a playful-positive-personal book on aging, *Going Like Sixty: A Lighthearted Look at the Later Years;* the other a juvenile on whales, *Sea Full of Whales.*

The two books indicate something else about subject matter. One is to make use of personal experience, to write about yourself. This was true of *Going Like Sixty.* It was also true of my favorite of all of my books, *Drug Store Days,* about my boyhood in the family drug store, and *Through Darkest Adolescence,* based on my observation of our children and their contemporaries. *Sea Full of Whales,* on the other hand—or fin—is an example of a subject of general interest that I knew nothing about to start with. But through reading many other books I was able to write a book that was acceptable to two experts engaged by my publisher. I didn't know *all* about whales, but I wrote in a special way and in some detail about what I myself had always wanted to know about whales but had been afraid to ask—or too lazy to learn.

Of my eleven books for children, most are playful-informational, and I have added to my own continuing education in gathering the material for them. Starting with a virgin mind, I spent long enough in the local libraries to write books in such alien fields as paleontology, history, biology, zoology, and cetology. But I have also written books that required no reading but came out of my own experience. A good example is *Animals on the Ceiling,* about the water stains on the ceiling in my bedroom that looked to me, when I was a child of six and my imagination was more far-ranging than it is now, like a turtle, a bear, a pony, and so on. I had my own zoo right above me.

Here was a small subject but a universal one. Most children have had a similar experience. The most touching response I had to the book was a letter sent me by an elementary school teacher in the ghetto of a big city. A girl in this teacher's class had written: "We have animals on our ceiling but the rich kids don't."

People, I have learned, are interested in reading about people. And the person you know best is yourself. Or you might include, as I did in my *Drug Store Days,* your relatives. It helps to have, as I did, some real oddballs among them.

So my suggestion, based on personal experience, is to write largely about the small, to look deeply into the overlooked, and to write about yourself and what is close to you. Or, by reading what others have written, make what was unfamiliar to you familiar. In this instance you can, to paraphrase Chaucer, "Gladly learn, and gladly write."

I have touched on this a bit already, but I have more to say. If you write, or want to write, you are probably already interested in words. But I suggest that you get even more interested in them. Words are the stock-in-trade of the writer. Words are what the writer builds with, as the stonemason builds with stones. I am a fanatic about words, surrounding myself with dictionaries and every few minutes looking up a synonym or an etymology. Millard Fillmore, who bought his first book—a dictionary—when he was nineteen, never became a writer, but he became President.

Words are the essence of all writing, but they are especially important in writing poetry. In fact, Coleridge once made this simple distinction: "Prose is words in the best order; poetry is the best words in the best order." A mother once took her son to W. H. Auden and asked him whether the boy had any chance of becoming a writer. "Does he like ideas?" Auden asked.

"Yes," the mother answered, "very much."

"That's good," Auden said. "But tell me, does he like words?"

"Oh, yes!" the mother exclaimed. "He *loves* words."

"Then," said Auden, "he may become a writer, even a poet."

But the words have to be put in the best order, and that involves style, or at least clarity. My advice here is to read—read the writers you admire, the writers you wish you could write like. I have never known a writer who was not also a reader. Once I met a writer who told me that he read for fifteen minutes every day, before starting to write, from a little book called *The Beauties of Shakespeare*. "It tones up my language," he said. "It starts the words flowing."

That suggests that you should, of course, read writers who are better than you are, especially in the fields or of the types you like and want to write. In a similar way, you learn golf or tennis by playing with players who are the best you can find to play with you—preferably the club pro. Robert Louis Stevenson said he "played the sedulous ape" to other writers. Don't worry too much about writing in the style of the great writers you read. Once you are on your way, you will write in a manner that reflects yourself. You can't help it. "The style is the man," as it was said long ago, though today we would be well advised to say "The style is the man or the woman," or "The style is the person."

In writing prose humor and satire, in both articles and books, I confess to having "played the sedulous ape" to Jonathan Swift (for instance using the irony of his *A Modest Proposal* in "The Depopulation Explosion," an article for *Playboy,* and at book length in *It All Started with Stones and Clubs,* a satire on war and weaponry), and to Mark Twain, whose writings I have come more and more to admire and learn from, and to Voltaire, whose *Candide* I try to read once a year.

As a background for writing light verse, I have read and analyzed (even as I have enjoyed) the superlative works of Arthur Guiterman, Samuel Hoffenstein, Dorothy Parker, Margaret Fishback, David McCord, Morris Bishop, Phyllis McGinley, Ogden Nash, and many another. From each I have borrowed tricks of style, the unusual handling of rhyme and meter, and the basic principle of writing enough but not too much.

Whether you are writing a poem, an article, a book for children, a play, or a novel, you may at first use too many words. If you do, bravely and boldly *cut*. A large part of revision is cutting. Cutting isn't easy at first, but it gets easier. Once an editor asked me to cut a book manuscript thirty percent. I cut it forty percent, and as I look at it now, I cannot recall a single word I took out. All I hope is that some day an editor doesn't ask me to cut my manuscript by one hundred percent.

I have had twelve publishers for my books and have written for more than two hundred magazines. It is not that I am restless. Some books require a certain type of publisher; some publishers require a certain type of book. As for magazines, not only do they come and go, but editors come and go, too. I could give you two long lists. One would be a list of magazines for which I once wrote that have gone out of business (and not, I hope, because of what I wrote for them). The other would be a list of magazines that have changed requirements or changed editors, the two often having the same result for me—losing me a market.

So, after all these years, I am still looking for markets. I do this in two ways, and I recommend both to you. One is to study the market lists in *The Writer* and at the back of this book. The other is to study the magazines themselves. I take many magazines, but I also spend many hours at the magazine stands, examining potential markets. My best time for doing this is while my wife is shopping in the supermarket, and I go through the magazines on the rack, looking for super markets myself!

Long ago, I learned to keep many pieces in the mail. I have just looked at my folder of "Pieces Out" and find I have sixty-four articles and verses in the hands of editors (where I hope most of them will stay). Nothing out, nothing sold. True, I have some regular markets that take whatever I write, but only a few of these, alas. I still get things back, but I make a sale almost every day.

You can imagine how eagerly I watch for the postman. He is my cash register. Some days, after I have opened the morning's mail, I am "high." Other days I am "low." But I have learned not to remain either euphoric or depressed for more than a few minutes.

Then back to the typewriter for another try. Writing, I discovered long ago, is a trying business. If at first you don't succeed. . . .

84

THE PRACTICE OF PLAYWRITING

By Mary C. Chase

You have asked me—what are the most important techniques for the beginning playwright to master? Well! Well! Well! First of all, is the beginner a playwright?

If so, he was born a playwright, with an instinct for the theater. If not, he cannot learn playwriting, as he could not learn to sing without a voice or to dance without an innate sense of rhythm.

He may have a desire and talent to spin stories and a need to communicate to others his sense of the wonder and beauty and terror of life; he may have understanding of character, a feel for narrative and style. He may have all of these qualities and yet not be a playwright. He may be a great artist, a superb intellect, a Titan of literature. He may be much, much more talented than a playwright and yet not be a playwright.

What then is a playwright? First, he is one who has a heightened awareness of the living presence of other human beings in the same room—a room seating five people or a theater seating five hundred. He has an awareness of creatures, animal creatures, a love and a fear of them; a knowledge of the banked fires of conflict between them and an almost guilty excitement in the desire to stir these fires into blaze; above all, he has a need to attract these animals, to please them, to entertain them, satisfy them and even uplift them. It is a social act, theater. And the playwright is closer to the actor than he is to the novelist; closer to the clown than to the professor; closer to the evangelist and the minister in the pulpit than he is to the scholar in the library.

If the writer has this extra dimension of sensitivity to the presence of others listening in the same room, he should fortify his instinct by studying the proven rules of dramaturgy. He should begin with Aristotle's *Poetics* and then go to William Archer's *Playmaking*. This is old-fashioned here and there but very, very sound. Then he should study the Greek plays, Shakespeare, Molière, Ibsen and O'Neill. Then he should study melodramas and perhaps try imitating one for practice.

The melodrama, while considered superficial in substance, is so dependent upon mounting suspense that it is an excellent form to study for construction. Several prize-winning modern plays are actually souped-up melodramas—even drawing on the past for the use of musical interludes. And whatever else melodrama may lack in the way of embellishments, it is always—theater.

The playwright should read Fielding's essay on comedy, Victor Hugo's essay on the art of preparation in the drama and Tolstoy's discussion of the drama in *What Is Art?*

Is he going to write comedies or dramas? He should learn that the main difference here is one of attitude: his own attitude toward a plot and characters; the attitude of the characters toward the plot and each other. If Hamlet, for instance, had been a milquetoast in the opening scene, and if the specter had tried to persuade him to forget about his father's murder and go back to sleep, the play would have had to zoom off into farce comedy.

At some point early, the playwright should decide that he is a playwright and get out of the library and into the theater—right where he is. He should begin to practice the techniques of the play form first with those around him—his friends, his family, his acquaintances.

When he tells a joke, a personal experience, an anecdote, he should observe the uses of the beginning, the middle, the end; how to arouse interest and hold it; how to satisfy the listener in concluding the story. He should watch carefully the change which comes in the telling of a story, say, to one person and then, as others join to listen; how the tempo accelerates, how he now condenses here or expands there, elaborates or cuts depending on the attention of the listeners. Telling stories aloud to children provides a superb laboratory in which the beginning playwright may practice theater techniques and learn to provoke interest—to hold it, make it rise, and then sum up. This audience is perfect for him, because children are even more impatient than adults and have not yet learned to conceal boredom. This is a primitive thing the playwright is doing while he is learning, and it fits the case. The theater itself is a primitive animal, a wonderful, wonderful thing.

When a writer writes a story, he is addressing a letter that is to be read and absorbed quietly by one person. The playwright is always addressing a group. He is interesting, rabble-rousing, clowning or inspiring—for the ear. He is doing this actually or in his imagination—always. Because even in the latter case he must be aware of others—listening!

The playwright must *wright* and not merely *write*. He must "wright" plays and scenes because he is primarily a builder and his job is to build scenes to play before a living audience.

When, after some practice in the telling of anecdotes, etc., he begins to feel a little more sure of himself with the rules, he must begin cautiously here and there to inject into these little shows and "tryouts" a bit of himself—certain of his own personal idylls, ideas, memories and dreams. These personal trial balloons may now and then excite, interest or bore his listeners. This will throw him into despair and shame. And it should. It must. But he must go on.

If something does strike fire from his audience—maybe it was an anecdote about an old aunt in Peoria—he must tell it again to another group. If it strikes fire again and still again, he will know he has something which interests people. Should he make a play out of this? Wait. Test it first with these questions. Ask—not if it will make a good play, or a bad play, a short play or a full-length play, but first—is it a play at all? Maybe it's a story or a novel. Think of the word play here as a verb, not as a noun. What would be "playing" against what? What forces against what other forces? For what stakes? What moments of change and crisis would be there to watch?

And be careful about using philosophical conclusions as the germ of a play. These can enrich a play but may not have enough vitality to initiate one. It has been my personal experience that plays which came into my mind as completed pieces of stage business always pleased an audience more than those written from a philosophical conclusion I had reached and then found a plot to illustrate.

A play is not a narrative in dialogue, like the talking picture which is acted out on a sound stage, filmed and shown later, coming across like scenes in memory. A play is an imitation of an action being performed in public, before other people sitting out there watching it happen—*now!*

Suppose the playwright decides he has a play. Where does he begin? At what point does he open the play? Stalk the game very carefully here. This is the only real choice the playwright has. After that he is bound by the laws of growth and the rules of dramatic progression. His choice here must be determined by his own instinct. He is on his own. And he trembles—rightly.

With his choice of the opening made, his chart of scenes set down, his acquaintance with his characters increased, he waits for the moment when his inner excitement propels him to the workroom to put down the dialogue in whatever scene he is now impelled to get moving. With every word he writes, he must hold in his consciousness the feeling of the actors on the stage and the presence of a living audience in the room with him. This inspires him to effects he had never calculated. He is amazed, awed, suspended in time, at one with the dramatists of the past. Have the shades of the past great playwrights come to stand behind his chair? Don't move. This is the theater— not Broadway. It is happening here—now. It is *playing!*

What happens to the play itself later will be determined at this point. If the writer's own heart does not pound—no one else's ever will. If he is not amused—nobody else will be—ever.

Eugene O'Neill was able to hold in his mind at the same time scenes and characters and background on a stage, and an audience watching these characters; he did this with such intensity that his plays can transcend bad acting and shabby productions. Once I saw a group of high school amateurs attempting one of his sea plays in the dingy auditorium of a women's club in Denver. Bad as the actors were—as the play went on, I felt the spray in my face. O'Neill had transcended the production and had brought me into his workroom where *he* was feeling the spray as he wrote.

When the playwright has a draft of his play which pleases him, he should not put it into an envelope and mail it to a producer—yet. He should try it out, reading it aloud to a group of three or more people in his home. He doesn't need to invite experts to these readings—just people. He should notice when, during the reading, the chairs scrape, the bracelets rattle, and the bodies shift positions; when there is a blessed stillness or wholehearted laughter. But he should never,

never, never listen to the friends who expound to him afterward on where the play went off and why. The friends don't know. The critics won't know. He must know. His audience has reacted or not reacted. The playwright watches, suffers, and learns why.

The late Frank Fay once told a young beginning comic who had met with a lukewarm reception, "Kid, you learn your trade through flop sweat. That means when you're doing it and you're dying and you know they don't like you and the sweat comes out on your brow. In that split second you learn more than in all the beforehand planning or theories. There's no other way."

What you learn from a fiasco in your living room or from a flop before an audience of a thousand in a theater—and the difference is only one of degree—you will make good use of.

Go back to your chart, your sequence of scenes, re-wright, re-build. Then read the play to another group. If you now hold them, try to form a contact with an acting company, amateur or professional, through a producer.

And don't ever let anybody tell you this is impossible for the beginner. It is not—not if he has a play that plays.

There is so little real theater in the true sense of the word: excitement, mounting interest, breathless waiting, a sense of fate and eternity outside the window or the joy of the comedy whisking the audience up and away from care. The world hungers for such experiences and goes patiently to the theater, time after time—waiting.

The theater is a mysterious, mystical place. And just as each play, no matter how much craft you learn, has within it a special secret which you alone must solve (perhaps in outright defiance of one of the rules of the craft you've learned), so each play has its own vitality and its own fate and will find its way somehow to the stage. Play your hunches about your work.

The theater is like war. The audience is your enemy to be overcome. At first it is ill-natured and skeptical and "show me." Your play is your plan of attack. You must meet your audience at the point where they are at this moment in time, interest them, hold them and try to lift them.

If your play fails and the audience wins, leaving the theater intact —unmoved, unamused—pay no attention to the notices explaining why. And don't pore over Sunday newspaper articles about your work or any other playwright's, measuring yourself and your plays against the weighty edicts handed down by journalists. These are the armchair generals leaning back to give opinions after the battle. They are around the theater but not "of" it. Nobody really understands the theater until he has risked everything for it. Until he himself has known "flop sweat."

If your play succeeds and the articles are full of raves explaining the victory—pay no attention. Take what you've learned here, too, sharpen your tools, and go back to work.

85

THE REWARDS OF PHOTO-JOURNALISM

By James Tallon

I'M HARDLY a wizard with words, but over four hundred articles tagged with my by-line have appeared in some fifty publications, and I must admit the credit for my success belongs to the field of photography. The only step I had taken to prepare for a writing career was a typing course in my freshman year of high school. And though I've always been interested in photography, I did not apply myself to it seriously until about a decade ago. After grinding hundreds of thousands of feet of film through various 8mm movie cameras, and getting zero satisfaction from it, I swapped the movie paraphernalia for a reliable twin-lens reflex still camera and a copy of *Where and How to Sell Your Pictures,* by Arvel W. Ahlers and Paul V. Webb (American Photographic Book Publishing Co., Inc., East Gate & Zeckendorf Blvds., Garden City, NY 11530). This book was a shot in the arm, and, following the authors' instructions, I put together my first picture story. If I had not done this, I might never have become a full-time free lancer.

Acting like a typical loving father, I exposed two rolls of 120 black-and-white film (twenty-four exposures) on my buckskin-garbed two-year-old daughter as she climbed about the ancient Indian apartment house, Wupatki, in Northern Arizona. Selecting eight negatives, I blew them up to 8x10 glossy prints, wrote captions and about a hundred words for a text block. Then I mailed the package to some publication whose name now escapes me and started eyeing the mailbox for the check.

The picture story came back with a standard printed rejection slip. Undaunted—remember that word—I mailed it out again. And again. And again—thirteen times in all. Ahlers and Webb insist that you must keep your work in the mails to sell it, but by the thirteenth try, I must admit it was hard to stick to their advice. However, this time a check arrived from an Arizona regional magazine. Not only did the editors like the piece, but they said they would like to see more of my material.

Fired by the sale of my very first work, I quickly produced a satire titled "The Art of Gunslinging." Again I exposed two rolls of film and selected eight shots for blow-up, but this time I pounded out 600 words—six times as much copy as for my first photo feature! The Arizona magazine bought the piece immediately, and sometime later I sold Canadian first rights to the *Toronto Star Weekly*.

Elated, I moved into the first stages of writer-photographer evolution, from referring to myself as being ninety-five percent photographer and five percent writer, to a point now where I feel about fifty-fifty. In fact, I recently did a 6,500-word manuscript for the Gulf Travel Club that included not a single photograph, and occasionally I produce short pieces without photos. But you can bet I have a go-ahead for pieces without photos before I even consider sending them.

By now you've possibly been reading between the lines. But if you want further proof of the pudding, study the article market listings. *Field & Stream* writes: ". . . photography (meaning none or poor) is a major cause of rejection." *Mechanix Illustrated* editors say: ". . . photos essential." *Modern Cycle*: ". . . acceptance depends on quality of photos." *Watersport*: ". . . photos will be needed for most articles." Once I heard an editor flatly state that as far as he was concerned, pictures make up fifty percent of the article.

The key to illustrating your manuscripts with top-quality photos hinges on several factors: 1) one or more 35mm cameras; 2) a wide-angle and a medium telephoto lens; 3) a little time spent in learning camera operation and darkroom techniques (less time than it takes to learn to drive an automobile skillfully); 4) a "reckless" consideration for film; 5) a strong desire to succeed as a writer-photographer.

My style has changed considerably since the "old days." At the outset, the text I wrote to accompany my pictures was radically edited before it appeared in print. But just recently an editor of the *Arizona Republic* Sunday Magazine commented, "We didn't have to lay a pencil to your alligator story." Very nice.

But perhaps the biggest change in my free-lance method is in the photography. Where once I cranked a miserly two rolls of 120 through the old twin-lens reflex, I now expose 200 to 300 frames—and sometimes as many as 1000—for a piece that may require only five to ten illustrations. Needless to say, the composition and human interest in my pictures have been upgraded to professional standards, if only through the law of averages. If you shoot enough pictures and change angles often, you will get reasonably good shots from the beginning. With practice you'll get a noticeable increase in usable frames. But always remember, it takes but a slight movement of your subject's eyes or mouth to change a dull picture to a lively one, so *quality* pictures may result from sheer *quantity*.

A number of things prompted this change in my photo techniques. First, was the desire to compete with the real pros. Second, I found the 120 cameras awkward to handle, especially the waist-level models. Sometimes I didn't find the action in the viewfinder until it was over. Then again, many big-format cameras are limited to non-interchangeable lenses. And those that feature interchangeable lenses are prohibitive in price to anyone but a well-to-do professional photographer or wealthy amateur, especially if he wants a nice complement of lenses and extras. In addition, 120 cameras with their twelve- and twenty-four-frame capacity have the nasty habit of running out of film when you need it most.

For writer-photographers who shoot for the printed page, the final product of 35mm cameras cannot only be excellent but often superior to work produced with some larger-format cameras! This stems from the 35mm camera's great versatility and wide range of lenses. It's fact, not opinion, that 35mm cameras are the most popular in the world.

When I give talks on how photography can increase sales for writers, I am frequently asked, "What camera should I buy?" There is no absolute answer to this except the best 35mm single-lens reflex you can afford. Single-lens reflexes are chosen over range-finder models simply because they are more versatile and the lenses more economical. You can pick up a good 35mm camera and a couple of lenses for less than the price of a new manual standard typewriter. And for the cost of a new electric typewriter, you can purchase everything you need to take and process high-quality pictures, if you shop wisely.

But don't put off buying equipment you need. Several years ago I coveted a Novoflex 400mm telephoto follow-focus lens, but procrastinated on the assumption I couldn't afford the $200 price tag. This was and *is* false economy. Crossing a ridge in Papago Park one evening, I saw the city of Phoenix spread dramatically against a spectacular sunset. A normal lens would lose the skyline entirely; a 400mm would retain the skyline and compress the sunset against it.

The next day I hesitantly dipped into my savings and ordered the lens. When it arrived I waited with saintly patience until about ten days later a similar sunset presented itself. One shot was used on the cover of *Arizona* Magazine and several inside. My first sale netted me nearly half the price of the lens, and since then many articles backed by pictures taken through the 400mm have gone to press that previously might not have made it.

By now you're getting the picture. But until now it's been a black-and-white one. Thirty-five-millimeter color presents a different story. With black-and-white film, you can send an editor a nice big 8x10 glossy print, which he generally reduces in size to fit the pages of his magazine. With 35mm color you must submit the transparency, which because of its small size is usually difficult to see and visualize as a color page.

What this all boils down to is that unless you have a confirmed market for 35mm color transparencies, I don't recommend you shoot them. For every color shot I expose, I trip the shutter across a hundred or more black-and-white frames. And after many years at this game I still find I sell about fifty black-and-white photos to one color. Essentially, good black-and-white prints teamed with a good manuscript have an excellent chance of selling, and more often than not the package fits better into the magazine's budget. The cost of speculative color shooting can be quite prohibitive to *your* budget, as well, when compared against overall sales. The exception to the rule is a red-hot situation which absolutely demands color, and you *think* it's sure to sell. Then, shoot away and don't spare the film.

For my own purposes I fit the type of color film to the situation, but I stay with Kodak Tri-X black-and-white film ninety-nine percent of the time. It gives me a telephoto-steady shutter speed of 1000 at f.11 for average daylight situations, and records images without flash under extremely poor light conditions. A four-stop error still allows you a printable negative. And the so-called grain is minimal, and rarely noticeable in an 8x10 print.

As an economy measure, struggling writer-photographers (or anyone else interested in photo economy) should load their own cassettes. In the old days, Eastman Kodak used to supply their 35mm film in re-usable cassettes, but found that all the photographers were "rolling their own", so they pack the film in cans that are destroyed when you open them. Now they charge 25c for cassettes that once were free. But at that, it beats the high cost of factory loads.

One hundred feet of bulk 35mm black-and-white film sells for about $7, discounted, and makes up into twenty rolls of approximately thirty-six exposures. This breaks down to about one cent per shot. And herein lies the most important tip I can pass on to you. *Besides equipment, the major difference between professional photographers and amateurs is the amount of film exposed.* To professionals, film is the cheapest part of the whole venture. Skill runs second!

You don't make prints of everything you shoot. The negatives are cut into six sections of approximately six each, and the entire roll contact-printed onto a single sheet of 8x10 glossy paper. When you submit ten sheets of these to an editor with your manuscript, you're sure to meet with a certain amount of favor. From the contacts, he'll mark—usually in red grease pencil—the blow-ups he'll need.

It's difficult to show the simplicity of camera operation and the fine art of arriving at nice 8x10 glossies without getting into a basic course in photo-journalism. But such things as shutter speeds and f stops quickly become as familiar as keys on your typewriter and easier to use (I don't make near as many mistakes with the former). Terms such as *developer* and *hypo* soon become as common as typewriter ribbon and carbon paper. The cost of your entire photographic package, including chemicals and enlarging papers, will probably be paid for by the first two or three sales—sales you might not have made otherwise.

Nearly every town has a high school or college that offers a course in photography, but you can learn from books as I did. And with a little practical experience you may back into photography the way I backed into writing.

86

Rx FOR COMEDY

By Neil Simon

The idea of a prescription for comedy is obviously ridiculous. What works for one playwright rarely works for another, and even the fact that a certain approach succeeded for a writer before does not mean that it will surely produce an amusing play for that same scribe a second time. The knowledge of this grisly reality gives me a healthy insecurity, which I consider a great asset. Insecurity encourages a writer to be open to criticism by competent professionals; it allows him to face up to the need to revise or rewrite. Of course, *everybody* cheerily tells a playwright how to repair his script and it takes cool courage and wondrous manners to endure the amateurs' well-meant advice. In Boston during the tryout of *The Odd Couple,* I had been up till four o'clock in the morning rewriting the third act—for the fifth time. Exhausted, I finally fell asleep on my typewriter. At seven A.M. a dentist from Salem, Mass., phoned to tell me how *he* would fix the third act. I thanked him and promised myself I would call him at five the next morning to tell him how I would fix his bridgework.

I happen to like rewriting, a good deal of which is often necessary after one sees how a scene actually "plays" on stage in rehearsal or tryout. Each chance to fix, polish and tighten is a glorious reprieve—something I never had in the urgent world of weekly television. I suppose the greatest problem the writer in the theater has is to face "those ferocious critics." My problem is even greater. I write my own critics' reviews as I'm writing my play. I place Walter Kerr just behind my right shoulder holding in his hand a big stick—with rusty nails. If I get verbose or careless or stretch for jokes, Mr. Kerr lets me have it right across the knuckles.

This article originally appeared in *Playbill* Magazine, January 1966. Reprinted courtesy of Playbill, Inc.

The jokes are a special hazard. In the first of 112 versions of *Come Blow Your Horn,* the opening five minutes of the play were crammed with good jokes—in fact, some of the best I had ever written—and the scene was terrible. The audience, knowing nothing of the characters or the situation, could not have cared less. Now I know enough to start with the characters. Where do they come from? In the case of *The Odd Couple,* from a party I attended in California. All the men there were divorced, all their dates were their new girl friends. Most of these men were sharing apartments with other divorced men because alimony payments forced them to save money. In *Barefoot* and *Come Blow Your Horn,* at least one or two characters in each play resembled, perhaps in speech patterns, mannerisms or personal outlook, someone I've actually known.

Looking back at what and how I write, I seem to begin a play with two people of completely opposite nature and temperament, put them in an intolerable situation, and let the sparks fly. The extra ingredient, and very important, is that they must both emphatically believe that their way of life is the right one. Then it's the playwright's job to support *both* those beliefs. As for form, I prefer my comedies in three acts. When I start, I write extensive notes for the first act, a sketchy outline for the second and nothing for the third. I'm rather curious myself as to what will happen in the third act. Sometimes I don't find out for certain until a week before we open on Broadway.

If there is anything remotely resembling a key to comedy in theater, I'd guess that it is for the writer, director and actors to apply one simple rule. Never treat it as a comedy. The actors and characters must treat their predicament as though their lives depended on it. Not an easy achievement, I admit. Play it too seriously and the laughs are gone. Play just the comedy and ditto. In casting, my preference is not to go with the "established comic" but with a good actor who understands comedy. Walter Matthau, Robert Redford and Mildred Natwick are among the best.

One question I'm asked quite often is if I consider myself funny. I suppose I apply my own personal humor to life in the same manner as I would in a play. I need a situation. Put me around a table with real funny men like Buddy Hackett or Jonathan Winters or Mel

Brooks and I fade like a shrinking violet. No fast repartee for me. I shine trapped in an elevator with six people and a German Shepherd licking my ear.

To me, the first ten minutes of a comedy are critical. The writer must (1) set up the rules and the situation, (2) catch the audience almost immediately. Once the rules are announced, farce, satire, straight comedy or whatever game you're playing, the audience will believe you so long as you stick to those rules and that game. I believe in starting the conflict in the opening minutes (e.g., the poker game in *Odd Couple*) and to be as theatrically arresting as possible. The idea of opening on an empty stage in *Barefoot* intrigued me. Then I begin with some new event in the life of our hero, something that has never happened to him before.

My writing routines are actually rather prosaic. No midnight oil burns in my lamp. I type in an office or at home, and put in a ten to five day with a short lunch break. I may do a complete draft of a play, use it as an outline and then set to work on a more finished version. I like to get into the writing quickly to "hear how the characters speak," for once I hear the speech patterns it is easier going. I ought to point out that my insecurity is such that even as I'm writing one play, I'm beginning to think ahead to the next. So if this one doesn't quite pan out, well. . . .

Once a play goes into rehearsal, my "normal" routine ceases and the midnight oil begins to burn. There seems to be less time for social obligations, children and—horror of horrors—the Giants' football games.

Do I need quiet when I'm working? It depends. If there are no problems in the script, they could be digging the new subway under my typewriter. But one day recently my two little girls were on the other side of the house playing jacks. And as the ball bounced softly on the thick rug, I ran from the study screaming at my wife, "Can't you keep those kids quiet?"

She looked at me with knowing affection and pity.

"I'm sorry the scene's not going well, Doc," she answered with ancient female wisdom.

If there's anything I can't stand, it's a smart aleck wife—who happens to be right.

87

REALITIES OF THE GREETING CARD MARKET

By Carl Goeller

WHAT is the outlook for the greeting card free-lance writer in the seventies? On the negative side, there have been some discouraging developments for free-lancers during the past year. The economic slump has not spared the greeting card industry, and there has been a good deal of belt-tightening on the part of editors of major companies as well as smaller ones. There are fewer purchases of borderline material—material that has merit but will take working over before it is publishable. This naturally hurts greeting card writers who specialize in ideas rather than in finished, craftsmanlike writing.

But, on the positive side, this is the most exciting period in greeting card history. Editors are competing for new ideas, new gimmicks, new products, and they're paying more than ever for what they buy. And they are buying ideas as well as words. To succeed in the greeting card field during the seventies, you have to be an idea man as well as a writer.

Who is going to make it in the next decade—and who isn't—and why? Here is my appraisal of what's in store for various kinds of greeting card writers in the seventies:

The conventional writer, who writes only conventional 4- and 8-line verse for serious occasions, is in trouble. In the sixties there were as many as ten rather good markets for straight verse; today there are fewer than five, and some of these are buying only a fraction of what they once did. One reason for this is that conventional verse is a reusable commodity—a popular verse can be modified and used with a dozen or more different designs throughout a card line, and these can last for years. Greeting card editors, therefore, don't need much new conventional verse, no matter how well written it may be. The writer who is convinced that conven-

tional verse is the only type he can do will have to content himself
with a limited income from his free-lancing.

Small greeting card publishers, as well as the large ones, are insisting on fresh, new approaches which will help get their wares into
stores handling more than one line. They are stressing originality,
especially in their studio card lines.

The ostrich sits behind the typewriter day and night, writing
card ideas by the dozens—conventional, humorous, juvenile and
studio ideas. He's been at it quite a few years and has been pretty
successful because he knows what the editors want. Or so he thinks!

But he hasn't been out into the greeting card departments recently; he hasn't been reading the trade magazines to see just what's
been happening in the industry. He's neglected the research end of
his job to the point that he doesn't even realize that there have been
more changes in the greeting card business in the last three years
alone than there were in the preceding twenty. As a result, he's
showing editors only a fraction of the kinds of material they really
want to see. Unless he removes his head from the sand—quickly—
the ostrich will find his hits becoming fewer and his misses becoming commonplace.

The in-tune writer does what the ostrich fails to do—he keeps in
tune with what's happening in the industry, and he slants his efforts
accordingly. He notices, for example, that the major publishers are
coming out every year now with many new groups of "promotions"
—series of cards with some unifying theme, either design or sentiment oriented. So, instead of simply sending one batch after another
of individual card ideas, he includes some interesting promotional
idea groups. One enterprising writer last year sold six promotional
ideas to several different companies, and each brought him a handsome check. He notices, too, the trends in copy which appeal most
to the consumer. For example, American Greetings' "Soft Touch"
cards—cards using mood photography and simple, meaningful copy,
all in prose—found immediate acceptance with the youth market,
and they sold over ten million cards in less than a year. Other
companies rushed into print with their imitations of Soft Touch . . .
and a writing market was born.

The creative idea person asks himself, "Why should my creative
efforts be limited to writing? Why not sell ideas as well as words?"

and he begins approaching the card companies in a new way. He begins selling them ideas for new products and new twists to existing products. Look at what the "card" industry is making and selling these days—books, puzzles, games, party items, toys, calendars, posters, badges, candles, candy, writing instruments, gift items . . . the list is endless. The idea person is aware of these, studies them, and then comes up with fresh new ideas for them. Only recently an idea man came up with an idea for a series of books which he presented and sold to a major card company for several thousand dollars. Another sold a series of games to one of the publishers and was well paid for them. The *very* creative idea person goes one step further. He researches a product before the card companies go into it, then gets in on the ground floor. How? By reading and shopping to see what's on the market and what isn't; by talking to clerks and store managers about what is in demand that they can't supply; and by creating something to meet that demand. The method by which he sells the idea to a manufacturer may well tax his creative ability more than coming up with it—but the results can be well worth it.

The analyst takes his writing and creating seriously enough to analyze his successes and failures. Someone once defined a professional as a person who doesn't make the same mistake twice. The analyst is a professional. He periodically reviews the cards he's sold to see what slant is hitting, and, perhaps as important, he reviews his rejections to see why he missed. Further, he is willing to ask the help of others—fellow professionals or even an editor—in determining *why*. If the editor likes his work in general and feels that he has something to contribute, he will be glad to comment and suggest improvements.

Which of the five different greeting card writers we've looked at are you? If you are *the conventional writer* or *the ostrich,* the seventies are going to be rough sledding, and you had better start now to enlarge your markets by trying other types of writing. If you are *the in-tune writer, the creative idea person,* or *the analyst,* you will find the greeting card market a real challenge, and an exciting and profitable one as well.

Five years ago, the greeting card market consisted of verse for conventional, humorous, and juvenile cards, and studio card gags—

period. Today, as we have already noted, it includes new products and new twists for old categories. Let's see what new twists are in demand.

Conventional cards: There is a great interest in simplified conversational verse which avoids the clichés which have been so reliable in past years. Forget about lines like "this card has come to say," "today and all year through," and "every thought prompts wishes." Every word and every line must count. Use ideas in your verses—design, sentiment tie-ins, fresh and interesting thoughts, and unusual verse formats. Don't always use verse. If you can put your thoughts into rhythmic, readable prose, do it. Keep your verse as brief as possible but have something to say.

Humorous cards: There's more emphasis now on cleverness and less on gimmick in humorous cards. This is a matter of economics as much as anything. All the companies are finding a real cost squeeze which makes mechanical gimmicks almost prohibitive except in the highest-priced cards. Separate pieces, too, which need to be attached, are costly because of the hand labor required. This means that words and art work are practically all an editor can use at 50¢ and under. Paper is still reasonably inexpensive, so many editors are receptive to novelty folds and unusual stock ideas (paper bags, etc.). There's a definite trend away from the old cornball type of humor and toward the more youthful, sophisticated approaches. Card ideas that were considered strictly for studio cards a few years back are now used on humorous cards with pictures of bunnies, dogs, cats, etc. A word of advice—you'll sell more humorous ideas if you think design as well as words. If your gag is accompanied by some clever designing, you're saving the editor and the art director some extra work, and they will appreciate it.

Juvenile cards: There is very little demand for straight juvenile verse. Most companies are interested in "idea cards"—things to do and play with, semi-educational, and easily designed. Don't talk down to the kids with your copy—they see lots of television and their vocabularies are much broader than ours were at that age. Some greeting card companies are buying stories, both for cards and for hardback books they are now publishing.

Studio cards: As previously noted, gags that used to appear only in studio lines have now spread to the humorous lines, and studio card editors are looking for more originality and youth-oriented copy. This doesn't mean hippie-type ideas, "cool" talk, drug-culture bits, and the like; it means humor that doesn't rely on slamming the recipient (today's kids are a sentimental bunch, no matter what they say), or getting drunk, or growing old (age gags just aren't cutting it in the studio card racks these days). Love is big—and so is sex— and little digs at the Establishment—and ecology, pollution, and the like. Not every company is moving its studio line in this direction, so don't rush out and throw away your pile of straight humor. There are some editors who still want that type. But be forewarned: most major greeting card publishers are heading in this direction (upon the advice of their research people).

Books: One of the hottest items to hit the card departments in the past three years has been the little hardback book. It was pioneered by American Greetings, and now more and more companies are building sizable book lines. There are several approaches which will bring checks from editors who find they have no backlog at all of this type of material. Here are a few:

Cute stuff—Girl-to-girl or girl-to-boy messages done in a cute, almost juvenile-sounding simplicity. These are especially strong in such subjects as love, friendship, "missing you," and in birthday messages. Some are in verse; most in very simple prose.

Humorous—Often these are collections of ideas that are taken from the studio card files, but on "missing you" compliments, love, birthdays, and get-well. Items must be short and quick. Long, involved humor goes nowhere.

Studio—These have been the weakest books, and consequently bring the greatest number of rejection slips. And yet, editors need them. The material should be timely, youth-oriented humor, usually girl-to-boy stuff.

Conventional—Many of these are similar to the old *Ideals* magazine—collections of very traditional, conventional verse and poetry. This is a very small market, but it's there if you have the right idea.

This is just the start of the book business for the major greeting card publishers. The next obvious step will be larger, high-priced books, and the ideas for them could just as well come from you as from their staff writers. Here's a prediction: By 1975, at least two of the card companies will be considered major book publishers. If you get in on the ground floor now . . . who knows—you may have some published books to your credit five years from now.

Novelties: Ceramic figures are big with a dozen publishers— the little characters that say, "I wuv you," "The devil made me do it," and so on. Watch the stores to see which companies are selling figurines, then send them ideas for new approaches—not just more of the same.

Calendars are a big item with many of the major companies. They have plenty of ideas for designed calendars, but they can use you for novelty approaches.

Posters are hot. The big companies wrote them off as a fad when they were introduced about five years ago (they did that with studio cards, too), but now they realize posters are here to stay, so they're going into the business. Submit some original ideas, and they'll sell.

Puzzles and games are relatively new to most card publishers, but destined to be big items. If you have the kind of complicated mind it takes to do puzzles, etc., send them to major companies —they're interested now.

The card companies are in the business of helping people communicate with one another—and who says that cards are the only way to do this? When you're thinking of items, products, gadgets, and copy for the greeting card field, keep that in mind. If you yourself use an unusual method of communicating with your friends or relatives, you may have the makings of a new product that will be of interest to the card companies.

To return, then, to the basic question posed in this piece, does the free-lance greeting card writer stand a chance in the seventies?

Yes, but he'll have to think of himself as more than just a greeting card writer. A better title might be creative communicator.

Yes, but he'll have to remember he's living in the seventies, and writing for the future decade, not the past.

Yes, but he's going to have to stay alert to the changing times and attitudes of the people. You're in for some exciting days, months, and years ahead as you become the complete creative communicator.

88

TELEVISION WRITING

By Edward Barry Roberts

In this electronic age, it well may be that the ability to write is the last thing expected of a television writer. For instance, in a popular Red Skelton show, in a skit called "Baby's First Birthday," there appeared this stage direction:

> In comes an attractive nurse in a short dress—she's carrying a birthday cake. NOTE (says the script): A split screen pre-taped—or Chromo-key her in and double hands to put cake on high chair tray.

The writer of the script wrote in that stage direction. My point is, before the writer could do his job, that is, use his writing talent to its expected value, he had to know what a split-screen pre-taped is, or what it means to Chromo-key the nurse in and double the hands that put the cake on the high chair tray. He had to know that he could solve a problem he faced by using the devices those two technical terms describe.

The writer's problem was this: Red Skelton, in baby clothes, was sitting in an out-sized highchair in order to put him in the right proportions for a proper baby. The nurse had to bring in his birthday cake. If she appeared in the same shot with Red, he'd be gigantic in relation to her, and the illusion of his being a proper baby would be destroyed. So, the writer suggested two possible methods: one, the split screen, which everyone has seen on televsion many times; the other, the Chromo-key method, which is much like the old motion picture "process shot," by which action can be superimposed on a background previously photographed through a color masking process which I'll not stick my neck out to describe.

In other words, writing for television today takes something more than being able to put words together. While all aspiring television playwrights need not expect to be faced with a split screen pre-taped, they should be aware of its technical possibilities, and, most important, they must be familiar with its writing rules and format requirements which the technical devices impose on the medium.

Early television scripts intended for live production (and for production live on tape) were written only on the left-hand side of the page, double-spaced, and only halfway across the page, leaving the right half blank.

The vacant half of the page was a notepad used by the technicians responsible for producing the script. The director used this space for stage business (note how the old terms survive—*stage* business), for his camera position, for cues, for any other memoranda he might wish to record. If that blank half page had not been available, there would have had to be *another* blank page adjoining the script to record the directors' and technicians' handwritten notes.

Dialogue is upper and lower case, and the names of the characters capitalized and centered above their speeches. The writer's stage directions and camera terms are capitalized in this format, merely to distinguish them from the dialogue. Also, regarding the double-spacing, sometimes the writer himself forgot that he had to keep in mind his transition scenes in live television production—those scenes which allowed the camera, the microphones, and the actors themselves to move from position to position without interfering with the flow of the drama on the viewer's TV screen.

In short, the generous spacing was to allow ease in reading and room for corrections when corrections might be needed—as well as for the actors to make those mysterious doodlings to themselves which are their own way of recording the instructions the director has given them.

After "live" production, there came "live on tape." I understand "live on tape" to mean that the play was recorded on magnetic tape, with the actual performance being continuous, as if it were on the air. The format does not look any different from that of a "live" script. However, there is one very important—even crucial—difference in a script written for tape production in this half-page format. The need for the writer to devise those all-important transition scenes—the cover scenes—was gone. The taping process, with the incredible machines doing the recording, could simply be stopped while the actors moved to the next set, changed costume or makeup, or had a coffee break. With magnetic tape recording, an actor could appear in swimming shorts on the beach, and a second later, could be in evening clothes in the ballroom, dancing with his lady love.

When magnetic tape recording came in, the playwright had to learn his technique all over again (actually, the technique was a lot easier) and such a change in technique inevitably changed the construction of his drama, allowing total freedom from internal time, as contrasted with *external* time—the allover length of his allowed time on the air. I have said many times, and it is not original with me, in television, *Time* is the overlord of everything—and I don't mean the magazine.

In my opinion, there is an enormous benefit to be gained by the television playwright from his mastering the technique of writing for live production. This benefit is the ability so to condense his material within the bed of Procrustes that establishes his time limits that he learns to tell a story better, more cleanly, more sparsely, with no excess words—assuming that he has a suitable story in the first place. By that I mean, I'd hate to see Proust's *Remembrance of Things Past* or one of Scott's Kenilworth novels reduced to the 54-minute length of an hour live program—or an hour filmed program, for that matter.

For television plays written for "live" production or in the "live" format for taping, the following table of *maximum* number of pages for dramatic scripts is generally accepted by television producers. This table is based on typing halfway across standard 8½″ × 11″ paper, using a typewriter with pica (12-point) type. If your typewriter has elite (much smaller) type, scale down the number of pages by roughly one-third, since with elite type you get much more on each page. (Should you wonder why an hour script is not twice the 40 pages of a half-hour script, but is instead 100 pages *maximum,* it's because of the difference in the handling of commercials and station identification time.)

15-minute script	20 pages
Half-hour script	40 pages
Hour script	100 pages
Hour-and-a-half script	150 pages

At the current stage of television production, I think that the playwright can safely assume that his play will be filmed, and write accordingly. Always I urge my television playwriting classes to "write with the camera" (that is, for dramatic visual effects), as well as with the typewriter.

A motion picture is a longitudinal mosaic of strips of film, in varying lengths, literally glued together—I believe the correct word is cemented—to form the complete motion picture. Each strip of film represents one scene of the writer's screenplay. Television plays for motion picture filming are written entirely across the page (the standard $8\frac{1}{2}" \times 11"$). For half-hour filmed plays, the average *maximum* number of shots—*every single shot described*—is 90. For hour-long filmed plays, the average number of shots—*every single shot described*—is 200. For motion pictures of indeterminate length —a movie that's "as long as it's long"—there is no numerical limit, although one surely will be set as filmed television plays come under television's severe over-all time limitations.

Ideally, each scene in the script describes the following: the size of the shot (medium shot, close up, follow shot, and so forth); the physical location of the shot (interior—the kitchen, exterior—the south forty acres, etc.); the lighting effect desired (day, night, twilight, gloom, sunrise); any possible movement of the camera (zoom in for a close-up); the actors in the shot—and any unusual business the writer dreams up—and any sound effects to be recorded directly or to be added.

Please notice that for convenience sake and for no other reason, *all directions concerning the camera are capitalized,* so that the cameraman and his assistants may pick out easily what the camera is required to do on a specified shot. Also, the *first time* they're mentioned in each shot, the names of all the actors involved in that scene are capitalized, so that the assistant director can round them up and have them ready.

And sound effects are capitalized so that the sound man can pick out his responsibilities in the shot. Any department of production, any technician in any department, certainly would be justified in thinking that his services are not required in a given scene if he fails to see his duties spelled out in capitals. And to prepare these duties— in capitals—is the playwright's responsibility. I repeat: all this capitalization is done for convenience, for utility, so that the technician involved in the scene can easily select what he's supposed to do.

It should be remembered that each specified *shot* requires a new and different *camera setup*. Inside a studio, that means balancing the lights so that there will be no different light values in closely connected scenes, unless such a difference is desired, and, if it is, it's the job of the playwright to indicate it; it means physically moving the *camera* around to a new place.

Tedious? Yes, but it's indispensable knowledge for the writer of scripts to be filmed. The first time I worked in a Hollywood studio, I was told by my supervisor that if I wrote ten shots a day, I was doing what was expected of me.

It is the screen playwright's duty to prepare all these scenes which, cemented together, end to end, make the complete motion picture. It's called, first, a rough cut. The editors—the cutters—have to keep track of the proper sequence. So at the start of each shot, a clapstick is used—an ordinary slate on which are written in chalk the scene number (supplied by the script), the name of the production, the director's name, usually; and the number of the "take," that is, the number of the time that the scene is being photographed.

The "slate" is called a "clapstick" because there's a hinged stick or clapper on top which is banged smartly at the beginning, producing a sharp knock which is a cue to the cutter—the editor—that the sound is functioning from that point on. And we get the familiar direction, "Lights! Camera! Speed! Action!" and the actors act.

You see, then, that the first process of putting a motion picture together, after it's been photographed, is an arithmetical process. And that's why you, the screen playwright, must number the shots as you write the drama and advance the story. I believe it's the practice in Hollywood nowadays among some producers not to number the shots until the final version of a script has been approved, to avoid messing up the sequence with divisions and subdivisions of numbers. You might like to know, too, that different rewrites are written on different colored paper, to show what's new.

I started with the writing of the finished script, because that's what most new writers think of, and dream of. Behind it in practice, however, lie several steps: first, usually, a synopsis of the proposed story which the writer must prepare. Most writers hate like the devil to write synopses; it's difficult to do and it's hard to keep a synopsis from being dull and sounding like a bunch of nothing. "And then she murders him, and then he kisses her"—the bold statement can so often produce the glazed look. It's also an art to read a synopsis and to detect the values and uniqueness of a story.

There's another kind of—well, synopsis—which is more than a synopsis. This more elaborate prose writing, which may include some dialogue, is a *treatment*. A producer may call on the writer to give him a treatment, which is a sort of road map of the planned production. The treatment shows how the story will be handled, will be developed. Say there is a ski sequence. Shall it be photographed in the Swiss Alps or in Aspen, Colorado? Shall the heroine wear a mink coat or a good cloth coat? Shall the lovers be shown reclining in the Waldorf Towers or in a hideaway on East 22nd Street? A treatment, then, is a detailed master scene arrangement in sequence showing the nature of the production and its handling. A friend wrote the screenplay of the original *Mutiny on the Bounty*. For several years, treatments of this story had been written, none of them satisfactory. Another friend tried to write the screenplay of the Kipling novel, *Kim*. She was never able to produce a satisfactory treatment which convinced the producer that a successful picture would result. *Kim* was not produced until years later and only when another writer did a successful treatment and screenplay.

A treatment can run to ten pages or a hundred, depending on the detail which the producer demands. Once upon a time I sold one which ran about eighty-five pages. This was the only form in which the producer saw the story. It was never done, but that's still another story.

I've mentioned master scenes—that a treatment can consist of a collection of master scenes in the proper sequence. A master scene is a scene which is a hunk of related action explained in narrative, stage directions, and/or in dialogue—or all three—which does not break down the content of the action into final detail—into camera shots, in the case of a movie. Many of the television playwrights adapting their own work into screenplays for the first time wrote master scenes because they did not know how to write separate camera shots which would make up the mosaic of a motion picture.

Sometimes a treatment is called a final script before dialogue.

And some really tough producers may insist on a scene-by-scene breakdown, before dialogue. This is real torture for the screen playwright, because it forces him to work out his story in the minutest detail without the help, the lift, the inspiration of the moment which comes from writing dialogue and which gives life and interest to the script.

Closely related to the scene-by-scene breakdown is the line-by-line breakdown. I once had to do it for a fiend of a producer. Here you describe in one declarative sentence after another the progression of the action of the complete picture.

Some brilliant and clever writers will prepare the complete shooting script—shots, dialogue, action all described—and hide it. Then they write the required scene-by-scene breakdown, based on the completed script. This is, I think, legitimate cheating, if you can get away with it, and if you hate, loathe and despise the task of writing any form of scene-by-scene breakdown.

Perhaps you know that sometimes when two writers are put on a script, one is the renowned author of the best-selling novel and the other is a skilled screenplay technician who knows nothing beyond how to write camera shots in acceptable terminology. If you are now, or plan to be, a renowned author, I urge you to learn how to write camera shots—continuity, as it's called—as soon as possible, for otherwise not only do you share the credit of the screen play with the technician, you also share the money.

Production of television drama has largely been concentrated in Hollywood, so much so that in New York, in the spring of 1967, the only assignment a high official of the Writers Guild with impressive credits could get was to write a documentary film for a fund-raising foundation combating a serious disease. Accordingly, he moved himself and his family to Hollywood, since he wished to continue writing for television. The much-touted "drama revivals" announced variously by the networks have not materialized; it is a matter of common knowledge that sponsors (who pay the bills) for drama are not easy to find; the costs of sponsorship have become astronomical; potential sponsors demand the prospect of the highest rating. Original dramas have not in the past always commanded such ratings.

In my opinion the "ratings" control more and more what will be telecast and what will not. "Spot" sponsorship—the numerous commercial interruptions of a program by perhaps as many as a dozen different sponsors, in the case of a full-length motion picture—has been created by economic necessity. These are the present facts of life which the television playwright must live with as long as he's writing for commercial television.

But—television is show business! It could change overnight. The agitation for change, which might come through Educational Television or "Public Television," is very great. The important thing for the individual beginning television playwright is to be ready with the indispensable knowledge of *how* to write a television play when his opportunity comes. (It might not be out of line to remark that the Broadway Theatre also is formidable in its difficulties for the unknown, unestablished playwright.) The best route to television (and Broadway) seems to lie through making a name, large or small, in some other medium—a paperback or hardcover novel; a play done off Broadway or off off Broadway, by a little theatre, a regional theatre, a university theatre, as a summer theatre tryout; or a television play on a local station; that is, any form of production of a writer's work which will set that writer apart.

In my opinion, the most reliable Market List for the television playwright is the Monthly Talent & Script Report issued by Television Index, Inc., 150 Fifth Avenue, New York, New York 10011. The cost per copy is $1.45 prepaid ($1.54 for New York residents). This report is as up-to-date as it is humanly possible to be in the world of television. It identifies markets and market conditions in all possible detail. It locates agents by name, address, kind of agent and telephone number. It is still highly desirable that you have an accredited agent; the report usually tells which agent will consider new material and new playwrights and which won't. To get a free list of the literary agents who are members of The Society of Authors' Representatives, write to the Society at 101 Park Avenue, New York, New York 10017. Enclose a self-addressed, stamped envelope.

With all its abrupt changes, through its vicissitudes, upheavals and contradictions, television, of course, is here to stay; and someone must write it. To write for television, you must know and be able to implement its fundamental principles.

89

OFF OFF BROADWAY

By Judith Gilhousen

I'll never forget that December night. It was cold, it was 2 A.M., and I sat in my living room, exhausted and shivering as I typed "The End" on the last page of my very first play. I was convinced every word was inspired, and the next day I sent the manuscript to two important producers. Two months later, the scripts came back, and the rejection letters said: "Your play is amusing and imaginative . . . however, it lacks . . . would like to see future scripts of yours. . . ."

It occurred to me that maybe I had something to learn about how to write a play, about marketing plays, and about the harsh realities of the theater.

As I began to study the current theatrical scene, I learned that rarely does an unknown playwright get a first play produced on Broadway. It's a matter of economics. The average cost to mount a Broadway drama or comedy is $200,000, and a musical, $500,-000. Because so much money is at stake, producers are unwilling to gamble on an unknown playwright. Generally, producers prefer, in this order: (1) playwrights who have already made a name for themselves on Broadway; (2) famous writers who have already made a name for themselves in other forms of writing; (3) playwrights who show promise from their productions Off Broadway or Off Off Broadway.

The situation Off Broadway is much the same. It wasn't always this way. Historically, the term "Off Broadway" was invented in 1952 when Tennessee Williams's *Summer and Smoke* opened in a Greenwich Village theater. It was the first time in thirty years for a hit show to be presented in a theater located away from the Broadway theater district. Hence, the term *Off* Broadway emerged.

In the fifties and early sixties, Off Broadway was known for its bold ideas and for its encouragement to new writers, many of whom (such as Edward Albee) moved upward into the main body of the theater.

Today, however, there is little difference between Broadway and Off Broadway. Again, it's economics. In the past, producers could gamble with new talents Off Broadway because shows then cost only $2,500 to $5,000. Today, an Off Broadway drama costs about $50,000, and a musical, $75,000. Because of this, Off Broadway plays today are written either by well-known playwrights, or by playwrights who have had a successful production Off Off Broadway.

For new playwrights, then, the best way to break into the business is through Off Off Broadway. The doors are open, and they're eager to discover new talent. It's a place where many of the now well-known playwrights received their first start. For example, Jason Miller, author of the award-winning Broadway hit, *That Championship Season*, had his first play produced in an Off Off Broadway theater.

After I received my rejection letters, I mailed my script to an Off Off theater. It was accepted, and five months later I experienced my first opening night. Since then, I've had another play produced, and I'm now a resident playwright with an Off Off Broadway theater.

Most people are probably unaware that Off Off Broadway is today the most productive theater in New York. It stages five to six hundred shows a year, compared to eighty for Broadway and Off Broadway combined. There are more than a hundred theaters, most of them non-profit organizations. Some are housed in storefronts, lofts, and coffeehouses, others in traditional theaters, or in churches. Most are small, and seat about seventy persons.

Many varieties of theater can be found in the Off Off Broadway movement. However, the majority of Off Off Broadway theaters are dedicated to producing new playwrights, and they present both traditional and experimental forms of drama. New plays range in subject matter from conventional to crazy, just as the quality of their physical productions ranges from excellent to poor.

In an otherwise shrinking market, Off Off Broadway provides

opportunities for a writer to showcase his work. Hopefully, an Off Broadway or Broadway producer will see your show and option it for a full commercial production. Most important, though, Off Off is a place to learn more about playwriting. You learn that what often *looks* good on paper does not always *sound* good on the stage.

For those of you interested in submitting plays to Off Off theaters, here are answers to questions you may have:

What kinds of plays do they want?
All kinds, including one acts. There is a preference for small casts (up to 6) over large casts.

Does the playwright get paid?
No. You either participate for the love of it, or you consider this the price you must pay along the way to your discovery. You invite agents, producers, and publishers' representatives to see your work and hope they will lead you into a paying market. Off Off Broadway is not the place to make money. Plays are mounted for $100 or less. Some of the best groups are funded by federal, state, and private foundations.

Is it necessary to attend rehearsals in New York?
No. But if you can, it's to your advantage, as you learn from the experience. Casting and rehearsals take four to five weeks, and the play has a limited run of 10 or 12 performances, usually on weekends, over a four- to six-week period.

Will your play be reviewed in New York?
Yes. Favorable reviews can help you obtain publication and/or a commercial production.

Do you need an agent?
No, not until you start making money.

Will you be required to sign a contract?
Sometimes. It amounts to promising them a small percentage of any future profits you may receive from the play they produce.

Must your play be copyrighted before you submit it?
No. But if it makes you feel more secure, copyright it. For applications, write to Register of Copyrights, Library of Congress, Washington, D.C. 20540.

How do you submit a play?

The manuscript should be in a binder. Attach a brief cover letter, addressed to the artistic director, saying you are offering the play for his consideration. You save postage by using the special fourth class manuscript rate. And always enclose a stamped, self-addressed envelope for return.

Although I've had two plays produced, neither has yet been picked up for a full commercial production. I feel certain, though, that the experience gained Off Off Broadway will eventually lead me, and others like me, into bigger and better markets.

OFF OFF BROADWAY THEATERS

Unless otherwise noted, the following theaters are interested in scripts of all types—one, two, and three act dramas, comedies, and musicals, both traditional and experimental in form. [Because of the instability of Off Off Broadway theaters, playwrights are urged to query the theaters in this list before submitting manuscripts.]

Actor's Place at St. Luke's—487 Hudson St., New York, NY 10014. John Cappelletti, Artistic Director.

The Actors' Unit—120 West 28th St., New York, NY 10001. Robert Capece, Artistic Director.

American Ensemble Co.—Box 5478, Grand Central Station, New York, NY 10017. Robert Petito, President.

American Theatre—106 East 14th St., New York, NY 10003. Richard Kuss, Artistic Director. Produces 5 plays a year, including classics.

Circle Theater—99 Seventh Ave. South, New York, NY 10014. Marshall Mason, Artistic Director. Produces 5 plays a year, including classics.

Courtyard Playhouse—39 Grove St., New York, NY 10014. Ken Eulo, Artistic Director. Prefers naturalistic plays.

The Cubiculo—414 West 51st St., New York, NY 10019. Philip Meister, Artistic Director. Prefers small cast, non-monumental plays. Produces 30 plays a year, including classics.

Joseph Jefferson Theatre Co.—1 East 29th St., Little Church Around the Corner, New York, NY 10016. Cathy Roskam, Artistic Director.

Manhattan Theatre Club—321 East 73rd St., New York, NY 10021. Lynne Meadow, Artistic Director.

New York Theater Ensemble—62 East 4th St., New York, NY 10003. Lucille Talayco, Artistic Director. Presents 30 new plays a year, many of them one-acts.

Playwright's Horizons—422 West 42nd St., New York, NY 10036. Louise Roberts, Artistic Director. Produces 24 new plays a year.

The Shade Company—230 Canal St., New York, NY 10013. Edward Berkeley, Director.

Theatre at St. Clement's—423 West 46th St., New York, NY 10036. Kevin O'Conner, Artistic Director. Produces 15 plays a year, including revivals.

Theatre at Noon—St. Peter's Gate Church, 116 East 56th St., New York, NY 10022. Miriam Fond, Artistic Director. Cabaret theater that entertains office workers at noon lunch hour.

Theatre for the New City—113 Jane St., New York, NY 10014. Crystal Field, Artistic Director. Prefers experimental theater.

Urban Arts Corps—26 West 20th St., New York, NY 10011. Vinnette Carroll, Artistic Director. Specializes in plays by Black playwrights.

Women's Interart Center—549 West 52nd St., New York, NY 10019. Margot Lewitin, Coordinator. Prefers feminist-oriented plays.

Workshop of the Players' Art—333 Bowery Ave., New York, NY 10003. Virginia Aquino, Artistic Director. Produces 15 to 20 new plays a year.

90

TRADE MAGAZINES—THE LARGEST MARKET

By Charles McIntosh

OVER 2500 magazines—the "trade press"—are listed in an advertising guide called *Business Publication Rates & Data*. Every one of them buys articles, often at better rates than many of the consumer magazines. More important, most of the trade publications are crying for competent writers—not supertalents, or even old hands in the game, but just capable, workaday writers.

Writing for trade magazines has augmented my income for years. Most of them pay promptly and publish quickly. While you spend years working on novels for major markets, trade journals offer you a field in which you can make money and gain experience.

The trade journal market is made up of a vast diversity of specialized journals catering to every conceivable occupation, from arts, banking and corsets, to tea, Venetian blinds, and welding. Most of them are give-aways to a "controlled" list of readers who purchase products or services in the realm of the magazine's professional interest. Circulation may be up to several hundred thousand. Advertisers try to reach the readers through paid ads, but readers read the magazine mostly for its editorial content. Therefore, the editors must be willing to pay writers well for material. Most trade magazines are put together with the same care and expense as are magazines of the caliber of *Esquire* or *Cosmopolitan,* for example. And the writer has to take the same pains with his writing as he would for mass-circulation magazines. Only the odds are different when you write for the trade publications: They're a hell of a lot better!

Assuming that you want to try this field, first get hold of a copy of *Business Publication Rates & Data* (Standard Rate and Data Service, Inc., publishers). You can't buy single monthly copies, so you're better off visiting any advertising agency to beg an old copy. (They throw them away when they're two or three months old, so they won't mind giving you an old one.) Anything up to a year old is fine for your purposes. Turn to the section labeled "Market Classifications," where approximately 575 kinds of occupations, businesses, and products are listed. This is where you'll do an hour or two of studying.

As you read each of the listings, ask yourself whether it fits in with any interests, experience, training, or knowledge you have. If, for example, you're familiar with electronics, computers, or dentistry, you have a head start in preparing yourself to write for the magazines in these fields. If you have no special background, there are still hundreds of publications which may be appropriate to you. Boating, amusements, gardening—even golf!—are some of the not-too-technical fields which you can try without having a graduate degree in the topic.

Once you have settled upon one or more categories of publication, turn to those sections and read carefully the "publisher's editorial statement" which describes each magazine. Here you'll learn how many articles are used each issue, frequency of publication, preferred subject matter, and the description of the typical reader. Also check the circulation and the single-insertion page rate for an ad. A publication with only five thousand circulation charging $200 per page won't pay nearly as much for a piece as will one with 90,000 circulation charging $2000 per page.

Make a list of from ten to twenty magazines you think you'd most like to write for—and would best be able to write for. Write to the editor of each, requesting one or two back issues. If you enclose a self-addressed, stamped envelope and explain that you are a writer interested in the possibility of submitting articles, most editors will be delighted to respond immediately.

At this point, though you haven't even seen a trade magazine, *you've done 50% of the most important work!* That being so, don't neglect your homework. You may have to look through several hundred publishers' statements, but what you hope to end up with finally are three or four magazines for which you can write regularly and remuneratively—*without rejections*. That alone should be a vital spur to your doing the work involved in finding the right trade magazines for your specialized experience, knowledge, and talents.

When you receive the sample copies, take a week or more to study them thoroughly from cover to cover, including the ads, to gain an understanding of the focus and style of the magazine. *Electronic Design* and *Electronics*, for example, at first seem to be similar, yet the first is engineering-oriented, while the second is much more newsy and informal. The ads differ accordingly.

After absorbing the ad content, read the articles, and then read them again. Here, you will get the real feel of the magazine. You will learn such things as the word length, number and types of diagrams and pictures used, and the general slant of the writing. Even more important, you will find out whether you feel comfortable with the style and approach of the articles.

You will probably find that the dozen or two magazines you first selected have dwindled to a handful that you think you might have a chance with. Fine. Now it's time to have a go at becoming a reliable writer for several of that "handful."

You could write a query, of course; however, I recommend that you pick a topic and write a full-length, completed article. There are some good reasons. The most important is that you'll really discover whether you have the ability, inclination, and knowledge to write for the magazines you've chosen. Writing one article is a cheap price to pay for learning that a certain magazine is not for you. After all, you plan to be writing for your selected list of magazines for a long time and hope to make a considerable amount of money from them.

Also, the writing of an article means that the editor will find out immediately that you're a) a serious "pro," and b) capable of turning out what he needs. If you had written only a query, you'd still have to write the article in any case and lose all that time waiting for the editor to tell you whether he's really interested in the idea you queried him about. Case in point: one magazine which *advertised* for writers received over 275 queries, and one completed article—mine. I got the job, because the editor didn't have to plow through those 275 query letters and outlines.

There's another thing—in a general, mass magazine, the variety of subject matter and treatment is extremely broad, so a query is almost mandatory. In a trade publication, the subject matter is much narrower, and the slant and length are fairly standard. This is why you pored over your sample copies so diligently—to understand what's wanted.

After you've sold your first article to a trade publication, you can follow it up with a short query which lists perhaps three or four possible subjects or ideas. Now, instead of writing one or two pages on each subject, you can write just a sentence or two. The editor already knows you're competent and can write what he wants. Eventually, you may be able merely to tell him you'd like to do a piece on such-and-such, skipping the outline, slant, and arguments for the importance of the subject to his magazine, etc. If the subject fits, you get an automatic go-ahead.

Think what this means! Instead of spending your time, energy, and easily-bruised ego on trying to *sell,* you'll be in the enviable, almost unbelievable position of spending your essence on *writing.*

It's for this reason that I consider it so important to winnow out the chaff and settle down to a few magazines for which you can really do good stuff. Because the writer-editor relationship is so vital, you may also have to do some extras. I have never hesitated to redo a piece, even if it involves a second, third, or fourth rewrite. I invest in trips up to one hundred miles, if it seems advisable to talk personally with an editor or do some checking, and I make a long-distance call without a quiver. On the other hand, I don't hesitate to ask for more money, if extra research or a field trip or photos are indicated or required. In more than a decade in this field, I have found that this attitude brings mutual respect. It is a refreshing experience, when one considers the usual lot of most writers who operate only in the general magazine field.

Once you are established with several trade publications, you can try to enlarge your area of writing. Here are some suggestions:

1. Attend trade shows in the appropriate fields. You will meet manufacturers who need articles and news releases written—for a fee.
2. Investigate the feasibility of a newsletter for the trade.
3. Contact trade associations about newsletters, lectures, articles.
4. See whether schools need part-time teachers in this subject.

5. Quote your credits to advertisers and propose you write their copy. If you have experience, you can even propose ads.
6. Suggest supplements or special booklets to your editors.
7. Investigate the correspondence-course-writing field.
8. Suggest interviews with prominent persons in the field.

How well does trade publication writing pay? Anything from $25 per piece up to over $1000 is the range. But I have generally found that a 1500-word article brings around $100—double that or more if it's done on assignment with perhaps a few photos.

This may not seem like much, but remember that the pieces are typically short and in a subject range that will become very familiar to you. You will also sell close to everything you write, and as time goes by, you will have few rewrites to do. The great time-taker, selling, will hardly occupy your time at all.

One final word. I have hinted that quality is just as necessary for a trade publication as for *Harper's* or *Redbook*. This is so true that you will find not only a great satisfaction from your articles on trade subjects, but you will also discover a great bonus treasure— your creative writing in other fields improves vastly! Terse, meaningful prose supplants rambling thought-forests. Organized plotting replaces shapeless stream-of-consciousness wanderings. The discipline and practice from your trade publication pieces help you achieve this.

PART III

THE EDITORIAL AND BUSINESS SIDE

91

HOW BOOK PUBLISHING DECISIONS ARE MADE

By A Managing Editor *

How do publishers (and their editors) find the books they eventually publish? To many writers the process may seem mysterious and even irrational, especially to those who have not been able to break into print. Yet the making of decisions at most book publishers has a logic of its own and is not likely to be capricious or inflexible. Publishers and editors are constantly looking for new voices, new ideas, new trends. Any business that in recent years has brought forth *The Whole Earth Catalog* and *Games People Play* and *The Exorcist* and *Hard Times* is scarcely standing still.

As an example of how books are acquired, let me cite the experience of my own firm. Last year we published ninety-five books of a general nature. They came to us in various ways.

Forty of these books were written by authors whom we had previously published. The category is self-explanatory and is evidence of a firm's strength and stability: many of our authors continue to publish with us over the years.

Thirty-one titles were submitted directly to the editors (not through literary agents) or were sought out by the editors. Editorial contacts played an important part in these acquisitions. A friend of an editor will recommend a manuscript. An editor meets a scholar at an academic convention. An editor learns that a prominent personality plans to write a book. An editor reads a magazine or newspaper article that suggests a full-length work. An editor thinks up an idea for a book and commissions the appropriate author to write it. An author may have heard about an editor through some form of publicity; frequently, in nonfiction books, the assistance of a particular editor is acknowledged.

---

* The author is senior editor of one of America's most distinguished book publishing companies.

Fourteen books were sent to our editors by literary agents on their own initiative. (Many titles in the first category were represented by agents.) There are about sixty literary agencies, almost all in New York City, that actively submit publishable manuscripts and are sought out by publishers. They range from one-man or -woman shops to organizations with a half dozen or more agents. Editors and agents lunch and drink and play tennis and poker with each other, and in several instances, agents are married to book editors. Thus many publishing relationships begin because an agent believes a particular author is suited to a particular editor.

Four titles were sent to us by foreign publishers, two in Britain, two in continental Europe. There is a considerable trading gap between American and foreign publishers: more American authors are published abroad than foreigners here. Nevertheless, American publishers actively search this market, because some famous writers have been first published abroad, for example, authors like Pasternak, Hammarskjöld, Heyerdahl, le Carré.

Two books were recommended by the firm's college textbook department. Most publishers have textbook divisions of varying sizes, but college travelers usually don't have the time or inclination to refer authors or books to editors in other parts of their company. However, this is an important area for editors to mine.

Two books were unsolicited, mailed to us unheralded and without recommendation. One was a suspense novel that sold moderately well. The other was a science book considered outstanding in its field. Although the author was chairman of his university department, he simply addressed the manuscript to "The Editors."

All of these books, whether by writers familiar or unfamiliar to the publisher, went through a decision-making process. This will differ from publisher to publisher, but there is a common thread to each system.

Depending upon a publisher's size, there will be one or two or three individuals who, because of management position or seniority or specialized knowledge, can make an affirmative publishing decision without consultation of colleagues. But in fact that does not often happen. The more enthusiasts behind a book from the beginning, the better its prospects when eventually published. It is as important for an editor to create an upbeat atmosphere for a book within a publishing house as it is to do so later among reviewers and prospective readers.

Nonfiction contracts are offered on the basis of certain varying amounts of material—an idea stated verbally to an editor, a letter, a comprehensive outline, a finished manuscript. In the case of fiction, most novels submitted to a publisher are complete. An established novelist can obtain a contract for an unwritten, or partially written novel. But such a commitment to an unknown author is not likely. Publishers too often have been burned by novels that began promisingly but concluded unsuccessfully.

QUESTIONS AND ANSWERS

Q. *Can you describe in more detail the actual procedure leading up to a publishing decision?*

A. As I said, the *modus operandi* varies from house to house. Some firms hold format meetings where an editor proposes a book, and it is approved or rejected by a management who may or may not have read the manuscript. The editor's track record and presentation may be crucial in such a situation. At another firm, it may simply be a matter of discussion between an editor and the editor-in-chief. Decisions in fiction are not usually complicated; a novel should either strike an editor strongly or not: a marginal reaction is probably the sign that a book shouldn't be taken on. A nonfiction proposal may require more discussion. If it's a cookbook, what's the competition? If it's a work of history, does it break new ground? An editor may have to read through other books on the topic to make such a judgment. If it's a biography, who else may be tackling the subject? (It's unfortunate that there's not a central registry where a publisher could check to ascertain whether a book about a particular subject is in preparation. Nasser and Solzhenitsyn, for example, are two world figures about whom there are currently too many books.) What are an author's qualifications in a particular field?

I should say that any author with a nonfiction proposal should thoroughly research the subject as to subject matter and competition. A very useful reference book is *Subject Guide to Books in*

Print, published by Bowker and available at many public libraries. It's a reasonably accurate compendium of what's been published.

Q. *Should a manuscript or query be submitted to the editor-in-chief of a publishing house or a lesser editor?*

A. Again, there would be different answers for different publishers. Obviously, the best situation for an author is for an editor-in-chief to be enthusiastic about a book. On the other hand, the top editor may be overburdened with management responsibilities, and unsolicited material is likely to be referred to other editors or assistants. A middle-level editor might have more time to deal with a book. But it is the practice in most publishing houses, if an author addresses a gardening book, for example, to the wrong editor, it will be passed on to the resident authority on the subject. Editors' names are listed in *Literary Market Place,* also a Bowker publication, and available in public libraries.

Q. *How much influence has a literary agent on publishing decisions?*

A. It depends on the agent; some are better than others. (The agent who submitted the most proposals and manuscripts to us last year did not make a single contract with us.) Obtaining a good agent is actually more difficult than finding a willing publisher. Most agents are small business persons who don't have the time or capacity to deal with new, unpublished authors. And it is a misunderstanding of the agent's function to reckon that intervention will guarantee a contract with a publisher. An editor's judgment has to be the controlling factor in a decision. A proposal submitted by a trusted agent will certainly have added weight in its corner, but that fact is rarely the main determinant in a publishing decision.

Q. *Does an unsolicited manuscript really have a chance?*

A. A few publishers now return such submissions unopened. But most houses are very much open to new and untried talent. I suspect that fewer unrecommended manuscripts are taken on these days, because most new writers are discovered by energetic editors before their books have been completed. Editors travel around the country and abroad, searching for new writers. And it is a rare author who doesn't have a friend at or remote connection with a publishing house—perhaps through a college teacher or a journalist. If a magazine publishes a good short story or article, the author is likely to receive several letters from editors inquiring whether there are any plans for a book.

Q. *Some authors feel that publishers and agents are cliquish, since most of them operate out of New York City. Is this true?*

A. In fact, only about a third of the authors we publish live in the Boston-New York-Washington complex, even though that is still generally regarded as the intellectual and cultural hub of the nation. I'm a great believer in regional publishing—we publish two or three authors whose books sell very well year after year in their home areas.

Q. *It's been written about before, but can you bring us up to date on the technical aspects of submitting a manuscript?*

A. Of course the pages should be typed double-spaced and legibly; occasionally we receive a handwritten manuscript, but it's unfair to ask an editor to read it. I don't mind a xerographic manuscript, as long as it's clear. I think that an explanatory letter, especially with a nonfiction proposal, is helpful background. Return postage (or International Reply Coupons, if abroad) is a simple matter of courtesy and protection. A strong cardboard box, the kind in which bond paper is sold, is useful. If an author doesn't hear from a publisher within six weeks (allowing two weeks for mailing both ways), he should write a follow-up letter of inquiry.

Q. *How often should a writer send out a manuscript?*

A. I think authors ought to keep trying. The history of publishing is replete with tales of editorial idiocy. *Auntie Mame* was rejected by at least fifteen publishers. Joyce Cary's *The Horse's Mouth* was turned down by seventeen, as was Irving Stone's *Lust for Life*. Beatrix Potter's *The Tale of Peter Rabbit* was returned by six houses. William L. Shirer's *The Rise and Fall of the Third Reich* was rejected by many publishers in outline form, even though Shirer was the author of two bestsellers. *The Day of the Jackal* was passed up by three or four New York publishers. If an author really believes in a manuscript he should submit it to at least ten publishers. If form rejections are the constant response, then perhaps the author should stop sending the book manuscript around until he carefully rereads it to see if improvements should be made before he resubmits it.

Q. *What kind of books are publishers looking for?*

A. Hardcover fiction is not selling well, but paperback novels are doing fine. There seems to be a price resistance to any novel over $6.95, unless the author is Wouk, Updike, Michener, Solzhenitsyn, etc. Books on hobbies and crafts are doing very well; frequently this field is a good one for a new author to make a sale. Many successful nonfiction titles concern the problems of society. Regional books that bring out the flavor of particular sections of America are flourishing. Interest in medicine and health seems stronger than ever.

Q. *How do you feel about the future of books?*

A. There are those who prophesy the demise of the book as entertainment and a learning tool. I can't pretend to know how strongly home facisimile and video recording will compete for the reader's time, but at the height of television's influence more people than ever are buying and reading books. And with the advent of the four-day week, there will be additional leisure time to divide among various pursuits. Further, the book is the most compact, convenient leisure product in existence. You can take it anywhere, except underwater. No, I don't think that the book is a dinosaur, any more than I think writers are going to stop writing.

92

THE MAN ACROSS THE DESK

By Samuel S. Vaughan

IF you write at book length, you could find yourself one day facing
a man (or woman) across a desk who announces himself as your
editor. A certain amount of confusion arises at times about what
one's editor is supposed to do for the writer, or do to the written
work.

If we confuse authors and, on occasion, our employers, perhaps
it is because your editor can turn out to be anything from a slightly
helpful acquaintance to a valuable friend to, at times, a deeply involved collaborator.

The thoroughly professional author, or the singular and striking
writer whose book is a work of art, may require little editing—that
is, little penciling on paper. The beginner, or the writer with ideas
but stylistic problems, or the stylist who lacks ideas, needs more
help. In every case, each book requires handling in the publishing
process.

One of the shocks ahead is that you might overhear the editor,
or someone around him, referring to what you have written as "his"
book—i.e., the editor's. *Whose* book? Good question. For if an
editor accepts your manuscript for publication, it becomes, to an
extent, his book, no matter how little work he does on it.

A unique pleasure of authorship is that a book, unlike a magazine
article or a play or a motion picture script, is first and last the
author's. It belongs to him; it is his, an individual creation in an
age of the collaborative arts and merger. But the editor's proprietary
interest, his assumption that it is "his" book, too, can work in your
best interest.

It is his book in the publishing house only. It is his judgment
that is on the line, his recommendation that the house take the risk.

This means that your editor will identify himself—and be identified personally—with your work in the small world of book publishing.

In practice, the process is more beneficent and less heavy-handed than it sounds. On a magazine, the editor seldom thinks of an article or story as his. He may, instead, think of it as the magazine's. Magazine editing is much rougher and more arbitrary (and sometimes better) than book editing. It is frequently done with little or no consultation with the original writer. A piece for *Time* becomes *Time's*. A story for *The New Yorker* or *Commentary*, especially after their skillful editing (and sometimes cutting and rewriting), can take on the tone and feel of a *New Yorker* or a *Commentary* piece.

But the book remains yours. It can be lightly edited, not edited, or extensively edited. The only tone and content it should have are whatever you finally agree to. In the center is your friendly neighborhood middleman, the editor, and while he is in the process of trying to bring you together with your readers out there somewhere he will tend to think of what you have written as, at least in part, his.

A great many words have been written in behalf of the writer. These few are in behalf of the editor, in the interests of peaceful coexistence.

Having disposed of any silly notion that it is only your fate which is hitched to your manuscript, let us see what to expect from the man or woman across the desk. The more you understand him, the more you are able to form a useful mutual assistance pact.

Your editor is usually an anonymous figure, a curious combination of ego and self-effacement. His job is somewhat akin to that of the director in the theater or in movies, but his hand is invisible and he is even less well known. His job, to begin with, is to represent the reader to you; to represent you in the publishing house; and to represent that publishing house to you. Eventually you will learn that any book has many people working for it and that even the quietest publication is the sum of a thousand separate actions and efforts.

It is reasonable to suggest that the job of the book editor is to edit books. Most of us understand that the editor also must seek out people with talent or intelligence or information, with special experience or celebrity or, now and then, genius (or with any combination of the above) who want to or can be persuaded to write at book length. If we can agree on those reasonable assumptions, we can give up reason for the next hour. Obviously, one would expect the editor to spend his day looking for writers and in reading and editing their works.

He does not. He spends his day in editorial meetings, discussing what was in the Sunday *Times*, filling out forms to accompany the transmission of manuscripts to production departments, badgering his colleagues in sales and advertising and publicity and art departments. An editor often spends his morning drinking coffee, his lunch time drinking seriously, and his afternoon repenting the lunch hour. Before becoming an editor, he assumed that his day would be taken up with writers, people with patches on their elbows who write books. Instead, he finds much of his day given over to lawyers, agents, PR men, people with patches on their eyes who negotiate contracts. Once in a while a good writer makes his way through the lines and into the office; the editor is usually so glad to see him that the writer mistakes enthusiastic noises of welcome for blanket approval of his manuscript.

Manuscript? The editor does work on manuscripts. But he spends much of his time in trying to take delivery of books contracted for before there was a manuscript.

Why isn't the manuscript ready? The main reason is that every book is more work than anyone intended. If authors and editors knew how much work was ahead, fewer contracts would be signed. Every book is beautiful before the contract. Every book, for the author, becomes a hate object in the middle of the writing. For the editor, it becomes a concrete necklace in the middle of editing. Both author and editor will recover the gleam in their eyes, will see it as the masterwork it is, when the manuscript is ready.

What else does your editor do with his day? He concerns himself with The List. Publishers spend countless hours worrying about the group of books they plan to release on a suspicious world. Endlessly we discuss the spring list, the fall list, the winter list. . . .

Everyone, perhaps especially you, knows that the fall is the best time to publish your book. After all, nobody reads in the summer. And the book will be out in time for the Christmas trade. No matter that the facts show January and June to be excellent months for book sales or August a good time to launch a best seller. Let's not let facts get in the way of launch or lunch. No matter that you delivered your manuscript in April, almost complete, that your editor didn't get to edit it for six weeks, and then spent most of three weeks doing so—leaving three months to make the fall. (Most books require about nine months from finished manuscript to publication day.) No matter—because you and your editor are not likely to make the publishing date decision anyhow. Other sensitive minds are at work on the problem.

They'll probably agree that fall is the best time for your book. (*"Fall?* You'd have to be out of your mind to release her fragile little book after September!") I mean spring. ("You some kind of guru, you want to do that kid's novel in May? Who reads in May?") Or do I mean winter? ("Come *on,* Sam—you don't do a political book in February. Everybody's going to the Bahamas in February; who cares for politics then?") Okay, how about shortly before Christmas? ("Now you're talking. Put that nice fat package on the list in time for Christmas, and we'll be swimming in money.") A publisher's Christmas is properly celebrated just after Labor Day; his idea of Christmas Eve is July 20. Any expensive volume must be published in time for the Christmas trade, we all know, or it will die. This is absolutely true. Except for the expensive volumes that are published in other seasons and sell nicely, while all those expensive, unsold volumes from the previous Christmas are still swimming back to the warehouse.

At any rate, the purpose of these glimpses into the philosophical life of your publishing house is to show something of what editors do when they're not actually editing.

Do editors edit? Yes, some editors do. At times we over-edit; some are lazy; some become virtual co-authors and now and then ghost writers.

What is editing? What should you expect your editor to do for, or to, your manuscript? He is, to start with, your first reader, a sympathetic but objective one. Make your mistakes in front of this reader; he will help you not to make them in public.

He should offer you comment, general and detailed, on style, structure, and substance. He should offer suggestions for improvement where appropriate. For a novel, he ought to respond to the characterizations, plotting, plausibility, length, pace, the title, and, if he understands it, your theme.

For a non-fiction work, many of the same comments apply, including characterization, oddly enough. People in books, all books, are important.

Behind every editor is, like the legendary woman behind every successful man, a copy editor. A first-rate copy editor is a godsend to the author and helps to make an honest man of the editor. The copy editor is responsible for your spelling, punctuation, grammar, and—though you should discuss this in advance—house style. (This includes such matters as rules for capitalization, the use of commas in series, which dictionary should be relied on as final authority, etc.) If you have special stylistic wishes, declare them in advance, before type is set. The copy editor will be on the lookout for inconsistencies, repetitions, and may do a certain amount of spot fact-checking. But neither the editor nor the copy editor is the researcher or the expert on your book: you are. If you have written a history of the Battle of Bourbon Station, don't expect your editors to check every fact. You, or they, should arrange for outside readings (sometimes called "vettings," although this also applies to legal check-readings, too) by experts, if required.

Why is your editor so slow? Because he has manuscripts to read that arrived before yours did. Because his fellow editors ask him to do second readings for them. Because he conducts an elaborate correspondence, his phone list is twenty-four names long at the moment, and an English publisher's cable is fighting it out with a California agent's telegram on top of a stack of memoranda, each headed URGENT, *Do Now*, or "Pass Quickly—by Hand." (At times, your editor would like to Pass Quickly—out.)

The time problem is not a matter of reading your manuscript—it is getting to read it. Your editor is slow because he needs time to think, because he cannot know positively things he has to assert flatly. ("Your Bill Breadloaf is brilliantly original. He will go on to become one of the titans." "Murray, people will be *breaking* into book stores to grab this book—how often do you get a rabbi who knows this much about the sex life of the Apostles?")

Your editor travels, seems to run around a good deal, may leave you feeling out of touch. Be of good cheer. Some of that traveling is in your behalf; he could be off to sales conferences, selling your book or talking to friends who are reviewers, agents, reprint or book club or movie people, advancing your reputation. As with agents, the editor with time on his hands to talk with you, to answer every letter and phone call promptly and at length, can be reassuring. But the one who is busy because he is successful may do something for your success, too, even if he does nothing for your ego by his glacial response to letters, manuscripts, or phone calls. Whatever the case, there are no perfect editors, agents, or publishing houses.

When does your editor edit? At night. When he is supposed to be buying a friend veal piccata, with a good, sensible, inexpensive wine. ("What a day I've had. Postponed my whole list from spring to fall.") Or when he is supposed to be helping his children with their homework ("New math? Is this kid in school or in an IBM branch office?")

Some editors read and edit in the office. But the more active your editor is, the less likely he is to spend the day editing. His is not simply an agreeable job, full of fun and excitement and gambles; publishing is a vocation—commanding, compelling, demanding. Editing itself is hard work, not the least of which is finding time and residual energy beyond publishing duties to edit.

There are other problems. Unless he has a surgeon's streak of sadism, the editor will be reluctant to put pencil to somebody else's paper unless he can see clearly that it can be, and how much it should be, improved. He may know what is wrong but not quite how to tell you. He may want to fix it himself but be unable to; some editors can write; others cannot. Either person can be an excellent editor.

He is often tempted to take more time with a manuscript than it is likely to be worth. And yet the least likely books are frequently among the ones that most intrigue him.

There is always the danger lurking out there of an alert reviewer. That reviewer can lay into the book when it is published, attacking its author and its editor. Once, years ago, I stuck my head into the office of Kenneth D. McCormick, Doubleday's editor-in-chief.

A book he had handled, on its way to best sellerdom, had been greeted in some quarters by questions rich in human charity. ("Why wasn't this miserable mess edited?" "What has happened to American editorial standards?" etc.)

"Ken," I said, a cub seeking enlightenment from a lion, "how do you feel when a book you've handled is one that a reviewer says needs editing?"

"I say to myself," Ken remarked, without looking up, "that he should have seen the book *before* I got it."

What about the relationship between you? Is your editor required to be your friend? Not always. Forced friendships work no better here than anywhere else. An editor and author can work together smoothly if they remain a little distant. In fact, a certain distance may be an asset. Relationships have broken down where the author and editor have become too close. When genuine friendship occurs, fine. It had better be genuine; it is certain to be tested.

Authors suspect that their editor has the best of both worlds. He works with words; he earns a regular salary, has an expense account, a secretary, and all that. In part, the author is correct. But (a) the words the editor works with belong to somebody else; (b) the salary is supplemented by an expense account because there are laws against malnutrition; (c) the secretary belongs to somebody else. (She vacations in Majorca and has promised her boss an introduction to Robert Graves if the editor ever goes abroad.)

Most people interested in books think that the editor lives with wooly-headed literary superstars, who are difficult to handle but are really lovable—underneath. Most of us live in wooly-headed perplexity, handling difficult problems, but we are really lovable—on the surface. We have the privilege of serving as the writer's friend, flack, devil's advocate, drinking buddy, financial adviser, lay analyst, sensor, and censor. Increasingly, we are asked to counsel him on and to invest in words he wishes to put on paper but has not. The editorial job has become, unlike the ancient age when one judged what one read, a job of making judgments on outlines, ideas, reputations, previous books, scenarios, "treatments," talk, and promises.

For every first novelist of promise there is an editor who has made fifty promises—about writers' futures. We are also trying to appraise not only the manuscript in question but what sort of books lie ahead. Serious publishers undertake to publish an author, not a book. We want to contract with a writer who will go on writing, not a man who is momentarily with book.

Is your editor well read? Once he was. He used to read a great deal, the good stuff. That was one of the reasons he got into the trade. Now he doesn't read a lot, he reads all the time. And everything is a modern classic in manuscript. His voluntary reading is drastically curtailed, and he suspects semi-literacy is creeping up on him.

One of the chief sacrifices he has made is the privilege of reading what he feels like reading. Does this have anything to do with you? Yes. He wants to like your book. Remember, if the going gets rough between you: *he wants to like your book*. Your success is, to a certain extent, his success.

You and the publishing house are linked by the royalty system; if the book sells, both the author and the house make out. Your editor, the man in the middle, does not profit as directly. But a publishing house, Mr. Alfred Knopf once wrote, is known by the company it keeps. An editor is known by the authors he gets and keeps. If he is critical of your work, try not to take it personally. There is a wrong time to eliminate the middle man.

In some respects, he will disappoint you. He deals with the intangible—with glimmers of talent and flashes of hope and with changing tastes. You want him to produce the concrete—sales and readers and dollars and advertisements full of praise for your name.

He has a limited amount of power, easily diffused, and little glamour, except the gilt by association with well-known authors. His power is arbitrary. He cannot command his colleagues or reviewers or the reader to react as you and he want them to. He can only try to present your work with intelligence and flair and conviction, to be persistent in your behalf, and yet to temper your expectations with his realism. He relies on a deep well of optimism that must spring eternal.

Daily, your editor faces fear and failure and frustration. His is a job of visions, some demented; of ideals, frequently compromised; of high standards, not always met. He has a chance to do some good in this world—and an equal opportunity to add to the meretricious trash that threatens to swamp the continent.

Why, then, is your editor apt to be a fairly cheerful man, younger than his years? Because his job allows him to, in fact requires him to, indulge his taste. He not only has opinions, he lives by them. His work permits him, a grown man, to tell other men or women that he likes their work, and (often, if not always) that he likes *them*. In a society where many people are too embarrassed or inhibited or sophisticated to admire openly someone else, where everyone is a critic, his job is to be positive, to pass on praise, and to appreciate.

There is another reason why your editor, dour as he may seem at times, is apt to be reasonably happy. A year or so ago I was working one evening, deep in a pile of manuscripts, when my oldest son stopped at the desk, regarded me evenly, and said: "What are you doing?"

It was a fair question. I'd asked Jeff as much twenty or thirty thousand times. I was pleased to be asked.

"I'm working on a translation, a marvelous book, a biography of Tolstoy," I said. Then I told him something of the riches of Leo Tolstoy's life and of Henri Troyat's book and explained a few of the niceties of editing translations.

After we talked, Jeff turned to go, to return to his own homework. But before he went up the stairs, he said simply: "You must learn a lot."

He was right and I was grateful to him for becoming one of my teachers, too. For a parade of people come into my life, and each one of them has something on his mind, something to say. If everything goes right, for a year or two I'll have the privilege of learning what they are so excited about or interested in, of becoming a temporary semi-expert in their field, and of helping them get it said. As anyone who buys a house becomes, for a time, a real estate specialist, I have been, once removed, an explorer, a novelist, an historian, a musician, a magician who can make other people laugh or stir them.

That is why, I suppose, when you come to face the man across the desk, he will—even if he has spent the morning arguing about ad budgets, reprint rights, civil rights, or whether the Extreme Left is more extreme than the Extreme Right—be very glad to see you sitting on the other side of the desk. The man or woman who can transform a box of typing paper into a living document is the most valuable visitor to the man who will help transform that manuscript into a book.

93

EDITING THE MYSTERY AND SUSPENSE NOVEL

By Joan Kahn

BEING a mystery book editor (which is what I am primarily, though I've edited a variety of books, including an etiquette book, biographies, poetry, art books and non-mystery fiction) is like being any old kind of an editor, except that it may be a little more fun, partly because the manuscripts one gets to read are usually above the general average and usually the author seems to have rather liked writing his book.

Though I have edited non-fiction happily, I am especially interested in fiction, in the novel, and I think that the best mystery/suspense fiction these days has many (or more) of the same qualities that make the good non-mystery novel good.

The novel, for me, is a piece of writing with a definite form, a form which has infinite variations, and gives the experimenter as much room as he needs. But a novel is a novel—it isn't a short story, or a prose poem, or an essay, or a form of biography or even a purge. In a novel the things an author saw or experienced, the emotions he felt, the information he acquired, and the ideas that came to him have been absorbed and digested and reproduced in a particular, if elastic, form—that of a novel.

A mystery novel is a novel. Once the mystery novel was fairly rigid in format, and the emphasis was primarily on detection and a puzzle. In the introduction to a 1932 book, *The Floating Admiral*, Dorothy L. Sayers (who, whether she knew it or not, widened the horizon of the detective mystery so successfully that her novels read as well today as they did when she wrote them—and Lord knows that seems to me to be no longer true of many of her contemporaries) said while talking about The Detection Club: "Its membership is confined to those who have written genuine detective stories (not adventure tales or 'thrillers')."

Genuine detective stories that are original and good are not readily available today, and Miss Sayers (who ultimately turned scornfully from all detective story writing, including her own, as her main interest became the field of religious writing), if she were still interested in the mystery novel today, might have agreed to widen the membership of The Detection Club and make it less restrictive.

The suspense novel label came into being to cover much of the widening mystery field (actually it is too generally used and often on some books not worthy of it). The suspense novel isn't limited to deductive mysteries and, in fact, some books under its free-wheeling label don't even have a detective (police or private) in them, and, though this is rare, sometimes don't include a murder.

But some of Miss Sayers' rules for Detection Club members could still be of use to today's suspense novelists: "Detectives must detect by their wits, without the help of accident or coincidence; the author must not invent impossible death rays and poison to produce solutions which no living person could expect; he must write as good English as he can, to keep the detective story up to the highest standard that its nature permits, and to free it from the bad legacy of sensationalism, claptrap and jargon."

At its best the present-day mystery novel often reaches, it seems to me, very high standards of writing, and it also is trying to explore a variety of new approaches to its story. But—and this time I quote Howard Haycraft quoting Somerset Maugham—"The reason that so many modern readers have turned to mystery fiction is that here, and here alone, they can be sure of a novel which tells a story."

The suspense novel tells a story, on many levels. We know that some of the levels appeal to Presidents of the United States, professors and provosts of colleges, lawyers and scientists. I think the average steady mystery reader is a lot brighter than the average man. The mystery is like caviar or a very good dry martini. At its best, only intelligent readers appreciate it. Today the mystery market is a vast one, reaching people who may not ordinarily be interested in book reading. Some of this vast market is the result of television and films which pluck characters out of books and return them in other mediums enticingly embodied in attractive actors and actresses.

I've been lucky, as an editor, in that I've been able to edit and publish what seem to me the best books I can find. I've never had to worry first about where or how big the market for the books will be, and I think Harper books have sold well enough to keep our authors fairly happy and to keep Harper's fairly happy, too, but how they would sell isn't what I thought about first. I feel that no writer or painter or musician should choose to enter his field primarily because he wants to make money. There are other fields in which one can make money faster and more easily and with far more certainty, though on the whole a writer has an easier time supporting himself than other creative people (there are more book buyers than there are concert goers or art collectors, and a book is easier to reproduce and to get to its audience).

To be a writer is hard work, but exciting work, even if one isn't sure one can make a living from it. To be an editor is hard work, too, and exciting work (and one does get a pay check), but publishing is a gambling game. We never *really* know what books are going to sell well—or sometimes even why a given book is selling.

I would like, as I'm sure every editor would, to find on my desk of a morning a manuscript that, when read, would have me saying, "Oh boy, is this a book!" And then I could dash around the House yelling, "Hey, you should see what *I* just found!" and the salesmen would all agree with me, and we'd turn the manuscript as fast as possible into a handsome book, and when the bookstores heard about the book, they'd take a lot of copies, and when the critics read the book they'd give it rave reviews, and when the public read the reviews, it would buy the book like mad. And then the book clubs and the reprint houses and the motion picture people would come storming in. Sometimes that does really happen. But not absolutely all the time, alas.

When it doesn't, then there is the need for an editor. An editor's job, as you probably know, is a lot of different things, Once he has decided to publish the book, he or she has to try to figure out (sort of guess) how many copies to print and what price to put on the book, and he has to consult the designer, and to worry about the jacket and the jacket copy, and the advertising and promotion, along with the various departments who watch over all these things.

But the most important thing an editor does, I think, is to help the author get his book into its best possible shape. To do this the editor has to be very gentle in part and very firm in part—and he must try to get into the author's mind and to understand what the author's intentions were as fully as he can. This is often especially hard if the editor and the author have never met (the author often lives far away) and the editor knows the author only through his manuscript and correspondence. Usually an author who has just finished a book is in a very touchy state: he's proud but defensive. The book was a part of him—for a long time his energies and his mind were devoted almost entirely to it. He must have loved it (or at least admired it) while he was working on it, or he couldn't have gone on working, and now that he's brought it into being he not only still loves it—but he's hoping it will go out and support him— and that it may also make him respected—or even famous.

An author who has just finished a book is often still infatuated with it; he hasn't the judgment he would have if he could put the book aside until time could take the rosiness out of his vision. Usually a writer can't afford to (or won't) wait for time. So he needs an editor, one who seems to understand him and to make sense to him. And the editor has to be able to respond with sensitivity, and sense, to the particular book of the particular author. To guide the author through the revision—sometimes minor, sometimes major—of the book he has written is a delicate (and often sometimes absolutely exhausting) job.

In fiction, the editor's hand must be as light and as accurate and knowledgeable as the hand of a very good surgeon as he probes the intricate network of veins and tissues, cutting away what should come out without cutting anything vital and making sure the patient will live, in a healthier condition. An author who needs the help of an editor to guide him through revisions must find the editor encouraging and reassuring as well as firm, because hard as writing often is, revision is often harder. And after the long hours at the typewriter, an author probably wants to lie down or to go dancing, or, if he's going to write, to start a completely new book.

One of the hardest things, I think, that an editor has to do (its not exactly easy on the author, either) is to turn down a book that seems to the editor so far below the author's level that publishing it won't do him any good. It's especially hard if one admires the author's work—and if the author has a reputation—because one knows that another publisher may very well take the book just to get the author and won't be concerned whether the publication of an inferior work a) will make the author sloppy and willing to do other inferior works later and b) will make the critics, bookstores and readers wonder if the author is really so hot. This is unlike the situation in other creative fields: a musician doesn't expect everything he writes to be heard, a playwright doesn't expect all his plays to be backed, a painter doesn't expect all his paintings to be hung and to be sold. Some manuscripts—even those of a good writer—*don't* work out, and, *very* hard though it is, these should be put aside. There's no easy sledding in writing or any of the arts. For artists in any field to depend upon their work to support them is a dangerous thing; it's much better to give the work a chance by doing something else for bread and butter—even if it means a double job.

I am a demanding editor—but I'm also a painstaking editor. I care about fiction and the mystery/suspense field. And I think *care* and *caring* pay off. I still, after a long time in it, find the field very exciting. I have made the usual, or perhaps more than usual, mistakes along the way; it would be a great help to be clairvoyant but I'm not. Sometimes I fail to reach an author I admire, and the author goes away and I'm saddened.

But the author-editor relationship is, I feel, a very close one, and it has to be an honest one. An author who doesn't trust my judgment and thinks I'm foolish would be even more foolish to keep on working with me. And I cannot fight wholeheartedly for a book I don't think is any good.

I've been very lucky in getting a good many good manuscripts from good authors. And I've never felt that suspense fiction was second-class fiction or should be so treated.

More and more readers are beginning to discover the quality and pleasure of today's suspense fiction, though I'm sorry to say it is still too often reviewed in little boxes and given short shrift. Too many people say simply that they never read suspense fiction. What, I wonder, if they like fiction, are they reading instead? Not too many general novels are superior to the better suspense novels as far as writing or general reading pleasure goes.

Occasionally a novel (or a non-fiction book) in the crime field shoots up on the best seller list and is wildly heralded, and I consider how much the readers of those books would enjoy other good —and sometimes better—books in the mystery field that they haven't bothered to notice the existence of, and I think, "Oh, hell, the idiots." But the situation is getting better all the time (I'm an optimist). I do believe that books, good books, in the suspense field are not only here to stay, but here to be noticed a lot more in time to come.

94

LEGAL RIGHTS FOR WRITERS

By Jeanne Pollett

Josh Billings once remarked that man's problem isn't so much the things he doesn't know, as the things he knows that aren't so.

Writers and photographers are no exception. Some of the most widely held beliefs about their legal rights and responsibilities have no foundation in law. Often the writer or the cameraman is on firmer legal ground than he thinks. He may worry about restrictions that simply don't exist. But sometimes he acts with false confidence, risking liability without realizing it.

Let's look at some of the legal principles important to those who write or take photographs for publication.

Use of the word "allegedly" or the naming of a source gives no legal protection to the writer.

There are perfectly valid reasons for a newsman to qualify a statement this way. The practice alerts the reader to the source and probable reliability of information. But it's no defense in a legal action.

"John Smith is alleged to have shot the victim" or "Police said John Smith fired the fatal shot" may literally be true, even though Smith was innocent and five hundred miles away at the time. But so far as the law of defamation is concerned, the words are the precise equivalent of the flat statement, "John Smith shot the victim." If John is innocent, he may bring a successful action for libel.

Inconsistently enough (and who ever said the law was consistent?), a retraction, to be legally effective, must be put forth as the writer's own statement. In the case of that shooting, it's not enough to say by way of retraction, "Police stated further investigation showed

John Smith had no connection with the shooting." The retraction must be a flat denial that Smith shot the victim.

Even reporting and denying a rumor may get the writer into a legal jam. An editorial stating, "This newspaper does not believe the report that Councilman Jones accepted any favor in return for changing his vote," may be treated as furthering a rumor that Jones did take a bribe. Courts say, perhaps somewhat unrealistically, that one may not escape liability for repeating a defamatory statement by adding that the writer does not believe it.

Recent court rulings regarding public figures have not abrogated the basic principles of libel law.

The cases of *New York Times* v. *Sullivan* and *Associated Press* v. *Walker,* and later pronouncements of the courts, do give writers considerably more leeway where public figures are concerned. But on the whole, the old concept of libel still stands:

> Libel is a malicious publication, expressed either in printing, writing, typewriting, or by signs and pictures, tending either to blacken the memory of one who is dead, or the reputation of one who is alive, and expose him to public hatred, contempt, or ridicule.

Truth is a defense to an action for libel. Under the more recent decisions, it doesn't have to be an absolute, every-i-dotted-and-every-t-crossed truth. But substantial accuracy is required. One cannot imagine a twentieth-century court holding it libelous to say a man had stolen two pigs when in truth he had stolen only one (although that rule used to be the law in England).

Mere name-calling is not actionable.

A writer isn't likely to become involved in this one except perhaps indirectly, in reporting a quarrel at a meeting, for example.

William L. Prosser, former dean of the University of California School of Law, puts it this way:

"The courts have held that mere words of abuse, indicating that the defendant dislikes the plaintiff and has a low opinion of him, but without suggesting any specific charge against him, are not to be treated as defamatory. A certain amount of vulgar name-calling is tolerated, on the theory that it will necessarily be understood to amount to nothing more."

Use of a person's name without his consent is not actionable.

Any working newsman has had the experience of watching an irate individual pound his desk, red-faced, and shout, "If you use my name again without my permission—I'll sue!"

The law doesn't give that kind of protection to even the most publicity-shy. So long as an event is newsworthy (and that's a broad definition indeed), the name of even a reluctant participant may appear in print. (A few states do prohibit publishing the identities of juvenile offenders or of victims of sex crimes.)

A newspaper or magazine may not be restrained from publishing— or required to publish—anything.

A surprisingly large number of otherwise well-informed persons will speculate whether a publication "should have been allowed" to print a controversial piece.

The First (freedom of the press) Amendment is construed as allowing no prior restraint on publication. After publication, writer and publisher are accountable for libel, invasion of privacy, or other actionable injury.

As to the reverse—the question whether a publication may be required to print a particular item or advertisement—the answer is a resounding "no." The question has in fact seldom even been raised. A publisher may reject anything (even crucial legal advertising) for any reason or for no reason but pure caprice.

A writer can get into trouble even if he sticks to facts which can be proved.

As we have seen, truth is ordinarily a complete defense to a civil action for libel. But a writer may risk suit on another ground— invasion of privacy—if he goes too far in exposing another's private life.

A typical example would be bringing up the fact that Joe Blow, who has for years lived a blameless life in the community, once was prosecuted for embezzlement. If Joe is running for county treasurer, his record is very much a matter of legitimate public concern. If he's simply going his own quiet way as a private citizen, digging into and publicizing his past may well be held to be actionable. Authors of factual police and detective yarns need be particularly aware of this problem.

The person who owns a photographic negative doesn't necessarily have the right to reproduce it.

There's a persistent belief among even professional photographers that ownership of a negative carries with it the right to reproduce the picture. The rule is neat, easily applied—and completely without legal foundation.

The test isn't who owns or holds the negative, but for whom the work was done. When a customer pays a commercial photographer to take a picture, it's the patron, not the cameraman, who owns the right to reproduce it. Conversely, an amateur or a professional photographer who takes a picture at his own expense owns the rights to it.

The same general rules govern publication of children's pictures as those of adults.

Another bit of photographic folklore has it that a minor child may not be photographed, or his picture printed, without his parents' consent.

The same rules govern the photographing of children as the portraying of adults. In general, any non-embarrassing picture taken in a public place can safely be used in the editorial pages of a magazine or newspaper. It's O.K. to photograph that schoolyard full of children without making the rounds of their parents with model release forms. (Commercial use of a picture, of either child or adult, in an advertisement or on a product is another matter entirely.)

A writer is not free to quote from letters and diaries that have come into his possession.

Just as ownership of a photographic negative does not carry with it a right to reproduce a picture, ownership of another person's letters or diaries does not imply the right to copy their contents.

A letter, once written, mailed, and delivered, belongs to the recipient. He may save it, destroy it, sell it, frame it and hang it on the wall. He is owner of the physical object—the paper and the ink. But literary property remains with the letter writer. The latter has what is called a common-law copyright, the same right an author has in his own unpublished manuscript.

An author who wants to quote from letters (even family letters) or diaries should first obtain permission. If the letter writer or the diarist has died, approval should be obtained from his heirs.

A writer may make limited use of copyrighted material.

Facts cannot be copyrighted. Otherwise research, writing, knowledge itself would come to a grinding halt. The *form of expression* of those facts is subject to copyright.

Even so, a writer may make fair use of material which has been copyrighted by others. Fair use has been described by Melville B. Nimmer, professor of law at the University of California at Los Angeles and authority on copyright law, as "copying by others which does not materially impair the marketability of the work which is copied."

The law does not specify a particular amount of copyrighted material that may be used.

Many persons in the book and music publishing industries firmly believe that up to eight bars of music (or lyrics) may be duplicated without risk.

Some countries do define fair use in mathematical terms, specifying for example that not more than eight bars may be taken from a piece of music, and not more than 1,000 words from a scientific or a literary work. There's no such specific rule in the United States.

A writer may use the title from another copyrighted work without infringement.

Titles are not subject to copyright. An author needn't search to see whether the one he has in mind has been used before.

But he shouldn't on that account dash off something under the name of *Everything You Always Wanted to Know About Sex but Were Afraid to Ask.* A title may be protected under another theory of law, unfair competition. If it's become identified with one writer's product in the public mind, the title may not be appropriated and used in such a way as to make a buyer think he's getting the first writer's work rather than another's.

There's no surefire way to avoid a lawsuit.

A writer or a photographer may be on firm legal ground, and still be sued.

Unfortunately, "Can they sue?" is an utterly meaningless question. Anybody can sue anyone, however groundlessly, if he can persuade a lawyer to take the case or if he follows the proper court procedure and files the action himself without benefit of counsel. He can sue, but he may be thrown out of court long before the action gets to the trial stage.

The sorting-out process occurs after the action has been brought. In the federal courts and in some states, the person being sued files a "motion to dismiss." Other states call the pleading a "demurrer." What it says in effect is, "Even though everything alleged in the complaint is true—and we're not admitting it except for purposes of argument—you still don't have a case."

Going back to the man who didn't want his name used without his permission: If he were to bring a lawsuit against the writer or the publisher, the defendant would demur and the court would say in effect: "Plaintiff has not suffered any wrong the law recognizes. Case dismissed."

95

RESEARCH AT UNCLE SAM'S BOOKSTORE

By Dee Stuart

SOMEONE once said that successful writing is 80% research and 20% rewriting. But what if you are tied to home or office and can't get away to do research? Or, if you are free to go, suppose there are no resources available?

As a beginning writer with two pre-schoolers, I hit these problems head-on while trying to research an article suggested by a friend.

"I'd love to grow gourds to make into decorative arrangements," she said. "But I've no idea how to grow them, much less preserve them."

Challenged, I, too, searched for information—with little success. Our garden book didn't cover gourds. My only other resource was the high school library. Encyclopedias were too general. The *Readers' Guide* turned up nothing. In my ignorance, I was pleased to find that nothing had been published on gourds. This would mean a plus value for my article. I soon learned there was a reason nothing had been written: No information was available.

Discouraged, I told a fellow writer I'd have to abandon the idea. Then she told me about "Uncle Sam's Bookstore."

This vast storehouse boasts approximately 27,000 different publications currently available for sale by the Superintendent of Documents, U. S. Government Printing Office, Washington, D. C. They range in price from 10¢ to $10.00 and up. Uncle Sam's Bookstore was as near as my mailbox.

We consulted my friend's list of publications and to my delight found two booklets on gourds. I promptly sent for them. A few weeks later I had more information about gourds than I could ever use.

Result? Two articles, two sales: "Gourds—Pretty and Practical," to *Popular Gardening*, and "Gourds Are for the Birds" to *Flower Grower*.

From then on, I resolved that Uncle Sam's Bookstore would be my first resource rather than a last resort.

A leaflet, "How to Keep in Touch with U. S. Government Publications," describes what's available. For the sake of convenience, Uncle Sam has broken down the listings into 47 subjects or areas of interest. For each subject there is a free list of titles and prices, revised approximately once a year to include newly-issued or still-popular publications for sale.

Among the free price lists are: *Home Economics, Geology, Fish and Wildlife, Occupations, National Parks, Forestry, American History, Plants, Weather, Astronomy and Meteorology,* and *Space, Missiles, the Moon, NASA,* and *Satellites.*

One list, *Consumer Information,* includes family finances, appliances, recreation, gardening, health and safety, food, house and home, child care, and clothing and fabrics. All of these subjects are gold mines of information for writers of home, garden and women's magazine features.

Government publications are a prime source of information from many points of view. Not only will you find material on ordinary subjects, such as gourds, but you can learn all about the newest discoveries in the fields of science, space, homemaking, and other areas that you may not be able to learn about anywhere else. The data is current, valid, authoritative, and the price is low.

These publications are ideal for supplementing previous research and for double-checking facts and accuracy. A woman I know who is working on a Civil War novel supplements her research by culling facts from the vast selection of National Park Service Civil War Historical Handbooks. Another friend who writes Indian stories for juvenile readers visited Bandelier National Monument in New Mexico. She absorbed the feel of the place and developed a story plot. But when she started writing, she found she needed more specific information. Since she lives on a ranch in Montana, miles from the nearest library, additional research could have been an unsolvable problem.

She scanned the Government Printing Office price list titled *Smithsonian Institution National Museum and Indians* and found

"Bandelier National Monument," 25¢. She ordered the booklet and from it gleaned information on the origins and life of the Indians who lived there. She added authenticity to later Indian stories with the aid of booklets on various tribes—without ever leaving home!

Our family camping trips from coast to coast have provided raw material for many travel stories. And GPO publications have served many times to jog my memory of sites we've seen and to add "nuts-and-bolts" to the articles that followed.

Recently we camped at Sylvan Lake, South Dakota. I took detailed notes on scenery and what to see and do. Later when I began writing a roundup piece on the Black Hills, I discovered I needed a few concrete facts to give the story depth and substance. I trekked down to the Government branch bookstore in Kansas City and found all the information I needed in brochures on Wind Cave National Park and Mount Rushmore. Result? A sale to *Midwest Motorist*.

The Government Printing Office operates branch bookstores across the country. In addition to the Kansas City branch there are stores in Boston, Chicago, Los Angeles, and San Francisco. Washington, D. C. alone boasts five. According to E. J. Brink, Bookstores Manager, branches are scheduled to open in Dallas and Atlanta. If you are lucky enough to live near one of Uncle Sam's bookstores, you may find that just browsing through the hundreds of publications on display will spark ideas for articles and stories. Some stores stock as many as 1400 publications.

But you don't have to live near a store. Merely perusing price list titles can turn you on. For example, a 10¢ pamphlet on John Muir, noted 19th-century scientist, author and conservationist, could be the inspiration for an article, short story or even a juvenile biography.

Writers of how-to articles find that the home economics publications offer a wealth of material. For instance, *Consumer Guides in Buying* includes "Be a Good Shopper" and "Money-saving Main Dishes."

Moneymaking ideas for young people—topics such as "Catfish Farming," "Raising Rabbits," "Mushroom Growing" and "Bee-Keeping for Beginners" could all be developed into salable articles.

If you need a few appropriate phrases for the American Field

Service student in your story to speak, send for a foreign phrase book. Uncle Sam has them—from Arabic to Tagalog.

Although U. S. Government publications are primarily a source of information, you are free to quote from them without asking permission—to give your article validity. U. S. Government publications are in the public domain. Be sure, however, that the government publication is *not a reprint* of copyrighted material; if it is, the copyright remains in force, and you will have to write for permission to the copyright owner to quote from it. A booklet of special interest to writers is "Copyright Laws of the U. S. of America," 45¢. Another helpful one is "The Seven Keys to Better Faster Typing," 50¢.

New titles appear monthly. A popular new release, "Search for Solitude," a 36-page color brochure, describes wilderness areas for the use and enjoyment and spiritual enrichment of the American people.

A recent GPO best seller, "Questions about the Oceans," 55¢, is designed to answer questions about oceanography and marine sciences. This 120-page book also answers such questions as, "Why is the ocean salty?" "Where do waves come from?" "How deep has man gone in the ocean?" It lists colleges and universities which offer oceanographic courses and tells who hires oceanographers. An imaginative writer could transform this material into a juvenile picture book, a science article for a children's magazine or a career article for young people.

Answers to the above questions and others in the 47 subject areas are yours for the asking. The first step is to send for the leaflet "How to Keep in Touch with U. S. Government Publications," describing the 47 categories or price lists. Then send for the price lists that interest you. From them choose the publications you want to buy. Fill in the order blank on the last page of the price list booklet and mail with your check or money order. Or you can use Special Documents Coupons sold in sets of 20 for $1 and good until used. Address all requests to: Superintendent of Documents, U. S. Government Printing Office, Washington, D. C. 20402.

The quickest way to order is to call or mail your request to the bookstore nearest you. If they stock what you want, they will ship it direct. If not, they will order it for you from Washington.

Thirty to forty thousand orders a day flood the Superintendent's office. Service is remarkable in the face of such a logistics nightmare. "In one section," Mr. Brink reports, "all the employees do is open mail, working sixteen hours a day in two shifts." A priority desk handles *bookstore* orders, all of which are shipped within forty-eight hours. If possible, place your order through a branch store to take advantage of this high-speed service.

The best way to keep informed about the avalanche of new and popular Government publications is to send for the free biweekly list of *Selected U. S. Government Publications*. The lists furnish a brief description of contents, price and an order blank. Take advantage of this service even if you think you don't need it. You'll be surprised at how many topics will interest you. Call the nearest bookstore and ask to be placed on the mailing list or send your request direct to Washington. Or, you may subscribe to the *Monthly Catalog,* a comprehensive listing of all publications issued by the departments and agencies of the U. S. Government each month, costing $6.00 a year.

Writers today need not be discouraged or put off by lack of opportunity for doing research. If you don't drive, if you are tied down with children or otherwise housebound, if you work eight hours a day and have no time to seek out information, if you live in the boondocks and no library is near you, or if you merely want to explore untapped resources, you will find Uncle Sam's bookstore a rich storehouse of knowledge just waiting for you to open the door.

96

LITERARY AGENTS

By James Oliver Brown

I speak on occasion to writers and aspiring writers, and the assumption is that I have a special knowledge of the questions such audiences ask. A few questions have been singled out as most recurring and this piece is devoted to them.

There is a lack of understanding on the part of inexperienced writers, and some experienced, of the functions of the East Coast literary agent who, while handling all rights and forms of writing, concentrates on the selling of rights to books and magazine stories and articles. The image of these agents is of rather grasping, ill-mannered, ill-bred parasites, who resist seeing and handling the works of writers, and who make the rounds of publishing houses, manuscripts in hand, persuading publishers to publish books. If females, they probably wear large flowered hats, and if males, they probably smoke cigars. I know of no such East Coast "book" literary agents.

A writer doesn't need an agent to sell a book for him here in this country. On the other hand his book will get closer attention if it has on it the imprint of a good agent. It might even sell bearing the agent's imprint where it would not have sold without such imprint, but such a sale would be rare, because manuscripts get read, regardless of who submits them. Reactions to writing are emotional, and the endorsement of an agent who is known for his taste and success might push the emotional scales in favor of the work. If I started telling an editor why he should like and buy a book, the editor would assume I was trying to get rid of a dud. The editor knows the James Brown imprint and for what it stands. He pays attention, in relation to that standing, whatever it might be in the mind of that particular editor.

The agent for "talent" (performers) and for all phases of the performance side of our business (stage, motion pictures, television) has a job of presentation different from that of the "book" agent, and the image of this kind of agent has had greater presentation by playwrights and novelists to the general public. Partly as a result of this exposure, the public has a wrong image of the "book" agent. In the performance side of the business, the buyer more than often has to be told. He has to be made to see how to blend everything together, the writing being only a part of the whole. The added factors are things such as casting, directing, stage designing. The "book" agent, on the other hand, usually presents the finished product. Ordinarily it doesn't need to be spoken about; it speaks for itself. I don't know of any of the literary agents on the performance side who wear hats and smoke cigars.

The literary agent performs a complex and varied function, which can't be too well defined. His function depends upon the kinds of writers he represents. I can speak only for my own operation. I'm a business manager-adviser, coordinator, protector of rights, exploiter of all rights to all writings of the writers I represent, such rights including book, magazine, dramatic, motion picture, radio, television, recording, translation. My important function as an agent is bringing in money for the writer, getting the most money possible in the interests of the writer, from every possible source. When an agent starts to work on a piece of writing, a story, an article, a book, whatever, he thinks of it in terms of all rights and gets it to the people who buy the rights, here and abroad. He is an expert in knowing the markets and having the organization to get to them.

The practices of the members of our agents' professional society, the Society of Authors' Representatives, are prescribed by reasonable and rigid rules. We don't advertise, and we don't live on reader's fees and editorial fees. We get clients from recommendations of people who know us, writers, editors, and others, and we live on a percentage take of the amount we take in from a sale. Theoretically, at least, if we don't sell we don't eat. Many, and I suspect, most "book" literary agents have independent incomes or some other subsidy such as rich or working spouses. A few of us actually live on 10% of our writers' earnings. This is not enough for much more than just modest, non-caviar, non-Rolls-Royce living.

I feel that if a written contract with one of my clients is necessary, I probably shouldn't have him for a client. On the other hand, if a simple letter agreement is signed stating what the relationship is anyway, I think it is in everyone's interests. I usually send such a document (if I happen to remember to do it) to a new client and leave it up to the client. They usually sign. Except in some situations where the interests of the writer were to be protected by doing it, I advise against the signing of an agency contract which goes beyond stating what the agent-client relationship is. An agency contract, for example, may provide that the agent will continue to handle the unsold rights to a property the agent has handled, should a writer leave the agent. This is not what would happen without the contract, and a writer should know this. Except in extraordinary cases, an agent should cease being the agent when the agency relationship ends. Rarely, if ever, is it in the writer's interests to have two agents working for him on different properties. The deserted agent is a deserted agent, alas, and has left only the right to receive monies and be paid under contracts with book publishers, etc., that he negotiated before the desertion. (Who cares about a deserted parasite?)

We members of the Society of Authors' Representatives feel that a writer does well to limit his search for an agent, to fit his particular needs, to the Society's membership of almost forty agents of the eighty-seven listed in the Manhattan Telephone Directory. There are at least one or two, and perhaps more, perfectly good agents, not members of the Society. One can consult a nationally known book publisher or magazine or The Authors Guild. By correspondence the author and agent can proceed to get together. I like to meet the people I take on, but not until I have read what they write to see whether they can write.

I consider it not in the writer's interest to be handled by different agents for different rights, but this is because in the operation of my office we handle everything and every right for our clients. We are represented abroad and on the West Coast by agents who carry on our work in these areas for us. We do not take on writers who divide their representation. Some perfectly reputable agents do, I am told. This is a matter of policy, having nothing to do with ethics; rather with efficiency. Commissions are 10% on U.S.A. rights and from 15% to 20% on foreign rights.

I have been asked whether a writer should pay his agent a commission on something the writer happens to place himself. If a writer questions the payment of a commission, but the agent feels he should receive this commission, I suggest a termination of the agency relationship at once since the agent should have his commission regardless of who makes the sale. A dispute of this sort sets up bad feeling not in the interests of the writer. A writer who questions the value of his agent by wanting to withhold his commission obviously is with the wrong agent. I cannot conceive of representing someone who thought I was not earning every commission on every sale. We are underpaid for the services we perform as it is. We can exist only by taking the low and high commissions on everything. Asking about *obligation* to pay a commission indicates a bad agency relationship or a misunderstanding of the agent's function. Agents often have little to do, for example, with the conferences which result in assignments to their writers of non-fiction articles by editors. Sometimes they don't know until a check arrives that there has been a conference. The agent earns his commission even here by the over-all services he performs in the over-all writing career of the writers on his list. The agent even earns it in the case of the arrived check by being sure that the pay is what it should be and that the contract of purchase is proper.

Most experienced professional writers indoctrinated in this country have a good relationship with their agents. Occasionally one runs into a writer who feels that he must be with an agent with whom he has no social life and, in fact, has an arm's length, challenging relationship. I'm sure these are fine relationships for the parties concerned. There's nothing wrong with them, ethically. The interesting thing is that the best agents, the most successful, those with the best reputations, seem not to have this kind of relationship with their clients.

Most agents of all kinds like writers and like to see manuscripts. A writer does not have to be published to get a hearing from most of the very best agents. Some of the largest successes I have had on my list have been first novels by previously unpublished writers, and an important part of my list is made up of successful writers with whom I have worked from the beginning of their published careers. A professional writer can be unpublished. He must know how to write and have that dedication which compels him to write and to consider writing as a primary function, even if, until he gets underway, he has to have a job to eat. We agents have a special sense of who is and who is not a "pro." One lady agent (and I'm told she is not being facetious, although I hope she is) claims that she can spot a writer by observing his wrists and ankles!

I'm looking now as I write this at a list of the members of the Society of Authors' Representatives. I know most of them, some better than others. Most of us are close friends. I once was an editor with a publisher, as several of us were, and got to know most of the members then. We also meet together regularly to discuss mutual problems. You can't go wrong with any of them as far as their qualifications and ability are concerned. You can go wrong as to personality. We all are pretty much alike in our attitudes toward the business, but we differ very much as people. It would be good if every writer deciding on an agent could meet several before making a decision. It saves a lot of trouble for both parties.

Good hunting to all of you. When you find the agent who inspires the best work from you, let him or her carry the ball. They will do it better than any writer can for himself. The agent knows his area of operation. And he can take the blame for any difficulties with a buyer of the writer's product. The agent is better equipped to get the buyer (publisher, producer, whatever) to do more for his client. One of the great functions of the agent is to act as a buffer and to see that love is maintained between the principals. Most people function better when they feel they are loved and that what they are doing is being appreciated. The wise writer will let his agent be the non-loved.

When I get to the end of my talks to writers, I get the questions. Down in one of the first few rows is a young man who asks the questions, "If I can place my novel myself, why do I need an agent?"

My reply, "As long as you ask that question, you don't. It's when you don't ask it that you will need an agent."

What do I mean? When this young man, I hope not too much later in his career, discovers that his career isn't as far along as it should be and realizes what a good agent can do for him, he's ready for an agent. The writer is alone in the world without an agent. He may be the kind of person incapable of working with an agent. There are some of those, and, alas, they usually don't get as far in the commercial world as they could if they were working with the experts in the competitive market place. The young man, now older, in trouble with contracts he has signed, checks with unread endorsements he has signed, out on too many tangents and limbs, without direction and proper counseling, without anyone to fight the battle for money, respect, proper promotion, proper printings and advertising, acceptable salable titles to his work, feeling alone and unwanted, realizes why placement of his work is a minor part of the function of the agent.

97

WRITERS, AGENTS, AND
MANUSCRIPT SALES

By Paul R. Reynolds

Why does the beginning author want an agent?

After collecting a certain number of rejection slips, the beginning writer is apt to wonder whether an agent can help him.

The beginning author hopes that the agent will sell a manuscript which the author himself could not sell. There is little if any basis for such a hope. Also the beginning writer wants someone to do the work of writing letters of submission to editors, to do the work of wrapping and mailing manuscripts. Finally, the beginner wants to avoid the unpleasantness of personally receiving a rejection slip.

However, once an author has attained a certain proficiency with the written word, there are areas where an agent can help him. Usually, but not always, the author at this stage in his career has made some sales through his own efforts.

What agent is the beginning writer likely to choose?

The beginning writer chooses someone he has heard about, namely a man or firm who advertises, a pseudo-agent. Off goes his manuscript to such pseudo-agent, one who "lunches with editors" or one whose clients "have made in some cases fabulous sales and in some cases modest ones" or one whose advertisements display testimonials of sales. By return mail comes a letter from the pseudo-agent asking the author for a check, sometimes for a large one, sometimes for a quite modest one. The beginning writer usually sends his check. Back comes a letter full of praise for the manuscript and with a request for more manuscripts accompanied by more checks. This process continues until the author runs out of money or out of patience. The author has made no sales.

The pseudo-agent makes his money by cashing checks from authors, not from commissions on sales of manuscripts. Some of these advertising sharks seldom if ever offer manuscripts to magazines or publishers for publication. If they do offer a manuscript to an editor, it is under a cloud. Editors, knowing that these pseudo-agents rarely have a publishable manuscript, start with a prejudice against their wares. Have some of these pseudo-agents made sales? Yes, but very infrequently. An author's chance of a sale is enhanced if he offers his manuscript himself and avoids the sponsorship of one of these literary spongers.

What about the legitimate agent?

The legitimate agent does not advertise. He makes his living from commissions on sales. This means that he must represent selling writers. There are several literary agents who sell more than two million dollars worth of literary property a year; a larger number whose sales are between one million and two million and many whose gross is a quarter of a million dollars up. These agents will have a staff of from three to twenty. Since a secretary in New York City receives at least $100 a week, successful authors are essential just for the agent to pay his overhead.

Most article writers should and do start writing pieces for the minor markets, for newspapers, trade magazines, regional publications, etc. Payment for an acceptable manuscript is usually small, but the number of markets is very large. No agent follows these markets or can make a living selling to them, and an author can do as well or better in this area on his own.

After one or more years writing for the very numerous minor markets, writers try to graduate to the high-paying, mass circulation magazines, and many are successful. Once a writer has made one or more sales to the mass circulation magazines such as *The Reader's Digest,* the *Post, McCall's,* etc., some of the legitimate literary agents will take the writer on as a client. The author will be helped some but still must do much of the selling work. Many writers at this stage continue to handle their own work. Authors who attain the steady success in the article field of a Richard Gehman, Joseph Wechsberg, or Geoffrey Hellman, can have any agent in the country. The above three writers do use agents.

What about the agent for short stories?

No agent will handle a writer whose short stories are published exclusively in the "little" magazines or in the small-paying markets. When a writer graduates to the high-paying, mass circulation magazines, some agents will take him on; some will not. The short story market has been continually contracting during the last ten years so that few writers seem to be able to make a living in this field.

What about the agent for television?

It is almost impossible to sell an original television script except through an agent of standing. Most of the buyers, partly for fear of lawsuits over alleged plagiarism, partly because of a lack of a staff of readers, will not consider scripts submitted by an unknown writer. Television script buying is more and more being done out on the Coast, and a Hollywood agent should be sought. This is a very technical field, very difficult to break into.

What about the agent and the play?

The newcomer in this field should try to get a play-broker, an agent who specializes in plays. Success in this field requires unusual skill and proficiency. Breaking into the amateur play market is difficult; surmounting Broadway is overwhelmingly difficult and here an agent is almost obligatory.

What about the agent in connection with sales of poetry?

No agent will handle poetry with the possible exception of the very big names. Ogden Nash or Richard Armour can certainly be helped with their books, but in the case of their magazine sales, it is doubtful if any agent can do any better than they can do themselves. Ogden Nash and Richard Armour both use agents.

What about the agent and writers of books?

Here perhaps is where the agent can be most helpful. A successful book, fiction or non-fiction, has so many rights to be promoted, publishers so differ in their ability to sell a particular type of book, the contracts they will proffer and the contracts that they can be induced to sign are at such variance that a good agent, although never essential, can be very helpful. The author of a specialized book such as a cookbook or a garden book has far less need for an agent. Here there are generally no rights of value involved other than American book publication rights. In the case of the general interest book, hard-cover or paperback or both, a good agent will make the author money over and above his commissions. One manuscript may involve many individual contracts. The above is true of the author's second or tenth or fortieth book; it is also true of a first book which is really good. All of the large agents have had one or more first novels or first non-fiction books which have been very successful.

Is it difficult for the new writer with a really good manuscript to obtain a good agent?

The answer is yes. It is sometimes said that it is easier to find a publisher than it is to find a good agent. Unless the agent believes or hopes that an author will make at least $5,000 a year, the agent is not interested. A book may earn a minimum of $500 to a maximum of $500,000 in the case of an enormous number one best seller. Will an agent read a first novel? The author can only write and ask. An agent is busy. He has only one pair of eyes. He knows that nine out of ten writers submit manuscripts before they have learned their trade, and hence submit second-rate manuscripts. With every new writer an agent is from Missouri. However, if there is any reason to believe that a first manuscript may be good, such as previous publication of the author's short pieces in minor markets, or such as a recommendation from one or more people who seem qualified to recognize a good manuscript, or perhaps just from the author's background, many of the agents will read it. The good agents are always looking for new talent. Of course an agent makes mistakes (just as publishers do) and may miss the good qualities of a manuscript, or the agent may like it and may be wrong, but if the agent reads the manuscript, likes it, and is right in his judgment, the author is off to the races. All kinds of interesting and profitable things will occur.

How should an author select an agent?

We have already spoken about the fee chargers, the advertising sharks, the literary spongers. Do not waste your money on them. The Society of Authors' Representatives, all of whose members are believed to be competent and reputable, publishes a short pamphlet which lists the members of the Society and their addresses. This pamphlet will be mailed by *The Writer*, 8 Arlington St., Boston, Mass. 02116, if you will ask for it and enclose a stamped, self-addressed envelope.

Really, how important is an agent?

No agent can sell any manuscript that an author cannot sell if the author is sufficiently persevering. If someone wants to buy, the agent may obtain more money; he has no magic, no influence in producing a sale. No writing career was ever made by an agent or blasted by the lack of an agent. Success in writing depends upon what is between the first and the last page of a manuscript. Learning to get the right material and to use it with the right words, learning the trade of a writer involves very hard work over a long period of time. The agent looms far larger in the minds of many writers than is justified. The agent cannot solve the writer's problems; continuous intensive work and the refusal to be beaten by discouragement usually can solve them.

98

A CONCISE GUIDE TO COPYRIGHT

A COPYRIGHT is a form of protection given by the law of the United States (Title 17, U.S. Code) to the authors of literary, dramatic, musical, artistic, and other intellectual works. The owner of a copyright is granted by law certain exclusive rights in his work such as:

a. the right to print, reprint, and copy the work.
b. the right to sell or distribute copies of the work.
c. the right to transform or revise the work by means of dramatization, translation, musical arrangement, or the like.
d. the right to record the work.
e. the right to perform the work publicly, if it is a literary, dramatic, or musical work.

Not all of the rights granted by the copyright law are without limitation. For example, in the case of musical compositions, the performance right is limited to public performances for profit. Likewise, recording rights in musical works are limited by the so-called "compulsory license" provision, which permits recordings upon payment of certain royalties, after the initial recording has been authorized by the copyright owner.

Writers often ask if they should copyright a manuscript before submitting it to a publisher for possible publication.

As outlined below under "Unpublished Works," such manuscripts as novels, short stories, poems, narrative outlines, etc., *cannot* be copyrighted before publication, but are protected by common law until publication. Plays, lectures, musical compositions, etc., may be copyrighted before they have been published, but here again it is not *necessary* to copyright such manuscripts before submitting them for publication, since they are also protected by common law.

WHAT CAN BE COPYRIGHTED

The copyright law (Title 17, U.S. Code) lists fourteen broad classes of works in which copyright may be claimed, with the provision that these are not to limit the subject matter of copyright. Within the classes are the following kinds of works:

Books (Class A). Published works of fiction and nonfiction, poems, compilations, composite works, directories, catalogs, annual publications, information in tabular form, and similar text matter, with or without illustrations, that appear as a book, pamphlet, leaflet, card, single page, or the like.

Periodicals (Class B). Publications, such as newspapers, magazines, reviews, newsletters, bulletins, and serial publications, that appear under a single title at intervals of less than a year. Also contributions to periodicals, such as stories, cartoons, or columns published in magazines or newspapers.

Lectures or similar productions prepared for oral delivery (Class C). Unpublished works such as lectures, sermons, addresses, monologs, recording scripts, and certain forms of television and radio scripts.

Dramatic and dramatico-musical compositions (Class D). Published or unpublished dramatic works such as the acting versions of plays for the stage, for filming, radio, television, and the like, as well as pantomimes, ballets, operas, operettas, etc.

Musical compositions (Class E). Published or unpublished musical compositions (other than dramatico-musical compositions) in the form of visible notation, with or without words. Also new versions of musical compositions, such as adaptations, arrangements, and editing when it represents original authorship. The words of a song, unaccompanied by music, are not registrable in Class E.

Maps (Class F). Published cartographic representations of area, such as terrestrial maps and atlases, marine charts, celestial maps, and such three-dimensional works as globes and relief models.

Works of art; or models or designs for works of art (Class G). Published or unpublished works of artistic craftsmanship, insofar as their form but not their mechanical or utilitarian aspects are concerned, such as artistic jewelry, enamels, glassware, and tapestries, as well as works belonging to the fine arts, such as paintings, drawings, and sculpture.

Reproductions of works of art (Class H). Published reproductions of existing works of art in the same or a different medium, such as a lithograph, photoengraving, etching, or drawing of a painting, sculpture, or other work of art.

Drawings or sculptural works of a scientific or technical character (Class I). Published or unpublished diagrams or models illustrating scientific or technical works, such as an architect's or an engineer's blueprint, plan, or design, a mechanical drawing, an astronomical chart, or an anatomical model.

Photographs (Class J). Published or unpublished photographic prints for filmstrips, slide films, and individual slides. Photoengravings and other photomechanical reproductions of photographs are registered in Class K.

Prints, pictorial illustrations, and commercial prints or labels (Class K). Published prints or pictorial illustrations, greeting cards, picture postcards, and similar prints, produced by means of lithography, photoengraving, or other methods of reproduction. A print or label, not a trademark, published in connection with the sale or advertisement of articles or merchandise also is registered in this class.

Motion-picture photoplays (Class L). Published or unpublished motion pictures that are dramatic in character, such as feature films, filmed or recorded television plays, short subjects and animated cartoons, musical plays, and similar productions having a plot.

Motion pictures other than photoplays (Class M). Published or unpublished nondramatic motion pictures, such as news films, travel films, nature studies, documentaries, training or promotional films, and filmed or recorded television programs or nontheatrical motion pictures having no plot.

Sound recordings (Class N). Published sound recordings, such as phonograph discs, tape cassettes and cartridges, player-piano rolls, and similar material in which a series of sounds are fixed. The copyright law covers only those sound recordings that are fixed and first published on or after February 15, 1972. Registration in Class N is not a substitute for registration for the music or other copyrightable matter recorded, and is not appropriate for a sound track when it is an integrated part of a motion picture.

What cannot be copyrighted

Even though a work does not fit conveniently into one of the fourteen classes, this does not necessarily mean that it is uncopyrightable. However, there are several categories of material which are generally *not eligible* for statutory copyright protection. These include among others:

a. Titles, names, short phrases, and slogans; familiar symbols or designs; mere variations of typographic ornamentation, lettering, or coloring; mere listings of ingredients or contents.

b. Ideas, plans, methods, systems, or devices, as distinguished from a description or illustration.

c. Works that are designed for recording information and do not in themselves convey information, such as blank forms to be used as time cards, account books, diaries, bank checks, score cards, address books, report forms, and the like.

d. Works consisting entirely of information that is common property and containing no original authorship. For example: standard calendars, height and weight charts, tape measures and rulers, schedules of sporting events, and lists or tables taken from public documents or other common sources.

e. The following types of unpublished works: books, short stories, poems, narrative outlines, prints, maps, reproductions of works of art, periodicals, commercial prints and labels, and sound recordings.

Who can claim copyright

Only the author or those deriving their rights through him can rightfully claim copyright. Mere ownership of a manuscript, painting, or other copy does not necessarily give the owner the right to copyright. In the case of works made for hire, it is the employer, and not the employee, who is regarded as the author.

There is no provision for securing a blanket copyright to cover all the works of a particular author. Each work must be copyrighted separately if protection is desired.

Minors may claim copyright. However, state law may regulate or control the conduct of business dealings involving copyrights owned by minors; for information on this subject, it would be well to consult an attorney.

UNPUBLISHED WORKS

An unpublished work is generally one for which copies have not been sold, placed on sale, or made available to the public. Unpublished works are eligible for one or the other of two types of protection:

a. *Common Law Literary Property.* This type of protection against unauthorized use of an unpublished work is a matter of state law, and arises automatically when the work is created. It requires no action in the Copyright Office. It may last as long as the work is unpublished, but it ends when the work is published or when statutory copyright is secured by registration.

b. *Statutory Copyright.* This is the protection afforded by the federal law upon compliance with certain requirements. Only the following types of work can be registered for statutory copyright before they have been published: musical compositions, dramas, works of art, drawings and sculptural works of a scientific or technical character, photographs, motion pictures, and works prepared for oral delivery. There is no requirement that any of these works be registered for statutory copyright in unpublished form, but there may be advantages in doing so. If they are registered in their unpublished form, the law requires that another registration be made after publication with the copyright notice affixed to the copies.

The following types of material *cannot* be registered for statutory copyright protection in unpublished form: books (including short stories, poems, and narrative outlines), prints, maps, reproductions of works of art, periodicals, commercial prints and labels, and sound recordings. These works secure statutory copyright by the act of publication with notice of copyright.

How to secure statutory copyright for an unpublished work

Statutory copyright for unpublished works is secured by registering a claim in the Copyright Office. For this purpose it is necessary to forward the following material:

Application Form. The appropriate form may be ordered from the Copyright Office. Forms are supplied without charge.

Copy. In the case of manuscripts of music, dramas, lectures, etc., one complete copy should accompany the application. It will be retained by the Copyright Office. For photographs, deposit one photographic print. Special requirements concerning pictures, and certain graphic and artistic works, are stated on the application forms.

Fee. The registration fee for unpublished works is $6, which should be sent in the form of a money order, check, or bank draft, payable to the Register of Copyrights. Do not send cash.

Published work

Published works are works that have been made available to the public in some way, usually by the sale or public distribution of copies. The copyright law defines the "date of publication" as "the earliest date when copies of the first authorized edition were placed on sale, sold, or publicly distributed by the proprietor of the copyright or under his authority. . . ."

No specific number of copies or method of distribution is required for a general publication. However, it is sometimes difficult to determine the dividing line between a general publication and a limited distribution (such as sending copies to agents, publishers, or some other limited group for a specific purpose). If you are in doubt about publication in a particular case, it may be advisable to consult an attorney.

The rights in a work will be permanently lost unless all published copies bear a notice of copyright in the form and position described below. When a work has been published without notice of copyright, it falls into the public domain and becomes public property. After that happens it serves no purpose to add the notice to copies of the work, and doing so may be illegal.

In the case of works that cannot be registered before publication, it is the act of publication with notice of copyright, rather than registration in the Copyright Office, that secures statutory copyright. While the Copyright Office registers claims to copyright, it does not grant copyright protection.

How to secure statutory copyright for a published work

The book or magazine publisher *and not the author* takes care of the copyright procedure in almost every case (exceptions are unpublished works eligible for statutory copyright, or privately printed works). In the case of a book, while the publisher takes care of the copyright procedure, the actual copyright should be taken out in the name of the author, and book contracts usually provide for this.

Three steps are taken to secure and maintain statutory copyright in a published work:

1. Produce copies with copyright notice. Produce the work in copies by printing or other means of reproduction. It is essential that all copies bear a copyright notice in the required form and position.
2. Publish the work.
3. Register the claim in the Copyright Office. Promptly after publication, the following materials should be sent to the Copyright Office:
   Application for Registration. The appropriate form duly completed. (This may be requested from the Copyright Office free of charge.)
   Copies. Two copies of the work as published.
   Fees. The registration fee for published works is $6. Fees sent to the Copyright Office should be in the form of a money order, check, or bank draft, payable to the Register of Copyrights.

Processing of the claim will be more prompt if the application, copies, and fee are all mailed in the same package.

The law requires that, after a work is published with the prescribed notice, two copies "shall be promptly deposited," accompanied by a claim of copyright (that is, an application for registration) and the registration fee.

THE COPYRIGHT NOTICE

Form of the Notice. As a general rule, the copyright notice should consist of three elements:

1. *The word "Copyright," the abbreviation "Copr.," or the symbol* ©. Use of the symbol © may have advantages in securing copyright in countries that are members of the Universal Copyright Convention.
2. The name of the copyright owner (or owners).
3. The year date of publication. This is ordinarily the year in which copies are first placed on sale, sold, or publicly distributed by the copyright owner or under his authority. However, if the work has previously been registered for copyright in unpublished form, the notice should contain the year date of registration for the unpublished version. Or, if there is new copyrightable matter in the published version, it is advisable to include both the year date of the unpublished registration and the year date of the publication.

These three elements should appear together on the copies. Example:

© John Doe 1973

Optional Form of Notice. A special form of the notice is permissible for works registrable in Classes F through K (maps; works of art, models or designs for works of art; reproductions of works of art; drawings or sculptural works of a scientific or technical character; photographs; prints and pictorial illustrations; and prints or labels used for articles of merchandise). This special notice may consist of the symbol ©, accompanied by the initials, monogram, mark, or symbol of the copyright owner, if the owner's name appears upon some accessible portion of the copies. A detachable tag bearing a copyright notice is not acceptable as a substitute for a notice permanently affixed to the copies.

Special Copyright Notice for Sound Recordings. The copyright notice for sound recordings consists of the symbol ℗ (the letter P in a circle), the year date of first publication of the sound recording, and the name of the copyright owner of the sound recording; e.g., ℗ 1973 Doe Records. The copyright notice for a sound recording should appear on the surface of the copies of the recording or on the label or container, in such manner and location as to give reasonable notice of the copyright claim.

Position of notice. For a book or other publication printed in book form, the copyright notice should appear upon the title page or the page immediately following. The "page immediately following" is normally the reverse side of the page bearing the title. For a periodical, the notice should appear upon upon the title page, upon the first page of text, or under the title heading. For a musical composition, the notice may appear either upon the title page or upon the first page of music.

DURATION OF COPYRIGHT

The first term of statutory copyright runs for twenty-eight years. The term begins on the date the work is published with the notice of copyright, or, in the case of unpublished works registered in the Copyright Office, on the date of registration. A copyright may be renewed for a second term of twenty-eight years if an acceptable renewal application and fee are received in the Copyright Office during the last year of the original term of copyright, which is measured from the exact date on which the original copyright began. Recent Acts of Congress have extended second-term copyrights that would have expired on or after September 19, 1962; however, these extensions have no effect on the time limits for renewal registration. For further information about renewal copyright and these extensions, write to the Copyright Office.

INTERNATIONAL COPYRIGHT

If a work is by an author who is neither a citizen nor a domiciliary of the United States, special conditions determine whether or not the work can be protected by U.S. copyright. Specific questions on this subject, and questions about securing protection for U.S. works in foreign countries, should be addressed to the Register of Copyrights, Library of Congress, Washington, D.C. 20540.

APPLICATION FORMS

The following forms are provided by the Copyright Office, and may be obtained free of charge upon request:

*Class A   Form A: Published book manufactured in the United States of America.

*Class A or B

Form A-B Foreign: Book or periodical manufactured outside the United States of America (except works subject to the ad interim provisions of the Copyright Law of the United States of America; see Form A-B Ad Interim).

Form A-B Ad Interim: Book or periodical in the English language manufactured and first published outside the United States of America and subject to the ad interim provisions of the Copyright Law of the United States of America.

*Class B

Form B: Periodical manufactured in the United States of America.

Form BB: Contribution to a periodical manufactured in the United States of America.

Class C   Form C: Lecture or similar production prepared for oral delivery.

Class D   Form D: Dramatic or dramatico-musical composition.

---

* Not to be used for unpublished material.

Class E

> Form E: Musical composition by an author who is a citizen or domiciliary of the United States of America or which is first published in the United States of America.
>
> Form E. Foreign: Musical composition by an author who is not a citizen or domiciliary of the United States of America and which is not first published in the United States of America.

*Class F   Form F: Map.

Class G   Form G: Work of art; model or design for work of art.

*Class H   Form H: Reproduction of a work of art.

Class I   Form I: Drawing or plastic work of a scientific or technical character.

*Class K

> Form K: Print or pictorial illustration.
>
> Form KK: Print or label used for article of merchandise.

Class L or M   Form L-M: Motion picture.

*Class N   Form N: Sound recording.

Form R: Renewal copyright.

Form U: Notice of use of musical composition on mechanical instruments.

TRANSFER OR ASSIGNMENT OF STATUTORY COPYRIGHT

A copyright may be transferred or assigned by an instrument in writing, signed by the owner of the copyright. The law provides for the recordation in the Copyright Office of transfers of copyright. The original signed instrument should be submitted for the purpose of recording. It will be returned following recordation. For the most effective protection, an assignment executed in the United States should be recorded within three months from the date of execution. Assignments executed abroad should be recorded within six months.

MAILING INSTRUCTIONS

Address. All communications should be addressed to the Register of Copyrights, Library of Congress, Washington, D.C. 20540.

Fees. Do not send cash. Fees sent to the Copyright Office should be in the form of a money order, check, or bank draft, payable to the *Register of Copyrights*.

Fee Schedule

All registrations (except renewals)	$6.00
All renewals	4.00
Additional certificates	2.00
Other certifications	3.00
Assignments, etc. (containing not more than 6 pages and not more than 1 title)	5.00
—Each additional page or title	0.50
Searches (hourly fee)	5.00

Mailing. Processing of the material will be more prompt if the application, copies, and fee are all mailed at the same time and in the same package.

LEGAL ADVICE

The Copyright Office cannot give legal advice. If you need information or guidance on matters such as disputes over the ownership of a copyright, obtaining royalty payments, or prosecuting possible infringers, it may be necessary to consult an attorney.

99

WHAT'S IN A PEN NAME?

BY DEBORAH N. KASSMAN

WHEN Queen Victoria told Charles Dodgson, author of *Alice's Adventures in Wonderland,* how much she liked his book and how eagerly she looked forward to reading something else he had written, he promptly sent her his *Syllabus of Plane Algebraical Geometry.* We do not know if the Queen was amused.

Dodgson would undoubtedly be amused, however, to learn that today, more than one hundred years after the publication of *Alice,* his pen name, Lewis Carroll, is famous throughout the English-speaking world. In fact, it is said that, with the exception of Shakespeare and the Bible, the most quoted works in the English language are *Alice* and its sequel, *Through the Looking Glass.*

Dodgson limited himself to one pen name. But most authors using pseudonyms generally find themselves in the position of William Sydney Porter, who had several pen names although he signed most of his stories O. Henry. Today, many authors erupt in a veritable rash of pen names: Don Ross, who abandoned the stage at the age of forty-nine to take up novel writing and has been described by *The New York Times* as "what must be one of the most formidable writing factories in this or any other hemisphere," uses Marilyn Ross (for Gothic novels), Rose Dana (for nurse books), Don Roberts (for Westerns), and Alice Gilmer, Ellen Randolph, and Jane Rossiter (for modern novels).

Sometimes, pen names are so well known that a reviewer could write, " 'Jeremy York' rises above his usual level and suggests one of John Creasey's better pseudonyms (perhaps 'Kyle Hunt') in *The Man I Killed.*" This pen name dropper knew, of course, about Mr. Creasey's twelve other pseudonyms, which include Gordon Ashe, J. J. Marric, Anthony Morton, Richard Martin, Robert Caine Frazer, etc. (Perhaps bowing to the inevitable in the case of Mr. Creasey, his publishers noted on the cover of one of his recent books, "A Mystery Novel by John Creasey as Anthony Morton." Another well-known pen name was acknowledged by the publishers in an advertisement of a new Ellery Queen mystery, giving the names of Manfred B. Lee and Fredric Dannay as the writing team behind this pseudonym.)

Often, however, even the critics are surprised by a pen name. "Some years ago I swore off reading all detective stories except those by Michael Innes," began *New York Times* critic Orville Prescott in a review. "Only the other day did I discover that Michael Innes is the pseudonym of J. I. M. Stewart, a distinguished scholar (author of *Character in Shakespeare's Plays* and a volume of the formidable *Oxford History of English Literature*) and also the author of six non-detective novels," continued the dumbfounded Mr. Prescott.

Why all these pen names? Is a pen name a good idea for a new author? There are many valid reasons why pen names are used.

1. Prolific authors sometimes use pen names simply because publishers do not want to flood the book market with many books by the same author in one year. Mr. Creasey, who completes about a dozen books a year, has three hardcover and many paperback publishers sharing his output in the United States. John Dickson Carr uses three names for his books: One publisher brings out his books under the name of John Dickson Carr; another publisher issues his books by "Carter Dickson," a pen name, and occasionally Mr. Carr has used Carr Dickson as another pseudonym. Erle Stanley Gardner writes mysteries for his publisher both under his own name and under his pen name, A. A. Fair. (Pen names are, obviously, especially widely used in the mystery and detective field, where a bonus mystery is sometimes offered to the reader: what is the *real* name of the author?)

2. Authors who have several different specialties sometimes want to use different names for each specialty. Leo C. Rosten uses his real name for serious work, the pen name Leonard Q. Ross for humor (*The Education of H*Y*M*A*N K*A*P*L*A*N*, etc.) and Leonard Ross, without the "Q," for his "melodramas" (he wrote the original story and screenplay for *Walk East on Beacon*). Bernard DeVoto wrote novels, history, and criticism under his own name, light

fiction under the name of John August, and light essays under the name of Cady Hewes. Willard Huntington Wright, who as S. S. Van Dine created the famous detective Philo Vance, noted, when he decided to leave literary criticism and become a writer of detective stories, "I rather feared ostracism if I boldly switched from esthetics and philologic research to fictional sleuthing, and so I hid behind an old family name (Van Dyne) and the Steam-Ship initials." Historical novelist Norah Lofts occasionally uses the pseudonym of Peter Curtis for suspense fiction (*No Question of Murder, The Devil's Own,* etc.).

3. Personal confessions and revelations are sometimes published under pseudonyms. *A Grief Observed,* reflections on the death of the author's wife, was signed N. W. Clerk. This name was a pseudonym for C. S. Lewis (*The Screwtape Letters,* etc.), who felt the book was so personal he should use another name. (The real name of the author was revealed by the newspapers only after Mr. Lewis died.) *The House of Tomorrow,* the diary of an unwed mother, was published under a pen name, as was *American Woman and Alcohol* by a now happily-married member of Alcoholics Anonymous.

4. Sometimes, an assumed name has already been used for other purposes. Rebecca West (author of *The Meaning of Treason,* etc.) was born Cicily Isabel Fairfield; when she began a brief stage career, she took as a stage name Rebecca West, the name of a woman in Ibsen's play *Rosmersholm,* and then used it as a pen name when she turned to writing.

5. A doctor, lawyer, or other professional person might use a pen name for non-professional writing to keep his two spheres of activity separate. Michigan Supreme Court Justice John Donaldson Voelker, especially well known for his bestselling *Anatomy of a Murder,* writes his novels under the pseudonym of Robert Traver. Sir Anthony Hope Hawkins wrote all of his books, including the famed *Prisoner of Zenda,* using his first and middle names as a pen name, Anthony Hope. Although he later regretted the pen name, he had decided to use it when he was a successful barrister and expected to continue his career as a lawyer. When *New York Times* art critic John Caraday was teaching art at the University of Virginia some

years ago, he wrote seven mystery novels under the pseudonym of Matthew Head because he wanted to use his own name solely for his art criticism.

6. Authors of non-fiction dealing with shocking or confidential material often do not use their real names because it might be unpleasant or even dangerous for them to do so. (Books by former members of secret organizations, ex-spies, etc., come in this category.) A recently published first novel about college professors and their wives—*Tell the Time to None* by Helen Hudson (a pen name) —might also be mentioned here. Declaring that the use of a pen name in this case "was clearly motivated by prudence," *Time* Magazine explained, " 'Helen Hudson' displays such knowledge of faculty politics . . . that it is obvious she occupies, or once occupied, her own glade in the groves of academe."

7. An author who has a name similar to another author's might use a pen name simply to avoid confusion. John P. Marquand's son decided to write under the name of John Phillips, rather than as John P. Marquand, Jr. Another "Jr." using a pen name is David E. Lilienthal, Jr., son of the former Atomic Energy Commissioner, who as "David Ely" has written two well-reviewed novels: *Seconds* and *The Tour*.

8. Sometimes the sex of an author is concealed by a pseudonym. Charlotte Brontë's *Jane Eyre* first appeared under the pseudonym Currer Bell, and Emily Brontë's *Wuthering Heights* originally was printed under the name Ellis Bell. George Eliot was the famous pen name of Mary Ann Evans, and George Sand the well-known pseudonym of Amandine Aurore Lucie Dupin. These women took pen names primarily because "female authors" were unpopular. Today, many women take pen names (or use initials plus last names) because they are writing sport, western or adventure fiction—and many men will not read such books or stories if they know the authors are women. Mary Grace Chute's popular Sheriff Olsen stories were therefore published under the by-line of M. G. Chute.

9. Pen names are widely used in television today. Sometimes a television playwright will be unhappy about the changes made in his script by other writers, producers, etc., and will therefore ask that

his name be dropped from the credits. But in these days of tapes and films, if a show is repeated and there is no writing credit, the producer does not have to pay a residual fee to the writer. Therefore, for his own protection, the playwright has a pen name registered with the Writers Guild of America. When he takes his real name off the script, his pen name is substituted—and when checks arrive at the Writers Guild office, made out to his pen name, they are forwarded to him. Ernest Kinoy, a former president of the Writers Guild, used B. Chweig on scripts that had been changed; another former Guild president, David Davidson, made use of his middle names, Albert Sanders. As one television playwright put it, "I use a pseudonym to protect my scripts. My name, to me, has value. It's all I've got."

(The Writers Guild of America—East and West—represents professional writers in the fields of radio, television and motion pictures.)

10. Throughout history, pen names have been used for political reasons, and the practice continues today, of course. Baroness Blixen of Rungstedlund, better known as world-famous fiction writer Isak Dinesen, wrote what the Germans considered a harmless Gothic romance during the time that the Nazis occupied Denmark. The book, which actually made use of quite subtle symbolism in presenting a parallel between the fictional villain and the Nazis, was published under the pen name Pierre Andrézel; after the war, the real name of the author was revealed. Frank O'Connor, the Irish short story writer, was born Michael John O'Donovan, and for political reasons assumed his mother's maiden name for his writing.

11. Sometimes, a pen name will be selected because several authors are involved in a collaborative effort, and listing all the names might prove cumbersome. The recent best-seller *Hurry, Sundown*, signed K. B. Gilden, was written by the husband-wife team, Katya and Burt Gilden. Other famous writing teams include Richard Wilson Webb and H. C. Wheeler (who use the names Q. Patrick, Patrick Quentin and Jonathan Stagge for their mystery novels).

12. Some business firms and government organizations do not permit employees to use their own names for writing *not* connected with their work. David Cornwell, who wrote best-selling spy novels

(*The Spy Who Came in From the Cold, The Looking-Glass War*) under the pen name John le Carré, had to use a pseudonym because he served in the British Foreign Office and thus came under Civil Service rules and restrictions. But the air of mystery surrounding Cornwell's experiences was considerably helped by the use of the pen name; even headlines in *The New York Times* after *The Spy* reached the best-seller list announced: SPY AUTHOR SHEDS UNDERCOVER POSE . . . Cornwell (Alias le Carré) Submits to Interrogation.

13. Many writers of juvenile books use pseudonyms (some authors of books for adults want to keep their writing for children quite separate). An astonishing number of pen names in the juvenile field are controlled by The Stratemeyer Syndicate, an organization founded by Edward Stratemeyer when dime novels were being replaced by the pulp magazines. Stratemeyer, who was writing The Rover Boys series under the pen name Arthur M. Winfield, contracted with various writers to turn out books on assignment, under specified pen names, for such popular juvenile series as The Bobbsey Twins, Tom Swift, The Hardy Boys, Nancy Drew, Honey Bunch, etc. In *My Father Was Uncle Wiggily,* Roger Garis describes how his mother and father worked for Stratemeyer: The titles, the pen name, and a sketchy outline were provided by Stratemeyer, and the author did the rest, receiving a flat payment of one hundred dollars for each book. Notes Mr. Garis (who also wrote for Stratemeyer):

> There was, in fact, a practical reason for writing a series under a fictitious name. If the writer died while the series was still continuing, it might be possible to find some other writer to carry it on. But if the author's own name were used, this would be impossible.

The Stratemeyer Syndicate still operates today—impressive evidence of the soundness of this particular use of pen names.

Should a new author use a pen name? In general, it is not advisable, but if a writer has a valid reason for wishing to write under a pen name, he should indicate this to an editor. However, the new author who wants to use a pen name must have excellent reasons for doing so; there are many disadvantages connected with pen names, and these may prove especially troublesome to him.

A major disadvantage is the attitude of editors toward pen names.

Simply put, editors are suspicious of writers who use pen names, and they have good reason for their distrust. Generally, editors feel an author should be proud to have his real name connected with his writing; if he is not, then perhaps the writing should not be published. This same editorial attitude extends even to letters published in a newspaper. Most newspapers will not publish any "Letter to the Editor" unless they know the real name of the author, and, in most instances, they dislike printing letters where the name of the writer must be witheld unless there is a very good reason for this. (Sometimes, the letters as published are *anonymous*—which the new *Random House Dictionary* defines as "without any name acknowledged as that of author. . . ." and sometimes the letters are *pseudonymous*, "bearing a false or fictious name.") A new writer who decides to use a pen name must be prepared to encounter editorial suspicions—and it may prove harder for him to have manuscripts accepted if editors are not in sympathy with his reasons.

Also, the writer using a pen name faces many complications, legal and otherwise. He may run into trouble trying to cash a check made out to his pen name (usually, the procedure here is for the author to endorse the check with his pen name and then his real name, and then deposit the check at a bank where he is known). Since many bankers question whether it is legally possible for an account to be opened for two names for one person, a writer might open an account only under his pen name. However, banks report that often legal troubles arise when an author dies, leaving a bank account under a pen name, and therefore they generally require full disclosure—a written document and means of verification—to be filed with the bank when an account under a pen name is opened.

If an author will be receiving correspondence addressed to him under his pen name, he should either arrange to have his real name appear on envelopes also (pen name, *in care of* real name), or else he should make sure his local post office and his mailman know about the pen name. The Post Office generally follows the rule that name has preference over address, *e.g.* an order addressed to R. H. Macy Company at Times Square in New York City will not be left at Times Square but will be delivered to Macy's at the correct address, Herald Square, New York City. The result may be that if the postal authorities do not know about a pen name, they may not leave a letter at the street address given but may simply return it to the sender.

Pen name complications may occur if an author uses a pseudonym only for writing, and has no bank account, etc., under that name. Certainly an author using a pen name should arrange to have his editor state in writing that his real name and his pen name belong to the same person.

If an author has decided to use a pen name, and his editor has agreed to cooperate, does this mean that the author's real name will remain a secret, known only to the author and the publishing firm? Not at all!

Of course, a copyright may be taken out under a pen name since the current Copyright Act does not forbid it. (The Copyright Office recognizes the common use of pseudonyms, and the standard application form even provides space for their insertion.) A married woman may take out a copyright under her maiden name, and, if proper legal arrangements are made, the copyright may also be taken out by someone designated by the author—for instance, the publisher.

However, many people are interested in bringing to light the real name of an author using a pen name. Reporters will often unearth an author's real name if a book has news value. (For many years the real identity of Mark Epernay, pseudonymous author of *The Mac-Landress Dimension* was not revealed by the publishers, although magazines and newspapers speculated and stated that Epernay was really John Kenneth Galbraith, Harvard economist and former United States Ambassador to India. Confirmation of this was definitely made by *The New York Times,* which explained that Galbraith had made up this pen name from Mark Twain and Epernay, Napoleon III's headquarters during the Franco-Prussian war.) Librarians make an effort find out the real name of an author so that they can assemble all material written by an author in one place in their catalogues, and they will indicate cross-references for the various names. This library practice is, of course, important to any researcher who may not know all the books written by the same author if a pen name has been used. Generally, courts have not considered it a violation of privacy when the real name of an author writing under a pen name is made known.

Is there any procedure an author must take before selecting and using a pen name? Most states do not require any legal steps. However, it would be advisable for the author to make a check of the names of other authors before selecting a name, so that he does not choose a pen name that is similar to the name of another writer. (The easiest way to do this is to check through the card catalogue of a fairly large library.)

Pen names are not protected by copyright. However, the laws relating to unfair competition may often provide protection for pseudonyms.

If an author decides that he must use a pen name, the name he has selected should appear on his manuscript under the story title as a by-line. The author's real name should appear in the upper left-hand corner of the first page of the manuscript, above the address; the pen name might be put in parentheses after the author's real name.

Though the use of a pen name can often cause unpleasant or troublesome complications for an author, there are some pleasant developments that may follow, also. A famous science-fiction writer reports that recently he was given a pile of science-fiction books to review. He was most interested when he discovered that one of the titles he was asked to appraise bore a familiar by-line: his own pen name!

100

MANUSCRIPT PREPARATION
AND SUBMISSION

By Joyce T. Smith

A MANUSCRIPT submitted for publication competes with hundreds of others which cross the editor's desk. It follows that the manuscript which is professional in appearance, easy to read, and is free of careless mistakes is more likely to receive better attention than those which do not meet these requirements. The rules of manuscript preparation are simple, but the writer who wishes to have his manuscript considered seriously by editors should follow them carefully. For the most part, the mechanical requirements for manuscripts are the same for all publishing houses and magazines. Publications which have special style requirements will usually send such information on request.

The basic and most important rule of manuscript preparation is: *The manuscript must be typed, double-spaced, on standard 8½ × 11 white paper, on one side of the page only.* Handwritten manuscripts, however legible, are not welcome.

TYPING

Any type face which is clear and easy to read is acceptable, and the typewriter may be standard or portable, manual or electric. The size of the type is also a matter of preference; either pica type or the smaller elite type is commonly used. Some of the unusual type faces now available on typewriters, while suitable for personal use, tend to become illegible on manuscripts. The type should always be clean, and the ribbon (black) should be in good condition, producing clear, legible type. Margins of one inch to an inch and a half should be left on both sides and at the top and bottom of the page.

Manuscripts should be typed on good white bond paper (8½ × 11).

Weights of 14 lbs., 16 lbs., or even 20 lbs. for short manuscripts, are acceptable. Avoid too thin a paper (onionskin, for example) or a very heavy weight (such as parchment), which are difficult to handle and to read. Remember, too, that paper especially treated for easy erasing is also easily smudged. For making carbon copies, inexpensive "second sheet" paper is available. But whatever paper is used, a writer should always make and keep a carbon copy of every manuscript, since occasionally a manuscript is lost. Copies made by Xerox or similar duplicating processes should not be submitted to an editor, though a writer may make such copies of the original for his own use.

The name and address of the author should be typed in the upper left- or right-hand corner of the first manuscript page. About one-third down the page, the title is typed in capital letters, followed a line or two below by the author's name. Leave a three-line space and begin the text.

Pages should be numbered consecutively in the upper right- or left-hand corner, followed by the author's surname or the title of the manuscript in full or abbreviated form. This helps identify a page that may become separated from the whole manuscript. The first page does not have to be numbered.

Although not essential, the approximate number of words in the manuscript may be typed in the corner of the first page opposite the author's name and address. The figure should be *only approximate,* and may be estimated to the nearest round number by multiplying the average number of words in a line by the average number of lines on a page, and then by multiplying that answer by the number of manuscript pages.

After the manuscript has been typed, the author should read it over carefully, not only for sense and factual errors, but also for typing, spelling, and grammatical errors. If a page has only one or two errors, the corrections may be made neatly in ink by crossing out the whole word and writing it correctly in the space immediately above. Or an omitted word or short phrase may be inserted in the space above, with a slant line or caret to indicate the exact place for the insertion. If lengthy insertions are necessary, the entire page (or sometimes several pages) should be retyped.

Since editors assume factual accuracy as well as correct spelling, punctuation, capitalization, and word usage, a final check of these "mechanics" of writing is essential before you send out your manuscript. Here are a few check points:

Enclose all direct quotations in quotation marks. Quotations within quoted material are indicated by single quotes. All quoted material must appear exactly as originally printed. Whether you are quoting the Bible, Shakespeare, a few lines from a poem that you remember (song lyrics, however brief, *always* require permission for quotation), recheck these before you send your manuscript out; do not rely on your memory.

When quoting material of more than three lines, indent the passage quoted, omit quotation marks except to indicate quoted dialogue, and type it single space. (If you wish to quote copyright material of more than a few words, it is advisable to obtain permission of the copyright owner.)

Dialogue is enclosed in quotation marks, with the words of each new speaker beginning a new paragraph.

Italics to indicate emphasis should be used sparingly for maximum effect, but there are some "rules" for italicizing. Book and play titles names of magazines and newspapers, and foreign words are generally italicized. (Titles of short stories, essays, poems, and other parts of books or longer works are enclosed in quotation marks.)

The pages of short manuscripts should be fastened with a paper clip. Do not pin, tie, bind, or staple the pages together in any other way. The pages of a book manuscript should be left loose and mailed in a box.

Book manuscripts

Follow general rules for manuscript preparation, and also include a title page (not required for short manuscripts) on which the title is typed in capital letters about half-way down the page. On the line immediately below type the word "By" and your name. The entire manuscript should be numbered consecutively from the first page to the last. (Do not number the pages of the individual chapters separately.) Begin each new chapter on a new page, typing the chapter number and chapter title (if any) about three inches from the top. Leave two or three spaces and then proceed with the text.

Sometimes the question of illustrations arises, especially in writing children's books. Most publishers assign artists after the manuscript is accepted. If the author has collaborated with an artist, then, of course, the text and sample illustrations may be submitted together. Similarly, if the author is also the artist, it is not advisable to submit *complete*, original illustrations, unless the publishers request you to do so.

SHORT ITEMS

Type poetry double-spaced, leaving three or four spaces between stanzas. Begin each new poem—no matter what its length—on a separate page, putting your name and address at the top right of each.

Fillers are also typed double-spaced, one to a page, with your name and address on each, and for fact fillers the source should be indicated. Because of the volume of manuscripts received, many magazines do not acknowledge or return fillers, but the author may assume that if he has not heard in three months, he may offer it for sale again.

Greeting card publishers sometimes have special specifications for the submission of verses or ideas, i.e., ideas should be submitted on 3 × 5 cards, one idea to a card, etc. Requirements for art work also vary greatly, and prospective contributors should check directly with the companies and should study manuscript market lists.

PLAY AND TELEVISION SCRIPTS

In typing dramatic material for the stage or for television, you must follow a special format. Specifications and illustrations for television scripts may be found in Chapter 93, "Television Writing Today." There are two commonly used styles in typing plays: (a) Type the names of the characters in capital letters at the left margin, followed by the dialogue in upper and lower case; (b) Type names of characters in capital letters at center of page. On next line, begin the speech at the left margin, in upper and lower case.

FOOTNOTES

Research publications and other scholarly works may require footnotes and bibliographies, and in typing these manuscripts, writers should follow standard accepted forms as given in the widely accepted reference manual, *A Manual of Style* (University of Chicago Press).

If the manuscript requires footnotes, type these in the body of the manuscript, immediately after the line to which the note refers, using a raised number or a symbol such as an asterisk in the text and correspondingly at the beginning of the footnote. Footnotes more than one line long should be typed single-space and set off from the text by a rule above and below it.

QUERY LETTERS

Before you submit a complete nonfiction manuscript—either article or book length—it is advisable to send a brief query letter to the editor describing the proposed article or book. The letter should also include information about the author's special qualifications for dealing with the particular subject, and for a book-length manuscript, an outline of the book and a sample chapter may be included. Otherwise, no covering letter is necessary when submitting a manuscript, though the writer may include a brief note simply indicating that the manuscript is submitted for possible publication. No amount of self-praise will bring about a sale if the manuscript is unsuitable, nor will the absence of a letter discourage an editor from accepting it. If you are submitting a manuscript following a positive response to your query letter, you may indicate this fact in a brief note accompanying it. For book manuscripts, a letter is often sent separately, stating that the manuscript has been mailed under separate cover.

REPORTS ON MANUSCRIPTS

Monthly or weekly magazines, as well as large publishing houses, may take several weeks—and often longer—to read and report on manuscripts. For bi-monthlies, quarterlies, some literary magazines, and small publishing houses with limited editorial staffs, two or more months may elapse before reports are made to authors.

If you have had no report on a manuscript after a reasonable time —six to eight weeks for a large company—you may write a brief, courteous letter inquiring about the status of your manuscript.

To save time and postage—and to approach the business of marketing manuscripts in a professional way—it is essential for free-lance writers to study editorial requirements of various publications as described in market lists and by examining the publications themselves. Read several issues of any magazine to which you may wish to submit material. Familiarize yourself with the types of books published by various publishers by browsing in a library or bookshop, and by watching their advertising.

It is common practice to submit a manuscript to only one publisher at a time. Although this may seem unfair and time-consuming, it is the only way to avoid the difficulties that may arise if, for example, two editors wish to buy the same manuscript. The same practice also applies to writing query letters—send only *one at a time*.

When submitting a manuscript, address it to the editor by name, if you know it, or to the editor of the particular part of the magazine— Fiction Editor, Articles Editor, Features Editor, etc., also by name, if possible, otherwise by title. The same is true for book publishers: Address your manuscript to the editor in charge of the particular division for which your book is suited: Juvenile Editor, Religious Editor, etc.

RIGHTS

As a rule, a writer submitting a manuscript to a magazine should not stipulate on his manuscript or in an accompanying letter what rights he is offering. Although most magazines buy only "First North American Serial Rights," some publications buy *all* rights as a matter of policy. It is therefore best to discuss what rights the magazine is interested in—and what limitations the writer may wish to set— *after* a manuscript is accepted.

First North American serial rights means that a magazine is buying the exclusive right to publish the material for the first time and only once. Purchase of *second serial rights* gives the magazine the right to reprint the material once after its original publication— twice in all. Some magazines buy *all periodical rights,* that is, the exclusive right to print and reprint the material here and abroad in magazine form. Generally, magazines buy only periodical rights, and all further rights—for television, motion pictures, book use, etc., belong to the author.

Books are handled quite differently, and if your book manuscript is accepted, you will receive a contract from the publishers outlining carefully the rights they are buying and those the author retains. These contracts are fairly standard throughout the industry, and writers may have confidence in the good faith of any reputable publishing company. When a writer has established an important reputation and achieved prestige and success, he may (directly or through his agent) be justified in negotiating with the publishers for higher royalties and other more liberal terms which he may want (and will often be able to arrange with the book or magazine publishers).

MAILING

Short manuscripts should be mailed flat in Manila envelopes. If the manuscript is only 3 or 4 pages in length, it may be folded twice, and sent in an ordinary long (#10) envelope. Book manuscripts should be sent loose, in a cardboard box, such as the kind typing paper comes in.

Under present postal regulations, manuscripts for books and periodicals may be mailed at the regular first-class mail rate, or, less expensively, by the Special Fourth Class Rate for Manuscripts; ask at your Post Office for this rate. Manuscripts or boxes sent by this rate must be marked Special Fourth Class Rate—Manuscript. If you wish to include a letter with a manuscript sent via the Special Fourth Class Rate, you may do so, provided you note on the outside of the box or envelope that first-class material is enclosed, and that you place additional first-class postage on the package.

Manuscripts sent at the Special Fourth Class Rate may also be insured at the post office.

A stamped self-addressed return envelope should always be enclosed when a manuscript is submitted to a publisher, in case the manuscript is rejected. If you are using the Special Fourth Class Rate, be sure that the return envelope is marked Special Fourth Class Rate—Manuscript.

PART IV

THE WRITER'S MARKETS

Where to Sell

This section of THE WRITER'S HANDBOOK is devoted to manuscript market information that will help writers sell their manuscripts. All information concerning the needs and requirements of markets comes directly from the editors of the periodicals, publishing companies, and television programs listed.

Although we have taken every precaution to have the information accurate, there will undoubtedly be some changes in the requirements listed as the needs of editors change from time to time. Therefore writers are advised to study recent issues of a publication before submitting any manuscripts to it. New magazines and television programs should always be checked carefully, since frequent changes occur in these markets.

FICTION MARKETS

This list is divided into three categories: general magazines; college, literary and little magazines; religious and denominational magazines. See *The Popular Market* for men's adventure fiction, confession stories, science fiction, mystery, western magazines. Juvenile fiction markets are listed under *Juvenile, Teen-Age and Young Adult Magazines*, and markets for book-length adult and juvenile fiction manuscripts are listed under *Book Publishers*.

GENERAL MAGAZINES

ADAM–8060 Melrose Ave., Los Angeles, CA 90046. Carlton Hollander, Editor.
 Hard-hitting, topical fiction, 1,000 to 3,000 words. Pays $50 to $150, on publication.

ALFRED HITCHCOCK'S MYSTERY MAGAZINE–850 Third Ave., New York, NY 10022.
 Original, well-written, well-plotted, plausible mystery, suspense, and crime stories, 1,000 to 10,000 words. No cheap sensationalism or actual crimes. Pays 5¢ a word, on acceptance.

AMA NEWS–American Motorcycle Association, Box 141, Westerville, OH 43051.
 Short fiction dealing with the positive aspects of motorcycling. Pays $1 per inch, on publication.

AMERICAN ART ENTERPRISES, INC.–21322 Lassen St., Chatsworth, CA 91311. George Bemos, Manuscript Editor.
 Fiction, 2,000 to 3,000 words, of interest to men: action-packed, with strong male-female relationships, eroticism, physical contact. Pays from $75.

THE AMERICAN SCANDINAVIAN REVIEW–127 East 73rd St., New York, NY 10021. Erik J. Friis, Editor.
 Short stories, 2,000 to 3,000 words, about Scandinavia. Photos and drawings. Pays $20 to $50.

ARGOSY–420 Lexington Ave., New York, NY 10017. Bert Randolph Sugar, Editor-in-Chief.
 Fiction, 3,000 to 5,000 words, with male viewpoint; condensed novels, 25,000 words. Pays $400 and up.

THE ATLANTIC ADVOCATE–Gleaner Bldg., Phoenix Sq., Fredericton, N. B., Canada.
 Not in the market for fiction at present time.

THE ATLANTIC MONTHLY–8 Arlington St., Boston, MA 02116. Robert Manning, Editor.
 One or two short stories an issue. High literary standards, considerable variety. Occasional stories up to 14,000 words. Pays on acceptance.

BLACK WORLD–820 South Michigan Ave., Chicago, IL 60605. Hoyt W. Fuller, Executive Editor.
 Short stories, to 3,900 words, on black life. Humorous stories particularly welcome. Pays about $100, on publication.

BOY'S LIFE–New Brunswick, NJ 08902. Robert E. Hood, Editor.
 For boys 10 to 17. Short fiction, 2,500 to 3,200 words, and short shorts 1,000 words, with strong plot and characterization, conflict, action, humor, or suspense. Pays from $350. Send for writer's guide.

BROADSIDE—21322 Lassen Street, Chatsworth, CA 91311. Arthur S. Long, Editor.
Strongly plotted fiction, 2,000 to 3,000 words, for men, centered on male-female relationships, eroticism, physical conflict, with adventurous action or sophisticated story line. Contemporary plots involving swinging, group sex, new life-styles, the drug scene. Welcomes short humor, to 2,000 words. Pays $85 and up, on acceptance.

CATS MAGAZINE—P.O. Box 4106, Pittsburgh, PA 15202. Jean Laux, Editor.
Some fiction about cats and their owners, 1,500 words. Photos or sketches when possible. "No fiction by feline writers." Pays 3¢ a word, on publication.

CAVALIER—316 Aragon Ave., Coral Gables, FL 33134.
Quality fiction, to 6,000 words, for young male readership with sophisticated and informed tastes. Pays up to $300, on publication.

CHATELAINE—481 University Ave., Toronto M5W 1AF, Ont., Canada. Doris Anderson, Editor; Almeda Glassey, Fiction Editor.
Fiction, 3,000 to 4,000 words, for women: social and human relations themes in modern women's lives and relationships; adventure family, some romance. Pays $400 and up.

CO-ED—Scholastic Magazines, Inc., 50 West 44th St., New York, NY 10036. Address Features Dept.
Stories up to 5,000 words for girls, 14 to 18, on problems of contemporary teen-agers: family, love, personal relationships, boy-girl situations. Humor welcome. Prefers fall, winter and spring rather than summer settings. Pays good rates, on acceptance.

COMMENTARY—165 East 56th St., New York, NY 10022. Norman Podhoretz, Editor.
Fiction of literary excellence, may have concrete social reference or Jewish interest. Pays about 7¢ a word, on publication.

THE COMPASS—Mobil Sales and Supply Corp., 150 East 42nd St., New York, NY 10017. R. G. MacKenzie, Editor.
Short stories and articles on the sea and deep sea trade, to 3,500 words. Pays up to $250. Query a must.

COSMOPOLITAN—224 West 57th St., New York, NY 10019. Helen Gurley Brown, Editor. Harris Dienstfrey, Fiction Editor.
Short-shorts, 1,500 to 3,000 words; short stories, 5,000 to 6,000 words, mystery novels and other condensed books, 30,000 words. Must have solid plot, sharp characterization, focus on man-woman relationship. Pays $1000 for short stories, $300 to $600 for short-shorts.

DELL CROSSWORD PUZZLES—245 East 47 St., New York, NY 10017. Kathleen Rafferty, Editor.
Short mysteries, 500 words, with clues so reader can figure out solution through general knowledge. Pays $25, on acceptance. Highly specialized needs, study publications before submitting.

THE ELKS MAGAZINE—425 West Diversey Parkway, Chicago, IL 60614. D. J. Herda, Articles Editor.
Short, humorous fiction of high quality and suitable for family reading. Also, mystery, suspense, detective stories. Send for sample copies. Payment $100 to $300, depending on length.

ELLERY QUEEN'S MYSTERY MAGAZINE—229 Park Ave. South, New York, NY 10003. Ellery Queen, Editor, Eleanor Sullivan, Managing Editor.
Quality detective, crime, mystery and spy fiction, 4,000 to 6,000 words. Needs suspense stories or straight detection. Pays 3¢ to 8¢ a word, on acceptance.

ESQUIRE—488 Madison Ave., New York, NY 10022. Don Erickson, Editor.
No longer considers unsolicited fiction manuscripts. Depends chiefly on solicited contributions and materials from literary agencies. Does not return manuscripts sent without stamped, self-addressed envelopes. Query letters only.

ESSENCE—300 East 42nd St., New York, NY 10017.
"The quality magazine for today's black woman." Query.

EXPLORING—Boy Scouts of America, North Brunswick, NJ 08902. Dick Pryce, Editor.
Published for coed Exploring Division of Boy Scouts, ages 15 to 20. Short stories, up to 2,500 words. Pays $300 to $500 on acceptance. Query.

FAMILY CIRCLE—488 Madison Ave., New York, NY 10022. Myrna Blyth, Fiction Editor.
Short stories of interest to women, 2,500 to 4,000 words, and short-shorts. Pays on acceptance.

FIELD & STREAM—383 Madison Ave., New York, NY 10017. Jack Samson, Editor.
Rarely uses fiction, but should be related to outdoor topics. Pays 20¢ a word, and up, on acceptance.

FLING—1485 Bayshore Blvd., Suite 400, San Francisco, CA 94124.
Fiction for adult male readers: serious stories examining off-beat relationships between the sexes, from 2,000 to 3,500 words; up-beat, humorous or satirical stories, 2,000 to 3,000 words. Sharp, contemporary dialogue important. Pays from $75 to $200.

GALLERY—116 East 27th St., New York, NY 10016. Joe Kelleher, Editor.
Fiction, to 4,000 words, to interest men. Pays $75 to $150 per 1,000 words, on publication.

GEM—303 West 42nd St., New York, NY 10036. Will Martin, Editor.
Contemporary, sex-related fiction, 500 to 1,500 words. Pays from $35 to $50, after acceptance. Same address and requirements for *The Swinger.*

GENESIS—120 East 56th St., New York, NY 10022. Eric Protter, Editor.
Fiction, 3,000 to 6,000 words, for men. Pays $350 and up.

GIRLTALK—380 Madison Ave., New York, NY 10017.
In the market for fiction, of interest to women, 2,000 words or less. Pays varying rates.

GLAMOUR—Conde Nast Building, 350 Madison Avenue, New York, NY 10017. Ruth Whitney, Editor-in-Chief; Phyllis Starr Wilson, Managing Editor.
Occasional quality fiction. Pays $750.

GOLF DIGEST—297 Westport Ave., Norwalk, CT 06856. Nick Seitz, Editor.
Unusual or humorous stories about golf, up to 2,000 words. Also golf "fables," 750 to 1,000 words. Pays from 20¢ per published word.

GOOD HOUSEKEEPING—959 Eighth Ave., New York, NY 10019. Naome Lewis, Fiction Editor.
"Attempting to be selective in processing unsolicited manuscripts. Some manuscripts are being returned unread. The beginner with a demonstrable talent and the experienced writer can be confident of being reviewed, however." Short stories, 2,000 to 1.000 words: serials: short-shorts. Pays top rates, on acceptance.

HARLEQUIN'S WOMAN–Harlequin Enterprises, Ltd., 240 Duncan Mill Rd., Suite 605, Don Mills, Ont., Canada M3B 1Z4. Beth McGregor, Editor.
Short stories and romances, 3,000 to 5,000 words. Pays varying rates, on acceptance.

HARPER'S BAZAAR–717 Fifth Ave., New York, NY 10022. Anthony T. Mazzola, Editor-in-Chief.
No unsolicited manuscripts accepted.

HUGHES RIGWAY–Hughes Tool Company, P.O. Box 2539, Houston, TX 77001. Address Tom Haynes.
Top-quality fiction, 2,000 to 2,500 words, in oilfield settings. Also character-revealing historical narratives about little-known incidents, heroes, or facts, of interest to oil and gas drilling personnel. Pays 10¢ per word, on acceptance. Reports in three weeks.

KNIGHT–Publisher's Service, Inc., 8060 Melrose Ave., Los Angeles, CA 90046. Jared Rutter, Editor.
Erotic fiction for men and women. Pays $60 to $300, on publication.

LADIES' HOME JOURNAL–641 Lexington Ave., New York, NY 10022.
Limited market. "We publish only first-rate fiction with which our readers can identify. Books, articles, and short stories are usually bought through recognized literary agents."

THE LADY GOLFER–P.O. Box 4725, Whittier, CA 90607. Charles G. Schoos, General Manager.
Golf-related fiction, 500 to 3,000 words. Pays $50 and up, on acceptance.

McCALL'S–230 Park Ave., New York, NY 10017. Helen DelMonte Fiction Editor.
Strong, memorable fiction (short stories, around 3,000 words, short-shorts, novel excerpts) that has depth, will make reader think, feel and respond. Pays top rates.

MADEMOISELLE–350 Madison Avenue, New York, NY 10017. Ellen A. Stoianoff, Fiction and Poetry Editor.
Non-formula short stories; accent on literary quality, 2,500 to 6,500 words. Pays from $300, on acceptance. Quality poems under 65 lines; payment from $25, on acceptance.

MAN TO MAN–280 Madison Ave., New York, NY 10016. Everett Meyers, Editor.
Strong, imaginative stories, 1,500 to 5,000 words, in modern mood, including man-woman relationship. No hackneyed, dull writing. Pays $75 and up, on publication. Same address and requirements for *Mr. Magazine* and *Sir!*

MIDSTREAM: A MONTHLY JEWISH REVIEW–515 Park Ave., New York, NY 10022. Ronald Sanders, Editor.
Fiction, to 8,000 words, of Jewish or general social and political interest. Pays 6¢ a word, on acceptance.

MIKE SHAYNE MYSTERY MAGAZINE–Renown Publications, 8230 Beverly Blvd., Los Angeles, CA 90048. Leo Margulies, Publisher. Cylvia Kleinman, Editor.
Good detective and mystery stories: 1,500-word short stories to 12,000-word novelettes. Pays 1¢ a word and up, on acceptance.

MR. MAGAZINE–See *Man to Man.*

MODERN MATURITY–215 Long Beach Blvd., Long Beach, CA 90801. Hubert Pryor, Editor.
Some short stories appealing to older readers. Pays from $50 to $500, on acceptance.

MS. MAGAZINE–370 Lexington Ave., New York, NY 10017. Address Fiction Manuscript Editor.
Fiction on topics relevant to women as people, not stereotypes. Pays top rates.

NRTA JOURNAL—215 Long Beach Blvd., Long Beach, CA 90801. Hubert C. Pryor, Editor.
Magazine of National Retired Teachers Association. Short stories, 500 to 2,500 words. Pays $50 to $500. Sample copy available.

THE NEW YORKER—25 West 43rd St., New York, NY 10036.
Short stories, 1,000 to 6,000 words. Humor and satire. Pays on acceptance.

OUI—Playboy Publications, Inc., 919 North Michigan Ave., Chicago, IL 60611.
For men 18 to 30. Short stories, 2,500 to 3,000 words. Pays from $500.

PENTHOUSE—909 Third Ave., New York, NY 10022. Gerard Van der Leun, Fiction Editor.
Sophisticated, sexy fiction, 3,000 to 5,000 words, on contemporary themes. Pays to 25¢ a word, after acceptance.

PLAYBOY—919 North Michigan Ave., Chicago, IL 60611. Hugh M. Hefner, Editor and Publisher. Robie Macauley, Fiction Editor.
Sophisticated, well-constructed fiction, 1,000 to 10,000 words. Strong plots and colorful writing important. Humorous fiction welcome. Serialized novels and novel excerpts published occasionally, but must be submitted through an agent. No poetry or plays. Pays $3,000 for lead stories, $2,000 standards, $1,000 for short, on acceptance. $1,000 bonuses for best story of year, best first appearance, and best longer work.

PLAYERS—8060 Melrose Ave., Los Angeles, CA 90046. Joe Nazel, Editor.
Fiction, 2,000 to 6,000 words, for black men. Pays from 5¢ a word, on publication.

PLAYGIRL—1801 Century Park East, Suite 2300, Los Angeles, CA 90067. Betty Ulius, Fiction Editor.
Fiction, 1,500 to 5,000 words, for today's woman, which explores complex relationship between the sexes: suspense adventure, humor, or romance. Pays from about $600, after acceptance.

POWDER—P.O. Box 359, Sun Valley, ID 83353.
Fiction, 800 to 1,500 words, on all aspects of the ski experience, including adventure and humor. Pays $25 to $100, on acceptance.

REDBOOK—230 Park Ave., New York, NY 10017. Anne Mollegen Smith, Fiction Editor.
Fresh, distinctive, intelligent stories for young married women. Welcomes unknown writers and unexpected themes, but always needs stories on basic themes of young couples, young parenthood. Literary quality and raised consciousness concerning women are both musts. Pays on acceptance, from $850 for short-shorts (1,800 words), $1,000 for short stories (about 5,000 words), $3,000 and up for novellas (12,000 to 25,000 words), and $7,500 for novels. Takes up to six weeks to read and report on manuscripts.

THE SATURDAY EVENING POST—1100 Waterway Blvd., Indianapolis, IN 46202. Address Fiction Editor.
Stories with structure, action, plot, character, 1,000 to 3,500 words, that lend themselves to illustration. No stream-of-consciousness writing. Payment determined by quality and length.

SCHOLASTIC SCOPE—Scholastic Magazines, Inc., 50 West 44th St., New York, NY 10036. Katherine Robinson, Editor.
Stories, 500 to 1,000 words for ages 15 to 18 with 4th to 6th grade reading level, dealing with interests of today's students, relationships between people, in family, job, school situations. Pays good rates, on acceptance.

SEVENTEEN—850 Third Ave., New York, NY 10022. Babette Rosmund, Fiction Editor.
Well-written fiction, adult in techniques and conception, but limited to situations involving adolescent experiences. Pays good rates, on acceptance.

SIR!—See *Man to Man.*

STAG—575 Madison Ave., New York, NY 10022. Noah Sarlat, Editor.
Fiction appealing to men, to 5,000 words, with strong sex element. Pays up to $350, on acceptance.

SUNSHINE MAGAZINE—Litchfield, IL 62506.
Wholesome, well-written short stories, to 1,250 words, with clearly defined plot and purpose, but with "moral" or lesson well concealed. Payment varies, on acceptance. Study magazine before submitting.

SURFER MAGAZINE—Box 1028, Dana Point, CA 92629. Steve Pezman, Editor.
Good, well-plotted fiction, 1,000 to 2,500 words, with authentic surfing theme. Pays 4¢ a word and up, on publication.

SWANK—717 Fifth Ave., New York, NY 10022.
Adventure, science fiction, 2,500, for blue-collar men. Pays to 5¢ a word. Query.

SWINGER—See *Gem.*

TEEN MAGAZINE—8831 Sunset Blvd., Los Angeles, CA 90069. Roxanne Cameron, Editor.
Fiction, 2,500 to 4,000 words, or 6,000-word two-part serials, depicting today's teen-age girl: mysteries, travel, adventure, humor, romance, social problems, etc. Pays $100 and up, on acceptance.

TENNIS ILLUSTRATED—630 Shatto Pl., Los Angeles, CA 90005. Gay Yellen, Editor.
Light fiction, to 1,000 words, on tennis. Pays 10¢ a word, on publication.

TODAY'S FAMILY—P.O. Box 31467, Dallas, TX 75231. Sherry Gish, Editor.
Fiction, with general family appeal, up to 3,000 words, but shorter preferred. Include word count with submissions. No multiple submissions or xeroxed manuscripts. Pays up to $50 the 28th of the month of issue. Enclose stamped, self-addressed envelope with all manuscripts and queries. Reports promptly.

TODAY'S SECRETARY—1221 Ave. of the Americas, New York, NY 10020. Ann Roberts, Editor.
Short, lively fiction, 800 to 1,000 words, with good story line. Wholesome subjects, settings. Pays $50, on acceptance.

VOGUE—420 Lexington Ave., New York, NY 10017. Grace Mirabella, Editor.
Rarely uses fiction and then only if high literary quality. Preferred length: about 2,000 words. Pays on acceptance. Send manuscripts to Leo Lerman, Consulting Feature Editor.

THE WESTERN PRODUCER—Box 2500, Saskatoon, Sask., Canada. R. H. D. Phillips, Editor.
Short stories, up to 2,500 words, on Western Canadian subjects, to interest intelligent farm and rural readers. Pays up to $75 a page, on acceptance.

WOMAN'S DAY—1515 Broadway, New York, NY 10036. Eileen Herbert Jordan, Fiction and Books Editor.
Quality short fiction, both humorous and serious. Pays top rates, on acceptance.

WOODMEN OF THE WORLD MAGAZINE—1700 Farnam St., Omaha, NE 68102.
Leland A. Larson, Editor.
Family-oriented fiction. Pays 2¢ a word, on acceptance.

YANKEE—Dublin, NH 03444. Judson Hale, Editor.
Fiction set in New England locale, not over 2,500 words. Pays $300 to $500.

COLLEGE, LITERARY AND LITTLE MAGAZINES

ALDEBARAN—Roger Williams College, Bristol, RI 02809. Lou Papineau, Editor.
Short stories, up to ten pages. Also excerpts from stories, novels. Include stamped,
self-addressed envelope. Pays in copies.

THE AMERICAN REVIEW—Bantam Books, 666 Fifth Ave., New York, NY 10019.
Theodore Solotaroff, Editor.
High-quality, contemporary fiction with fresh, articulate writing and thought. Buys
first rights only. Manuscripts must be accompanied by stamped return envelope.

THE ANTIGONISH REVIEW—St. Francis Xavier University, Antigonish, N. S., Canada.
R. J. MacSween, Editor.
Short stories, 1,800 to 2,500 words.

ANTIOCH REVIEW—P.O. Box 148, Yellow Springs, OH 45387. Paul Bixler, Editor.
Quality fiction, 2,000 to 6,000 words. Pays $8 per printed page, on publication.

APHRA—Box 893, Ansonia Station, New York, NY 10023.
Short stories, up to 6,000 words, with feminist orientation. Study magazine carefully
for special slant. Pays in copies.

ARARAT—628 Second Ave., New York, NY 10016. Leo Hamalian, Editor.
Publication of the Armenian General Benevolent Union of America. Short stories,
1,000 to 5,000 words, on Armenian experience in America. Pays $30 to $50, on
publication.

ARIZONA QUARTERLY—University of Arizona, Tucson, AZ 85721. Albert F.
Gegenheimer, Editor.
Fiction up to 3,500 words. No payment. Annual awards.

THE ARK RIVER REVIEW—911 Lombard St., Philadelphia, PA 19147. Jonathan Katz,
Editor.
Short fiction. Pays $3 per page. Annual awards.

ASIA CALLING—845 Via de la Paz, Pacific Palisades, CA 90272. Mary Ellen Hawk
Saunders, Editor.
Adult fiction, 500 to 2,000 words, from and about the Orient—especially China,
Korea, India, Japan. No payment.

BACHY—Papa Bach Bookstore, 11317 Santa Monica Blvd., West Los Angeles, CA
90025.
Serious fiction. Pays $2 per page on publication.

BALL STATE UNIVERSITY FORUM—Ball State University, Muncie, IN 47306. Merrill
Rippy and Frances Mayhew Rippy, Editors.
Short stories, 500 to 4,000 words. Pays in copies.

THE BERKELEY BARB—Box 1247, Berkeley, CA 94701. Jim Schreiber, Managing
Editor.
Short, biting, satirical fiction, on current events, 50 to 1,000 words. Pays 50¢ per
column inch, on publication.

BEYOND BAROQUE–1639 West Washington Blvd., Venice, CA 90291.
Experimental fiction, to 7,500 words.

BLACK MARIA: WOMEN SPEAK–815 West Wrightwood Ave., Chicago, IL 60614.
Pro-women short stories, experimental fiction, to 3,500 words. Pays in copies. Study magazine before submitting.

BLACK TIMES: VOICES OF THE NATIONAL COMMUNITY–Box 10246, Palo Alto, CA 94303. Frank Lee Downe, Fiction Editor.
Fiction, to 4,000 words, which celebrates efforts and achievements of individuals and groups in black America. Pays in copies. Study magazine before submitting.

BOSTON UNIVERSITY JOURNAL–775 Commonwealth Avenue, Boston, MA 02215.
High-quality fiction, 2,500 to 6,000 words. Pays in copies.

BOUNDARY 2–SUNY-Binghamton, Binghamton, NY 13901.
Journal of postmodern literature. Short stories, sections from longer fictional works, criticism of contemporary literature, any length. Prefers "experimental work which is working against the 'early modern' grain."

THE CALIFORNIA QUARTERLY–100 Sproul Hall, University of California, Davis, CA 95616. Elliot L. Gilbert, Editor.
Fiction, under 8,000 words. Black-and-white graphics. Pays in copies and subscriptions, on publication.

THE CANADIAN FICTION MAGAZINE–Box 46422, Station G, Vancouver, B.C. V6R 4G7, Canada.
Fiction, to 5,000 words: novel excerpts, short stories, experimental fiction. Pays $3 per page, on publication.

THE CARLETON MISCELLANY–Carleton College, Northfield, MN 55057. Wayne Carver, Editor.
Literary short stories "in which something interesting happens." Pays on publication. Reports in 4 to 6 weeks.

CAROLINA QUARTERLY–Box 1117, Chapel Hill, NC 27514. Jeff Richards, Editor.
Innovative, well-crafted short fiction, to 8,000 words, by young writers, as well as new work by more established writers. Excerpts from longer works are considered. Pays $3 per printed page. Address Fiction Editor, and enclose stamped, self-addressed envelope.

CHELSEA–Box 5880, Grand Central Station, New York, NY 10017.
Original and translated stories. Pays in copies.

THE CHICAGO REVIEW–University of Chicago, Chicago, IL 60637. Thomas Joyce, Editor.
Well-written fiction, traditional or experimental. No length requirements.

CIMARRON REVIEW–Oklahoma State University, Stillwater, OK 74074. Jeanne Adams Wray, Managing Editor.
Fiction of high quality on contemporary life. Pays in copies.

THE COE REVIEW–G.M.U. Box 328, 1220 First Ave., Cedar Rapids, IA 52402. Mike Magrath, Editor.
High quality fiction. Pays in copies.

THE COLORADO QUARTERLY–Hellems 134, University of Colorado, Boulder, CO 80302. Paul Carter, Editor.
Quality fiction, 2,000 to 4,000 words.

CONFRONTATION–English Dept., Long Island University, Brooklyn, NY 11201. Martin Tucker, Editor.
High-quality fiction of all types, 750 to 6,000 words. Pays on publication. Reports in six weeks.

DASEIN–G.P.O. Box 2121, New York, NY 10001. Percy Johnston, Editor.
Fiction of high quality, 2,000 to 3,000 words. Drawings and photos.

THE DeKALB LITERARY ARTS JOURNAL–DeKalb College, 555 Indian Creek Drive, Clarkston, GA 30021.
Fiction of any length. Pays in copies.

DESCANT–Texas Christian University, T.C.U. Sta., Fort Worth, TX 76129. Betsy Colquitt, Editor.
Fiction, to 6,000 words. Pays in copies.

EPOCH–245 Goldwin Smith Hall, Cornell University, Ithaca, NY 14850.
Fiction of high literary quality. Pays in copies.

EVENT–Dept. of English, Douglas College, Box 2503, New Westminster, B.C., Canada. Robert W. Lowe, Editor.
Short stories, novellas, any length. Photography, graphics. Token payment after publication.

THE FALCON–Belknap Hall, Mansfield State College, Mansfield, PA 16933. T. E. Porter, Fiction Editor.
Contemporary short stories and excerpts from novels, 2,000 to 6,000 words; originality essential. Pays in copies. Usually reports within 30 days.

FICTION–English Dept., C.C.N.Y., Convent Ave., and 138th St., New York, NY 10031. Mark J. Mirsky, Editor,
High-quality, serious fiction.

FICTION INTERNATIONAL–Dept. of English, St. Lawrence University, Canton, NY 13617. Joe David Bellamy, Editor and Publisher.
Especially receptive to innovative forms or rich personal styles, originality, and the ability to create living characters. Any length. Pays $25 to $150. Usually reports in less than two months.

THE FIDDLEHEAD–Dept. of English, University of New Brunswick, Fredericton, N.B., Canada.
High quality fiction, 2,500 words. Pays about $5 per published page, on publication. Strong Canadian preference.

FOLIO–Box 31111, Birmingham, AL 35222.
Short fiction and poetry. Pays in copies.

FORUM–University of Houston, Houston, TX 77004. Dr. William L. Pryor, Editor.
Literary short stories of moderate length. Pays in copies.

FOUR QUARTERS–LaSalle College, Philadelphia, PA 19141. John Keenan, Editor.
Character-centered stories that offer some revelation. No slicks. Pays up to $25, on publication.

THE GAR–Box 4793, Austin, TX 78765. Hal Wylie and Carolyn Cates Wylie, Editors.
Short stories; photos and drawings. Pays in copies.

THE GEORGIA REVIEW–University of Georgia, Athens, GA 30602. John T. Irwin, Editor.
Short fiction. Pays on publication.

GREEN RIVER REVIEW–c/o Raymond Tyner, Editor, Box 56, University Center, MI 48710.
Short stories, to 3,000 words. Pays in copies.

THE GREENFIELD REVIEW–Greenfield Center, NY 12833. Joseph Bruchac III Editor.
Some very short fiction. Pays in copies.

GREEN'S MAGAZINE–P.O. Box 313, Detroit, MI 48231.
Fiction, 1,500 to 4,000 words, and some short poetry. Pays $3 to $25 on publication. Stamped, self-addressed envelope required.

THE GREENSBORO REVIEW–University of North Carolina, Greensboro, NC 27412.
Fiction, to 5,000 words. Pays in copies.

HAWAII REVIEW–2465 Campus Rd., University of Hawaii, Honolulu, Hawaii 96822. Ms. Chris Cooke, Editor.
Fiction, 1,400 to 5,200 words. Pays $30 per short story, on publication.

HUDSON REVIEW–65 East 55th St., New York, NY 10022. Frederick Morgan, Editor.
Quality fiction up to 10,000 words. Pays 2½¢ a word.

HUDSON RIVER ANTHOLOGY–Vassar College, Poughkeepsie, NY 12601.
Poetry and fiction to reflect and encourage literary trends in Hudson Valley. Pays in copies.

INLET–Dept. of English, Virginia Wesleyan College, Norfolk, VA 23502. Bruce Guernsey, Editor.
Short fiction accepted from September 1 to March 1. Pays in copies.

THE IOWA REVIEW–EPB 453, The University of Iowa, Iowa City, IA 52240.
Short stories, poems, prose poems. Pays $1 a line for poetry, $10 per page for fiction, on publication.

JESTURE MAGAZINE–Public Relations Office, Thomas More College, Box 85, Covington, KY 41017.
Short stories, to 2,500 words. Experimental and/or meditative works appreciated. Pays in copies.

KANSAS QUARTERLY–Dept. of English, Kansas State University, Manhattan, KS 66506.
Fiction. Pays in copies.

KARAMU–English Dept., Eastern Illinois University, Charleston, IL 61920. Allen Neff, Editor.
Quality stories, 2,000 to 7,000 words, using traditional or experimental forms. Pays in copies. No manuscripts read between June and September.

THE LAKE SUPERIOR REVIEW–Box 724, Ironwood, MI 49938.
Fiction, 2,000 words. Pays in copies.

THE LITERARY REVIEW–Fairleigh Dickinson University, Rutherford, NJ 07070. Charles Angoff, Editor.
Fiction of outstanding literary quality. Pays in copies.

THE LITTLE MAGAZINE–P.O. Box 207, Cathedral Station, New York, NY 10025. David G. Hartwell, Editor.
Fiction, to 5,000 words. Pays in copies.

THE MAINE REVIEW–c/o William Kenda, 265 Stevens, University of Maine, Orono, ME 04473.
Short stories and excerpts from novels, 2,000 to 10,000 words. Pays in copies.

THE MALAHAT REVIEW–University of Victoria, P.O. Box 1700, Victoria, B.C., V8W 2Y2, Canada. Robin Skelton, Editor.
High quality stories, 2,000 to 5,000 words. First English translations of work from Latin America, Continental Europe, and Asia. Pays $25 per 1,000 words. Photos or drawings in groups of 12 to 16. Pays $10 each.

THE MASSACHUSETTS REVIEW–Memorial Hall, University of Massachusetts, Amherst, MA 01002. L. R. Edwards, John H. Hicks, M. T. Heath, Editors.
Short fiction. Modest payment.

MIRROR NORTHWEST–Humanities Div., Bellevue Community College, Bellevue, WA 98007.
Fiction. Best to submit December through February. Pays in copies.

MISSISSIPPI REVIEW–Southern Station, Box 37, Hattiesburg, MS 39401. Gordon Weaver, Editor.
High quality fiction, 5,000 words. Pays $3 per printed page, on publication.

MOVING OUT–Box 26, U.C.B. Wayne State University, Detroit, MI 48202.
Feminist magazine. Fiction, 250 to 3,000 words, about women. Pays in copies.

MUNDUS ARTIUM: A Journal for International Literature and the Arts–Ellis Hall, Ohio University, Athens, OH 47701. Rainer Schulte, Editor-in-Chief.
Fiction, poetry, art reproductions.

NEW LETTERS–University of Missouri, Kansas City, MO 64110.
Extremely high-quality fiction. Pays $100 per story. No unsolicited manuscripts: query first and enclose stamped, self-addressed postcard. Closed May 15 to Sept. 15, annually.

NEW ORLEANS REVIEW–Loyola University, New Orleans LA 70118.
Quality short stories, poetry. Pays $50 for fiction, $10 for poems.

THE NEW RENAISSANCE–9 Heath Rd., Arlington, MA 02174.
Short stories, excerpts from novels, quality poetry. Pays up to $25 for fiction after publication. Manuscripts will not be returned unless accompanied by a stamped, self-addressed envelope.

NEWLETTERS–1639 West Washington Blvd., Venice, CA 90291. George Drury Smith, Editor.
Fiction, to 5,000 words, primarily by West Coast writers. Pays in copies.

NIMROD–Dept., of English, University of Tulsa, Tulsa, OK 74104. Francine Ringold, General Editor. Katherine Anne Porter, William Peden, Advisory Fiction Editors.
Quality fiction of any length. Pays in copies or $5 and up. International distribution.

NOCTURNE–LaGuardia Hall, Brooklyn College, Brooklyn, NY 11210. Ilene Becker, Editor.
Fiction to 2,500 words, poetry, photography, artwork, traditional or experimental. Pays in copies.

THE NORTH AMERICAN REVIEW–University of Northern Iowa, Cedar Falls, IA 50613.
No length, content, or style limitations, but only highest quality fiction considered. Pays minimum of $10 per published page. Address manuscripts to Fiction Editor.

NORTHWEST REVIEW–University of Oregon, Eugene, OR 97403. Michael Strelow, Managing Editor.
Highest quality fiction and poetry. Payment varies.

THE OHIO REVIEW–Ellis Hall, Ohio University, Athens, OH 45701.
Short stories, about 5,000 words, and poetry. Pays $5 per page and up, plus copies.

ONE–P.O. Box 1347, New Brunswick, NJ 08903. Paul Freeman, Editor and Publisher.
Fiction of all lengths and kinds: mystery, science fiction, experimental and character pieces. Pays in copies.

OYEZ!–Roosevelt University, 430 South Michigan Ave., Chicago, IL 60605.
Fiction. Pays in copies.

PARIS REVIEW–45-39 171 Pl., Flushing, NY 11358.
Quality fiction. Address manuscripts to Fiction Editor and enclose stamped, self-addressed envelope. Pays on publication.

PARTISAN REVIEW—Rutgers, 1 Richardson St., New Brunswick, NJ 08903.
Fiction and verse. Manuscripts held at least 3 months. Pays 1½¢ a word, on publication.

PHOEBE: The George Mason Review—George Mason University, 4400 University Dr., Fairfax, VA 22030. Ann Elizabeth Poe, Editor.
Short fiction, to 6,500 words. Pays in copies.

PRAIRE SCHOONER—201 Andrews Hall, University of Nebraska, Lincoln, NE 68508. Bernice Slote, Editor.
Short stories, up to 5,000 words. Not confined to regional themes. Pays in copies, reprints, and prizes.

PRISM INTERNATIONAL—c/o Creative Writing, University of British Columbia, Vancouver, B.C., Canada V6T 1W5.
Fiction, up to 5,000 words, and short plays. Pays $5 per magazine page, on publication.

PROTEUS—1004 North Jefferson St., Arlington, VA 22205. Frank Gatling, Editor.
Fiction, excerpts from novels, any length. Pays in copies. Reports in one to six weeks.

PYSCHOLOGICAL PERSPECTIVES—595 East Colorado Blvd., Suite 503, Pasadena, CA 91101. J. M. Sellery, Associate Editor.
Fiction, from 5,000 to 7,000 words. Not interested in vignettes or short shorts. Psychological emphasis creatively developed is essential. Pays in copies.

PYRAMID—39 Eliot St., Jamaica Plain, MA 02130. Ottone Riccio, Editor.
Experimental fiction. Pays $3 to $20 per published page, plus copies and subscription.

QUARTERLY REVIEW OF LITERATURE—26 Haslet Ave., Princeton, NJ 08540. T. Weiss, Editor.
Short stories of high literary quality.

QUARTET—1119 Neal Pickett Drive, College Station, TX 77840. Richard Hauer Costa, Editor.
Quality short stories under 4,000 words preferred, but exceptional longer stories will be considered. Well-made, coherent experimental stories.

RED CEDAR REVIEW—Dept. of English, Morrill Hall, Michigan State University, East Lansing, MI 48823. Dennis Pace, Editor.
Fiction, especially experimental, and portions of novels, from 4,000 to 8,000 words. Pays in copies. Query.

THE REMINGTON REVIEW—505 Westfield Ave., Elizabeth, NJ 07208. Joseph A. Barbata, Fiction Editor.
Fiction 1,500 to 10,000 words. Quality material of any school. Xerox and carbon copies returned unread. Must address appropriate editor and enclose stamped, addressed envelope. Interested in new writers. Pays in copies.

RIVERSIDE QUARTERLY—Box 14451, University Sta., Gainesville, FL 32604. Leland Sapiro, Editor.
Science fiction and fantasy, under 3,500 words preferred. Pays in copies.

ROANOKE REVIEW—English Dept., Roanoke College, Salem, VA 24153. Robert R. Walter, Editor.
Quality short stories, and poetry. Pays in copies. Published twice per year Fall (Nov. or Dec.) and Spring (May or June).

SALT LICK—Box 1064, Quincy, IL 62301. James Haining and Dan Castelaz, Editors.
Fiction, any length. Drawings, photos, collages. Pays in copies.

THE SAVAGE—1049 West Taylor St., Chicago, IL 60607.
Avant-garde short fiction, to 2,000 words. Pays in copies.

SECOND COMING—Box 31246, San Francisco, CA 94131. A. D. Winans, Editor.
Prefer avant-garde, experimental, short-short stories, 500 to 1,500 words, but will look at longer material if outstanding. Pays in copies.

THE SENECA REVIEW—Box 115, Hobart and William Smith Colleges, Geneva, NY 14456. James Crenner, Ira Sadoff, and William Burtis, Editors.
Quality short stories. Pays $25 per story, on publication.

SEWANEE REVIEW—Sewanee, TN 37375. George Core, Editor.
Fiction of highest literary quality, to 8,000 words. Pays $10-$12 a printed page.

SHANTIH—P.O. Box 125, Bay Ridge Station, Brooklyn, NY 11220. John S. Friedman and Irving Gottesman, Editors.
All types of fiction, especially experimental stories, to 3,000 words. Possible payment.

THE SMITH—5 Beckman St., New York, NY 10038. Harry Smith, General Editor; Sidney Bernard, Roving Editor.
Fiction, 500 words to novella length. Encourages new writers, but has very high standards. Modest payment, plus copies.

SNOWY EGRET—220 East College Ave., Westerville, OH 43081. William T. Hamilton, Fiction Editor.
Short stories or self-contained portions of novels, up to 10,000 words, on man and nature. Pays $2 a page, on publication.

SONOMA REVIEW—Box 1016, Petaluma, CA 94952. Joseph Jeremy, Editor.
Short stories, excerpts from novels, to 2,000 words. Pays in copies.

SOUTH CAROLINA REVIEW—c/o English Dept., Clemson University, Clemson, SC 29631.
Short stories of 3,000 to 5,000 words. Pays in copies.

SOUTH DAKOTA REVIEW—Box 111, University Exchange, Vermillion, SD 57069. John R. Milton, Editor.
Fiction, any length, with emphasis on Western setting. Open to experimental and non-regional fiction, as well. Pays in copies.

SOUTHERN HUMANITIES REVIEW—Auburn University, Auburn, AL 36830.
Short stories, 3,500 to 5,000 words. Pays in copies.

SOUTHERN REVIEW—Drawer D, University Sta., Baton Rouge, LA 70803. Donald E. Stanford and Lewis P. Simson, Co-Editors.
Fiction, 4,000 to 8,000 words, of lasting literary merit. Pays minimum of 3¢ a word, on publication. Stamped, self-addressed envelope required with all submissions. Allow 2 to 3 months for editorial decisions.

SOUTHWEST REVIEW—Southern Methodist University, Dallas, TX 75275. Margaret L. Hartley, Editor.
Stories, 3,000 to 5,000 words, emphasizing characterization. Pays on publication.

STONECLOUD—c/o Dan Ilves, Editor, 1906 Parnell Ave., Los Angeles, CA 90025.
Short stories, to 5,500 words. Stamped, self-addressed envelope must be enclosed for return of manuscript. Pays in copies.

THE STUDENT—127 Ninth Ave. North, Nashville, TN 37234. Norman Bowman, Editor.
Light features and short stories with collegiate flavor. Pays 2½¢ a word, on acceptance.

SUNDAY CLOTHES: A Magazine of the Arts—Box 66, Hermosa, SD 57744. Linda Hasselstrom, Editor.
Fiction, up to 6,000 words. Pays in copies.

THE SUNSTONE REVIEW—P.O. Box 2321, Santa Fe, NM 87501. Jody Ellis, Editor. William Farrington, Manuscript Editor.
Short stories, to 1,500 words. Pays in copies.

13th MOON—30 Seaman Ave., New York, NY 10034. Ellen Marie Bissert, Editor.
Short stories by women, to 5,000 words. Pays in copies.

THREE SISTERS—Box 969, Georgetown University, Washington, DC 20067.
Fiction, poetry, any length. Also black-and-white 8½ x 10 glossy photos, and drawings. Pays in copies. Query.

TRANSATLANTIC REVIEW—Box 3348, Grand Central St., New York, NY 10017. Joseph McCrindle, Editor.
Short stories of literary quality, 2,000 to 5,000 words. No criticism. Payment is arranged. Self-addressed stamped envelope required.

TRIQUARTERLY—University Hall, 101 Northwestern University, Evanston, IL 60201.
Fiction for international audience. No length or subject limits. Payment varies, on publication.

THE UNIVERSITY OF DENVER QUARTERLY—The University of Denver, Denver, CO 80210. Burton Feldman, Editor.
Fiction, no length limit. Pays $5 per printed page. Stamped, self-addressed envelope must be included.

THE UNIVERSITY OF PORTLAND REVIEW—University of Portland, Portland, OR 97203. Thompson M. Faller, Editor.
Occasional fiction which makes significant statement about contemporary scene, 500 to 2,500 words. No payment.

THE UNIVERSITY OF WINDSOR REVIEW—Dept. of English, University of Windsor, Ontario, Canada. Eugene McNamara, Editor. Alistair MacLeod, Fiction Editor.
Limited amount of fiction, 2,500 to 5,000 words. Pays in copies and offprints. Send manuscripts with international reply coupons to The Editor.

THE UNSPEAKABLE VISIONS OF THE INDIVIDUAL—Box 439, California, PA 15419. Arthur W. Knight, Glee Knight, Editors.
Experimental and mainstream fiction. Black-and-white photos, drawings, collages. Pays by arrangement.

UP FROM UNDER—339 Lafayette St., New York, NY 10012.
Feminist magazine for working class women. Fiction, 1,000 to 10,000 words, about women's experiences, problems. No payment.

THE VILLAGER—135 Midland Ave., Bronxville, NY 10778. D. Timmerman, Editor.
Fiction, up to 2,000 words. No payment.

VIRGINIA QUARTERLY REVIEW—1 West Range, Charlottesville, VA 22903.
Fiction of high literary standard, 3,000 to 5,000 words.

WASCANA REVIEW—c/o English Dept., University of Regina, Regina, Saskatchewan, Canada S4S OA2.
Short stories, 2,000 to 6,000 words, and poetry, 4-100 lines. Pays $3 per page for fiction, $10 for verse, after publication.

WEBSTER REVIEW—Webster College, Webster Groves, MO 63119. Nancy Schapiro, Harry J. Cargas, Editors.
Fiction, and English translations of contemporary fiction. Pays in copies.

WEST COAST REVIEW–Simon Fraser University, Burnaby, B.C., Canada V5A 1S6. Fiction, especially experimental writing, 1,000 to 3,000 words. Pays $5 on acceptance.

WESTERN HUMANITIES REVIEW–University of Utah, Salt Lake City, UT 84112. Jack Garlington, Editor. High-quality fiction of any length. Pays $75 to $100.

WIND–RFD Route No. 1, Box 810, Pikeville, KY 41501. Quentin R. Howard, Editor. Short stories under 3,000 words. Will publish longer ones if outstanding. Pays in copies.

WISCONSIN REVIEW–Box 777, Dempsey Hall, University of Wisconsin, Oshkosh, WI 54901. Fiction, short critical essays.

YALE REVIEW–1902A Yale Station, New Haven, CT 06520. J. E. Palmer, Editor; Mary Price, Managing Editor. Limited market for highest-grade short stories.

RELIGIOUS AND DENOMINATIONAL MAGAZINES

BRIGADE LEADER–Christian Service Brigade, P.O. Box 150, Wheaton, IL 60187. Paul Heidebrecht, Managing Editor. Short stories, talks, role plays, games, feature activities for men to use in boys' club meetings, to 1,200 words. Pays 3¢ a word and up. Send for author's guideline packet and questionnaire for specific assignments.

CAMPUS LIFE–Box 419, Wheaton, IL 60187. Philip Yancey, Editor. For teen-agers and young adults 16 to 19. Fiction, 1,500 words, to interest Christian youth. Pays from $100 to $200.

THE CANADIAN MESSENGER–833 Broadview Ave., Toronto M4K 2P9, Ont., Canada. Rev. F. J. Power, S.J., Editor. Short stories, 1,800 to 2,000 words, with Catholic tone, about daily life and problems of men and women. Seeks humorous stories. Pays 2¢ a word, on acceptance. Address Mrs. M. Pujolas.

CATHOLIC RURAL LIFE–3801 Grand Ave., Des Moines, IA 50312. Msgr. J. G. Weber, Editor. Fiction with spiritual emphasis and rural background. Pays $20 to $30, shortly after acceptance. Submissions without return postage not returned.

CATHOLIC WORLD–1865 Broadway, New York, NY 10023. Robert J. Heyer, Managing Editor. Fiction, 2,000 words, reflecting religious concern about modern problems. Each issue is thematic; sample themes are: Arts and Religion; Sanctity of Life, Family; New Feminine Identity; Economic Morality; Advent. Pays $75 and up, on publication.

CHRISTIAN LIFE MAGAZINE–Gundersen Dr. and Schmale Rd., Wheaton, IL 60187. Robert Walker, Editor. Fiction, 1,500 to 2,500 words, on significant problems faced by Christians today, solved by character action. Pays up to $150, on publication.

COLUMBIA–Box 1670, New Haven, CT 06507. Elmer Von Feldt, Editor. Official journal of Knights of Columbus. Fiction, from Christian viewpoint, 1,000 to 3,000 words, for Catholic family. Pays $100 to $300, on acceptance.

COMMENTARY–165 East 56th St., New York, NY 10022. Norman Podhoretz, Editor. Fiction of high intellectual quality. Pays on publication.

THE COMPANION–15 Chestnut Park Rd., Toronto, Ont. M4W 1W5, Canada. Rev. Leo Linder, O.F.M. Conv., Editor.
Fiction, 1,200 to 1,500 words. Pays 2¢ a word, on acceptance.

CONQUEST–6401 The Paseo, Kansas City, MO 64131. Dan Ketchum, Editor.
Church of the Nazarene. For teenagers. Religious short stories, to 2,500 words. Pays 1½¢ and up per word for prose, on acceptance.

CONTACT–302 U.B. Building, Huntington, IN 46750. Stanley Peters, Editor; Lois Breiner, Assistant Editor.
United Brethren in Christ. Christ-centered fiction and articles for teens and adults, 1,200 to 1,500 words. Pays ¾¢ a word and up, on acceptance.

THE EVANGEL–999 College Ave., Winona Lake, IN 46590. Vera Bethel, Editor.
Free Methodist. Fiction, 1,500 to 2,000 words, on Christian answer to contemporary problems. Pays 2¢ a word for prose, on acceptance.

FACE-TO-FACE–201 Eighth Ave. South, Nashville, TN 37203. Mrs. Sharilyn S. Adair, Editor.
United Methodist. Fiction, 2,500 to 3,000 words, on problems and concerns of 15- to 18-year-olds. Pays 3¢ a word on acceptance. Query.

FRIAR: THE MAGAZINE OF CATHOLIC OPTIMISM–Butler, NJ 07405. Rev. Rudolf Harvey, O.F.M., Editor.
Light and humorous fiction, to 2,000 words, preferably on Catholic or Franciscan themes. Pay varies, on acceptance.

GOSPEL CARRIER–Pentecostal Church of God of America, P.O. Box 850, Joplin, MO 64801.
Short stories, 1,500 to 1,800 words, that emphasize some point about Christian living. Pays ½¢ per word, quarterly. Send stamped, self-addressed envelope for sample.

HOME LIFE–127 Ninth Ave. North, Nashville, TN 37234. George W. Knight, Editor.
Southern Baptist. Fiction, to 2,000 words, on children's growth, family inter-relationships, etc. "Professional in depth but popular in style." Human-interest shorts, 200 to 500 words. Pays 2½¢ a word, on acceptance. Writer's guide available on request.

JEWISH FRONTIER–575 Sixth Ave., New York, NY 10011. Dr. Judah J. Shapiro, Editor.
Fiction related to Judaism. Pays 2¢ a word, on publication.

LIVE–1445 Boonville Ave., Springfield, MO 65802. Gary Leggett, Adult Editor.
Sunday school paper for adults. Fiction, 1,500 to 2,000 words, on how to put Bible principles into action in everyday living. Pays on acceptance. Samples and "Suggestions for Writers" sheet sent on request.

LOGOS JOURNAL–185 North Ave., Plainfield, NJ 07060. Alden West, Editor.
Charismatic, evangelical Christian. Some fiction, to 2,500 words.

THE LOOKOUT–8121 Hamilton Ave., Cincinnati, OH 45231. Jay Sheffield, Editor.
Good, clean stories, 1,000 to 1,400 words, with a punch. Pays monthly; usual rate $35. Sample suggestions to authors on request.

LUTHERAN STANDARD–426 South Fifth St., Minneapolis, MN 55415. Dr. George H. Muedeking, Editor.
Fiction, to 1,300 words, related to the church or Christian life. Pays 2¢ a word and up, on acceptance.

MATURE YEARS–201 Eighth Ave. South, Nashville, TN 37203. Daisy D. Warren, Editor.
United Methodist. For older adults. Humorous and other short stories, 1,200 to 1,500 words, especially with Christmas or Thanksgiving settings. Pays 3¢ a word, on acceptance.

MIDSTREAM: A MONTHLY JEWISH REVIEW–515 Park Ave., New York, NY 10022. Ronald Sanders, Editor.
Fiction of Jewish or general social and political interest, to 8,000 words. Pays 6¢ a word, on acceptance.

MOODY MONTHLY–820 LaSalle St., Chicago, IL 60610. Jerry B. Jenkins, Managing Editor.
Contemporary Christian short stories, 1,500 to 2,500 words. Pays 5¢ a word, on acceptance. Query.

OUR FAMILY–Box 249, Dept. E, Battleford, Sask., Canada S0M OE0. Rev. A. J. Materi, O.M.I., Editor.
Fiction, 1,000 to 3,000 words, for Catholic family readers. Pays 2¢ a word.

THE PENTECOSTAL EVANGEL–Gospel Publishing House, 1445 Boonville, Springfield, MO 65802. Robert C. Cunningham, Editor.
Publication of Assemblies of God, fellowship of Protestant evangelical Pentecostal churches. Religious material only. Some fiction, (e.g., Christmas), 1,500 to 1,800 words. Pays 1¢ per word and up, upon publication. Sample copy on request.

PURPOSE–610 Walnut Ave., Scottdale, PA 15683. David E. Hostetler, Editor.
Fiction, to 1,200 words, on Christians working through problems and confronting issues aided by faith. Pays 2¢ a word. "No pious or sweet stuff considered." Sample copies on request.

QUEEN–40 South Saxon Avenue, Bay Shore, NY 11706. Rev. James McMillan, S.M.M., Editor.
Fiction, preferably with Marian theme. Rates vary, on acceptance.

THE RECONSTRUCTIONIST–15 West 86th St., New York, NY 10024. Dr. Ira Eisenstein, Editor.
Fiction, 2,000 to 3,000 words, dedicated to advancement of Judaism. Pays $20 to $25, on publication.

REVIEW FOR RELIGIOUS–612 Humboldt Bldg., 539 N. Grand Blvd., St. Louis, MO 63103.
Fiction for religious men and women. Pays $5 per printed page, on publication.

ST. ANTHONY MESSENGER–1615 Republic St., Cincinnati, OH 45210. Rev. Jeremy Harrington, O.F.M., Editor.
Catholic family magazine. Fiction with Christian background. Pays 6¢ a word and up.

THE SIGN–Monastery Place, Union City, NJ 07087. Rev. Augustine P. Hennessy, C.P., Editor.
Short stories of general or religious interest, to 4,000 words. Pays $200 to $300, on acceptance.

VISTA–Box 2000, Marion, IN 46952.
Fiction for adults, 1,500 to 2,500 words, on following Christ in today's world. Serials of 6 to 8 chapters. Pays 2¢ per word, on acceptance.

WORKING FOR BOYS–601 Winchester St., Newton Highlands, MA 02161. Send manuscripts to Brother Jason, CFX, Associate Editor, 800 Clapboardtree St., Westwood, MA 02090.
For teenagers and parents. Fiction, to 1,000 words. Sample copy available on request.

THE POPULAR MARKET

The popular market includes the magazines which used to be called the "pulps": men's magazines, detective and mystery, science fiction, confession and romance magazines. Both fiction and nonfiction needs of these magazines are listed here. Most of the popular magazines are fiction primarily, although a number of the detective and adventure magazines want only factual material. Publishers of paperback books also have a continuing need for western, mystery, science fiction, love and adventure novels, and writers should consult the list of *Paperback Book Publishers* for their requirements.

MEN'S MAGAZINES

ADAM—8060 Melrose Ave., Los Angeles, CA 90046. Carlton Hollander, Editor.
Well-written nonfiction, 1,000 to 3,000 words, on social themes, human sexuality, personalities. Sexy humor and satire. Hard-hitting, topical fiction. Pays $50 to $150, on publication.

AMERICAN ART ENTERPRISES, INC.—21322 Lassen St., Chatsworth, CA 91311. George Bemos, Manuscript Editor.
Publisher of men's magazines. Articles, 2,000 to 3,000 words, on today's morality, with stimulating photos. Action packed fiction with strong male-female relationships, eroticism, physical conflict. Pays $80 and up; $10 for cartoons.

ARGOSY—420 Lexington Ave., New York, NY 10017. Bert Randolph Sugar, Editor-in-Chief.
Nonfiction, to 3,000 words, on men's adventures. Fiction, 3,000 to 5,000 words, with male viewpoint; condensed novels, 25,000 words. Pays $400 and up. Query on historical and topical subjects.

ARMY TIMES—475 School St, S.W., Washington, DC 20024. Gene Famiglietti, Editor.
Articles on military service. Cartoons. Pay varies.

BROADSIDE—21322 Lassen St., Chatsworth, CA 91311. Arthur S. Long, Editor.
Well-researched, factual articles, 2,000 to 3,000 words, for men: sex, expose, sports, adventure, etc. Humor. Action-packed fiction. Pays $85 and up, on acceptance. Same address and requirements for *Nightcap* and *Showpiece*.

CAVALIER—316 Aragon Ave., Coral Gables, FL 33134. Nye Willden, Managing Editor.
Quality fiction and illustrated nonfiction of interest to hip young men, 3,000 to 6,000 words. Pays to $300 for fiction, on publication.

DARING—see *Wildcat.*

ESQUIRE—488 Madison Ave., New York, NY 10022. Don Erickson, Editor.
Articles, 1,500 to 5,000 words, for sophisticated audience. Strong need for humor. Pays top rates, on acceptance. No longer considers unsolicited fiction. Query first.

FLING—1485 Bayshore Blvd., Suite 400, San Francisco, CA 94124.
Fiction, 3,000 to 4,000 words; nonfiction, to 5,000 words, to entertain sophisticated men. Short humor, satire. Photos. Pays $75 to $150 per 1,000 words, on publication. Query.

GALLERY—116 East 27th St., New York, NY 10016. Joe Kelleher, Editor.
Fiction, to 4,000 words; nonfiction, to 5,000 words, to entertain sophisticated men. Short humor, satire. Photos. Pays $75 to $150 per 1,000 words, on publication. Query.

GEM—303 West 42nd St., New York, NY 10036. Will Martin, Editor.
Sex-related fiction and articles, 500 to 1,500 words. Pays after assignment. Same address and requirements for *The Swinger.*

GENESIS—120 East 56th St., New York, NY 10022. Eric Protter, Editor.
Articles, 2,500 to 6,000 words, with sexual orientation; profiles, exposes, interviews. Fiction, 3,000 to 6,000 words. Pays $350 and up. Query.

GENTLEMEN'S QUARTERLY (GQ)—488 Madison Ave., New York, NY 10022. Jack Haber, Editor.
Queries only; no fiction, poems, or cartoons. Unsolicited manuscripts returned unread.

KNIGHT—Publisher's Service, Inc., 8060 Melrose Ave., Los Angeles, CA 90046. Jared Rutter, Editor.
Articles on human sexuality; interviews. Erotic fiction for men and women. Pays $60 to $300, on publication.

MALE—575 Madison Ave., New York, NY 10022. Carl Sifakis, Editor.
Articles, 4,000 to 6,000 words: true adventures with exotic backgrounds; exposes; profiles of unusual men; World War II and contemporary cold war stories. Pays to $600, on acceptance. Query. Same address and requirements for *Men.*

MAN TO MAN—280 Madison Ave., New York, NY 10016. Everett Meyers, Editor.
Modern fiction, 1,500 to 5,000 words, with man-woman relationships. Articles, 2,000 to 5,000 words, on contemporary trends: sex, travel, art, entertainment, etc. Pays $75 and up, on or before publication. Same requirements for *Mr. Magazine* and *Sir!*

MEN—See *Male.*

MODERN MAN—8150 North Central Park Ave., Skokie, IL 60076. Donald Stahl, Editor.
Dramatic, humorous, or documentary articles, 2,000 words, on sex. Query.

MR. MAGAZINE—See *Man to Man.*

NIGHTCAP—See *Broadside.*

OUI—919 North Michigan Ave., Chicago, IL 60611. Peter McCabe, Articles Editor.
Published by *Playboy*, for men 18 to 30. Articles and short stories, 2,500 to 5,000 words. Pays to $1200. Short pieces for "Openers" section. Pays $50 to $100.

P.O.P. MAGAZINE—919 Filley St., Lansing, MI 48906. Jack Dinley, Editor.
Articles, 1,200, for men: adventure, sports, racing, etc., with black-and-white photos. Pays $200, on publication.

PENTHOUSE—909 Third Ave., New York, NY 10022. James Goode, Executive Editor.
Sophisticated, sexy fiction, 3,000 to 5,000 words; general-interest or hard-hitting controversial articles, to 6,000 words. Pays $750 per feature article, on acceptance.

PENTHOUSE FORUM—909 Third Ave., New York, NY 10022. Marlene Deverell-Van Meter, Executive Editor.
Articles, 1,500 to 2,500 words, on contemporary emotional, psychological, medical, sexual scenes, conflicts, problems, innovations. Pays $200 to $400.

PLAYBOY—919 North Michigan Ave., Chicago, IL 60611. Sheldon Wax, Managing Editor; Geoffrey Norman, Articles Editor; Robie Macauley, Fiction Editor.
Sophisticated, well-plotted fiction of all kinds, 1,000 to 10,000 words (average, 4,000). Articles on topics of interest to urban men, 4,000 to 8,000 words. Humor and satire welcome. Pays to $3,000.

PLAYERS—8060 Melrose Ave., Los Angeles, CA 90046. Joe Nazel, Editor.
Articles, 1,000 to 4,000 words, with photos, for black men: interviews, travel, business, entertainment, sports. Fiction, 2,000 to 6,000 words, humor, satire, movie, theatre, record reviews, 100 to 500 words. Pays from 5¢ a word, on publication.

SAGA—333 Johnson Ave., Brooklyn, NY 11206. Martin M. Singer, Editor.
Nonfiction, 4,000 to 5,000 words, for men: adventure, interviews and profiles of newsworthy figures, humor, travel, hunting, fishing, sports, war (World War II or later); photo essays on action sports, dangerous pastimes. Pays from $250.

SHOWPIECE—See *Broadside*.

SIR!—See *Man to Man*.

STAG—575 Madison Ave., New York, NY 10022. Noah Sarlat, Editor.
Articles, to 7,000 words, on personalities, true adventure, exposes, etc. Pays to $500, on acceptance, $10 to $25 for single photos, to $50 a page for picture stories.

SWANK—717 Fifth Ave., New York, NY 10022.
Articles, 2,500 to 4,000 words, on personalities, sports, politics, interviews, sex and behavior. Sophisticated fiction, 1,800 to 3,500 words. Pays $250 to $350 for fiction, $300 for non-fiction. Query with outline.

THE SWINGER—See *Gem*.

TRUE—21 West 26th St., New York, NY 10016.
High-quality, topical, insightful articles for men; adult adventure. Articles, 1,000 words, for columns: sports, finance, behind-the-scenes views of reporting in various media. Pays $300. Pays $25 per item for "Strange But True," $50 for "True News" items. Pays $750 and up for major features. Query with example of published work.

WILDCAT—235 Park Ave. South, New York, NY 10003. Dan Sontup, Editor.
Fiction and articles, 2,000 to 3,000 words, serious or humorous, about modern relationships and encounters between young men and women, presented in a credible manner. Pays to $125, on acceptance. Same address and requirements for *Daring*.

DETECTIVE AND MYSTERY MAGAZINES

(Fact and Fiction)

ALFRED HITCHCOCK'S MYSTERY MAGAZINE—850 Third Ave., New York, NY 10022.
Original, well-written, well-plotted mystery, suspense and crime fiction, 1,000 to 10,000 words. No cheap thrills; "now" feeling preferred. Pays 5¢ a word, on acceptance.

ARMCHAIR DETECTIVE—3656 Midland, White Bear Lake, MN 55110. Allen J. Hubin, Editor.
Nonfiction relevant to mystery and detective fiction field: biographical sketches, critiques, book reviews, etc. No payment.

BEST TRUE FACTS—See *Official Police Detective*.

CONFIDENTIAL DETECTIVE CASES—235 Park Ave. South, New York, NY 10003.
B. R. Ampolsk, Editor.
Action- and emotion-filled, true fact detective cases, 3,500 words with photos, with woman as principal character. Pays on acceptance. Same address and requirements for *Crime Detective*. Query.

CRIME DETECTIVE—See *Confidential Detective Cases*.

DEADLINE DETECTIVE—See *Official Police Detective*.

EIGHTY-SEVENTH PRECINCT MAGAZINE—See *The Executioner Mystery Magazine.*

ELLERY QUEEN'S MYSTERY MAGAZINE—229 Park Ave. South, New York, NY 10003. Ellery Queen, Editor; Eleanor Sullivan, Managing Editor.
Quality detective, crime, mystery and spy fiction, 4,000 to 6,000 words. Needs suspense stories or straight detection. Pays 3¢ to 8¢ a word, on acceptance. "We invite new as well as name writers to submit."

THE EXECUTIONER MYSTERY MAGAZINE—8730 Sunset Blvd., Los Angeles, CA 90069. Leonard J. Ackerman, Editor.
Mystery fiction, 3,000 to 12,000 words. Pays 2¢ a word. Same address and requirements for *87th Precinct Mystery Magazine.*

FRONT PAGE DETECTIVE—See *Inside Detective.*

INSIDE DETECTIVE—1 Dag Hammarskjold Plaza, 245 East 47th St., New York, NY 10017. James W. Bowser, Editor.
Timely, true fact detective stories, 3,500 to 4,500 words with photos, stressing suspense and detective work, characterization and emotion. Pays $200 and up, on acceptance. Current crime shorts, to 1,500 words. Pays $25 to $50. No fiction. Same address and requirements for *Front Page Detective.*

MASTER DETECTIVE—235 Park Ave. South, New York, NY 10003. A P. Govoni, Editor.
Chiefly current cases, but a few older, solved cases, with strong human motivation and considerable amount of detective work. Detailed treatment required. Authentic photos must be available as illustrations. Pays to $200 for 5,000 to 6,000 words; extra for photos. No fiction. Query.

MIKE SHAYNE MYSTERY MAGAZINE—8230 Beverly Blvd., Los Angeles, CA 90048. Leo Margulies, Publisher. Cylvia Kleinman, Editor.
Good detective and mystery stories, from 1,500-word short-shorts to 12,000-word novelettes. Pays 1¢ a word and up, on acceptance.

OFFICIAL DETECTIVE STORIES—235 Park Ave. South, New York, NY 10003. A. P. Govoni, Editor.
Fact detective stories on current investigations, strictly from the investigator's point of view, 5,000 to 6,000 words. Pays $200; extra for photos. No fiction. Query.

OFFICIAL POLICE DETECTIVE—P.O. Box 26872, Tempe, AZ 85282. Tommy Kay, Editor.
Articles, 2,500 to 3,500 words, with photos, of true-crime police investigative work. Prefer murder cases, with sexually oriented crime, after trial. No fiction. Pays 1¢ to 2¢ per word, extra for photos, on acceptance. Also buys crime photos (query). Same address and requirements for *Special Detective, Deadline Detective, Best True Facts,* and *True Crime Detective.*

SPECIAL DETECTIVE—See *Official Police Detective.*

STARTLING DETECTIVE—Globe Communications Corp., 1440 St. Catherine St. West, Montreal, Canada, H3G I52. Dominick A. Merle, Editor.
Current sensational United States crimes, 3,000 to 6,000 words, with photos. Detail police investigation leading to arrest. No fiction. Pays $125 to $225.

TRUE CRIME DETECTIVE—See *Official Police Detective.*

TRUE DETECTIVE—235 Park Ave. South, New York, NY 10003. A. P. Govoni, Editor.
Current headline police cases, from 5,000 words, with considerable amount of detective work, strong human motivation. Authentic photos must be available. Some older cases are used in special series and double-length features. Pays to $200; extra for photos. No fiction. Query.

TRUE POLICE CASES–Globe Communications Corp., 1440 St. Catherine St. West, Montreal, Canada H3G I52. Dominick A. Merle, Editor.
Factual, sensational crimes throughout United States, 3,000 to 6,000 words, with photos. No unsolved cases or "oldies." Pays $125 to $225.

WESTERN MAGAZINES

THE AMERICAN WEST–599 College Ave., Palo Alto, CA 94306. Ed Holm, Managing Editor.
Short articles, 1,000 words, about unusual people, places or events in Old West. Constructed around full-page illustration furnished by author. Pays $75.

FRONTIER TIMES–See *True West.*

FRONTIER WEST–Reese Publishing Co., 235 Park Ave. South, New York, NY 10003. Art Crockett, Editor.
Historical and biographical articles, 2,500 to 5,000 words, with photos. Pays $75, extra for photos, on publication.

GOLD!–Western Publications, Inc., Box 3338, Austin, TX 78764.
Articles, 750 to 6,000 words, on treasures, lost mines, etc. Give sources, except for personal experiences. Photos welcomed; returned after publication. Pays 2¢ a word, on acceptance. Query.

OLD WEST–See *True West.*

TRUE WEST–Western Publications, Inc., P.O. Box 3338, Austin, TX 78764. Joe A. Small, Publisher; Pat Wagner, Editor.
Articles, 750 to 4,000 words, on true incidents of Old West (1830–1910). Source list required unless first-hand account. Good photos help greatly; returned after publication. Pays 2¢ a word, on acceptance. Query. Same address and requirements for *Frontier Times* and *Old West.*

THE WESTERN HORSEMAN–3850 North Nevada Ave., Colorado Springs, CO 80901. Chuck King, Editor.
Articles, 1,500 words, with black-and-white photos, by experienced horsemen. Pay varies, on acceptance.

WESTERN TREASURE–1440 West Walnut St., Compton, CA 90220. Ray Krupa, Managing Editor.
Articles about searches for lost, buried and sunken treasures using metal detectors, etc. Historical articles on early American inhabitants, places to look for treasure. Pays 2¢ a word, $5 for pictures, up to $100, on publication.

WESTERNER–Behn-Miller Publishers, Inc., 16001 Ventura Blvd., Encino, CA 91316. Robert Wolenik, Editor.
Historical, western adventure articles, 3,500 words. First-person factual accounts preferred. Photos and drawings required. Pays 3¢ a word, $10 a photo, on publication.

SCIENCE FICTION AND FANTASY MAGAZINES

ALGOL: A MAGAZINE ABOUT SCIENCE FICTION–P. O. Box 4175, New York, NY 10017. Andrew Porter, Editor.
Articles, 1,000 to 10,000 words, on writing science fiction and on science-fiction writers. Interviews with authors, editors, and others involved in sf. Artwork with fantastic or sf themes. Pays 1¢ per word, on acceptance.

ANALOG: SCIENCE FICTION & FACT—350 Madison Ave., New York, NY 10017. Ben
  Bova, Editor.
  Science fiction, with human characters against background of believable future or
  alien environment. Short stories, 3,500 to 7,500 words; novelettes, 10,000 to 20,000;
  serials, to 70,000 words. Short fact articles, giving modern facts with probable future
  developments, 3,500 to 5,000 words. Pays to 4¢ a word; 5¢ a word for short stories,
  on acceptance. Query first on novels and fact articles.

FANTASY & SCIENCE FICTION—P.O. Box 56, Cornwall, CT 06753. E. Ferman,
  Editor.
  Imaginative fiction, supernatural or scientific, from short-shorts to (very rarely)
  serialized novels. Pays 2¢ a word, on acceptance. Pays 1¢ a word for one use only of
  reprints that are not from science fiction magazines. At present chiefly needs *real
  science* fiction and well-plotted fantasy. Light material in either category always
  welcome.

GALAXY MAGAZINE—235 East 45th St., New York, NY 10017. James Patrick Baen,
  Editor.
  Science fiction, based on problems arising from situations and environments that are
  extensions of present scientific knowledge or hypotheses, or demonstrate acquaintance with them. No fantasy. Short stories, to 7,200 words; novelettes, to 17,000
  words; novellas, to 20,000 words, usually, but not always, by arrangement. Pays by
  arrangement or on publication.

IF SCIENCE FICTION—Merged with *Galaxy*.

THE LITERARY MAGAZINE OF FANTASY AND TERROR—Box 89517, Zenith, WA
  98188. Jessica Amanda Salmonson, Editor.
  Epic and hard-core fantasy, tales of terror and the supernatural. Pays in copies,
  subscriptions and ½¢ to 1¢ a word (to $100), on acceptance.

POLLUTION CONTROL JOURNAL—144 West 12th Ave., Denver, CO 80204.
  Science fiction, 2,500 to 3,000 words, incorporating pollution theme. Pays 3¢ a
  word, on publication.

RIVERSIDE QUARTERLY—Box 14451, University Station, Gainsville, FL 32604.
  Leland Sapiro, Editor.
  Science fiction and fantasy, under 3,500 words preferred. Pays in copies.

WEIRDBOOK—Box 35, Amherst Branch, Buffalo, NY 14266. W. Paul Ganley, Editor.
  Supernatural, horror and fantasy adventure fiction, to 10,000 words; poetry, to 15
  lines. No straight science fiction. Pays $1 and up per printed page, on publication.

CONFESSION, ROMANCE MAGAZINES

BRONZE THRILLS—Good Publishing Co., 1220 Harding St., Fort Worth, TX 76102.
  Mrs. Edna K. Turner, Editor.
  Confession stories, 5,000—8,000 words, with black interest. 8 x 10 black-and-white
  glossy prints. Pays on acceptance. Same address and requirements for *Hep, Jive* and
  Soul Confessions.

HEP—See *Bronze Thrills*.

HERS—IPC Magazines, Ltd., Room 1705, 205 East 42nd St., New York, NY 10017. British romance magazine. First-person stories, 5,000 to 8,000 words, of an emotional, romantic, realistic nature. Pays good rates, on acceptance.

INTIMATE STORY—575 Madison Ave., New York, NY 10022. Jane Bernstein, Editor. First-person stories with appealing narrator, to 6,500 words, on love, courtship, marriage and family problems, resolved in meaningful manner. Needs stories on teenagers and exciting current news events. No nonfiction. Pays to $180, after acceptance.

JIVE—See *Bronze Thrills*.

MODERN LOVE—See *Real Confessions*.

MODERN ROMANCES—1 Dag Hammarskjold Plaza, New York, NY 10017. Rita Brenig, Editor.
Good first-person stories, to 7,000 words, for wives and daughters of blue-collar class, with emphasis on plot and characterization. Pays 5¢ per printed word.

MY CONFESSION—See *True Secrets*.

MY ROMANCE—See *True Secrets*.

PERSONAL ROMANCES—757 Madison Ave., New York, NY 10022. Johanna Roman Smith, Editor.
Confession stories, 2,000 to 6,500 words, told in strong, up-to-date terms by young marrieds, singles and teenagers, on emotional, sexual and family conflicts and the search to resolve personal problems. Pays on acceptance.

REAL CONFESSIONS—355 Lexington Ave., New York, NY 10017. Ruth Beck, Editor. First-person confession stories, to 7,000 words, told by female narrator in romantic, exciting, tragic or frightening situation growing out of relationship with parents, lovers, husbands, children. Original stories, timely, action-packed, credible, in colloquial style, with much dialogue. Pays on acceptance. Same address and requirements for *Modern Love*.

REAL ROMANCES—21 West 26th St., New York, NY 10010. Ardis Sandel, Editor. Sexy, realistic, well-plotted, first-person confession stories, to 7,500 words, with good characterization and convincing motivation. Needs teen-age, courtship and young married stories. Some male viewpoint; no racial themes. Pays $100 to $150, on publication. Same address and requirements for *Real Story* and *Uncensored Confessions*.

REAL STORY—See *Real Romances*.

SECRET STORY—See *True Secrets.*

SOUL CONFESSIONS—See *Bronze Thrills.*

TRUE—IPC Magazines Ltd., Room 1705, 205 East 42nd St., New York, NY 10017.
British romance magazine. First-person stories, 3,000 to 6,000 words, with drama, emotion, credibility and high moral tone. Pays on acceptance.

TRUE CONFESSIONS—205 East 42nd St., New York, NY 10017. Helen Vincent, Editor.
Woman-told confessions, 2,500 to 12,000 words, with strong emotional conflict and intriguing, suspenseful situations involving man-woman relationships. Special non-fiction feature each month, which must be well-researched. Pays good rates, on acceptance.

TRUE EXPERIENCE—205 East 42nd St., New York, NY 10017. Lydia E. Paglio, Editor.
Realistic, insightful first-person stories, 4,000 to 8,000 words (short shorts to 2,000 words), with lively characters, on family life, love, courtship, health, religion, behind-the-headlines topics. Pays 3¢ a word.

TRUE LOVE—205 East 42nd St., New York, NY 10017. Erma E. Benedict, Editor.
Fresh, realistic first-person stories, to 8,000 words. "Avoid conventional type of confession story." Pays 3¢ a word.

TRUE ROMANCE—205 East 42nd St., New York, NY 10017. Jean Press Silberg, Editor.
True-to-life stories of romance, family life, 1,500 to 10,000 words. Fillers, 300 words for columns: "My Personal Recipe for Happiness," "How We Met," "One Moment That Changed My Life." Short letters from readers for "Between Us." Pays 3¢ a word for stories, $10 for fillers, on acceptance; $5 for published letters.

TRUE SECRETS—575 Madison Ave., New York, NY 10022. Cara Sherman, Editorial Director.
First-person stories, 1,500 to 7,000 words, focusing on romantic or emotional problems such as sex, love, teen-age romance, children, etc. Should have realistic resolution. Also mystery-gothic confessions. Pays to $150. Same address and requirements for *My Romance, Secret Story, My Confession, Intimate Romances,* and *Intimate Secrets.*

TRUE STORY—205 East 42nd St., New York, NY 10017. Sue Hilliard, Editor.
First-person stories, 3,000 to 8,000 words, mirroring hopes, fears, drama and humor of life today. Articles of general interest to women, 1,500 to 3,000 words. Pays 5¢ a word and up, on publication.

UNCENSORED CONFESSIONS—See *Real Romances.*

ARTICLE MARKETS

The magazines in this list are in the market for free-lance articles. The list is divided into the following categories: general magazines; college, literary and "little" magazines; religious and denominational magazines; magazines devoted to sports, outdoors, travel, cars, etc.; home and garden or women's magazines; trade and business magazines; and specialized magazines.

Only the largest trade and business publications which particularly want to see free-lance material are listed, and a selected list is given of highly specialized magazines in such fields as education, agriculture, science, etc. Writers who are able to write articles in a particular technical or business field can find the names of thousands of other specialized magazines in N. W. Ayer and Son's *Directory of Newspapers and Periodicals,* which is available in most libraries and contains an index according to classification. Since Ayer's *Directory* does not list editorial requirements, writers should query these magazines before submitting manuscripts.

Juvenile article markets are listed under *Juvenile, Teen-Age and Young Adult Magazines,* and markets for popular or pulp articles (men's true adventure stories, true detective stories, etc.) are listed under *The Popular Market.*

GENERAL MAGAZINES

ADAM—8060 Melrose Ave., Los Angeles, CA 90046. Carlton Hollander, Editor.
 Articles, 1,000 to 3,000 words, on social themes, human sexuality, and personalities. Sexy humor and satire. Pays $50 to $150, on publication.

ADAM FILM WORLD—Same address as *Adam.*
 Articles dealing with film erotica.

ALLIED PUBLICATIONS, Inc.—P.O. Box 23505, Fort Lauderdale, FL 33307.
 Articles on home and family interests, travel, secretaries to famous personalities, art, for beauticians, business executives, secretaries. Pays 5¢ a word, on acceptance; $5 for photos or cartoons.

AMERICAN ASTROLOGY—2505 North Alvernon Way, Tucson, AZ 85712.
 Articles to 3,000 words on popular astrology, serious study material. Pays on publication.

AMERICAN BAR ASSOCIATION JOURNAL—1155 East 60th St., Chicago, IL 60637. Richard B. Allen, Editor.
 Nonfiction, 3,000 to 3,500 words, on law, legal history, public affairs, political science. No payment. Query.

AMERICAN HERITAGE—1221 Ave. of Americas, New York, NY 10020. Oliver Jensen, Editor.
 Limited amount of free-lance material on American history and historical figures, 3,000 to 6,000 words. No rewrites, local history, or fictionalizing. Check index of back issues before submission. Pays $150 and up, on acceptance.

AMERICAN HOME—641 Lexington Ave., New York, NY 10022.
 General-interest articles on home subjects, to appeal to young families. Home improvement articles on remodeling, redecorating, maintenance, etc. Before-and-after stories and how-to stories. Pays on acceptance. Query.

AMERICAN LEGION MAGAZINE—1345 Ave. of the Americas, New York, NY 10019. Robert B. Pitkin, Editor.
 Articles on national and international affairs. American history and military history. Query.

THE AMERICAN-SCANDINAVIAN REVIEW–18 East 73rd St., New York, NY 10021. Erik J. Friis, Editor.
Articles, 2,000 to 3,000 words, about Scandinavia and Scandinavians in America. Photos and drawings. Pays about $75, on acceptance.

THE AMERICAN SCHOLAR–1811 Q St. N.W., Washington DC 20009. Carol Brann, Associate Editor.
Nontechnical articles and essays on current affairs, the American cultural scene, politics, the arts, religion and science, 3,000 to 4,000 words. Pays $250, on acceptance.

AMERICAN WAY–American Airlines, 633 Third Ave., New York, NY 10017. John Minahan, Editor and Publisher.
General-interest articles, 1,500 to 2,000 words. Pays $200 to $500, after acceptance.

AMERICAN WEST–599 College Ave., Palo Alto, CA 94306.
Researched, well-illustrated articles, 3,000 to 5,000 words, on the American West, past, present, and future. Pays $100 to $300, on acceptance. Query.

AMERICANA–American Heritage Society, 1221 Ave., of the Americas, New York, NY 10020. Michael Durham, Editor.
Articles, 1,000 to 2,000 words with photos and/or illustrations, on historical subjects the reader can participate in: travel to historic places, crafts, collecting, decorating and living in old houses, gardening, cooking, etc. Pays $150 to $250, on acceptance. Query.

AMERICAS–General Secretariat of the Organization of American States, Washington, DC 20006. Guillermo de Zendegui, Editor-in-Chief. Address articles to Mrs. Flora L. Phelps, Editor, English edition, or to Mr. Juan Villaverde, Editor, Spanish edition.
Illustrated articles, 3,000 words, with "hemisphere-wide appeal." Pays $60 to $75, on acceptance. Query.

ANIMAL CAVALCADE–11926 Santa Monica Blvd., Los Angeles, CA 90025.
Articles, 1,500 words, with photos, for pet owners on pet health problems, care, nutrition, grooming, training. Pays to $35 for articles, and $5-$20 for photos, on publication.

ANIMAL KINGDOM–Zoological Park, Bronx, NY 10460.
Articles on mammals, birds, reptiles, fishes, conservation, 2,500 words, with 8 x 10 glossies and/or 35 mm color. No articles on pets or tame animals. Pays $75 to $300, on acceptance.

ANIMALS–M.S.P.C.A., 180 Longwood Ave., Boston, MA 02115. Richard H. Cowan, Editor.
Official publication of the Massachusetts Society for the Prevention of Cruelty to Animals. Articles, to 2,000 words, viewing animals from cultural perspective. Pays 2¢ a word, on publication. Query.

ARGOSY–420 Lexington Ave., New York, NY 10017. Seth Masia, Articles Editor. Bert Sugar, Editor.
Men's magazine. Articles, to 3,000 words with photos, on adventure, outdoor recreation and leisure activities – camping, nature, hunting, archeology, exploration, etc. Pays $250 to $3,000. Query.

THE ATLANTIC–8 Arlington St., Boston, MA 02116. Robert Manning, Editor.
Highest quality articles on public issues, politics, social sciences, education, business, criticism, literature, and the arts. Pays about $100 per *Atlantic* page.

THE ATLANTIC ADVOCATE—Gleaner Bldg., Phoenix Sq., Fredericton, N.B., Canada. H. P. Wood, Editor.
Prefers regional articles about Eastern Canada, but also considers general-interest articles, especially unusual, well-researched pieces. Photos. Pays by negotiation.

BC OUTDOORS—Box 900, Postal Station A, Surrey, B.C., Canada. Art Downs, Editor.
Articles, 2,000 to 3,000 words with black-and-white photos, of topical, historical, outdoor and general interest, about people and places of British Columbia and the Yukon. Hunting, fishing, travel, wildlife and boating pieces on same region. Pays $50 to $100, on acceptance.

BETTER HOMES AND GARDENS—1716 Locust St., Des Moines, IA 50336. James A. Autry, Editor.
Articles, 250 to 1,000 words, on travel, health, cars, projects with "before" and "after" snapshots. Pays top rates, on acceptance. "Direct the manuscript to the department where the story line is strongest."

BLACK STARS—820 South Michigan Ave., Chicago, IL 60605.
Articles on black entertainers, their personal lives, careers and future intentions. Articles are assigned. Query.

BLACK WORLD—820 South Michigan Ave., Chicago, IL 60605. Hoyt W. Fuller, Executive Editor.
Articles, to 3,500 words, on blacks or black life: think pieces, controversy, figures out of black history, essays on black literature and black literary figures, dissent.

BON APPETIT—5900 Wilshire Blvd., Los Angeles, CA 90036.
Devoted to fine food, wines, travel, entertaining, restaurants, new products and culinary equipment. Travel articles, 1,200 to 1,500 words, should mention specific restaurants, hotels, resorts, foods, and wine. Pays 10¢ per word, $25 per color photo, $10 for black-and-white photo.

BOSTON GLOBE MAGAZINE—*Boston Globe,* Boston, MA 02107. Robert Levey, Editor.
General interest articles, 1,000 to 5,000 words, photo essays. Pays $150 to $200 for articles, $150 for photo-layouts, $100 to $150 for covers, on publication. Query.

BUYWAYS—1000 Sunset Ridge Rd., Northbrook, IL 60062. Anne Springhorn, Editor.
Articles, 500 to 2,500 words, on how to shop, how to save, money management, taxes, legal advice; travel pieces with emphasis on budget. Pays 10¢ to 20¢ a word, on acceptance. Query.

CALIFORNIA HIGHWAY PATROLMAN—1225 8th St., Suite 150, Sacramento, CA 95814. Joseph L. Richardson, Editor.
Lively articles with photos on transportation safety, driver education, California travel, and old California. Pays 1½¢ a word, $2.50 per photos or illustration, $10 for cartoons. Sample copy available.

CAMPAIGN INSIGHTS—Suite 408, Petroleum Bldg., Wichita, KS 67202. Hank Parkinson, Publisher.
Articles, 800 to 1,000 words, describing political techniques that lead to campaign wins on all levels of government. Pays 5¢ a word, on acceptance. Query.

CAMPING JOURNAL—229 Park Ave. South, New York, NY 10003.
Articles to 2,500 words, on camping (routes, campsite locations, facilities, person-alities, adventure or uniqueness of an area), with 20 top-quality transparencies. Camp-skills articles and short, how-to articles. Pays $150 and up for feature articles, $100 and up for camp-skills articles, $50 and up for how-to articles, on acceptance. Query.

THE CANADIAN MAGAZINE–The Canadian Star Weekly, Simpson Tower, 401 Bay St., Toronto 1, Ont., Canada. Alan Walker, Managing Editor.
Controversial, thought-provoking articles on timely topics with Canadian appeal, to 2,000 words. Profiles, sports, human-interest, adventure, entertainment page articles. Pays 10¢ a word and up, on acceptance.

CAPPER'S WEEKLY–616 Jefferson St., Topeka, KS 66607. Dorothy Harvey, Editor.
Articles, 300 to 500 words: human-interest, personal experience, historical. Pay varies, on publication.

CARTE BLANCHE–3460 Wilshire Blvd., Los Angeles, CA 90010. J. Walter Flynn, Editor and Publisher.
Travel, dining and entertainment articles directed to family audience as well as professional men and women. No fiction.

CATS–P.O. Box 4106, Pittsburgh, PA 15202.
Unusual experience articles about cats; factual articles on veterinary medicine advances, cats in art, literature, or science, humorous pieces, 1,000 to 2,000 words. "We stay away from cats that talk, unless it is to Paul Gallico," Full-color cover (pays $75) and black-and-white Picture of the Month contest photos ($20). Pays 3¢ a word, extra for photos.

CAVALIER–316 Aragon Ave., Coral Gales, FL 33134.
Articles, 2,500 to 5,000 words, appealing to hip young males with informed and sophisticated tastes. Pays $200 and up, on publication.

CHATELAINE–481 University Ave., Toronto, Ont., Canada. Doris Anderson, Editor.
Articles, 3,500 words, of interest to women, on controversial subjects, outstanding and colorful personalities, and on personal interest topics in medical, psychological and emotional fields. Pays $300 and up, on acceptance.

CHEVRON USA–P.O. Box 6227, San Jose, CA 95150. Marian May, Editor.
Articles, 500 to 1,500 words, on travel in western, southern and eastern U.S., family activities (hobbies, crafts, outdoor sports, etc.), wildlife, conservation. Pays 15¢ a word, $25 for black-and-white photos, $50 to $200 for color, on acceptance.

THE CHRISTIAN SCIENCE MONITOR–One Norway St., Boston, MA 02115. John Hughes, Editor.
Articles for travel, education, homemaking, science, environment, consumer pages, etc. Humorous or human-interest articles for People page; literary essays, 400 to 800 words, for Home Forum; guest columns, to 800 words, for editoral page. Rates vary.

CIRCLE K MAGAZINE–101 East Erie Street, Chicago, IL 60611. Carl L. Stach, Executive Editor.
Articles, 800 to 2,000 words, of interest to college students, especially about social action, political issues, leadership, group dynamics. Pays on acceptance; extra for photos.

CIVIL LIBERTIES REVIEW–22 East 40th St., Room 1020, New York, NY 10016. Walter J. Green, Managing Editor.
Articles, 1,200 to 7,000 words, on civil liberties controversies and "frontier" issues, for civil liberties professionals, activists and concerned lay people. Artwork and photos. Pay varies, on acceptance. Query.

COLORADO–7190 West 14th Ave., Denver, CO 80215. David Sumner, Executive Editor.
Exciting adventure, current or historical, about people in Rocky Mountain West, from 2,500 to 3,000 words, preferably with photos or artwork. Pays 10¢ a word, on acceptance.

COLUMBIA–Box 1670, New Haven, CT 06507. Elmer Von Feldt, Editor.
Official journal of Knights of Columbus. Illustrated articles, 1,000 to 3,000 words, on science, history, sports, current events, religion, education and art. Short humorous pieces to 1,000 words. Pays $100 to $300, on acceptance.

COMMENTARY–165 East 56th St., New York, NY 10022. Norman Podhoretz, Editor.
Articles, 5,000 to 7,000 words, on the contemporary scene, here and abroad: profiles, Jewish affairs, social sciences, community life, religious thought, cultural activities. Pays about 3½¢ a word.

COMMONWEAL–232 Madison Ave., New York, NY 10016. James O'Gara, Editor.
Catholic. Articles on political, social, religious and literary subjects, up to 3,000 words. Pays 2¢ a word, on acceptance.

THE CONTINENTAL MAGAZINE–Room 961, World Headquarters, Ford Motor Co., Dearborn, MI 48121. Robert M. Hodesh, Editor-in-Chief.
Sophisticated service articles, 1,300 to 1,500 words, on travel, entertainment, shopping, collecting, cuisine, for the well-to-do. Pays on acceptance. Query.

CORONET–7950 Deering Ave., Canoga Park, CA 91304. Catherine N. Cooke, Managing Editor.
General-interest articles, 1,500 words; consumer affairs, health, self-improvement, politics, business success, human-interest, sex-related, etc. Pays $200 and up. Query.

COSMOPOLITAN–224 West 57th St., New York, NY 10019. Helen Gurley Brown, Editor. Walter Meade, Managing Editor. Roberta Ashley, Articles Editor.
Magazine for young, active, career women. Articles, to 5,000 words, and shorter features, 1,000 to 2,500 words, which tell readers how to improve and enjoy their lives. Pays roughly $750 and up for full-length articles, less for short features. Other payment by arrangement. Query.

CRAWDADDY–72 Fifth Ave., New York, NY 10011.
Rock and roll interviews, celebrity pieces, politics and culture, 1,000 to 2,000 words, to appeal to readers 18 to 30. Pay varies, on publication. Query.

CREATIVE LIVING–747 Third Ave., New York, NY 10017. Robert H. Spencer, Editor.
Articles, 800 to 2,000 words, on how to use leisure time creatively: profiles of people involved in satisfying spare-time activities, with specific examples to explain motivation and philosophy of these individuals. Pays $50 to $400, on acceptance. Editorial requirements sheet available.

THE CRISIS–NAACP, 1790 Broadway, New York, NY 10036. Henry Lee Moon, Editor.
Articles, 3,000 words, on the problems and achievements of black people, and the status of race relations in the U.S. and abroad. Pays in copies.

DESERT MAGAZINE–Palm Desert, CA 92260. William Knyvett, Editor.
Illustrated features, especially travel, about the Southwest, including history, ghost towns, lost mines and nature, 500 to 2,000 words. Pays 2¢ a word; $35 for cover color transparencies (2¼ x 2½ or 4 x 5), up to $25 for other photos, on publication.

DIVERSION–Box 215, Bear Tavern Rd., Titusville, NJ 08560. Willard Clark, Editor.
For physicians, dentists, veterinarians as consumers. Articles, 300 to 3,000 words, on travel, sports, hobbies, recreation, entertainment, food. Color illustrations. Pays $200 and up. Query.

DIXIE-ROTO—*The Times-Picayune,* 3800 Howard Ave., New Orleans, LA 70140. Sunday supplement. Terence P. Smith, Editor.
Factual feature articles, with Louisiana-Mississippi background. Pays $40 and up for articles. Pays $20 for Deep South anecdotal, true stories with dramatic interest, usually set in past, 750 to 1,000 words. Sample copies on request. Query.

DOG WORLD—10060 West Roosevelt Rd., Westchester, IL 60153. George Berner, Publisher.
Technical material of interest to professional dog breeders, exhibitors, and judges.

EARLY AMERICAN LIFE—Box 1831, Harrisburg, PA 17105. Robert G. Miner, Editor.
Illustrated articles, 1,000 to 4,000 words, on early American life: arts, crafts, furnishings and architecture. Pays $25 to $200, on acceptance. Query.

EBONY—820 South Michigan Ave., Chicago, IL 60605. Herbert Nipson, Executive Editor.
Photo-feature material primarily on American blacks, with emphasis on achievement, civil rights, human interest. Pays $150 and up, on acceptance.

THE ELKS MAGAZINE—425 West Diversey Pkwy., Chicago, IL 60614. D. J. Herda, Articles Editor.
Authoritative, in-depth articles, 3,000 words, on timely, appealing topics: business, money management, profiles of industries, ecology, etc. Pays $400 and up. Shorter articles, informative or lightly entertaining, up to 2,000 words: hunting, fishing, science, history, etc. Pays $100 to $300, on acceptance. Sample copies available. Query.

ENCORE—515 Madison Ave., New York, NY 10022. Ida Lewis, Publisher and Editor.
Articles, 1,500 words, on contemporary topics: fashion, travel, politics, penal reform. Movie and book reviews. Pays on publication. Query.

ENVIRONMENT—438 North Skinker Blvd., St. Louis, MO 63130. Sheldon Novick, Editor.
Factual articles, 5,000 to 7,000 words, presenting technical information in layman's terms on environment pollution, effects of technology. Pays $100. Query.

ESQUIRE—488 Madison Ave., New York, NY 10022.
Articles, 1,500 to 5,000 words, with depth of insight and strong impact, to interest intelligent adult audience. Particular interest is "revelatory, newsworthy lead pieces" and 1,000-word one-pagers about major problem or dramatic piece of news. Pays $350 to $1,000, on acceptance. Query.

FAMILY CIRCLE—488 Madison Ave., New York, NY 10022. Babette Ashby, Articles Editor.
High-quality articles on all "service" subjects, including advice about marriage problems, financial and psychological insights to help women. Human interest stories with personal significance for readers.

FAMILY HEALTH—545 Madison Ave., New York, NY 10022.
Articles, under 3,000 words, and photo-essays, on health, beauty, physical fitness, marriage, child care, nutrition, health-oriented consumerism, personal experiences. Submit outline first. Pays $500 and up for major articles, on acceptance.

FAMILY MAGAZINE—Army Times Publishing Co., 475 School St. S.W., Washington, DC 20024. Jim Scott, Managing Editor.
Supplement to *Army Times, Air Force Times, Navy Times.* Articles, 800 to 3,000 words, with black-and-white or color photos when possible, on any subject related to military men and families. Pays on publication.

FAMILY WEEKLY—641 Lexington Ave., New York, NY 10022. Mort Persky, Editor-in-Chief. Reynolds Dodson, Managing Editor.
Sunday Supplement. Unsolicited articles not welcome. Queries and article ideas are welcome and should be sent to Mr. Dodson. Pays on acceptance.

FATE–Clark Publishing Co., Highland House, 3500 Western Ave., Highland Park, IL 60035. Mary M. Fuller, Editor.
Documented, fact articles and stories up to 3,000 words, on strange and mysterious happenings. Pays 3¢ a word. Pays $5 on publication for true, first-person accounts of psychic or unexplainable experiences, to 300 words, for "True Mystic Experiences" and "My Proof of Survival."

FLING–1485 Bayshore Blvd., Suite 400, San Francisco, CA 94124.
Articles for adult male readers, 2,500 to 6,000 words. Controversial and offbeat themes. Careful research, authenticated case histories, strong point of view required. No self-help, sports, travel. Pays $100 to $200, on acceptance. Query.

FLORIDA SPORTSMAN–4025 Ponce de Leon Blvd., Coral Gables, FL 33146. Bill Hallstrom, Executive Editor.
Fishing, boating, and camping articles, 800 to 1,500 words, on Florida, Bahamas, Caribbean and West Indies. Heavy on how-tos. Black-and-white glossy prints or color transparencies with articles. Pays $50 and up, on publication. Query.

FOCUS/MIDWEST–Box 3086, St. Louis, MO 63130. Charles L. Klotzer, Editor.
Controversial regional and national articles, 900 to 3,000 words, of concern to readers in Midwest, on political, social and cultural issues, especially urban problems in Chicago, St. Louis, and Kansas City. No taboos. Pays on publication.

FORD TIMES–Ford Motor Company, The American Rd., Dearborn, MI 48121. William E. Pauli, Managing Editor.
Articles, 1,200 to 1,500 words, relating to American life: motor travel, sports, fashion, vacation ideas, reminiscence, portraits of big cities and small towns, the arts, Americana, nostalgia, the outdoors. Pays $250 and up. Query.

FOREIGN SERVICE JOURNAL–2101 E St. N.W., Washington, DC 20037. Shirley Newhall, Editor.
Professional journal of foreign affairs. Articles on American diplomacy and foreign affairs, or material of interest to Americans representing United States abroad. Few travel articles, generally experiences of foreign affairs officers. Pays on publication.

THE FREEMAN–Foundation for Economic Education, Irving-on-Hudson, NY 10533. Paul L. Poirot, Editor.
Nonfiction, to 3,000 words, on economic, political, and moral philosophy behind concepts of private property, limited government, competitive bargaining and voluntary exchange. Pays 5¢ a word, on publication.

FRIENDS–30400 Van Dyke, Warren MI 48093.
Photo-articles on travel, recreation, sports, personalities, etc. Photos must tell story. Writers' guide available on request. Pays $75 to $150 per page, depending on photos, on acceptance. Query.

FRONTIER TIMES–Western Publications, Box 3338, Austin, TX 78764. Pat Wagner, Editor.
Researched, accurate stories, to 5,000 words, on events in the Old West, 1840 to 1915. Must not be fictionalized. Source list should accompany manuscript. Photos welcome; returned after publication. Pays 2¢ a word on acceptance. Same address and requirements for *True West* and *Old West*. Query.

FRONTIERS–Academy of Natural Sciences, 19th St. and The Parkway, Philadelphia, PA 19103. Nancy Steele, Editor.
Articles, 1,000 to 2,000 words, on natural history and ecology, with black-and-white photos when available. Pays $15 per published magazine page.

GAMBLERS WORLD–527 Madison Ave., New York, NY 10022. Lawrence Bernard, Editor.
How-to articles about recreational gambling. Varying rates, on acceptance. Query.

GEM—G & S Publications, Inc., 303 West 42nd St., New York, NY 10036. Will Martin, Editor.
Articles on any contemporary theme, preferably sex-oriented, from 500 to 1,500 words. Pay varies, generally after assignment to specific issue. Same address and requirements for *The Swinger.*

GENESIS—120 East 56th St., New York, NY 10022. Eric Protter, Editor.
Articles, 2,500 to 6,000 words, with sexual orientation; exposes; profiles; interviews. Pays $350 to $750.

GENTLEMEN'S QUARTERLY—488 Madison Ave., New York, NY 10022. George Mazzei, Managing Editor.
Hip, sophisticated, male-oriented features about personalities, travel, good living, sports, etc. No fiction; no poetry. Query letter *must* precede unsolicited manuscripts; otherwise returned unread. Pays shortly after acceptance.

GLAMOUR—350 Madison Ave., New York, NY 10017. Ruth Whitney, Editor-in-Chief. Phyllis Starr, Managing Editor.
Lively, well-written service articles, 2,000 to 3,000 words, for young women, on all aspects of life and topics of current interest. Pays $300 to $700.

GOOD HOUSEKEEPING—959 Eighth Ave., New York, NY 10019. Elizabeth Pope Frank, Articles Editor.
Informative, absorbing articles for women. Articles usually written on assignment, but queries considered. Especially interested in dramatic first-person experiences in fields of human relations, individual achievement, practical living, romance, and social techniques. Pays top rates, on acceptance. "Better Way" occasionally buys research reports on news of practical interest about women's activities.

GOURMET—777 Third Ave., New York, NY 10017. Earle R. MacAusland, Editor and Publisher.
Articles, 2,500 to 3,000 words — reminiscences, travel, and other facets of good living — for sophisticated audience interested in fine food and wines. Recipes purchased only as part of articles. No short features, profiles of living persons, reports on festivals or wine tastings, or specific restaurant recommendations. Gourmet Holidays feature is written by staff writers only. Send manuscripts to Gail Zweigenthal, Managing Editor. Pays on acceptance.

GRIT—Williamsport. PA 17701. Kenneth D. Loss, Feature Editor.
Human-interest, inspirational articles, 300 to 800 words, occasionally to 2,500 words: personalities, small towns, patriotism, etc. All articles accompanied by black-and-white photos (pays $10 each) or color transparencies ($25 each) with identifying captions. Pays 5¢ a word; for illustrations with captions that stand alone, pays $7.50 for black-and-white photos and $30 for color transparencies; on acceptance.

GUIDE TO EARNING EXTRA INCOME—363 7th Ave., New York, NY 10001. Mel Shapiro, Editor.
Articles, from 1,000 words with photos, on spare- and full-time income opportunities. Pays from $50, on publication.

HARPER'S BAZAAR—717 Fifth Ave., New York, NY 10022. Anthony T. Mazzola, Editor-in-Chief.
No unsolicited manuscripts accepted.

HARPER'S MAGAZINE—2 Park Ave., New York, NY 10016. Robert Shnayerson, Editor-in-Chief.
Timely articles, 2,000 to 5,000 words, on social, political, economic, cultural aspects of American life. Foreign reporting. Pays on acceptance. Query.

HOLIDAY—1100 Waterway Blvd., Indianapolis, IN 46206. Kathryn Klassen, Managing Editor.
Articles on travel and free-time subjects, 1,500 to 2,000 words. Pays on publication.

HORIZON—1221 Ave. of the Americas, New York, NY 10020. Shirley Tomkievicz, Editor.
Articles on the arts and historical subjects related to the contemporary world. Pays on acceptance.

HOW-TO—964 North Pennsylvania St., Indianapolis, IN 46204. John J. Sullivan, Editor.
Detailed do-it-yourself articles, any length, with step-by-step instructions, on home maintenance and repair, home improvement projects, gardening, etc. Accompanying photos. Pays $100 and up per published page, on acceptance. Query. Send for writer's guide.

HUMAN BEHAVIOR—12031 Wilshire Blvd., Los Angeles, CA 90025.
Articles, 1,500 to 4,000 words, with photos, relating to new developments in social sciences and human behavior research. Pays $150 to $500. Query.

THE HUMANIST—923 Kensington Ave., Buffalo, NY 14215. Paul Kurtz, Editor.
Journal of humanist and ethical concern. Articles, 2,000 to 4,500 words, on social and moral issues. Query.

INFANTRY—Box 2005, Fort Benning, GA 31905. Professional journal of U.S. infantryman.
Articles, 2,000 to 5,000 words, on military organizations, weapons, equipment, tactics, techniques and leadership. Welcomes civilian contributions. Writers' guide sent on request. Pay varies, on publication. Query.

JURIS DOCTOR, MAGAZINE FOR THE NEW LAWYER—730 Third Ave., New York, NY 10017. Wendy Lyon Moonan, Editor.
Feature articles, to 2,000 words, on new developments in the legal profession; profiles of outstanding young lawyers. "Muckraking" pieces, 2,500 words, on conflicts of interest, legal fees, the organized bar. Pays $300 and up for investigative articles. $150 and up for profiles, on acceptance. Query with outline and sample of published work.

KEYNOTER—101 East Erie St., Chicago, IL 60611. Carl L. Stach, Executive Editor.
Articles, 800 to 2,000 words, of interest to high school students, particularly on ecology, human relations and community action. Pays on acceptance; extra for photos.

KIRKLEY PRESS, INC.—Box 200, Timonium, MD 21093. Walter Kirkley, Editor.
Material to motivate employees, on ambition, initiative, honesty, cooperation, etc. Pays $35 for articles of 350 to 400 words; $200 to $300 for booklets of 2,000 to 2,400 words. Sample sent on request.

THE KIWANIS MAGAZINE—101 East Erie, Chicago, IL 60611. David B. Williams, Executive Editor.
In-depth articles on domestic problems and developments in United States and Canada, and on topics of social, economic and educational interest, 2,500 to 3,500 words. Value placed on good research, wide use of examples, authoritative quotes. No fiction or short material. Pays up to $500, on acceptance.

LADIES' HOME JOURNAL—641 Lexington Ave., New York, NY 10022. Dick Kaplan, Executive Editor.
Exciting, accurate, tightly-written articles of interest to contemporary women. Magazine works principally with well-known writers.

LADY'S CIRCLE—21 West 26th St., New York, NY 10010. Evan Frances, Editor.
Articles, 2,000 to 2,500 words, on changing life-styles, travel in U.S., service pieces for homemakers, personal-experience pieces by homemakers on solving practical, day-to-day problems. Pays $125, more for photos, on publication.

LEATHERNECK—Box 1918, Quantico, VA 22134. Ronald D. Lyons, Managing Editor.
Current articles, 1,500 to 3,000 words, with photos, about U.S. Marines. Pays to $300, on acceptance. Query.

LEISURETIME MAGAZINE—Box 11626, Santa Ana, CA 92711. Ann Terrill, Editor.
Sunday news supplement. Articles, 600 to 2,500 words, on unique untravelled places, with black-and-white glossies. Occasional feature material. Pay varies. Query.

THE LION—York and Cermak Rds., Oak Brook, IL 60521. Robert Kleinfelder, Senior Editor.
Factual, informative articles, 1,500 to 2,000 words, to interest business and professional men. Pays 10¢ a word and up. Photo features on Lions Club projects.

LISTEN—6840 Eastern Ave. N.W., Washington, DC 20012. Francis A. Soper, Editor.
Illustrated articles, 500 to 1,500 words, on all phases of narcotics problem, including alcohol, emotional balance and mental health. Especially interested in youth-slanted features with positive approach, showing better way of life than dependence on drink and drugs. Pays 2¢ to 4¢ a word, on acceptance.

LITHOPINION—113 University Place, New York, NY 10003. Jim Hoffman, Editorial Consultant.
Articles, 2,000 to 4,000 words, on history, culture, politics, society; profiles, interviews, satire, exposes, nostalgia, by "recognized professionals with extensive credits in national magazines." Pays $750, within two weeks of acceptance. Query.

LIVELY WORLD—Caldwell Communications, Inc., 747 Third Ave., New York, NY 10017. Robert H. Spencer, Editor.
Articles, 800 to 3,000 words, on U.S. and foreign travel, relevant to Marriott Hotel locations, focusing on the people, history and social issues; sports, leisure, business, personal finance, food, profiles, sophisticated humor. Pays $50 to $400, more for color transparencies, on publication. Non-returnable writing samples and list of published credits must accompany query or manuscript. Send for writer's guide.

THE LOOKOUT—Seamen's Church Institute, 15 State St., New York, NY 10004. Carlyle Windley, Editor.
Fact-filled articles, 200 to 1,000 words with photos, on the sea; merchant marine, sea oddities and phenomena, tall but "true" sea tales. Pays $25 to $40.

McCALL'S—230 Park Ave., New York, NY 10017. Helen Markel, Articles Editor.
Timely features and articles on all subjects, 2,500 to 3,500 words. All service articles staff-written. Pays top rates, on acceptance.

MACLEAN'S MAGAZINE—481 University Ave., Toronto, Ont., Canada.
Canadian-slanted articles on entertainment, sports, politics, business, etc., 2,000 to 3,000 words. Submit full outline first.

MADEMOISELLE—420 Lexington Ave., New York, NY 10017. Mary Cantwell, Managing Editor.
Articles of general interest to literate young women, on controversial or timely subjects, 1,500 to 4,000 words. Pays on acceptance. Query.

MALE—575 Madison Ave., New York, NY 10022. Carl Sifakis, Editor.
Powerful, dramatic articles, 5,000 to 6,000 words, appealing to men; exposes; profiles of adventurous men, both contemporary and World War II; stories of survival, escape, heroic deeds set in exotic backgrounds. Pays to $500, on acceptance; considerably more for 15,000-word book-lengths of particular appeal. Prefers detailed query. Same address and requirements for *Men*.

MAN TO MAN—See *Mr. Magazine.*

MANKIND—8060 Melrose Ave., Los Angeles, CA 90046. Alvaro Cardona-Hine, Editor.
Articles, 2,000 to 4,000 words, on historical incidents, in lively, enjoyable style. Pays from $150, on publication. Query with outline.

MAN'S MAGAZINE–919 Third Ave., New York, NY 10022. Phil Hirsch, Editorial
    Director.
    Tautly written adventure features, exposes, sports, crime, military, historical, medical
    and service pieces, 4,000 to 6,000 words. Pays $200 to $500, on acceptance.

MARRIAGE & FAMILY LIVING–St. Meinrad, IN 47577.
    Articles, to 2,500 words, for married adults on their problems, aspirations, etc. Pays
    5¢ a word.

MEDIA & CONSUMER–Box 850, Norwalk, CT 06852. Francis Pollock, Editor.
    Critical, investigative articles, 1,000 to 3,000 words, on journalism and advertising as
    they affect consumer. Photos. Moderate pay, on publication. Query.

MEN–See *Male.*

MIDNIGHT–1440 St. Catherine St. West. Montreal 107, Quebec, Canada. Joan Leblanc,
    Editor-in-Chief.
    Hard-hitting, factual articles, 500 to 1,000 words, with photos: exposes, celebrity
    interviews, consumer articles. Pays $50 to $175, on acceptance.

MIDSTREAM: A MONTHLY JEWISH REVIEW–515 Park Ave., New York, NY 10022.
    Ronald Sanders, Editor.
    Quality articles, fiction, and book reviews for general readers. Pays 6¢ a word, on
    acceptance.

MILITARY LIFE/MALE CALL–W. B. Bradbury Co., 6 East 43rd St., New York, NY
    10017. Will Lieberson, Editor.
    Male-oriented articles, 700 to 1,000 words, with military slant, on sports and
    adventure. Pays $75, on acceptance. Query.

MINNESOTA AAA MOTORIST–7 Travelers Trail, Burnsville, MN 55337. Ronald D.
    Johnson, Editor.
    Articles, 800 to 1,500 words, on travel, motoring, car care and related subjects.
    8 x 10 black-and-white photos of travel scenes, usually with articles. Pays $150 and
    up for articles, $15 per photos, $75 for front cover color photos, $15 per cartoon, on
    acceptance.

MR. MAGAZINE–280 Madison Ave., New York, NY 10016. Everett Meyers, Editor.
    Articles, 2,000 to 5,000 words, on contemporary trends in travel, music, sex, art
    forms, unusual entertainment, and other activities of interest to men. Good 8 x 10
    glossy photos will help sell articles. Pays $100 minimum for articles; extra for
    pictures used, on publication. Same address and requirements for *Man to Man* and
    Sir!

MODERN MAN–Publisher's Development Corp., 8150 North Central Park Blvd.,
    Skokie, IL 60076. Donald Stahl, Editor.
    Articles, 2,000 words, on all areas of sexual exploration, approached in dramatic,
    humorous, or documentary style, with emphasis on human side of sex. No taboos.

MODERN MATURITY–215 Long Beach Blvd., Long Beach, CA 90802. Hubert Pryor,
    Editor.
    Service articles, to 2,000 words, on living, food, health, employment, for persons
    over 55 years. Nostalgia, inspirational articles, personality pieces, Americana,
    interpretations of the current scene. Pays $50 to $500, on acceptance; $15 up for
    black-and-white photos, and $50 up to color photos. Special fees for covers.

MODERN PEOPLE NEWSWEEKLY–11058 Addison St., Franklin Park, IL 60131.
    Articles, 500 to 800 words with black-and-white photos, on health, consumer
    protection, the occult, true-life adventures, star interviews. Pays $20 and up, within
    two weeks of acceptance.

MONEY—Time & Life Bldg., Rockefeller Center, New York, NY 10020. William Simon Rukeyser, Managing Editor.
Articles, 2,000 to 3,000 words, on investments, consumer affairs, careers, taxes, household budgets and estate planning. Pay varies. Query with brief outline.

MONTANA: THE MAGAZINE OF WESTERN HISTORY—Montana Historical Society, 225 North Roberts, Helena, MT 59601. Mrs. Vivian A. Paladin, Editor.
Documented nonfiction, 3,500 to 6,000 words, about Old West or frontier West. Include research sources. No contrived dialogue or trite rewriting of standard incidents. Pays 1½¢ a word and up, on acceptance. Query.

MS.—370 Lexington Ave., New York, NY 10017.
Reporting, interviews, personal experiences on women's changing self-image and status, up to 3,000 words. Pays competitive rates. Query.

THE NATION—333 Sixth Ave. New York, NY 10014. Carey McWilliams, Editor.
Articles on matters of current interest, 2,000 to 2,500 words. Pays 2¢ a word, on publication. Query.

NATION'S CITIES—1620 Eye St. N.W., Washington, DC 20006. Allen E. Pritchard, Jr. Editor.
Articles, to 1,000 words, for city and town officials, on municipal government and urban affairs. Pays $100, on acceptance. Query.

NATIONAL ENQUIRER—Lantana, FL 33462. Nat Chrzan, Editor.
Factual, in-depth articles of any length based on personal interviews on subjects appealing to mass audience: fresh slants on topical news stories, medical "firsts," scientific breakthroughs, human drama, personality profiles, self-help and how-to articles, occult and psychic fields, government waste of taxpayers' money. Pays $125 and up; extra for good photos. Query.

THE NATIONAL GUARDSMAN—1 Massachusetts Ave. N.W., Washington, DC 20010. Luther L. Walker, Editor.
Articles, 2,000 to 4,000 words, exclusively on the military, both air and ground, combat lessons, current development. Pays 3¢ and up per published word, on publication.

NATIONAL GEOGRAPHIC—17th and M Sts. N.W., Washington, DC 20036. Gilbert M. Grosvenor, Editor.
First-person articles, 2,000 to 4,000 words (8,000 words maximum), on travel, exploration, mountaineering, seafaring, archaeological discoveries, natural history, important or unusual industries, occupations, advances in science, notable festivals and folkways. Manuscript, especially of adventure in hard-to-reach place, has better chance of acceptance if accompanied by original color transparencies, preferably 35 mm or larger, of high quality and interest. Pays $1,500 to $3,000. Separate payment for photographs. Query. Leaflets available on photographic and writing needs.

NATIONAL HUMANE REVIEW—Box 1266, Denver, CO 80201. Mrs. Eileen F. Schoen, Editor.
Human-interest articles, 1,000 to 2,000 words, demonstrating humane treatment of animals and prevention of cruelty to animals. Include dramatic incident. Photo stories with captions. Pays 1½¢ a word, on publication.

THE NATIONAL STAR—730 Third Ave., New York, NY 10017.
Topical articles, 300 to 2,000 words, for broad family readership, on controversial political, social and moral issues, changing life-styles, human-interest pieces, sports, women's features. Pay varies.

NATURAL HISTORY MAGAZINE–Central Park West at 79th St., New York, NY 10024.
The Journal of the American Museum of Natural History. Articles, to 3,500 words, by experts on anthropology and natural sciences for intelligent reader. Usually requires good color photos. Pays $500. Query.

NEW ENGLAND GALAXY–Old Sturbridge Village, Sturbridge, MA 01566. Catherine Fennelly, Editor.
Articles, 2,000 to 3,000 words, on New England, particularly episodes of political and social history. Pays $75 to $150, on publication. Query.

THE NEW REPUBLIC–1244 19th St. N.W., Washington, DC 20036. Gilbert Harrison, Editor-in-Chief; David Sanford, Managing Editor.
Features on political, social, economic, and cultural subjects, 2,000 words or less. Pays by arrangement.

NEW TIMES–One Park Ave., New York, NY 10016. Jonathan Z. Larsen, Editor.
Articles, 1,500 to 4,000 words, on current or controversial subjects; profiles of newsmakers; exposes. Pays $200 to $500. Query.

THE NEW YORK TIMES MAGAZINE–Times Sq., New York, NY 10036. Max Frankel, Editor.
Sunday magazine. Timely articles, approximately 3,500 words, based on specific news items, forthcoming events, anniversaries, trends. Pays $850; $500 for short articles, 1,000 to 2,000 words, on acceptance. No poetry.

THE NEW YORKER–25 West 43rd St., New York, NY 10036.
Factual, historic, and biographical material in "Profiles," "Reporter at Large," "That Was New York," "Annals of Crime," "Onward and Upward with the Arts," etc. Pays good rates, on acceptance. Address The Editors. Query.

OCEANS–125 Independence Dr., Menlo Park, CA 94025. Don Greame Kelley, Editor.
Articles, to 5,000 words with photos, on marine life (biology and ecology), oceanography, man-sea history, geography, undersea exploration, etc. Limited use of travel, adventure, sport fishing, diving, and boating subjects. Pays 3¢ to 6¢ a word, on publication; $5 to $50 for color transparencies or black-and-white. Negotiate cover photos. Overstocked; query.

OLD WEST–See *Frontier Times.*

OPTIMIST MAGAZINE–4494 Lindell Blvd., St. Louis, MO 63108. Gary Adamson, Editor.
Optimist-oriented articles. Pays $75, on acceptance. Query. Cartoons, color photos for cover; pays $5.

OUI–919 North Michigan Ave., Chicago, IL 60611. Peter McCabe, Editor.
Published by Playboy Enterprises for men 18 to 30. Entertaining articles, 2,500 to 5,000 words, especially with international flavor. Pays $1,200. Query.

OUTDOOR WORLD–24198 West Bluemound Rd., Waukesha, WI 53186. D'Arlyn Marks, Associate Editor.
Unusual nonfiction, outdoor activity stories and in-depth articles on personal observations of wildlife, with photos; also arts, crafts, Indians and foreign lands. No hunting or fishing. Pays $200 to $250 for major articles with photos; $75 to $150 for short pieces with photos. Query.

OUTDOORS–*Sunday Oregonian,* 1320 S.W. Broadway, Portland, OR 97201. J. R. Bianco, Editor.
Articles, 800 words with black-and-white photos, on outdoor activities in Pacific Northwest. Pays $40, plus $15 per photo, the 10th of each month.

P. O. P.–919 Filley St., Lansing, MI 48906.
Articles, 1,200 words, of general interest to male readers, on adventure, sports, antique cars, racing, etc. Two black-and-white photos must accompany each manuscript. Pays $200, 15 days after publication.

PAGEANT–205 East 42nd St., New York, NY 10017. Nat Perlow, Editor.
Articles on health, medicine, humor, current social trends, how-to's, etc. Pay varies. Query.

PARADE–733 Third Ave., New York, NY 10017.
National Sunday newspaper magazine. News-related lead articles on important general-interest subjects, to 2,500 words. No spot news. Shorter stories of interest or service to families. Pays well, on acceptance. Query Articles Editor.

PARENTS' MAGAZINE–52 Vanderbilt Ave., New York, NY 10017. Genevieve Millet Landau, Editor-in-Chief.
Articles, 2,500 words, on children's physical and mental growth and development, family and marriage relationships, community activities, baby care, health and education. Prefers colloquial style with quotes from experts. Pays on acceptance. Query with outline.

PEN–444 Sherman St., Denver, CO 80203. Jean Blair Ryan, Editor.
Articles, to 1,800 words, of interest to government employees on career goals, government services and programs; travel, animals, sports, human interest, history, personalities. Pays 5¢ per word, on acceptance; $5 per 8 x 10 black-and-white glossy photo, $10 if used for cover. Sample copy available.

PENTHOUSE–909 Third Ave., New York, NY 10022. James Goode, Executive Editor; Ken Gouldthorpe, Managing Editor.
General-interest or hard-hitting controversial articles, to 6,000 words; sexually-oriented nonfiction and humor, to 5,000 words. Pays $250 per 1,000 words, on acceptance.

PENTHOUSE FORUM–909 Third Ave., New York, NY 10022. Marlene Deverell-VanMeter, Executive Editor.
Articles, 1,500 to 2,500 words, on contemporary emotional, psychological, medical, and sexual conflicts, problems or innovations. Pays $200 to $400.

PETROLEUM TODAY–1801 K St. N.W., Washington, DC 20006. Cynthia Riggs Stoertz, Editor.
Articles of broad general interest on oil industry: oil products, personalities, history, operations, cars, etc. Pays good rates. Query.

PHILADELPHIA INQUIRER, TODAY MAGAZINE–Broad and Callowhill Sts., Philadelphia, PA 19101. Scott DeGarmo, Editor.
Local interest features, "how-to-cope" articles on contemporary problems, 500 to 2,000 words. Pay varies, on publication. Query.

PLAYBOY–919 North Michigan Ave., Chicago, IL 60611. Geoffrey Norman, Articles Editor.
Top-quality light and serious nonfiction, 4,000 to 8,000 words, on subjects with appeal to largely male audience: science, politics, sports, etc. Pays $3,000 for lead articles.

PLAYGIRL–1801 Century Park East, Suite 2300, Los Angeles, CA 90067. Marin Scott Milan, Editor-in-Chief.
Personal essays, 1,000 to 1,500 words, by professional writers, on any aspect of the human condition, and written in contemporary anecdotal style, for sophisticated young women. Pays $300 to $500.

POINTS–465 West Milwaukee, Detroit, MI 48202.
Articles, 700 to 900 words with color transparencies, on hobbies, sports and travel for families. Pays $100 to $400. Query.

POPULAR ARCHAEOLOGY–Box 4211, Arlington, VA 22204.
Non-technical articles, to 2,000 words on archaeological subjects. Pays 4¢ a word, $5 per black-and-white captioned photo, on publication. Query.

POPULAR SCIENCE MONTHLY–380 Madison Ave., New York, NY 10017. Herbert P. Luckett, Editor-in-Chief.
Factual articles, to 2,000 words, on new, useful products for yard, home, car, workshop, boat, or outdoor activities. Black-and-white photos and illustrations to accompany articles. Pays about $150 per page. Query.

PRESENT TENSE: THE MAGAZINE OF WORLD JEWISH AFFAIRS–165 East 56th St., New York, NY 10022. Murray Polner, Editor.
Serious reportage and analysis of international developments that concern Jews; memoirs, profiles of Jewish life abroad; 3,000 to 5,000 words with black-and-white photos if available. Pays on acceptance. Query.

THE PROGRESSIVE–408 West Gorham St., Madison, WI 53703. Erwin Knoll, Editor.
Articles, 1,000 to 3,500 words, on political, social, economic and international problems. Occasional light features and profiles. Pays $75 to $150, on acceptance.

PSYCHIC–680 Beach St., San Francisco, CA 94109.
Straightforward, entertaining approach to psychic phenomena, parapsychology, consciousness research. Factual articles, pro and con, on phenomena of the inner man. No fiction or personal experiences. Pays up to $350. Query.

RAILROAD MAGAZINE–420 Lexington Ave., New York, NY 10017. Freeman Hubbard, Editor.
Articles, 2,000 to 3,000 words, on any phase of railroading, in U.S. or Canada, combining technical information with human interest and anecdotes. Pays 5¢ a word, on acceptance. Query with title and qualifications for handling subject.

RAMPARTS–2749 Hyde St., San Francisco, CA 94109.
Serious reviews, 1,000 to 2,000 words, of books, movies, plays and records with social or political dimension. Pays 5¢ per published word. Query.

READER'S DIGEST–Pleasantville, NY 10570. Hobart Lewis, Chairman and Editor-in-Chief.
Articles of outstanding merit in field of personal experience and "Dramas in Real Life." Pays $3,000 for articles in "First Person" category. Submit query or outline, highlighting especially wide applicability and high readability. Pays top rates.

REAL WEST–Charlton Publications, Inc., Charlot Bldg., Derby, CT 06418.
Articles, 1,000 to 3,000 words on pioneering experiences in West during late 19th and early 20th centuries. Pays 2¢ a word, on acceptance. Photos must be available.

REDBOOK–230 Park Ave., New York, NY 10017.
Practical articles, 500 to 5,000 words, on home, health, husband-wife, parent-child relationships, etc., for young women. Pays top rates, on acceptance. Query with outline.

RELAX–136-138 North Montezuma, Prescott, AZ 86301. Richard J. Voelkel, Editor.
Articles, 2,000 to 2,500 words, on travel, hobbies, sports, for physicians. Include names and photos of doctors when possible. Pays $250 to $300, on publication. Query with outline.

RETIREMENT LIVING–150 East 58th St., New York, NY 10022. J. Wandres, Managing Editor.
Articles, 1,000 to 1,500 words, with photos, on needs and activities of those planning or beginning retirement: health, hobbies, housing, community activities, job opportunities, financial planning; particuarly personal-experience articles by experts. Pays $50 to $125 for articles, on acceptance. Pays $10 for black-and-white photos, $25 for color, up to $150 for color cover photos, on publication. Writer's guide available; query.

ROLL CALL: THE NEWSPAPER OF CAPITOL HILL–428 8th St. S.E., Washington, DC 20003.
Factual, breezy articles–history, human-interest, grass-roots political lore, material involving Congress, political changes, good satire or political humor. Must have strong political or Congressional angle. Slow reports. Prestige high, rates low.

ROSICRUCIAN DIGEST–Rosicrucian Park, San Jose, CA 95191. Gerald Bailey, Editor.
Features, to 2,500 words, on mysticism, the arts, inspiring biographies, significant scientific progress and achievements. Pays 2¢ a word, on acceptance.

THE ROTARIAN–1600 Ridge Ave., Evanston, IL 60201. Willmon L. White, Editor.
Articles, 1,200 to 2,000 words, of interest to business and professional men, on international, social and economic problems, ethics of business, community and family betterment, humor, travel. Pays first-class rates, on acceptance. Query.

Rx SPORTS AND TRAVEL–447 South Main St., Hillsboro, IL 62049. Harry Luecke, Editor.
Articles, 1,500 to 3,000 words, on sports, recreation, leisure, and unusual places to travel, of interest to physicians. Profiles of physicians with unique hobby. Pays to $350 for articles with 35mm color transparencies or black-and-white photos. Query.

SAGA–333 Johnson Ave., Brooklyn, NY 11206. Martin M. Singer, Editor.
Nonfiction only, 4,000 to 5,000 words, of interest to men: first-person adventure, sports, hunting and fishing, exploration, travel, cars, people in the news, entertainment, etc. Accompanying photos help sale. Rates begin at $300, with periodic increases and additional payment for lead articles.

THE SATURDAY EVENING POST–1100 Waterway Blvd., Indianapolis, IN 46202. Frederic A. Birmingham, Managing Editor.
Articles, 2,500 to 3,000 words, on education, the arts, science, politics, etc. Photo-stories. Pay varies. Query with outline.

SATURDAY NIGHT–52 St. Clair Ave. East, Toronto, Ont., M4T IN4, Canada. Robert Fulford, Editor.
Articles, to 3,000 words, of general interest to Canadians, on current affairs, economics, literature, etc. Pays to $400, on publication.

SATURDAY REVIEW/WORLD—488 Madison Ave., New York, NY 10022. Norman Cousins, Editor.
Articles, 1,000 to 3,000 words. Pays $500 to $750, less for short pieces. Query with outline.

SCOUTING MAGAZINE—North Brunswick, NJ 08902. Walter Babson, Editor.
Articles, 500 to 1,000 words, on Scouting, for adult Scout leaders. Pays $25 to $75 per magazine page, on acceptance. Query.

SEA CLASSICS MAGAZINE—7950 Deering Ave., Canoga Park, CA 91304. Jim Scheetz, Editor.
Unusual, original action articles, 1,000 to 3,500 words, with previously unpublished photos, on maritime history, especially wartime periods. Pays to $150, on publication. Sample copy and guidelines available.

SENIOR WORLD—7840 Mission Center Court, Suite 201, San Diego, CA 92108. Len Hansen, Editor.
Personality profiles, 250 to 650, and photo features on active senior citizens, over age 55. Modest pay negotiable. Query.

SEPIA—1220 Harding St., Box 2257, Fort Worth, TX 76101.
Articles, to 3,000 words with black-and-white photos, color transparencies or other illustrations, of interest to blacks: personalities, blacks in unusual jobs, news, controversy, entertainment, sports, history, medicine, religion, education, oddities. No essays or poetry. Pays $125 to $250, more if color is used for cover, on acceptance. Query.

SEXOLOGY—200 Park Ave. South, New York, NY 10003. Martin Sage, Editor.
Well-researched articles, including first-person reports, on all aspects of sexuality: medical, sociological and personal, 1,750 to 2,000 words. Pays $125 to $250, on acceptance. Send query or brief outline.

SHOWCASE—Chicago Sun-Times, 401 North Wabash Ave., Chicago, IL 60611. Herman Kogan, Editor.
High-quality articles, profiles, and interviews in field of serious and lively arts, to 1,500 words. Pays to 10¢ a word, on acceptance. Query.

SIGNATURE—260 Madison Ave., New York, NY 10016. Robin Nelson, Managing Editor. Josh Eppinger, Executive Editor.
Articles to interest Diners Club cardholders—affluent, well-traveled business people: on travel, sports, business, entertainment, social issues, profiles of interesting men and women. Pays on acceptance. Query.

SINGLE LIFE—225 Kearny St., Suite 200, San Francisco, CA 94108. Al Pellegrini, Editorial Director.
Articles, 1,000 to 1,500 words, of interest to single people. No poetry. Pays 2¢ a word, $5 per photo. $10 per cartoon, on publication.

SIR!—See *Mr. Magazine*.

SMALL WORLD—Volkswagen of America, 818 Sylvan Ave., Englewood Cliffs, NJ 07632. Jonathan Fisher, Editor.
Articles, 600 to 1,400 words, with color transparencies, to do with Volkswagen or Volkswagen owners: personality pieces on well-known VW owners, inspirational or human-interest stories with VW tie-in, travel, VW lore, humor. No poetry. Pay $100 per page for text and photos; $250 for covers, on acceptance. Query. Sample copy and writer's guide available.

SMITHSONIAN MAGAZINE—Arts and Industries Bldg., 800 Jefferson Dr., Washington, DC 20560. Edward K. Thompson, Editor.
Articles on wildlife, the environment, art, science, cultural history. Study magazine before querying the editor.

SOUTHERN ISRAELITE–390 Courtland St. N.E., Atlanta, GA 30303. Adolph Rosenberg, Editor.
All material staff written, at present.

SPORT MAGAZINE–641 Lexington Ave., New York, NY 10022.
New angles on current controversies and personalities in major spectator sports; articles about college athletes, 2,500 to 3,500 words. Pays $350 to $750 and up. Query.

SPORTS ILLUSTRATED–Rockefeller Center, New York, NY 10020. Patricia Ryan, Articles Editor.
Sports-related material: short, off-the-news features, 1,000 to 2,000 words; humor, personality, or reminiscence; long pieces, 2,000 to 5,000 words, on major personalities, or sporting subjects. Pays from $250 for short features used regionally to $750 and up for long pieces, on acceptance.

STAG–575 Madison Ave., New York, NY 10022. Noah Sarlat, Editor.
Articles, to 5,000 words: personality pieces, true adventures, exposes, etc. Pays to $500 for articles, on acceptance; to $25 for single photos, to $50 per page for picture stories.

SUCCESS UNLIMITED–The Arcade Bldg., 6355 Broadway, Chicago, IL 60660. Arlene Canaday, Executive Editor.
Inspirational and self-help articles, to 1,800 words, with photos, stressing positive mental attitude. Personality pieces about well-known people who exemplify success through perseverance and hard work. Pays $100, on publication. Query.

SWANK–717 Fifth Ave., New York, NY 10022.
Articles, 2,500 to 4,000 words, on personalities, sports, politics, interviews, sex and behavior. Pays $300 to $450. Query with outline.

THE SWINGER–See *Gem.*

TV GUIDE–Radnor, PA 19088. Roger J. Youman, Managing Editor.
Articles on television topics. Pays on acceptance. Query.

TWA AMBASSADOR–1999 Shepard Rd., St. Paul, MN 55116. James Morgan, Editor.
Articles, 1,000 to 2,500 words with color 35mm or larger photos, on travel, humor, sports, business, personalities, and "modern living," for international audience. Pays to $600, on acceptance. Query. Send for writer's guide.

TODAY'S SECRETARY–1221 Ave. of Americas, New York, NY 10020. Ann Roberts, Editor.
Articles on *young* secretaries, 1,000 to 1,500 words, with candid photos; brief articles, 500 to 800 words, on human relations, communications, self-improvement, career tips, office techniques and trends. Pays $75 to $150. Query.

TOWN & COUNTRY–717 Fifth Ave., New York, NY 10022. Frank Zachary, Editor.
Articles for high-income readership, on medicine, finance, personalities, social customs; humor, satire. Pays from $300, on acceptance. Query with outline.

TRAVEL & LEISURE MAGAZINE–61 West 51st St. New York, NY 10019. Mr. Caskie Stinnett, Editor-in-Chief.
For holders of American Express Cards. Sophisticated articles, 2,500 to 3,000 words, on travel and the good life. Pay varies. Most articles on assignment; query first.

TROPIC–*The Miami Herald,* 1 Herald Plaza, Miami, FL 33101. John Parkyn, Editor.
Professional, general-interest articles, 1,000 to 4,000 words, for sophisticated reader. Especially interested in personality pieces. Pays to $300. Query.

TRUE—21 West 26th St., New York, NY 10016.
High-quality, topical, insightful articles for men: adult adventures and in-the-news stories. Columns, 1,100 words, on sports, finance, and behind the scenes pieces on reporting by various media. Pays $750 and up for major features, $300 for columns. Query with example of published work.

TRUE WEST—See *Frontier Times.*

TUESDAY AT HOME—625 North Michigan Ave., Chicago, IL 60611. Sharon Shaw, Associate Editor.
Family-oriented articles, 2,000 words, for black, urban homemaker. Pays $350, six weeks after acceptance. Query.

TUESDAY MAGAZINE—625 North Michigan Ave., Chicago, IL 60611. Walter L. Lowe, Jr., Associate Editor.
Articles, 2,000 words, for black, urban audience. Pays $350, six weeks after acceptance. Query.

UNDERSTANDING—Box 206, Merlin, OR 97532. Dr. Daniel W. Fry, Editor.
Articles, to 1,000 words, on extrasensory perception and related phenomena; how to create better understanding among peoples of the earth. Pays 1¢ a word, on publication.

US MAGAZINE—W. B. Bradbury Co., 6 East 43rd St., New York, NY 10017.
Articles, 1,000 to 1,200 words with black-and-white photos, of interest to military wives and families stationed overseas. Pay varies. Query.

VFW MAGAZINE—Broadway at 34th, Kansas City, MO 64111.
Published by Veterans of Foreign Wars of U. S. Timely and factual articles, 1,000 words, on any subject of national interest; ways to cope with problems of daily living; how-tos, personalities, sports, and historical pieces. Pays 5¢ to 10¢ a word, on acceptance; extra for photos.

VIVA—909 Third Ave., New York, NY 10022. Bette-Jane Raphael, Editor.
Lively, well-researched articles, 2,500 to 4,000 words, on problems that face modern women: social, sexual, economic, emotional, etc.; first-person experience pieces. Humor welcome. Pays $250 to $1,000. Query.

VOGUE—350 Madison Ave., New York, NY 10017. Leo Lerman, Feature Editor.
Articles, to 2,000 words, of general interest on the arts, music, medicine, travel; original comment of interest to intelligent reader. Pays good rates, on acceptance. Query.

THE WASHINGTON MONTHLY—1028 Connecticut Ave. N.W., Washington, DC 20036. Charles Peters, Editor.
Investigative articles, 1,500 to 5,000 words, illuminating processes of government, good and bad. Pays 5¢ to 10¢ a word, on publication. Query.

WEEKDAY—20 North Wacker Drive, Chicago, IL 60606.
Informative articles, 200 to 1,000 words, on meeting everyday problems—consumer buying, legal problems, community affairs, real estate, education, human relations, etc. Pays $10 to $40, on acceptance.

WEEKEND MAGAZINE—231 St. James St. West, Montreal H2Y 1M6, Que., Canada. Sheena Paterson, Managing Editor. Frank Lowe, Editor.
Limited market for articles, to 2,000 words, and photo features, on subjects of Canadian interest. Pay varies, on acceptance. Query.

WEIGHT WATCHERS MAGAZINE—W/W Twenty-first Corp., 635 Madison Ave., New York, NY 10022. Matty Simmons, Editor. Edythe K. Tomkinson, Feature Editor. General-interest articles, 500 to 2,750 words. Include word count with manuscript. No "how-to-get-thin" or dieting pieces. Pays $15 to $400, on acceptance. Query.

WESTWAYS—Box 2890, Terminal Annex, Los Angeles, CA 90051. Frances Ring, Associate Editor.
Articles, 1,000 to 3,000 words, and photo essays on western U.S., Canadian and Mexican activities, natural science, travel personality profiles, contemporary events, history, etc. Pays 10¢ a word and up, on acceptance; $25 and up for black-and-white photos; $25 to $200 for color transparencies. Query.

WOMAN'S DAY—1515 Broadway, New York, NY 10036. Geraldine Rhoads, Editor. Address Rebecca Greer, Articles Editor.
Serious or humorous articles, 1,500 to 3,500 words, on subjects of interest to women; marriage, child care, family health, money management, vacations, education, leisure activities, etc. Short service or inspirational pieces of 400 to 750 words on all subjects. Top rates, on acceptance.

WOMEN'S ALMANAC—1430 Massachusetts Ave., Cambridge, MA 02138. Holly A. McClellan, Editor.
Articles, 1,500 to 2,500 words with photos, on women's needs and interests: adult education, employment, child care and education, woman and law, finance, consumerism, etc. Pays 5¢ to 10¢ a word, on publication.

WOODMEN OF THE WORLD MAGAZINE—1700 Farnam St., Omaha, NE 68102. Leland A. Larson, Editor.
General interest articles on history, travel, outdoor and indoor sports, do-it-yourself, science, television, movies, household tips, etc. Pays 2¢ a word, on acceptance; $8 per black-and-white photo, $20 per black-and-white cover photo and per color photo, up to $100 per color cover photo.

YANKEE—Dublin, NH 03444. Judson D. Hale, Editor.
Articles with New England locale, to 3,000 words, with black-and-white photos and/or 4 x 5, 2¼ square, or 35 mm color transparencies. Pays $25 to $400; average $250 to $300.

THE YANKEE GUIDE TO THE NEW ENGLAND COUNTRYSIDE—143 Newbury St., Boston, MA 02116. Georgia Orcutt, Editor.
Articles, 500 to 2,000 words, with photos, on family activities and recreation in New England. Short features, two printed pages long. Pays $50 to $200, on publication. Query.

COLLEGE, LITERARY, AND LITTLE MAGAZINES

AMERICAN JOURNAL OF POLITICAL SCIENCE—Wayne State University Press, Detroit, MI 48202. Address John H. Kessel, Editor, Dept. of Political Science, Ohio State University, Columbus, OH 43210.
Articles, to 6,000 words, addressed to professional concerns of political scientists. Query. Pays in reprints.

AMERICAN QUARTERLY—Box 1, Logan Hall, University of Pennsylvania, Philadelphia, PA 19174. Bruce Kuklick, Editor.
Careful studies of any aspect of U.S. culture from interdisciplinary viewpoint, 3,000 to 5,000 words; notes, 1,000 to 2,000 words; reviews, 200 to 2,000 words. No payment.

THE AMERICAN REVIEW—Bantam Books, 666 Fifth Ave., New York, NY 10019. Theodore Solotaroff, Editor.
High-quality essays showing fresh, articulate writing and thought. Send complete manuscript with stamped return envelope. Reports in about four weeks.

ANTIOCH REVIEW—P.O. Box 148, Yellow Springs, OH 45387. Paul Bixler, Editor.
Primarily interested in non-fiction of social comment, and some literary criticism, 3,000 to 7,000 words. Pays $8 per printed page, on publication.

ARARAT—628 Second Ave., New York, NY 10016. Leo Hamalian, Editor.
Publication of Armenian General Benevolent Union of America. Articles, 1,000 to 5,000 words, on some aspect of Armenian experience in America. Pays $30 to $60, on publication.

ARIZONA QUARTERLY—University of Arizona, Tucson, AZ 85721. Albert F. Gegenheimer, Editor.
Literary essays, Southwestern regional material, articles of general interest. No payment. Annual awards.

ARTS IN SOCIETY—University Extension, University of Wisconsin, 610 Langdon St., Madison, WI 53706.
Articles, 2,500 to 3,500 words, on teaching and learning of the arts; aesthetics and philosophy; social analysis; significant examples of creative printing as an art medium. Pays honorarium on publication.

ASIA CALLING—845 Via de la Paz, Pacific Palisades, CA 90272. Mary Ellen Hawk Saunders, Editor.
Articles from and about the Orient on customs, traditions, political and social changes, etc., 500 to 1,500 words. No payment.

BACHY—Papa Bach Bookstore, 11317 Santa Monica Blvd., West Los Angeles, CA 90025.
Serious nonfiction; black-and-white photos and drawings. Pays $2 per page on publication. Query.

BALL STATE UNIVERSITY FORUM—Ball State University, Muncie, IN 47306. Merrill Rippy and Frances Mayhew Rippy, Editors.
Articles of general interest in any field, 500 to 4,000 words. Pays in copies.

THE BERKELEY BARB—Box 1247, Berkeley, CA 94701. Jim Schreiber, Managing Editor.
Articles, 1,000 words, on people affected by oppressive institutions, typifying pressing social issues, of interest to San Francisco Bay area readers. Pays 50¢ per column inch, on publication.

THE BLACK COLLEGIAN—3217 Melpomene Ave., New Orleans, LA 71025. Kalamu ya Salaam, Managing Editor.
Articles, to 2,000 words, on conditions or experiences of black students. Pays on publication.

BOOKS ABROAD—The University of Oklahoma, Norman, OK 73069. Ivar Ivask, Editor.
Essays and analyses of contemporary world literature and literary figures. Writer must be competent in foreign language of his subject. No payment. Query.

BOSTON UNIVERSITY JOURNAL—775 Commonwealth Ave., Boston, MA 02115.
Articles on any subject, literary criticism, photographs. Pays in copies.

BUCKNELL REVIEW—Bucknell University, Lewisburg, PA 17837. Harry R. Garvin, Editor.
Scholarly articles in letters, arts and sciences. Pays in copies and offprints.

THE CALIFORNIA QUARTERLY–100 Sproul Hall, University of California, Davis, CA 95616. Elliot L. Gilbert, Editor.
Criticism, to 8,000 words; black-and-white graphics. Pays in copies and subscriptions, on publication.

THE CANADIAN FORUM–56 Esplanade St. East, Toronto 1, Ont., Canada. Michael Cross, Managing Editor.
Articles of interest to Canadians, on current events, politics, art, etc., 1,500 to 2,000 words. Pays in copies.

THE CENTENNIAL REVIEW–110 Morrill Hall, Michigan State University, East Lansing, MI 48823. Dr. David Mead, Editor.
Articles, 2,000 to 3,000 words, on sciences and humanities. Pays by subscription.

THE CHICAGO REVIEW–The University of Chicago, Chicago, IL 60637. Thomas Joyce, Editor.
Essays, interviews, book reviews, of any length.

CIMARRON REVIEW–Oklahoma State University, Stillwater, OK 74074. Jeanne Adams Wray, Managing Editor.
Articles, 1,500 to 3,500 words, of opinion, comment, observation in all humanistic fields: history, philosophy, sociology, economics, political science, etc. Pays in copies.

THE COE REVIEW–G. M. U. Box 328, 1220 First Ave., Cedar Rapids, IA 52402. Mike Magrath, Editor.
Literary essays. Pays in copies.

COLORADO QUARTERLY–Hellems 134, University of Colorado, Boulder, CO 80302. Paul Carter, Editor.
Nontechnical articles, 4,000 words, for general reader, but preferably written by specialists in humanities, sciences, economics, politics, Western problems and history.

CONFRONTATION–English Dept., Long Island University, Brooklyn, NY 11201. Martin Tucker, Editor.
High quality literary essays up to 2,500 words. Pays on publication. Query.

DASEIN–G.P.O. Box 2121, New York, NY 10001. Percy Johnston, Editor.
Serious nonfiction on scholarly subject (film, esthetics, social philosophy).

THE DE KALB LITERARY ARTS JOURNAL–DeKalb College, 555 Indian Creek Drive, Clarkston, GA 30021.
Personal, expository essays, of any length. Pays in copies.

DESCANT–Texas Christian University, T.C.U. Sta., Fort Worth, TX 76129. Betsy Colquitt, Editor.
Critical articles on modern literary works and philosophy, to 3,000 words. Pays in copies.

DIMENSION–Dept. of Germanic Languages, University of Texas, Box 7939, Austin, TX 78712. A. Leslie Willson, Editor.
Translations of contemporary writing in German, poetry and prose of various lengths. Modest payment. Query.

EIGHTEENTH-CENTURY STUDIES–Dept of English, University of California, Davis, CA 95616.
Scholarly and critical essays on aspects of eighteenth-century culture, to 6,500 words. No payment.

EVENT–Dept. of English, Box 2503, New Westminster, B. C. Canada. Robert W. Lowe, Editor.
Reviews, essays, to 3,500 words; graphics, photography. Token payment after publication.

FLORIDA QUARTERLY–University of Florida, 330 Reitz Union, Gainesville, FL 32601.
Poetry, prose, translations. No payment.

FORUM–University of Houston, Houston, TX 77004.
Articles for scholars and intelligent laymen, on letters, science, and the arts. Pays in copies.

FOUR QUARTERS–La Salle College, Philadelphia, PA 19141. John Keenan, Editor.
Critical articles, 1,500 to 6,000 words, on particular authors or individual works; think pieces on history, politics, the arts. Literate style, free of jargon. Pays up to $25, on publication.

THE FREE LANCE–6005 Grand Ave., Cleveland, OH 44104. Casper L. Jordan and R. Atkins, Editors.
Short critical essays. Experimental, avant garde only. Pays in copies. Query first.

THE GAR–Box 4793, Austin, TX 78765. Hal Wylie and Carolyn Cates Wylie, Editors.
Articles, essays, photos, drawings. Pays in copies.

THE GEORGIA REVIEW–University of Georgia, Athens, GA 30602. John T. Irwin, Editor.
Articles in general field of humanities. Pays on publication.

HUDSON REVIEW–65 East 55th St., New York, NY 10022. Frederick Morgan, Editor.
Essays on literature, the arts, general cultural subjects; criticism and reviews. Pays 2½¢ a word.

INVISIBLE CITY–Red Hill Press, 6 Gabriel Dr., Fairfax, CA 94930. John McBride and Paul Vanyelisti, Editors.
Reviews, translations, statements. No payment.

THE IOWA REVIEW–EPB 453, University of Iowa, Iowa City, IA 52240. Thomas R. Whitaker, Editor.
Critical essays. Pays $10 per page, on publication.

JOURNAL OF UNIVERSITY STUDIES (formerly *New University Thought*)–Box 7431, Detroit, MI 48202. Otto Feinstein, Managing Editor.
Articles on foreign and domestic politics, student problems, academic subjects; literary and film criticism; reviews, 3,000 to 12,000 words. No payment.

JOURNAL OF THE WEST–1915 South Western Ave., Los Angeles, CA 90018. Lorrin L. Morrison and Carroll Spear Morrison, Editors.
Scholarly, documented articles, 2,500 to 7,500 words, on historical, geographical, and archeological aspects of western United States. Reviews of current books on Western history. Illustrative photos and maps. Pays in reprints.

KANSAS QUARTERLY–Dept. of English, Kansas State University, Manhattan, KS 66506.
Articles and criticism on history, sociology, art and folklore of Midwest or High Plains area. Pays in copies. Query.

THE LITERARY REVIEW–Fairleigh Dickinson University, Rutherford, NJ 07070. Charles Angoff, Editor.
Sketches and imaginative essays about literature, of any length. Pays in copies.

THE MALAHAT REVIEW–University of Victoria, Victoria, B. C. Canada. Robin Skelton, Editor.
High-quality articles, 2,000 to 5,000 words. First English translations of work from Latin America, Continental Europe, and Asia. Pays $25 per thousand words for prose. Photos or drawings in groups of 12 to 16, $10 each.

MAN-ROOT—Box 982, South San Francisco, CA 94080. Paul Mariah, Richard Tagett, Editors.
Contemporary poetry, criticism, translations, any length. Pays in copies. Query.

MARK TWAIN JOURNAL—Kirkwood, MO 63122. Cyril Clemens, Editor.
Articles, 6,000 to 8,000 words, on American and foreign authors. No payment. Query.

MASSACHUSETTS REVIEW—Memorial Hall, University of Massachusetts, Amherst, MA 01002. L. R. Edwards, John H. Hicks, M. T. Heath, Editors.
Literary criticism and articles on public affairs, intellectual disciplines. Small payment.

MIDWEST QUARTERLY—Kansas State College, Pittsburg, KS 66762. Rebecca Patterson, Editor.
Analytical and speculative scholarly articles, 2,000 to 4,000 words, on any topic of contemporary interest. No payment.

MONTHLY REVIEW—62 West 14th St., New York, NY 10011. Paul M. Sweezy and Harry Magdoff, Editors.
Serious nonfiction, 2,500 words, on politics and economics from independent socialist viewpoint. Pays $25 to $50, on publication.

MOSAIC—208 Tier Bldg., University of Manitoba, Winnipeg, Canada R3T 2N2.
Scholarly, lively articles about 5,000 words, on relationship between literature and various social, critical, and philosophical themes.

NEW ENGLAND QUARTERLY—Hubbard Hall, Brunswick, ME 04011. Herbert Brown, Editor.
Historical, biographical, and critical articles on New England life and letters, about 5,000 words. No payment. Query.

NEW LETTERS—University of Missouri at Kansas City, Kansas City, MO 64110.
High-quality articles and essays, 1,200 to 4,000 words. Modest payment. No unsolicited manuscripts: query first and enclose stamped, self-addressed postcard. Closed May 15 to Sept. 15, annually.

NEW ORLEANS REVIEW—Loyola University, New Orleans, LA 70118.
Scholarly, scientific, or general-interest nonfiction, to 6,000 words, plus book reviews. Pays $50 for articles.

THE NEW RENAISSANCE—9 Heath Rd., Arlington, MA 02174.
Provocative, controversial articles, on national or international politics or sociology, well-researched and written with style. Quality essays and criticism (literary, theatre, film). Reports in 8 to 10 weeks. Query first. Pays up to $40, after publication.

NEW UNIVERSITY THOUGHT—See *Journal of University Studies.*

THE NEW YORK QUARTERLY—Columbia University Club, 4 West 43rd St., Room 603, New York, NY 10036. William Packard, Editor.
Poetry magazine. Critical essays with technical emphasis on craft of poetry, helpful to practicing poets. Pays in copies. Study magazine and query before submitting.

NEWLETTERS—1639 West Washington Blvd., Venice, CA 90291. George Drury Smith, Editor.
Articles, to 5,000 words, primarily by west coast writers, on publishing crisis; current literary critique, news of western literary scene. Pays in copies. Query first.

THE NORTH AMERICAN REVIEW—University of Northern Iowa, Cedar Falls, IA 50613. Robley Wilson, Jr., Editor.
Articles on contemporary affairs, especially ecological. Most are commissioned; query first. Pays $10 per printed page and up.

THE OHIO REVIEW—Ellis Hall, Ohio University, Athens, OH 45701.
Essays, to 6,000 words, on interdisciplinary subjects in humanities, for learned but not specialized readers. Pays $5 a page and up, plus copies.

OYEZ!—Roosevelt University, 430 South Michigan Ave., Chicago, IL 60605.
Essays, prose, and graphics. Pays in copies.

PARTISAN REVIEW—Rutgers, 1 Richardson St., New Brunswick, NJ 08903.
Nonfiction. Manuscripts held at least 3 months. Pays 1½¢ a word, on publication.

PERSONALIST—School of Philosophy, University of Southern California, Los Angeles, CA 90007. John Hospers, Editor.
Articles on philosophy. No word limit. No payment.

PHOEBE: THE GEORGE MASON REVIEW—George Mason University, 4400 University Dr., Fairfax, VA 22030. Ann Elizabeth Poe, Editor.
Essays, book reviews, interviews, to 3,500 words. Pays in copies. Include cover letter with manuscript. Query first.

PRAIRIE SCHOONER—201 Andrews Hall, University of Nebraska, Lincoln, NE 68508. Bernice Slote, Editor.
Criticism bearing on contemporary American scene. Pays in copies, reprints, and prizes.

PRISM INTERNATIONAL—c/o Creative Writing, University of British Columbia, Vancouver, B.C., Canada V6T 1W5.
Literary essays, to 5,000 words. Pays $5 per magazine page, on publication.

PROTEUS—1004 North Jefferson St., Arlington, VA 22205. Frank Gatling, Editor.
Reviews and criticism, any length. Pays in copies. Reports in one to six weeks.

PYRAMID—39 Eliot St., Jamaica Plain, MA 02130. Ottone M. Riccio, Editor.
Articles and essays on experimental writing, preferably in that style. Pays $3 to $20 per published page, on publication, plus copies and subscription.

QUEEN'S QUARTERLY—Queen's University, Kingston, Ontario, Canada.
Literary and general interest articles. Written by specialists for educated general reader. Pays $3 per page, on publication. Query.

REVIEW—Center for Inter-American Relations, 680 Park Ave., New York, NY 10021.
Essays and reviews, 800 to 1,000 words, original or in translation, on Latin American literature in translation. Photos or drawings. Pays $20 to $35, on publication. Query first.

THE RUFUS—P.O. Box 75982, Los Angeles, CA 90075. Patricia Ann Bunin, Editor.
Essays on current poetry modes and movements, 500 to 1,000 words. Pays in copies and cash awards. Query.

SALT LICK—Box 1064, Quincy, IL 62301. James Haining and Dan Castelaz, Editors.
Articles, essays, reviews, of any length. Drawings, photos, collage, etc. Pays in copies.

SEWANEE REVIEW—Sewanee, TN 37375. George Core, Editor.
Literary articles of high quality, chiefly critical. Pays $10 to $12 a printed page.

SMALL PRESS REVIEW—Box 1056, Paradise, CA 95969. Len Fulton, Editor.
News, reviews, essays about the small press and little magazines worldwide.

THE SMITH—5 Beekman Street, New York, NY 10038. Harry Smith, General Editor; Sidney Bernard, Roving Editor.
Nonfiction of almost all kinds, "except the Reader's Digest type of sentimentality." Modest payment on acceptance, plus copies on publication.

SNOWY EGRET–205 South Ninth St., Williamsburg, KY 40769. Humphrey A. Olsen, Editor.
Articles up to 10,000 words on naturalists and nature subjects from literary, artistic and philosophical viewpoints, including fiction, biography, criticism, and essays. Pays $1 per magazine page, on publication.

SOCIETY–Rutgers University, New Brunswick, NY 08903. June Cannell Birnbaum, Managing Editor.
Articles on social science research for broad general public as well as social science community. Authors preferably in social sciences or services, or having intimate working familiarity with field. Query.

THE SOUTH ATLANTIC QUARTERLY–Duke University Press, College Station, NC 27708. Oliver W. Ferguson, Editor.
Current-interest, historical, and literary articles, on English and American literature, about 8 to 12 printed pages.

SOUTH DAKOTA REVIEW–Box 111, University Exchange, Vermillion, SD 57069. John R. Milton, Editor.
Articles to about 5,000 words. Regional emphasis preferred. Must be professional in quality. Pays in copies.

SOUTHERN HUMANITIES REVIEW–Auburn University, Auburn, AL 37830.
Essays and articles, 3,500 to 5,000 words. Pays in copies.

SOUTHERN REVIEW–Drawer D, University Sta., Baton Rouge, LA 70803. Donald E. Stanford and Lewis P. Simpson, Co-editors.
Essays, 4,000 to 8,000 words, of lasting literary merit. Pays from 3¢ a word, on publication. Stamped, self-addressed envelope required. Reports in 3 months.

SOUTHWEST REVIEW–Southern Methodist University, Dallas, TX 75275. Margaret L. Hartley, Editor.
Articles, 1,500 to 4,000 words. Pays on publication. Query.

THE STUDENT–127 Ninth Ave. North, Nashville, TN 37234. Norman Bowman, Editor.
Articles on spiritual and moral concerns of contemporary college students and on practical aspects of campus life; lighter pieces with collegiate flavor. Pays 2½¢ a word, on acceptance.

STUDIES IN AMERICAN FICTION–Dept. of English, Northeastern University, Boston, MA 02115. James Nagel, Editor.
Reviews, 750 words, scholarly essays on American fiction, 1,200 to 6,300 words. No payment.

SUNRISE–Box 271, Macomb, IL 61455. Bill Knight, Editor.
Nonfiction, 1,000 to 3,000 words: Concert, record, film, and book reviews; "leftist" political analyses; personality interviews; general counter-cultural news and features. Photos of live music appearances. Payment varies, on publication. Query first.

THE TEXAS QUARTERLY–Box 7517, University Sta., Austin, TX 78712. Harry Ransom, Editor.
Lively, factual essays in humanities, science, and social sciences, written for literate general reader, crossing academic lines. Query with summary.

TRIQUARTERLY–University Hall 101, Northwestern University, Evanston, IL 60201.
Articles for international audience. No length of subject limits. Primarily a review of arts, letters, and opinion. Payment varies, on publication.

THE UNIVERSITY OF DENVER QUARTERLY–The University of Denver, Denver, CO 80210. Burton Feldman, Editor.
Literary, cultural essays and articles, book reviews; any length. Stamped self-addressed envelope must accompany manuscript. Pays $5 per printed page.

THE UNIVERSITY OF PORTLAND REVIEW—University of Portland, Portland, OR 97203. Thompson M. Faller, Editor.
Articles and essays, 500 to 2,500 words, of scholarly interest. No payment.

THE UNIVERSITY OF WINDSOR REVIEW—Dept. of English, University of Windsor, Ontario, Canada.
Articles 3,500 to 5,000 words, on arts and sciences, politics, and social sciences. Pays in copies. Include Canadian postage or international reply coupons for return of manuscript.

THE UNSPEAKABLE VISIONS OF THE INDIVIDUAL—Box 439, California, PA 15419. Arthur Winfield Knight and Glee Knight, Editors.
Essays of literary interest. Black-and-white photos, line drawings, collages. Pays by arrangement.

VIRGINIA QUARTERLY REVIEW—1 West Range, Charlottesville, VA 22903.
Serious essays and articles on literary, scientific, political, and economic subjects, 3,000 to 6,000 words. Pays $5 a page (about 350 words), on publication.

WEST COAST REVIEW—Simon Fraser University, Burnaby, B. C., Canada V5A 1S6.
Nonfiction with focus on creativity, 1,000 to 3,000 words. Pays $5 on acceptance.

WESTERN FOLKLORE—University of California Press, Los Angeles, CA 90024.
Folklore material of the world, academically oriented, 2,000 to 3,000 words. Fillers. No creative writing. No payment. Address D. K. Wilgus, Editor, Folklore and Mythology Group, University of California, Los Angeles, Calif. 90024.

WESTERN HUMANITIES REVIEW—University of Utah, Salt Lake City, UT 84112. Jack Garlington, Editor.
Articles on art, politics, world affairs, music, cinema, and literary criticism. Interdisciplinary approach. Pays $75 to $100.

WIN MAGAZINE—Box 547, Rifton, NY 12471. Maris Cakars, Editor.
Nonfiction, 1,000 to 2,000 words: political material on struggle for peace and freedom.

WORKING PAPERS—Cambridge Policy Studies Institute, 123 Mt. Auburn St., Cambridge, MA 02138. John Case and Nancy Lyons, Managing Editors.
Essays, to 5,000 words, on political, economic and social alternatives; book reviews on similar topics, to 2,500 words. Pays $100 per article, $50 per review, one month before publication.

YALE REVIEW—1902A Yale Station, New Haven, CT 06520. J. E. Palmer, Editor; Mary Price, Managing Editor.
Limited market for a variety of highest-grade articles, 2,000 to 4,500 words. Pays on publication.

RELIGIOUS AND DENOMINATIONAL MAGAZINES

A.D.—Presbyterian Life Edition and United Church Herald Edition, 1840 Interchurch Center, 475 Riverside Dr., New York, NY 10027. J. Martin Bailey, Editor.
Articles, to 2,500 words, of general interest to church members, and of particular interest to members of United Church of Christ and United Presbyterian Church in U.S. Pays $35 to $150, on acceptance. Reports in one month. Query.

AMERICA—106 West 56th St., New York, NY 10019. Donald R. Campion, S.J., Editor.
Nonfiction, 1,000 to 1,500 words, on current events, social criticism, international and domestic problems, family life, literary trends. Pays $50 to $75, on acceptance.

AMERICAN BIBLE SOCIETY RECORD—1865 Broadway, New York, NY 10023. Clifford P. Macdonald, Managing Editor.
Material related to purposes and work of American Bible Society—translating, publishing, distributing. Pays on acceptance. Query.

THE AMERICAN ZIONIST—4 East 34th St., New York, NY 10016. Elias Cooper, Editor.
Articles, 2,000 words, on Israel, Middle East, Jewish issues in United States or elsewhere. Pays $50 to $100 per article, on publication.

ANNALS OF ST. ANNE DE BEAUPRE—Basilica of St. Anne, Quebec, Canada. Eugene Lefebvre, C.SS.R., Editor. Address Jean-Claude Nadeau, C.SS.R., Managing Editor.
Articles, 1,500 to 1,800 words, of general Catholic interest. Articles on St. Anne. Photos, and illustrations. Pays 1½¢ to 2¢ a word, on acceptance.

BAPTIST HERALD—North American Baptist General Conference, 7308 Madison St., Forest Park, IL 60130. Dr. R. J. Kerstan, Editor.
Nonfiction, 800 to 1,600 words, photos or drawings. Pays about $5 for 800 words, after publication.

BAPTIST LEADER—Valley Forge, PA 19481. V. Alessi, Editor.
Articles on church school work, 750 to 1,600 words. Photos to illustrate articles, or pictures of interest. Pays 2¢ a word and up, on acceptance.

BRIGADE LEADER—Christian Service Brigade, P.O. Box 150, Wheaton, IL 60187. Paul Heidebrecht, Managing Editor.
Articles of practical help and interest to Christian men. Talks, role plays, games, feature activities for men to use in boys' club meetings, to 1,200 words. Articles, photos, with evangelical Christian emphasis, for men helping boys. Pays 3¢ a word and up. Send for author's guideline packet and questionnaire for specific assignments.

CAM—General Council of the Assemblies of God, 1445 Boonville, Springfield, MO 65802.
Articles, 1,500 to 2,000 words, of religious significance or practical help to Pentecostal Christians at secular colleges or universities. Pays 1¢ to 2¢ a word.

THE CANADIAN MESSENGER—833 Broadview Ave., Toronto M4K 2P9, Ont., Canada. Rev. F. J. Power, S.J., Editor.
Articles, 1,800 to 2,000 words, with Catholic tone, about daily life and problems of men and women. Pays 2¢ a word, on acceptance. Address Mrs. M. Pujolas.

CATHOLIC DIGEST—P.O. Box 3090, St. Paul, MN 55165.
Articles, 2,000 to 2,500 words, on Catholic and general subjects, but is 95% reprint in content. Fillers for special departments; see magazine. Pays to $200 for original articles, $50 and up for reprints; $4 to $50 for fillers. Address Articles Editor.

CATHOLIC LIFE—9800 Oakland Ave., Detroit, MI 48211. Robert C. Bayer, Editor.
Articles, 600 to 1,200 words, on Catholic missionary work in Hong Kong, Bangladesh, India, Burma, Japan, Latin America, Africa, the Philippines, and underdeveloped nations around world. Accompanying photos or drawings. Pays 2¢ a word, $20 for photos, on publication.

CATHOLIC RURAL LIFE—3801 Grand Ave., Des Moines, IA 50312. Msgr. J. G. Weber, Editor.
Short articles, with black-and-white photos. Pays $20 to $30, shortly after acceptance. Submissions without return postage not returned.

CATHOLIC WORLD—1865 Broadway, New York, NY 10023. Robert J. Heyer, Managing Editor.
Articles, to 2,000 words, on national and international events, politics, science, literature, etc. Each issue is thematic. Pays $75 and up, on publication. Query.

THE CHAPLAIN—Suite N200, 3900 Wisconsin Ave., N.W., Washington, DC 20016. Edward I. Swanson, Editor.
Interdenominational professional journal for chaplain-ministers in military service, Veterans Administration hospitals and Civil Air Patrol. Articles, 1,500 to 2,000 words, on chaplaincy history, biography, and program; preaching, worship, theology, church school, etc. Pays 1½¢ to 2¢ a word.

CHICAGO STUDIES: AN ARCHDIOCESAN REVIEW—Box 665, Mundelein, IL 60060. Scholarly articles, 5,000 to 6,000 words, on scripture, theology, liturgy, catechetics, canon law, and philosophy. Payment varies. Address The Editors.

CHORAL PRAISE—See *The Church Musician.*

THE CHRISTIAN ATHLETE—Fellowship of Christian Athletes, 812 Traders National Bank Bldg., 1125 Grand Ave., Kansas City, MO 64106. Gary Warner, Editor.
Articles, to 2,500 words, on sports in relation to faith, profiles of Christian athletes and coaches. Pays $25 for major article, on publication.

CHRISTIAN BOOKSELLER—Gunderson Dr. and Schmale Rd., Wheaton, IL 60187.
Trade magazine for Christian booksellers, publishers, suppliers. Articles, 800 to 1,500 words, with photos, on operating religious book and supply stores: management, sales techniques, success stories, trends in religious book trade. Pays $25 to $50 for articles with photos, on publication. Query.

THE CHRISTIAN CENTURY—407 South Dearborn St., Chicago, IL 60605. James M. Wall, Editor.
Ecumenical. Articles, with religious angle, 1,500 to 2,500 words, on political and social issues, international affairs, culture and the arts, etc. Pays 2¢ a word, on publication.

CHRISTIAN HERALD—Chappaqua, NY 10514. Kenneth L. Wilson, Editor.
Interdenominational. Articles and personal-experience pieces, to 2,500 words, on current social issues, subjects with religious or moral implications. Pays $100 and up for full-length nonfiction; $10 and up for short pieces.

CHRISTIAN LIFE MAGAZINE—Gundersen Dr. and Schmale Rd., Wheaton, IL 60187. Robert Walker, Editor.
Articles, 1,500 to 2,500 words, on evangelical subjects; trends in missions, Christian organizations, churches; practical aspects of successful Christian living; Christian personalities in politics, sports or entertainment. Photos. Pays up to $150, on publication.

CHRISTIAN LIVING—Mennonite Publishing House, Scottdale, PA 15683. J. Lorne Peachey, Editor.
Articles on application of Christian faith to family life and marriage. Prefers anecdotal, first-person style. Pays on acceptance.

CHRISTIANITY AND CRISIS—537 West 121st St., New York, NY 10027. Wayne H. Cowan, Editor.
Founded by Reinhold Niebuhr. Articles, 1,000 to 4,000 words: political, social, and theological commentary and analysis from Protestant, ecumenical perspective. Small cuts and photos. Pays to $50 for full-length articles, on publication.

CHRISTIANITY TODAY—1014 Washington Bldg., Washington, DC 20005. Harold Lindsell, Editor-Publisher.
Doctrinal, devotional, and interpretive essays, 1,500 to 2,500 words, from evangelical Protestant perspective, for students of Bible, ministers, and laymen. Pays $75 to $100.

CHURCH ADMINISTRATION—127 Ninth Ave. North, Nashville, TN 37234. George Clark, Editor.
Southern Baptist. Articles, 750 to 1,500 words, on administrative topics: planning,

staffing, organization, financing, facilities, communication, pastoral ministries, etc. Pays 2½¢ per usable word, on acceptance.

THE CHURCH HERALD–630 Myrtle St. N.W., Grand Rapids, MI 49504.
Official magazine of Reformed Church in America. Articles, 800 to 1,400 words, on Christianity and culture, Christianity's relationship to government and politics, communication between generations, marriage and the home, race relations, abortion, drug and alcohol addiction, etc. Open to new ideas on Bible, church and religion-related subjects. Pays 2½¢ a word and up.

CHURCH MANAGEMENT: THE CLERGY JOURNAL–115 North Main St., Mt. Holly, NC 28120. Norman L. Hersey, Editor.
Articles, 500 to 1,800 words, on Protestant church administration, education, worship, law, building, etc. Pays $10 and up per article.

THE CHURCH MUSICIAN–127 Ninth Ave. North, Nashville, TN 37234. W. M. Anderson, Editor.
For Southern Baptist music leaders. Articles, 500 to 2,000 words, on church music. Biographical sketches of musicians. Pays about 2¢ a word, on acceptance. Same address and requirements for *Gospel Choir* and *Choral Praise* (for adults) and *Opus One* and *Opus Two* (for teenagers).

THE CHURCHMAN–1074 23rd Ave. North, St. Petersburg, FL 33704. Edna Ruth Johnson, Editor.
Independent journal of religion with liberal views. Articles to 1,000 words on current social scene. No payment.

COLUMBIA–Box 1670, New Haven, CT 06507. Elmer Von Feldt, Editor.
Official journal of Knights of Columbus. Articles, 1,000 to 3,000 words, for Catholic layman and family, on current events, social problems, Catholic apostolic activities, education, topics of general interest. Pays $100 to $300, on acceptance.

COMMENTARY–165 East 56th St., New York, NY 10022. Norman Podhoretz, Editor.
Articles of general or Jewish interest. Book reviews. Pays on publication.

COMMONWEAL–232 Madison Ave., New York, NY 10016. James O'Gara, Editor.
Catholic. Articles, to 3,000 words, on political, religious, social, and literary subjects. Pays 2¢ a word, on acceptance.

THE COMPANION–15 Chestnut Park Rd., Toronto, Ont. M4W1W5, Canada. Rev. Leo Linder, O.F.M. Conv., Editor.
Articles, 1,200 to 1,500 words, on current national and international subjects, moral and social issues, and inspiration for better Christian living, with photos and drawings, if possible. Pays 2¢ a word, on acceptance.

THE CONGREGATIONALIST–801 Bushnell St., Beloit, WI 53511. Louis B. Gerhardt, Editor.
Articles, 800 to 1,200 words preferred, 2,000 maximum, emphasizing the free church and moral and spiritual concepts. Pays $20 to $50 per article.

CONGRESS BI-WEEKLY–15 East 84th St., New York, NY 10028. Herbert Poster, Editor.
Topical articles, 1,500 to 2,500 words, fact or opinion, on issues of interest to liberal Jewish readers. Book reviews, movies, plays of Jewish interest. Pays $60 to $75 an article, $25 to $50 for reviews, on publication.

CONQUEST–6401 The Paseo, Kansas City, MO 64131. Dan Ketchum, Editor.
Church of the Nazarene. For teenagers. Devotional, Bible study, Christian guidance articles, to 1,200 words. Pays 1½¢ and up, on acceptance.

CONTACT–302 U.B. Building, Huntington, IN 46750. Stanley Peters, Editor; Lois Breiner, Assistant Editor.
United Brethren in Christ. Christ-centered articles for teens and adults. True stories of notable Christians, 1,200 to 1,500 words; devotional articles, 500 to 1,000 words. Pays ¾¢ a word and up, on acceptance.

CROSS AND CROWN: A SPIRITUAL QUARTERLY–1909 South Ashland Ave., Chicago, IL 60608. J. J. McDonald, O.P., Editor.
Doctrinal, Biblical, liturgical, ecumenical, and biographical articles, 3,000 to 4,000 words, on spiritual life. Pays 1¢ a word, on publication.

DAILY BLESSING–P.O. Box 2187, Tulsa, OK 74105. Oral Roberts, Editor.
Simply-written, daily devotionals, 300 words, using lively, timely illustrations followed by link with Scripture truth, summed up to give guide and blessing for the day. Pays $5 to $15 for articles; $35 to $75 for scenic color photos; $7.50 to $10 for black-and-white. Writer's guide and sample on request.

DAILY MEDITATION–Box 2710, San Antonio, TX 78299. Ruth S. Paterson, Editor.
Inspirational, self-improvement, nonsectarian religious articles, 650 to 2,000 words, showing path to greater spiritual growth, or on God's mysterious ways; new Mayan archaeological discoveries. Pays ½¢ to 1¢ a word, on acceptance. Seasonal material six months in advance.

DECISION–Billy Graham Evangelistic Association, 1300 Harmon Place, Minneapolis, MN 55403. Sherwood E. Wirt, Editor.
Articles, 2,000 words with photos, testimonials on Christ as Savior and deeper Christian life. Pay varies, on publication.

THE DISCIPLE–Box 179, St. Louis, MO 63166. James L. Merrell, Editor.
Disciples of Christ bi-weekly. 150-word devotional meditations. Articles related to enrichment of Christian life and church's involvement in society. Pays $5 to $15, on acceptance.

THE EDGE–6401 The Paseo, Kansas City, MO 64131. Norman J. Brown, Editor.
Church of the Nazarene. Short articles on Christian education. Pays $20 per 1,000 words, on acceptance.

ENGAGE/SOCIAL ACTION–100 Maryland Ave. N.E., Washington, DC 20002.
Articles, 2,000 to 2,500 words, on social issues and problems, for United Methodist and United Church of Christ local leaders in social concerns; photographs. Pays $50, on publication.

THE EPISCOPALIAN–1930 Chestnut St., Philadelphia, PA 19103.
Articles, 500 to 2,000 words, of interest to Protestant Episcopal Church members. Photos and art work. Pay varies.

ETC.–6401 The Paseo, Kansas City, MO 64131. J. Paul Turner, Editor.
Church of the Nazarene. Devotional, Bible study, and Christian guidance articles, to 1,200 words, for young adults. Pays 1½¢ per word and up, on acceptance.

ETERNITY–1716 Spruce St., Philadelphia, PA 19103. William J. Petersen, Executive Editor.
Articles, to 2,000 words, with special religious interest. Pays $15 to $65, on acceptance. Query.

EUCHARIST–194 East 76th St., New York, NY 10021. Rev. William J. O'Halloran, S.S.S., Editor.
Explains function of Catholic layman in post-conciliar Church. Articles, 500 to 2,000 words, to instill Eucharistic spirituality, inspire prayer and apostolic activity, and explore private devotion in relation to liturgy and Vatican II. Pays 2¢ a word on publication.

THE EVANGEL—999 College Ave., Winona Lake, IN 46590. Vera Bethel, Editor.
Free Methodist. Nonfiction, 1,500 to 2,000 words, on Christian answer to contemporary problems. Human-interest articles, 1,000 to 2,000 words. Pays 2¢ a word, on acceptance.

EVANGELICAL BEACON—1515 East 66th St., Minneapolis, MN 55423. George Keck, Editor.
National magazine of Evangelical Free Church of America. Articles, 800 to 1,750 words, on religious topics, personal testimonies. Pays 2¢ per word, on publication.

FACE-TO-FACE—201 Eighth Ave. South, Nashville, TN 37203. Mrs. Sharilyn S. Adair, Editor.
United Methodist. Illustrated articles, 1,200 to 1,500 words, on problems and concerns of 15-to-18 year-olds. Pays 3¢ a word, on acceptance. Query.

FRIAR: THE MAGAZINE OF CATHOLIC OPTIMISM—Butler, NJ 07405. Rev. Rudolf Harvey, O.F.M., Editor.
Articles, to 3,000 words, on general and religious topics. Payment varies, on acceptance.

FRIENDS JOURNAL—152-A North 15th St., Philadelphia, PA 19102. James Lenhart, Editor.
Articles on religious and social concerns, to 1,500 words. No payment. Query.

GOSPEL CARRIER—Pentecostal Church of God of America, P.O. Box 850, Joplin, MO 64801.
Articles, 500 to 800 words, that emphasize some point about Christian living. Pays ½¢ per word, quarterly. Send stamped, self-addressed envelope for sample.

GOSPEL CHOIR—See *The Church Musician.*

GOSPEL HERALD—Scottdale, PA 15683. Daniel Hertzler, Editor.
Mennonite. Articles, to 1,500 words, on Christian experience and concerns. Pays to 2¢ a word, on acceptance.

GUIDEPOSTS—747 Third Ave., New York, NY 10017. Dina Donohue, Senior Editor.
Inspirational magazine for all faiths. Simple, anecdotal articles in first-person, on applying faith to everyday life. Pays $25 to $50 for short articles, 250 to 750 words, $100 to $200 for articles, 750 to 1,500 words.

HIS—5206 Main St., Downers Grove, IL 60515.
For Christian university students, graduates, faculty. Articles on Christian living on campus; relationship of Christianity to current life, culture, and problems; biography and missionary work. All material oriented to Scriptures. Pays 2¢ a word, on acceptance.

HOME LIFE—127 Ninth Ave. North, Nashville, TN 37234. George W. Knight, Editor.
Southern Baptist. Articles, (perferably first-person, personal experience), to 2,000 words, on children's growth, family interrelationships, etc. "Professional in depth but popular in style." Human-interest shorts, 200 to 500 words. Pays 2½¢ a word on acceptance. Writer's guide available on request.

INSIGHT—6856 Eastern Ave. N.W., Washington, DC 20012. Michael A. Jones, Editor.
For Seventh-day Adventist upper high school and college-age readers. True-life narratives and articles, to 1,800 words. Parables and other shorts which make spiritual point without moralizing. Art on assignment. Pays 2¢ to 4¢ a word, upon acceptance; $7.50 for 8 x 10 glossies. Sample copies and "Information for Writers" available upon request. Query.

INTERACTION–3558 South Jefferson, St. Louis, MO 63118. Earl Gaulke and Paul Pallmayer, Co-Editors.
Popularly-written articles, to 2,000 words, of educational or inspirational nature, to aid part-time and full-time teachers of Christian faith. Pays $20 to $50.

JEWISH DIGEST–P.O. Box 57, Heathcote Station, Scarsdale, NY 10583. Bernard Postal, Editor.
Nonfiction, to 1,800 words, with Jewish themes: historical, biographical, travel and humor. Pays 1¢ per word, after acceptance. Query.

JEWISH FRONTIER–575 Sixth Ave., New York, NY 10011. Dr. Judah J. Shapiro, Editor.
Articles, 2,500 to 4,000 words, on Judaism, Zionism, Israel, and labor in U.S. or abroad. Pays 2¢ a word, on publication.

KEY TO CHRISTIAN EDUCATION–Standard Publishing, 8121 Hamilton Ave., Cincinnati, OH 45231. Marjorie Reeves, Editor.
Articles, all lengths, with photos, on teaching tips, methods, success stories; inspirational material; for workers in field of Christian education. Payment varies, on acceptance.

LIBERTY MAGAZINE–6840 Eastern Ave. N.W., Washington, DC 20012. Roland R. Hegstad, Editor.
Timely articles, to 2,500 words, with photos, on religious freedom and church-state relations in U.S., Canada, and around world. Pays 3¢ to 4¢ a word, on acceptance. Query.

THE LIGUORIAN–Liguori, MO 63057.
Published by Redemptorist Fathers. Articles, 500 to 1,500 words, on Christian values related to modern life. Black-and-white glossies with articles. Pays 7¢ a word, on acceptance. Reports in four to six weeks.

LIVE–1445 Boonville Ave., Springfield, MO 65802. Gary Leggett, Adult Editor.
Sunday school paper for adults. Articles, 1,000 to 1,500 words, on how to put Bible principles into action in everyday living. Pays on acceptance. Samples and "Suggestions for Writers" sheet sent on request.

THE LIVING LIGHT–Our Sunday Visitor, Inc., 1312 Mass. Ave. N.W., Washington, DC 20005. Rev. Charles McDonald, Editor.
In-depth theoretical and practical articles, 1,500 to 4,000 words, on current trends and problems in religious education and related fields. Pays 2½¢ a word, on publication.

LOGOS JOURNAL–185 North Ave., Plainfield, NJ 07060. Alden West, Editor.
Articles, to 3,000 words, on aspect of charismatic-evangelical Christian life; personal, reportive, humorous, or educational. Photos and drawings; pays $5 and up. Pays 5¢–7¢ per word on publication for articles.

THE LOOKOUT–8121 Hamilton Ave., Cincinnati, OH 45231. Jay Sheffield, Editor.
News-type articles, 1,000 to 1,400 words. Pays monthly; usual rate $35. Sample suggestions to authors on request.

THE LUTHERAN–2900 Queen Lane, Philadelphia, PA 19129. Albert P. Stauderman, Editor.
Articles, to 2,000 words, on Christian ideology, personal religious experience, Christian family life, church and community. Photographs helpful. Pays $75 to $250. Query.

LUTHERAN STANDARD–426 South Fifth St., Minneapolis, MN 55414. Dr. George H. Muedeking, Editor.
Articles, 500 to 1,300 words, on church or Christian life; social, economic, or

political issues in light of Christian principles; human-interest items; personality articles. Pays 2¢ a word and up, on acceptance.

THE MARIAN—4545 West 63rd St., Chicago, IL 60629. P. P. Cinikas, M.I.C., Managing Editor.
Articles on religion, morals, Christian culture, and social problems. Query.

MARRIAGE AND FAMILY LIVING—St. Meinrad, IN 47577. John J. McHale, Editor.
Interviews, personal experience, humor, etc., 1,500 to 3,000 words, dealing with relationship between husband and wife. Some verse; photos on assignment only. Pays 5¢ per word, on acceptance.

MARYKNOLL—Maryknoll Fathers, Maryknoll, NY 10545.
Articles, to 1,500 words: profiles of mission people, socio-economic studies of mission countries, personal experiences on development-mission work abroad. Pays to $150 for unillustrated and black-and-white photo articles; to $200 for color photo features; $10 and up for single photos. Query.

MESSAGE—Southern Publishing Association, Box 59, Nashville, TN 37202. W. R. Robinson, Editor.
Black family magazine. Articles, to 2,500 words, on moral issues, mental health, temperance, inspirational and patriotic themes, nature, juvenile delinquency, the Bible, religious liberty, marriage and the home. Pays to $35, on acceptance.

MIDSTREAM: A MONTHLY JEWISH REVIEW—515 Park Ave., New York, NY 10022. Ronald Sanders, Editor.
Quality articles and book reviews for general readers. Pays 6¢ a word, on acceptance.

THE MIRACULOUS MEDAL—475 East Chelten Ave., Philadelphia, PA 19144. Rev. Donald L. Doyle, C.M., Editorial Director.
Articles, to 2,000 words, within framework of Catholic teaching, but not necessarily religious. Pays 2¢ a word and up, on acceptance. No reprints. No unsolicited articles or editorial viewpoints of a religious or political nature.

MOODY MONTHLY—820 North LaSalle St., Chicago, IL 60610. Jerry B. Jenkins, Managing Editor.
Contemporary, Christian articles, 1,500 to 2,500 words, of spiritual significance. Pays 5¢ a word, on acceptance. Query.

MUSART—National Catholic Music Educators Association, Inc., Riggs Bldg., Suite 228, 7411 Riggs Rd., Hyattsville, MD 20783. Sister Jane Marie Perrot, D.C., Editor.
Articles of general musical interest, 1,200 to 2,000 words, with photos. Especially interested in articles on music in renewed liturgy of Catholic Church.

NATIONAL CATHOLIC EDUCATIONAL ASSOCIATION MOMENTUM—Suite 350, One Dupont Circle N.W., Washington, DC 20036. Carl Balcerak, Editor.
Articles, 1,500 to 3,000 words, on outstanding programs, issues, and research in education. Book reviews, 500 to 1,500 words. Pays 2¢ per word; photos $5. Query.

THE NATIONAL JEWISH MONTHLY—B'nai B'rith, 1640 Rhode Island Ave. N.W., Washington, DC 20036. Charles Fenyvesi, Editor.
Shorts, 200 to 800 words; articles, 1,000 to 3,500 words, of contemporary Jewish interest. Pays 5¢ to 10¢ a word, on publication. Additional payment for dramatic photographs to illustrate articles.

NEW WORLD OUTLOOK—475 Riverside Drive, New York, NY 10027. Arthur J. Moore, Jr., Editor.
Articles, 1,500 to 2,500 words, on Christian missions, home and abroad; world events and Christian activities. Photos. Pays 3¢ a word.

OMI MISSIONS—The Oblate Fathers, Box 96, San Antonio, TX 78291.
Catholic. Mission stories of Oblate Fathers in Texas, Mexico or Philippines, 1,000 to 1,600 words. Pays about 1¢ to 2¢ a word.

OPUS ONE—See *The Church Musician.*

OPUS TWO—See *The Church Musician.*

OUR FAMILY—Box 249, Dept. E, Battleford, Sask., Canada SOM OEO. Rev. A. J. Materi, O.M.I., Editor.
Challenging contemporary articles, 1,000 to 3,000 words, for Catholic family readers, on modern society, family, marriage, youth, national and international affairs; religious, psychological and moral problems. Pays 2¢ a word.

OUR SUNDAY VISITOR—Huntington, IN 46750.
Articles, 1,000 to 1,200 words, on personalities, Catholic lay groups, philosophy, theology. Pays $75 to $100 per article, $10 to $20 for cartoons. Buys all rights.

PASTORAL LIFE—Canfield, OH 44406. Rev. Victor Viberti, S.S.P., Editor.
Articles for priests and ministers on pastoral activities, needs, trends, problems and contemporary issues. Book reviews of interest to clergymen. Pays 3¢ a word and up. Query.

THE PENTECOSTAL EVANGEL—Gospel Publishing House, 1445 Boonville, Springfield, MO 65802. Robert C. Cunningham, Editor.
Publication of Assemblies of God, fellowship of Protestant evangelical Pentecostal churches. Religious material only. Personal experience articles, 500 to 1,000 words. Black-and-white photos and full-color transparencies. Pays 1¢ per word and up, upon publication. Sample copy on request.

PEOPLE—1312 Massachusetts Ave. N.W., Washington, DC 20005. Patricia A. Lantz, Editor.
Features on current ideas and action programs in community, state, national, and international affairs as well as those of family and church. Photography, illustrations, cartoons. Pays 2¢ per word for articles, $10 to $50 for photos.

PRESENT TENSE: THE MAGAZINE OF WORLD JEWISH AFFAIRS—165 East 56 St., New York, NY 10022. Murray Polner, Editor.
Serious reportage and analysis of international developments that concern Jews; memoirs; profiles of Jewish life abroad; 3,000 to 5,000 words, with black-and-white photos if available. Pays on acceptance. Query.

THE PRIEST—1111 North Richmond St., Chicago, IL 60622.
Contemporary articles, to 2,500 words, on life and ministry of priests, current theological developments, liturgy, pastoral theology, Sacred Scripture, etc., for priests and seminarians.

PURPOSE—610 Walnut Ave., Scottdale, PA 15683. David E. Hostetler, Editor.
Hard-hitting articles (with photos, preferred), 350 to 1,000 words, on Christians working through problems and confronting issues aided by faith; historical, biographical, scientific, and recreational material. Pays 2¢ a word; $5 to $25 for photos. "No pious or sweet stuff considered." Sample copies on request.

QUAKER LIFE—Friends United Meeting, 101 Quaker Hill Drive, Richmond, IN 47374. Fred Wood, Editor.
Nonfiction, 600 to 1,500 words. No payment.

QUEEN—40 South Saxon Avenue, Bay Shore, NY 11706. Rev. James McMillan, S.M.M., Editor.
Published by Montfort Fathers, to foster devotion to Mary. Fact articles, 1,000 to 2,000 words, on any activity that stresses importance of devotion to Mary. Rates vary, on acceptance.

THE RECONSTRUCTIONIST—15 West 86th St., New York, NY 10024. Dr. Ira Eisenstein, Editor.
Articles, 2,000 to 3,000 words, dedicated to advancement of Judaism. Pays $20 to $25, on publication.

REVIEW FOR RELIGIOUS—612 Humboldt Bldg., 539 N. Grand Blvd., St. Louis, MO 63103.
Nonfiction for religious men and women. Pays $5 per printed page, on publication.

ST. ANTHONY MESSENGER—1615 Republic St., Cincinnati, OH 45210. Rev. Jeremy Harrington, O.F.M., Editor.
Catholic family magazine. Articles, 2,500 to 3,500 words, on outstanding personalities, major movements in Church, education, personal living (labor, leisure, art, psychology, spirituality). Human-interest and humor articles, photos, picture stories. Pays 6¢ a word and up. Query.

SCIENCE OF MIND—Science of Mind Publications, 3251 West 6th St., Los Angeles, CA 90020.
Inspirational articles, 1,500 to 2,000 words, on metaphysical aspects of science, philosophy and religion, that help reader with problems of daily life. Pays varying rates, on publication.

SH'MA—Box 567, Port Washington, NY 11050. Eugene B. Borowitz, Editor.
Articles, all lengths, on ethics, Jewish social strategy, legalization of homosexuality, Zionism, etc. No payment.

THE SIGN—Monastery Place, Union City, NJ 07087. Rev. Augustine P. Hennessy, C.P., Editor.
Current events and religious articles, 1,000 to 3,000 words, of interest to Catholics. Pays $200 to $300, on acceptance.

SIGNS OF THE TIMES—Pacific Press Publishing Association, 1350 Villa St., Mountain View, CA 94042. Lawrence Maxwell, Editor.
Seventh-day Adventist. Devotional articles, to 800 words.

SOCIAL JUSTICE REVIEW—3835 Westminster Pl., St. Louis, MO 63108. Harvey J. Johnson, Editor.
Articles, 2,000 to 4,000 words, on social problems in light of Catholic social teaching, and current scientific studies. Pays 1¢ a word, on publication.

SPIRITUAL LIFE—2131 Lincoln Rd., N.E., Washington, DC 20002. Rev. Christopher Latimer, O.C.D., Editor.
Professional religious journal. Religious essays, 3,000 to 5,000 words, of expository nature on spirituality in contemporary life. No first-person accounts. Pays $40 and up, on acceptance.

SUNDAY DIGEST—850 North Grove Ave., Elgin, IL 60120. Darlene Petri, Editor.
Articles, to 1,800 words, with black-and-white photos, on application of Christian faith to current problems, the Christian home, interpersonal relationships, Christian personalities, and Protestant church work. Pays 3¢ per word and up, on acceptance. Sample copy and editorial requirements booklet on request.

THEOLOGY TODAY—Box 29, Princeton, NJ 08540. Hugh T. Kerr, Editor.
Social, religious, and theological articles, 5,000 to 7,000 words, on some aspect of contemporary life from religious perspective; literary analysis. Shorter articles, to 1,500 words. Pays $35 to $50 per article, on publication.

THESE TIMES—Southern Publishing Association, Box 59, Nashville, TN 37202. K. J. Holland, Editor.
Family magazine. Articles, to 2,500 words, on moral issues, mental health, temperance, inspirational and patriotic themes, nature, juvenile delinquency, the Bible, religious liberty, marriage and the home. Pays to 10¢ a word, on acceptance.

THE THOMIST–487 Michigan Ave. N.E., Washington, DC 20017. Rev. Nicholas Halligan, O.P., Editor-in-Chief.
Scholarly articles on philosophy and theology. Reviews of books in field.

THOUGHT–Fordham University Press, Fordham University, Bronx, NY 10458. Rev. Joseph E. O'Neill, S.J., Editor.
Scholarly articles on world of culture and ideas from Christian viewpoint, on questions of permanent value and contemporary interest. No payment. Query.

TODAY'S CHRISTIAN MOTHER–8121 Hamilton Ave., Cincinnati, OH 45231. Wilma L. Shaffer, Editor.
Articles, 600 to 1,000 words, on problems and pleasures of mothers of preschool children, showing Christian principles in action. Material for fathers' pages, and creative children's activities. Payment varies.

TRIUMPH–278 Broadview Ave., Warrenton, VA 22186. Michael Lawrence, Editor.
In-depth historical and theological articles; discussions of current affairs, ecclesiastical and secular, in relation to Catholicism. Book reviews usually by assignment. Artwork. Pays on publication.

THE UNITED CHURCH OBSERVER–85 St. Clair Ave. East, Toronto 7, Ontario, Canada. A. C. Forrest, Editor.
Factual articles, 1,500 to 2,500 words, on religious trends, human problems, personalities. Cartoons with church angle. Pays $50 and up per article, before publication. Query.

UNITED EVANGELICAL ACTION–Box 28, Wheaton, IL 60187. Dr. Billy A. Melvin, Executive Editor.
Official publication of National Association of Evangelicals. Articles, 1,500 to 2,500 words, on religious, social, and political problems in evangelical context. Pays 2¢ to 5¢ a word, on publication. Query.

UNITED SYNAGOGUE REVIEW–3080 Broadway, New York, NY 10027. Rabbi Alvin Kass, Editor.
Articles, 1,000 to 1,500 words, on synagogues, Jewish worship services, ritual, etc.

UNITY MAGAZINE–Unity School of Christianity, Lee's Summit, MO 64063. James A. Decker, Editor.
Inspirational and metaphysical articles, 500 to 2,500 words. Pays 2¢ a word and up, on acceptance.

THE UPPER ROOM–1908 Grand Ave., Nashville, TN 37203.
Meditations on Bible texts, 250 words, with illustrations, including prayer and Thought for the Day. Pays $7, on publication.

THE VINEYARD–8 Ravenna St., Asheville, NC 28803. Daniel Gorham, Editor.
Religious/political articles, 500 to 600 words, pointing out faults and follies of human element in Church. Pays about $25 per article, on publication.

VISTA—Box 2000, Marion, IN 46952.
Devotional and biographical articles; photo features. Pays 2¢ per word, on acceptance.

THE WAY—Mennonite Publishing House, Scottdale, PA 15683. Paul M. Schrock, Editor.
Fast-moving, personal-experience articles, 300 to 1,500 words, showing how faith in God gives meaning and purpose to life. Pays 2¢ a word, on acceptance.

WAY: CATHOLIC VIEWPOINTS—109 Golden Gate Ave., San Francisco, CA 94102. Rev. Simon Scanlon, O.F.M., Editor.
Articles, 1,700 to 2,200 words: personality profiles showing how one person's efforts can help create better world for others; current social, artistic, cultural trends. Photos help. Pays $25 to $50, on acceptance. Sample copies on request.

WORKING FOR BOYS—601 Winchester St., Newton Highlands, MA 02161. Address Brother Jason, CFX, Associate Editor, 800 Clapboardtree St., Westwood, MA 02090.
For teenagers and parents. General articles, to 1,000 words. Sample copy available on request.

WORSHIP—St. John's Abbey, Collegeville, MN 56321. Rev. Aelred Tegels, O.S.B., Editor.
Articles on Christian worship in its theological, historical, psychological, and sociological aspects. Pays 2¢ a word for commissioned articles, on publication.

SPORTS, OUTDOORS, RECREATION AND CONSERVATION

AERO MAGAZINE—P.O. Box 1184, Ramona, CA 92065. Marvin Patchen, Editor.
Factual articles, any length, with photos, related to aircraft ownership, from single engine to light business jet, general aviation aircraft. Pays $25 to $50 per printed page, on publication. Query.

AIR PROGRESS—8490 Sunset Blvd., Los Angeles, CA 90069. David B. Noland, Jr., Editor.
Articles, 1,500 to 2,000 words, on aviation, of interest to private pilots. Pays $200 to $400 for articles, $35 to $200 for photos, on acceptance.

THE AMERICAN FIELD—222 West Adams St., Chicago, IL 60606. William F. Brown, Editor.
Yarns about hunting trips and upland bird-shooting experiences. Short articles, to 1,500 words, on breeding and training hunting dogs, and pointer and setter field trials. Features, to 3,500 words. Conservation of game resources and restoration of game emphasized. Pay varies, on acceptance.

AMERICAN FORESTS—1319 18th St. N. W., Washington, DC 20036. James B. Craig, Editor.
Well-documented factual articles, to 1,800 words, with photos, on outdoor subjects; environmental needs, how-to camping trailer vacations, horseback trips, hiking. 4 x 5 transparencies of outdoor subjects for cover. Pays 5¢ to 10¢ a word, on publication.

THE AMERICAN HUNTER—1600 Rhode Island Ave. N.W., Washington, DC 20036. Ken Warner, Editor.
Articles, 1,000 to 1,025 words, on hunting in America. Top rates, on acceptance.

THE AMERICAN RIFLEMAN—1600 Rhode Island Ave. N.W., Washington, DC 20036. Ashley Halsey, Jr., Editor.
Factual articles on use and enjoyment of sporting firearms. Pays on acceptance.

AMERICAN YOUTH—Ceco Publishing Co., Warren Plaza, 30400 Van Dyke, Warren, MI 48093. Robert M. Girling, Editor.
General Motors publication. "Upbeat" articles, about 1,000 words, for 16- to

18-year-olds. Pays $200 to $500, on acceptance. Request specification sheet before querying.

ARCHERY–Rt. 2, Box 514, Redlands, CA 92373. Dan Gustafson, Editor.
Articles, 1,000 to 2,500 words, on bow-and-arrow hunting and fishing, fun and appeal of field archery (not target archery); interviews with field archery personnel. Fillers, humor, jokes; photos, drawings with articles. Pays to $50 per published page, on publication. Query.

ARCHERY WORLD–534 North Broadway, Milwaukee, WI 53202. Glenn Helgeland, Editor.
Articles, 1,000 to 3,000 words, with black-and-white photos, on all aspects of archery, for hunters and competitive shooters, beginners and professionals. Semi-technical pieces, how-to, short photo-feature tips. Color transparencies for cover. Pays $35 and up, $10 for individual photos, on or near acceptance.

ARGOSY–420 Lexington Ave., New York, NY 10017. Bert Sugar, Editor.
Articles, from 2,500 words, on adventure, science, exploration, outdoors, recreation. Query Ernie Baxter, Managing Editor. Book condensations, fiction and nonfiction. Query Joanne Schmidt, Senior Editor. Pays $400 to $1,000 for articles, extra for photos, on publication.

AUTO RACING DIGEST–See *Baseball Digest.*

BC OUTDOORS–Box 900, Postal Station A, Surrey, B.C., Canada V3S 4P4. Art Downs, Editor.
Articles, 2,500 to 3,000 words, on hunting, fishing, travel, boating, hiking, nature, wildlife, in British Columbia and Yukon. Pays $40 to $60, $4 for 5 x 7 black-and-white photos, on acceptance. Query.

BACKPACKER–28 West 44th St., New York, NY 10036. William G. Kemsley, Editor.
Articles, 1,500 words with photos on what to do on a backpacking trip, where to go, how to get there; family backpacking trips in U.S.; profiles of great naturalists of past; short pieces on care and treatment of equipment; interviews with prominent outdoor figures; photo essays; cartoons; poetry. Pays to $200 for articles, $100 per page for color photos, $25 to $50 for black-and-white, on publication.

THE BACKSTRETCH–19363 James Couzens Highway, Detroit, MI 48235. Ruth LeGrove, Editor.
Published by United Thoroughbred Trainers of America. Feature articles with photos, for thoroughbred horsemen and fans. Pays after publication.

BASEBALL DIGEST–1020 Church St., Evanston, IL 60201. John Kuenster, Editor.
Articles, 800 to 1,200 words, on baseball and players. Pays on publication. Query. Same address and requirements for *Auto Racing Digest, Basketball Digest, Football Digest,* and *Hockey Digest.*

BASKETBALL DIGEST–See *Baseball Digest.*

BAY AND DELTA YACHTSMAN–2019 Clement Ave., Alameda, CA 94501. H. W. Chamberlain, Associate Publisher.
Articles, to 1,200 words, with photos, on boating: how-to pieces. First-person fiction, humor, to 3,000 words. Pays about 2¢ to 2½¢ per word; $3 for black-and-white photos, 5 x 7 up, with captions, on publication. Query.

BICYCLING!–119 Paul Dr., San Rafael, CA 94903. Gail Heilman, Editor.
Articles and fiction, 500 to 3,000 words, for cycling enthusiasts, on touring or racing bicycles here and abroad. Humor, photos, drawings. Pays $1 per column inch, $7.50 for black-and-white photos, $50 for cover color transparencies, on publication.

BIG BOOK OF WRESTLING–See *Wrestling Guide.*

BIKE WORLD—Mountain View, CA 94040. George Beinhorn, Editor.
Articles on bicycle touring, racing, training, physiology, bicycling and new life styles, technical information, for active riders. Related fiction, any length. Black-and-white photos, primarily of touring. Pays $5 and up per published page; $2.50 per inside photo, $40 per cover slide, on publication.

BOATING—One Park Ave., New York, NY 10016. Richard L. Rath, Editor.
Articles, 1,000 to 1,500 words with illustrations, on all aspects of boating, fresh and salt water; adventure, navigation, boating skills, seamanship, and how-to projects. No fishing, water-skiing, or skin-diving material. Pays good rates, on acceptance.

BOW & ARROW—Box HH, 34249 Camino Capistrano, Capistrano Beach, CA 92624. Chuck Tyler, Editorial Director.
Practical articles, 1,200 to 2,600 words, with black-and-white or color photos, on bow-hunting, target archery, historical pieces, do-it-yourself projects. Pays $50 to $150, on acceptance. Same address and requirements for *Gun World.*

BOWLING—5301 South 76th St., Greendale, WI 53129. Edward J. Baur, Editor.
Articles, to 1,000 words with photos, on bowling, emphasizing league or tournament bowling in ABC-sanctioned competition. Popular treatment. Pays $35 to $100, on acceptance. Query.

BUFFALO!—P.O. Box 822, Rapid City, SD 57701. Dana C. Jennings, Editor.
Articles, to 2,500 words, on buffalo history, legend, how-to pieces on care, managing and marketing buffalo, with photos. Fiction, 500 to 1,000 words, poems; cartoons, fillers, on buffalo. Pays $15 to $25 for articles and fiction, $3 to $5 for photos, $5 for poems and cartoons, on acceptance. Query.

CAMPING AND TRAILERING GUIDE—P.O. Box 1014, Grass Valley, CA 95945. George S. Wells, Editor-in-Chief.
Articles, 1,200 to 2,000 words and illustrations, on boating and wilderness trips, family camping and trailering, first-person camp-travel pieces, how-to articles, technical tips. Travel pieces, 300 to 800 words, with 2-3 photos. Pays from $40 for feature articles, $25 for short articles, $10 for cartoons, on acceptance.

CAMPING JOURNAL—229 Park Ave. South, New York, NY 10003. Andrew J. Carra, Editor.
Short how-to articles with step-by-step captioned photos or line drawings. Articles, to 2,500 words, with color transparencies or 8 x 10 black-and-white glossy photos. Pays from $75 for how-to articles, from $150 for travel features; from $150 for covers, on acceptance. Query.

CAMPING MAGAZINE—5 Mountain Ave., North Plainfield, NJ 07060. Howard P. Galloway, Editor and Publisher.
Articles, to 1,500 words, on children's camps and social agency administration and operation; leadership training; education, guidance, group work; building and equipment; food and feeding programs. Shorts, 750 words. Photos. No payment.

CANADA RIDES—2920 11th St. S.E., Calgary, Alberta, Canada T2G 3G8. Mary Jo Birrell, Editor.
Articles, to 1,500 words, with some relationship to horses or horse industry: human interest, technical, or on Canadian historical events. Pays 4¢ a word, on publication.

CAR AND DRIVER—One Park Ave., New York, NY 10016. Stephan Wilkinson, Editor.
Articles to 2,500 words, for knowledgeable enthusiasts, on Detroit or foreign car

manufacturers, autosports, new developments in cars, safety on highways, profiles of outstanding automotive designers, executives, racers, personalities. Pays to $1,000, on acceptance.

CAR CRAFT—8490 Sunset Blvd., Los Angeles, CA 90069. John Dianna, Editor.
Articles and photo features, any length, on unusual street machines, drag cars, racing events, technical pieces. Clear and imaginative photos, with captions and concise story copy. Color sheet and drag race action photos. Pays from $100 per page, on acceptance.

CAROLINA SPORTSMAN—P.O. Box 2581, Charlotte, NC 28202. Sidney L. Wise, Editor.
Fiction and articles, 1,000 to 1,500 words, on outdoor sports (hunting, fishing, boating, camping, riding, backpacking, etc.) in North and South Carolina. Glossy black-and-whites, 8 x 10; line drawings with stories. Pays 1¢ to 2¢ per word, on publication.

CAVALIER—316 Aragon Ave., Suite 209, Coral Gables, FL 33134. Nye Willden, Managing Editor.
Unusual features, 3,000 to 4,500 words, with black-and-white contact sheets and/or 35 mm transparencies, on sports or outdoors. Pays about $300, extra for photos, one month before publication. Query.

COMPETITION PRESS & AUTOWEEK—Box A, Reno, NV 89506. Russell R. Goebel, Publisher.
Weekly newspaper on motor sports. Automotive news items and features to 1,200 words. Pays $1 per column inch, $5 for photos, $10 for cartoons, on publication. Query.

CRUISING WORLD—P.O. Box 452, Newport, RI 02840. Murray Davis, Editor and Publisher.
Informative articles, 500 to 3,500 words with photos, on technical and enjoyable aspects of cruising under sail: specific cruises, people, general interest. Pays $50 to $300, on publication.

CYCLE GUIDE—1440 West Walnut St., Compton, CA 90220. Carol P. Neill, Managing Editor.
Articles, 2,000 to 4,000 words, technical pieces, short stories, photos, or miscellany, relating to motorcycles. Pays from $50 per page, on publication.

CYCLE WORLD—1499 Monrovia Ave., Newport Beach, CA 92663. Bob Atkinson, Editor.
Accurate, technical and feature articles, 1,500 to 2,500 words, for motorcycle enthusiasts. Humor, fiction, photos. Pays $75 to $100 per page, on publication. Query.

DIVERSION—Box 215, Bear Tavern Road, Titusville, NJ 08560. William Clark, Editor.
Articles, 300 to 3,000 words with color photos, on sports, travel and recreation, for physicians, dentists, veterinarians, and their families. Pay varies, on acceptance. Query.

THE ECONOMICAL DRIVER—363 7th Ave., New York, NY 10001. Mel Shapiro, Editor.
Articles, 500 to 2,500 words, on economical operation of automobiles, safety, economy travel. Pays $50 to $150, on publication.

ENTHUSIAST—Harley-Davidson Motor Co., Inc., P.O. Box 653, Milwaukee, WI 53201. T. C. Bolfert, Editor.
Articles, to 3,000 words, cartoons, photo-stories, photos of motorcycle racing, tours, etc., featuring Harley-Davidson cycles. Pays 5¢ a word, $7.50 to $15 per photo, on publication.

FAMILY HOUSEBOATING—23945 Craftsman Rd., Calabasas, CA 91302. Bill Estes, Editor.
Articles, to 2,000 words, on houseboats, waterways suitable for houseboating, personal experience and how-to pieces. Photos. Pays $50 to $150, on publication.

FIELD & STREAM—383 Madison Ave., New York, NY 10017. Jack Samson, Editor.
Articles, 1,500 to 2,500 words, with photos. Occasional fiction. Pays from 20¢ a word, on acceptance.

FISH AND GAME SPORTSMAN—P.O. Box 1654, Regina, Sask., Canada. Red Wilkinson, Editor.
Articles, to 2,500 words, on fishing, hunting, camping, outdoor trips and experiences in Alberta and Saskatchewan; how-to pieces on coverage area. Photos. Pays $40 to $150, on publication, or on acceptance if article not used in three-month period.

FISHING IN VIRGINIA—P.O. Box 305, Alexandria, VA 22313. Send mss. to Robert E. Lee, Editor, 1637 East Jefferson St., Rockville, MD 20852.
Articles, to 2,000 words, on "how, when and where" of fishing in Virginia, offshore Virginia, or Chesapeake Bay area. 6 to 8 photos with article. Pays to $150, on publication.

FISHING WORLD—51 Atlantic Ave., Floral Park, NY 11001. Keith Gardner, Editor.
Factual articles, 1,500 to 3,000 words, with color photos, for sports fishermen, on angling in particular areas, fresh and salt water; how-to pieces. Pays $200 for articles with photos, $75 for color transparencies for cover, on acceptance.

FLORIDA SPORTSMAN—4025 Ponce de Leon Blvd., Coral Gables, FL 33146. Bill Hallstrom, Executive Editor.
Lively, informative articles, 800 to 1,500 words, on fishing, camping, boating and hunting in Florida and Islands. How-to pieces; no "fish stories." Emphasis on conservation. Pays $50 to $100, on publication.

THE FLYFISHER—4500 Beach Drive S.W., Seattle, WA 98116. Steve Raymond, Editor.
Articles, 2,000 to 3,000 words, on fly fishing: technique, literature, lore, history and conservation, for sophisticated anglers. Black-and-white glossies, preferably 8 x 10, with article; sketches, cartoons, maps. Pays $50 to $150, on publication. Query.

FOOTBALL DIGEST—See *Baseball Digest.*

FUR-FISH-GAME—2878 East Main St., Columbus, OH 43209. A. R. Harding, Editor.
Illustrated articles, 2,000 to 2,500 words, on hunting, fishing, camping, trapping, etc. Pays 1½¢ to 3½¢ a word, on acceptance.

GARCIA FISHING ANNUAL—329 Alfred Ave., Teaneck, NJ 07666. Robert E. Stankus, Editor.
Yearly publication for international rod and reel sport fishing. Articles, 1,000 to 3,000 words with photos, on angling. Pays $100 to $300, on acceptance.

GOLF DIGEST—297 Westport Ave., Norwalk, CT 06856. Nick Seitz, Editor.
Articles, 500 to 2,000 words, on golf: personalities, special events, instruction (especially authorized by golf professional), remarkable feats, humor, etc. Fillers, photos, cartoons, Pays from 20¢ a word for articles, $50 for cartoons, on acceptance. Query.

GOLF JOURNAL—Chilton Co., Chilton Way, Radnor, PA 19089. Joe Schwendeman, Editor.
Official magazine of the United States Golf Association. Articles, 500, to 4,000 words, and poetry, relating to golf: personalities, features, history, rules. fillers and humor. Pays on publication. Query.

GOLF MAGAZINE—380 Madison Ave., New York, NY 10017. John M. Ross, Editor-in-Chief.
Articles, 1,500 words with photos if possible, of national interest to golfers. Short

articles, to 500 words. Pays to $500 for full-length articles; $75 to $200 for short articles; $75 for cartoons.

GOLF USA—P.O. Box 2102, Jackson, MS 39205. Paul Tiblier, Editor.
Features, with illustrations, on golfers, country clubs, golf resorts. Pay varies, on publication.

GUN DIGEST AND HANDLOADER'S DIGEST—20604 Collins Road, Marengo, IL 60152. John T. Amber, Editor.
Factual, well-researched articles, to 5,000 words, on guns and shooting equipment. Hunting material acceptable if it contains considerable information on guns and ammunition. Black-and-white illustrations. Pays 7¢ to 12¢ a word, on acceptance. Query.

GUN WORLD—See *Bow and Arrow.*

GUNS—8150 North Central Park Blvd., Skokie, IL 60076. J. Rakusan, Editor.
Articles, 1,500 to 2,500 words, on methods of shooting for target, military, self-defense, hunting, history or design of guns. Gunsmithing tips. Photos and illustrations. Pays about 5¢ a word, on publication. Query.

GUNS & AMMO—8490 Sunset Blvd., Los Angeles, CA 90069. Howard French, Editor.
Technical articles, 1,500 to 2,000 words, on guns, ammunition, target shooting, gunsmithing, etc. General articles on guns and accessories. Captioned photos required. Fillers on guns. Pays from $50, on publication.

GUNSPORT & GUN COLLECTOR—711 Penn Ave., Pittsburgh, PA 15222. E. B. Matesevac, Associate Editor.
Articles on new sports equipment and/or guns. Query.

GYMNAST—410 Broadway, Santa Monica, CA 90401. Glenn Sundby, Publisher.
Gymnast news; competitions, instructions, personalities, with many photos; fillers. No payment.

HANDBALL—4101 Dempster St., Skokie, IL 60076. Mort Leve, Editor.
Articles, 200 to 400 words, photos, cartoons, fillers, 30 to 40 words, on handball and handball players. No payment.

HANG TEN'S SPORTING WORLD—P.O. Box 1028, Dana Point, CA 92629. Steve Pezman, Editor.
Action-oriented articles, to 3,000 words, on participation sports and personalities: surfing, skiing, bikes, off-road, climbing. Black-and-white or color photos. Pays 5¢ to 10¢ a word, $10 to $40 for black-and-white photos, $25 to $100 for color, on publication. Query.

HOCKEY DIGEST—See *Baseball Digest.*

HOCKEY ILLUSTRATED—333 Johnson Ave., Brooklyn, NY 11206. Jim McNally, Editor.
Articles, 1,500 to 2,000 words, on hockey players. Fiction, 1,000 to 1,500 words, fillers, puzzles, short humor. Black-and-white 8 x 10 glossies or 35 mm color slides, with articles. Pays $100 for articles, $150 for cover photo, $50 to $75 for interior color photos. Query.

HORSE, OF COURSE—Temple, NH 03084. R. A. Greene, D.V.M., Editor.
Photo-illustrated, how-to articles, 600 to 2,000 words, on basics of horse ownership, training, riding, care; profiles of horses or people with horse-related occupations. No news items or dated material. Black-and-white and color photos. Pays from $50, on publication.

HORSEMAN—5314 Bingle Rd., Houston, TX 77018. Tex Rogers, Editor.
Articles, 2,000 to 3,000 words, on techniques of western horsemanship, horse

management. Photos required. Pays 4¢ per word, $6 per photo, on acceptance. Query.

HORSEMEN'S JOURNAL—Suite 317, 6000 Executive Blvd., Rockville, MD 20852. R. Anthony Chamblin, Publisher. Don Meredith, Editor.
In-depth articles, 500 to 3,000 words, reflecting inside knowledge of thoroughbred (flat) racing. Pays $25 to $100.

HOT ROD—8490 Sunset Blvd., Los Angeles, CA 90069. Jim McCraw, Editor.
How-to pieces and articles, 500 to 5,000 words, on auto mechanics, hot rods, track and drag racing, hill climbing, other hot rod competitions. Photo-features on custom or performance-modified cars. Glossy photos and cover transparencies. Pays to $100 per page, on publication.

HUNTING—Petersen Publishing Co., 8490 Sunset Blvd., Los Angeles, CA 90069.
How-to articles on practical aspects of hunting. 15 or more glossy black-and-white photos or color transparencies required with articles. Pays $200 to $300 for articles, to $75 for color photos. Guidelines sent on request.

HUNTING DOG—Box 330, Dept. A1, Greenfield, OH 45123. George R. Quigley, Managing Editor.
Articles, from 1,000 words, on sporting dogs and outdoors, with art or black-and-white photos. Pays 2¢ per word, $5 for photos, on publication.

INVITATION TO SNOWMOBILING—Snowsports Publications, 1500 East 79th St., Minneapolis, MN 55420. John A. Ehlert, Editor.
Articles, 500 to 1,000 words, on snowmobile events, places to go, personalities; mechanical features. Scenic black-and-white photos or color transparencies of snowmobiles in action. Cartoons. Pays $30 per printed page, on publication. Query.

KARATE ILLUSTRATED—1845 Empire, Burbank, CA 91504.
Articles, 200 to 3,000 words, on karate, kung-fu, tae kwon do, kendo, and related arts, with illustrations and photos. Seeks stringers in U.S. Pay varies, on acceptance.

KENDALL SPORTS TRAIL—Kendall Sports Division, 20 Walnut St., Wellesley Hills, MA 02181. John S. O'Neill, Editor.
Articles, to 2,500 words, for high school and college athletic directors, business managers, coaches, trainers, equipment managers, student trainers, team physicians, on all aspects of athletic department and sports management: legal problems, equipment purchasing, athletic training, sports medicine, etc. Pays 5¢ per word for articles, $25 for photos, on publication. Query.

THE LADY GOLFER—P.O. Box 4725, Whittier, CA 90607. Charles G. Schoos, General Manager.
Golf articles, 500 to 3,000 words, on personalities, sidelights, instruction. Related fiction, 500 to 3,000 words, golf poems, fillers, jokes, humor, puzzles. Pays $50 to $150 for short articles, $35 to $50 for cartoons, on acceptance.

LAKELAND BOATING—412 Longshore Dr., Ann Arbor, MI 48107. David R. Kitz, Editor.
Articles, 1,000 to 2,000 words, on powerboating, outboarding, sailing in Great Lakes region and inland waters in Middle West. Illustrated features on major boating events in area. Pays on publication. Query.

THE LIVING WILDERNESS—Wilderness Society, 1901 Pennsylvania Ave. N.W., Washington, DC 20006. Richard C. Olson, Editor.
Articles, narratives, book reviews, to 5,000 words, on environment and wilderness. Wilderness poetry. Slides of wilderness—no manufactured structures visible—drawings, maps. Pay varies, on publication. Query.

MASSACHUSETTS WILDLIFE—Mass. Division of Fisheries and Game, Field Headquarters, Westboro, MA 01581. Ted Williams, Managing Editor.
Articles, with black-and-white photos, on wildlife and general environmental and conservation issues. No pay.

MODERN CYCLE—7950 Deering Ave., Canoga Park, CA 91304. Len Weed, Editor.
Articles, 1,000 to 2,500 words, and photo-features, for motorcycle enthusiasts, trail pieces with maps and scenic photos of riders operating cycles; how-to's with photos for "Maintenance Tips" section. Pay varies for articles; $5 for photos, on publication. Query.

MOTORBOAT—38 Commercial Wharf, Boston, MA 02110. Joseph Gribbins, Editor.
Articles, 1,500 to 2,500 words, on powerboats: design, construction, power, equipment, use. Technical pieces on new developments in powerplants, construction, maintenance products, improvements. Color cover photo. Pays $250 to $400 for articles, $300 for cover photo, on acceptance. Query.

MOTOR BOATING AND SAILING—224 West 57th St., New York, NY 10019. Peter R. Smyth, Editor.
Informative and entertaining articles, 1,000 to 5,500 words with illustrations, on power boat cruising, sailing; technical, practical how-to pieces. Cartoons. Pays on acceptance.

MOTOR TREND—8490 Sunset Blvd., Los Angeles, CA 90069. Eric Dahlquist, Editor.
Articles, 1,000 to 2,000 words, on foreign and domestic autos, past, present and future, racing, events, how-to pieces, character sketches. Black-and-white and color photos. Pays from $350 for major features, on acceptance.

MOTORCYCLIST—Petersen Publishing Co., 8490 Sunset Blvd., Los Angeles, CA 90069. Tony Murphy, Editor.
Articles, 1,000 to 3,000 words with photos. Action motorcycle black-and-white and color photos. Pay varies, on acceptance. Query.

MOTORHOME LIFE—23945 Craftsman Rd., Calabasas, CA 91302. Art Rouse, Editor.
Articles, to 2,000 words with photos, on motorhomes, self-propelled recreational vehicles, travel, how-to pieces. Pays $50 to $150, on publication.

MOUNTAIN GAZETTE—2025 York St., Denver, CO 80205. Mike Moore, Editor.
Articles, 1,000 to 2,500 words, with 8 x 10 black-and-white photos, on mountaineering, skiing, and other outdoor recreation; environment, wilderness preservation. Fiction, 500 to 5,000 words. Pays $50 to $200 for articles, $10 to $50 for photos, on acceptance.

THE NATIONAL BOWLERS JOURNAL AND BILLIARD REVUE—Hemingway Professional Building, 1825 North Lincoln Plaza, Chicago, IL 60614. Mort Luby, Jr., Editor.
Trade, or consumer articles, 1,200 to 2,000 words with photos, on facet of bowling or billiards with national interest. Cartoons with bowling or billiard theme. Pays $50 to $75 for articles; $5 for cartoons, on publication.

NATIONAL PARKS AND CONSERVATION MAGAZINE—1701 18th St. N.W., Washington, DC 20009. Eugenia Horstman Connally, Editor.
Illustrated articles, 1,500 to 2,000 words on environmental problems and plans to solve them; national parks and monuments; endangered species of plants and animals; outdoors and wildlife appreciation and protection; natural history; etc. Photos of park and wildlife. Pays $75 to $100, on acceptance.

NATIONAL POLICE GAZETTE—520 Fifth Ave., New York, NY 10036. Nat K. Perlow, Editor.
Articles 1,500 to 2,000 words, on sports and theatrical personalities; adventure stories; fishing and hunting experiences; fact detective cases; fraud exposes. Pays 5¢ a word, on publication. Query.

NATIONAL WILDLIFE AND INTERNATIONAL WILDLIFE–534 North Broadway, Milwaukee, WI 53202. Bob Strohm, Managing Editor.
Articles, 1,000 to 2,500 words that are or can be illustrated, on wildlife, conservation, environmental quality. Black-and-white photos. Pay varies, on acceptance. Query, with photos.

NATURAL HISTORY MAGAZINE–Central Park West at 79th St., New York, NY 10024. Alan Ternes, Editor.
Articles, 2,500 to 3,500 words, by specialists on natural sciences, geology, astronomy, anthropology, environment, with basic scientific point. Photos. Pays $500 for full-length articles, $150 for cover photos, $100 per page for color; $50 for black-and-white.

NATURE CANADA–46 Elgin St., Ottawa K1P 5K6, Ontario, Canada.
Informational articles, 1,000 to 2,000 words with photos or sketches, on natural science, conservation, with Canadian slant. Pays 5¢ per word, on publication.

NEVADA OUTDOORS AND WILDLIFE REVIEW–P.O. Box 10678, Reno, NV 89510.
Factual articles on fish and game, history, boating, related to Nevada.

NEW MEXICO WILDLIFE–State Capitol, Dept. of Game and Fish, Santa Fe, NM 87501. J.D. Crenshar, Editor.
Articles, 800 to 3,000 words, on outdoors, hunting, fishing, camping, conservation, in New Mexico. How-to pieces with New Mexican slant. Cartoons on hunting, fishing, camping; photos and drawings on New Mexican wildlife. Pays $5 to $10 for photos with articles; $7.50 for drawings, on acceptance.

NORTHEAST OUTDOORS–95 North Main St., Waterbury, CT 06702. John Florian, Editor.
Tabloid format. Articles, from 800 words, on camping: tips, places to camp and visit while camping in northeast, recreational vehicle hints; hunting, fishing, skiing; recreation; nature; etc.; in northeast U.S. Pays from $25, on publication.

NORTHWEST SKIER–P.O. Box 5029, University Station, Seattle, WA 98105. Robert B. Hinz, Editor.
Fiction, 250 to 2,500 words; articles, 250 to 3,500 words, on skiing in Pacific Northwest. Pays from 75¢ per column inch, on publication.

ODYSSEY–300 South Wacker Dr., Chicago, IL 60606. Jerry Reedy, Editorial Director.
Detailed, travel-oriented articles, 2,000 to 2,500 words with color photos, on national parks, recreation areas, etc. Shorter pieces, 1,000 to 2,000 words, on ecology, conservation, and outdoor activities (hiking, camping, sports). Pays about 10¢ a word, on acceptance. Query with samples of published work.

OUTDOOR INDIANA–Dept. of Natural Resources, Indianapolis, IN 46204. Herbert R. Hill, Editor.
Articles to 2,000 words, on Indiana subjects. Photos. Pays 2¢ per work, on publication.

OUTDOOR LIFE–380 Madison Ave., New York, NY 10017. Chet Fish, Editor-in-Chief.
Articles on hunting and fishing and related subjects. Pays top rates, on acceptance. Query.

OUTDOORS–Outdoors Bldg., Columbia, MO 65201. Lee Cullimore, Editor.
Informative, objective articles, to 1,200 words, with 8 x 10 black-and-white photos, on recreation, with emphasis on boating. Pays $35 to $100, on acceptance.

OUTDOORS–*Sunday Oregonian*, 1320 S.W. Broadway, Portland, OR 97201. J. R. Bianco, Editor.
Articles, to 800 words with black-and-white photos, on outdoor activities in Pacific Northwest: fishing, skiing, camping, etc. Pays $40 per article; $10 per photo, tenth of each month.

OUTDOORS IN GEORGIA—Dept. of Natural Resources, Room 719, 270 Washington, St. S.W., Atlanta, GA 30334. T. Craig Martin, Editor.
Articles, 1,200 to 1,800 words with black-and-white and color photos on environment, historic sites or areas, hunting and fishing in Georgia. Pays from $35 for articles, from $50 for 35 mm color transparencies on acceptance. Query.

P. O. P—919 Filley St., Lansing, MI 48906. Jack Dinley, Editor.
Articles about 2,000 words with two black-and-white photos, on sports, adventure, antique cars, etc., for male readers. Pays $200, 15 days after acceptance.

PV4—CBS Publications, 1499 Monrovia Ave., Newport Beach, CA 92663. Thomas L. Bryant, Editor.
How-to articles, 2,500 words, on off-road driving or camping with pickups, vans or four-wheel drive vehicles. Jokes on off-road driving or camping, travel or racing photos. Pays $50 per page, on acceptance. Query.

PARACHUTIST—U.S. Parachute Association, Box 109, Monterey, CA 93940. Charles W. Ryan, Editor.
Articles on sport parachuting; cartoons; photos. Pays in copies.

PENNSYLVANIA ANGLER—Pennsylvania Fish Commission, P.O. Box 1673, Harrisburg, PA 17120. J. F. Yoder, Editor.
Articles, 750 to 2,500 words with 8 x 10 black-and-white glossy photos, on fresh water fishing, recreational boating, and camping in Pennsylvania. Pays $50 to $75 for single page spreads; $75 to $100 for double-page, to $125 for cover transparencies (verticals only), 35 mm up.

PENNSYLVANIA GAME NEWS—Game Commission, Harrisburg, PA 17105. Bob Bell, Editor.
Articles, to 2,500 words with black-and-white glossy photos, on outdoor subjects, excluding fishing and hunting. Pays from 3¢ per word, and from $5 per photo, on acceptance.

POOL 'N' PATIO—3923 West 6th St., Los Angeles, CA 90020. Fay Coupe, Editor.
Articles, 500 to 1,500 words, for owners of residential swimming pools. Pays 5¢ per word, on acceptance.

POPULAR HOT RODDING—Argus Publishers Corp., 131 South Barrington Pl., Los Angeles, CA 90049. Lee Kelley, Editor.
Articles, any length, on cars and car mechanics. Photos and drawings. Pays top rates for field, on publication. Query.

POPULAR SCIENCE MONTHLY—380 Madison Ave., New York, NY 10017. Herbert P. Luckett, Editor-in-Chief.
Factual articles, to 2,000 words with black-and-white photos or illustrations, on new, useful products for home, yard, car, boat, workshop, or outdoor activities. Pays about $150 per magazine page, on acceptance. Query.

POWDER—P.O. Box 359, Sun Valley, ID 83353. Dave Baldridge, Contributing Editor.
Articles, 800 to 1,500 words, on all aspects of deep powder ski experience: adventure, personalities, humor, opinion pieces, mountain enjoyment and appreciation. Related fiction and poetry. Pays $25 to $100 for prose, $5 to $25 for photos, on acceptance.

POWERBOAT—Nordco Publishing, Inc., P.O. Box 3842, Van Nuys, CA 91407. Bob Brown, Editor.
Articles, to 1,500 words with eight or ten 8 x 10 glossy photos (including negatives), for powerboat owners, on outstanding achievements, water-skiing competition; non-technical how-to pieces. Pays about $50 per page, on publication.

PRIVATE PILOT—GHP Publications, Box 296, Encinitas, CA 92024. Dennis Shattuck, Editor.

Technically sound, true-experience articles, technical analyses, technique discussions, 1,000 to 4,000 words, for aviation enthusiasts. Photos. Pays $25 to $250, on publication. Query.

RAILROAD MAGAZINE—420 Lexington Ave., New York, NY 10017. Freeman Hubbard, Editor.
Technical, informative articles, 2,000 to 3,000 words, on railroading, with human interest and anecdotes, U.S. and/or Canadian locale. Locomotive pieces, "no hobby-type articles." Photos with articles. Pays 5¢ a word, on or before publication. Queries answered immediately.

RELAX—136-138 North Montezuma, Prescott, AZ 86301. Richard J. Voelkel, Editor.
Sports articles, 2,000 to 2,500 words with photos, for physicians. Include names of doctors in manuscripts when possible. Pays $250 to $300, on publication. Query with outlines.

RUDDER—Fawcett Publications, Inc., 1515 Broadway, New York, NY 10036. Martin Luray, Editor.
Well-researched how-to articles, to 2,000 words, on boating. Photos. Pays $100 to $250, on acceptance. Query.

Rx SPORTS AND TRAVEL—447 South Main St., Hillsboro, IL 62049.
Articles, 1,500 to 3,000 words, for physicians, on participation sports and travel, profiles of physicians with unusual sports achievements; how-to pieces on sports. Fillers, 250 to 750 words; participation sport tips, humorous sports events, etc. Black-and-white and color photos with articles; candid shots of physicians in sports for column. Pays to $350, on acceptance. Query.

SAGA—333 Johnson Ave., Brooklyn, NY 11206. Martin M. Singer, Editor.
Articles, 3,500 to 4,000 words, with color or black-and-white photos, on adventure (in first person); sports, profiles or new aspects of game. Pays from $300, on acceptance.

SAIL—38 Commercial Wharf, Boston, MA 02110. Keith Taylor, Editor.
Articles, 1,500 to 2,000 words with black-and-white or color photos, on sailing, sailboats, sailboat equipment, etc. Pays $75 to $350, on publication.

SALMON TROUT STEELHEADER—P.O. Box 02112, Portland, OR 97202. Frank W. Amato, Editor.
Accurate articles, 750 to 2,500 words with 5 to 10 black-and-white photos, on salmon, trout, and steelhead fishing in western states. Cartoons. Pays $15 to $60 for articles, on publication.

SALT WATER SPORTSMAN—10 High St., Boston, MA 02110. Frank Woolner, Editor.
How-to articles, 2,500 to 3,000 words, on salt water sport fishing on Atlantic, Gulf, and Pacific coasts of North, Central, and South America. Glossy action photos of salt-water sport fishing, color transparencies for cover. Pays 5¢ and up a word, on acceptance.

SCOUTING MAGAZINE—North Brunswick, NJ 08902. Walter Babson, Editor.
Articles, 1,500 words, on news, program ideas, policy interpretations, youth and adult leadership hints, patriotism, health, safety, Scouting's role in development of boys; book reviews; how-to pieces.

SCRUMDOWN—Rugby Press, Ltd., 157 East 87th St., New York, NY 10028. A. Jon Prusmack, Editor/Publisher.
Articles and reports, to 2,500 words, on rugby: events, tournaments, social and cultural background of sport. Related fiction, to 1,000 words. Pay varies. Query.

SEA—Suite 200, 2706 Harbor Blvd., Costs Mesa, CA 92626. Harry Monahan, Editor.
Separate northwest and southwest editions. How-to articles, about 2,000 words, on boat operation; cruising destinations in 13 western states. Humor, cartoons,

black-and-white and color photos. Pays 5¢ to 10¢ per word for articles, $150 for cover photo, $50 to $125 for interior photos, $10 for black-and-white with articles. Query.

SHOOTING TIMES—News Plaza, Peoria, IL 61601. Alex Bartimo, Executive Editor.
Articles, 2,000 to 2,500 words with photos, on guns and pistols, hunting and shooting, black powder, reloading, conservation, gunsmithing. Pay varies, on acceptance. Query.

SKATING—178 Tremont St., Boston, MA 02111. Barbara R. Boucher, Editor.
Articles, to 1,500 words, on amateur ice figure skating, skating clubs, personalities, opinions, skating's relation to other sports. Photos of skating. Pays 2½¢ a word, $25 minimum; $5 per photo, on publication.

SKI MAGAZINE—380 Madison Ave., New York, NY 10017. John Fry, Editor.
Articles, 1,300 to 2,00 words with photos or drawings, on skiing. Pays $75 to $200, on acceptance. Query.

SKI RACING—Paper House, Inc., 1801 York, Denver, CO 80206. Gaylord Guenin, Managing Editor.
Interviews, articles, and reports, to 2,000 words, on national and international ski competitions. Fillers, short humor, black-and-white action drawings, cartoons and photos, on skiing. Pays from $1 per column inch for articles, from $10 for photos, on publication.

SKIER—22 High St., Brattleboro, VT 05301. Kay Scanlan, Editor.
Official publication of Eastern Ski Association. Articles on skiing; personality, human interest, ski techniques, ski history, etc. Photos; cartoons. Pays $35 for articles without photos, $50 with photos, on publication.

SKIING MAGAZINE—Ziff-Davis Publishing Co., One Park Ave., New York, NY 10016. Al Greenberg, Editor.
Articles, 1,000 to 3,000 words, on skiing: travel, personality profiles, humor, history, technique, reminiscence. Short pieces, from 800 words. Pays $100 to $500.

SKIN DIVER MAGAZINE—8490 Sunset Blvd., Los Angeles, CA 90069. Jack McKenney, Editor.
Articles, 1,000 to 2,000 words with illustrations on skin diving activities, equipment, or personalities. Black-and-white photos, 8 x 10 glossies; color, 35 mm, 2¼ x 2¼, or 4 x 5 transparencies; line drawings, sketches, charts. Pays $35 per page for editorial copy and photos, $100 for cover photos, $10 for cartoons, on publication.

SKY DIVER MAGAZINE—P.O. Box 1024, La Habra, CA 90631. Lyle Cameron, Editor.
Fiction and non-fiction, any length, photos and drawings, technical miscellany: humor, jokes, puzzles. No payment unless exceptional.

SKYSURFER MAGAZINE—P.O. Box 872, Worcester, MA 01613. John F. Wellsman, Editor.
Historical, technical, general and news articles, 200 to 1,200 words, on skysurfing, hand gliding, man-augmented soaring, man-powered airplanes. Related fiction, same lengths. Fillers, humor, poetry, drawings. No payment.

SMITHSONIAN—Arts and Industries Bldg., 900 Jefferson Dr., Washington, DC 20560. Edward K. Thompson, Editor.
Articles, 700 to 4,000 words, on wildlife, environment, science (hard and natural), art, history, for members of Smithsonian. Pay varies, on acceptance. Query.

SNOWMOBILE WEST—P.O. Box 896, Idaho Falls, ID 83401. D. Brent Clement, Editor.
Articles, 1,200 words with photos, on snowmobiling in the western states. Pays 3¢ a word. Query.

SNOTRACK—534 North Broadway, Milwaukee, WI 53202. Bill Vint, Editor.
Photo-articles, 700 to 2,000 words, on snowmobiling activities, race events, rallies, trail rides, family activities; how-to pieces. Humor, cartoons. Black-and-white inside photos, color cover photo. Pays to $100 for photo-articles, $100 for cover photo, on acceptance. Query.

SPECIAL-INTEREST AUTOS—215 River Rd., Grandview-on-Hudson, NY 10960. Richard C. Taylor, Editor.
Articles, 2,500 to 3,500 words with photos, about unusual or classic automobiles. Pays about $100 per magazine page, on acceptance.

SPORT—641 Lexington Ave., New York, NY 10022. Don Kowet, Managing Editor.
Human interest or controversial articles, 2,000 to 3,000 words, on important figures and events in spectator sports. Pays $350 to $1,000 on acceptance. Query.

SPORTS AFIELD—250 West 55th St., New York, NY 10019. Lamar Underwood, Editor.
Articles, 500 to 2,000 words, on hunting and fishing, conservation, nature, travel, camping, personal experience; photo-features; how-to pieces. Humor, fiction. Color or black-and-white photos. Pays top rates, on acceptance.

SPORTS AFIELD FISHING ANNUAL—250 West 55th St., New York, NY 10019.
How-to and personal experience articles, 3,000 words with photos, on fishing. How-to fillers. Pays from $400, on acceptance. Query. Same address and requirements for *Sports Afield Hunting Annual,* except articles are on hunting.

SPORTS ILLUSTRATED—Rockefeller Center, New York, NY 10020. Pat Ryan, Editor.
Articles, 1,000 to 2,000 words, on sporting events or sports personalities prior to 1965, from new perspective. Short sports features, 600 to 2,000 words; humor, reminiscences, personality profiles. Pays from $250 for short features, $250 to $400 for "Yesterdays," from $750 for long articles, on acceptance.

SPORTS TODAY—919 Third Ave., New York, NY 10022. Herb Gluck, Managing Editor.
Hardhitting articles, 1,500 words, on top pro athletes. Pays $100 within a month of publication.

THE SPORTSWOMAN—P.O. Box 2611, Culver City, CA 90230. Marlene Jensen, Editor.
Articles, 1,000 to 2,000 words, on unusual sports; interviews with women sports stars. Cartoons, photos. Pays $75 to $100 for articles, $25 for cartoons, $25 for photos, on publication. Query.

STREET CHOPPER—1132 N. Brookhurst, Anaheim, CA 92801. Steve Stillwell, Editor.
Technical articles, 4,000 words with 5 x 7 or 8 x 10 black-and-white glossies, on motorcycles. Pays $50 per published page.

SURFER MAGAZINE—Box 1028, Dana Point, CA 92629. Steve Pezman, Editor.
Light fiction, 1,000 to 2,500 words, and articles, 5,000 words, on surfing theme, from experts' point of view. Fillers, short humor, black-and-white or color photos of surfing. Verse. Pays 4¢ a word and up, on publication.

SWIMMING WORLD—8622 Bellanca Ave., Los Angeles, CA 90045. Al Schoenfield, Publisher. Bob Ingram, Editor.
Articles, from 500 words, for high school, collegiate, and national competitive swimmers, on nutrition, body building, diet, technique, competitive swimming, diving, water polo; profiles of swimming-meet winners. Pay varies, on acceptance.

TENNIS—297 Westport Ave., Norwalk, CT 06856. Shepherd Campbell, Editor.
Instructional articles, features, profiles of tennis stars, 500 to 2,000 words. Fillers, humor, etc. Photos and drawings. Pays $50 to $100 for articles, from $10 for fillers and humor, on publication. Query.

TENNIS ILLUSTRATED—630 Shatto Pl., Los Angeles, CA 90005. Gay Yellen, Editor.
Instructional, humorous, tournament and personality articles, on all aspects of tennis. Light fiction, to 1,000 words, on tennis; verse, fillers. Pays 10¢ a word, on publication. Query.

TENNIS U.S.A.—c/o Chilton Co., Chilton Way, Radnor, PA 19089. Robert L. Gillen, Editor.
Articles, 500 to 3,000 words, on tennis personalities, events, fashion, travel, equipment; instructional pieces. Humorous poetry, 5 to 25 lines, fillers, cartoons, puzzles, on tennis theme. Pays $50 to $350, on acceptance. Query.

TRACK AND FIELD NEWS—Box 296, Los Altos, CA 94022. Jon Hendershott, Garry Hill, Editors.
Track and field features, profiles, any length. Fillers, humor, photos and drawings. Pay negotiable on publication. Query.

TRAIL CAMPING—20813 Hart St., Canoga Park, CA 91306. Don Maxwell, Editorial Director.
First-person personal experience articles, 1,500 to 4,000 words, with black-and-white or color photos, on hiking, backpacking, canoeing, etc., to interest experienced wilderness travelers. Fiction, 500 to 1,000 words; poetry, cartoons. Pays 3¢ a word and up for articles, to $10 for 8 x 10 black-and-white glossies, to $35 for color prints and transparencies; $10 per cartoon, and $5 per poem, on publication.

TRAILER BOATS—P.O. Box 6697, 1512 West Magnolia Blvd., Burbank, CA 91506. Ralph Poole, Editor.
Technically accurate articles, 1,500 to 2,500 words, on boat, trailer or car maintenance and operation, new boats and towing cars, skiing, fishing, cruising. Boat-oriented fillers, humor. Pays 7¢ to 10¢ a word, on publication. Query.

TRAILER LIFE—23945 Craftsman Rd., Calabasas, CA 91302. Arthur J. Rouse, Editor and Publisher.
Articles, to 2,500 words with black-and-white and four-color photos, on trailering, truck campers, motorhomes, hobbies, etc.; how-to pieces. Pays to $175, on publication. Send for editorial guide.

TREASURE—7950 Deering Ave., Canoga Park, CA 91304. Bob Grant, Editor.
Articles, 500 to 3,500 words, on treasure hunting: "treasures" discovered, products to use in hobby, how to use or build equipment, etc., particularly on areas other than Western states and Florida. 8 x 10 glossy prints. Pay varies on publication. Same address and requirements for *Treasure Search*.

TREASURE SEARCH—See *Treasure*.

TROUT—737 South Sparks St., State College, PA 16801. Alvin R. Grove, Editor.
Articles, 800 to 2,500 words, with 8 x 10 black-and-white photos, on trout management and related conservation projects. Pays $25 to $50 per article, $5 per photo, $25 for cover photo, on publication. Query.

TRUE—21 West 26th St., New York, NY 10016.
Articles, to 3,000 words, on sports. Pays $200 to $1,000. Query.

TURF AND SPORT DIGEST—511-13 Oakland Ave., Baltimore, MD 21212. Les Woodcock, Editor and Publisher.
Colorful articles, 1,500 to 4,000 words, on careers of national turf personalities, playing the races, human interest. Pays $60 to $100 for articles, $40 for system pieces, on publication. Query.

VIRGINIA WILDLIFE—4010 West Broad St., Richmond, VA 23230. Harry Gillam, Editor.
Articles, about 1,500 words, on Virginia hunting, fishing, boating, nature, photo features on nature subjects; humorous outdoor episodes. Fiction, about 1,500 words, on animals. Pays 1½¢ per word, $7.50 per photo. Query.

WATER SKIER—7th St. and Ave. G, S.W., Winter Haven, FL 33880. Thomas C. Hardman, Editor.
Off-beat articles and photo features on water skiing. Pay varies, on acceptance.

WATERSPORT—Boat Owners Council of America, 534 North Broadway, Milwaukee, WI 53202. Glenn Helgeland, Editor.
Articles and photos of outboard motor boating, canoeing, sailing, water skiing, personalities, boat camping, fishing, shell collecting, etc. No "cruise plan" or mechanical "how-to" pieces. Pays $50 to $400 for stories with photos, $15 to $50 for black-and-white photos; $35 to $75 for inside color photos; $100 for cover photos, on publication. Query.

THE WESTERN HORSEMAN—3850 North Nevada Ave., Colorado Springs, CO 80901. Chan Bergen, Assistant Editor.
Articles, about 1,500 words with photos, on care and training of stock horses; historical pieces. Pay varies, on acceptance. Query.

WESTWAYS—Box 2890 Terminal Annex, Los Angeles, CA 90051. Francis Ring, Associate Editor.
Articles, 700 to 2,500 words, on western U.S., Canadian and Mexican activities: natural science, travel, history, etc. Verse, to 45 lines. Pays 10¢ a word on acceptance, for articles; $25 per black-and-white photo, $25 to $200 for color photos, $25 and up for poems, on publication. Query.

WHEELS AFIELD—8490 Sunset Blvd., Los Angeles, CA 90069. Robert T. Kovacik, Editor.
Articles, to 2,000 words, with recreational vehicle slant; how-to pieces for campers. Illustrations should accompany articles. Pays about $50 per page, on acceptance.

WOMENSPORTS—1660 South Amphlett Blvd., San Mateo, CA 94402. Rosalie Muller Wright, Editor.
Sports articles 3,000 to 4,000 words, on personalities, trends, events, opinions, travel, of interest to women. Short pieces, to 1,500 words; technical articles. Pays $100 to $500 for articles, more with photos, within 30 days of acceptance. Query.

WOODALL'S TRAILER TRAVEL—3500 Western Ave., Highland Park, IL 60035. Jerry Pinkham, Editor.
Articles, 300 to 3,000 words, on family camping, travel, outdoor living, how-to pieces on updating, maintaining, utilizing recreational vehicles. Pays to 10¢ a word, on acceptance. Query, with photos or illustrations.

WORLD TENNIS—385 Madison Ave., New York, NY 10017. Ronald Bookman, Editor.
Knowledgeable features and instruction articles, 1,000 to 2,000 words with photos, on tennis; photos of tournament action. Pay varies, on publication. Query.

WRESTLING GUIDE—Jalart House, Inc., P.O. Box 642, Scottsdale, AZ 85252. Tommy Kay, Editor.
Profile or dressing room articles, 800 to 3,000 words with black-and-white photos, on pro or amateur wrestling stars, wrestling fan clubs, big matches. Pays $15 to $35 for articles, $40 for color transparencies for cover, 90 days before publication. Same address and requirements for *Big Book of Wrestling*.

YACHTING—50 West 44th St., New York, NY 10036. William W. Robinson, Editor.
Articles on recreational boating (sail and power), history; technical pieces on yachting.

THE YANKEE GUIDE TO THE NEW ENGLAND COUNTRYSIDE—143 Newbury St., Boston, MA 02116. Georgia Orcutt, Editor.
Articles, 2,000 words, on unusual New England activities. No history or descriptions of specific places. Black-and-white or color photos. Pays $50 to $200. Query with outline.

HOME AND GARDEN; WOMEN'S MAGAZINES

ALLIED PUBLICATIONS, INC.—P.O. Box 23505, Fort Lauderdale, FL 33307. Marie Stilkind, Associate Editor.
General, noncontroversial articles, with black-and-white photos, on home and family interests; travel; beauty; decorating; hobbies and art techniques, methods, new ideas and materials; profiles of noted artists and secretaries of famous people; how-tos; pieces of interest to hairstylists. Pays 5¢ a word, $5 per photo, on acceptance.

AMERICAN BABY—575 Lexington Ave., New York, NY 10022. Judith Nolte, Editor.
Articles, 400 to 1,500 words, to help new and expectant parents, and pieces on child care for ages on month to three years, from 400 to 1,500 words. Pay varies.

AMERICAN HOME—641 Lexington Ave., New York, NY 10022.
Short, informative articles on home service subjects: decorating, remodeling, entertaining, gardening. No fiction, poetry. Most features staff-written. Query first.

THE AMERICAN ROSE MAGAZINE—P.O. Box 30,000, Shreveport, LA 71130. Harold S. Goldstein, Editor.
Articles for home gardener with interest in roses; new products, varieties, experiments readers can try. Fillers. No payment.

THE ANTIQUES JOURNAL—P.O. Box 88128, Dunwoody, GA 30338. John Mebane, Editor.
Factual articles with illustrations, to 2,500 words, on antiques and collectible objects. Query.

BABY CARE—52 Vanderbilt Ave., New York, NY 10017. Mrs. Maja Bernath, Editor.
Articles, to 1,800 words, on infant care, emotional and physical development, husband-wife-baby relationships, seasonal topics. Short features, to 1,000 words, with humorous narrative or reflective approach. Some cartoons and short poetry. Pays $10 for "Family Corner" (to 100 words), $25 for "Focus on You" (to 500 words), $50 to $125 for features, on acceptance.

BABY TALK—66 East 34th St., New York, NY 10016. Eve Hammerschmidt, Editor.
True-experience pieces, 500 to 1,000 words, by mother or father, on baby, baby care, family relations, etc. "Your Opinion" department uses short articles expressing a point of view.

BETTER HOMES AND GARDENS—1716 Locust St., Des Moines, IA 50336. James A. Autry, Editor.
Articles on home and family entertainment, money management, health, travel, cars. All other material staff-written. Pays top rates, on acceptance. Query with outline.

BLACK MARIA: WOMEN SPEAK—815 West Wrightwood Ave., Chicago, IL 60614.
Feminist quarterly: short stories, nonfiction, poetry, graphics. Pays in copies. Publishes women only.

BRIDE'S—350 Madison Ave., New York, NY 10017. Barbara Donovan Tober, Editor-in-Chief.
Articles, 1,000 to 3,000 words for nearly-weds, newly-weds, their family and friends, on personal communication, sexual adjustment. All other material staff-written. Pays $200 to $500. Query Peyton Bailey, Articles Editor.

BUDGET DECORATING—699 Madison Ave., New York, NY 10021. Connie Dodds Devitt, Editor-in-Chief.

Articles with photos on home decorating and remodeling (exterior and interior), do-it-yourself and how-to projects, constructive crafts, and money-saving tips. Query.

CAPPER'S WEEKLY—616 Jefferson St., Topeka, KS 66607. Dorothy Harvey, Editor.
Articles, 300 to 500 words: human interest, personal experience, historical. Poetry, to 15 lines, on nature, home, family. Letters on women's interests for "Heart of the Home"; jokes, cartoons. Pay varies, on publication.

CHATELAINE—481 University Ave., Toronto, Ont., M5W 1A7, Canada. Doris Anderson, Editor.
Fiction, 3,000 to 4,000 words, with woman interest: romance, family, and social and human relations themes. Articles, 3,000 words, on controversial subjects, famous names, current social problems of interest to Canadian women. True personal experience articles, $300; $600 for articles; $400 and up for fiction; $25 to $150 for fillers, on acceptance.

THE CHRISTIAN HOME—201 Eighth Ave. South, Nashville, TN 37202. Florence A. Lund, Editor.
Educationally sound articles, 1,000 to 2,000 words, for parents (may be humorous). Pays 2½¢ a word, 50¢ a line for poetry, on acceptance.

THE CHRISTIAN SCIENCE MONITOR—One Norway St., Boston, MA 02115. John Hughes, Editor. Nan Trent, Woman's Editor. Phyllis Hanes, Food Editor.
Articles on homemaking, food, fashion, family and children, consumerism, women of achievement, and issues affecting women. Pay varies.

THE CONSUMER GAZETTE—466 Lexington Ave., New York, NY 10017. Bill Wolf, Editor.
Brief, how-to articles with strong consumerist stance, on money saving in the home, gardening, fashion, sporting goods, hobbies and pet care. Pays $25 to $200, on publication.

COSMOPOLITAN—224 West 57th St., New York, NY 10019. Helen Gurley Brown, Editor. Walter Meade, Managing Editor, Harris Dientsfrey, Fiction Editor.
Magazine for young career women. Articles, to 4,000 words, and shorter features, 1,000 to 2,000 words, on issues affecting women. Fiction: short-shorts, 1,500 to 3,000 words; short stories, 5,000 to 6,000 words; mystery and other novels; condensed books, 30,000 words. Must have solid plot, sharp characterization, focus on man-woman relationships. Pays $1,000 to $1,500 for full-length articles, $100 for short stories, $300 to $600 for short-shorts.

EARLY AMERICAN LIFE—Box 1831, Harrisburg, PA 17105. Robert G. Miner, Editor.
Illustrated articles, 1,000 to 4,000 words, on early American life, including arts, crafts, furnishings and architecture. Pays from $25 to $200, on acceptance. Query.

ESSENCE—300 East 42nd St., New York, NY 10017.
"The magazine for today's black woman." Query.

EXPECTING—52 Vanderbilt Ave., New York, NY 10017. Mrs. Maja Bernath, Editor.
Articles, 700 to 1,800 words, for expectant mothers on prenatal development, husband-wife relationships, etc.; medical pieces by R.N.'s and M.D.'s. No fiction. Pays $50 to $125, on acceptance; slightly higher for professionals in medical fields.

FAMILY CIRCLE—488 Madison Ave., New York, NY 10022. Arthur Hettich, Editor.
Articles on health, finances and consumer affairs, jobs, food, gardening, family relationships, travel. Pay varies.

THE FAMILY FOOD GARDEN—Rt. 1, Box 877, McCourtney Rd., Grass Valley, CA 95945. George S. Wells, Publisher.
Practical articles with black-and-white photos or color transparencies, on home gardening, raising livestock. Nominal payment, on publication.

THE FAMILY HANDYMAN—235 East 45th St., New York, NY 10017.
Non-technical, step-by-step articles, to 1,000 words, with black-and-white photos, on home improvement, repair and maintenance for do-it-yourselfers. How-to garden articles. Pays $40 to $100. Shorts, 100 to 300 words, on expert tips or shortcuts for do-it-yourselfers. Pays $5 to $15, on publication.

FAMILY HEALTH—545 Madison Ave., New York, NY 10022.
Articles, to 3,000 words, and photo-essays, on health, beauty, physical fitness, marriage, child care, nutrition, health-oriented consumerism, personal experiences. Pays $500 and up for features, on acceptance. Query with outline.

FAMILY HOUSEBOATING—23945 Craftsman Rd., Calabasas, CA 91602. Bill Estes, Editor.
Articles, 500 to 2,000 words, with black-and-white photos, color transparencies, maps, on all phases of houseboating. Pays on publication.

FAMILY WEEKLY—641 Lexington Ave., New York, NY 10022. Mort Persky, Editor-in-Chief. Rosalyn Abrevaya, Women's Editor.
Sunday supplement. Short, lively articles with emphasis on prominent individuals, family help and advice. Queries only; no unsolicited manuscripts.

FLOWER & GARDEN MAGAZINE—4251 Pennsylvania, Kansas City, MO 64111. Rachel Snyder, Editor-in-Chief.
Articles, to 1,500 words, with good photos, on indoor and outdoor gardening; may have regional emphasis. Pays 3¢ a word and up, on acceptance.

GIRLTALK—380 Madison Ave., New York, NY 10017.
Fiction, articles, 2,000 words or less, of interest to women. Short, humorous poems, fillers. Only one manuscript per month from any author. Pay varies.

GLAMOUR—350 Madison Ave., New York, NY 10017. Ruth Whitney, Editor-in-Chief.
Helpful, informative articles, humorous or serious, on all aspects of young woman's life—medicine, mental health, social, economic and emotional problems. (Fashion and beauty material staff-written.) Unusual career stories; entertainment. Short features, 1,500 to 3,000 words, stressing personal viewpoint or experience. Pays $300 and up.

GOOD HOUSEKEEPING—959 Eighth Ave., New York, NY 10019. John Mack Carter, Editor; Betty Frank, Articles Editor.
Dramatic, first-person experience articles in fields of human relations, individual achievement, practical living, romance, social techniques. "Better Way" occasionally buys research reports on news of practical interest about women's activities, jobs, etc. Pays top rates, on acceptance.

GOURMET—777 Third Ave., New York, NY 10017. Gail Zweigenthal, Managing Editor.
Articles, 2,500 to 3,000 words, on food, travel, good living, for sophisticated audience interested in fine foods and fine wines. Recipes only in connection with articles. No short features or fillers. Pays on acceptance.

HARLEQUIN'S WOMAN—Harlequin Enterprises, Ltd., 240 Duncan Mill Rd., Suite 605, Don Mills, Ont., Canada M3B 1Z4. Beth McGregor, Editor.
Upbeat articles, 2,000 to 4,000 words, on overcoming personal problems, travel, cooking, personal experiences; inspirational material. Short stories, romances, 3,000 to 5,000 words. Short poetry. Pay varies, on acceptance. Query for articles.

HORTICULTURE—300 Massachusetts Ave., Boston, MA 02115. Edwin F. Steffek, Editor.
Authoritative articles on gardening or horticulture, 500 to 1,200 words. Pays 3¢ a word, after publication.

HOUSE & GARDEN—350 Madison Ave., New York, NY 10017. Denise Otis, Associate Editor.
Articles on decorating, entertaining, do-it-yourself crafts. Rarely buys unsolicited articles.

HOUSE BEAUTIFUL—717 Fifth Ave., New York, NY 10022. Wallace Guenther, Editor.
Interested in seeing detailed outlines for proposed articles. Submit to Linda Downs, Senior Editor.

HOW-TO—964 North Pennsylvania St., Indianapolis, IN 46204. John J. Sullivan, Editor.
Detailed, do-it-yourself articles with photos, on home maintenance, home repair, home improvement projects, gardening, etc. Pays $100 and up per published page, on acceptance. Query. Send for writer's guide.

LADIES' HOME JOURNAL—641 Lexington Ave., New York, NY 10022.
Limited market. "We have no set requirements—except those of quality—for editorial material. However, at the present time most of our articles are staff-written or assigned through recognized literary agents."

THE LADY GOLFER—P.O. Box 4725, Whittier, CA 90607. Charles G. Schoos, General Manager.
Articles, 500 to 3,000 words, with photos, on golf, golfing personalities, golf instructions (by professionals). Golf-related fiction, 500 to 3,000 words, poems, fillers, jokes, humor, and puzzles. Pays $50 and up for articles and fiction, $35 to $50 for cartoons, on acceptance.

LADY'S CIRCLE—21 West 26th St., New York, NY 10010. Evan Frances, Editor.
Articles, 2,000 to 3,000 words, with at least two black-and-white photos, to interest homemakers. Pays $125 and up, on publication.

LADYCOM—520 North Michigan Ave., Chicago, IL 60611. Anne Taubeneck, Editor.
Articles, to 2,000 words, for military wives between 21 and 35, in the U.S. and overseas. Pays $50 to $100, after acceptance. Query.

LUTHERAN WOMAN—2900 Queen Lane, Philadelphia, PA 19129.
Short stories, 1,000 to 2,000 words, on growth and change in people; occasional short poems. Pays $25 to $40, on publication.

McCALL'S—230 Park Ave., New York, NY 10017. Robert Stein, Editor.
Timely articles, 3,000 words, on all subjects. Well-written, distinguished fiction. Short reportorial pieces, 300 to 800 words, for "Right Now" section. Pays top rates, on acceptance.

MADEMOISELLE—350 Madison Ave., New York, NY 10017. Mary Cantwell, Managing Editor. Ellen A. Stoianoff, Fiction Editor.
High-quality short stories and articles, 1,200 to 6,500 words, for young women 18 to 25. Pay varies for articles; $300 and up for fiction, on acceptance.

MOBILE LIVING—Box 1418, 1323 Main St., Sarasota, FL 33578. Ward H. Patton, Jr., Publisher. Frances Neel, Editor.
Articles, 500 to 1,000 words, for travel trailer and camper owners, on travel clubs, vacation trips in trailers or campers. Pays 1¢ a word, on publication. Query.

MODERN BRIDE—One Park Ave., New York, NY 10016. Robert W. Houseman, Editor.
Articles, from 1,500 words, on etiquette, marriage, the home, honeymoon travel, for both bride and groom. Pays on acceptance.

MODERN MATURITY—215 Long Beach Blvd., Long Beach, CA 90801. Hubert Pryor, Editor.
Service articles on housing, food, health, employment, hobbies, for persons over 55. Also nostalgia, inspirational articles, personality pieces, Americana, personal accounts. Short stories. Pays $50 to $500, on acceptance; $15 and up for black-and-white photos, from $50 for color.

MOTHERS' MANUAL–176 Cleveland Dr., Croton-on-Hudson, NY 10520. Beth Waterfall, Editor.
Authoritative articles for expectant parents and parents of babies from birth to six years. Pays on publication.

MOTORHOME LIFE–23945 Craftsman Road, Calabasas, CA 91602. Bill Estes, Editor.
Articles, 500 to 2,000 words, with both black-and-white photos and color transparencies, on all phases of motorhomes only. Pays on publication.

MOVING OUT–169 Mackenzie Hall, Wayne State University, Detroit, MI 48202.
Feminist magazine. Short stories, essays about women, short poetry, interviews with prominent women. Pays in copies.

MS.–370 Lexington Ave., New York, NY 10017. Patricia Carbine, Editor-in-Chief and Publisher; Gloria Steinem, Editor.
Address Manuscript Editor. Articles and fiction on topics relevant to women as people, not stereotypes.

NATIONAL ANTIQUES REVIEW–Box 619, Portland, ME 04104. Lillian F. Potter, Editor.
Articles, to 1,500 words, with photos, relating to prices of antiques: auction, show, flea market coverage. Collecting tips, aids to identification and advice on collectibles old and new. Pays $25 per article, $1 to $2 per photo, after publication. Query.

NEW WOMAN–P.O. Box 24202, Fort Lauderdale, FL 33307.
Articles to interest top-level business and professional women. Pay varies. Query.

ORGANIC GARDENING AND FARMING–Emmaus, PA 18049. M. C. Goldman, Managing Editor.
Articles, to 2,500 words, on organic agriculture; biological control of pests; compost, and natural fertilizers; etc. Pays $50 to $200 for articles with photos or illustrations, $25 to $50 for fillers, on preparation for use. Send for writer's guide.

PARENTS' MAGAZINE–52 Vanderbilt Ave., New York, NY 10017. Genevieve Millet Landau, Editor-in-Chief.
Articles, 2,000 words, on physical, emotional and mental development of infants, school children, and adolescents; family relationships; adults in the community. Lively, readable articles on important research in medicine, science, education. Prefers colloquial style with quotes from experts. Pays on acceptance.

PERFECT HOME–427 6th Ave., S.E., Cedar Rapids, IA 52400. Donna Nicholas Hahn, Editor.
Photographic coverage of moderate-cost homes, remodeling projects, unusual decorating, etc., with brief captions and professional-quality photos. Also 500-word editorials on "What Home Means to Me," by nationally known figures; pays $50. Query.

PLAYGIRL–1801 Century Park East, Suite 2300, Century City, Los Angeles, CA 90067. Marin Scott Milam, Editor-in-Chief.
Pertinent, in-depth articles of interest to contemporary women; fiction, 1,000 to 7,500 words on any subject. Humor and satire. Pays $300 to $1,000, after acceptance. Query.

REDBOOK–230 Park Ave., New York, NY 10017.
Practical articles, 500 to 5,000 words, for young women, on home, health, husband-wife, parent-child relationships, etc. Fiction with basic themes of love, marriage, parenthood, jobs, or on social and moral questions, etc. Pays $1,000 and up for short stories, $850 for short-shorts (1,400 to 1,600 words), $3,000 and up for novellas (12,000 to 25,000 words), $7,500 for full-length novels, on acceptance.

THE SECRETARY–2440 Pershing Rd., G-10, Kansas City, MO 64108. Mrs. Shirley S. Englund, Editor and Publishing Manager.

Articles, 800 to 2,000 words, on office procedures, secretarial skills, administrative responsibilities, and human relations. Pays on publication.

SPHERE—500 North Michigan Ave., Chicago, IL 60611. Joan Leonard, Editor.
Imaginative, how-to women's interest articles. Queries only.

SUNSET MAGAZINE—Menlo Park, CA 94025. Proctor Mellquist, Editor.
No free-lance material at present.

TEXAN WOMAN—P.O. Box 1267, Austin, TX 78767.
Articles, to 1,500 words, short stories, to 2,500 words, poetry, and news with Texas tie-in or origin, and showing new slant on women or having strong images of women. Pays in copies.

13TH MOON—30 Seaman Ave., New York, NY 10034. Ellen Marie Bissert, Editor.
Short stories, 5,000 words, poetry, reviews of books by women. Pays in copies.

THREE SISTERS—Box 969, Georgetown University, Washington, DC 20067.
Fiction and poetry by women. Black-and-white 8½ x 10 glossy photos, and drawings. Pays in copies.

TODAY'S CHRISTIAN MOTHER—8121 Hamilton Ave., Cincinnati, OH 45231. Wilma L. Shaffer, Editor.
Articles, 600 to 1,200 words, showing Christian principles applied in home training of children. Material for father's page, ideas for creative children's activities. Pay varies.

TODAY'S SECRETARY—1221 Ave. of Americas, New York, NY 10020. Ann Roberts, Editor.
Articles, 1,000 to 1,500 words with photos, for women, ages 16 to 21, on young secretaries, new office techniques and trends, self-improvement, etc. Lively fiction, 500 to 1,000 words, dealing with secretaries' business lives; rarely uses romance. Pays $50 for fiction, $60 to $150 for articles. Query or send outline.

TRAILER LIFE—23945 Craftsman Rd., Calabasas, CA 91602.
Articles, 500 to 2,000 words, with both black-and-white photos and color transparencies, on all phases of trailering, motor homes, truck campers, how-to, etc. Editor's Guide available. Pays good rates, on publication.

UP FROM UNDER—339 Lafayette St., New York, NY 10012.
Fiction and nonfiction, 1,000 to 10,000 words, for working-class women, about women's experiences, their problems and how they overcame them. Cartoons, photos. No payment.

VIVA—909 Third Ave., New York, NY 10022. Bette-Jane Raphael, Articles Editor.
Articles, 2,500 to 5,000 words, on problems that face modern women: social, sexual, economic, emotional, etc. Humor welcome. Pays $250 to $1,000. Query.

VOGUE—350 Madison Ave., New York, NY 10017. Grace Mirabella, Editor-in-Chief. Leo Lerman, Consulting Features Editor.
Articles, to 1,500 words, on women and their interests and problems, the arts, travel, medicine and health. Rarely buys unsolicited manuscripts. Pays good rates, on acceptance.

WEIGHT WATCHERS MAGAZINE—635 Madison Ave., New York, NY 10022. Edythe K. Tomkinson, Feature Editor.
General-interest articles, humor, travel pieces, how-to's. No health or diet articles. Pays on acceptance.

THE WOMAN—235 Park Ave. South, New York, NY 10003. Diana Lurvey, Editor.
First-person articles dealing with today's world, from viewpoint of married or once-married woman. No fiction or poetry. Pays $50, on acceptance.

WOMAN'S DAY—1515 Broadway, New York, NY 10036. Geraldine E. Rhoads, Editor. Rebecca Greer, Articles Editor. Eileen Herbert Jordon, Fiction Editor.
Serious, human-interest, and some humorous articles, to 3,500 words, on marriage, child rearing, family health, interpersonal relationships, money management, leisure activities. Quality short stories. Pays top rates, on acceptance. Query on nonfiction.

WOMAN'S LIFE TODAY (formerly *Woman's Life*)—261 Fifth Ave., New York, NY 10016. Diana Willis, Editor.
Articles, 500 to 1,500 words, for women, on new products, full- or part-time careers and business opportunities; humor, interviews, profiles, how-to pieces. Pays $20 to $40; $2.50 per black-and-white glossy photo, on publication.

WOMAN'S WORLD—Ideal Publishing Corp., 575 Madison Ave., New York, NY 10022. Holly Garrison, Editor.
Handicraft how-to articles for women, with black-and-white photos. Pays $50 to $150, on publication. Query. Sample copies 25¢.

WOMEN: A JOURNAL OF LIBERATION—3028 Greenmount Ave., Baltimore, MD 21218.
Fiction and nonfiction, to 3,000 words; poetry, artwork, photos, relevant to women's liberation. No payment.

WOMEN'S ALMANAC—Armitage Press, Inc., 1430 Massachusetts Ave., Cambridge, MA 02138. Holly A. McLellan, Editor.
Articles, 1,500 to 2,500 words with photos, on women's needs and interests: adult education, child care and education, consumer close-ups, finances, health, women and law, women at work, etc. Pays about 5¢ to 10¢ a word on publication. Query.

WOMENSPORTS—1660 South Amphlett Blvd., San Mateo, CA 94402. Rosalie Muller Wright, Editor.
Sports articles, 3,000 to 4,000 words, on personalities, trends, events, opinions, travel, adventure, of interest to women. Technical and short pieces, to 1,500 words. Pays $50 to $300, more with photos, after publication.

THE WORKBASKET—4251 Pennsylvania, Kansas City, MO 64111. Mary Ida Sullivan, Editor.
Articles, 500 to 700 words, on how specific women have improved their home environment. Concise, how-to articles on women's homecrafts. Short items, to 200 words, on women who make extra money, for "Women Who Make Cents." Pays $5, on acceptance.

WORKBENCH—4251 Pennsylvania, Kansas City, MO 64111. Jay W. Hedden, Editor.
Detailed, how-to articles with 8 x 10 black-and-white glossy photos and drawings, for do-it-yourselfers and home owners. Pays $75 to $200 per published page, on acceptance. Send for sample copy and editorial requirements sheet.

SPECIALIZED MAGAZINES

HEALTH

ACCENT ON LIVING—P.O. Box 726, Bloomington, IL 61701. Raymond C. Cheever, Editor.
Articles on rehabilitation of the handicapped, success stories, self-help devices. Humorous articles about physical disabilities; articles dealing constructively with prejudice against the handicapped. Pays up to $50, on publication.

AMERICAN BABY—10 East 52nd St., New York, NY 10022. Judith Nolte, Editor.
Articles for new and expectant parents, on care of babies one month to three years old, from 400 to 1,500 words. Payment varies.

AMERICAN FAMILY PHYSICIAN—American Academy of Family Physicians, 1740 West 92nd St., Kansas City, MO 64114. Walter H. Kemp, Publisher.
Articles, 1,600 to 3,200 words, on clinical medicine, with photos or drawings. Pays from $100, on publication. Query.

AMERICAN JOURNAL OF NURSING—10 Columbus Circle, New York, NY 10019. Thelma M. Schorr, R.N., Editor.
Articles on nursing subjects, 1,500 to 2,000 words, with photos. Pays $20 per printed page, on publication. Query.

DENTAL ECONOMICS—P.O. Box 1260, Tulsa, OK 74101. Richard Henn, Editor.
Articles on business side of dental practice, and money management, 1,200 to 1,500 words, with photos. Pays on acceptance.

THE EXCEPTIONAL PARENT—P.O. Box 101, Back Bay Annex, Boston, MA 02117. Stanley D. Klein, Ph.D., Editor.
Articles, 600 to 3,000 words, giving practical guidance, in layman's language, for parents of disabled children. Pays up to 5¢ a word, on publication. Query.

EXPECTING—Parents' Magazine Enterprises, Inc., 52 Vanderbilt Ave., New York, NY 10017.
Guide for expectant mothers. Medical articles by R.N.'s and M.D.'s, and personal experience pieces, 700 to 1,500 words. Pays from $50 to $125, on acceptance. Slightly higher rates for specialists, such as M.D.'s.

FAMILY HEALTH—1271 Ave. of the Americas, New York, NY 10022.
Articles, about 3,000 words, personal experience pieces, and photo essays, on health, nutrition, child care, marriage, etc. Shorter pieces on beauty and physical fitness. Submit outline first. Pays on acceptance.

HEALTH—212 East Ohio St., Chicago, IL 60611. Mary Anne Klein, Assistant Editor.
Articles with photos on health and medicine for layman, 1,000 to 1,750 words. Cartoons on medical subjects. Pays 4¢ a word, $5 a photo, and $7.50 a cartoon.

HOSPITAL PROGRESS—1438 South Grand Blvd., St. Louis, MO 63104. Robert J. Stephens, Editor.
Official journal of Catholic Hospital Association. Hospital management and administration features, 1,500 to 5,000 words. Pays $1 per column inch, on publication, or by arrangement. Query first.

LIFE AND HEALTH—6856 Eastern Ave. N.W., Washington, DC 20012. Dr. Mervyn G. Hardinge, Editor.
Well-researched, documented, human-interest articles, up to 2,000 words, on health, emphasizing prevention, for laymen. Pays $50 to $150, six weeks after acceptance.

MEDICAL COMMUNICATIONS—School of Journalism, Ohio University, Athens, OH 45701. Byron T. Scott, Editor.
Articles, 1,500 to 3,000 words, on new approaches to medical communications in any medium. Pays in copies, on publication.

MEDICAL OPINION—575 Madison Ave., New York, NY 10022. Patrick Flanagan, Editor.
Articles to interest general practitioners, on medical topics—political, clinical, cultural, personal, 1,000 to 2,000 words. Prefer M.D. by-line. Pays from $150 to $250, on acceptance. Query first.

MD—30 East 60th St., New York, NY 10022. Michael Fry, D.Sc., Managing Editor.
Not in the market at the present time.

PHYSICIAN'S MANAGEMENT–757 Third Ave., NY 10017. Gene Balliett, Editor.
Financial and office-management magazine for physicians. Writer's guidelines free on request to editor.

PRACTICAL PSYCHOLOGY FOR PHYSICIANS–Harcourt Brace Jovanovich Publications, 757 Third Ave., New York, NY 10017. Robert McCrie, Editor.
Informative, practical articles on sociological and behavioral topics, to help physicians in their practice. Pays 5¢ to 15¢ a word, extra for photos used with articles, on acceptance. Query.

RN MAGAZINE–Oradell, NJ 07649.
Articles, preferably by R.N.'s, on subjects of interest and practical value to nurses, up to 2,000 words. Emphasis on nursing guidelines in clinical care. Pays up to 10¢ a word, on acceptance. Query.

STRENGTH AND HEALTH–P.O. Box 1707, York, PA 17405. Bob Karpinski, Editor.
Articles, 1,500 words and up, on weightlifting, physical fitness, sports. Also, color transparencies of couple engaged in physical fitness activity, with article. Pays $50 and up for articles, on publication; $100 for transparencies.

SWEET 'N LOW–436 West Colorado Blvd., Glendale, CA 91204. Connie O'Kelley, Editor.
Articles, 1,000 to 3,000 words, on nutrition and related breakthroughs, exercise, diet, physical and mental health. Also general-interest features, short poetry and cartoons related to dieting and exercise. Pays various rates. Query first.

TIC–P.O. Box 407, North Chatham, NY 12132. Joseph Strack, Editor.
Articles, 800 to 3,000 words, on subjects of interest to dentists: building practice, patient management, improving office procedures, etc. Photos, cartoons about dentistry. Pays on acceptance.

TODAY'S HEALTH–535 North Dearborn St., Chicago, IL 60610. Bard Lindeman, Editor-in-Chief.
Family articles, 2,500 to 4,000 words, on nutrition, medicine, recreation, child development, ecology and other health-related problems, self-help, health angles on major news events and personalities, documented pieces crusading for healthier living. Medical articles must be scientifically accurate. Pays from $750 to $1,000. No unsolicited manuscripts; query.

EDUCATION

THE ACEHI JOURNAL/LA REVUE ACEDA (formerly *Canadian Teacher of the Deaf*)–Box 308, Amherst, Nova Scotia, Canada. Russell Fisher, Editor.
An English/French journal published by the Association of Canadian Educators of the Hearing Impaired. Articles, up to 2,000 words, with black-and-white photos (including author) on professional work with hearing impaired children and adults. Pays in copies.

ACADEMIC THERAPY–1539 Fourth St., San Rafael, CA 94901. John Arena, Editor.
Articles by professionals in the field of learning disabilities. No payment.

AMERICAN EDUCATION–400 Maryland Avenue S.W., Washington, DC 20202. Leroy V. Goodman, Editor.
Informative articles, 1,000 to 3,000 words, preferably with photos, on current

developments in education — preschool through college, adult and vocational education, teacher training. Activities reported must involve Federal education programs. For educators, school and college administrators, parents, civic leaders. Pay scale varies. Query first, with lead paragraph and outline.

AMERICAN SCHOOL & UNIVERSITY–134 North 13th St., Philadelphia, PA 19107. James R. Russo, Editor.
Articles and case studies dealing with design, construction, operation, maintenance, and equipping of school and college plants, 1,200 to 1,500 words. Pays $25 per published page. Query.

AMERICAN SCHOOL BOARD JOURNAL–National School Boards Association, State National Bank Plaza, Evanston, IL 60201.
Articles on problems of school administration and local control of education. Query.

ATHLETIC JOURNAL–1719 Howard St., Evanston, IL 60202. John L. Griffith, Editor.
Technical articles on interscholastic athletics by coaches and athletic directors only, to 1,500 words, with photos. Pays $20, on publication.

CHANGE–NBW Tower, New Rochelle, NY 10801. George W. Bonham, Editor.
Reports, 1,500 to 2,000 words, on programs, people, or institutions of higher education. Sophisticated, intellectual essays, 5,000 to 6,000 words, on issues of major interest to higher education today. Pays $150 for reports, $350 for essays, on acceptance.

CHILDREN'S HOUSE–Box 111, Caldwell, NJ 07006. Kenneth Edelson, Editor.
Articles, 800 to 2,500 words, based on research, anecdote or experience, on the child: comprehensive coverage of Montessori, innovative or controversial programs in education or special ed.; alternative schools, health, sex, juvenile crime, etc. Photos and drawings. Payment negotiable. Query.

CROFT TEACHER'S SERVICE–100 Garfield Ave., New London, CT 06320. Bill Palmer, Editor.
Lesson plans, 1,800 words, in science, social studies, mathematics, and English, for grades K-12. Send for author's briefing paper. Pays $60, on publication.

EDCENTRIC–Center for Educational Reform, Box 10085, Eugene, OR 97401.
High-quality articles, 2,000 to 3,000 words, and reviews of books on radical social and educational change. Poetry, short humor, graphics. No payment. Study magazine and query first.

ELEMENTARY SCHOOL JOURNAL–5835 Kimbark Ave., Chicago, IL 60637. Richard E. Hodges, Editor.
Articles, 2,000 to 4,000 words, with black-and-white photos, on education: classroom procedure, supervision, and school administration. No payment.

FORECAST FOR HOME ECONOMICS (Teach Edition of Co-ed)–50 West 44th St., New York, 10036. Edie McConnell, Editor.
Articles, to 1,500 words, of professional interest to home economics teachers, by specialists in the field. Rates vary, depending on quality and photos.

FOUNDATION NEWS–888 Seventh Ave., New York, NY 10019.
Articles, to 2,500 words, on field of grant-making foundations. Pays $300 to $400, on acceptance. Mostly written on assignment by people in field. Query first.

THE HORN BOOK MAGAZINE—585 Boylston St., Boston, MA 02116. Paul Heins, Editor.
Articles, 600 to 2,000 words, for librarians, teachers, parents, and others interested in pleasure reading of children and field of children's literature. Pays 1¢ a word, on publication. Query.

THE INDEPENDENT SCHOOL BULLETIN—National Association of Independent Schools, 4 Liberty Sq., Boston, MA 02109. Blair McElroy, Editor.
Articles, around 2,500 words, on elementary or secondary education in general, independent schools in particular. Pays in copies.

INDUSTRIAL EDUCATION—1 Fawcett Pl., Greenwich, CT 06830. Howard Smith, Editor.
Administrative and instructional material for vocational, industrial arts, and technical education classes, 1,000 to 2,000 words, with photos and drawings. Pays $15 to $20 per magazine page, on publication.

INSTRUCTOR—7 Bank St., Dansville, NY 14337. Ernest Hilton, Editor.
Articles by teachers on elementary school teaching. Short stories for primary and middle grades, 400 to 600 and 500 to 1,000 words, short plays, and poems. Payment varies. Query on articles.

LEARNING—530 University Ave., Palo Alto, CA 94301. Frank McCulloch, Editor.
Well-written articles for elementary school teachers on techniques, materials, research, philosophy, public affairs; book reviews. Pays $150 to $500 for articles, $50 to $100 for reviews, depending on length.

LEARNING TODAY—P.O. Box 956, Norman, OK 73069. Howard Clayton, Editor.
Articles on education, 2,000 words, with photos.

MISSOURI ENGLISH BULLETIN—Missouri Association of Teachers of English, Northeast Missouri State University, Kirksville, MO 63501. Hubert T. Moore, Managing Editor.
Articles, to 500 words, on teaching techniques, new methods (e.g., games to teach new concepts), research, language arts, humor for junior and senior high teachers. Book reviews, poetry. Pays in copies.

THE NATIONAL ELEMENTARY PRINCIPAL—NAESP, 1801 North Moore St., Arlington, VA 22209.
Articles, 3,000 to 3,500 words, on school administration, instruction, etc. Query first. Pays in copies.

PARKS & RECREATION—National Recreation and Park Association, 1601 North Kent St., Arlington, VA 22209. Charles B. Fowler, Editor.
Articles, 2,000 words, and short articles, 400 to 500 words, on individual or group recreation, park programs, crafts, camping, playground and community activities, hobbies, conservation. Photos when possible. No payment.

PHI DELTA KAPPAN—8th St. and Union Ave., Box 789, Bloomington, IN 47401. Stanley Elam, Editor.
Articles on education, 1,000 to 4,000 words. Cartoons on education issues. Fees negotiated—$25 to $250. Query first.

THE READING TEACHER—International Reading Association, 800 Barksdale Rd., Newark, DE 19711. Dr. Lloyd W. Kline, Editor.
Nonfiction about reading and instruction in reading. Good quality photos of classroom situations. Occasional topical cartoons. Pays in copies.

SCHOOL REVIEW–5835 Kimbark Ave., Chicago, IL 60637. Benjamin D. Wright, Editor.
Articles on research, theory, innovations, and philosophical inquiry in education and related disciplines; personal experience articles on teaching, learning, administration; education book reviews. No payment.

SCIENCE AND CHILDREN–National Science Teachers Association, 1201 16th St. N.W., Washington, DC 20036. Phyllis R. Marcuccio, Editor.
Informational articles, 800 to 1,200 words, to assist elementary school science teacher. No payment.

TEACHER–1 Fawcett Pl., Greenwich, CT 06830. Howard S. Ravis, Managing Editor.
Features for kindergarten, primary, intermediate, and junior high school teachers, on curriculum and methods, classroom-tested units, new teaching strategies, up to 1,500 words. Pays 1¢ a word and up.

TODAY'S CATHOLIC TEACHER–2451 East River Rd., Suite 200, Dayton, OH 45439. Ruth A. Matheny, Editor.
For Catholic elementary and high school teachers, administrators, school boards, and teachers of religious education (CCD). Articles, 600 to 800 words, and 1,200 to 2,000 words, on Catholic schools and teaching, parent-teacher relationships, innovative teaching, guidance testing, etc. Pays $15 to $75, on publication.

WILSON LIBRARY BULLETIN–950 University Ave., Bronx, NY 10452.
Articles, 1,000 to 3,000 words, on library-related material, education, and "informed commentary on a topic of current or enduring interest to librarians." Special library news reports of national interest, and 900 word opinion pieces on library issues for "Overdue" column. Photos of library displays and unusual activities; color slides or original artwork for cover. Pays $35 and up for articles; $10 for display photos, $100 for cover artwork. Study copies.

AGRICULTURE

AMERICAN AGRICULTURALIST-RURAL NEW YORKER–DeWitt Bldg., Ithaca, NY 14850. Gordon L. Conklin, Editor.
Articles on farm subjects in Northeast (New York, New Jersey, northern Pennsylvania, and New England states). Pays on acceptance.

AMERICAN FRUIT GROWER–Willoughby, OH 44094. E. G. K. Meister, Publisher.
Articles, to 750 words, with photos, on how commercial grower overcomes specific production or marketing problems. Pays about 2¢ a word, on acceptance or publication; $3 and up per photo. Same address and requirements for *American Vegetable Grower.*

AMERICAN VEGETABLE GROWER–See *American Fruit Grower.*

BIG FARMER–Big Farmer, Inc., 131 Lincoln Highway, Frankfort, IL 60423. Bob Moraczewski, Editor.
Challenging articles to 1,500 words, for and about high income commercial farmers, especially on money, markets and merchandising. Dramatic, top-quality photos essential. Short items on new cost-cutting money-making ideas for farmers. Pays on acceptance.

DAIRY GOAT JOURNAL—Box 1908, Scottsdale, AZ 85252. Kent Leach, Editor.
How-to articles, 250 to 750 words, for those interested in dairy goats. Photos or drawings. Pays 1½¢ per word, on publication. Query first.

FARM FUTURES—Market Communications, Inc., 534 North Broadway, Milwaukee, WI 53202. Royal Fraedrich, Editor.
Articles, up to 1,500 words, on successful experience with marketing agricultural commodities; how producers of corn, wheat, soybeans, cattle or hogs use commodities futures markets in managing and marketing their commodity. Payment varies, 30 to 60 days after acceptance. Query with outline.

FARM JOURNAL—Washington Sq., Philadelphia, PA 19105. Lane Palmer, Editor.
Articles, 500 to 1,500 words with photos, on new ideas in farming to increase profit, save time, or improve living. Occasional humor. Must have thorough background in subject to write meaningful material for today's business farmer. Pays 10¢ to 15¢ per word, on acceptance. Query.

FARM SUPPLIER—Mt. Morris, IL 61504. Ray Bates, Editor.
Articles, 600 to 1,200 words, and photos, on selling feed, fertilizer, agricultural chemicals, farm supplies, etc., through retail farm trade outlets. Strong emphasis on product news. Also articles on small business management. Pays about 7¢ a word, on acceptance.

THE FURROW—Deere & Company, John Deere Rd., Moline, IL 61265. George Sollenberger, Editor, North America.
Mostly staff-written. Buys occasional illustrated articles of specialized interest to farmers. Reports promptly.

THE GEORGIA FARMER—500 Plasamour Dr. N.E., Atlanta, GA 30324. Elmo Hester, Editor.
Illustrated features and shorts, up to 1,200 words, for Georgia farm family readership. Pays on publication.

THE KENTUCKY FARMER—Kellwood Bldg., Box 645, Bowling Green, KY 42101.
How-to farming articles, about Kentucky farmers only. Photos. Payment varies, on publication.

MICHIGAN FARMER—4415 North Grand River, Lansing, MI 48906.
Articles on Michigan farming and rural situations; problems of Michigan farmers and their families. Pays $5 to $10 per printed column, on acceptance.

THE NATIONAL FUTURE FARMER—Box 15130, Alexandria, VA 22309. Wilson Carnes, Editor.
For high school members of Future Farmers of America. Nonfiction, up to 1,000 words, on vocational, educational, social, and recreational interests. Success stories about members, and up-to-date agricultural information. Pays up to 4¢ a word, on acceptance. Cartoons, $7.50.

NORDEN NEWS—Norden Laboratories, 601 West Cornhusker Highway, Lincoln, NE 68521. Patricia Pike, Editor.
Articles, 1,200 to 1,500 words, on surgical or treatment techniques in veterinary medicine. Jokes relating to veterinary medicine, and photos. Pays $100 for feature articles, and $7.50 per published photo, on publication.

ORGANIC GARDENING AND FARMING—Emmaus, PA 18049. M. C. Goldman, Managing Editor.
Articles, 1,000 to 2,500 words, with photos, on gardening or farming livestock, houseplants, conservation, ecology, environmental action, etc., stressing natural gardening techniques: use of organic and ground mineral fertilizers, mulching, composting, biological insect control, etc. Home handicraft, landscaping, orcharding, fruits, wildlife. Pays $50 to $150; extra for photos. Author's Handbook and sample copy sent on request.

POULTRY MEAT, THE MAGAZINE FOR THE BROILER BUSINESS–Cullman, AL 35055. Charles Perry, Editor.
Articles, 1,200 to 2,000 words, with photos, giving broiler production, processing, and marketing information. Pays $40 to $100, on acceptance.

POULTRY TRIBUNE–Mt. Morris, IL 61054. Milton R. Dunk, Editor.
Egg production, processing, and marketing stories, 200 to 1,000 words, Pays to 8¢ a word, on acceptance.

SUCCESSFUL FARMING–1716 Locust St., Des Moines, IA 50336. Dick Hanson, Editor.
Farm articles, with emphasis on management, farming operations, and experience pieces. Helpful hints for farm shops. Pays various rates.

WALLACES FARMER–Des Moines, IA 50305. Alvin F. Bull, Editor.
Short features, 600 to 700 words, on Iowa; interviews on farming methods, practices, equipment. Pays 4¢ to 5¢ per published word; $10 for cartoons; $7.50 to $15 for black-and-white photos; $50 to $100 for color transparencies. Mostly staff-written. Query first.

THE WESTERN PRODUCER–446 2nd Ave. North, Sask., Canada. R. H. D. Phillips, Editor.
Short stories and articles, up to 2,500 words, on western Canadian subjects, with black-and-white or color photos, to interest intelligent farm and rural readers. Pays up to $75 a page for articles, on acceptance, and $5 to $35 for photos.

THE WYOMING STOCKMAN FARMER–110 East 17th St., Cheyenne, WY 82001. Pat Stuart, Editor.
Factual features, historical or current, on agriculture in Wyoming-western Nebraska-Rocky Mountain area, to 500 words, with black-and-white photos. Pays various rates, on publication.

PERFORMING ARTS, FINE ARTS, BROADCAST/FILM, PHOTOGRAPHY, HOBBIES, CRAFTS, COLLECTING

ACQUIRE–170 Fifth Ave., New York, NY 10011. Mr. R. Rowe, Editor.
Articles, 750 to 3,000 words, on collectibles: porcelain, medallic art, plates, *objets d'art*, modern Americana, etc. Study magazine before submitting. Pays $75 to $250, on publication. Query first.

AFTER DARK, THE MAGAZINE OF ENTERTAINMENT–10 Columbus Circle, New York, NY 10019. William Como, Editor.
Covers whole entertainment scene, including theatre, films, TV, dance, opera, pop music, happenings, travel. Reviews, feature articles on regional theatres, people in entertainment field, etc. Photos, drawings, occasional fillers. Pays $15 to $25; $5 to $25 for photos, on publication.

AMERICAN RECORDER–141 West 20th St., New York, NY 10011. Daniel Shapiro, Editor.
Articles, 1,000 to 5,000 words, of interest to recorder players, about instrument itself, or music of medieval, renaissance, baroque, or contemporary period for recorder. Pays in copies.

THE ANTIQUE DEALER–1115 Clifton Ave., Clifton, NJ 07013. Stella Hall, Editor.
Articles, 1,200 to 2,000 words, on trends, pricing, retailing hints, "hard news" stories, in antiques trade. Longer features by authorities informing general dealers about special fields. Pays 4¢ a word for articles, $30 per page for longer features, on publication; $5 per photo. Query.

ANTIQUES JOURNAL—P.O. Box 88128, Dunwoody, GA 30338. John Mebane, Editor.
Factual, well-researched, illustrated articles about antiques, to 2,000 words. Original professional photos required. Query first.

ARTS IN SOCIETY—University Extension, University of Wisconsin, 610 Langdon St., Madison, WI 53706.
Articles, 2,500 to 3,500 words, on teaching and learning of the arts; aesthetics and philosophy; social analysis; significant examples of creative printing as an art medium. Pays honorarium upon publication.

ARTS MAGAZINE—23 East 26th St., New York, NY 10010.
Articles, 1,000 to 2,000 words, on art and architecture, reviews of painting and sculpture exhibitions, book reviews. Pays on publication.

AUDIO—134 North 13th St., Philadelphia, PA 19107. Eugene Pitts III, Editor.
Semi-technical articles of interest to hi-fi equipment enthusiasts, music lovers, and audio professionals. Pays $35 a page, on publication.

BLUEGRASS UNLIMITED—P.O. Box 111, Burke, VA 22015. Peter V. Kuykendall, Editor.
Articles, 2,000 words, on all aspects of bluegrass music, including personalities and events. Pays 1¢ to 1½¢ a word, $20 per black-and-white cover photo, $10 per inside photo, after publication. Query.

BROADCASTER—77 River St., Toronto M5A 3P2, Ontario, Canada. Doug Loney, Editor.
Canadian-oriented articles, 500 to 2,000 words, illustrating how various communicators conduct their business; controversies, inventions, innovations of broadcast engineers; profiles or interviews of successful men and women, industry and technical news in layman's language. Pays from $25, on acceptance. Query.

CAMERA 35—American Express Publishing Corp., 61 West 51st St., New York, NY 10019. Jim Hughes, Editor. Bob Nadler, Technical Editor.
Illustrated, instructional articles, 800 to 3,900 words, dealing with practice and technique of serious photography. Payment varies, on publication.

CB MAGAZINE—250 Park Ave., New York, NY 10017. Leo G. Sands, Editor.
Technical articles and case histories, 1,000 to 3,000 words, about use of two-way citizens band radio. Payment varies.

THE CHURCH MUSICIAN—127 Ninth Ave. North, Nashville, TN 37234.
Southern Baptist. Articles, 500 to 1,000 words, on church music, administration, leadership, inspiration, and musicians; cartoons with musical touch. Pays about 2¢ a word, on acceptance.

THE CLASSIC COLLECTOR—711 South Saint Asaph St., Alexandria, VA 22314. William Carmichael, Editor.
Articles, 1,500 to 4,000 words, on collectibles and fields of collecting. Pays 3¢ a word, on publication. Query first with outline.

COLLECTOR'S WORLD—P.O. Box 919, Kermit, TX 79745. Reta Field, Editor.
Articles, 1,500 to 2,500 words, with photos, on valuable antiques, collectibles, bottles, missing art, archeological and historical treasures. Pays 3¢ a word, on publication.

CRAFT HORIZONS—44 West 53rd St., New York, NY 10019. Rose Slivka, Editor-in-Chief.
High-quality nonfiction on craft-art-design fields—ceramics, weaving, wood, metal, 500 to 2,000 words. Payment varies. Query.

CREATIVE CRAFTS MAGAZINE—P.O. Box 700, Newton, NJ 07860. Sybil C. Harp, Editor.
How-to features, 200 to 1,500 words, with good quality black-and-white photos, on

adult handicrafts of all types. Must tell how authors themselves do craft work. No interview articles. Pays various rates, on publication.

DANCE MAGAZINE–10 Columbus Circle, New York, NY 10019. William Como, Editor.
Personalities, ideas, informed commentary on best in all kinds of dancing.

DANCE PERSPECTIVES–29 East 9th St., New York, NY 10003. Selma Jeanne Cohen, Editor.
Monographs, 15,000 to 20,000 words, on critical or historical aspects of dance. Specialized knowledge of field essential. Pays $250, on acceptance. Query.

DESIGN–1100 Waterway Blvd., Indianapolis, IN 46202. Barbara L. Albert, Editor.
Arts and crafts articles, 1,000 to 1,500 words, for junior high to college level art teachers and students, artists and craftsmen on: discovering design or art elements in surroundings; unusual art projects; useful, challenging crafts; innovative teaching methods. Black-and-white photos or artwork necessary with articles. Pays up to $75, on publication.

THE DRAMA REVIEW–School of the Arts, New York University, 32 Washington Place, New York, NY 10003. Michael Kirby, Editor. Paul R. Ryan, Executive Editor.
Articles and photos on theatre, film, dance, TV, music: criticism, theory, history. Historically significant plays. Pays 2¢ a word on publication.

DRAMATICS–College Hill Station, Box E, Cincinnati, OH 45224. Dennis Klasmeier, Editor.
Practical, informal articles, 1,500 to 2,500 words, on high school, college, community, and professional theatre; one-act plays for high school production. Articles on playwriting, technical innovations, theatre exercises and games, classroom projects, acting, directing, filming, mime, puppetry, improvisation, play production. Photos desired. Pays up to $50 on publication.

EXHIBIT–P.O. Box 2305, Fort Lauderdale, FL 33307. Marie Stilkind, Editor.
Articles, to 900 words with photos, on commercial or fine art: how-tos and step-by-step demonstrations of art techniques and methods; profiles of outstanding artists; new ideas in art. Pays 5¢ per accepted word, $5 per photo, on acceptance.

THE FAMILY HANDYMAN–235 East 45th St., New York, NY 10017.
Non-technical, step-by-step articles, to 1,000 words, with black-and-white photos, on home improvement, repair, and maintenance for do-it-yourselfers. Pays $40 to $100, on acceptance. Shorts, 100 to 300 words, with or without photos and rough drawings, on expert tips or shortcuts. Pays $5 to $15, on acceptance.

THE FILM JOURNAL–Box 9602, Hollins College, VA 24020. Thomas R. Atkins, Editor and Publisher.
Critical articles, scholarly essays about films of all types, stressing relationship between movies and contemporary culture. Interviews with important directors, book reviews; artwork and poetry related to movies. Query first on longer pieces.

FILM QUARTERLY–University of California Press, Berkeley, CA 94720.
Reviews of films, historical and critical articles, production projects, etc., up to 5,000 words. Pays 1½¢ a word, on publication. Approach very specialized. Authors must be familiar with magazine. Query.

GEMS AND MINERALS–P.O. Box 687, Mentone, CA 92359. Jack R. Cox, Editor.
Articles with photos or drawings, telling how to collect, identify, cut, clean and display gemstones and minerals. Also how-tos of jewelry making, field trips with

maps. Pays 50¢ per column inch or $15 per page. Query first. Stamped return envelope essential.

GUITAR PLAYER MAGAZINE–348 North Santa Cruz Ave., Los Gatos, CA 95030.
Articles, 1,500 to 2,500 words, on guitarists, guitars, guitaring. How-tos are staff-written. Pays $50 to $70; $10 to $20 for photos.

HAM RADIO–Greenville, NH 03048. James R. Fisk, Editor.
Technical and home-construction articles on amateur radio, up to 2,500 words. No operating news or fiction. Pays up to 5¢ per word, on acceptance. Query helpful.

HI-FI CAMERA WORLD–W. B. Bradbury Co., 6 East 43rd St., New York, NY 10017.
Technical articles for beginning or would-be camera and stereo buffs. Pay varies. Query.

HIGH FIDELITY–Great Barrington, MA 01230. Leonard Marcus, Editor.
Articles about music, records, and sound reproduction for knowledgeable record collectors, 2,500 to 3,000 words. Pays on acceptance. Query.

INDUSTRIAL PHOTOGRAPHY–750 Third Ave., New York, NY 10017.
Articles any length, for industrial photographers or communications executives, on techniques and trends in professional photography, audiovisuals, motion pictures, video-tape. Pays on publication. Query.

INSECT WORLD DIGEST–Box 428, Latham, NY 12110. Ross Arnett, Editor.
Illustrated articles, to 3,500 words, in field of entomology, to interest entomologists conservationists, the educated public. Pays up to 5¢ a word for articles, $10 for black-and-white photos, $20 and up for 35mm color transparencies. Query first.

JOURNAL OF POPULAR FILM–Bowling Green, State University, 101 University Hall, Bowling Green, OH 43403.
Articles, to 3,000 words on popular films, directors, genres, the film industry, "filmographies" and bibliographies. Pays in copies and offprints.

LEICA PHOTOGRAPHY–15 Columbus Circle, New York, NY 10023.
Articles on 35mm photo techniques, Leica cameras and equipment, 750 to 1,500 words. Photos taken with Leica cameras and lenses. Pays on publication. Query.

McCALL'S NEEDLEWORK & CRAFTS MAGAZINE–230 Park Ave., New York, NY 10017. Eleanor Spencer, Managing Editor.
Original, made up handicraft items in variety of techniques with directions for making them. Pays in ratio to originality and quality.

MAINE ANTIQUE DIGEST–RFD 3, Box 76A, Waldoboro, ME 04572. Samuel Pennington, Editor.
Authoritative, entertaining articles, anecdotes, and interviews on antiques market in New England, include black-and-white photos. Pays $25, on acceptance. Study magazine; query.

MAKE IT WITH LEATHER–Box 1386, Fort Worth, TX 76101. Earl F. Warren, Editor.
How-to articles on leathercraft, to 2,000 words, with quality Ektachrome color photos (print film and black-and-white also accepted if good quality) and diagrams. Pays from $10 to $50 per printed page, extra for artwork, on publication. Write for sample copy.

MODEL AIRPLANE NEWS–White Plains Plaza, 1 North Broadway, White Plains, NY 10601. Walter L. Schroder, Publisher; Arthur F. Schroeder, Editor.
Scientific or technical articles and photos on model aviation. Construction projects with drawings, photos, directions. Pays on publication.

MODEL RAILROADER–1027 North 7th St., Milwaukee, WI 53233. Linn H. Westcott, Editor.
Articles on construction or operation of model railroads, with photos of layout and equipment. Firsthand knowledge essential. Pays on acceptance. Query.

MUSIC OF THE AVANT GARDE–See *Source: Music of the Avant Garde.*

MUSIC EDUCATORS JOURNAL–Music Educators National Conference, Suite 601, 8150 Leesburg Pike, Vienna, VA 22180. Malcom E. Bessom, Editor.
Articles, 2,000 to 3,000 words, on music education, contemporary music, American music, the arts in general, aesthetics; humorous pieces on music and music education. Pays in copies. Query.

MUSICAL AMERICA–1 Astor Plaza, New York, NY 10036.
Authoritative, nonfiction feature material of musical interest, 1,000 to 1,500 words.

MUSICAL NEWSLETTER–654 Madison Ave., Suite 1703, New York, NY 10021. Patrick J. Smith, Editor.
Articles, to 4,000 words, on classical music, and occasionally jazz, rock, folk. Quality writing–no straight reviews or interviews. Pays 10¢ a word, on acceptance. Query.

NATIONAL ANTIQUES REVIEW–Box 619, Portland, ME 04104. Lillian Potter, Editor.
Articles to 1,500 words with photos, on prices of antiques; auction, show, flea market coverage. Collecting tips, aids to identification, advice on collectibles old and new. Pays $25 per article, $2 per picture. Query first.

NEWSPAPER COLLECTOR'S GAZETTE–2164 East Broadmor, Tempe, AZ 85282. Barbara Stuhlmuller, Editor.
Articles, to 2,500 words, on history of journalism, early newspapers, newsmen, newspaper collecting. Pays to $15, on acceptance. Send return envelope for specification sheet. Query.

OLD BOTTLE MAGAZINE–Box 243, Bend, OR 97701. Shirley Asher, Editor.
Articles to 2,000 words on bottle collecting. Well-researched material on specific company, bottle, or personality. Articles illustrated with black-and-white photos preferred. Pays $20 per published page; for photos with captions and drawings submitted separately, on acceptance. Study recent issues.

OPERA NEWS–The Metropolitan Opera Guild, 1865 Broadway, New York, NY 10023. Robert Jacobson, Editor.
Articles on all aspects of today's lyric theatre; pre-publication chapters of books, humorous anecdotes, 600 to 3,500 words. Pays 8¢ a word and up.

PERFORMING ARTS REVIEW–Law-Arts Publications, 453 Greenwich St., New York, NY 10013. Dr. Joseph Taubman, Editor.
Articles of professional or scholarly quality, 1,000 to 2,000 words, on management and legal aspects of arts organizations, and creative process. Some short poetry. No payment.

PLAYBILL–151 East 50th St., New York, NY 10022. Joan Rubin, Editor.
Short, sophisticated articles on theatre or general subjects of interest to the theatre-going public, 800 to 2,000 words, with photos. Pays $100 to $300.

POPULAR CERAMICS–6011 Santa Monica Blvd., Los Angeles, CA 90038. William H. Geisler, Publisher.
Step-by-step instructional articles on hobby ceramics, 800 to 1,000 words, with photos.

POPULAR PHOTOGRAPHY MAGAZINE–One Park Ave., New York, NY 10016.
Articles, 500 to 2,000 words, for amateur photographer, how-tos with illustrations. For queries, include one-page outline, plus two or three representative pictures. Pays $75 and up for complete word-and-picture articles; $10 for illustrated "Photo Tips." Contributors must know photography.

PROFITABLE CRAFT MERCHANDISING–News Plaza, Peoria, IL 61601. Mike Jeffries, Editor.

Articles, with 8 x 10 black-and-white photos, on successful craft retailers; how-to projects with new crafts; store management techniques; craft trade shows, conventions, and better consumer shows. Pays $45 to $125, on publication. Query.

THE PURPLE THUMB–P.O. Box 423, Van Nuys, CA 91408. S. B. Taylor, Editor.
Articles on making wine and beer at home, growing grapes, history and traditions of wine and beer. Pays $5 per photo and up to $25 per article, on publication. Query.

R/C MODELER MAGAZINE–P.O. Box 487, Sierra Madre, CA 91024. Don Dewey, Editor.
How-to magazine for model aircraft hobbyists. Technical and semi-technical articles on radio controlled model aircraft. Pays $25 to $400, 30 days after publication. Query first, and ask for sample copy.

RAILROAD MODEL CRAFTSMAN–P.O. Box 700, Newton, NJ 07860. J. Anthony Koester, Managing Editor.
How-to features on scale model railroading: cars, structures, operation, scenery, traction, narrow gage locos, layout building, etc. Some prototype railroading. Authors must be railroad modelers. Pays promptly on publication.

RELICS–P.O. Box 3338, Austin, TX 78764. Pat Wagner, Editor.
Articles, 500 to 2,000 words on American frontier relics, historical Americana, amateur collecting. Photos and drawings returned after publication. Pays 2¢ a word, on acceptance. Query first.

ROCK AND GEM–Behn-Miller Publishers, Inc., 16001 Ventura Blvd., Encino, CA 91316.
Knowledgeable, lapidary, how-to articles, rockhound field trips, to 2,000 words, with photos. Pays $40 per printed page, on publication.

ROCKHOUND–P.O. Drawer L, Conroe, TX 77301. John H. Latham, Editor.
Articles, 100 to 3,500 words, on mineral collecting sites: what's collected there, exact location, road and local conditions, etc. Include photos to illustrate articles. Pays 2¢ per word, $5 per photo, on acceptance. Sample copy available. Query.

SHOWCASE–Chicago *Sun-Times,* 401 North Wabash Ave., Chicago, IL 60611. Herman Kogan, Editor.
Articles, profiles, interviews, up to 1,500 words, on serious and lively arts. Pays up to 10¢ a word, on publication.

THE SILENT PICTURE–First Media Press, 6 East 39th St., New York, NY 10016.
Articles, to 1,500 words, on silent films; film reviews, film book reviews, interviews with silent film personalities. Payment varies. Query.

SOURCE: MUSIC OF THE AVANT GARDE–2101 22nd St., Sacramento, CA 95818. Stanley G. Lumetta, Editor.
Scores and articles on newest ideas in music. Pays royalty rates. Query.

STEREO QUARTERLY–State Rd., Great Barrington, MA 01230.
Factual articles, to 4,000 words, on stereo music systems and related equipment, articles relating music and musicians to current scene, recordings; humor; descriptions and photos of attractive installations. Pays up to 10¢ a word, on acceptance. Query.

SUNDAY CLOTHES: A MAGAZINE OF THE FINE ARTS–51 Sherman St., Deadwood, SD 57732. Linda Hasselstrom, Editor.
Articles, to 6,000 words, on fine arts; interviews, book and movie reviews, fiction, poetry, black-and-white graphics and photos. Pays in copies.

SUPER-8 FILMAKER—PMS Publishing Co., 145 East 49th St., Suite 6B, New York, NY 10017. Joyce Newman, Editor.
Feature articles, 3,000 to 4,500 words: how-tos; Super-8 programs, organizations, productions, special applications of Super-8 eqiupment. Pays $70 to $100. Short pieces, 500 to 2,500 words: film technique how-tos, film book reviews, tips. Pays $25 to $75. Query first.

TV RADIO MIRROR—205 East 42nd St., New York, NY 10017. Patricia Canole, Managing Editor.
Articles, 3,000 words, on television celebrities and how they cope with their problems. Pay varies. Send query or outline.

TAKE ONE—Box 1778, Station B, Montreal, Quebec, Canada H3B 3L3. Peter Lebensold, Editor.
Articles, interviews, reviews related to film. Small payment.

THEATRE DESIGN AND TECHNOLOGY—U.S. Institute for Theatre Technology, 245 West 52nd St., New York, NY 10019. Thomas S. Watson, Editor.
Articles, 1,000 to 1,500 words, on theatre design and technology. Performing arts book reviews: contact editor. No payment. Query.

WESTART—Box 1396, Auburn, CA 95603.
Artists' newspaper primarily concerned with current news items in West Coast arts field. Occasionally buys features of exceptional interest, 350 to 500 words on fine arts and crafts. Black-and-white photos desirable. No hobbies. Pays 30¢ per column inch, on publication.

WINE WORLD—15101 Keswick St., Van Nuys, CA 91405. Jerry Vonne, Editor.
Articles for wine consumer, on wines, history, selecting and serving wine, vintners, cellars, etc. Black-and-white photos, some color. Pays up to $250 per article, on publication. Query first.

WOMAN'S WORLD—Ideal Publishing Corp., 575 Madison Ave., NY 10022. Holly Garrison, Editor.
How-to articles. Each issue devoted to single theme: needlework, knitting, food, gardening, money-saving crafts, etc. Pays $50 to $150, more with black-and-white glossy photos, on publication. Query.

THE WORKBASKET—4251 Pennsylvania, Kansas City, MO 64111.
How-to articles, 300 to 500 words, on women's home crafts, with good black-and-white photos and clear instructions. Pays 4¢ per word, on acceptance. "Women Who Make Cents" column uses short instructions for specific item women can make and sell (including selling price). Pays $5 per item, on acceptance.

THE WORKBENCH—4251 Pennsylvania, Kansas City, MO 64111. Jay W. Hedden, Editor.
Do-it-yourself articles with emphasis on home workshop, home improvement, home maintenance. Pays $75 per published page for complete article with photos and/or drawings; $100 and up for assignments.

TECHNICAL AND SCIENTIFIC

THE AOPA PILOT—7315 Wisconsin Ave., Bethesda, MD 20014.
First-person, how-to and human-interest articles, with photos, on private and business aviation. Articles for beginning and experienced pilots to promote safer, enjoyable flying through increased knowledge and pilot proficiency. Pays up to $300, on acceptance; $15 for black-and-white photos. Query.

AIR PROGRESS—437 Madison Ave., New York, NY 10022. Richard B. Weeghman, Editor.

Articles and photos on aviation subjects. Pays $100 to $500 per article, on acceptance.

COMPUTER DECISIONS—50 Essex St., Rochelle Park, NJ 07662. Hesh Wiener, Editor.
Articles, 800 to 4,000 words, on generic uses of computer systems, and on more effective ways to use data processing systems. Pays $30 to $50 per published page.

ELECTRONICS ILLUSTRATED—See *Mechanics Illustrated*.

ENVIRONMENT—438 North Skinker Blvd., St. Louis, MO 63130. Sheldon Novick, Editor.
Factual articles, 3,000 to 4,000 words, with technical information in laymen's terms on environment pollution effects of technology. Pays $100. Submit brief proposal first.

ENVIRONMENTAL QUALITY MAGAZINE—10658 Burbank Blvd., North Hollywood, CA 91601. Richard Cramer, Editor.
Articles, 2,000 to 4,000 words, on all aspects of physical environment, with black-and-white photos or color transparencies. Pays varying rates, on publication. Query.

THE LIVING WILDERNESS—1901 Pennsylvania Ave., N.W., Washington, DC 20006.
Articles, to 5,000 words, on wilderness experiences, studies, wildlife, environmental concerns, conservation. Outstanding nature photos, black-and-white and color. Rates vary. Query first.

MECHANIX ILLUSTRATED (including *Electronics Illustrated*)—1515 Broadway, New York, NY 10036. Robert G. Beason, Editor.
Articles with strong lead, or on controversial subjects. Pays $300 and up for features, 1,500 to 2,500 words; $75 to $300 for short articles or picture sets of one or two pages; up to $400 for how-to projects; $10 to $20 for useful tips with photo or drawing, $5 if unillustrated; $10 to $30 for single photos with captions.

NEW ENGINEER—MBA Enterprises, 555 Madison Ave., New York, NY 10022. Steven S. Ross, Editor.
Articles, 1,500 to 5,000 words, on engineering profession, technical projects of wide interest, common ground between engineering and other professions. Query. Pays $50 per published page, on acceptance.

PACIFIC DISCOVERY—California Academy of Sciences, Golden Gate Park, San Francisco, CA 94118. Bruce Finson, Editor.
Natural history articles, 1,500 to 3,000 words, with extensive photo coverage, addressed to scientists and seriously interested laymen. Pays 5¢ a word, $10 a picture, on publication. Query.

POPULAR ELECTRONICS—One Park Ave., New York, NY 10016. Arthur P. Salsberg, Editor.
State-of-the-art reports and feature articles on modern electronics technology, for seriously-interested electronics hobbyist, technician, and engineer with avocational interest in electronics. Pays up to $350 for feature-length articles and up to $500 for construction articles.

POPULAR MECHANICS MAGAZINE—224 West 57th St., New York, NY 10019. Jim Liston, Editor.
Features on scientific, mechanical, and industrial subjects, with action or adventure elements; occasional articles on subjects of general interest to men, including sports, automotive, and housing fields. How-to pieces on craft projects and shop work. Good illustrations required. Photo shorts with up to 250 words of copy and one or two photos. Pays $300 to $500 for top-quality features, occasionally higher; $12 and up for shorts.

POPULAR SCIENCE MONTHLY–380 Madison Ave., New York, NY 10017. Hubert P. Luckett, Editor.
Timely material on new developments in applied science and technology, with photos, to 2,000 words. Short illustrated articles describing new inventions and products. Photo layouts up to five pages, in black-and-white.

PROBE THE UNKNOWN–5455 Wilshire Blvd., Los Angeles, CA 99036. Sergio Ortiz, Editor.
Well-documented, objective articles, 2,500 to 5,000 words, with photos, on cases of psychic phenomena. Study magazine closely. Pays up to 10¢ per word. Send query and outline.

RADIO-ELECTRONICS–200 Park Ave. South, New York, NY 10003. Larry Steckler, Editor.
Practical, technical articles on all areas of electronics, electronics servicing; 2,000 to 3,000 words, authoritative, easy to read, interesting, with 8 x 10 black-and-white glossies. Pays good rates, on acceptance.

SCIENCE DIGEST–224 West 57th St., New York, NY 10019.
Scientifically accurate articles, about 1,500 words, for average reader, in any of the sciences; photo-essays; human-interest photos. Timeliness helps. Occasional cartoons. Pays from $50 for 1-pagers to $350 for top features. Query on all article ideas.

SEA FRONTIERS–The International Oceanographic Foundation, 10 Rickenbacker Causeway, Virginia Key, Miami, FL 33149. F. G. Walton Smith, Editor.
Articles for laymen on recent scientific advances and discoveries related to the sea, 2,000 words. General articles on interesting life or phenomena of the sea, economic and industrial applications of marine sciences. Illustrations, black-and-white, or preferably, color photographs, required. Pays 5¢ a word and up, on acceptance. Query.

TRADE AND BUSINESS MAGAZINES

AERO–Box 1184, Ramona, CA 92065. Marvin Patchen, Editor.
Factual articles, any length, with photos, on upgrading skills and technical know-how, for pilots and owners of aircraft from single engine to light business jet. Pays $45 to $50 per printed page. Query.

AIR FORCE MAGAZINE–1750 Pennsylvania Ave. N.W., Washington, DC 20006. John Frisbee, Executive Editor.
Articles, 1,500 to 3,000 words, on military aviation and aerospace; current, historical and semi-technical subjects. Short pieces, 250 words, on true-life experiences in Air Force life. Pays 7¢ a word for articles, $10 for true items, on acceptance. Query.

AMERICAN BICYCLIST AND MOTORCYCLIST–461 Eighth Ave., New York, NY 10001. Stan Gottlieb, Editor.
Articles, 1,500 to 2,800 words, on successful bicycle dealers, covering sales and/or repair practices. Pays from 3¢ a word, $5 a photo, on publication. Query.

AMERICAN COIN-OP–500 North Dearborn St., Chicago, IL 60610. Bob Harker, Editor.
Articles, from 250 words, with photos of interior and exterior of shops, on successful coin-operated laundries and drycleaners: attracting customers, increasing profits, equipment, maintenance, security, etc. Pays 3¢ to 5¢ a word, $5 per photo, on publication. Query.

AMERICAN DRYCLEANER–500 North Dearborn, Chicago, IL 60610. Paul T. Glaman, Editor.
Well-documented case histories on development by cleaners of important programs in merchandising, production, etc. Photos. Pays 3¢ and up a word, on publication.

AMERICAN LAUNDRY DIGEST—500 North Dearborn, Chicago, IL 60610. Ben Russell, Editor.

Articles, 300 to 2,500 words, on operation of hospital and hotel laundries, uniform rental laundries, linen supply plants, and self-service laundries: production, management, marketing, merchandising, advertising, promotion. Pays from 3¢ per word and $5 per photo, two weeks before publication; $5 per cartoon, on acceptance. Query.

AMERICAN PAINTING CONTRACTOR—2911 Washington Ave., St. Louis, MO 63103. Erwin L. Below, Editor.

Technical, descriptive articles with photos, to 2,500 words, on residential and commercial decorating, industrial maintenance painting; management of painting and decorating business. For professional painting contractors, architects, plant maintenance engineers. Pays 5¢ a word and up, on publication; extra for usable photos.

AMERICAN ROOFER AND BUILDING IMPROVEMENT CONTRACTOR—221 Lake St., Oak Park, IL 60304. J. C. Gudas, Editor.

Timely articles, 600 words, on sales, case histories, manufacturing, estimating of roofing, siding, and building improvement; contractor pieces on neighborhood newspaper items. Pays 3¢ a word and up, on publication.

AMUSEMENT BUSINESS—1719 West End Ave., Nashville, TN 37203. Tom Powell, Editor.

Articles, any length, for owners, operators, managers, booking agents, of mass-audience amusement enterprises: fun parks, fairs, stadiums, circuses, tourist attractions, etc. Pay varies; made monthly. Query.

THE ANTIQUE DEALER—1115 Clifton Ave., Clifton, NJ 07013. S. Hall, Editor.

Articles, 1,200 to 2,000 words, on national and international news trends in antique business. Features by authorities in specific fields. Pays $30 a page, on publication.

THE APOTHECARY—401 Commonwealth Ave., Boston, MA 02215. Lee Tamis, Managing Editor.

Serious, educational articles, 1,000 to 5,000 words, on pharmacy and other health sciences. Photos. Modest payment, on acceptance.

AQUARIUM INDUSTRY—Toadtown, Magalia, CA 95954. Bob Behme, Editor.

Articles, 300 to 1,000 words, for members of industry, on business, improving sales, trade news; experience pieces on hobby. Pays from $30, on acceptance.

AREA DEVELOPMENT MAGAZINE—114 East 32nd St., New York, NY 10016. Albert H. Jaeggin, Editor.

Instructive articles for top executives of manufacturing companies, on industrial and office facility planning (site selection, plant relocation, and expansion, plant design, landscaping, financing, etc.). Pays $40 per printed page, including photos, display heads. Query.

AUDECIBEL—20361 Middlebelt Rd., Livonia, MI 48152.

Articles, 200 to 2,000 words, on hearing aids, sound, and related topics, for hearing specialists. Pays 1¢ to 2¢ a word, on acceptance. Send for writer's "Fact Sheet."

AUTO GLASS JOURNAL—1929 Royce Ave., Beloit, WI 53511. Richard L. Sine, Editor.

Interviews, 500 to 1,000 words, with photos, on successful auto glass replacement shops. Pays 5¢ a word, on publication.

AUTO TRIM NEWS—129 Broadway, Lynbrook, NY 11563. Nat W. Danas, Editor.

Articles, to 1,000 words, with photos, on successful management and merchandising in auto trim shops or departments, seat cover specialty stores, or by installation specialists. How-to pieces, 300 to 400 words, on specific aspect of work, marine or aircraft upholstery, or recreational vans. Pays $30 per published page, on publication.

BARRON'S—22 Cortlandt St., New York, NY 10007. Robert M. Bleiberg, Editor.

Business and finance articles of national interest, 1,200 to 2,500 words. Pays from $500, on publication. Query.

BATH PRODUCTS MERCHANDISING—76 S.E. 5th Ave., Delray Beach, FL 33444. Bill Dogan, Editor.
Articles, 1,000 to 1,500 words, with black-and-white photos, on merchandising and display techniques for buyers of bathroom accessories in department stores, variety stores, discount stores, chain stores and boutiques. Pay negotiable. Query.

BICYCLE DEALER SHOWCASE—P.O. Box 2830, Newport Beach, CA 92663. Steve Ready, Editor.
Well-researched, timely articles, 1,000 to 1,500 words, for bicycle dealers, on business and selling, news, service and repair, with strong technical slant. Black-and-white photos. Pays $50 to $75, on publication.

BIG FARMER—Big Farmer, Inc., 131 Lincoln Highway, Frankfort, IL 60423. Bob Moraczewski, Editor.
Challenging articles, 1,500 words, with dramatic photos, for and about high-income commercial farmers. Short pieces on new, cost-cutting, money-making ideas. Pays $75 to $300, on acceptance.

BLACK ENTERPRISE—Earl G. Graves Publishing Co., 295 Madison Ave., New York, NY 10017. Robert J. Imbriano, Managing Editor.
Articles, about 2,000 words, with photos, on black businesses, businessmen, and related topics. Pays from $300, on acceptance. Query.

BOATING INDUSTRY—205 East 42nd St., New York, NY 10017. Dave Kendall, Senior Editor.
Business articles, 1,000 to 1,500 words, on boating dealers. Pays 4¢ to 5¢ a word, $5 to $10 for photos, on publication. Query.

BROADCAST ENGINEERING—1014 Wyandotte, Kansas City, MO 64105. Ron Merrell, Editor.
Practical, engineering-management oriented articles, 1,000 to 2,800 words, on cable TV, broadcasting educational radio and TV, recording studios. Engineer's Exchange column for short cuts and equipment modification. Photos of unique communications situations. Pays $75 to $200 per article; $10 to $25 for column, on acceptance. Query.

BURROUGHS CLEARING HOUSE—Box 418, Detroit, MI 48232. Norman E. Douglas, Managing Editor.
Articles, 1,800 to 2,000 words, for finance officers in banks, corporate management and insurance companies, on lending, investment management, controllership, personnel, etc. Pays 10¢ a word, on acceptance. Query.

BUSINESS AND COMMERCIAL AVIATION—Ziff-Davis Publishing Co., 1 Park Ave., New York, NY 10016. Archie Trammell, Editor.
Articles, 2,500 words, with photos, for semi-pro and professional pilots, on use of privately owned aircraft for business transportation. Pays $100 to $500, on acceptance.

BUSINESS DIGEST OF FLORIDA—P.O. Drawer 23729, 4602-A N.E. 6th Ave., Ft. Lauderdale, FL 33334. Mary W. Lathrop, Editor.
Articles, to 1,200 words, on business management, new products, economy, business trends. Pays $25 per printed page, on publication.

BUSINESS GRAPHICS—7373 North Lincoln Ave., Chicago, IL 60646. Roy D. Conradi, Editor.
Articles, 1,600 words, for management, on in-house reproduction, business forms, microfilm, copiers, printing equipment, word processing, mail management, photocomposition. Pays $50 per article, on publication. Query.

BUSINESS OPPORTUNITIES–1328 Garnet Ave., San Diego, CA 92109. Wayne Wakefield, Editor.
Articles, 1,500 to 2,500 words, on building personal wealth through real estate, investments, business ventures; practical ways for saving money or cutting taxes; business and investment opportunities in U.S. and Canada. Pay varies, on acceptance. Query.

BUSINESS AND SOCIETY REVIEW–870 7th Ave., New York, NY 10019. Theodore Cross, Editor.
Articles, 2,000 to 6,000 words, on economic, sociological or business material on U.S. society. Pays infrequently. Query.

BUSINESS WORLD–P.O. Box 1234, Rahway, NJ 07065. Gretchen Mirrielees, Editor.
Career-related articles, 1,200 to 2,500 words, for graduating college students, on business: interviews with executives, first-person accounts of young people on the rise, business and social responsibility, environment. Life-style pieces, 300 to 1,200 words, with practical information on life-insurance, credit cards, consumerism, budget travel, apartment hunting, etc. Two issues (*Business World for Women*) on careers for women from business and liberal arts backgrounds. No payment.

CAMPGROUND AND RV PARK MANAGEMENT–P.O. Box 1014, Grass Valley, CA 95945. Bob Behme, Editor.
Detailed articles, 300 to 1,200 words with black-and-white photos, on phase of park owner's business operation. Pays to $50, on publication.

CAMPGROUND MERCHANDISING–20-21 Wagaraw Rd., Fair Lawn, NJ 07410. Martin Dowd, Co-Publisher.
Articles, 1,500 words, quoting managers of campground recreation vehicle parks on what equipment and merchandise they sell to RV'ers. Pays 4¢ per word for articles, $10 per black-and-white photo.

CANDY AND SNACK INDUSTRY–777 Third Ave., New York, NY 10017. Mike Lench, Editor.
Illustrated features, 1,000 to 1,250 words, on production and promotion of national candy and snack firms and local retail manufacturers. Short news pieces. Pays 5¢ a word, $5 for photos, on publication. Query on plant stories.

CANNER PACKER–875 N. Michigan Ave., Chicago, IL 60611.
Articles for canned, frozen, dry food industries, on industry problems, labor, herbicides and insecticides, etc. Pays $25 per printed page, including photographs. Query.

CARS & TRUCKS–2000 K St. N. W., Washington, DC 20006.
National Automobile Dealers Association magazine. Ray A. Sullivan, Publisher. Dealer member management case histories, 750 to 2,000 words, with photos. Pays on acceptance. Query.

THE CATTLEMAN–410 East Weatherford, Fort Worth, TX 76102. Paul W. Horn, Editor.
Articles, of 1,500 to 2,000 words, on southwest cattle-raising. Pay varies, on publication.

CERAMIC SCOPE–Box 48643, Los Angeles, CA 90048. Mel Fiske, Editor.
Articles, 1,000 to 1,500 words, on business operations of hobby ceramic studies: merchandising, promotion, layout, display, inventory systems, record keeping, studio management on retail or wholesale level. Photos of studios. Pays 2¢ a word, $5 a photo, on acceptance. Query.

CHAIN SAW AGE–3435 N.E. Broadway, Portland, OR 97232. Norman Raies, Publisher.
Merchandising features, to 500 words, on dealers, distributors and users of chain

saws; unusual uses for chain saws, etc. Pays 2½¢ a word, extra for photos, on publication. Query.

CHEMICAL WEEK–1221 Ave. of the Americas, New York, NY 10020. Patrick McCurdy, Editor-in-Chief.
News pieces of chemical business signficance, to 200 words. Pays $3.50 per column inch, minimum of $5 per item. Query.

CHRISTIAN BOOKSELLER–Gundersen Dr. and Schmale Rd., Wheaton, IL 60187. W. T. Bray, Editor.
Anecdotal articles, 1,200 to 1,500 words with photos, on successful advertising programs, sales promotions, remodeling projects, store fronts, of retail outlets of religious books. Pays $25 to $50, on publication.

CLEANING MANAGEMENT–710 West Wilson Ave., Glendale, CA 91209. Charles F. Wheeler, Jr., Publisher.
Instructive articles, 1,000 words, for cleaning and maintenance personnel, on improving efficiency, increasing economy, upgrading performance. No case histories. Pays from 3¢ a word, $5 for photos, on publication.

COINAMATIC AGE–60 East 42nd St., New York, NY 10017. Jack J. Gubala, Editor.
Factual articles, 1,000 to 1,500 words, with 3 to 6 glossy photos, on ingenuity of store owner in coin laundry and drycleaning. Include complete list of all trade-named equipment. Pays 3¢ a word and up, $10 for first three photos, $5 per each additional photo used, on publication. Query.

COMMERCIAL CAR JOURNAL–Chilton Way, Radnor, PA 19089. James D. Winsor, Editor.
Knowledgeable articles, any length, on truck and bus fleet operation and maintenance. Pays from $50, on acceptance. Query.

COMMUNICATION NEWS–402 West Liberty Dr., Wheaton, IL 60187. Bruce Howat, Editor.
Technical articles, 500 to 1,500 words, on developments in voice, signal and data communications; news, case histories, how-to pieces. Pays 3¢ per word, $7.50 per photo, on publication.

COMPUTER DECISIONS MAGAZINE–50 Essex St., Rochelle Park, NJ 07662. Hesh Wiener, Editor.
Articles, 800 to 4,000 words, on generic uses of computer systems, social, economic and political aspects of computing. Pays $30 per published page. Query.

CONCRETE CONSTRUCTION–P.O. Box 321, Addison, IL 60101. William H. Kuenning, Editor.
Technical articles, 1,500 to 2,000 words, on constructing with concrete on site (not precast). Pay varies. Query.

CONCRETE PRODUCTS–300 West Adams St., Chicago, IL 60606. William J. Blaha, Editor.
Articles, about 1,400 words, on production methods, processes, distribution, marketing of ready-mix concrete block, pipe and precast and prestress concrete. Pays 3¢ a word, extra for photos, on acceptance. Query.

CONSUMER ELECTRONICS PRODUCT NEWS–St. Regis Publications, 25 West 45 St., New York, NY 10036. Kathleen Lander, Editor.
Lively articles, 500 to 2,000 words, on sales training and merchandising techniques for people in consumer electronics field (hi-fi, calculators, telephone accessories, tape, etc.). Pay varies, on acceptance. All articles on assignment. Query with sample of work.

CONTRACTOR–Berkshire Common, Pittsfield, MA 01201. Seth Shepard, Editor.
Articles, 1,000 to 2,000 words, for major plumbing, heating and air conditioning

contractors; news pieces on labor, industry trends, legal actions, associations, etc. Pays 15¢ a printed line.

CRAFT HORIZONS–44 West 53rd St., New York, NY 10019. Rose Slivka, Editor.
Articles with photos on professional handcrafts and craftsmen: weaving, ceramics, metal working, woodworking, etc. Pays to $100, after publication. Query.

CREDIT AND FINANCIAL MANAGEMENT–475 Park Ave. South, New York, NY 10016. James J. Andover, Editorial Director.
Articles, 2,000 words, on business credit, financial and business conditions, management policies and techniques in manufacturing, wholesaling, and service companies.

CURTAIN, DRAPERY & BEDSPREAD MAGAZINE–Columbia Communications, 370 Lexington Ave., New York, NY 10017. Ruth L. Lyons, Editor.
Articles, to 1,500 words, with 3 to 8 photos, on merchandise, merchandising or promotional techniques. Pieces, 250 words, on trends, fashions. Pays 5¢ a word, $5 per photo with caption, on publication. Query.

CYCLE AGE–Babcox Publications, Babcox Bldg., 11 South Forge St., Akron, OH 44304. Gary L. Gardner, Editor.
Articles, 1,250 words, on marketing and retailing motorcycles; technical business-oriented pieces on cycle repair, maintenance and customizing, profiles of industry leaders. Black-and-white photos of races, machine shops, retailing situations. Pay varies, on publication. Query.

DAIRY HERD MANAGEMENT–P.O. Box 67, Minneapolis, MN 55440. George Ashfield, Editor.
Articles, 50 to 2,000 words with photos, on large dairy operations and innovative techniques and equipment used by major U.S. dairymen. Fillers, clippings. Pays $10 to $150, on acceptance. Query.

DAIRY INDUSTRY NEWS–176 Alexander St., Princeton, NJ 08540. William G. Reddan, Editor.
New articles on dairy marketing industry. Newspaper experience preferred. Pays monthly. Query.

DE/JOURNAL–450 East Ohio, Chicago, IL 60611. Stephen J. Shafer, Editor.
Articles, to 3,000 words, on plumbing, heating, air conditioning, process piping, etc. Photos. Pays $20 to $35 per published page, on publication.

DEFENSE TRANSPORTATION JOURNAL–1612 K St. N.W., Washington, DC 20006. G. W. Collins, Publisher.
Articles, 1,500 to 3,000 words, reporting and analyzing concepts, trends and developments in domestic and international transportation industry. Pays to $150, on publication.

DELI NEWS–Box 706, Hollywood, CA 90028. Michael Scott, Editor.
Articles, 700 to 2,000 words, on delicatessen and dairy departments of supermarkets. Related humorous fiction, photos, and cartoons. Pays $15 to $40 for articles, $5 to $10 for cartoons and photos, on acceptance.

DENTAL MANAGEMENT–Box 3285, Stamford, CT 06905. M. J. Goldberg, Editor.
Articles, to 2,000 words, on taxes, insurance, offices, etc., of interest to dentists. No technical or clinical material. Pays 10¢ to 15¢ a word, on acceptance. Query.

THE DISCOUNT MERCHANDISER–641 Lexington Ave., New York, NY 10022. Nathaniel Schwartz, Editor.
Articles on innovations in mass-merchandising techniques and ideas for discount stores. Pays to $150 for articles, $7.50 for photos, on acceptance. Query.

THE DISPENSING OPTICIAN—1980 Mountain Blvd., Oakland, CA 94611. Robert L. Pickering, Editor.
Articles, 750 to 2,000 words, on operation of optical dispensing businesses. Nothing on optometrists or retail operations with eye examination services. Pays 4¢ a word, $7.50 for photos, on acceptance. Query.

DRIVE-IN FAST SERVICE—757 Third Ave., New York, NY 10017. Freda Barry, Editor.
Articles, with photos, on fast food restaurants: advertising, how-to pieces, executive profiles, management. Fillers with photos on promotional gimmicks. Pays 5¢ to 7¢ a word, $5 to $7 for photos. Query.

DRUG TOPICS—496 Kinderkamack Rd., Oradell, NJ 07649. David W. Sifton, Editor.
News pieces, 500 words, with photos, on retailers and associations in retail drug field. Merchandising features, 1,000 to 1,500 words; query. Pays $5 to $25 for leads, $25 to $50 for pieces, $50 to $200 for features, on acceptance.

EARNSHAW'S INFANTS' AND CHILDREN'S REVIEW—393 Seventh Ave., New York, NJ 10001. Janet Morgan, Managing Editor.
Articles on promotions, fashions shows, business-building ideas in infants', children's, boys' and subteen departments. Pays $75 per published article. Query.

EASTERN AUTOMOTIVE JOURNAL—P.O. Box 373, Cedarhurst, NY 11516. Stan Hubsher, Publisher.
Wholesaler-oriented articles, 1,000 to 1,500 words with three to five black-and-white photos, on automotive replacement parts trade from Maine to Virginia. Pay negotiable, on publication. Query.

EDITOR & PUBLISHER—850 Third Ave., New York, NY 10022. Robert U. Brown, Editor.
Articles, to 1,200 words, with photos, on newspapers and newspapermen—news preferred. Pay varies, after publication. Query.

ELECTRICAL CONTRACTOR—7315 Wisconsin Ave., Washington, DC 20014. Larry C. Osius, Editor and Publisher.
Articles, 1,000 to 1,500 words, with photos, on construction techniques and/or management techniques for electrical contractors. Pays $60 per published page, before publication. Query.

ELECTRONIC TECHNICAL DEALER—1 East First St., Duluth, MN 55802. J. W. Phipps, Editor.
Articles, 1,500 to 2,500 words, for radio and communications service technicians and dealers, on successful dealers, CCTV, sound systems, MATV, two-way radio, etc. Cartoons. Pays $25 per estimated magazine page; $7.50 per cartoon, on acceptance.

ENERGY NEWS—P.O. Box 1589, Dallas, TX 75221.
Articles, to 1,000 words, on natural gas industry for management-level persons. Pays 10¢ per published word, within a month after publication.

FARM AND POWER EQUIPMENT MAGAZINE—2340 Hampton Ave., St. Louis, MO 63139. Glenn S. Hensley, Editor.
Articles, to 1,500 words, with photos, on retailers selling light industrial power equipment and farm implements. Pays to $300, on acceptance. Query.

FEED INDUSTRY REVIEW—3055 North Brookfield Rd., Brookfield, WI 53005. Bruce W. Smith, Publisher.
Feature articles, with photos, 1,200 to 2,500 words, on full-scale manufacturing of brand-name feeds. Immediate replies to queries.

FENCE INDUSTRY—461 Eighth Avenue, New York, NY 10001. Ben Newman, Editor.
Articles and interviews with dealer-erectors on fence industry topics: history, gross volume, etc.; on-the-job pieces. Pays $5 to $10 for photos; about 4¢ per word. Query.

FINANCIAL EXECUTIVE–633 Third Ave., New York, NY 10017. Carl Cerminaro, Editor.
Articles, 3,000 to 4,000 words, on business and finance. No payment. Query.

THE FISH BOAT–P.O. Box 52288, 624 Gravier St., New Orleans, LA 70152. William A. Sarratt, Editor.
Articles on commercial fishing, promotion and merchandising of seafood products. Short items on commercial fishermen and boats. Include specifications and equipment. Pay varies, on acceptance. Query.

FISHING GAZETTE–461 Eighth Ave., New York, NY 10001. Robert J. Burns, Editor.
Articles, to 2,000 words, with photos, on commercial fisheries, fishing boat construction, fish processing plants, freezing plants. No game fishery material. Pay varies. Query.

FLOORING MAGAZINE–757 Third Ave., New York, NY 10017. Michael Korsonsky, Editor.
Articles, 1,500 words, for floor covering industry, on merchandising, display, advertising, promotion, distribution. Photos with negatives. Pays 5¢ to 10¢ per word, on acceptance. Query.

FLORIST–900 West Lafayette, Detroit, MI 48226. Frank J. Baccala, Editor.
Articles, to 1,000 words, with 8 x 10 black-and-white glossy photos, on retail flower shop business improvement. Pays 5¢ a word, and $7.50 per photo.

THE FOOD BROKER–436 West Colorado St., Glendale, CA 91204. D. David Dreis, Editor.
Articles on activities, views, merchandising techniques of food brokers. Query.

FOOD MANAGEMENT–Harcourt Brace Jovanovich, 757 Third Ave., New York, NY 10017. William Patterson, Editor.
Articles, 2,000 to 3,000 words, with 35 mm color slides, on institutional food service at schools, colleges, hospitals, nursing homes, and in-plant. Pays to 10¢ a word, on acceptance. Query.

FOOD MARKETER–2700 Cumberland Pkwy., Suite 500, Atlanta, GA 30339. Beth Souther, Editor.
Articles, 1,000 to 2,500 words, on wide range of food industry interests including natural and organic foods, poultry industry, nutrition labeling, as they relate to retail and wholesale food marketing. Pay varies, on publication. Query.

THE FOREMAN'S LETTER–Bureau of Business Practice, 24 Rope Ferry Rd., Waterford, CT 06385. Frank L. Berkowitz, Editor.
Interviews, to 750 words, with black-and-white close-up photos, on successful employee leadership practices of industrial supervisors and foremen. Pays 7¢ to 8½¢ per usable word, on acceptance; additional for photos. Similar requirements for newsletters directed to construction and public utilities supervisors. Query.

FURNITURE AND FURNISHINGS–1450 Don Mills Rd., Don Mills, Ontario, Canada M3B 2X7. Ronald H. Shuker, Editor.
Retail merchandising and management articles with photos, for retailers, buyers, decorators, contract salesmen, distributors and manufacturers' representatives on distribution and sales of furniture, floor coverings, draperies, lamps, accessories, with Canadian slant. Pay varies, on publication.

GAS APPLIANCE MERCHANDISING–1 E. First St., Duluth, MN 55802. Zane Chastain, Editor/Associate Publisher.
Articles, with photos, 500 to 1,200 words, on gas appliance dealer operations and promotional activities; display, special projects, etc. Pays 5¢ per word; $5 to $7 per photos, on acceptance. Query.

GASOLINE NEWS–100 North Grant St., Columbus, OH 43215. Paul Hendershot, Editor.
Trade paper for service stations. Clippings on service station, car wash, and snowmobile industries. Pays 50¢ per clipping, on publication. Query.

GIFT AND TABLEWARE REPORTER–1515 Broadway, New York, NY 10036. Jack McDermott, Editor.
Illustrated merchandising articles and news items, 300 to 500 words, for giftware and tableware retail buyer. Pays $25 to $40 for articles with photos, on acceptance. Query.

GIFTS AND DECORATIVE ACCESSORIES–51 Madison Ave., New York, NY 10010. Phyllis Sweed, Editor.
Merchandising features, 1,500 to 3,000 words, with photos, on promotions, display techniques, design features, business activities, of retailer shops for gifts, social stationery, and greeting cards. Pays to $50, extra for photos, on publication.

GLASS DIGEST–15 East 40th St., New York, NY 10016. Oscar S. Glasberg, Editor.
Case histories, 1,200 to 1,500 words, of building projects and glass/metal dealers, distributors, storefront and glazing contractors. Pays 3½¢ to 5¢ per word, $5 for photos, on publication.

GOLF SHOP OPERATIONS–297 Westport Ave., Norwalk, CT 06856. James McAfee, Editor.
Case histories, 200 to 800 words, of successful golf shop operations; new ideas on merchandising, display, bookkeeping, etc. Short pieces on golf professionals. Pays $50 to $100, on publication.

GRAPHIC ARTS MONTHLY–7373 No. Lincoln Ave., Chicago, IL 60646. Dr. Paul J. Hartsuch, Editor.
Technical articles, 2,500 to 3,000 words, on printing industry. Pays 3¢ per word, on acceptance. Query.

GROCERY COMMUNICATIONS–436 West Colorado St., Glendale, CA 91204. Brad McDowell, Editor.
Articles, any length, with black-and-white photos, for grocery store retailers, on effective merchandising techniques, with human-interest slant. Pays $50 to $100. Query.

HANDBAGS AND ACCESSORIES–80 Lincoln Ave., Stamford, CT 06904. Renee Prowitt, Editor.
Articles and features, any length, with photos, for handbag and accessory buyers: unique store displays, retail promotions, profiles of designers and manufacturers. Pays $50 for short articles, $100 and up for major features with photos, on publication. Query.

HARDWARE AGE–Chilton Way, Radnor, PA 19089. Jon P. Kinslow, Editor.
Articles on unique merchandising methods in hardline outlets. Photo features. Pays on acceptance.

HARDWARE MERCHANDISER–7300 North Cicero Ave., Chicago, IL 60646. W. P. Farrell, Editor.
Articles, to 1,000 words, with black-and-white photos, on hardware marketing; general and specific merchandising of lines in hardware stores, discount stores, mass merchandisers, home centers.

HEALTH FOODS BUSINESS–225 West 34th St., New York, NY 10001. Georgette Manla, Editor.
Articles, 1,500 words with photos, on managing health food stores or departments in larger stores: security, health cosmetics, advertising, etc. Pays $25 per published page. Query.

HEATING/PIPING/AIR CONDITIONING–10 South LaSalle St., Chicago, IL 60603. Robert T. Korte, Editor.
Articles, to 5,000 words, on heating, piping and air-conditioning systems in industrial plants and large buildings; engineering information. Pays $30 per printed page, on publication.

HOME AND AUTO–757 Third Ave., New York, NY 10017.
Articles on merchandising methods of auto supply stores, home and auto stores and other mass-merchandisers. Photos of novel display materials. Pay varies. Query. Unsolicited manuscripts not returned.

HOMESEWING TRADE NEWS–129 Broadway, Lynbrook, NY 11583. Nat Danas, Editor.
Articles, 750 to 1,000 words, with 2 to 4 photos, for fabric shop owners, department store buyers, in home-sewing field. Pays $35 to $50, on publication. Query.

HOSPITAL SUPERVISOR'S BULLETIN–681 Fifth Ave., New York, NY 10022.
For hospital supervisors of nonmedical areas. Interview-based articles, 900 to 1,400 words, on solving problems, and methods of "getting things done through others." Pays $25 a printed page, $7.50 for cartoons, on acceptance. Query. Send for editorial requirements.

HOTEL & MOTEL MANAGEMENT–845 Chicago Ave., Evanston, IL 60202. Bob Freeman, Editor.
Articles, 1,000 to 2,000 words, on management subjects. Pays 6¢ a word, on acceptance. Query.

THE INLAND PRINTER/AMERICAN LITHOGRAPHER–300 West Adams St., Chicago, IL 60606. R. H. Green, Editor.
Articles on plant management and operation, shop technique, sales, design. Query.

THE JEWELERS' CIRCULAR-KEYSTONE–Chilton Way, Radnor, PA 19089. George Holmes, Editor.
Articles, 200 to 1,500 words, with photos, on phase of retail jewelry store merchandising or operation. Shorts, 200 to 300 words, on single activity that built sales or cut costs. Pays $10, on acceptance.

JOBBER & WAREHOUSE EXECUTIVE–53 West Jackson Blvd., Chicago, IL 60604. James Halloran, Editor.
Articles, 800 to 1,200 words, with photos, for management personnel in automotive wholesaling firms. Pay varies.

KIRKLEY PRESS, INC.–Box 200, Lutherville, MD 21093. Address Walter Kirkley.
Articles, 400 words and 2,200 to 2,400 words, that promote better on-the-job employee relations, and higher personal efficiency. Pays $40 for folders and $200 to $300 for booklets. Query with lead-in material.

KITCHEN BUSINESS–1515 Broadway, New York, NY 10036. Patrick Galvin, Editor.
Case histories, 500 to 2,000 words, with photos, on management or merchandising procedures of successful dealers in cabinets, or built-in products for kitchens plants making plastic-surfaced kitchen cabinets or countertops. Pays $50 first printed page, $30 per succeeding page, on acceptance. Query.

KITCHEN PLANNING–757 Third Ave., New York, NY 10017. Freda Barry, Editor.
Articles, 750 to 1,500 words, with photos and blueprints, for designers, architects consultants, on new commercial and industrial kitchens. Pays 7¢ to 10¢ a word, $5 to $7.50 per photo, on acceptance. Query.

KNITTING INDUSTRY–44 East 23rd St., New York, NY 10010. Perry Antoshak, Editor.
Articles, 1,500 to 2,000 words, with photos, on manufacturing processes in knitting industry; outerwear, underwear, hosiery, packaging. Pays $1 per inch and $5 per photo, after publication. Query.

LP-GAS MAGAZINE–1 East First St., Duluth, MN 55802. Zane Chastain, Editor Associate Publisher.
Articles, 750 to 2,000 words, with photos, on LP-Gas dealer operation: marketing, management, etc. Pays to 7¢ a word, $5 to $10 per photo, on acceptance. Query.

LAWN & GARDEN MARKETING–1014 Wyandotte St., Kansas City, MO 64105. Wendall J. Burns, Editor.
Articles and photo-featues, 600 to 1,200 words, with 5 x 7 black-and-white glossies on management, for retailers of landscaping and gardening supplies, outdoor power and recreational equipment. Pays $100 to $125 for articles, $35 to $50 for photo-features, on acceptance.

MADISON AVENUE MAGAZINE–Unique Communications, Inc., 545 Madison Ave., New York, NY 10022. Jenny Greenberg, Publisher.
Feature articles on advertising and marketing. No payment.

MAINE ANTIQUE DIGEST, INC.–R.F.D. 3, Box 76A, Waldoboro, ME 04572. Samuel Pennington, Editor.
Lively, authoritative articles on antiques market in New England. Black-and-white photos. Pays to $25, on acceptance.

MANAGE–9933 Alliance Rd., Cincinnati, OH 45242. Ralph Vines, Editor.
Articles, 1,500 to 2,200 words with photos and illustrations, on management and/or supervision. Pays 3¢ to 5¢ a word, on acceptance, $10 for cartoons.

MARKING INDUSTRY–18 East Huron Street, Chicago, IL 60611. A. W. Hachmeister, Editor.
Technical or sales material on manufacture and distribution of steel stamps, checks badges, seals, etc., in U.S. or Latin America. Pays on acceptance.

MILITARY REVIEW–U.S. Army Command and General Staff College, Fort Leaven-worth, KS 66027. Col. J. H. Chitty, Jr., Editor-in-Chief.
Articles, 2,500 to 6,000 words, to stimulate military thinking on tactics, history, military forces, strategy, etc. Pays about $50, on publication. Query.

MILK HAULER AND FOOD TRANSPORTER–221 N. LaSalle St., Chicago, IL 60601. Douglas D. Sorenson, Editor.
Success stories, with photos, on transporters who haul cheese and other dairy products, liquid sugar, molasses, citrus juice and other edible foods. Pays about $35 per article, $5 each for sharp black-and-white photos, on acceptance. Query. Reports in 2 to 3 weeks.

MODEL DEALER–249 Freeport Blvd., Reno, NV 89510. James Sunday, Editor.
Articles for dealers and distributors of hobby models – aircraft, boat, car, rocket, train – and accessories, on retailing: controlling inventory, expansion, increasing sales and efficiency, etc. Pays $40 per 1,000 words, on publication. Query.

MODERN HEALTHCARE–230 West Monroe St., Chicago, IL 60606. Ted Isaacman, Editor.
Articles, 2,500 words, for health care professionals, on issues in management of health care institutions: finance, building design, new technology, etc. Pay varies. Query.

MODERN PACKAGING–1221 Ave. of the Americas, New York, NY 10020. Thomas M. Jones, Editor.
Articles, to 1,000 words, with tables, charts, graphs or photos, for packers of consumer, industrial or military products. Pays $30 per published page on publication. Query.

MODERN TIRE DEALER–P.O. Box 5417, 77 North Miller Rd., Akron, OH 44313. Charles Slaybaugh, Editor.

Merchandising management and service articles, 1,000 to 1,500 words, with photos, on independent tire dealers and retreaders. Pays 7¢ a word and up, on publication.

MOTOR—1790 Broadway, New York, NY 10019. J. Robert Connor, Editor.
Articles, 750 to 1,500 words with glossy photos, on particular repair shop, or service station's success in merchandising automotive accessories. (TBA). Pays on acceptance. Query.

MOTOR/AGE—Chilton Publ., Chilton Way, Radnor, PA 19089. Gerald V. Haddon, Editor.
Merchandising and management articles, 1,500 words, with photos, for managers of automotive repair outlets (new car dealers, garages, service stations). Pays $50 to $70, on acceptance. Query.

MOTOR IN CANADA—1077 St. James St., Box 6900, Winnipeg, Man., Canada. Ralf Neuendorff, Editor.
Merchandising and service articles, 250 to 1,000 words, for automotive trade in Western Canada. Pays $1.50 per column inch, extra for pictures, on publication.

MOTORCYCLE DEALER NEWS—P.O. Box 288, South Laguna, CA 92677. Mead P. Miller, Editor.
Articles, 700 to 1,500 words with black-and-white glossy photos, on current trends in motorcycle industry and solutions to dealers' problems. Fillers on merchandising ideas, cartoons. Pays $50 to $100, on publication. Query with outline.

NATIONAL BOWLERS JOURNAL AND BILLIARD REVIEW—1825 North Lincoln Plaza, Chicago, IL 60614. Mort Luby, Jr., Editor.
Articles, 1,200 to 1,500 words, with photos, on promotions which increased business for bowling and billiard proprietors. Pays $50 to $60, on publication.

NATIONAL BUSINESS WOMAN—2012 Massachusetts Ave., N.W., Washington, DC 20036. Lola S. Tilden, Editor.
Articles, to 1,200 words, for business and professional women, on career development, opportunities, responsibilities, etc. Pays 3¢ a word, on acceptance. Manuscripts without postage not returned.

NATIONAL LIVESTOCK PRODUCER—733 North Van Buren, Milwaukee, WI 53202. Frank Lessiter, Editor.
Articles, any length, for livestock producers in U.S. Pays about $100 per article, on acceptance. Query.

THE NATIONAL PUBLIC ACCOUNTANT—1717 Pennsylvania Ave. N.W., Washington, DC 20006. Stanley H. Stearman, Editor.
Articles, 1,800 to 5,000 words, on accounting taxation, bookkeeping, data processing, business administration, and professional development. No payment.

NATIONAL SKI AREA NEWS—1801 York St., Denver, CO 80206. William Grout Editor.
Factual articles, 500 to 2,000 words, with black-and-white prints or contact sheets with negatives, on ski instructors handling specific problems. News items for ski area operators. Pays 10¢ a word, on publication. Query.

NATION'S CITIES—1620 Eye St. N.W., Washington, DC 20006. Allen E. Pritchard, Jr., Editor.
Articles, to 1,000 words, for city and town officials in U.S., on municipal government and urban affairs: finances, management, crime prevention, etc. Pays $100 per article, on acceptance. Query.

THE NEW ENGLAND BUSINESS JOURNAL—777 Country Way, North Scituate, MA 02060. Alan Greenblatt, Editor.
Lively articles, 500 to 1,200 words, on business, finance, stock and money markets, personalities, humor. Pay varies, on publication. Query.

NEW YORK BUSINESS—301 East 48th St., New York, NY 10017. Charles Tannen, Editor.
How-to articles, 1,000 to 5,000 words, for top executives on all aspects of doing business in New York City. Pay varies.

NORTHERN HARDWARE TRADE—5901 Brooklyn Blvd., Suite 203, Minneapolis MN 55429. Betty Braden, Managing Editor.
Case history articles, 800 to 1,000 words, on unusual hardware stores and promotions in Northwest — from Michigan to California, Oregon and Washington; south from Canadian border through Missouri. Pays 4¢ a word, $5 per photo, on publication. Query.

OCCUPATIONAL HAZARDS—614 Superior Ave. West, Cleveland, OH 44113. Peter J. Sheridan, Editor.
Articles, 500 to 2,000 words, on industrial safety, health, fire prevention, and security. Related cartoons and photos. Pays 3¢ a word and up, on publication; $3 for photos and illustrations, $5 for cartoons, on acceptance.

OFFICE PRODUCTS—Hitchcock Building, Wheaton, IL 60187. Thomas J. Trafals, Editorial Director.
Illustrated merchandising articles, any length, for and about office supply, machine, and furniture dealers. Pays from $25 per printed page, including pictures, on acceptance. Query.

OFFICE SUPERVISOR'S BULLETIN—681 Fifth Ave., New York, NY 10022. Margaret Green, Editor.
Interview-based articles, 900 to 1,350 words, for first- and second-line supervisors, on solving problems, and methods of "getting things done through others." Pays $35 per 450 words, $7.50 for cartoons, on acceptance. Query. Send for editorial requirements.

THE OPTICAL JOURNAL AND REVIEW OF OPTOMETRY—203 King of Prussia Rd., Radnor, PA 19087. John F. McCarthy, Editor.
Articles, to 1,500 words, on optometric practice and ophthalmic optical work; investing and economics for optometrists. Pays 60¢ per published inch, on publication. Query.

PACKAGE ENGINEERING—5 South Wabash Ave., Chicago, IL 60603. R. Bruce Holmgren, Editor.
Articles, 1,000 to 2,000 words, on technical and operational packaging field: engineering, production, research and development, testing, purchasing, management. Pays $25 per published page, on publication. Query.

PACKING AND SHIPPING—437 East 5th St., Plainfield, NJ 07060. C. M. Bonnell, Jr., Editor.
Illustrated articles, about 1,000 words, on physical distribution, industrial packing, handling, shipping-room practice. Short items. Pay varies, on publication.

PAPER, FILM AND FOIL CONVERTER—200 South Prospect, Park Ridge IL 60068. Peter Rigney, Editor.
Articles, 2,500 to 5,000 words, or photo essays on converter processes, production, product development. No payment.

PAPERBOARD PACKAGING— 777 Third Ave., New York, NY 10017. Joel J. Shulman, Editor.
Articles, any length, on paperboard mill, corrugated container, folding carton, setup boxes, related activities. Pays $50 per 1,000 words, on publication. Query with outline.

PET DEALER— 225 West 34th St., New York, NY 10001. Fred Rackmil, Editor.
How-to articles, 1,000 words, on specialty pet shops or departments, grooming,

selling techniques, etc. Black-and-white photos. Pays $25 per published page, on acceptance. Query.

PETROLEUM TODAY– 1801 K St. N.W., Washington, DC 20006. Cynthia Riggs Stoertz, Editor.
Articles, 500 words, or 1,200 to 2,000 words, on oil industry issues of general interest: energy crisis, Alaska pipeline, environment, deep water ports, personalities, etc. Pays from $200, on publication. Query.

PETS/SUPPLIES/MARKETING– One East First St., Duluth, MN 55802. Paul A. Setzer Editor.
Articles, 1,500 to 2,000 words, with 4 to 6 8 x 10 black-and-white glossies with captions, for pet and pet product retailers, wholesalers, and manufacturers of pet supplies, on successes of quality pet shops. Short pieces with photos, on new products, merchandising or display ideas. Pays 5¢ per published word, $6 to $7.50 per black-and-white photo, $12.50 to $15 for color. Query.

PHOTO MARKETING– 603 Lansing Ave., Jackson, MI 49202. James L. Crawford, Managing Editor.
Articles, about 500 words, on camera store and finishing plant successes in particular area: promotion, advertising, personnel management, etc. Pays 5¢ to 7¢ per printed word, $5 to $7.50 per published photo, on publication.

PHYSICIAN'S MANAGEMENT– 757 Third Ave., New York, NY 10017. Gene Balliett, Editor.
Articles, 400 to 2,000 words, for doctors, on office management, socio-economic subjects, interviews. Black-and-white photos with captions; color slides. Pays 5¢ to 20¢ a word for articles, $25 to $75 for black-and-white photos with articles, $75 to $150 for color slides, on acceptance. Query.

POOL NEWS– Leisure Publication, 3932 West Sixth St., Los Angeles, CA 90020. Fay Coupe, Editor.
News pieces on swimming pool industry. Pays 5¢ a word, $5 per photo. Query.

POULTRY TRIBUNE– Mt. Morris, IL 61054. Milton R. Dunk, Editor.
Business articles, 200 to 1,000 words, on egg production, processing, and marketing. Pays 6¢ to 8¢ a word, on acceptance. Query.

POWER ENGINEERING–1301 South Grove Ave., Barrington, IL 60010. John Papamarcos, Editor.
Specialized articles, 1,000 to 2,400 words, on design, construction, operation and maintenance of large power facilities for industry and utilities. Pays $40 per published page, on acceptance.

PRINTING MANAGEMENT– 106 Benton Rd., Paramus, NJ 07652. Jeremiah E. Flynn, Editor.
Articles, 1,000 to 3,000 words, on management, marketing and technical problems and resolutions, for commercial printers with offset and letterpress facilities. Pays from $35 per page, after publication. Query.

PRODUCTION MAGAZINE–Bramson Publishing Co., P.O. Box 101, Bloomfield Hills, MI 48013. Robert F. Huber, Editor.
Articles, 300 to 3,000 words, with photos, on improved mass production metalworking operations. Pay varies, on acceptance.

PROFITABLE CRAFT MERCHANDISING– News Plaza, Peoria, IL 61601.
Articles, 1,000 to 1,500 words, with photos, for small independent retailers, on store management techniques: sales, displays, accounting systems, store arrangement, etc., profiles of successful craft retailers; how-to pieces on craft projects and new techniques. Pays $45 to $250. Query.

PROGRESSIVE GROCER–708 Third Ave., New York, NY 10017. Edgar B. Walzer, Editor.
Factual articles, to 2,500 words, on supermarket management, operations, merchandising, and promotion. Shorts, 100 to 200 words, on sales and promotion ideas. Photos. Pays $10 and up per black-and-white photo and caption, $25 for color transparencies, on acceptance. Article rates vary.

PURCHASING– 221 Columbus Ave., Boston, MA 02116. Robert Haavind, Editor.
Articles, 1,200 to 1,500 words, on buying techniques in industrial purchasing departments, supply situations, industry personalities, recycling etc. Photos, charts, illustrations. Pays about $50 per printed page.

RVB (RECREATIONAL VEHICLE BUSINESS)–3000 France Ave. South, Minneapolis, MN 55416. Jerry Hoffman, Editor.
Case history articles on snowmobiles, ATV, trail and mini-bike dealers. Query.

RADIO AND TELEVISION WEEKLY–145 Ave. of the Americas, New York, NY 10013. Cy Kneller, Editor.
News on activities of radio, television, and electronic wholesale distributors and retail dealers. Pays $2 per inch, end of month after publication. Query.

RADIO-ELECTRONICS–200 Park Ave. South, New York, NY 10003. Larry Steckler Editor.
Technical articles, 1,500 to 3,000 words, on electronic equipment and maintenance; servicing TV, hi-fi, audio, AM and FM, CB, and other communications equipment; construction projects on electronics devices; general interest items. Pays $50 to $500, on acceptance. Send for Guide to Writing.

RECREATIONAL VEHICLE RETAILER– 23945 Craftsman Rd., Calabasas, CA 91302. Art Rouse, Publisher; Denis Rouse, Editor.
Articles, 2,000 to 3,500 words, with black-and-white photos, on selling and servicing recreational vehicles, success in increasing profits in dealer business, opening new demographic markets. Pays to $100 for articles with photos, on publication.

REFRIGERATED TRANSPORTER–1602 Harold St., Houston, TX 77006.
News articles, with illustrations, on transportation under refrigeration, by for hire and private motor carriers. Pays from $50 and up per printed page.

RENT ALL–Harcourt Brace Jovanovich, 1 East First St., Duluth, MN 55802. Roy Johnson, Editor.
Business articles, 1,000 to 1,500 words with 6 to 8 photos, on rental field. Pays 7¢ a word, $6.50 per photo with caption, on acceptance. Query.

RESERVE LAW– 2440 Freedom Dr., San Antonio, TX 78217. Otto Vehle, Editor.
Articles and fiction, 100 to 1,000 words with photos, on law enforcement, primarily on volunteers such as Auxiliary or Reserve Law Enforcement Officers. Fillers and short humor. Pays to $50, for articles and fiction, $10 for fillers, to $100 for color cover photos, $10 to $25 for other photos, on publication. Query.

RESORT MANAGEMENT– 1509 Madison Ave., P.O. Box 4169, Memphis, TN 38104. Allen J. Fagans, V.P./Editor.
Case histories, 1,000 to 1,500 words, on successful resort operation and management programs: attracting and entertaining guests, saving money, servicing bar, kitchen, housekeeping, front desk departments. Pays to $75 for articles, $5 for black-and-white photos, on publication. Query with outline. Reports in two weeks.

ROCK PRODUCTS– 300 West Adams St., Chicago, IL 60606. Sidney Levine, Editor
Articles, from 1,000 words, on production methods in construction minerals fields: cement, lime, gypsum, sand and gravel, crushed stone, slag, and lightweight aggregates. Pays $35 per published page, after publication.

SELLING SPORTING GOODS–717 North Michigan Ave., Chicago, IL 60611. Thomas B. Doyle, Managing Editor.
Articles, 1,000 to 1,200 words, with black-and-white photos, on retail sporting goods stores with outstanding promotions, advertising, merchandising, training programs, etc. Pays on acceptance, $50 to $100 per article. Query.

SHOPPING CENTER WORLD–461 8th Ave., New York, NY 10001. Davis Crippen, Editor.
Articles, to 2,5000 words, on new developments in shopping center design, construction, and operation: sites, financing, etc. Pays to $200, on publication. Query.

SKIING TRADE NEWS– One Park Ave., New York, NY 10016. William Grout, Editor.
How-to articles, 1,500 words, with black-and-white photos, on making profits in retail ski shops. Brief news items on new developments in ski equipment retailing. Pays 10¢ a word, on publication.

SNACK FOOD MAGAZINE– Harcourt Bldg., Duluth, MN 55802. Jerry Hess, Editor.
Articles, 1,200 to 1,400 words, for snack food industry, on trade news, personalities, promotions, ad campaigns, production and packaging, etc. Related short pieces, photos. Pays 5¢ to 7¢ per word used, $5 to $7 per photo used, on acceptance.

THE SOUTH MAGAZINE– Trend Publications, Inc., P.O. Box 2350, Tampa, FL 33601. Harris H. Mullen, Publisher.
Articles, 500 to 3,500 words on southern business: companies, people, successes and failures, urban problems and solutions. Pays $50 to $300, on acceptance. Query.

SOUTHERN HARDWARE– 1760 Peachtree Rd., Atlanta, GA 30309. Ralph E. Kirby, Editor.
Articles, 800 to 1,000 words, on merchandising activities and operational methods of specific Southern hardware retailers. Pays $40 per printed page and up, on acceptance. Query.

SOUVENIRS AND NOVELTIES–20-21 Wagaraw Rd., Fair Lawn, NJ 07410. Martin Dowd, Editor.
Articles, 1,500 words, quoting souvenir shop managers on items that sell well, display ideas to improve sales, problems in selling souvenirs and novelties, and industry trends. Pays from $1 per published inch, $10 for black-and-white photos.

SPECIALTY SALESMAN– 307 North Michigan Ave., Chicago, IL 60601. Jane Bjoraas, Editor.
Articles, 300 to 1,200 words, for independent salesperson selling to homes, stores, industries and business. Pays 3¢ a word, on acceptance.

THE SPECTATOR– 203 King of Prussia Rd., Radnor, PA 19089. T.J. Casper, Editor.
Articles, 1,200 to 2,000 words with black-and-white photos, on insurance and financial management. Pays $50 to $100, on acceptance.

SPORTING GOODS DEALER– 1212 North Lindbergh, St. Louis, MO 63166. Roland Burke, Managing Editor.
Articles, about 500 words, on news, merchandising ideas, personalities. Photos of sporting goods stores and people. Pays from 2¢ a word for articles, $5 per photo, on publication.

SUPERVISION– 424 No. Third, Burlington, IA 52601. G.B. McKee, Editor.
Self-help articles, 1,500 to 2,000 words, for management executives: supervisors, foremen, and production managers. Pays 2¢ a word, on publication. Query.

TENNIS INDUSTRY– 915 N.E. 125th St., Suite 2C, North Miami, FL 33161. Michael Keighley, Editor.
Articles, 1,000 to 2,000 words, on business end of tennis; tennis products, new court

surfaces, recreational center planning, costs of creating and operating tennis complexes at schools, etc. Pays 5¢ a word, on publication. Query.

TEXTILE SERVICES MANAGEMENT–P.O. Box 4021, Mountain View, CA 94040. Stanley Daly, Editor.
Articles, any length, on drycleaning and/or laundry, linen supply, industrial laundering, garment rental, etc. Query. Pay varies.

TEXTILE WORLD– 1175 Peachtree St. N.E., Atlanta, GA 30361. L.A. Christiansen, Chief Editor.
Articles, 1,000 to 3,000 words, with photos, on technology of manufacturing and finishing textiles, increasing textile-mill efficiency, modernizing, management techniques, marketing, etc. Pay varies, on acceptance.

TRAILER/BODY BUILDERS–1602 Harold St., Houston, TX 77006. Paul Schenck, Editor.
Articles on engineering, sales, and management ideas for truck body and truck trailer manufacturers. Pays from $50 a printed page, on acceptance.

TRAINING– One Park Ave., New York, NY 10016. Harold Littledale, Editor.
Articles, 1,500 to 2,000 words, on how organizations (excluding schools) train employees. Pays 5¢ a word, on acceptance. Query.

THE WELDING DISTRIBUTOR– 5811 Dempster St., Morton Grove, IL 60053. Don Jefferson, Editor.
Articles, 1,000 to 3,500 words, on selling welding and safety equipment and supplies, merchandising, running small business, keeping records, personal and personnel management. Cartoons and photos. Pays 2½¢ per word, on publication.

WESTERN OUTFITTER– 5314 Bingle Rd., Houston, TX 77018.
Articles, to 1,500 words, with photos, on merchandising western wear and equipment; tips on retail sales and promotion of familiar items. Pays 4¢ per word, $6.50 per picture, on publication. Query.

WESTERN PAINT REVIEW– 1833 West 8th St., Los Angeles, CA 90057. E.C. Ansley, Editor.
Articles, 1,000 to 2,000 words, with 3 to 4 photos, on paint and painting industries in 13 Western states. Pays 4¢ per word and $3 per photo, on publication. Query.

WINES & VINES– 703 Market St., San Francisco, CA 94103. Philip Hiaring, Editor/Publisher.
Articles, about 1,000 words, with photos, for wine industry, emphasizing marketing. Pays 3¢ a word, on acceptance.

WOODWORKING & FURNITURE DIGEST–Hitchcock Bldg., Wheaton, IL 60187. R.D. Rea, Editor.
Articles, 1,200 to 1,600 words, with photos, on management, production, and engineering in industries using wood as primary material, case history manufacturing pieces. No sawmill, logging, paper industry or forestry pieces. Pays $35 to $50 per published page. Query.

WORLD COFFEE & TEA–McKeand Publications Inc., 636 First Ave., West Haven, CT 06516. J.J. Martino, Editor.
First person pieces from overseas areas producing coffee and tea. Pays $200 per page. Query.

WORLD OIL–Gulf Publishing Co., P.O. Box 2608, Houston, TX 77001. R. W. Scott, Editor.
Engineering and operations articles, 3,000 to 4,000 words, on petroleum industry exploration, drilling or producing. Photos or drawings with engineering articles. Pays from $25 per printed page. Query.

TRAVEL

AFRICA REPORT— 833 U.N. Plaza, New York, NY 10017. Anthony Hughes, Editor.
Articles, 1,000 to 4,000 words with photos, on African current affairs and life-styles, travel in Africa, based on solid research. Pays $40 to $150, on publication.

AIRFAIR INTERLINE MAGAZINE—9800 South Sepulveda Blvd., Suite 520, Los Angeles, CA 90045. Crista C. Gillette, Editor.
For airline employees. Travel articles, 1,000 to 1,500 words with black-and-white photos, with specific details on shopping, sightseeing, dining, etc., including current prices, addresses. Pays to $75, within 30 days of publication.

ALOFT— 2701 South Bayshore Dr., Miami, FL 33133. Karl Y. Wickstrom, Editor.
National Airlines' in-flight magazine. Articles, 1,300 words, with fresh approach to cities along National route: offbeat angles on places to go, shopping, dining. Pays $150 to $200. Query.

ARIZONA HIGHWAYS— 2039 West Lewis St., Phoenix, AZ 85009. Joseph Stacey, Editor.
Overstocked through 1975. Queries only.

AWAY— ALA Auto and Travel Club, 888 Worcester St., Wellesley, MA 02181. Gerard J. Gagnon, Editor.
Articles, 1,000 and 1,200 words, on travel, travel-related subjects (photo hints, tipping, etc.), tourist attractions, auto trips, and outdoor activities, with New England slant. No hunting pieces. Light, non-seasonal articles, 600 to 800 words. Black-and-white photos, 5 x 7 or 8 x 10, with articles; photo-essays. Pays 10¢ a word, on acceptance. $5 to $10 per photo on publication. Query.

BON APPETIT—5900 Wilshire Blvd., Los Angeles, CA 90036.
Devoted to fine food, wines, travel, entertaining, restaurants, new products and culinary equipment. Travel articles, 1,200 to 1,500 words, should mention specific restaurants, hotels, resorts, foods, and wine. Pays 10¢ per word, $25 per color photo, $10 for black-and-white photo.

BRANIFF PLACE—15383 N.W. 7th Ave., Miami, FL 33169. Seymour Gerber, Editor and Publisher.
Braniff airlines in-flight magazine. Travel articles, 750 to 2,000 words, on Braniff destination cities and personalities in these cities; accompanied by color transparencies (35mm, 2¼, or 4 x 5). Pays $125 to $250.

BUYWAYS—1000 Sunset Ridge Rd., Northbrook, IL 60062. Anne Springhorn, Editor.
Official publication of the National Association of Consumers and Travelers (NACT). Travel articles, 500 to 2,500 words, emphasizing budget. Seasonal materials should be submitted 4 months ahead. Pays 10¢ to 20¢ a word, on acceptance. Query.

CHEVRON USA—P.O. Box 6227, San Jose, CA 95150. Marian May, Editor.
Articles, 500 to 1,500 words, on travel in western, southern and eastern states. Humorous anecdotes, 100 to 250 words, and cartoons. Pays 15¢ a word and up, on acceptance. $35 for black-and-white photos, $50 to $200 for color.

CHICAGO TRIBUNE (Travel Section)—Tribune Square, Chicago, IL 60611. Kermit Holt, Travel Editor; Alfred S. Borcover, Associate Travel Editor.
Descriptive travel articles, 800 to 1,200 words, with photos. Pays $40 to $100 for articles; $50 for page 1 color photos, on acceptance.

CLIPPER MAGAZINE—East/West Network, Inc., 5900 Wilshire Blvd., Suite 300, Los Angeles, CA 90036. James Clark, Editor.
Articles, 1,000 to 1,500 words, on international travel along Pan Am route system. Pays $150 to $200 within 60 days of acceptance. See *PSA Magazine.*

THE CONTINENTAL MAGAZINE—Room 956, Central Office Bldg., Ford Motor Company, Dearborn, MI 48121. Robert M. Hodesh, Editor-in-Chief.
Sophisticated service articles, 1,300 to 1,700 words, on travel, entertainment, shopping, sports, for well-to-do. Pays on acceptance. Query.

CONTINENTAL TRAILWAYS MAGAZINE—Suite 409, 1500 Jackson, Dallas, TX 75201. John F. McCormick, Editor.
Articles, 400 to 800 words, with photos, giving general information on an area or special travel event. Pays $50 per article, $35 per black-and-white photo, $50 for color, on publication.

COSMOPOLITAN—224 West 57th St., New York, NY 10019. Helen Gurley Brown, Editor.
First-person narratives, 2,500 to 3,000 words, about vacation spots within possible price range of singles. Accompanying candid 35 mm photos. Pay varies. Query Roberta Ashley, Articles Editor.

DESERT MAGAZINE—Palm Desert, CA 92260. Bill Knyvett, Editor.
Illustrated features about travel in the West, 500 to 2,500 words. Pays 2¢ a word on publication, $5 and up for photos.

DISCOVERY—Allstate Motor Club, Northbrook, IL 60062. Alan Rosenthal, Editor.
Articles, 1,500 to 2,500 words, with photos: first-person accounts of weekend or vacation trips, occasional humor pieces related to the motoring scene. Pays $100 to $400, on acceptance.

ENTHUSIAST—Harley-Davidson Motor Co., P.O. Box 654, Milwaukee, WI 53201. T. C. Bolfert, Editor.
Emphasis on photo-journalism. Fiction and articles, to 2,500 words, on motorcycling subjects. Travel pieces, particularly about places not readily accessible by car. Pays 5¢ a word, $7.50 to $15 per photo, on publication.

FLIGHTIME—See *PSA Magazine*.

FORD TIMES—Ford Motor Co., The American Rd., Dearborn, MI 48121. William E. Pauli, Managing Editor.
Articles, to 1,500 words, to interest young adults: recreation and travel related to car ownership, little-known places to visit. Humor. Pays $250 and up, on acceptance. Query.

HOLIDAY—1100 Waterway Blvd., Indianapolis, IN 46202. Kathryn Klassen, Managing Editor.
Articles on travel and leisure subjects, 1,000 to 2,000 words. Pays on publication. Query.

IRELAND OF THE WELCOMES—590 Fifth Ave., New York, NY 10036. Elizabeth Healy, Editor.
Irish cultural, sporting and tourism events, 1,200 to 2,000 words, with black-and-white glossy photos. Pay varies.

LIVELY WORLD—Caldwell Communications, Inc., 747 Third Ave., New York, NY 10017. Robert H. Spencer, Editor.
For in-room use at Marriott hotels. Articles, 800 to 3,000 words, on U.S. and foreign cities and countries, focusing on people, history and social issues. Color photo features. Pays $50 to $400, on publication; extra for color transparencies. Send for writer's guide.

THE LUFKIN LINE—P.O. Box 849, Lufkin, TX 75901. Virginia R. Allen, Editor.
Articles, 1,000 to 1,200 words, on travel in U.S. and Canada, with 8 to 10 color photos or transparencies. Pays $50 for articles, $25 for color transparency used on cover; on acceptance.

MAINLINER—See *PSA Magazine*.

MEXICAN WORLD—2617 East Hennepin Ave., Minneapolis, MN 55413.
Articles, fiction and poetry, any length, on Mexico as seen by tourist, to increase understanding of Mexican culture and people. Pay varies. Query.

THE MIDWEST MOTORIST—3917 Lindell Ave., St. Louis, MO 63108.
Articles, 1,000 to 2,000 words with black-and-white photos, on travel and transportation for midwest readership. Pays $50 to $200, on acceptance. Sample copies on request.

MINNESOTA AAA MOTORIST—7 Traveler's Trail, Burnsville, MN 55337. Ron D. Johnson, Editor.
Articles, 800 to 1,200 words, on domestic and foreign travel, motoring, car care, safety; outdoor recreation and related subjects. Pays $150 and up for articles, $15 and up for photos, $15 for cartoons, on acceptance.

MOTOR NEWS—Auto Club Dr., Dearborn, MI 48126.
Colorful articles, 800 to 2,000 words, on American tourist destinations, with information on costs, trip planning, good and bad points; interested in pieces with Michigan slant. Photos. Pays $100 and up, on acceptance.

MOTORLAND—150 Van Ness Ave., San Francisco, CA 94101. William C. Ellis, Editor.
Articles, 800 to 2,000 words with black-and-white or color photos, on western travel or with fresh approach to popular foreign travel destination.

NATIONAL GEOGRAPHIC—17th and M Sts., N.W., Washington, DC 20036. Gilbert M. Grosvenor, Editor.
First-person narratives on geography (travel, exploration, natural history, archaeology, etc.), 2,000 to 8,000 words; shorter lengths (2,000 to 4,000 words) very desirable. Pays $1,500 to $3,500 and up, on acceptance; good original color transparencies greatly increase chance of acceptance and amount paid. Writer's guide available. Query.

NATIONAL MOTORIST—65 Battery St., San Francisco, CA 94111. Jim Donaldson, Editor.
Illustrated articles, 500 to 1,100 words, for California motorist, on motoring in the West, care care, motor travel techniques, roads, interesting people and places in western U.S., outdoor subjects, etc. Pays 10¢ a word and up; $15 and up per black-and-white photo; $25 and up per color transparency; on acceptance.

THE NEW YORK TIMES—Times Square, New York, NY 10036. Robert W. Stock, Travel Editor.
Travel articles, 1,000 to 2,500 words, with realistic coverage. Query first, indicating specific subject, approach, time and purpose of visit (no articles based on sponsored trips), authors' credentials. Pays 10¢ a word, $50 per black-and-white photo used.

NORTHLINER— 1999 Shepard Rd., St. Paul, MN 55116. James Carney, Editor.
In-flight magazine for North Central Airlines. Articles, 1,000 to 2,000 words, with 35 mm color transparencies, on travel, business, personalities and humor in North Central route area. Cartoons; no poetry. Pays $50 to $400, on acceptance. Query. Sample copy on request.

NORTHWEST— *Sunday Oregonian,* 1320 S.W. Broadway, Portland, OR 97201. J.R. Bianco, Editor.
Articles, to 1,500 words, with black-and-white photos, on travel in Pacific Northwest. Pays $40 per magazine page, plus $15 per photo, 10th of each month.

ODYSSEY— 300 South Wacker Dr., Chicago, IL 60606. Jerry Reedy, Editorial Director.
Gulf Travel Club magazine. Articles, 2,500 words, on travel destinations. Shorter pieces, 1,000 words: travel economizing how-tos, tips, profiles of little-known towns or areas, outdoor activities, etc. Pays about 2¢ a word, on acceptance. Query.

PSA, THE CALIFORNIA MAGAZINE— East/West Network, Inc., 5900 Wilshire Blvd., Suite 300, Los Angeles, CA 90036. Thomas Shess, Editor.
Pacific Southwest Airlines in-flight magazine. Seeks travel, business articles of 1,500 words, with photos, to interest business travelers. Pays on publication. Same address and requirements for Allegheny Air System *Executive,* Continental Airlines *Flightime,* Delta Air Lines *Sky,* Pan Am *Clipper,* Hughes Airwest *Sundance,* and United Air Lines *Mainliner.*

PASTIMES—720 Fifth Ave., New York, NY 10019. Thomas Humber, Editor.
Eastern Airlines in-flight magazine. Non-controversial articles, 2,000 words, on Eastern destinations; interesting hobbies, people, occupations, events. Pays $50 to $200, on publication. Query.

RX SPORTS AND TRAVEL— 447 South Main St., Hillsboro, IL 62049. Harry Luecke, Editor.
Articles, 1,500 to 3,000 words, on sports, recreation, leisure and unusual places to travel, of interest to physicians, with or without a doctor involved. Profiles of physicians with unique hobby. Pays to $350 for articles with 35 mm color transparencies or black-and-white photos. Query.

SIGNATURE— 260 Madison Ave., New York, NY 10016. Josh Eppinger, Executive Editor.
Sophisticated, offbeat travel articles, to 2,500 words, on foreign and domestic travel. Articles must reflect writer's motivation and presence. Avoid "destination" pieces. Offbeat sports, business and social impact articles for affluent audience. Pays $600. Query.

SKY—See *PSA Magazine.*

SUNDANCE—See *PSA Magazine.*

TWA AMBASSADOR— 1999 Shepard Rd., St. Paul, MN 55116. James Morgan, Editor.
TWA in-flight magazine. Travel articles, 1,000 to 2,500 words, with color transparencies (35 mm or larger), with specific angle; "no where-to-eat, where-to-stay pieces." Also humor, sports, business, personalities, modern living. International readership. Pays to $600, on acceptance. Query. Writer's guide available on request.

TRAVEL— Travel Bldg., Floral Park, NY 11001. Robert H. Rufa, Editor.
Personal-experience travel articles, 1,500 to 2,000 words, on places to visit, what to see and do, with costs and prices wherever appropriate. Photos necessary: 35 mm or larger original color transparencies or black-and-white prints. Pays $150 to $300, on acceptance, depending on photos. Query.

TRAVEL AGE WEST— 582 Market St., San Francisco, CA 94104. Martin B. Deutsch. Editor.
Articles, 800 to 1,000 words, with photos, on any aspect of travel useful to travel agents. Include names, addresses, prices of places described. Pays $1.50 per column inch, at end of month of publication. Query.

TRAVEL AND LEISURE—61 West 51st St., New York, NY 10019. Caskie Stinnett, Editor-in-Chief.
For holders of American Express Cards. Sophisticated articles, 2,500 to 3,000 words, on travel and the good life. Pays $500 to $1,500. Articles on assignment. Query.

TRAVEL TRAILER—Woodall Publishing Co., 500 Hyacinth Place, Highland Park, IL 60035. Jerry Pinkham, Editor.
Articles, 1,200 to 2,500 words with photos, on specific, recreational vehicle-related travel experiences, including information about routes, costs, recreational opportunities and facilities, scenic and historical attractions. Pays to 10¢ a word, on acceptance. Query. Send for free copy and writer's guide.

WESTERN'S WORLD–141 El Camino Dr., Suite 110, Beverly Hills, CA 90212. Frank
    M. Hiteshew, Editor.
    Western Airlines in-flight magazine. Travel and special-interest articles, 1,500 to
    2,000 words, on the West: artists, food, sports, ecology, etc. Pays 10¢ a word, on
    publication. Query.

CITY AND REGIONAL MAGAZINES

The following list gives a representative sample of the many city and regional magazines
published across the country. These publications offer writers an excellent market for all
types of material – general-interest articles, travel features, photo-features and fillers
with photos, and even, occasionally, short stories.
    City magazines, usually published by chambers of commerce, are particularly
interested in articles and features that build local pride, focusing on business, history,
local politics, and cultural and urban affairs.
    It's essential for writers to query editors of these publications before sending
completed manuscripts, and to enclose a list of photos available, or even a few sample
prints or transparencies. Always study past issues of these magazines carefully to learn
what has been used recently, and to determine a magazine's style and slant.

ACCENT/GRAND RAPIDS–Accent Organization, Inc., 3120 Hall S.E., Grand Rapids,
    MI 49506. Anne Frahm, Editor.
    Articles, 2,500 to 5,000 words, on Grand Rapids: local business, cultural, political
    and community interests. Pays $25 to $75, on publication. Query.

ADIRONDACK LIFE–Willsboro, NY 12996. Lionel A. Atwill, Editor.
    Articles, 750 to 2,000 words, on artists, personalities, history, events, unusual trips,
    collectibles, geography, wildlife, etc., related to Adirondacks. Color transparencies,
    35mm or larger, black-and-white prints, 4 x 5 or larger, or drawings must accompany
    articles. Pays $75 to $100 per article, $30 for color photos, and $10 for
    black-and-white photos, on publication. Query.

ALABAMA REVIEW–History Dept., Auburn University, Auburn, AL 36830. Malcolm
    C. McMillan, Editor.
    Historical, scholarly material on Alabama and southern region.

ALASKA GEOGRAPHIC–Alaska Geographic Society, Box 4-EEE, Anchorage, AK
    99509.
    Quarterly magazine of Alaska Geographic Society. Informative articles without
    scientific terminology on geographic subjects – adventure, exploration, geology,
    biology, resources and their uses – in areas with physical or economic relationship to
    Alaska (northern Canada, Siberia, Japan), with color photos. Pays to $500, on
    publication. Query The Editors.

ALASKA JOURNAL–422 Calhoun, Juneau, AK 99801. R. N. DeArmond, Editor.
    Soundly researched articles on Alaska and Yukon history, 500 to 5,000 words, with
    black-and-white and color photos, and articles on Alaska artists. Pays about 2¢ a
    word, on publication. Query.

ALASKA, THE MAGAZINE OF LIFE ON THE LAST FRONTIER–Box 4-EEE,
    Anchorage, AK 99509. Bob Henning, Editor and Publisher.
    Authentic articles, to 3,000 words, on all aspects of life in Far North, preferably by
    residents. Color or black-and-white photos desirable. No fiction or poetry. Pays $10
    to $100, on publication.

THE AMERICAN WEST–599 College Ave., Palo Alto, CA 94306. George Pfeiffer III,
    Editor.
    Articles on western history, natural history, conservation, environment, 2,500 to
    4,000 words. Pays to $300, 30 to 60 days after acceptance. Query.

ARIZONA—Arizona *Republic,* 120 East Van Buren St., Phoenix, AZ 85004. Bud DeWald, Editor.
Articles, 500 to 2,500 words; short fillers and humor, photos and drawings, and cartoons. All material except cartoons must be on subjects related to Arizona. Pays $25 to $175, on scheduling for publication.

ARIZONA AND THE WEST—University of Arizona Press, Library 308, University of Arizona, Tucson, AZ 85721. Harwood P. Hinton, Editor.
Scholarly articles on history of trans-Mississippi West, and edited original documents, 4,000 to 6,000 words. Accompanying photographs and maps. No payment.

ARIZONA HIGHWAYS—2039 West Lewis Ave., Phoenix, AZ 85009. Joseph Stacey, Editor.
Queries only.

ATLANTA JOURNAL AND CONSTITUTION MAGAZINE—Box 4689, Atlanta, GA 30302. Andrew Sparks, Editor.
Nonfiction feature material, 800 to 1,500 words, on subjects of regional interest. Pays on publication. Query.

THE ATLANTIC ADVOCATE—Gleaner Bldg., Phoenix Sq., Fredericton, N.B., Canada. James D. Morrison, Editor.
Prefers regional articles about Eastern Canada, but also considers general-interest articles, especially unusual, well-researched pieces with photos. High-quality fiction, for family reading, to 2,000 words. Poetry overstocked at present. High quality color scenic photos, all seasons, for covers. Pays 5¢ a word, on publication.

AUSTIN— Austin Chamber of Commerce, Box 1967, Austin, TX 78767. Ann B. Marett, Editor.
Articles, 800 to 1,500 words, on Austin. Local photos. No fiction or cartoons. Rates negotiable. Query.

BALTIMORE MAGAZINE— Baltimore Chamber of Commerce, 22 Light St., Baltimore, MD 21202. James F. Waesche, Editor.
Articles, to 3,500 words, on metropolitan area problems, institutions, attractions and personalities. Special emphasis on topics of interest to Baltimore business community. Pays to $200. Some photos. Query essential.

THE BEAVER— Hudson's Bay House, Winnipeg, Manitoba, Canada, R3C 2R1. Mrs. Helen Burgess, Editor.
Fillers, 700 to 1,500 words, and factual, well-written articles, 3,000 words, on historical or modern aspects of Canadian northwest and Arctic regions and their people with photos or drawings. Pays about 5¢ a word, on acceptance.

BERKELEY BARB— Box 1247, Berkeley, CA 94701. Jim Schreiber, Editor.
Weekly newspaper. Vivid, fast-paced, accurate articles, 1,000 words, about people caught up by oppressive institutions, typifying pressing social issues, of interest to San Francisco Bay Area readers. Pays 50¢ per column inch, on publication.

BIRMINGHAM— Birmingham Area Chamber of Commerce, 1914 Sixth Ave. North, Birmingham, AL 35203.
Articles of local and regional interest, 1,500 to 3,000 words. Photos on assignment. Pays on publication. Query.

BLADE SUNDAY MAGAZINE (formerly *Toledo Blade Sunday Magazine)*—Toledo, OH 43660. Mike Tressler, Editor.
Toledo-area material: in-depth personality stories, current news angles, non-fiction, to 4,000 words, preferably with photos or drawings. Pays $35 to $75, $5 to $50 per photo or drawing, on publication. Query.

BOSTON MAGAZINE— 38 Newbury St., Boston, MA 02116.
Not in the market for freelance material.

BUCKS COUNTY PANORAMA– 50 East Court St., Doylestown, PA 18901. Carla Coutts, Editor.
Regional articles and fiction, 2,000 to 5,000 words, oriented toward Bucks County, on historical or contemporary subjects. Photos or illustrations appreciated. Pays $10 to $15, on publication.

BUFFALO SPREE MAGAZINE– P.O. Box 38, Buffalo, NY 14226. Richard G. Shotell, Editor.
Stimulating essays, 2,000 to 4,000 words, exploring contemporary social, philosophical, artistic and environmental concerns. Occasional fiction, 2,000 to 4,000 words. High-quality, experimental poetry, 2 to 52 lines. Pays $75 for lead article or story, $1.00 per line for poetry with $20 maximum.

CALIFORNIA JOURNAL– 1617 10th St., Sacramento, CA 95814. Ed Salzman, Editor.
Well-written, expert, objective and analytical articles on California state government and politics, of varying length. Pays by arrangement. Study back issues and query.

CALIFORNIA TODAY– 750 Rider Park Dr., San Jose, CA 95131. Fred Dickey, Editor.
Sunday magazine of San Jose *Mercury-News*. Articles and photo-features with California tie-in, to reflect the "good life," with strong emphasis on sports, outdoors, leisure home. No fiction or poetry.

CANADIAN GEOGRAPHICAL JOURNAL– 488 Wilbrod St., Ottawa, Ont., Canada K1N 6M8. David Maclellan, Editor.
Articles and pictorial features about Canada, 2,000 to 3,000 words. Some foreign material accepted. Photos essential. Pays on publication.

CHARLOTTE MAGAZINE–P.O. Box 15843, Charlotte, NC 28210. Betty Hill Folts, Editor.
Articles, 500 to 3,000 words with photos, on business, personalities, unusual lifestyles or hobbies of people in North Carolina, preferably within Charlotte-Metrolina area. Also articles on ex-Charlotteans who have achieved some fame or are engaged in some unusual occupation. Fillers, to 750 words; small line drawings. Pays to $150, for features; $30 to $75 for shorter articles, on publication.

CHEVRON USA– P.O. Box 6227, San Jose, CA 95150. Marian May, Editor.
Articles, 500 to 1,500 words, on travel in western, southern and eastern states, family activities, wildlife, conservation. Humorous anecdotes, 100 to 250 words; cartoons. Pays 15¢ a word, $35 for black-and-white photos, $50 to $200 for color, on acceptance.

CHICAGO– 500 North Michigan Ave., Chicago, IL 60611. Allen H. Kelson, Editor.
Nonfiction and fiction related to Chicago, 1,000 to 5,000 words. Pay varies, on the first of the month of publication. Query.

CHICAGO HISTORY– Clark St., at North Ave., Chicago, IL 60614. Isabel Grossner, Editor.
Articles, 4,500 words, on historical matters of Chicago area. Pays $250, on acceptance. Query.

CINCINNATI– 120 West Fifth St.,Greater Cincinnati Chamber of Commerce, Cincinnati, Ohio 45202.
Articles about Greater Cincinnati—people, places and things and broader articles of interest to Cincinnati residents, 800 to 1,800 words. Pays 6¢ per word, on publication.

CLEVELAND– 1740 Chester Ave., Cleveland, OH 44114. Michael Roberts, Editor.
Articles, 75 to 8,000 words, for or about Clevelanders or the Cleveland area. Pays 10¢ a word, on publication.

COAST MAGAZINE– 291 South La Cienega Blvd., Beverly Hills, CA 90211. Colman Andrews, Editor.

General-interest articles, 2,000 to 3,000 words, emphasizing California culture, society, and politics. Pay varies, 2 to 4 weeks after publication.

COLORADO MAGAZINE– 7190 West 14th Ave., Denver, CO 80215.
Exciting adventure, both current and historical, about people and events in Rocky Mountain West, from 1,500 to 3,000 words with photos. Pays 12¢ a word, on acceptance.

COLUMBUS DISPATCH SUNDAY MAGAZINE– Columbus, OH 43216. Robert K. Waldron, Editor.
Articles, to 1,800 words, with strong Ohio slant. Pays from 3¢ a word, $5 for photos, tenth of month after publication.

COMMONWEALTH– Virginia State Chamber of Commerce, 611 East Franklin, Richmond, VA 23219. James S. Wamsley, Editor.
Articles, 1,500 to 3,000 words, with sophisticated Virginia slant. No stock history or routine travel pieces. Pays about 5¢ a word. Query.

CONTEMPORARY– The Denver *Post,* Denver, CO 80201. Dick Martin, Editor.
Sunday supplement. News features, 500 to 1,500 words, with photos and drawings, keyed to Rocky Mountain area preferably. Submissions must be exclusive to *Contemporary* in Colorado-Wyoming-New Mexico area. Pays $20 to $75, $7.50 for photos used, on publication. Using very limited number of freelance articles at this time. Query.

COUNTRY JOURNAL– Box 870, Manchester Center, VT 05255. Richard Ketchum, Editor.
Articles, 250 to 3,000 words, on how-to of country living, and serious reporting of issues affecting rural New England life; real estate, conservation, nature, communities, history; photography. Pay varies, on acceptance.

DALLAS– 1507 Pacific Ave., Dallas, TX 75201.
Dallas metro-interest articles and features, 4,000 words, to explore Dallas environment, heritage, growth, and human resources. Query first – all articles written on assignment. Pays $150 and up, on acceptance. Uses Dallas writers only.

DAYTON, U.S.A.– Dayton Area Chamber of Commerce, 111 West First St., Dayton, OH 45402. Kathleen Turner, Editor.
Published bi-monthly for community decision makers in business, industry, education and home. Article length, 2,000 to 3,000 words. Photographs or drawings to illustrate articles or as feature spread. No payment. Query.

DESERT MAGAZINE– Palm Desert, CA 92260. Bill Knyvett, Editor.
Illustrated features, 500 to 2,500 words, about the West and travel in this area. Pays 2¢ a word, $5 and up for photos, on publication.

THE DES MOINES SUNDAY REGISTER PICTURE–*Des Moines Register and Tribune,* 715 Locust St., Des Moines, IA 50304.
Articles and photos about Iowa and Iowans, to 1,000 words. Pays on publication; a minimum of $15 for black-and-white photos and $25 for color transparencies.

DETROIT– Detroit Free Press, 321 West Lafayette Blvd., Detroit, MI 48231. Rogers Worthington, Editor.
Articles, 1,000 to 2,500 words, on Detroit metropolitan area and Michigan, including personality profiles. Pays $100 to $200 per article, on acceptance. Query.

THE DETROITER– 150 Michigan Ave., Detroit, MI 48226. William Hinds, Editor.
Articles, 1,200 to 2,000 words, with photos, on sports, personalities, history, science, medicine and cultural activities, as they affect Detroiters. Pay varies. Query.

DISCOVER– *Sunday Bulletin,* 30th and Market Sts., Philadelphia, PA 19101. Jack Wilson, Editor.

Articles, 300 to 1,500 words, with black-and-white photos, relevant to lifestyle of Greater Philadelphia area. Pays varying rates.

DOWN EAST– Camden, ME 04843. Duane Doolittle, Editor.
Articles, 1,500 to 2,500 words, on subjects related to Maine. Pays 3¢ a word and up, $5 to $10 for black-and-white photos, $15 to $25 for color, on acceptance.

THE DULUTHIAN– Chamber of Commerce, 220 Medical Arts Building, Duluth, MN 55802.
Articles, 750 to 1,500 words, on Duluth area: people, business developments, some civic and social problems or activities and some outdoor or area sports interests. No payment.

EMPIRE MAGAZINE– The Denver *Post,* P.O. Box 1709, Denver, CO 80201. Carl Skiff, Editor.
Articles, 500 to 2,500 words, with strong regional peg about people, events, history, adventure, issues. Photos may help sell article. Pays about 5¢ a word, on acceptance. Query.

FIESTA– 140 North Federal Hwy., Boca Raton, FL 33432.
Informative articles, 1,000 to 2,000 words, on people, places, events in southern Florida, with emphasis on cultural, social and historical aspects of region. Pays by arrangement.

FLORIDA TREND– P.O. Box 2350, 1306 West Kennedy Blvd., Tampa, FL 33601.
Articles about Florida business and businessmen, to 3,000 words. Photos. Rates negotiable, average 6¢ a word. Query.

THE FLORIDIAN– St. Petersburg *Times,* Box 1121, St. Petersburg, FL 33731.
In-depth Florida features – personality profiles, controversial subjects in medicine, law, education, politics. Short, well-researched pieces, 800 to 1,500 words, on nature, wildlife, science, crime, history. Photos and line drawings. Pays $50 to $150, more for exceptional material, on acceptance. Query.

FOCUS-MIDWEST– Box 3086, St. Louis, MO 63130. Charles I. Klotzer, Editor.
Controversial regional and national articles, 900 to 3,000 words, of direct concern to readers in Midwest, particularly Missouri and Illinois, on political, social and cultural issues, especially urban problems in Chicago, St. Louis, and Kansas City. No taboos. Pays on publication.

FRONTIER TIMES– See *True West.*

GOLDEN GATE NORTH– P.O. Box 3028, Santa Rosa, CA 95403.
In-depth articles, 1,500 words, on local and regional issues and personalities, interviews; photo-features, black-and-white photos. Pays 5¢ a word and $10 per photo, on publication.

HOUSTON BUSINESS JOURNAL– 5314 Bingle Rd., Houston, TX 77018. Mike Weingart, Editor.
Articles, to 3,000 words, on business news from Houston area. Pays $1.50 per column inch, $5 per cartoon, on publication.

INCREDIBLE IDAHO– Room 108, Capitol Bldg., Boise ID 83720. Dorine Goertzen, Editor.
Illustrated articles on Idaho, 1,000 to 2,500 words, and poems. Photos should be either 5 x 7 or 8 x 10 black-and-white glossies, or 2¼ x 2¼ to 4 x 5 color transparencies. Pays in copies. Query essential.

JACKSONVILLE MAGAZINE– P.O. Box 329, Jacksonville, FL 32201. Tom Ellis III, Editor.
Articles on Jacksonville area, 1,500 to 6,000 words; some photos, transparencies. Pays on publication. Query.

LONG ISLAND FORUM– P.O. Box 215, West Islip, NY 11795. Carl A. Starace, Editor.
Non-fiction, to 2,400 words, on Long Island history and folklore. Photos only when accompanying article. No payment. Query.

LOS ANGELES MAGAZINE– 352 North Rodeo Dr., Beverly Hills, CA 90210. Geoff Miller, Editor.
Topical articles, of particular relevance to active, affluent Southern Californians, to 2,500 words. Some photo stories and humor. Pays 5¢ to 10¢ a word, on publication. Query.

LOUISVILLE– 300 West Liberty St., Louisville, KY 40202. Betty Lou Amster, Editor.
Articles, 1,000 to 2,000 words, on community problems, Louisville business success stories, for business leaders of Louisville metropolitan area. Some photos and art. Pays $35 and up, on acceptance. Query.

MAINE ANTIQUE DIGEST– RFD 3, Box 76A, Waldoboro, ME 04572. Samuel Pennington, Editor.
Authoritative, entertaining articles, anecdotes, and interviews, on antiques market in New England; include black-and-white photos. Pays $25, on acceptance. Study magazine; query.

MARYLAND–2525 Riva Rd., Annapolis, MD 21401. M. E. Dougherty, Editor.
Well-researched articles, 600 to 2,000 words, on life in Maryland: agriculture, culture, economic, ethnics, human interest, travel, portraits of interesting Marylanders. Pays 6¢ a word, $20 per 8 x 10 black-and-white glossy photo, $25 per 35mm or 2¼ x 2¼ color transparency, on publication. Write for writer's guide.

MIAMI MAGAZINE–2825 Oak Ave., Miami, FL 33133. Gaeton Fonzi, Editor.
Articles, any length, which view with clarity, wit, and style all facets of South Florida lifestyle. Pay varies, on publication.

MIDWEST MAGAZINE–Chicago *Sun-Times,* Chicago, IL 60611.
Articles, 1,800 words, topical, preferably geared to Chicago and Chicago area interests. Pays $75 to $300. Query.

MISSOURI LIFE–1209 Elmerine Ave., Jefferson City, MO 65101. W. R. Nunn, Editor.
Articles, 1,500 to 3,000 words, with photos, on Missouri: history, scenery, commerce, culture, people. Some photo essays, original art on Missouri theme. Pays $50 for articles with color illustrations, $35 for pieces with black-and-white photos. Query.

MONTANA MAGAZINE OF THE NORTHERN ROCKIES–Box 894, Helena, MT 59601. Rick Graetz, Editor.
Articles, with black-and-white photos, on Montana: history, personalities, recreation, life in general. Pays by arrangment. Query.

MONTANA: THE MAGAZINE OF WESTERN HISTORY–Montana Historical Society, 225 North Roberts, Helena, MT 59601. Mrs. Vivian A. Paladin, Editor.
Well-written articles, 3,500 to 6,500 words, on history of American West, preferably lesser-known facets. Must be documented. Authentic photos, drawings, or engravings. Pays 1½¢ a word. Query.

NEBRASKALAND–Nebraska Game and Parks Commission, 2200 North 33rd St., Lincoln, NE 68503. Lowell Johnson, Managing Editor.
Articles on Nebraska: people, hunting, fishing, environment, travel, tourism, outdoors and history with 2¼ x 2¼ transparencies preferred, 35 mm or 4 x 5 acceptable. No payment.

NEVADA HIGHWAYS AND PARKS–State of Nevada Dept. of Highways, Carson City, NV 89701.
Articles, 1,000 to 2,500 words, with Nevada angle – historical, scenic, etc. – accompanied by black-and-white glossies, 4 x 5 or 2¼ x 2¼ transparencies. Pays 5¢ to 8¢ a word, $10 to $40 for photos, on scheduling.

NEW ENGLAND GALAXY—Old Sturbridge Village, Sturbridge, MA 01566. Catherine Fennelly, Editor.
Well-written nonfiction, to 3,000 words, preferably historical. New England material only. Pays $75 to $150, on publication. Query. Poetry, to 32 lines, and photos or drawings.

THE NEW ENGLANDER—Dublin, NH 03444. Bradford W. Ketchum, Jr., Editor.
Articles, 2,000 to 4,000 words with black-and-white glossy photos, describing New England business and public affairs: real estate, manufacturing, education, insurance, commercial fishing, transportation, agriculture, travel and recreation, politics, and government. Pays $50 up per published page. Query.

NEW HAMPSHIRE PROFILES—P.O. Box 68, Hanover, NH 03755. Peter E. Randall, Editor.
Nonfiction, to 2,000 words, on country living, history, nostalgia pertinent to New Hampshire. 8 x 10 black-and-white photos, 35 mm or larger transparencies related to N.H. Especially interested in photo essays. Pay varies, on publication. Query.

NEW JERSEY LIFE (formerly *Suburban New Jersey Life*) — Box 40, Maplewood, NJ 07040. Carlette Winslow, Editor.
New Jersey oriented articles, 2,000 to 3,000 words, with photos. Pays $25 to $100.

NEW MEXICO MAGAZINE—113 Washington Ave., Santa Fe, NM 87503. Sheila Tryk, Editor.
High-quality nonfiction, 250 to 2,000 words, on specific New Mexico subjects, Black-and-white and color photos, 35mm and up, of New Mexico locales and activities. Pays $25 to $300 for articles, $150 to $300 for photo assignments. Query.

NEW NORFOLK—475 St. Paul's Blvd., P.O. Box 327, Norfolk, VA 23501. Susan S. Phillips, Editor.
Articles, 500 to 3,000 words on business, civic or metropolitan-oriented topics in southeastern Virginia. Pays $25 to $150, on publication.

NORTH COUNTRY ANVIL—Box 37, Millville, MN 55957. Jack Miller, Editor.
Fiction and articles, 1,500 to 3,000 words, on individual and social struggles, alternative ways of living and thinking. Verse. Writers from upper midwest given special consideration. Pays in copies.

NORTHWEST—1320 S.W. Broadway, Portland, OR 97201. Sunday supplement magazine of the *Sunday Oregonian.* J. R. Bianco, Editor.
Articles, to 1,500 words: on profiles of individuals, social commentary in Pacific Northwest, and regional-interest subjects. Black-and-white photos with articles. No hunting articles. Pays $40 per magazine page, $15 per black-and-white photo, on 10th of each month. Stamped, self-addressed envelopes must accompany all manuscripts.

OKLAHOMA TODAY—Will Rogers Memorial Bldg., State Capitol, Oklahoma City, OK 73105. Bill Burchardt, Editor.
Articles on Oklahoma topics, to 1,500 words. Study past issues carefully before querying. Pays 5¢ a word, on publication.

OLD WEST—See *True West.*

OREGON HISTORICAL QUARTERLY—Oregon Historical Society, 1230 S.W. Park Ave., Portland, OR 97205. Thomas Vaughan, Editor.
Nonfiction, 1,000 to 20,000 words on North Pacific regional history of all kinds: diaries, recollections, etc. Interested in new material and new interpretations pertinent to Pacific Northwest, its role in U.S. and West. Illustrated articles welcome (both photos and drawings). Pays in ten copies.

OUTDOORS—1320 S.W. Broadway, Portland, OR 97201. Sunday supplement magazine of the *Sunday Oregonian.* J. R. Bianco, Editor.
Articles, to 800 words, on wildlife, outdoor sports of every kind, packing trails and

places, and any other type of outdoor activity of interest to residents of Northwest. Pays $40 per magazine page, $15 for each black-and-white photo used, on the 10th of each month.

PACIFIC SEARCH—715 Harrison St., Seattle, WA 98109. Harriet Rice, Editor.
Articles, to 2,400 words on wildlife, environment, and history of Pacific Northwest. Black-and-white and color photos. Pays from 3¢ to 10¢ a word. No payment for photos. Query.

PENINSULA LIVING—901 Marshall St., Redwood City, CA 94063. J. A. Gallagher, Editor.
Articles, 250 to 1,500 words, on Northern California subjects: regional travel, adventure, personalities, history, etc. Pays about 4¢ to 5¢ a word, on tenth of month after publication. Query.

PEOPLE AND PLACES—Box 47, Grand Marais, MI 49839. Rose Mary Bridger, Publisher.
Concise, warm, human-interest pieces, well-researched articles on regional subjects; nostalgia; articles on outdoors and crafts, to 1,000 words, with black-and-white photos if possible. Short stories, poetry, cartoons, humor, and fillers to 250 words. Pays in copies.

PHILADELPHIA—1500 Walnut St., Philadelphia, PA 19102. Alan Halpern, Editor.
Nonfiction, 1,000 to 5,000 words, dealing specifically with Philadelphia metropolitan area. Mostly staff-written. Pays $50 to $500, on acceptance. Query.

PHILADELPHIA INQUIRER TODAY MAGAZINE—400 North Broad St., Philadelphia, PA 19101. Scott DeGarmo, Editor.
Nonfiction, 500 to 3,500 words, on local subjects. Accompanying photos or drawings. Pay varies, on publication. Query.

PHOENIX MAGAZINE—4707 North 12th St., Phoenix, AZ 85014. Anita J. Welch, Editor.
Articles, 1,000 to 2,500 words, with photos and/or drawings, on Phoenix region. Pays from $50 up, on publication. Query.

PITTSBURGH RENAISSANCE—4802 Fifth Ave., Pittsburgh, PA 15213. Joyce Cher-ones, Editor.
Articles, 3,500 words, and shorter pieces, 650 words, on subjects of interest to western Pennsylvania readers. Pays $75 to $200 for features, $50 for shorter pieces, on publication.

THE PORTLAND OREGON JOURNAL—Portland, OR 97201.
Articles of all types, of regional interest, 1,200 words. Pays $25 to $35.

REAL WEST—Charlton Bldg., Derby, CT 06418. Edward Doherty, Editor.
Nonfiction only, 2,000 to 4,000 words; illustrations essential. Especially interested in pioneering experiences in the West around turn of century. Pays 2¢ a word, on acceptance.

THE RHODE ISLANDER—Providence Sunday *Journal,* Providence, RI 02902. Douglas R. Riggs, Editor.
Anecdotal articles, 1,000 to 1,500 words, on southern New England subjects. Pays $50 to $200, on publication.

ROLL CALL: THE NEWSPAPER OF CAPITOL HILL—428 8th St., S.E., Washington, DC 20003.
Magazine for professional politicians, office holders, and political scientists. Articles, 250 to 1,000 words, must be authoritative and accurate; anti-congressional slant is out. Historical pieces with topical significance, personality pieces, humor; good satire, 500 to 1,000 words, most wanted, but not on "issues." Pays on acceptance. Slow reports. Prestige high, payment low.

THE ST. LOUISAN—6306 Clayton Rd., St. Louis, MO 63117.
Articles on St. Louis food and restaurants, people, arts, medicine, environment, education, etc., of interest to residents of Greater St. Louis area. Black-and-white photos and photo-features (captions and copy must be included). Pay varies, after publication. Query.

SAN ANTONIO MAGAZINE—Chamber of Commerce, P.O. Box 1628, San Antonio, TX 78296. Sandra Brown, Editor.
Articles on San Antonio or immediate surrounding area. Pays from 3¢ a word, on publication. Query.

SAN FRANCISCO—120 Green St., San Francisco, CA 94111. Michael Parrish, Managing Editor.
Features and profiles 1,000 to 3,000 words, of Bay Area subjects and personalities that are new, significant, interesting, and written about with style. Subject matter is open. Cartoons. Pays $50 to $250 for articles, from $15 for cartoons, on publication. Query.

SAN FRANCISCO BUSINESS—Greater San Francisco Chamber of Commerce, 465 California St., San Francisco, CA 94104. Jim Haynes, Editor.
Articles, 1,500 words, on business or area subjects. No payment. Query.

SANDLAPPER: THE MAGAZINE OF SOUTH CAROLINA—P.O. Box 1668, Columbia, SC 29202. Bob W. Rowland, Editor.
Articles, to 2,500 words with photos, on people, places, things and events in and about South Carolina. Short fiction and poetry with strong South Carolina ties. Pays $20 to $100 at end of month of publication; $6 for black-and-white photos, $12 for color. Query. Reports within six weeks.

SEATTLE BUSINESS—Seattle Chamber of Commerce, 215 Columbia St., Seattle, WA 98104.
Bimonthly. Special but not exclusive emphasis on business-related items keyed to western Washington readers. Socio-economic aspects of modern living and regional human-interest features. Query.

SEATTLE TIMES SUNDAY MAGAZINE—Box 70, Seattle, WA 98111. Larry Anderson, Editor.
Articles on Pacific Northwest, 800 to 1,200 words. Accompanying illustrations. Pays $35 to $75, on publication. Query.

SEAWAY REVIEW—3750 Nixon Rd., Ann Arbor, MI 48105. Jacques LesStrang, Editor.
Articles, 500 to 3,000 words, with photos, on Great Lakes water transportation, ports, economics, ships; St. Lawrence Seaway activity, history, and romance. Cartoons; drawings on assignment. Pays $50 to $150, on publication. Buys ship photos, black-and-white and color.

SOUTH CAROLINA MAGAZINE—Box 89, Columbia, SC 29202. Sidney L. Wise, Editor.
Articles, 1,000 to 2,000 words with black-and-white photos, about South Carolina and South Carolinians, past and present. Modest pay, on publication. Query.

THE SOUTH MAGAZINE—Trend Publication, Inc., P.O. Box 2350, Tampa, FL 33601. Harris H. Mullen, Publisher. Roy B. Bain, Editor.
Articles, 1,500 to 3,500 words, on companies, people's successes and failures related to business in the South, and pieces on urban problems and their solutions. Pays $50 to $300, on acceptance. Query.

SOUTHERN EXPOSURE—Institute for Southern Studies, Box 230, Chapel Hill, NC 27514.
Well-documented, investigative pieces, book reviews, historical analyses, opinion pieces, 2,000 to 6,000 words, on political, economic, and cultural affairs related to the South. Fiction, 1,500 to 5,000 words dealing with life in the South. Pays $50.

SOUTHLAND SUNDAY MAGAZINE–Long Beach *Independent Press-Telegram,* 6th and Pine, Long Beach, CA 90844. James M. Leavy, Editor.
Articles, 500 to 3,000 words, mainly on southern California subjects. Some light humor, photos with articles. Pays 5¢ a word, on acceptance.

THE STATE–Box 2196, Raleigh, NC 27602. Bill Wright, Editor.
Features, 500 to 1,500 words, on subjects related to North Carolina. Pays $10 to $35, on acceptance.

SUBURBAN NEW JERSEY LIFE–See *New Jersey Life.*

SUNDAY NEW YORK NEWS MAGAZINE– *Sunday News,* 220 East 42nd St., New York, NY 10017. Richard C. Lemon, Editor.
Articles, 500 to 2,500 words, with photos, on New York subjects (preferably people). Pays $150 to $750, on acceptance.

SUNSET MAGAZINE–Menlo Park, CA 94025. Proctor Mellquist, Editor.
Uses very little freelance material as background for staff-written articles on Western food, homes, crafts, travel, garden subjects. Original solutions to small problems of houses and garden management. Material accepted only from people in circulation area. Pay varies, on acceptance. Query.

TEXAS METRO–Drawer 5566, Arlington, TX 76011. Dr. Dora Daugherty Strother, Editor.
Brief articles, with photos, on travel, better living and investment. Particularly interested in recipes for "Recipes of the Southwest" section. Pays 3¢ a word, $1 per recipe, $5 for color photos, $2 for black-and-white photos, and $50 for cover. Query a must.

TEXAS MONTHLY–P.O. Box 1569, Austin, TX 78767. Lyn Van Dusen, Managing Editor.
Articles, 2,000 to 8,000 words, on Texas, its residents and subjects of interest to them. Pay varies, on acceptance.

TEXAS PARADE–P.O. Box 12037, Capitol Station, Austin, TX 78711. Kenneth Lively, Editor.
Business articles, 1,500 to 2,000 words, with strong Texas slant. Photos or drawings. Pays from $35 per printed page, 10th of month following publication. Query.

THIS IS WEST TEXAS–West Texas Chamber of Commerce, Box 1561, Abilene, TX 79604. J. L. Martin, Editor.
Illustrated articles, 1,500 to 2,000 words, on scenic, historical, industrial, educational subjects, etc., oriented to West Texas area.

TOLEDO BLADE SUNDAY MAGAZINE–See *Blade Sunday Magazine.*

TORONTO LIFE–159 Front St. East, Toronto, Ont. MSE 1B3, Canada. Alexander Ross, Editor.
Largely staff-initiated; contributors must be very familiar with Toronto. Articles, 1,000 to 2,500 words. Pays $150 to $400. Query essential.

TOWN AND COUNTRY JOURNAL–101½ Mill St., Coudersport, PA 16915. Ms. G. Miller, Editor.
Articles, 1,500 to 5,000 words with photos, on northern Pennsylvania and southern New York: local personalities, history, points of interest, antiques, etc. Real estate tips, profiles of people who have "gone back to the earth," etc. Fiction; poetry to 20 lines. Pays $5 to $15, on publication; $5 each for black-and-white "country scene" photos.

TRENTON–Trenton-Mercer County Chamber of Commerce, 104 N. Broad St., Trenton, NJ 08608.
Articles, 500 to 1,500 words, about interesting people in Mercer County area. No fiction. Pays $25 to $50 for articles, $10 for fillers, puzzles, games. Query.

TROPIC—*The Miami Herald,* 1 Herald Plaza, Miami, FL 33101. John Parkyn, Editor.
Professionally written, general-interest articles, 1,500 to 3,000 words, on topics appealing to South Florida readers. Especially interested in high-quality personality profiles. No family situation material. Pays to $300, on publication. Query.

TRUE WEST—P.O. Box 3338, Austin, TX 78764. Pat Wagner, Editor.
Nonfiction articles about the West, 1845-1910, first-hand accounts or otherwise, 500 to 3,500 words. Documentary, essay style not encouraged but material must be accurate and accompanied by sources. Photos with articles welcome. Originals returned after publication. Pays from 2¢ a word, on acceptance. Query. Same requirements for *Frontier Times* and *Old West.*

TULSA—Metropolitan Tulsa Chamber of Commerce, 616 South Boston Ave., Tulsa, OK 74119. Larry P. Silvey, Editor.
Primarily for area businessmen but with general community slant. In-depth, people-oriented articles, 800 to 1,600 words, on Tulsa and vicinity. Articles must be factual, must tell all sides of question if topic is controversial or provocative. Uses some accompanying illustrations. Pays $25 to $75, on publication. Query.

UPCOUNTRY—Eagle Publishing Co., Pittsfield, MA 01201. William H. Tague, Managing Editor.
Articles, 500 to 2,500 words with photos, on rural and small town New England: problems faced by city people who move to country; land management and development; social, educational, political, economic, environmental and other contemporary issues; hunting, fishing, non-motorized outdoor recreation and sports, rural do-it-yourself ideas. First person accounts and nostalgia generally not appropriate. Short, humorous stories, 1,500 words, on country life. Pay varies, on acceptance.

UTAH HISTORICAL QUARTERLY—Utah Historical Society, 603 East South Temple, Salt Lake City, UT 84102. Stanford J. Layton, Managing Editor.
Well-researched, documented scholarly articles on history of Utah and related regions, to 7,500 words. Accompanying photos and illustrations. Pays in copies.

VERMONT LIFE—61 Elm St. Montpelier, VT 05602.
Factual articles on Vermont, 2,000 words. Accompanying photos. Pays 10¢ a word, on acceptance. Query.

THE WASHINGTONIAN—1218 Connecticut Ave. N.W., Washington, DC 20036. Laughlin Phillips, Editor.
Articles, 1,000 to 4,000 words, on any subject with strong Washington flavor, to stimulate, assist, and/or entertain intelligent, well-informed Washingtonians. Pays 7¢ to 10¢ a word, on publication. Query first.

WEEKEND MAGAZINE—231 St. James St., West Montreal H2Y 1M6, Quebec, Canada. Frank Lowe, Editor.
Articles and essays, 1,500 to 2,500 words, of interest to Canadians. Pays $400 to $750.

THE WESTERN PRODUCER—446 2nd Ave. North, Saskatoon, Sask., Canada. R. H. D. Phillips, Editor.
Short stories and articles, to 2,500 words with color or black-and-white photos, on western Canadian subjects, for intelligent farm and rural readers. Pays to $75 a page, $5 to $35 for photos, on acceptance.

WESTERN RESERVE MAGAZINE—Box 243, Garrettsville, OH 44231. Mary Folger, Editor.
Historical and contemporary articles on Ohio's Western Reserve, 600 to 2,400 words. Fillers on little-known, off-the-beaten path Western Reserve history. Pays $50, on publication.

WESTWAYS–Box 2890, Terminal Annex, Los Angeles, CA 90051. N. J. Kockler, Executive Editor.
Articles, 800 to 2,500 words, on western U.S., Canadian, and Mexican activities: natural science, travel, history, profiles of individuals, towns, regions, etc. Verse, to 45 lines. Pays from 10¢ a word on acceptance for articles; $25 and up for color photos. Query.

WISCONSIN TRAILS–P.O. Box 5650, Madison, WI 53705. Mrs. Jill Dean, Editor.
Articles, 1,500 to 3,000 words, relating to Wisconsin: history, industry, personalities, recreational possibilities, etc. Articles should inform as well as entertain. Pays $50 to $200, $10 for black-and-white photos, $50 for color transparencies 2¼ x 2¼ or larger, $100 for cover photos and centerspreads. Also publishes books. Query.

WONDERFUL WEST VIRGINIA–Information and Education Division, Dept. of Natural Resources, Charleston, WV 25305. Edward R. Johnson, Editor.
Articles, 1,200 words, relating to West Virginia: on nature, conservation, natural resources, hunting, fishing, hiking, caves, mountain climbing, forestry, water resources, wildlife, state parks, winter sports, outdoor lore. Fillers; black-and-white photos of native animals and 4 x 5 color transparencies of scenes in West Virginia. Query. No payment.

YANKEE–Dublin, NH 03444. Judson D. Hale, Editor.
Articles and short stories with New England locale and/or people, to 2,000 words. Black-and-white or color photos. Pays $200 to $400 for feature articles, $300 to $500 for fiction.

THE YANKEE GUIDE TO THE NEW ENGLAND COUNTRYSIDE–143 Newbury St., Boston, MA 02116. Georgia Orcutt, Editor.
Biannual guidebook. Articles, 500 to 2,000 words, with photos, on interesting and unusual activities in New England. Short features, two printed pages long. Pays from $50 to $200. Query a must.

HOUSE MAGAZINES AND COMPANY PUBLICATIONS

House magazines (also called company publications) are published by a company or corporation to promote good will, familiarize readers with the company's services and products, and interest customers in these products. A large percentage of the material published in house organs is frankly promotional–but editors also look for general-interest articles, travel or regional features, humor, and, surprisingly enough, some short stories. These magazines are also an excellent market for photographs.

The house magazines on the following list represent only a sampling of the many publications in the field. For a complete listing of house magazines–both those that buy free-lance material and those that do not–see the *Gebbie House Magazine Directory*, published by National Research Bureau, Inc. (424 North Third St., Burlington, IA 52601), available in most libraries.

AIR LINE PILOT–Air Line Pilots Association International, 1625 Massachusetts Ave. N.W., Washington, DC 20036. C. V. Glines, Editor.
Aviation-oriented articles, to 3,000 words, stressing pilot's point of view. Need safety articles on aircraft, airports and equipment, and articles on air transport history. Pilot profiles of ALPA Members. Payment varies, on publication.

BAUSCH & LOMB FOCUS–1400 North Goodman St., Rochester, NY 14602. Ralph I. Fiester, Editor.
Articles about new or novel methods in science teaching, or interesting applications of scientific optical instruments, 3,000 words. Accompanying photos. Before submitting, write for pamphlet S-301, "How to Write for Bausch & Lomb *Focus*." Pays 3¢ a word, $5 per photo.

THE BOLEX REPORTER–Paillard Inc., 1900 Lower Road, Linden, NJ 07036.
Short technical articles and photographs on moviemaking, and travel articles including moviemaking details, preferably featuring Bolex cameras. Pays $50 per published page. Query.

THE CARAVANNER–Guerin, Johnstone, Gage, Inc., 600 South Commonwealth Ave., Suite 901, Los Angeles, CA 90005. Frank Quattrocchi, Public Relations.
Articles about pleasant, interesting, or unusual use of Airstream travel trailers, 500 to 2,000 words. Articles must be illustrated by one or more black-and-white photographs of the Airstream used. "We are looking for articles about happy people, not hardware." Pays on acceptance. Query.

CHANNELS OF BUSINESS COMMUNICATION–Northwestern Bell Telephone Co., Roðm 910, 100 South 19th St., Omaha, NE 68102. Gerald T. Metcalf, Editor.
Case-history articles, 500 to 1,200 words, on how specific businessmen in Northwestern states use communication to best advantage (data transmission, computer-to-computer, etc.); articles about communications in the broader sense. Aimed at 50,000 business leaders in Iowa, Minnesota, Nebraska, North and South Dakota. Artwork or photos should accompany articles if possible; cartoons. Pays $150 and up for articles, $20 and up for cartoons. Allow one month for reply. Query.

THE COMPASS–Mobil Sales and Supply Corp., 150 East 42nd St., New York, NY 10017. R. G. MacKenzie, Editor.
Short stories and articles, up to 3,500 words, on the sea and deep sea trade, with historical twist where needed. Items should have international flavor, since magazine is distributed world-wide. Color photos should accompany manuscripts wherever possible. Rates depend on length and photos, and are up to $250. Query.

THE CONTINENTAL MAGAZINE–Room 956, World Headquarters, Ford Motor Company, Dearborn, MI 48121. Robert M. Hodesh, Editor-in-Chief.
High-quality service articles, 1,300 to 1,700 words, for well-to-do, sophisticated audience, on travel, entertainment, shopping, sports. Pays on acceptance. Query.

ENTHUSIAST–Harley-Davidson Motor Co., P.O. Box 653, Milwaukee, WI 53201. T. C. Bolfert, Editor.
Emphasis on photo-journalism. Fiction and articles, to 2,500 words, on motorcyling subjects featuring Harley-Davidson products. Travel stories, particularly about places not readily accessible by car. Pays 5¢ a word, $7.50 to $15 per photo, on acceptance.

FLAGSHIP NEWS–American Airlines, Inc., 633 Third Ave., New York, NY 10017. Bill Hunter, Editor.
Distributed to American Airlines employees and travel agents. Articles of varying lengths on humorous or unusual incidents on board American Airlines planes, or features about destination cities on the AA system. Emphasis on employee angle. Most photos assigned through regional public relations bureaus. Pays varying rates, within 30 days of publication.

FORD TIMES–Ford Motor Co., The American Rd., Dearborn, MI 48121. William E. Pauli, Managing Editor.
Articles, to 1,500 words, on recreation and travel related to car ownership; humor, little known places to visit. Especially interested in articles for young adults. Pays $20 and up, on acceptance. Query.

FORD TRUCK TIMES–420 Lexington Ave., New York, NY 10017. Warren Weith, Editor.
Articles, around 1,500 words, of interest to truck owners: how-tos, business-success, unusual ways people have fun with Ford trucks, direct product sell. Illustrated with color photos. Pays $100 to $300, on publication. Write for editorial and photographic requirements pamphlet. Query.

FRIENDS—30400 Van Dyke, Warren, MI 48093. Alexander Suczek, Editor.
Photo-articles and photos with captions. Articles on travel, with route and recreation information, sports, personalities, unusual news or recreational events, human-interest articles and stories on use of Chevrolet cars and trucks. Both color and black-and-white photos used; write for information on submitting. Pays from $75 to $150 a page, including photos. Query first with outline and photo situations.

THE FURROW—John Deere, John Deere Rd., Moline, IL 61265. George R. Sollenberger, Editor, North America.
Nonfiction and humor, to 1,500 words, with emphasis on researched agricultural-technical features and rural social- and economic-trend features. Pays to $400, on acceptance.

GAYLORD TRIANGLE—Gaylord Bros., Inc., P.O. Box 61, Syracuse, NY 13201. W. F. Hogan, Advertising Manager.
Brief articles about new company products, and testimonial photos and write-ups showing products in use.

GO GREYHOUND—Greyhound Tower, Phoenix, AZ 85077. Donald L. Behnke, Editor.
Travel articles, 600 to 800 words, accompanied by color photos. Pays $300 for articles with photos. Query.

GOING PLACES—American Express Co., 65 Broadway, New York, NY 10006. Barbara Ross, Editor.
Travel articles, on assignment only. Payment varies, on acceptance. Query.

HANG TEN'S SPORTING WORLD—Box 1028, Dana Point, CA 92629. Steve Pezman, Editor.
Action-oriented, informative articles, on sporting events and personalities from expert viewpoint, up to 3,000 words. Participation and recreational sports stressed. Pays 5¢ a word, $10 to $40 for black-and-white photos, $25 to $100 for color, on publication. Query.

HARVEST—Campbell Soup Co., Campbell Place, Camden, NJ 08101.
Articles with company tie-in, or of general food industry nature—agricultural developments, product use, health and nutrition, food research. Candid color transparencies that help to tell story are essential: either 35mm or 2¼ x 2¼. Payment on acceptance, by arrangement. Requirement sheet and sample on request. Query.

HUGHES RIGWAY—Hughes Tool Co., P.O. Box 2539, Houston, TX 77001. Address Tom Haynes.
For persons in oilfield drilling business. Fiction and non-fiction, to 2,500 words, especially historical narratives of little known incidents or facts. Pays 10¢ a word, on acceptance.

ILLINOIS CENTRAL GULF NEWS—Illinois Central Gulf Railroad, 233 North Michigan Ave., Chicago, IL 60601. A. R. Lind, Editor.
Articles, to 1,500 words, with pictures and captions on Illinois Gulf Railroad only. Cover shots of ICG freight trains and scenes along its lines. Pays $25 for articles, on acceptance.

IMPERIAL OIL FLEET NEWS—111 St. Clair Ave. West, Toronto, M5W1K3, Ont., Canada. Gordon R. McKean, Editor.
Articles, 1,000 to 3,000 words, of interest to tankermen, preferably with modern or historical Canadian angle. Photos to illustrate articles. Pays $40, on publication. Query.

INLAND—Inland Steel Co., 30 West Monroe St., Chicago, IL 60603. Sheldon A. Mix, Managing Editor.
Imaginative articles, essays, commentaries, any length, of special interest in Mid-West: humor, history, folklore, sports, etc. Pays about $300, on acceptance. Sample issues available on request.

THE IRON WORKER—Lynchburg Foundry, A Mead Co., Lynchburg, VA 24505. F. T. Hausman, Editor.
In-depth, well-documented, factual, historical articles, Virginia-related Americana, 3,500 to 5,000 words. Payment varies, on acceptance. Query.

KENDALL SPORTS TRAIL—The Kendall Co., Sports Division, 20 Walnut Street, Wellesley Hills, MA 02181. John S. O'Neill, Editor.
For high school and college athletic administrators. Articles, to 2,500 words, and photos on all phases of athletic department and sports management: game and personnel management, finance, sports medicine, coaching, athletics administration, etc. Pays 5¢ a word, $25 for photos, on publication.

LIVELY WORLD—Caldwell Communications, Inc., 747 Third Ave., New York, NY 10017. Robert H. Spencer, Editor.
For in-room use at Marriott Hotels. Articles, 800 to 3,000 words, on U.S. and foreign travel, focusing on people, history and social issues; sports, leisure, business, personal finance, food profiles, sophisticated humor. Pays $50 to $400, more for accompanying color transparencies, on publication. Non-returnable writing samples and list of published credits must accompany query or manuscript. Send for writer's guide.

THE LOOKOUT—Seamen's Church Institute of New York, 15 State St., New York, NY 10004. Carlyle Windley, Editor.
Articles, to 1,000 words, relating to old and new merchant marine: oddities, adventure, factual accounts, unexplained phenomena. Uses art with article. Occasional short verse. No fiction or technical pieces. Pays up to $40 for articles, $20 for black-and-white cover photos, on publication.

THE LUFKIN LINE—P.O. Box 849, Lufkin, TX 75901. Virginia R. Allen, Editor.
Articles on travel in United States and Canada, 1,000 to 1,200 words, with minimum of eight color transparencies or prints. Pays $50, on acceptance; $25 for 4 x 5 color transparencies for inside front cover.

MARATHON WORLD—Marathon Oil Co., 539 South Main St., Findlay, OH 45840. Richard Atcheson, Editor.
Petroleum- and business-oriented narrative approach preferred, reportorial rather than analytic; current issues and events. Pays $150 to $500 for feature-length articles. Request sample copy. Query a must.

THE MODERN WOODMEN—Modern Woodmen of America, Mississippi River at 17th St., Rock Island, IL 61201. Robert E. Frank, Editor.
Juvenile fiction and general-interest fiction and non-fiction, 1,500 to 2,000 words, strongly plotted, with accurate foreign or historical setting when used. 8 x 10 black-and-white glossies with manuscripts. Pays $25 and up for fiction and articles, more with photos.

NEW DIMENSIONS—International Correspondence Schools, Scranton, PA 18515.
Articles, for middle- and upper-management officials, 1,000 to 3,000 words, on new methods, systems, techniques, etc., with special emphasis on industrial training and development. Accompanying photos encouraged. Pays $6 to $10 per page.

OUR SUN—1608 Walnut St., Philadelphia, PA 19103. Ray L. Enderle, Editor.
Petroleum industry-related articles, 500 to 1,500 words. Most material internally generated. Query.

OUTDOORS—Outdoors Bldg., Columbia, MO 65201. Lee Cullimore, Editor.
Informative articles, to 1,200 words, accompanied by 8 x 10 black-and-white photos, on recreational subjects, with emphasis on boating. Pays $35 to $100, on acceptance.

POINTS—465 West Milwaukee, Detroit, MI 48202.
Illustrated, how-to articles, 700 to 1,200 words, on family activities, stressing little-known or unusual ideas: semi-technical articles concerning collecting, nature

study, etc.; hobbies; women's features; arts and crafts; sports. Pays $100 to $400 for articles with photos. Query.

PRINTING SALESMAN'S HERALD—Champion Papers, 245 Park Ave., New York, NY 10017. Michael P. Corey, Editor.

Knowledgeable articles about buying and selling of printing, 500 to 2,500 words, to help to make printing salesmen more effective and useful members of their profession. Pays from $50 to $75 per article, on acceptance.

THE RECORD—Fireman's Fund American Insurance Companies, 3333 California St., San Francisco, CA 94119. William F. Lawler, Editor.

Submissions accepted May 1 to September 1. Short stories (about 3,000 words), short-shorts, anecdotes, and poetry, with strong Christmas theme. Will consider only tight, well-presented material with original twist. Pays on acceptance, from $300 for stories, $75 for short-shorts, $25 for anecdotes, and $10 for poetry.

SEVENTY SIX MAGAZINE—Union Oil Co. of California, Box 7600, Los Angeles, CA 90051. Steve Milakov, Editor.

Articles, 750 to 1,750 words, to dramatize company's operations in terms of participating employees. Emphasis on anecdotes and quotes. No dealer stories. No fillers or poetry. Pays 10¢ to 30¢ a word, extra for photos, on acceptance. Samples and writer's kit on request. Query.

SHELL NEWS—Shell Oil Co., Box 2463, Houston, TX 77001. J. H. Powers, Manager of Publications.

Petroleum industry-related articles, 1,000 to 2,000 words. Pays average of 15¢ a word, about 30 days after acceptance. While almost entirely staff-written, free lancers who specialize in oil business are needed in various parts of country. Query.

SPERRY NEW HOLLAND—Division of Sperry Rand Corp., New Holland, PA 17557. Michael A. Balas, Editor.

Articles, 1,000 to 1,500 words, about farmers and farm operations, mentioning Sperry New Holland equipment only as used in farm operation. Black-and-white action photos and 4 x 5 or 2¼ x 2¼ color transparencies must accompany articles. Pays on publication.

TEXACO TEMPO—Texaco Canada Ltd., 90 Wynford Dr., Don Mills, Ontario, Canada.

Articles relating to Canadian oil industry in some way, with Texaco Canada interest preferred, 800 to 1,200 words, and photos. Pays from $100 to $150, plus photo costs, on acceptance.

THINK—International Business Machines Corp., Armonk, NY 10504. C. B. Hansen, Editor.

In-company magazine. Business/management-related articles, 2,000 to 3,000 words. Pays competitive rates. Query.

TILE AND TILL—Eli Lilly and Company, Indianapolis, IN 46206.

Management and scientific articles about pharmacy, by qualified writers. Query.

POETRY MARKETS

The following list is divided into four categories: general magazines; college, literary, little magazines and magazines which use only poetry; religious or denominational magazines; and greeting card markets. Each tends to use a certain type of poetry, but many poems may meet the requirements of markets in more than one of the groups. Markets for both serious and light verse are included in each category.

In addition to the markets listed here, many daily and weekly newspapers use occasional verse. Though they may not specifically seek poetry from free-lance writers, the papers often print verse submitted to them, especially on holidays and other special occasions.

The markets for juvenile poetry are listed under *Juvenile, Teen-Age and Young Adult Magazines* and markets for book-length poems or collections of poems are under *Book Publishers.*

GENERAL MAGAZINES

THE AMERICAN LEGION MAGAZINE–1345 Ave. of the Americas, New York, NY 10019.
   Humorous verse, to 16 lines, No serious poetry. Pays $10 and up, on acceptance. Submit to "Parting Shots" Editor.

THE AMERICAN-SCANDINAVIAN REVIEW–127 East 73rd St., New York, NY 10021. Erik J. Friis, Editor.
   Verse, 10 to 30 lines, about Scandinavia. Pays $5 to $10, on acceptance.

THE AMERICAN SCHOLAR–1811 Q St. N.W., Washington, DC 20009. Joseph Epstein, Editor.
   Poetry, to 60 lines. Pays $35 to $75, on acceptance.

THE ATLANTIC–8 Arlington St., Boston, MA 02116. Peter Davison, Poetry Editor.
   Highest quality. Limited market; prints only three or four poems an issue. Special interest in young poets. Occasionally prints light verse. Payment varies, on acceptance.

THE ATLANTIC ADVOCATE–Gleaner Bldg., Phoenix Sq., Fredericton, N.B., Canada.
   Poetry related to Canada's Atlantic provinces. Pays $2 per column inch. Query first.

BABY CARE–52 Vanderbilt Ave., New York, NY 10017. Maja Bernath, Editor.
   Poetry, to 24 lines. Pay varies, on acceptance.

BLACK TIMES: VOICES OF THE NATIONAL COMMUNITY–Box 10246, Palo Alto, CA 94303. I. Odus, Poetry Editor.
   Poetry, to 10 lines, Pays in copies.

BREEZY–See *Humorama, Inc.*

CARTOON PARADE–See *Humorama, Inc.*

CATS MAGAZINE–P.O. Box 4106, Pittsburgh, PA 15202. Jean Laux, Editor.
   Poems, preferably light, about cats, to 30 lines. Pays 30¢ a line, on publication.

CHATELAINE–481 University Ave., Toronto, Ont., Canada. Doris Anderson, Editor.
   Short verse, to 25 lines. Pays to $30, on acceptance.

CHILD LIFE–1100 Waterway Blvd., P.O. Box 567B, Indianapolis, IN 46206. Jane E. Norris, Editor.
   Poetry for children 7 to 11. Pays 25¢ a line, on publication.

CHILDREN'S PLAYMATE–1100 Waterway Blvd., P.O. Box 567B, Indianapolis, IN 46206. Beth Wood Thomas, Editor.
Humorous poetry for children 3 to 8. Pays about 3¢ a word, $5 minimum, on publication.

THE CHRISTIAN SCIENCE MONITOR–1 Norway St., Boston, MA 02115. Henrietta Buckmaster, Editor, "The Home Forum."
Fresh, vigorous, clearly focused poems of high literary standard. Subjects may vary widely, but not be downbeat. Pay varies, on acceptance.

COMEDY MAGAZINE–See *Humorama, Inc.*

COSMOPOLITAN–224 West 57th St., New York, NY 10019. Jo Hynes, Poetry Editor.
Magazine for young, active career women. Poetry about personal relationships. Pays from $25, on acceptance.

ESQUIRE–488 Madison Ave., New York, NY 10022. Don Erickson, Editor.
No longer considers unsolicited poetry manuscripts. Query letters only.

ESSENCE–300 East 42nd St., New York, NY 10017. Sharyn J. Skeeter, Fiction and Poetry Editor.
Poetry, to 40 lines. Pays $25 and up, after publication.

FAMILY CIRCLE–488 Madison Ave., New York, NY 10022. Arthur M. Hettich, Editor.
Poetry and light verse, to 20 lines. Pays from $10, on acceptance.

FARM WIFE NEWS–733 North Van Buren, Milwaukee, WI 53202. Carol Haiar, Editor.
Poetry with rural flavor. Pays $10 to $20, after acceptance.

FUN HOUSE–See *Humorama, Inc.*

GAZE–See *Humorama, Inc.*

GEE WHIZ–See *Humorama, Inc.*

GIRLTALK–380 Madison Ave., New York, NY 10017.
Humorous poems, 4 to 8 lines. Pays $10.

GOLF DIGEST MAGAZINE–297 Westport Ave., Norwalk, CT 06856. Kathy Jonah, Poetry Editor.
Humorous verse, 4–8 lines, on golf subjects. Pays $10 to $20, on acceptance.

GOLF MAGAZINE–380 Madison Ave., New York, NY 10017. John M. Ross, Editor.
Light or humorous verse, to 25 lines, on various aspects of golf. Pays $25 and up, on acceptance.

GOOD HOUSEKEEPING–959 Eighth Ave., New York, NY 10019.
Good, serious poetry on subjects of interest to women. Send to Poetry Editor. Send short, light verse to Gay Norton, Assistant Editor, for Light Housekeeping page. Pays $5 a line and up, on acceptance.

GOURMET MAGAZINE–777 Third Ave., New York, NY 10017.
Light verse with sophisticated food angle. Avoid mention of dieting, calories, etc. Pays on acceptance.

HARLEQUIN'S WOMAN–Harlequin Enterprises, Ltd., 240 Duncan Mill Rd., Suite 605, Don Mills, Ont., Canada M3B 1Z4.
Short poetry.

HARPER'S MAGAZINE–2 Park Ave., New York, NY 10016. Address Poetry Editor.
Poetry, to 40 lines. Pays about $2 a line, on acceptance. Manuscripts returned within two months if accompanied by stamped return envelope. "Please don't submit poems more frequently than twice a year."

THE HARTFORD COURANT—285 Broad St., Hartford, CT 06101. Malcolm L. Johnson, Poetry Column Editor.
Verse, to 50 lines. Pays in copies.

HUMORAMA, INC.—100 North Village Ave., Rockville Centre, NY 11570. Ernest N. Devver, Editor.
Breezy, fast, humorous erotic verse from 4 to 48 lines. Pays 60¢ a line, before publication. Same address and requirements for *Jest, Laugh Riot, Laugh Digest, Comedy, Stare, Zip, Fun House, Romp, Joker, Gaze, Gee-Whiz, Breezy, Quips,* and *Cartoon Parade.*

JEST—See *Humorama, Inc.*

JOKER—See *Humorama, Inc.*

LADIES' HOME JOURNAL—641 Lexington Ave., New York, NY 10022.
Not in the market for poetry at present.

LADY GOLFER—P.O. Box 4725, Whittier, CA 90607. Charles G. Schoos, General Manager.
Poems on golf. Pays $35 to $50, on acceptance.

LAUGH DIGEST—See *Humorama, Inc.*

LAUGH RIOT—See *Humorama, Inc.*

LEATHERNECK—Box 1918, Quantico, VA 22134. Ronald D. Lyons, Managing Editor.
"Magazine of the Marines" published monthly for enlisted members of U.S. Marine Corps. Marine-oriented poetry. Pays from $10 on acceptance.

McCALL'S MAGAZINE—230 Park Ave., New York, NY 10017.
Some poetry and light verse, 4 to 20 lines. Top rates. Address Poetry Editor.

MS.—370 Lexington Ave., New York, NY 10017.
Poetry of high quality, not necessarily with feminist content. Pays $75, on acceptance.

MADEMOISELLE—350 Madison Ave., New York, NY 10017. Ellen A. Stoianoff, Fiction and Poetry Editor.
Outstanding poetry of high literary quality, to 65 lines. Pays from $25, on acceptance.

MAINE LIFE—RFD 1, Liberty, ME 04949. David E. Olson, Editor.
Poetry on Maine. Query.

MODERN BRIDE—One Park Ave., New York, NY 10016. Cele G. Lalli, Executive Editor.
Short verse appealing to bride and groom. Pays on acceptance.

NRTA JOURNAL—215 Long Beach Blvd., Long Beach CA 90801. Hubert C. Pryor, Editor.
National Retired Teachers Association publication. Short verse. Pays from $10.

THE NATION—333 Sixth Ave., New York, NY 10014. Carey McWilliams, Editor. Grace Schulman, Poetry Editor.
Poetry of high literary quality.

NEW-ENGLAND GALAXY—Old Sturbridge Village, Sturbridge, MA 01566. Catherine Fennelly, Editor.
High quality poetry, to 30 lines, of New England interest. Pays $50, on publication.

NEW YORK TIMES MAGAZINE—229 West 43rd St., New York, NY 10036.
Not currently in the market for poetry.

THE NEW YORKER—25 West 43rd St., New York, NY 10036.
Light verse (topical, satirical or humorous) and serious poetry. Pays top rates, on acceptance. Address "The Editors."

THE OHIO MOTORIST—6000 South Marginal Road, Cleveland, OH 44103. A. K. Murway, Editor.
Short humorous poems on motoring, automotive and vacation topics (foreign and domestic), preferably 4 to 6 lines. Pays $6 to $8, on acceptance.

OREGONIAN VERSE—*The Oregonian,* Portland, OR 97201. Howard McKinley Corning, Editor.
Weekly column. Short, objective verse of high quality, to 24 lines. Rarely uses religious, humorous, or personal mood poetry. Submit seasonal poems several weeks in advance. Pays $5 per poem, 10th of month following publication.

PEN—444 Sherman St., Denver, CO 80203.
Humorous poetry and light verse, to 16 lines. No obscure "far-out" poetry. Some serious poems, for holiday issues. Pays 50¢ a line, on acceptance.

PEOPLE AND PLACES—Box 47, Grand Marais, MI 49839. Rose Mary Bridger, Editor.
Short poetry of all kinds. Pays in copies.

PLAYBOY—919 North Michigan Ave., Chicago, IL 60611. Address Party Jokes Editor.
Light verse, poetry. Pay varies, on acceptance.

PRE-VUE—P.O. Box 20768, Billings, MT 59102. Virginia B. Hansen, Editor.
Poetry, Pays 50¢ a line.

QUIPS—See *Humorama, Inc.*

QUOTE MAGAZINE—P.O. Box 4073, Station B, Anderson, SC 29621.
Light verse, to 4 lines, of value to ministers, toastmasters, club leaders and other public speakers. Pays from $1, on publication. Free sample copy. Include return postpaid envelope.

THE RHODE ISLANDER—75 Fountain St., Providence, RI 02902. Laurence J. Sasso, Jr., Poetry Editor.
Poetry, to 20 lines. Pays $20, on publication.

ROLL CALL: THE NEWSPAPER OF CAPITOL HILL—428 Eighth Street, S. E., Washington, DC 20003.
Light, humorous satire on Congress or politics, not on issues. Pays on acceptance.

ROMP—See *Humorama, Inc.*

THE ROTARIAN—1600 Ridge Ave., Evanston, IL 60201. Willmon L. White, Editor.
Humorous or philosophical verse. Pays fair rates.

ROUNDUP—The Denver *Post,* P.O. Box 1709, Denver, CO 80201. Walter Hall, Editor, "Poetry Forum."
Poetry, to 20 lines, by Rocky Mountain area poets. Pays $2, on acceptance.

RURAL ELECTRIC MISSOURIAN—2722 East McCarty St., Jefferson City, MO 65101. Don Yoest, Editor.
Short poetry, 5 to 12 lines, with rural flavor, or human interest. Pays $5 up, on acceptance.

THE SATURDAY EVENING POST—1100 Waterway Blvd., Indianapolis, IN 46202. Frederic A. Birmingham, Managing Editor.
Short poetry, no restrictions on form. Light verse especially in demand for "Post Scripts" pages. Pay varies.

SATURDAY REVIEW—488 Madison Ave., New York, NY 10022.
No unsolicited poetry accepted.

SEVENTEEN–850 Third Ave., New York, NY 10022.
Poetry, to 20 lines, by teens. Pays to $25. Allow 8 weeks for response. Stamped self-addressed envelope required for return.

STARE–See *Humorama, Inc.*

SURFER MAGAZINE–Box 1028, Dana Point, CA 92629. Steve Pezman, Editor.
Poetry on surfing. Pays $10 to $20, on publication.

TENNIS USA–Chilton Co., Chilton Way, Radnor, PA 19089. Robert L. Gillen, Editor.
Light verse, 5 to 25 lines, on tennis. Pay varies, on acceptance.

TENNIS ILLUSTRATED–630 Shatto Pl., Los Angeles, CA 90005. Gay Yellen, Editor.
Poetry on tennis. Pays on publication.

UNDERSTANDING–P.O. Box 206, Merlin, OR 97532. Dr. Daniel W. Fry, Editor.
Poetry, to 36 lines, expressing good will among all peoples of the earth. Pays 40¢ a line, on publication.

WESTWAYS–P.O. Box 2890, Los Angeles, CA 90051. Frances Ring, Associate Editor.
Serious, high-quality verse, to 24 lines, preferably with Western mood or theme; e.g., travel, history, conservation or contemporary events. Uses 10 to 12 poems each year; pays $25 minimum, on acceptance. Heavily overstocked at present. Please submit no more than five poems for consideration.

YANKEE–Dublin, NH 03444. Judson D. Hale, Editor. Jean Burden, Poetry Editor.
Serious poetry of high quality, to 30 lines. Pays $25 per poem, on publication. Annual awards.

ZIP–See *Humorama, Inc.*

COLLEGE, LITERARY, AND POETRY MAGAZINES

AMANUENSIS–Dept. of English, Room 1215, University of Kentucky. Lexington, KY 40506. Philip Mitchum, Editor.
Poetry. Pays in copies.

AMERICAN POETRY REVIEW–401 South Broad St., Philadelphia, PA 19147.
Poetry, short stories, essays. Newspaper format. Pays in Copies.

THE ANTIGONISH REVIEW–St. Francis Xavier University, Antigonish, N.S., Canada. R. J. MacSween, Editor.
Quality poetry on any subject. Pays in copies.

THE ANTIOCH REVIEW–P.O. Box 148, Yellow Springs, OH 45387. Ira Sadoff, Poetry Editor.
Quality poetry. No light or inspirational verse. Especially interested in new good poets. Pays $8 a poem or per page for longer poems.

APHRA–Box 893, Ansonia Station, New York, NY 10023.
Good poetry with feminist slant. Study magazine. Pays in copies. Overstocked.

ARIZONA QUARTERLY–University of Arizona, Tucson, AZ 85721. Albert F. Gegenheimer, Editor.
Poetry. No payment; annual award.

THE ARK RIVER REVIEW–911 Lombard St., Philadelphia, PA 19147. Jonathan Katz, Editor.
Contemporary and experimental poetry. Pays 20¢ a line

ASPEN LEAVES–Box 3185 Aspen, CO 81611. Indira Singh, Editor.
Poetry. Pays in copies, awards.

ATARAXIA—Box 8032, Athens, GA 30601.
Poetry. Pays in copies.

BACK ROADS—Box 543, Cotati, CA 94928. Stella Nathan, Editor.
Poetry, to 2 pages. Pays in copies.

BALL STATE UNIVERSITY FORUM—Ball State University, Muncie, IN 47306. Merrill
Rippy and Frances Mayhew Rippy, Editors.
Poetry, 4 to 200 lines. Pays in copies.

BARDIC ECHOES—1036 Emerald Ave. N.E., Grand Rapids, MI 49503. Clarence L.
Weaver, Editor.
Poetry in any form, to 40 lines; shorter poems preferred. Reports in one to three
months. Language in bad taste not acceptable. Pays in copies. Overstocked till
Sept. 1975.

BELOIT POETRY JOURNAL—Box 2, Beloit, WI 53511.
Quality poetry of any length, experimental or traditional. Occasional special
chapbooks. Pays in copies. Study magazine before submitting.

BERKELEY BARB—Box 1247, Berkeley, CA 94701. Jim Schreiber, Editor.
Poetry on social issues, 2 to 100 lines. Pays 50¢ per column inch, $5 minimum, on
publication.

BEST FRIENDS—1709 Cagua Dr., N.E., Albuquerque, NM 87110.
Poetry, any length, by women only. Pays in copies.

BEYOND BAROQUE—P.O. Box 806, Venice, CA 90291.
Avant-garde poetry.

BITTERROOT—Box 51, Blythebourne Station, Brooklyn, NY 11219. Menke Katz,
Editor.
Quarterly poetry magazine.

BLACKFISH—1851 Moore St., Burnaby, 2 B.C., Canada. B. T. Brett and Allan Safarik,
Co-editors.
Poetry, of high quality, any length. Pays in copies. Enclose international reply
coupons with manuscript.

BOSTON UNIVERSITY JOURNAL—775 Commonwealth Ave., Boston, MA 02215.
Poetry. Pays in copies.

BOX 749—Box 749, Old Chelsea Station, New York, NY 10011. David Ferguson,
Editor.
Poetry, any length. Pays in copies.

BROADSIDE SERIES—12651 Old Mill Place, Detroit, MI 48238. Dudley Randall,
Editor.
Black poetry, one page or less. Pays $10 a poem, on publication. Sample copies 50¢.
Also publishes *The Broadside Annual*, an anthology of poems by black poets never or
seldom published before. Pays $10 per poem.

CANADIAN FORUM—56 Esplanade East, Toronto, Canada. Michael S. Cross, Managing
Editor. Tom Marshall, Poetry Editor.
Poetry, any length. Pays $8 per poem, plus copies.

CAPE ROCK JOURNAL—Southeast Missouri State College, Cape Girardeau, MO 63701.
R. A. Burns, Editor.
Poetry of any length, form and subject. Pays in copies. Query.

CAROLINA QUARTERLY—Box 1117, Chapel Hill, NC 27514. Jeff Richards, Editor.
High quality poems of any length, form, subject, by well-known and new poets.

CHELSEA—Box 5880, Grand Central Station, New York, NY 10017. Sonia Raiziss, Editor.
Original and translated poems of high quality. Pays in copies.

CHICAGO REVIEW—The University of Chicago, Faculty Exchange Box C, Chicago, IL 60637. Curt Matthews, Poetry Editor.
Verse, verse translations, and verse plays. Sample copy, $1.95. No manuscript accepted without stamped, self-addressed envelope.

CHOMO-URI—Feminist Arts Program, Everywoman's Center, Goodell Hall, University of Massachusetts, Amherst, MA 01002.
Poetry which offers alternative views of woman's role in society. Pays in copies.

CIMARRON REVIEW—Oklahoma State University, Stillwater, OK 74074. Jeanne Adams Wray, Managing Editor.
Verse, any length, particularly poetic commentary on contemporary society. Pays in copies.

THE COLD MOUNTAIN REVIEW—Appalachian State University, English Department, Boone, NC 28608. R. T. Smith, Editor.
Serious poetry, any length. Parody, translation, verse in Old English language and prosody. No inspirational or patriotic verse. Pays in copies.

CONNECTIONS—Bell Hollow Rd., Putnam Valley, NY 10579. Toni Ortner Zimmerman, Editor.
Modern poetry, one page, especially by women.

THE COOPERATOR—17819 Roscoe Blvd., Northridge, CA 91324.
Poetry, to 40 lines, which fosters emergence of new universal person, civilization based upon unity in diversity among all peoples. Pays in copies.

CORBAN—970 Van Buren, Eugene, OR 97402. Carole J. Monsma, Editor.
Poetry, any length. Pays in copies. Include stamped, self-addressed envelope.

CRAZY HORSE—Southwest Minnesota State College, Marshall, MN 56258. Philip Dacey, Editor.
Quality modern poems of any length, subject and style. Stamped, self-addressed envelope must accompany manuscripts for return. Prompt reply. Pays in copies.

CREATIVE MOMENT—See *Poetry Eastwest.*

CUTBANK—Dept. of English, University of Montana, Missoula, MT 59801. Robert Wrigley, Editor.
Poetry of all lengths. Pays in copies.

DARKWATERS—Box 22246, Seattle, WA 98100.
Poetry on issues relevant to Third World People. Pays in copies.

THE DeKALB LITERARY ARTS JOURNAL—DeKalb College, 555 Indian Crrek Drive, Clarkston, GA 30021. Mr. Gayle Goodwin, Editor.
Original, unpublished poetry by established and beginning writers. Pays in copies. No carbon, Xeroxes, or dittoes.

DESCANT—Texas Christian University, T. C. U. Sta., Fort Worth, TX 76129. Betsy Colquitt, Editor.
Poetry, any length; short poetry preferred. Pays in copies.

DOGSOLDIER—East 323 Boone, Spokane, WA 99202. William Hudson, Editor.
Poetry, any length, any style. Pays in copies.

DRAGONFLY: A QUARTERLY OF HAIKU—4102 N.E. 130th Pl., Portland, OR 97230. Lorraine Ellis Harr, Manuscripts Editor.
Classical/traditional haiku preferred (not necessarily 5-7-5). Cash and book awards each issue. Include stamped, self-addressed envelope.

EDCENTRIC—P.O. Box 10085, Eugene, OR 97401.
Poetry, any length, relating to radical social and educational change. No payment.

EPOCH—245 Goldwin Smith Hall, Cornell University, Ithaca, NY 14850. Baxter
Hathaway, Editor.
Verse, to 4 pages; of high quality; not necessarily experimental, but expressive of
contemporary experience. Pays in copies.

EPOS—Rollins College, Winter Park, FL 32789. Address manuscripts to Evelyn Thorne,
Crescent City, FL 32012.
Poetry, to 2 pages. Pays in copies. Prompt reports.

ESSENCE—26 Fowler St., New Haven, CT 06515. Joseph Payne Brennan, Editor.
Lyric poems, to 20 lines, with impact and originality. Must send stamped return
envelope. Pays in copies.

EVENT—Dept. of English, Douglas College, P.O. Box 2503, New Westminster, B.C.,
Canada. Robert Lowe, Editor.
Quality poetry, any length. Pays in copies.

EXILE—193 Church St., Toronto, 205, Canada. B. Callaghan, Editor.
High-quality poetry. Pays $20 to $50 per poem, on acceptance.

EXTENSIONS—P.O. Box 383, Cathedral Station, New York, NY 10025. Suzanne
Zavrian and Joachim Neugroschel.
Experimental poetry and translations. Pays in copies. See magazine before submit-
ting.

THE FALCON—Mansfield State College, Mansfield, PA 16933. W. A. Blais, Poetry
Editor.
Poetry, any length. No traditional, inspirational or light verse. Pays in copies. Include
stamped, self-addressed envelope. See sample copy before submitting.

THE FAULT—41186 Alice Ave., Fremont, CA 94538. Terrence Ames, Editor.
Poetry. Pays in copies.

THE FIDDLEHEAD—Dept. of English, University of New Brunswick, Fredericton, N.B.,
Canada. Kent Thompson, Editor.
High quality poetry, preferably short. Emphasis on Canadian writing. Pays about $5
per page, on publication.

FIELD—Rice Hall, Oberlin College, Oberlin, OH 44074.
Poetry, any length, of highest quality, by established and unknown poets. Pays $15
per page, on publication. Study sample issue before submitting.

THE FILM JOURNAL—Box 9602, Hollins College, VA 24020. Thomas R. Atkins,
Editor and Publisher.
Poetry on movies. Pays in copies.

FORUM—University of Houston, Houston, TX 77004. William Lee Pryor, Editor;
Archibald Henderson, Poetry Editor.
Quality poetry, to 50 lines. Pays in copies.

FOUR QUARTERS—LaSalle College, Philadelphia, PA 19141. John Keenan, Editor.
Poetry, under 30 lines preferred. $5 honorarium (except for 3-line fillers), on
publication.

FREE LANCE—6005 Grand Ave., Cleveland, OH 44104. Casper L. Jordan and Russell
Atkins, Co-editors.
Experimental philosophy. Poetry of any length. Avant-garde material. Pays in copies.

FRONT STREET TROLLEY—2507 Forde Ave., Nashville, TN 37215. Molly McIntosh,
Editor.
Serious and satirical poetry, any length. Prefers Southern writers. Pays in copies.

GALLIMAUFRY–359 Frederick, San Francisco, CA 94117. Mary L. MacArthur, Editor.
Poetry, any length. Pays in copies.

GEORGIA REVIEW–University of Georgia, Athens, GA 30602. John T. Irwin, Editor.
Poetry, any length. Pays 50¢ per line, on publication.

GHOST DANCE–ATL, Michigan State University, Lansing, MI 48823.
Fresh, innovative, eclectic poetry. Especially interested in computer-language experimentation. Pays in copies.

GRAVIDA–P.O. Box 76, Hartsdale, NY 10530. Lynne Savitt, Managing Editor.
Quality poetry. Pays in copies.

THE GREEN RIVER REVIEW–Box 56, University Center, MI 48710. Raymond Tyner, Editor.
Poetry to 500 lines. Translations. Pays in copies.

GREEN'S MAGAZINE–P.O. Box 313, Detroit, MI 48231. David Green, Editor.
Poetry, to 30 lines. Pays $2 to $3 per poem, on publication. Include stamped, self-addressed envelope with submission.

THE GREENFIELD REVIEW–Greenfield Centre, NY 12833. Joseph Bruchac III, Editor.
Contemporary poetry, any length, by established poets, new and third world writers. Translations. Pays in copies.

HAWAII REVIEW–2465 Campus Rd., University of Hawaii, Honolulu, HI 96822. Christine Cook, Editor.
Poetry, any length.

HAWK AND WHIPPOORWILL RECALLED–c/o Joyce W. Webb, 53 South Midvale Blvd., Madison, WI 53705.
Poetry, to 30 lines. Include stamped, self-addressed envelope. Pays in copies.

HIRAM POETRY REVIEW–P.O. Box 162, Hiram, OH 44234. David Fratus, Editor.
Quality poetry, any length. Pays in copies and subscription.

HUDSON RIVER ANTHOLOGY–Vassar College, Poughkeepsie, NY 12601. David Elliott Hartman, Editor.
Poetry, any length, Pays in copies.

INLET–Dept. of English, Virginia Wesleyan College, Norfolk, VA 23502. Bruce H. Guernsey, Editor.
Annual. Poetry, to 50 lines, accepted from September 1 to March 1. Pays in copies. Reports in one month.

THE IOWA REVIEW–EPB 453. The University of Iowa, Iowa City, IA 52240.
Poetry and prose poems. Pays $1 a line, on publication.

JEAN'S JOURNAL QUARTERLY–Box 15, Kanona, NY 14856. Jean Calkins, Editor.
Verse, any style and length. Cash awards.

JESTURE–Public Relations Office, Thomas More College, Box 85, Covington, KY 41017.
Bi-yearly. Poetry. Pays in copies. Reports November and April.

KAMADHENU MAGAZINE–Dept. of English, Washington State University, Pullman, WA 99163. G. S. Sharat Chandra, Editor.
Contemporary poetry, to 100 lines, of excellent quality. Reviews and translations. Encourages minority groups. Pay varies, on publication.

KANSAS QUARTERLY–Dept. of English, Kans. State University, Manhattan, KS 66506.
Poetry of all types. Pays in copies. Annual poetry prize.

KARAMU—English Department, Eastern Illinois University, Charleston, IL 61920. Allen Neff, Editor; Carol Elder, Poetry Editor.
Quality poetry with clear imagery and strong tone, 4 to 60 lines. No translations. No manuscripts read between June and September. Pays in copies.

LIBERA—516 Eshleman Hall, University of California, Berkeley, CA 94720.
Poetry, any length, by women. Pays in copies.

THE LITERARY REVIEW—Fairleigh Dickinson University, Rutherford, NJ 07070. Charles Angoff, Editor.
Poetry of high literary quality, any length. Pays in copies.

THE LITTLE MAGAZINE—P.O. Box 207, Cathedral Station, New York, NY 10025. David G. Hartwell, Editor.
Poetry, any length. Pays in copies.

LONG ISLAND REVIEW—Box 10, Cambria Heights, NY 11411. Stephen Sossaman, Edward Faranda, Editors.
Poetry, any length. Pays in copies.

LOON—P.O. Box 11633, Santa Rosa, CA 95406. D. L. Emblen, Richard Speakes, Richard Welin, Editors.
Poetry, and short, thoughtful essays on poetics. Pays in copies.

THE LYRIC—Bremo Bluff, VA 23022. Ruby Altizer Roberts and John Nixon, Jr., Editors.
Traditional, high quality poetry. Prefers optimistic viewpoint. No payments; cash prizes, and annual college contest.

MACABRE—26 Fowler St., New Haven, CT 06515. Joseph Payne Brennan, Editor.
Verse, to 30 lines, on eerie, macabre, supernatural subject matter. No science fiction or light verse. Pays in copies. Manuscripts sent without stamped, self-addressed envelopes will not be returned.

MADRONA—4332 4th N.E., #3, Seattle, WA 98105. Charles Webb, Editor.
Poetry, any length, of high literary quality. Translations, prose poems. Pays in copies.

MICHIGAN QUARTERLY REVIEW—3032 Rackham Bldg., University of Michigan, Ann Arbor, MI 48104. Radcliffe Squires, Editor.
Poetry, 4 to 30 lines; some longer. Pays 50¢ to $1 a line, on acceptance. Stamped, self-addressed envelope required.

THE MIDWEST QUARTERLY—Kansas State College, Pittsburg, KS 66762. Rebecca Patterson, Editor.
Serious poetry of all types, 50-line maximum. Pays in copies.

MISSISSIPPI REVIEW—Department of English, Southern Station, Box 37, University of Southern Mississippi, Hattiesburg, MS 39401. Gordon Weaver, Editor.
Poetry of high quality, any length. Pays $5 per poem.

MOONS AND LION TAILES—Lake Street Station, Box 8434, Minneapolis, MN 55408.
Lyrical poetry, essays, translations. Pays in copies for poetry, $9 per page for translations, prose. Query for essays.

MOVING OUT—Box 26, U.C.B., Wayne State University, 169 Mack Hall, Detroit, MI 48202.
Feminist literary magazine. Short poetry. Pays in copies.

MUNDUS ARTIUM—Ellis Hall, Ohio University, Athens, OH 45701. Rainer Schulte, Editor.
Journal of international literature and arts. International bilingual poetry. Highly conceptual quality manuscripts, not descriptive material.

MUSTANG REVIEW—P.O. Box 9007, Denver, CO 80209. Karl Edd, Editor.
   Semiannual. Metaphoric poetry, preferably 12 to 20 lines. Pays in copies.

THE NANTUCKET REVIEW—Box 1444, Nantucket, MA 02554.
   Poetry, any form, to 300 lines, of distinctive style and tone. Pays in copies.

NEW COLLAGE MAGAZINE—P.O. Box 1898, Sarasota, FL 33578. A. McA. Miller,
   General Editor.
   Expressive poems, with clear imagery and strong tone. No taboos. Pays in copies.

NEW ORLEANS REVIEW—Loyola University, New Orleans, LA 70118.
   Innovative poetry. Pays $10, on publication.

THE NEW SALT CREEK READER—1720½ C St., Lincoln, NE 68502.
   Poetry. Pays in copies.

NEW WORLD HAIKU—Heliopolis Press, Box 256, San Fernando, CA 91340. Joseph
   Earner, General Editor.
   Haiku and senryu poetry. Pays in copies.

NEW YORK QUARTERLY—P.O. Box 2415, Grand Central Station, New York, NY
   10017.
   Considers poetry of all schools, genres. Critical essays on craft and technique of
   poetry, query first. Photos, interviews staff-written. Pays in copies.

NIMROD—University of Tulsa, Tulsa OK 74104.
   Poetry, originals and translations, of highest quality. Pays in copies.

NOCTURNE—LaGuardia Hall, Brooklyn College, Brooklyn, NY 11210.
   Poetry. Pays in copies.

NORTH AMERICAN REVIEW—University of Northern Iowa, Cedar Falls, IA 50613.
   Peter Cooley, Poetry Editor.
   Highest quality poetry only. Pays 50¢ a line, on publications.

NORTHERN LIGHT—University of Manitoba Press, 605 Fletcher Argue Bldg.,
   University of Manitoba, Winnipeg, Canada R3T 2N2.
   Poetry, preferably by young Canadian writers. Reviews, 1,000 to 2,000 words, of
   recent Canadian poetry. Pays in copies.

OYEZ—430 South Michigan Ave., Chicago, IL 60605.
   Innovative poetry which reflects new trends and directions in both content and
   technique. Pays in copies. Stamped, self-addressed envelope must be included.

PAINTBRUSH—Box 3353, University Station, Laramie, WY 82071. B. M. Bennani,
   Editor.
   Semi-annual. High-quality poetry and translations.

THE PAINTED BRIDE QUARTERLY—527 South St., Philadelphia, PA 19147.
   Poetry by experienced poets, to 3 pages. Pays in copies.

PARTISAN REVIEW—Rutgers, 1 Richardson St., New Brunswick, NJ 08903. William
   Phillips, Editor.
   Poetry, any length, Pays 40¢ per line, on publication. Manuscripts held for
   consideration for at least four months.

PEBBLE—118 South Boswell Ave., Crete, NE 68333. Greg Kuzma, Editor.
   Poems, any length, essays on poetry, poetry book reviews. Pays in copies.

PENNY DREADFUL—c/o English Dept., Bowling Green University, Bowling Green, OH
   43403.
   Poetry of highest quality. Pays in copies.

PERSPECTIVES: A LITERARY OCCASIONAL–Dept. of English, State University of
  New York, Potsdam, NY 13676.
  Poetry. Submit at least 3 poems. Pays in copies.

PHOEBE: THE GEORGE MASON REVIEW–George Mason University, 4400 University
  Dr., Fairfax VA 22030.
  Poetry, 10 to 50 lines. Pays in copies.

POEM–Box 1247, West Station, Huntsville, AL 35807. Robert L. Welker, Editor.
  Highest quality poetry, any length.

POET LORE–Box 350, Westport, CT 06880.
  Conventional and experimental poetry of all types, original and translations. Verse
  plays. Pays in copies. Annual prizes for best poem published in five categories:
  Narrative, Descriptive, Subjective, Translation and Love.

POETRY–1228 N. Dearborn Pkwy., Chicago, IL 60610. Daryl Hine, Editor.
  Poems on any theme. Very high standard. Pays $1 a line, on publication.

POETRY EASTWEST–Box 391, Sumter, SC 29150. Syed Amanuddin, Editor.
  Poetry and translations of recent poetry, to 30 lines. Pays in copies. Same address
  and requirements for *Creative Moment.*

POETRY FORUM–P.O. Box 1470, Tustin, CA 92680. George S. Cook, Publisher.
  Poetry no longer than 1 page. Pays in copies.

POETRY NEWSLETTER–Dept. of English, Temple University, Philadelphia, PA 19122.
  Richard O'Connell, Editor.
  High quality poetry and translations, not necessarily restricted to modern period.
  Pays in copies.

POETRY NORTHWEST–University of Washington, Seattle, WA 98195. David Wagoner,
  Editor.
  Poetry. Pays in copies and year's subscription.

POETRY/PEOPLE–P.O. Box 264WR, Menomonee Falls, WI 53051.
  Poetry. Emphasis on good graphics and new writers. Pays in cash awards.

POETRY VIEW–1125 Valley Rd., Menasha, WI 54952. Dorothy Dalton, Editor.
  Serious poetry, to 24 lines, with fresh use of language. Free verse preferred. Light
  verse, 4 to 8 lines. No religious and overly sentimental poetry. Pays $4 per poem,
  month following publication. Reports in 2 to 3 months.

PORT TOWNSEND JOURNAL–933 Tyler St., Port Townsend, WA 98368. Ms. Cheryl
  Van Dyke, Editor.
  Annual. Traditional or experimental poetry, any length. Pays in copies.

PRAIRE SCHOONER–Andrews Hall 201, University of Nebraska, Lincoln, NE 68508.
  Bernice Slote, Editor.
  Good verse of any style and reasonable length. Pays in copies, reprints and prizes.

PRISM INTERNATIONAL–c/o Creative Writing, University of British Columbia,
  Vancouver 8, B.C., Canada.
  Poetry of high quality, any length. Pays $5 per magazine page, on publication.

PROTEUS–1004 N. Jefferson St., Arlington, VA 22205. Frank Gatling, Editor.
  Poetry, any length and style. Experimental if literate. Pays in copies. Reports in 1 to
  6 weeks.

PSYCHOLOGICAL PERSPECTIVES—595 East Colorado Blvd., Suite 503, Pasadena, CA 91101.
Quality poems with contemporary and psychological point of view. Send to J'nan M. Sellery, Poetry Editor, c/o Department of Humanities. Harvey Mudd College, Claremont, CA. 91711.

PUDDINGSTONE—539 Waterfront Cove #201, Virginia Beach, VA 23451. John Coward, Editor.
Quality poetry of all forms, any length. Pays in copies and awards.

QUARTERLY REVIEW OF LITERATURE—26 Haslet Ave., Princeton, NJ 08540. T. Weiss, Editor.
30th Anniversary Retrospective issues. No manuscripts considered until September 1976.

QUARTET—1119 Neal Pickett Dr., College Station, TX 77840. Richard H. Costa, Editor.
Poetry for highly literate audience. Pays in copies.

THE REMINGTON REVIEW—505 Westfield Ave., Elizabeth, NJ 07208. Dean Maskevich, Editor.
Quality poetry, to 100 lines, of any school. Interested in new writers. Xerox and carbon copies returned unread. Pays in copies.

ROANOKE REVIEW—English Dept., Roanoke College, Salem, VA 24153. R. R. Walter, Editor.
Quality poetry in all forms. Pays in copies.

ST. ANDREWS REVIEW—St. Andrews Presbyterian College, Laurinburg, NC 28352. Ronald H. Bayes, Editor.
Poetry. Pays in copies and awards.

SALTILLO—Box 2638, Santa Fe, NM 87501. William Kloefkorn, Poetry Editor.
Poetry. Pays in copies.

SEVEN—21½ North Harvey (Terminal Arcade), Oklahoma City, OK 73102. James Neill Northe, Editor.
Well-written, original poems, any form; free verse only if genuine and not chopped prose. Pays $4 per poem, on acceptance. Study magazine. Query.

SEWANEE REVIEW—Sewanee, TN 37375. George Core, Editor.
Serious poetry, to 60 lines, of highest quality. Pays about 60¢ per line, on publication.

SHAMAN—47 Fletcher St., Kennebunk, ME 04043. Dora Sherwood, Editor.
Serious, quality poetry in all forms, on all subjects. Pays $5 per page, on acceptance.

SHANTIH—P.O. Box 125, Bay Ridge Station, Brooklyn, NY 11220. John S. Friedman and Irving Gottesman, Editors.
Original poetry and translations. No payment.

SHENANDOAH—Box 722, Lexington, VA 24450. Dabney Stuart, Poetry Editor.
Poetry. Pay varies, on publication. Study magazine before submitting. No mss. considered June through Oct.

SILO—Bennington College, Bennington, VT 05201.
Poetry, any length. Pays in copies. Self-addressed, stamped envelope required for return of mss.

THE SMALL POND MAGAZINE—10 Overland Dr., Stratford, CT 06497. Napoleon St. Cyr, Editor.
Poetry, to 100 lines, any subject, any style. Pays in copies.

THE SMITH—5 Beekman St., New York, NY 10038. Harry Smith, General Editor.

Poetry of any length. Special interest in young and unknown poets. Modest payment on acceptance, plus copies.

SNOWY EGRET—17 Usher Rd., West Medford, MA 02155. Alan Seaburg, Poetry Editor.
High-quality poetry related to natural history, any length, any form. Pays from $2 per magazine page, on publication.

SOUTH AND WEST—1520 South 26th St., Fort Smith, AR 72901. Sue Abbott Boyd, Editor.
All types of poetry, to 40 lines; vignettes, book reviews. Pays $250 in annual awards. Overstocked.

THE SOUTH CAROLINA REVIEW—c/o English Department, Clemson University, Clemson, SC 29631.
Poems of any length. Pays in copies.

SOUTH DAKOTA REVIEW—Box 111, University Exchange, Vermillion, SD 57069. John R. Milton, Editor.
Always overstocked but will still consider outstanding poetry. Prefers longer than 20 lines. Pays in copies.

SOUTHERN HUMANITIES REVIEW—Auburn University, Auburn, AL 36803.
Poems, to 2 pages. Pays in copies.

SOUTHERN POETRY REVIEW—Dept. of English, North Carolina State University, Raleigh, NC 27607. Guy Owen, Editor.
Serious poems, shorter lengths preferred. No light verse, inspirational or nature poetry. Pays in copies.

SOUTHERN REVIEW—Drawer D, University Sta., Baton Rouge, LA 70803. Donald E. Stanford and Lewis P. Simpson, Co-editors.
High-quality poetry on serious subjects. Pays $20 per page, on publication. Manuscripts submitted without stamped, self-addressed envelopes will not be returned. Allow 1 to 2 months for editorial decision.

SOUTHWEST REVIEW—Southern Methodist University, Dallas, TX 75275. Margaret L. Hartley, Editor.
Short verse and occasional longer pieces. Pays $5 per poem, on publication.

THE SPARROW—103 Waldron St., West Lafayette, IN 47906.
High-quality poems and translations, any style, any length. Essays on poetics. Pays in copies. Offers one $25 prize for a poem in each issue. Also publishes *Vagrom Chap Books*.

SPECTRUM—U.C.S.B., Box 14800, Santa Barbara, CA 93107.
Literary annual published at University of California at Santa Barbara. Poetry of reasonable length, primarily by college students. Pays in copies. Deadline is January 15.

SPIRIT—Seton Hall University, South Orange, NJ 07079. David Rogers, Editor.
Semiannual. Poetry of all forms and lengths.

SUMUS—The Loom Press, 500 West Rosemary St., Chapel Hill, NC 27514. Kip Ward, Editor.
Poetry, any length. Pays in copies, occasional awards.

SUNDAY CLOTHES: A Magazine of the Arts—Box 66, Hermosa, SD 57744. Linda Hasselstrom, Editor.
Poetry, any length. Pays in copies, subscription.

THE SUNSTONE REVIEW—P.O. Box 2312, Santa Fe, NM 87501. Jody Ellis, Editor.
High quality poems, any length. Pays in copies. Manuscripts without stamped, self-addressed envelopes not returned.

TALL WINDOWS—1515 West 10th St., Topeka, KS 66604.
Poetry, any length, form, subject. Pays in copies.

THREE SISTERS—Box 969, Georgetown University, Washington, DC 20007. Mary Morrison, Editor.
Poetry, any length. Pays in copies.

TWIGS—Pikeville College Press, Pikeville, KY 41501.
Poetry, 28 lines preferred. Pays in copies and awards. Send poetry to Editor Lillie D. Chaffin, Box 42, Meta Sta., Pikeville, KY.

UNIVERSITY OF DENVER QUARTERLY—University of Denver, Denver, CO 80210. Burton Feldman, Editor.
Quality verse, any length. Pays $10 per page.

UNIVERSITY OF WINDSOR REVIEW—Dept. of English, University of Windsor, Ont., Canada. John Ditsky, Editor.
Poetry. Pays in copies.

THE UNSPEAKABLE VISIONS OF THE INDIVIDUAL—Box 439, California, PA 15419. Arthur Winfield Knight and Glee Knight, Editors.
Poetry, any length, any style. Pay varies. Include stamped, self-addressed envelope for return of submission.

VAGABOND—P.O. Box 879, Ellensburg, WA 98926. John Bennett, Editor.
Poetry, any length. Pays in copies.

THE VILLAGER—135 Midland Ave., Bronxville, NY 10708. Mrs. Ted W. Proudfoot, Editor.
Short verse. No payment.

VIRGINIA QUARTERLY REVIEW—1 West Range, Charlottesville, VA 22903. Charlotte Kohler, Editor.
Poetry of high literary quality, by nationally known poets and promising newcomers.

WASCANA REVIEW—c/o English Dept., University of Regina, Regina, Saskatchewan, Canada S4S 0A2.
Poetry, 4 to 100 lines. Pays $10, after publication.

WAVES—York University, Room S-713, Ross Bldg., 4700 Keele St., Downsview, Ont. M3J 1P3, Canada.
Tri-annual. Modern poetry, 4 to 200 lines. Some French manuscripts considered. Black-and-white artwork. Pays in copies.

WEST COAST REVIEW—Simon Fraser University, Burnaby 2, B. C., Canada.
Verse, any length. Pays from $5, on acceptance.

WESTERN HUMANITIES REVIEW—University of Utah, Salt Lake City, UT 84112. Jack Garlington, Editor.
High-quality poetry, any length. Single poems or groups. Pays $35 per poem, on acceptance.

WESTERN POETRY—3253 Q San Amadeo, Laguna Hills, CA 92653. Joseph Rosenzweig, Editor.
Poetry and light verse, to 20 lines. Not limited to western themes. Pays in copies and awards, after publication.

WIND—RFD Route No. 1, Box 810, Pikeville, KY 41501. Quentin R. Howard, Editor.
Poems to 30 lines. Pays in copies. Stamped, self-addressed envelopes required.

THE WINDLESS ORCHARD—6718 Baytree Dr., Ft. Wayne, IN 46825. Robert Novak, Editor.
Poetry, about one page or less. Pays in copies.

WISCONSIN POETRY MAGAZINE–P.O. Box 187, Milwaukee, WI 53201. A. M. Sterk, Editor.
High quality poetry, and accompanying art work. No payment, frequent prizes, radio readings of best poems.

WISCONSIN REVIEW–Box 177, Dempsey Hall, University of Wisconsin, Oshkosh, WI 54901.
Poetry, to 50 lines. Pays in copies.

THE WORMWOOD REVIEW–P.O. Box 8840, Stockton, CA 95024. Marvin Malone, Editor.
Poems and prose poems, to 400 lines; any style, tone, subject. Pays in copies. Stamped, self-addressed envelope should accompany submissions.

YALE REVIEW–1902A Yale Station, New Haven, CT 06520. J. E. Palmer, Editor.
Exceptional poetry, to 200 lines. Pays on publication.

YES, A MAGAZINE OF POETRY–Smith Pond, R.D. 1, Avoca, NY 14809. Virginia Elson and Beverlee Hughes, Editors.
Quality poetry of all types. Pays in copies. Stamped, self-addressed envelope must accompany manuscripts.

RELIGIOUS AND DENOMINATIONAL MAGAZINES

ALIVE! FOR YOUNG TEENS–Christian Board of Publication, Beaumont and Pine Blvd., St. Louis, MO 63166.
Suitable short poetry. Pays 25¢ per line, on acceptance.

THE AMERICAN ZIONIST–4 East 34th St., New York, NY 10016. Elias Cooper, Editor.
Poetry on themes relevant to Israel, Middle East, Jewish issues in United States or elsewhere. Pays on publication.

CAM–General Council of the Assemblies of God, 1445 Boonville, Springfield, MO 65802.
Poetry of religious significance or practical help to Pentecostal Christians at secular colleges or universities. Pays 20¢ a line.

CATHOLIC WORLD–1865 Broadway, New York, NY 10023. Robert J. Heyer, Managing Editor.
Verse, 3 to 22 lines. Pays on publication.

THE CHRISTIAN ATHLETE–Fellowship of Christian Athletes, 812 Traders National Bank Bldg., 1125 Grand Ave., Kansas City, MO 64106. Gary Warner, Editor.
Free verse, any length. Pays on publication.

THE CHRISTIAN CENTURY–407 South Dearborn St., Chicago, IL 60605. James M. Wall, Editor.
Ecumenical. Verse, to 20 lines. No payment.

CHRISTIAN HERALD–Chappaqua, NY 10514. Kenneth L. Wilson, Editor.
Interdenominational. Occasional short verse.

CHURCH MANAGEMENT–115 North Main St., Mt. Holly, NC 28120. Norman L. Hersey, Editor.
Two- or three-verse poems of interest to Protestant ministers. No payment.

COMMONWEAL–232 Madison Ave., New York, NY 10016. James O'Gara, Editor.
Catholic. Serious poetry of high quality. Pays 40¢ a line, on acceptance.

CONQUEST–6401 The Paseo, Kansas City, MO 64131. Dan Ketchum, Editor.
Church of the Nazarene. Devotional and inspirational poetry, to 20 lines. Pays 15¢ a line, on acceptance.

DAILY MEDITATION–Box 2710, San Antonio, TX 78299. Ruth S. Paterson, Editor.
Some inspirational verse. Pays 14¢ a line, on acceptance.

DECISION–Billy Graham Evangelistic Association, 1300 Harmon Place, Minneapolis,
MN 55403. Sherwood, E. Wirt, Editor.
Devotional poetry, 5 to 8 lines, for "Quiet Heart" column. Pays on publication.

THE DISCIPLE–Box 179, St. Louis, MO 63166.
Disciples of Christ. Pays $2.50 to $5 for poetry, on acceptance.

THE EVANGEL–999 College Ave., Winona Lake, IN 46590. Vera Bethel, Editor.
Free Methodist. Serious poetry, 8 to 12 lines. Pays 25¢ a line, on acceptance.

EVANGELICAL BEACON–1515 East 66th St., Minneapolis, MN 55423. George Keck,
Editor.
National magazine of Evangelical Free Church of America. Poetry. Pays on
publication.

FACE-TO-FACE–201 Eighth Ave. South, Nashville, TN 37202.
United Methodist. Poetry, traditional and avant-garde, 30 to 150 lines. Pays 25¢ a
line, on acceptance.

GOSPEL CARRIER–Pentecostal Church of God of America, P.O. Box 850, Joplin, MO
64801.
Poems, 12 to 16 lines. Pays quarterly. Send stamped, self-addressed envelope for
sample.

GOSPEL HERALD–Scottdale, PA 15683. Daniel Hertzler, Editor.
Mennonite. Poetry, to 10 lines, on Christian experience and concerns. Pays $5, on
acceptance.

HOME LIFE–127 Ninth Ave., North, Nashville, IN 37234. George W. Knight, Editor.
Southern Baptist. Short, lyrical poems with family angle; some humorous verse. Pays
on acceptance.

MATURE YEARS–201 Eighth Ave. South, Nashville, TN 37203. Daisy D. Warren,
Editor.
United Methodist. For older adults. Poetry, to 12 lines. Pays $1 per line.

THE MIRACULOUS MEDAL–475 East Chelten Ave., Philadelphia, PA 19144. Rev.
Donald L. Doyle, C.M., Editorial Director.
Catholic. Verse, to 20 lines, preferably about the Virgin Mary. Pays 50¢ a line and up,
on acceptance.

NEW WORLD OUTLOOK–475 Riverside Dr., New York, NY 10027. Arthur J. Moore,
Jr., Editor.
Occasional poetry, to 16 lines.

OUR FAMILY–Box 249, Dept. E, Battleford, Sask., Canada SOM OEO. Rev. A. J.
Materi, O.M.I., Editor.
Verse for Catholic family readers.

PURPOSE–610 Walnut Ave., Scottdale, PA 15683. David E. Hostetler, Editor.
Inspirational poetry, 3 to 24 lines, of Christian orientation. Prefers free verse poems
that deal with people's problems and indicate source of solution or comfort. "No
pious or sweet stuff considered." Pays $5 to $15. Sample copies on request.

QUAKER LIFE–Friends United Meeting, 101 Quaker Hill Dr., Richmond, IN 47374.
Appropriate verse, 10 to 30 lines. Pays in copies.

THE RECONSTRUCTIONIST–15 West 86th St., New York, NY 10024. Dr. Ira
Eisenstein, Editor.
Poetry dedicated to the advancement of Judaism. Pays on publication.

THOUGHT–Fordham University Press, Fordham University, Bronx, NY 10458. Rev.
   Joseph E. O'Neill, S.J., Editor.
   Catholic, scholarly publication. Verse. No payment.

UNITY MAGAZINE–Unity School of Christianity, Lee's Summit, MO 64063. James A.
   Decker, Editor.
   Poetry, to 20 lines. Pays 50¢ a line and up, on acceptance.

VISTA–Box 2000, Marion, IN 46952.
   Devotional poetry on following Christ in today's world. Pays 25¢ a line, on
   acceptance.

THE WAY–Mennonite Publishing House, Scottdale, PA 15683. Paul M. Schrock, Editor.
   Inspirational poems, 4 to 12 lines. Pays $5, on acceptance.

THE GREETING CARD MARKET

AMBERLEY GREETING CARD CO.–P.O. Box 37902, Cincinnati, OH 45327. Herb
   Crown, Editor.
   Humorous studio greeting card ideas, for birthday (general and relative), illness,
   hospital, friendship, anniversary; wedding, birth, and other congratulations; please
   write, miss you, travel, thank you, retirement, apology, goodbye, promotion, new
   home, new car, expectant parents. Risque humor. No conventional verse or seasonal
   cards. Motto ideas and bumper stickers; promotional concepts. Pays from $15 per
   idea, on acceptance. Reports in 30 days. Include stamped, self-addressed envelope
   with submissions.

AMERICAN GREETINGS CORPORATION–10500 American Rd., Cleveland, OH
   44144.
   Fresh ideas for humorous or juvenile cards, promotions and books. No conventional
   verse. Address S. H. McGuire, Editorial Director, Editorial Department. Short
   messages, not poetic, and not humorous or risque in tone, for Soft Touch, on love,
   missing you, think of you and friendship themes. Address Myra Zyrkle. Studio cards
   by professionals. Address Jack Clements. Pays top rates, on acceptance. Include
   stamped, self-addressed envelope with submissions.

BARKER GREETING CARD CO.–Rust Craft Park, Dedham, MA 02026. Address
   Studio Card Editor.
   Fresh ideas for Studio and Novelty greeting cards, Everyday and Seasonal lines.
   Special interest in ideas using attachment or mechanical action. Also seeks greeting
   card promotion ideas. Pays from $25, bonus for attachment and mechanical ideas.
   Monthly Market Letter sent on request when stamped, self-addressed envelope is
   included.

DAVID PRINTS–P.O. Box 502, Miller Place, NY 11764. R. David Cox, President.
   Ideas, artwork and copy for general occasion cards with honest good humor,
   intelligence and sophistication. No studio cards.

D. FORER & CO., INC.–511 East 72nd St., New York, NY 10021.
   Whimsical everyday ideas, all titles. $15 and up per idea. Designs for cute Everyday
   and whimsical Christmas lines. Stamped, self-addressed envelope must be enclosed for
   return.

FRAN MAR GREETING CARDS, LTD–630 South Columbus Ave., Mt. Vernon, NY 10550.
  Greeting card copy, preferably no more than 4 lines – cute, short and whimsical, preferably not verse, with appeal to teen and college market; no juvenile copy. Birthday (general and relative), get well, anniversary and friendship cards, and special titles. Pays $10 per idea within 30 days. Reports promptly. Stamped, self-addressed envelope must be enclosed. Query.

FRAVESSI-LAMONT, INC.–11 Edison Place, Springfield, NJ 07081. Address Editor.
  Short verses, mostly humorous; studio cards with witty prose. Sentimental verses. No Christmas material. Payment varies, on acceptance.

GALLANT GREETINGS CORPORATION–2725 West Fullerton, Chicago, IL 60647.
  Ideas for humorous and sensitivity greeting cards. Pays $12.50 to $20 per idea, in sixty days.

GIBSON GREETING CARDS, INC.–2100 Section Rd., Cincinnati, OH 45237.
  Outstanding studio, humorous, and general material. Minimum rates: $25 for humor; $50 for studio. Verse, $3 per line; "cute" and "soft" or sentimental ideas, $20; small books, $100, on acceptance. Address Editorial Dept. and enclose stamped, return envelope. Reports in ten days. Buys exclusive rights. Studio and humorous newsletter available on request.

HALLMARK CARDS, INC.–Kansas City, MO 64141. Ken DeVore, Contemporary Editor.
  Contemporary card copy that expresses strong new ideas. General greeting card ideas on assignment only. No art work. Pays $25 to $50 per idea. *Hallmark Editions:* No free lance material at this time for gift books. *Hallmark General Verse & Prose:* Submissions from previously published writers. *Humorous Illustrated Dept.* considers all free-lance ideas. Write Charles Church, Editor, for guide sheet and needs list before submitting.

KEEP 'N TOUCH GREETING CARDS–Happy Thoughts, Inc., P.O. Box 337, Stoughton, MA 02072. Rosalie Lapriore, Editor and Art Department.
  A studio line that is punchy, cheerful and complimentary. Sophisticated studio cards that say something nice in a humorous way. Ideas for Sensitivity Lines and for art. No common cartoons, conventional poetry, sarcasm, off-color cards, or overly sweet "hearts and flowers" ideas. Ideas should by typed on 3 x 5 cards or sketched in black-and-white in studio card form. Pays $15 to $20 for art, $12 to $15 per idea, $25 and up for art and idea combined, on publication. Newsletter available to contributors. Enclose self-addressed, stamped envelope.

ALFRED MAINZER, INC–39-33 29th St., Long Island City, NY 11101. Arwed H. Baenisch, Art Director.
  Everyday, Easter, Christmas, Mother's Day, Father's Day verses. Pay varies.

MILLER DESIGNS–9 Ackerman Ave., Emerson, NJ 07630. Joseph Schulman, Editor.
  Short, simple ideas for sophisticated animal cards: birthday, anniversary, get well, Valentine's Day, Christmas, Easter. Include stamped, self-addressed envelope. Reports in two weeks. Pay varies.

MISTER B GREETING CARD CO.–3500 N.W. 52nd St., Miami, FL 33142. Alvin Barker, Editor.
  Humorous, risque or novelty ideas and serious conventional or sentimental material, no more than 4 lines. Material for anniversary, birthday, Mother's Day, St. Patrick's Day, Christmas, get well, miss you. No Easter or religious material. Illustration optional. Pay varies.

NORCROSS, INC.–950 Airport Rd., West Chester, PA 19380. Nancy Lee Fuller, Creative Department.
  Conventional, Inspirational, Informal, Soft Line, Humorous, Studio, and Juvenile

cards: conversational verse; light, complimentary contemporary prose, 2, 4, or 8 lines for general and relative cards. Pays $1.50 to $3 per line for regular verse, $25 and up for humor and studio ideas, on acceptance. Submit copy on 3 x 5 cards (unless gag depends on illustration or dummy) with writer's name and address on each card, and include self-addressed, stamped envelope. Seasonal schedule available on request. Reports within three weeks.

NOVO CARD PUBLISHERS, INC.—3855 Lincoln Ave., Chicago, IL 60613.
Humorous, cute, studio, novelty greeting cards for all occasions, with "real comic punch or kick." Partial to ideas with double meaning. Verse and art combinations. No sentimental verse. Submit ideas in rough sketch. Address Editor. Pays $15 per idea, 10 days after acceptance.

THE PARAMOUNT LINE, INC.—Box 678, Pawtucket, RI 02862. Dorothy Nelson, Editor.
Humorous ideas and rough dummies; ideas for sensitivity or prose cards; four and eight line verses, both everyday and seasonals. Copy for "Images," both everyday and seasonals. Prefers material that is conversational and casual rather than sentimental. Family captions especially welcome. Reports and pays promptly. Pay varies.

REED STARLINE CARD CO.—3331 Sunset Blvd., Los Angeles, CA 90026. Reed Stevens, Editor.
Short, humorous studio card copy, conversational in tone, with message, for sophisticated adults; no verse or jingles. Everyday copy, with emphasis on birthday, friendship, get well, anniversary, thank you, travel, leaving, congratulations. Submit material for Fall holidays in December; for Valentine's Day and St. Patrick's Day in March; and for Easter, Mother's Day, Father's Day, and graduation in July. Submit each idea on 3 x 5 card. Include self-addressed, stamped envelope. Pays $40 per idea, on acceptance.

ROTH GREETING CARDS—P.O. Box 1455, 7900 Deering Ave., Canoga Park, CA 91304. Charles Roth, Editor.
Ideas for humorous studio cards, both everyday and holiday, may be submitted throughout year. Pays $40 for each original studio idea, on acceptance. Ideas for humorous plaques and "Thoughts of Love" line. Submit each idea on 3 x 5 card and enclose stamped, self addressed envelope. Promotional ideas for greeting cards, stationery and other printed paper products.

RUST CRAFT GREETING CARDS, INC.—Rust Craft Park, Dedham, MA 02026. Address Editor-in-Chief.
$10 and up for informal cards with strong illustration possibilities, $10 and up for imaginative prose sentiments (one or two lines), $25 for studio card ideas, $25 and up for humorous cards, and $30 for juvenile novelties. Pays $50 and up for book ideas, sixteen pages, one or two lines per page; with birthday, illness, friendship, love, inspirational themes—general or humorous. Pays on acceptance. Replies promptly. Market letter available on request; send stamped, self-addressed envelope.

THOUGHT FACTORY—P.O. Box 5515, Sherman Oaks, CA 91413.
Greeting cards, note cards and prints of turn-of-the-century artwork. Pay varies.

UNITED CARD CO.—1101 Carnegie, Rolling Meadows, IL 60008. Ed Letwenko, Creative Director.
Humorous contemporary studio greeting cards, with seasonal or year-round application. Submit in any form, but no finished art work. Pays from $25 and $50 per idea, on acceptance. Reports in about three weeks.

VAGABOND CREATIONS—2560 Lance Dr., Dayton, OH 45409. George F. Stnaley, Jr., Editor.
Birthday, everyday, Valentine, Christmas, and graduation studio card copy in good taste with surprise inside punch line. Humor slanted to younger age group with no

references to age itself. Mild risque humor with double entendre acceptable. Seasonal material may be submitted at any time. Ideas for buttons and motto postcards. Pays $10, on acceptance.

WARNER PRESS PUBLISHERS–Anderson, IN 46011. Mrs. Dorothy Smith, Verse Editor.
Creators of *"Sunshine Line"* and *"Regent Line."* Religious greeting card verse, from 4 to 6 lines, with suggested Scripture text for each verse (no extra pay for texts). Sensitivity or prose cards if religious in nature. Begins reading Everyday sentiments September 1st, Christmas sentiments, November 1st. Pays $1 a line on acceptance.

FILLERS AND HUMOR

Included in this list are those magazines which are noted for their excellent filler departments, plus a cross-section of other representative publications that use fillers. However, almost all magazines use some type of filler material, and writers can find dozens of markets by studying sample copies of magazines at a library or newsstand.

Many magazines do not return filler material. In such cases, writers can assume that ninety days is a long enough period to wait; after that, a filler may be submitted to another market.

ALASKA, MAGAZINE OF LIFE ON THE LAST FRONTIER–Box 4-EEE, Anchorage, AK 99509.
Short features with photos on Alaska by Alaskans.

ALIVE! FOR YOUNG TEENS–Christian Board of Publication, St. Louis, P.O. Box 179, MO 63166.
Suitable cartoons, puzzles, brainteasers, word games, short poetry.

THE AMERICAN FIELD–222 West Adams St., Chicago, IL 60606.
Short fact items and anecdotes on outdoor sports, field trails for bird dogs. Pay varies, on acceptance.

AMERICAN FRUIT GROWER–37841 Euclid Ave., Willoughby, OH 44094.
Short, personal-experience pieces, 200 to 500 words, on commercial production and/or selling of fruit. Pay varies.

AMERICAN LEGION MAGAZINE–1345 Ave. of the Americas, New York, NY 10019.
Original anecdotes (to 300 words), epigrams, humorous and light verse (to 16 lines). Pays $2.50 per line for verse, $10 per epigram, $20 per anecdote. Address "Parting Shots" Editor.

THE AMERICAN ROSE MAGAZINE–P.O. Box 30,000, Shreveport, LA 71130.
Magazine for home gardeners. Fillers. No payment.

AMERICAN VEGETABLE GROWER–37841 Euclid Ave., Willoughby, OH 44094.
Fact items, 200 to 500 words with black-and-white photos, on commercial production of vegetables: spraying, fertilizing, irrigating, machinery, innovative ideas. Pays $10 to $20, on acceptance.

THE AMERICAN WEST–599 College Ave., Palo Alto, CA 94306. Ed Holm, Managing Editor.
"Collector's Choice," 1,000 words, plus illustration, about unusual people, places or events in Old West. Pays $75.

ARGOSY–420 Lexington Ave., New York, NY 10017.
Anecdotes, 250 words, for "Adventure" column: drama, humor or news on hunting, fishing, outdoors, camping, crime, cars, etc. Pays $15 to $20.

ARIZONA–120 East Van Buren St., Phoenix, AZ 85004.
Sunday roto magazine of *The Arizona Republic.* Short fillers, humor, cartoons, related to Arizona. Pays before publication.

THE ATLANTIC—8 Arlington St., Boston, MA 02116.
Sophisticated humorous or satirical pieces, 1,000 to 3,000 words. Some light poetry. Study magazine before submitting. Payment rates vary, on acceptance.

BABY CARE—52 Vanderbilt Ave., New York, NY 10017. Mrs. Maja Bernath, Editor.
Short items for columns: "Focus on You" (500 words), pays $25; "Family Corner" (100 words), pays $10. Also some short poetry, cartoons.

BABY TALK—66 East 34th St., New York, NY 10016.
Short features on child care.

BITS AND PIECES—Box 746, Newcastle, WY 92701. Mabel E. Brown, Editor.
Fillers, 500 to 1,000 words, on history of Wyoming and surrounding states. Source must be given. Pays in copies.

BOY'S LIFE—North Brunswick, NJ 08902.
Short how-to features, 750 words maximum, on hobbies, crafts, science, outdoor skills.

CAMPING AND TRAILERING GUIDE—P.O. Box 1014, Grass Valley, CA 95945.
Occasional one-picture how-tos, 300 to 800 words, on travel objectives, with information about camping at the scene or close by. Pays $25, on publication.

CARTOON PARADE—See *Humorama, Inc.*

CATALYST—Christian Board of Publication, Box 179, St. Louis, MO 63166.
For senior high school students. Poems, cartoons. Pays 25¢ a line to 20 lines, by arrangement for longer lengths; $6 and up for cartoons.

CATHOLIC DIGEST—P.O. Box 3090, St. Paul, MN 55165.
For "Hearts Are Trumps," original accounts, under 300 words, of true cases where unseeking kindness was rewarded. For "Open Door," true incidents by which persons were brought into the Church. For "The Perfect Assist," original reports of tactful remarks or actions. For "People Are Like That," true accounts illustrating goodness of human nature. Pays $50 per item. Amusing tales of parish life for "In Our Parish." Pays $20 per item. Pays $4 for "Flights of Fancy," picturesque figures of speech, and for "Signs of the Times," amusing signs. Give exact source. Regular jokes and fillers, average payment $10. All payment on publication. Submissions not acknowledged or returned.

CATS—P.O. Box 4106, Pittsburgh, PA 15202.
Poems, preferably light, about cats, to 30 lines. Pays 20¢ a line, on acceptance.

CHANGING TIMES: *The Kiplinger Magazine*—1729 H St. N.W., Washington, DC 20006.
Original, unpublished epigrams, topical quips, one or two sentences, for "Notes on These Changing Times." Pays $10 per item.

CHATELAINE—481 University Ave., Toronto M5N 1V5, Ont., Canada.
Pays $25 to $150 for humorous fillers, $10 to $25 for light verse, on acceptance.

CHEVRON USA—P.O. Box 6227, San Jose, CA 95150.
Humorous anecdotes, 100 to 250 words, on travel in the U.S., West, family activities, sports. Cartoons. Pays $25 for anecdotes, $50 for cartoons, on acceptance.

CHILD LIFE—1100 Waterway, Box 567B, Indianapolis, IN 46206.
For children 7 to 11. Verse, puzzles, games, mazes, tricks. Pays about 3¢ a word for prose, 25¢ a line for poetry, on publication.

CHILDREN'S PLAYMATE–1100 Waterway Blvd., P.O. Box 567 B, Indianapolis, IN 46206.
For children 3 to 8. Verse, puzzles, games, mazes, tricks. Pays about 3¢ a word for prose, about 25¢ a line for poetry, on publication.

CHORAL PRAISE–See *Church Musician.*

THE CHRISTIAN ADVENTURER–Messenger Publishing House, P.O. Box 850, Joplin, MO 64801.
Weekly Sunday school paper for teen-agers. Inspirational fillers, Bible puzzles. Pays ½¢ a word, on publication.

CHRISTIAN HERALD–40 Overlook Dr., Chappaqua, NY 10514.
Poems, 4 to 24 lines, church bulletin board photos with significant messages, 500-word personal experiences with a point, unusual original anecdotes. Pays $5 to $15.

THE CHRISTIAN HOME–201 Eighth Ave. South, Nashville, IN 37202.
United Methodist. Material on almost any subject related to family living, 800 to 1,000 words. Seasonal, inspirational, or humorous verse, to 16 lines. Pays 50¢ a line for poetry, $10 to $15 for prose, on acceptance.

CHRISTIAN LIFE–Gundersen Dr. and Schmale Rd., Wheaton, IL 60187.
News items, 100 to 200 words, with human interest, on trends, ideas, personalities, events of interest to Christians today; also photos. Pays on publication.

CHURCH MUSICIAN–127 Ninth Ave. North, Nashville, TN 37234. W. M. Anderson, Editor.
For Southern Baptist music leaders. Fillers with musical touch. Pays about 2¢ a word, on acceptance. Same address and requirements for *Gospel Choir* and *Choral Praise* (for adults), and *Opus One* and *Opus Two* (for teenagers).

CLIMB–Warner Press Inc., Publication Board of the Church of God, Anderson, IN 46011.
Church school paper for junior boys and girls. Puzzles, cartoons, ideas for family fun, things to make and do, brief meditations, photo essays. Pays $7.50 per thousand words, on acceptance.

COLORADO MAGAZINE–7190 West 14th Ave., Denver, CO 80215. James Sample, Managing Editor.
For "Alpinehaus," articles to 1,000 words, on mountain homes in Rocky Mountain West, with photos. Pays $150. Pays $75 for "Out-of-the-Way-West" 750-word articles about unusual spots off main highways in Rocky Mountain states. Occasional short "sidebar" pieces on skiing, ski touring, safety, to accompany full-length articles. Queries welcome.

COLUMBIA–Box 1670, New Haven, CT 06507.
Official journal of Knights of Columbus. Short humor or satire features, to 1,000 words, and captionless cartoons. Pays up to $100 for short humor, $25 for cartoons, on acceptance.

CONFIDENTIAL CONFESSIONS–Dauntless Books, Inc., 1120 Ave. of Americas, New York, NY 10036.
Fillers, to 700 words, on marriage, courtship, personality, child care. Pays 3¢ a word and up, on acceptance. Same address and requirements for *Daring Romances, Exciting Confessions, Revealing Romances* and *Secrets.*

DAVID C. COOK PUBLISHING CO.–850 North Grove Ave., Elgin, IL 60120.
Puzzles, games, cartoons, how-to features, anecdotes about famous people, word origins, etc., for junior through adult Protestant evangelical Sunday schools. Pays 2¢ to 4¢ a word.

CORONET—7950 Deering Ave., Canoga Park, CA 91304. Catherine Nixon Cooke, Editor.
Short, humorous anecdotes about children for "Things Our Kids Tell Us." Puzzles, brainteasers; submit to Puzzle Editor. Pays $5.

CREEM—P.O. Box P-1064, Birmingham, MI 48012. Robert Duncan, Acquisitions Editor.
Offbeat news times, to 500 words, and cartoons. Pay varies.

CURRENT COMEDY—See *Orben's Current Comedy.*

CYCLE WORLD—1499 Monrovia Ave., P.O. Box 1757, Newport Beach, CA 92663.
Humor of interest to motorcycle enthusiasts, 1,500 to 2,000 words. Racing reports, 400 to 600 words, with photos; cartoons; news of motorcycle industry, legislation, trends. Pays $75 to $100 per page, on publication.

DIXIE-ROTO— *The Times-Picayune,* New Orleans, LA 70140.
Humorous, original shorts involving children from Louisiana or Mississippi for "Bright Talk." Pays $2 to $3. Documented historical anecdotes related to the south. Pays $20.

DOWN EAST—Camden, ME 04843.
True anecdotes and stories about Maine, to 300 words, for "It Happened Down East." Pays $5. Recollections of Maine incidents, to 300 words with black-and-white photo, for "I Remember," $10. "Room With a View," 850-900 words, pays $35. Amusing or informative observations of contemporary Maine, which lend themselves to editorial comment, for "North by East" section. Payment is determined by length and on acceptance.

EBONY—820 South Michigan Ave., Chicago, IL 60605.
For "Speaking of People," items to 200 words, on blacks in jobs heretofore closed to blacks. Material must describe job, how obtained, training, etc. Human-interest angle helpful. Pays $20 and up.

THE ELKS MAGAZINE—425 West Diversey Pkwy., Chicago, IL 60614. D. J. Herda, Editor.
Good, general-interest humor, traditional, tongue-in-cheek, or experimental, tastefully slanted to family audience, 1,500 to 3,000 words. No fillers. Pays 10¢ a word, and up.

THE EMPIRE MAGAZINE—*Denver Post*, Denver, CO 80201.
Weekly supplement. Photo-illustrated fillers on subjects of interest to Rocky Mountain readers. Pays about 4¢ to 5¢ a word, plus $10 per black-and-white photo.

EVENT—Baptist Sunday School Board, 127 Ninth Ave. North, Nashville, TN 37234.
For Southern Baptist youth. Puzzles, cartoons, poetry to 16 lines. Pays $5 to $15.

EXPECTING—52 Vanderbilt Ave., New York, NY 10017. Mrs. Maja Bernath, Editor.
"Happenings," anecdotes about pregnancy. Sophisticated light verse. Pays $10 per item; $5 for verse.

FAMILY CIRCLE—488 Madison Ave., New York, NY 10022. Babette Ashby, Articles Editor.
Back-of-book features, to 1,500 words: short humor, how-to and inspirational items. Pays to $500. Fillers, 50 to 75 words, on informative ideas to better everyday life. Pays $10.

THE FAMILY FOOD GARDEN—Rt. 1, Box 877, McCourtney Rd., Grass Valley, CA 95945. George S. Wells, Publisher.
Fillers, cartoons relating to home food gardening; some recipes. Nominal payment, on acceptance.

THE FAMILY HANDYMAN—235 East 45th St., New York, NY 10017.
Shorts, 100 to 300 words, with or without photos or rough drawings on expert tips or shortcuts for do-it-yourselfers. Pays $5 to $15, on acceptance.

FATE—Clark Publishing Co., 500 Hyacinth Pl., Highland Park, IL 60035.
Fact fillers, to 200 words, on strange, psychic, or unexplained happenings. Pays $1 to $3. True stories, to 300 words, on psychic or mystic personal experiences. Pays $10.

FIELD AND STREAM—383 Madison Ave., New York, NY 10017.
Short features on unusual outdoor subjects, basically how-to, up to 1,000 words. Humorous articles, to 2,000 words. Pays $250 and up, on acceptance for fillers; more for humor.

FUN HOUSE—See *Humorama, Inc.*

GARCIA FISHING ANNUAL—329 Alfred Ave., Teaneck, NJ 07666. Robert E. Stankus, Editor.
Humorous pieces on fishing. Pays on acceptance.

GAZE—See *Humorama, Inc.*

GIRLTALK—380 Madison Ave., New York, NY 10017.
Fillers and short, humorous verse for women. Pays 8¢ a word.

GOLF—380 Madison Ave., New York, NY 10017.
Fillers and short humor on golf. Pays $50 on acceptance.

GOLF DIGEST MAGAZINE—297 Westport Ave., Norwalk, CT 06856.
Short fact items, anecdotes, quips, jokes, light verse pertaining to golf. True humorous or odd incidents, up to 200 words. Pays $15 and up, on acceptance.

GOOD HOUSEKEEPING—959 Eighth Ave., New York, NY 10019. Robert M. Liles, Features Editor.
Pays $5 and up a line for light verse. Very short humorous prose items for humor page and back of book fillers. Pays from $10 to $100.

GOSPEL CARRIER—Messenger Publishing House, P.O. Box 850, Joplin, MO 64801.
Weekly adult Sunday school paper. Inspirational fillers. Pays ½¢ a word, on publication.

GOSPEL CHOIR—See *Church Musician.*

GOURMET MAGAZINE—777 Third Ave., New York, NY 10017.
Light verse with a sophisticated food or drink angle. Pays on acceptance.

GUIDEPOSTS—747 Third Ave., New York, NY 10017. Dina Donohue, Senior Editor.
Anecdotal fillers, to 250 words, with spiritual or inspirational point. Pays $10 to $25.

HARDWARE AGE—Chilton Way, Radnor, PA 19089. Jon P. Kinslow, Editor.
Fillers and photos, describing unique or successful hardware store operations. Cartoons on hardware retailing. Pays $10 and up.

HOME LIFE—127 Ninth Ave. North, Nashville, TN 37234. George Knight, Editor.
Southern Baptist. First-person, personal-experience fillers, 100 to 500 words, related to family relationships. Pays 2½¢ a word, on acceptance.

HOSPITAL PHYSICIAN—550 Kinderkamack, Oradell, NJ 97649.
"Here's How I Do It," "What's Wrong with This Patient?" "Your Next Step?" and "Pediatricks," by *doctor* readers. Pays $50.

HOW-TO—964 North Pennsylvania St., Indianapolis, IN 46204. John J. Sullivan, Editor.

Simple, "how-to" fillers on home maintenance, home repair, home improvement projects, gardening, etc. Pays $15 to $50, on acceptance.

HUMORAMA, INC.–100 North Village Ave., Rockville Centre, NY 11570.
Topical satire. epigrams, humorous fillers, up to 600 words. Light verse, up to 24 lines. Pays $1.50 for one-line fillers, 50¢ a line for verse, 4¢ a word for prose, just before publication. Same address and requirements for *Joker, Pop Cartoons, Pop Jokes, Cartoon Parade, Laugh Riot, Quips, Stare, Gaze, Fun House, Zip, Cartoon Fun & Comedy.*

HUNTING–Petersen Publishing Co., 8490 Sunset Blvd., Los Angeles, Ca 90069.
Fillers on how-to aspect fo hunting. Pays $50.

JACK AND JILL–1100 Waterway Blvd., P.O. Box 567B, Indianapolis, IN 46206. William Wagner, Editor.
For children 5 to 12. Poems, short plays, puzzles, games, science and craft projects. "For Carpenters Only," articles, 250 to 500 words, on woodworking. Instructions for all activities should be clearly written, accompanied by models or diagram sketches, and list of materials and tools needed. Pay varies, on publication.

THE JEWELERS' CIRCULAR-KEYSTONE–Chilton Company, Radnor, PA 19089.
Shorts, 200 to 300 words, focusing on a single activity that built traffic and sales or cut costs for a jeweler or jewelry department. Pays $10, on acceptance.

JOKER–See *Humorama, Inc.*

LADY'S CIRCLE–21 West 26th St., New York, NY 10010.
Fillers, 600 words, with photos, on women who overcame obstacles to get to top in any area of employment for "Women Who Never Say Never." "Sound-Off" department pays $10. "Cut-Out Cookbook" pays $5 per recipe.

LADY GOLFER–P.O. Box 4725, Whittier, CA 90607. Charles G. Schoos, General Manager.
Golf-related fillers, jokes, humor, puzzles. Pays $35 to $150, on acceptance.

LAUGH RIOT–See *Humorama, Inc.*

LOGOS JOURNAL–185 North Ave., Plainfield, NJ 07060. Alden West, Editor.
Charismatic, evangelical Christian publication. Fillers, short humor, puzzles. Pays $2 to $15, on publication.

McCALL'S–230 Park Ave., New York, NY 10017.
Fillers, 150 words, on "Survival in the Suburbs" for "Right Now" column. Pays $50. Manuscripts are not returned. Include address and telephone number with submissions.

MAKE IT WITH LEATHER–Box 1386, Fort Worth, TX 76101.
"Tips and Hints," problem/solution format pertaining to leathercraft. Pays $10.

MALE–575 Madison Ave., New York, NY 10022.
Jokes of interest to men. Submissions cannot be returned. No poetry. Pays $5 per joke, on acceptance. Same address and requirements for *Men, Man's World,* and *True Action.*

MAN'S WORLD–See *Male.*

MARRIAGE AND FAMILY LIVING (formerly *Marriage*)–St. Meinrad, IN 47577.
For "Two Ring Circus," short jokes, anecdotes, to 150 words, on husband-wife, parent-child relationships. Original best, but if published before, must indicate source. Pays $5 on publication. Manuscripts not acknowledged or returned.

MATURE YEARS–Methodist Publishing House, 201 Eighth Ave. South, Nashville, TN 37202.
For older adults. Poems, cartoons, puzzles, jokes, anecdotes, to 300 words. Pays 3¢ per word, on acceptance.

MECHANIX ILLUSTRATED–1515 Broadway, New York, NY 10036.
Single photos with captions, tips with rough drawings, or unillustrated tips for shortcuts in shop, garage, or home for "It's New," "Home & Shop Shorts," "Freddie Fumbles" (cartoon strip), "Ask Rufus," "Inventions Wanted" (ideas for inventions from readers), with "MIMI" (unusual new products shown with girl "product tester"). Cartoons and short fillers, to 500 words. Rates: Captioned photos, $30; tips with drawing, to $25; unillustrated tip, $15; cartoons, $35, "Inventions Wanted" ideas, $5; "Freddie Fumbles" ideas, $15; fillers, $75.

MEN–See *Male.*

MODERN BRIDE–One Park Ave., New York, NY 10017.
Poems, short humorous pieces, 500 to 1,500 words, directed to the about-to-be or newly married bride. Pays on acceptance.

MODERN MATURITY–215 Long Beach Blvd., Long Beach, CA 90802. Hubert C. Pryor, Editor.
For "Tips Worth Considering," money-saving ideas, how-to and craft tips, no medical and legal. Quotes from people over 54. For "Fun Fare," crossword puzzles, pays $50; quizzes, problems, cryptograms, etc., $20; riddles, brain-teasers, etc., $5. Prefers seasonal material; send 6 months ahead.

MODERN PEOPLE NEWSWEEKLY–11058 West Addison St., Franklin Park, IL 60131.
Fillers, 25 to 250 words, on health, consumer protection, the occult, oddities, etc. Pays $2 to $25 within three weeks of acceptance.

MODERN PHOTOGRAPHY–130 East 59th St., New York, NY 10022.
Photographic how-tos, 250 to 300 words. Pays $15 to $20 for text and photograph, on acceptance.

MOTOR BOATING & SAILING–224 West 57th St., New York, NY 10019.
Short items of strong boating or water sports interest, including anecdotes, humor, news, shorts, fillers, cartoons. Pays competitive rates, on acceptance.

NRTA Journal–215 Long Beach Blvd., Long Beach, CA 90801. Hubert C. Pryor, Editor.
Short verse, humor, "Find-the-Word" and crossword puzzles, tips, how-to and crafts, cartoons, for older readers. Pays $5 to $50.

NATIONAL ENQUIRER–Lantana, FL 33462.
Short humorous fillers, original or well-selected quotation (give source), witticisms, anecdotes, tart comments on the human condition. Pays $15. Submit to Fillers Editor.

NATIONAL GUARDSMAN–1 Massachusetts Ave. N.W., Washington, DC 20001.
True Army and Air Force anecdotes for "Tales from the Troops." Pays $10, on publication.

NATIONAL LAMPOON–635 Madison Ave., New York, NY 10022.
No unsolicited manuscripts.

NATIONAL REVIEW–150 East 35th St., New York, NY 10016.
Conservative political journal. Short prose satire, to 900 words. Pays $35 to $75, on publication.

THE NATIONAL STAR–730 Third Ave., New York, NY 10017.
Newsy, topical, unusual stories and photos, for broad family readership. Pay varies.

NEBRASKALAND–2200 North 33rd St., Lincoln, NE 68503. Lowell Johnson, Editor.
Verse of interest to Nebraska residents; no payment. Cartoons, preferably on outdoor subjects; pays $5.

THE NEW YORKER–25 West 43rd St., New York, NY 10036.
Amusing mistakes printed in newspapers, books, magazines, etc. Entertaining, true anecdotes. Pays $5 and up, on acceptance; extra payment for headings and/or tag lines.

THE OHIO MOTORIST–6000 South Marginal Rd., Cleveland, OH 44103.
Short humorous poems, 4 to 6 lines, on motoring, automotive and vacation topics (foreign and domestic). Pays $6 to $8.

OKLAHOMA RANCH AND FARM WORLD–Box 1770, Tulsa, OK 74102.
Sunday supplement of Tulsa *Sunday World*. Farm, suburban, homemaking pieces, to 800 words, with photos. Pays $10 per column, on publication. Query.

ON THE LINE–Mennonite Publishing House, Scottdale, PA 15683.
Children's story paper. Light verse, 8 to 24 lines, cartoons, human-interest photos with brief explanations. Pays $3.50 and up for puzzles, quizzes; verse, $4 to $8; photo features $75.0 to $15. Sample copies available on request.

OPUS ONE and OPUS TWO–See *Church Musician.*

ORBEN'S CURRENT COMEDY (formerly *Current Comedy*)–801 Wilmington Trust Bldg., Wilmington DE 19801. Send manuscripts to Robert Orben, 2510 Virginia Ave. N.W., Apt. 701-N, Washington, DC 20037.
Original, funny, performable one-liners and brief jokes on news, fads, trends, topical subjects. Pays $3, at end of month. No material returned without stamped, self-addressed envelope.

ORGANIC GARDENING AND FARMING–Emmaus, PA 18049.
Fillers, 100 to 500 words, on actual garden experiences; how-tos, solution of problems, etc. Material for various departments, news items. Pays $25 to $50, before publication.

THE ORPHAN'S MESSENGER–P.O. Box 288, Jersey City, NJ 07303.
Humorous fillers, 90 to 100 words, and verse, 4 to 40 lines in length. Pays 1¢ per word, on acceptance.

OUTDOOR LIFE–380 Madison Ave., New York, NY 10017.
Short, instructive or informative items, hints on hunting, fishing, camping gear, boats, similar outdoor equipment. Often uses one photo or sketch. Pays on acceptance.

PARENTS MAGAZINE–52 Vanderbilt Ave., New York, NY 10017.
Imaginative, humorous children's sayings for "Out of the Mouths of Babes"; pays $5 per item; short items on sensible solution of problem in child care or family relations (allowances, nap-taking, eating problems, etc.) for "Family Clinic"; pays $10 per item, on publication.

PLAYBOY–919 North Michigan Ave., Chicago, IL 60611.
Buys jokes for $50; "After Hours" items (brief amusing paragraphs on topical subjects), $50 to $350. Address Party Jokes Editor or After Hours Editor.

PLAYGIRL–1801 Century Park, East, Suite 2300, Century City, Los Angeles, CA 90067.
Fillers, 500 to 800 words, humor, satire, to interest contemporary women. Cartoons. No jokes.

POP JOKES–See *Humorama, Inc.*

POPULAR PHOTOGRAPHY–One Park Ave., New York, NY 10016.
Pays $10 for each illustrated "Photo Tips" department item, on publication.

POPULAR SCIENCE MONTHLY–380 Madison Ave., New York, NY 10017.
Short fact items and hints, with glossy photos or rough sketches, for departments: "Taking Care of Your Car;" "Short Cuts and Tips" (home shop hints, techniques); ideas for "Wordless Workshop." Pays $25, on acceptance.

PROBE THE UNKNOWN—1874 West Empire Ave., Burbank, CA 91504. Leslie D. Zerg, Associate Editor.
Short news items on psychic phenomena for "Psychic News and Enigmas." Pay varies, on publication. No material returned unless accompanied by self-addressed, stamped envelope.

PROCEEDINGS—U.S. Naval Institute, Annapolis, MD 21402. Clayton R. Barrow, Jr., Editor.
Short, humorous anecdotes to interest naval and maritime readers. Pays $25, on acceptance.

QUIPS—See *Humorama, Inc.*

READER'S DIGEST—Pleasantville, NY 10570.
"Life in These United States," "Humor in Uniform," "Campus Comedy," "All in a Day's Work," pays $200 for previously unpublished anecdotes, on publication. "Toward More Picturesque Speech," $25 to first contributor. For "Laughter, the Best Medicine," "Personal Glimpses" and other anecdotes, $10 per *Digest* two-column line for originals, $25 for reprints. Watch magazine for announcements of other departments. No fillers acknowledged or returned.

ROLL CALL—428 8th St. S.E., Washington, DC 20003.
Short humorous items concerning Congress and Congressmen, anecdotes, puzzles, quips on political subjects. Pays on acceptance.

ROTARIAN—1600 Ridge Ave., Evanston, IL 60201. Willmon L. White, Editor.
Humorous articles, 1,200 words, for business and professional men. Pays top rates. Query.

SAN FRANCISCO—120 Green St., San Francisco, CA 94111.
Cartoons. Pays $25 and up, on publication.

THE SATURDAY EVENING POST—1100 Waterway Blvd., Indianapolis, Ind. 46202. Frederic A. Birmingham, Managing Editor.
Short humor pieces, 1,500 to 2,000 words, cartoons, light verse for "Post Scripts," short quizzes (boxed and illustrated), two-paragraph anecdotes. Pays varies.

THE SENTINEL—Organizations Services Corp., 1616 Soldiers Field Rd., Boston, MA 02135.
Official publication of Massachusetts Police Association. Some appropriate humorous shorts and fillers. Pays on publication.

SEVENTEEN—850 Third Ave., New York, NY 10022.
Fashion and service magazine for teen-age girls. Fillers, to 500 words, for "Mini-Mag" news section. Short articles by writers under 20 for "In My Opinion"; pays $100. Fact and fiction. 20 to 200 words, for "Free For All"; pays to $40. Photos, cartoons, poetry by teens. Pay varies, on acceptance.

SICK—919 Third Ave., New York, NY 10022. Paul Laikin, Editor.
Zany articles that fit magazine's format. No lengthy prose pieces. Pays within a month of acceptance.

SKIING MAGAZINE—One Park Ave., New York, NY 10016.
Short articles, 500 to 1,000 words, on skiing of the past, personal anecdotes, humorous vignettes. One-paragraph fillers on skiing oddities. Articles, 1,200 to 1,500 words, for "Letters From" column, detailing skiing experience in distant place. Pays 10¢ a word and up, on acceptance.

SMALL WORLD–Volkswagen of America, 818 Sylvan Ave., Englewood Cliffs, NJ
    07632.
    Anecdotes, up to 100 words, about Volkswagen owners' experiences; cartoons,
    humorous color transparencies about Volkswagens. Pays $15 and up, on acceptance.

SNOTRACK–534 North Broadway, Milwaukee, WI 53202. Bill Vint, Editor.
    Official magazine of United States Snowmobile Association. Short humor and
    cartoons. Pays $15 to $25 for single cartoon; other payments vary.

SPORTS AFIELD–250 West 55th St., New York, NY 10019.
    Unusual, useful tips and gimmicks, 100 to 700 words with photos, on hunting,
    fishing, camping, boating, shooting. Pays $50 to $400, on acceptance.

STARE–See *Humorama, Inc.*

SUNDAY DIGEST–850 North Grove Ave., Elgin IL 60120. Darlene Petri, Editor.
    Christian publication. Original anecdotes to 500 words, inspirational or humorous.
    Pays $20 to $25. Timely vignettes (submit seasonal material twelve months in
    advance), quotations, to 300 words. Pays up to $15. Short pithy, original poems,
    jokes, epigrams pinpointing Christian virtues or frailties. Pays $2.50 to $5. All
    payment on acceptance. Material returned only if stamped, self-addressed envelope is
    enclosed.

SUNSET–Lane Publishing Co., Menlo Park, CA 94025.
    Uses almost no free-lance material.

SURFER MAGAZINE–Box 1028, Dana Point, CA 92629.
    Humor, humorous poems, cartoons, news items, to 50 words with photos, on surfing.
    Pays 4¢ to 10¢ a word, on publication.

TV GUIDE–Radnor, PA 19088.
    Short humor pertaining to television for one-page "TV Jibe" feature. Items should fit
    on one *TV Guide* page; some longer humor (to two pages) accepted. Pay varies.

TABLE TALK–5161 River Rd., Washington, DC 20016. Martin Buxbaum, Editor.
    Original puzzles, jokes, essays, riddles, and personal anecdotes. No poetry. Pays 2¢ a
    word, $5 minimum.

TENNIS USA–Chilton Co. Chilton Way, Radnor, PA 19089. Robert L. Gillen, Editor.
    Tennis-related cartoons, jokes, puzzles, fillers. Pays to $25, on acceptance.

TODAY'S CHRISTIAN MOTHER–8121 Hamilton Ave., Cincinnati, OH 45231. Wilma
    L. Shaffer, Editor.
    Fillers for father's page; creative children's activities; brief suggestions from parents
    on methods of building Christian home for "Happenings at Our House"; quips, short
    poems. Pay varies, on acceptance.

TRAILER BOATS–P.O. Box 6697, 1512 West Magnolia Blvd. Burbank, CA 91510.
    Ralph Poole, Editor and Publisher.
    Boat-oriented fillers, humor, jokes. Pays 7¢ to 10¢ a word, on publication.

TRUE–21 West 26th St., New York, NY 10016.
    Men's magazine. Brief news items not overexposed in the media. Pays $50.
    Humorous, unusual events in sports; unusual recipes or food ideas. Pays to $300. No
    filler jokes, experiences or anecdotes.

TRUE ACTION–See *Male.*

TRUE CONFESSIONS–205 East 42nd St., New York, NY 10017.
    Fillers, 300 to 800 words, of interest to young wives, for "Feminine Side of Things"
    column. Pays $50 and up, on acceptance.

TRUE ROMANCE—205 East 42nd St., New York, NY 10017. Jean Press Silberg, Editor.
Short personal-experience items for columns: "How We Met," "One Moment That
Changed My Life," "My Personal Recipe for Happiness." Watch for new features.

TRUE STORY—P.O. Box 1448. Grand Central Station, New York, NY 10017.
Short, humorous or inspirational personal experiences for "Women Are Wonderful";
features on home and children; light verse. Pays 5¢ a word.

TRUE TREASURE—P.O. Drawer L, Conroe, TX 77301.
Magazine about lost mines, buries or sunken treasure. Fillers, 100 to 250 words, for
"Treasure Nuggets." Pays $12.50.

WEIGHT WATCHERS MAGAZINE—635 Madison Ave., New York, NY 10022.
Humor, jokes, quizzes and cartoons. No poetry or puzzles. Pays on acceptance.

WESTART—Box 1396, Auburn, CA 95603.
Artists' newspaper. Short features, current news items, 350 to 500 words, of
exceptional interest in the field of crafts and fine arts. No hobbies. Pays 30¢ per
column inch, on publication.

WOMAN'S DAY—1515 Broadway, New York, NY 10036.
For "Neighbors," items relating some family experience which will benefit others,
and brief practical suggestions for homemakers. Pays $25 for each letter published,
$5 for suggestions. Photos welcome.

THE WORKBASKET—4251 Pennsylvania, Kansas City, MO 64111.
How-to articles, 200 to 400 words, with completed models or good black-and-white
photos, and clear instructions. Pays 2¢ a word. Short instructions, including selling
price, on item women can make and sell, for "Women Who Make Cents." Pays $5, on
acceptance.

YACHTING MAGAZINE—50 West 44th St., New York, NY 10036. William W.
Robinson, Editor.
Occasional short fillers and anecdotes. Nominal pay, on publication.

YANKEE MAGAZINE—Dublin, NH 03444.
Items, to 400 words, about New England's small business and/or hobbies. Pays $15.
Unusual articles, humorous stories, 500 to 2,500 words, with black-and-white photos
if possible, related to New England. Pays $25 to $400; $15 to $25 per photo.

YOUNG MISS—52 Vanderbilt Ave., New York, NY 10017.
How-to hints, especially things to make with odds and ends, to 100 words, for young
teen-age girls. Pays $5, on acceptance.

YOUNG MUSICIANS—127 Ninth Ave. North, Nashville, TN 37234. Jimmy R. Key,
Editor.
Puzzles, games, quizzes, relating to church music for children, ages 9-11, and
illustrated material on making simple instruments, sound experiments. Much material
written on assignment.

YOUR TIME—4825 North Scott, Schiller Park, IL 60176.
Fillers on unusual used of leisure time, or on new products in entertainment and
recreation fields. Pay varies, on publication.

ZIP—See *Humorama, Inc.*

JUVENILE, TEEN-AGE AND YOUNG ADULT MAGAZINES

Magazines for both children and teen-agers are listed here. Markets for book-length juvenile fiction and nonfiction are listed under *Book Publishers*.

JUVENILE MAGAZINES

A.D.–United Church Herald Edition and Presbyterian Life Edition, 1840 Interchurch Center, 475 Riverside Dr., New York, NY 10027. J. Martin Bailey, Editor.
Adult publication, but also uses stories for children, ages 6 to 10, 700 to 800 words and "Fun for Families" activities material. Pays on acceptance.

AMERICAN RED CROSS YOUTH NEWS–American National Red Cross, Washington, DC 20006.
Stories, 1,000 to 1,200 words, for children through sixth grade: fantasy, mystery, adventure, science fiction, history, biography, seasonal material, contemporary U.S. children. Accurate, up-to-date articles on ecology, wildlife, science. Realistic photo essays of children in this country and others.

THE BEEHIVE–201 Eighth Ave. South, Nashville, TN 37203.
For grades four through six. Stories, to 700 words. Some poetry. Pays 2¢ to 3¢ a word for prose, 50¢ a line for poetry.

CHILD LIFE–1100 Waterway Blvd., P.O. Box 567B, Indianapolis, IN 46206. Jane E. Norris, Editor.
For children 7 to 11. Fiction to 1,200 words. Beginner reading material, 400 to 500 words. Nature and science articles, 600 to 900 words. Games, puzzles, projects, etc. Short plays for classroom and living room production. Pays about 3¢ a word for stories, about $2.50 per photo and $5 per transparency, and 25¢ a line for verse, on publication. Reports in 8 to 10 weeks. No queries; send completed manuscript.

CHILDREN'S PLAYMATE–1100 Waterway Blvd., P.O. Box 567B, Indianapolis, IN 46206. Beth Wood Thomas, Editor.
For children ages 3 to 8. Fiction, to 600 words. Humorous stories and poems preferred. Make-its or crafts requiring minimum of adult guidance, with clear, brief instructions. Simple science articles and/or easy experiments. Monthly "All About . . ." features, 300 to 500 words, on interesting people, animals, events, etc. Pays about 3¢ per word, on publication. Submit seasonal material 8 months in advance. Reviews articles in 8 to 10 weeks. Stamped, self-addressed envelope required for return. Writer's guide sent on request.

THE CHRISTIAN SCIENCE MONITOR–One Norway St., Boston, MA 02115. John Hughes, Editor.
Puzzles, quizzes, news features, occasional story, 500 to 600 words, for children 12 years and under, weekly. Pays $10 to $50. No serials. Address "Editor for Children."

THE CHURCH HERALD–630 Myrtle St. N.W., Grand Rapids, MI 49504.
Official magazine of Reformed Church in America. Children's stories, 500 to 700 words. Pays 2½¢ a word and up.

CRICKET–Open Court Publishing Co., Box 100, La Salle, IL 61301.
Fiction and articles, 200 to 2,000 words, poems to 100 lines, plays, puzzles, riddles, directions for craft projects, for children 6 to 10. Pays to 25¢ per word for prose, to $3 a line for poetry.

CRUSADER–1548 Poplar Ave., Memphis, TN 38104. Lee Hollaway, Editor.
Southern Baptist. For boys, ages 6 to 11. Fiction and non-fiction, to 1,000 words, with black-and-white photos when possible; hobbies, games, handicrafts, nature articles. Pays 2½¢ a word, from $5 per photo, on acceptance.

DASH—Christian Science Brigade, Box 150, Wheaton, IL 60187.
For boys 8 to 11. Articles on Christian life-style, youth scene, current issues, interpersonal relationships, general interest. Photos and photo essays; cartoons. Pays 3¢ a word up, $7.50 per cartoon, varying rates for photos, on publication. Address Managing Editor. Send for writer's guide.

DISCOVERIES (formerly *Junior Discoveries*)—6401 The Paseo, Kansas City, MO 64131. Ruth Henck, Editor.
For grades 3 to 6. Fiction, up to 1,200 words, with Christian emphasis, Bible background. Features, 500 to 800 words, on nature, travel, history, crafts, science, devotional, biographical topics. Cartoons. Poetry, 4 to 20 lines. Pays 2¢ per word for prose, 25¢ a line for poetry, on acceptance.

DISCOVERY—Light and Life Press, Winona Lake, IN 46590. Vera Bethel, Editor.
Fiction, 1,800 to 2,000 words, for 8- to 11-year-olds. Also how-to-do-it features, 500 to 1,000 words, and verse. Seasonal material wanted. Pays 2¢ a word for prose; 25¢ a line for poetry, after acceptance.

EXPLORE—Christian Board of Publication, Box 170, St. Louis, MO 63166. Norman Linville, Editor.
For early elementary grades. "How-to" articles and featues, to 400 words. (Include source of information.) Short stories, to 600 words; poems, to 12 lines; illustrated puzzles. Pays on acceptance. For specifications and sample copies, send 25¢.

THE FRIEND—50 East North Temple, Salt Lake City, UT 84150. Mrs. Lucile C. Reading, Managing Editor.
Stories to 1,000 words, with character-building ideals; suspense, adventure, holiday, humor. "Tiny tot" stories, 300 to 500 words. Needs stories and verse for younger children, older girls, and on international holidays. Pays from 3¢ a word up for prose; 25¢ to 50¢ a line for poetry; on acceptance.

FUN FOR MIDDLERS—See *Rainbow*.

THE GOOD DEEDER—Box 15, Berrien Springs, MI 49103. Shirlee Ingram, Editor.
For children 10 to 14. Inspirational, character-building short stories, 750 to 1,500 words. Pays 1¢ a word, on publication. Send stamped return envelope for a sample copy.

HIGHLIGHTS FOR CHILDREN—803 Church St., Honesdale, PA 18431. Caroline C. Myers, Managing Editor.
Stories for children, 3 to 12, under 1,000 words. Humor, struggle, self-sacrifice for an ideal preferred. Needs easy-to-read stories, 400 to 600 words, with strong plot; urban settings or characters from American ethnic groups. Overstocked on verse. Pays 6¢ a word and up, on acceptance.

HUMPTY DUMPTY'S MAGAZINE—52 Vanderbilt Ave., New York, NY 10017. Ruth Craig, Editor.
For children, 3 to 8. Read-Aloud Stories, to 900 words, with third- or fourth-grade vocabulary. Tell-Me Stories, to 1,000 words, for parents to read to child. Picture Stories for Beginning Readers, usually on assignment. Pays $50 for prose, $10 for verse (4 to 12 lines), on acceptance. Write for requirements sheet.

THE INSTRUCTOR—Instructor Park, Dansville, NY 14437. Ernest Hilton, Editor.
Short stories, 400 to 600 words for primary, 500 to 1,000 words for middle grades, for teachers to read aloud. Plays for classroom use, short poems. Pay varies.

IT'S OUR WORLD—Pontifical Association of the Holy Childhood, 800 Allegheny Ave., Pittsburgh, PA 15233. Thomas F. Haas, Editor.
Articles, 600 to 800 words, for elementary school students. Stories about children in other countries or with religious or moral lesson. Pays $25 and up.

JACK AND JILL—1100 Waterway Blvd., Box 567B, Indianapolis, IN 46206. William Wagner, Editor.
For children 5 to 12. Short, factual articles: on nature, science, other aspects of child's world. Longer features: "My Father (or My Mother) Is a . . .," first-person stories of life in other countries, historical, biographical pieces. Accompanied by 35mm color transparencies when appropriate. Short stories, 500 to 1,200 words, serials, 1,200 words per installment: realistic stories, fantasy, adventure. Short plays, puzzles, jokes, poems, games, songs, science projects, creative construction projects. Pays 3¢ a word, $2.50 per black-and-white photo; $5 for color, on publication. Stamped, self-addressed envelope required for return of manuscript. Write for writer's guide.

JET CADET—8121 Hamilton Ave., Cincinnati, OH 45231. Dana Eynon, Editor.
Sunday school weekly for children 8 to 11. Christian character-building (not "preachy") stories, 900 to 1,200 words, of young teen-agers in situations involving mystery, animals, sports, adventure, school, travel, relationships with parents and friends. Two-part serials to 2,000 words. Articles, 400 to 500 words, on hobbies, animals, nature, life in other lands, sports, seasonal subjects, with religious emphasis. Poems, to 12 lines. Pays 25¢ to 35¢ a line for poetry, up to 1½¢ a word for stories and articles, on acceptance.

JUNIOR DISCOVERIES—See *Discoveries*.

THE KINDERGARTNER—Graded Press, 201 Eighth Ave. South, Nashville, TN 37202. Mrs. Arba O. Herr, Editor.
United Methodist church-related paper for kindergarten. Stories to 300 words. Poems, simple activities. Pay varies, on acceptance.

MY JEWELS—Union Gospel Press, Box 6509, Cleveland, OH 44101.
Sunday school magazine with evangelical emphasis for children 6 to 8. Articles and fiction, 400 to 500 words; biographies of Christians; how-to articles; fillers, puzzles, poems, quizzes. Pays 2¢ a word, $5 per color slide, $3 per black-and-white glossy photos accompanying article, 35¢ a line for poetry, from $2.50 for puzzles. Writer's guide and samples on request. Same address and requirements for *My Pleasure*.

MY PLEASURE—See *My Jewels*.

NATIONAL GEOGRAPHIC WORLD—National Geographic Society, 17th and M Sts., N.W., Washington, DC 20036.
Photo-articles for readers from 8 to 12. Query before submitting photos or text. Also, puzzles, mazes, games, humor. Pays $150 per page for photos, prorated according to size used.

NURSERY DAYS—Graded Press, 201 Eighth Ave. South, Nashville, TN 37202. Mrs. Jo Risser, Editor.
United Methodist story paper for nursery children, 2 to 4. Stories, 250 words, on church, family, friends, God's word, Bible, Jesus. Poems, 4 to 8 lines. Pays on acceptance.

ON THE LINE—616 Walnut Ave., Scottdale, PA 15683. Helen Alderfer, Editor.
Weekly story paper for children 10 to 14. Stories and articles, 750 to 1,000 words, that help children see God at work in the world around them. Poetry, quizzes, puzzles, and cartoons. Pays to 3¢ a word, less for second rights. Sample copies and "When You Write" leaflet free on request.

OUR LITTLE FRIEND–Pacific Press Publishing Assoc., 1350 Villa St., Mountain View, CA 94042. Louis Schutter, Editor.
Seventh-day Adventist weekly for children 2 to 6. Stories, 500 to 1,000 words, "slanted to our religious standards." Verse 8 to 12 lines, puzzles, photos, drawings. Pays 1¢ a word for stories, 10¢ a line for verse.

PLAYS, THE DRAMA MAGAZINE FOR YOUNG PEOPLE–8 Arlington St., Boston, MA 02116. Carol Kountz, Managing Editor.
One-act plays, suitable for production by young people from 7 to 17. Plays with one set preferred. Uses comedies, skits, farces, melodramas, dramatized classics, dramatized folk tales and fairy tales, dramas, puppet plays, creative dramatics material. Seeking Bicentennial plays. Manuscript specification sheet on request. Pays good rates, on acceptance.

PRIMARY TREASURE–Pacific Press Publishing Assoc., 1350 Villa St., Mountain View, CA 94042. Louis Schutter, Editor.
Seventh-day Adventist weekly for children 7 to 9. Stories, 500 to 1,500 words; "must be slanted to our religious standards." Verse (8 to 12 lines), puzzles, photos, drawings. Query on serials. Pays 1¢ a word for stories, 10¢ a line for verse.

QUEST–Box 179, St. Louis, MO 63166. Lee Miller, Editor.
For older elementary children. Short stories, to 1,000 words, and verse, to 16 lines. Feature articles, to 600 words (include source). No fantasy. Strong emphasis on developing values. Pays on acceptance.

RAINBOW (formerly *Fun For Middlers* and *Whenever Whatever*) – American Baptist Board of Education and Publication, Valley Forge, PA 19481. Gracie McCay, Editor.
Fiction and articles, 800 to 1,000 words, for children 8 to 11. Biographies, projects, poetry, puzzles, prayers, cartoons, art and writings by children. Pays to 3¢ a word, on acceptance.

RANGER RICK'S NATURE MAGAZINE–Publisher's Services, Inc., 1518 Walnut St., Philadelphia, PA 19102. Trudy Dye Farrand, Editor.
Articles, to 900 words, to help young people enjoy nature: on nature, natural science, conservation, or environmental problems. Pays $5 to $250, shortly before publication.

ROADRUNNER–See *Wow*.

STORY FRIENDS–Mennonite Publishing House, Scottdale, PA 15683. Alice Hershberger, Editor.
For children 4 to 9. Stories, 350 to 900 words, relating Christian faith to everyday experiences in family, school, church, community life; to God's creation, special days, current issues; to building friendship with people of all races, caring and sharing in others' needs. Bible-based quizzes, riddles, activities. Poetry, photo stories. Pays to 3¢ a word for stories, to $5 per poem, on acceptance.

THREE/FOUR—See *The Vine.*

TRAILS—Box 788, Wheaton, IL 60187. Sara Robertson, Editor.
Published by Pioneer Girls for girls 8 to 12. High-quality short stories and articles, to 2,000 words, consistent with Christian teaching. Photos, games, cartoons, quizzes, crafts. Pay varies, on acceptance.

UNION GOSPEL PRESS—See *My Pleasure* and *My Jewels.*

THE VINE (formerly *Three/Four*)—201 Eighth Ave. South, Nashville, TN 37203. Betty M. Buerki, Editor.
Weekly magazine for third and fourth graders. Short stories, about 1,000 words, poetry, puzzles, quizzes. Short informational articles. Pays 3¢ a word for stories; 50¢ to $1 a line for poetry.

WEE WISDOM—Unity Village, MO 64065. Jim Leftwich, Editor.
Character-building magazine for boys and girls. Short, action, adventure stories; science, nature stories, projects; creative craft ideas. About 750 words. Avoid sermonizing.

WHENEVER WHATEVER—See *Rainbow.*

WONDER TIME—6401 The Paseo, Kansas City, MO 64131. Elizabeth B. Jones, Editor.
For children 6 to 8. Fiction, 200 to 750 words, with Christian emphasis. Features, 200 to 500 words; nature, travel, simple crafts, Bible background. Poetry, 4 to 16 lines. Pays 2¢ a word for prose; 25¢ a line and up for verse, on acceptance.

WOODMEN OF THE WORLD MAGAZINE—1700 Farnam St., Omaha, NE 68102. Leland A. Larson, Editor.
Stories, 400 to 1,200 words, for children 8 to 16. Pays 2¢ a word, on acceptance.

WOW (formerly *Roadrunner*)—American Baptist Board of Educational Ministries, Valley Forge, PA 19481. Roger Price, Editor.
Weekly publication for children 6 to 7. Fiction, 300 to 400 words, with simple vocabulary. Puzzles, articles, short poetry, projects, cartoons, Bible verses. Prayers, art and writings by children. Pays to 3¢ a word, on acceptance.

YOUNG CRUSADER—1730 Chicago Ave., Evanston, IL 60201. Michael Vitucci, Editor.
Character-building and temperance stories, 600 to 850 words, for children 6 to 12. Pays ½¢ a word, on publication.

YOUNG WORLD—1100 Waterway Blvd., P.O. Box 567B, Indianapolis, IN 46206. Johanna Bradley, Editor.
For young people 10 to 14. Fiction, to 1,800 words, and articles, to 1,200 words, on contemporary situations — young people in community action, sports, entertainments, etc. Articles on popular sports and entertainment personalities, crafts, fashion or beauty, family, music. Some verse. Pay varies for poetry and puzzles, $2.50 for black-and-white photos accompanying articles, $5 for color transparencies; about 3¢ a word for prose, on publication. Stamped, self-addressed envelope required for return.

TEEN-AGE, YOUNG ADULT MAGAZINES

ALIVE!—Christian Board of Publication, Beaumont and Pine Blvd., St. Louis, MO 63166. Darrell Faires, Editor.
Fiction, 1,200 to 1,600 words, for junior high youth. First-person articles, to 1,500 words, on outstanding youth, projects and activities, with photos. Cartoons. Puzzles, word games, brain-teasers, and poetry to 16 lines. Pays 2¢ a word for prose, extra for photos and illustrations. Pays 25¢ a line for poetry, $6 for cartoons. Query for articles.

AMERICAN GIRL–830 Third Ave., New York, NY 10022. Cleo Paturis, Editor.
Published by Girl Scouts for all girls 12 to 16. Nonfiction, 500 to 1,500 words, covering teen-age interests. Fiction 1,000 to 2,000 words: mystery, adventure, school and family life, sports, careers, friendship and romance, etc. Query for articles.

AMERICAN NEWSPAPER BOY–915 Carolina Ave. N.W., Winston-Salem, NC 27101. Charles Moester, Editor.
Light fiction, 1,800 to 2,000 words, mystery, character-building and adventure stories for newsboys, 14 to 17. Inspirational articles, editorials, articles on newspaper routes. Pay varies, about $10 to $25.

BOY'S LIFE–New Brunswick, NJ 08902. Robert E. Hood, Editor.
For boys 10 to 17. Short fiction, 2,500 to 3,200 words, and short shorts, 1,000 words, with strong plot and characterization, conflict, action, humor, or suspense. Articles, 500 to 1,500 words with photos; photo-features showing "how-to" in crafts, hobbies, nature, camping, etc. Query for non-fiction. Pays from $350 for fiction, from $150 for non-fiction. Write for writer's guide.

CAMPUS LIFE–Box 419, Wheaton, IL 60187. Philip Yancey, Editor.
For 16 to 19 age group. Fiction and articles, about 1,500 words; stories of outstanding Christian young people; factual pieces on teen-age life. Need photo-stories of teens in wholesome, unique activities. Cartoons for teens. Pays 3¢ a word and up. Most articles assigned; query.

CATALYST–Christian Board of Publication, Beaumont and Pine Blvd., St. Louis, MO 63166. Jerry O'Malley, Editor.
Articles on religion or social issues, or what high school youth are doing in these areas. Fiction, 1,000 to 1,200 words, for intelligent, concerned teens. Poetry to 16 lines. Cartoons and photos. Humor, especially satire. Pays 1½¢ a word and up for prose, 25¢ a line for poetry, $6 and up for cartoons.

CONTACT–44 East Franklin St., Room 302, Huntington, IN 46750. Stanley Peters, Editor.
United Brethren in Christ. Christ-centered fiction and articles for teens and adults, true stories of notable Christians, to 1,500 words. Pays 1¢ for first and simultaneous rights; ¾¢ a word for second rights.

CRAWDADDY–72 Fifth Ave., New York, NY 10011.
Rock and roll interviews, celebrity pieces, politics and culture, 1,000 to 2,000 words, to appeal to readers from ages 18 to 30. "Hip" humor and high-quality fiction. Pay varies, on publication. Query.

DIRECTIONS '80–University Communications, Inc., Box 1234, Rahway, NJ 07065. Gretchen Mirrielees, Editor.
Career-related articles, 1,500 to 3,500 words, for high school juniors and seniors. Fillers, short humor, cartoons on unusual, interesting careers. Pay varies, on acceptance.

ENCOUNTER–The Wesleyan Church, Box 2000, Marion, IN 46952.
For teen-agers 15 to 18. Fiction, 2,500 words, with Christian emphasis. Serials, 6 to 8 chapters, 800 to 2,500 words per chapter. Nonfiction, 500 to 1,500 words: personal witness, devotional, informational. Poems, 4 to 16 lines. Pays 2¢ a word for prose, 25¢ a line or poetry.

ETC.—6401 The Paseo, Kansas City, MO 64131. J. Paul Turner, Editor.
Denominational tabloid for 18- to 24-year-olds. Religious and non-religious articles, 500 to 1,200 words. Poetry, to 20 lines. Pays from 2¢ a word, on acceptance.

EVENT—Baptist Sunday School Board, 127 Ninth Ave. North, Nashville, TN 37203. Linda Lawson, Editor.
For Southern Baptist youth, 12 to 17. Stories, 1,000 to 3,000 words, and articles, to 1,500 words. Contemporary poetry, any length. Pays 2½¢ a word for all rights, for prose, slightly more for poetry, on acceptance.

EXPLORING—Boy Scouts of America, North Brunswick, NJ 08902. Dick Pryce, Editor.
Articles, to 2,500 words and photo-features, for teen-agers: careers, education, current issues, music, sports, clothes, outdoor adventure, cars, human relationships. Short stories, to 2,500 words, and some cartoons. Pays $300 to $500, on acceptance. Query.

FACE-TO-FACE—201 Eighth Ave., South, Nashville, TN 37202. Sharilyn Adair, Editor.
United Methodist. Free-verse poetry and mood prose relating to faith and human existence. No straight moralism. Pays 25¢ a line and up.

FOR TEENS ONLY—235 Park Ave. South, New York, NY 10003. B. J. Lange, Editor.
Short stories, 4,000 words, with realistic characters, dialogue and situations, relevant to teen-age lives. Pays $50, on acceptance.

FREEWAY—Scripture Press Publications, 1825 College Ave., Wheaton, IL 60187. Anne Harrington, Editor.
For ages 15 to 19. Nonfiction, to 2,000 words, about young people who have experienced dramatic, life-changing encounter with Christ, or overcome danger, frustration, etc., by relying on faith in Christ. Photos help. Query first. Top-notch fiction. Pays to $60, on acceptance, more for photos. Samples and writer's tips packets available on request.

GRIT—Williamsport, PA 17701. Kenneth D. Loss, Feature Editor.
Articles, black-and-white photos and color transparencies on personalities and small towns for Teen pages. Pays on acceptance.

HICALL—1445 Boonville Ave., Springfield, MO 65802. Jim Erdmann, Youth Editor.
Material with evangelical emphasis for young people 12 to 19. Fiction, 1,200 to 1,500 words. Non-fiction, 500 to 1,000 words: Christian biography, true stories from mission fields, features for teens. Pays on acceptance.

HIGH—Harvest Publications, 1233 Central, Evanston, IL 60201. David Olson, Editor.
Illustrated articles, 500 to 1,000 words, on evangelical Christian ideas, persons and activities. Fiction, 1,000 to 1,500 words, for teens. Pays 4¢ a word and up, $5 and up per photo, on acceptance. Query. Write for samples and writers guide.

LIGHTED PATHWAY—1080 Montgomery Ave., Cleveland, TN 37311. Clyne W. Buxton, Editor.
Religious fiction and nonfiction, 400 to 1,200 words, for young people. Pays ½¢ per word, on acceptance; $2 for photos used with articles.

MY DELIGHT–Union Gospel Press, Box 6509, Cleveland, OH 44101.
Sunday school magazine with evangelical emphasis for teens 13 to 17. Fiction, 1,000 to 1,500 words; biographies; how-tos; fillers, puzzles, poems, quizzes. Pays 2¢ a word, $5 per color slide, $3 per black-and-white glossy photo accompanying article, 35¢ a line for poetry, from $2.50 for puzzles. Writer's guide and sample copy available on request.

THE NATIONAL FUTURE FARMER–Box 15130, Alexandria, VA 22309. Wilson Carnes, Editor.
Written for high school students of vocational agriculture, average age 17. Nonfiction, to 1,000 words, on activities of Future Farmers of America, new developments in agriculture, and leadership and citizenship subjects. Pays to 4¢ a word, on acceptance. Cartoons, $7.50.

PROBE–1548 Poplar Ave., Memphis, TN 38104. Mike Davis, Editor.
Brotherhood Commission of Southern Baptist Convention. For boys 12 to 17. Photo-features on sports personalities; articles, to 1,500 words, on teen problems, current events. Pays 2½¢ a word, $5 to $10 each for photos, on acceptance.

REACHOUT–Light and Life Press, Winona Lake, IN 46590. Verna Bethel, Editor.
Short stories, 1,800 to 2,000 words, for young teens, religious in tone. Human interst, hobby, and career articles, 800 to 1,500 words, fillers, some poetry. Seasonal material wanted. Pays 2¢ per word.

REFLECTION–Box 788, Wheaton, IL 60187. Sara Robertson, Editor.
Published by Pioneer Girls for girls 13 to 18. High-quality short stories and articles, to 2,000 words, consistent with Christian teaching. Photos, cartoons, crafts, quizzes, games. Pay varies, on acceptance.

ROLLING STONE–625 Third St., San Francisco, Calif. 94107. Jann Wenner, Editor.
Not in the market at present.

SCHOLASTIC SCOPE–Scholastic Magazines, Inc., 50 West 44th St., New York, NY 10036. Katherine Robinson, Editor.
For ages 15 to 18, with 4th to 6th grade reading level. Stories of 500 to 1,000 words and plays up to 3,000 words, dealing with interests of today's students, relationships between people (international, adult-teen-age, employer-employee, male-female, etc.) in family, job, school situations. Also realistic stories, written from viewpoint of member of minority group, not necessarily focusing on race relations. No crime fiction. Pays good rates, on acceptance.

SEVENTEEN–850 Third Ave., New York, NY 10022. Babette Rosmund, Fiction Editor.
Well-written fiction, adult in technique and conception, but limited to situations involving young people, adolescent "growing up" experiences. Pays good rates, on acceptance.

SPRINT–Scholastic Magazines, Inc., 50 West 44th St., New York, NY 10036. Vicky Chapman, Editor.
Short stories, 300 to 500 words, written at second grade level for remedial reading students, 9 to 11. Wants fast-moving plots, lots of action, on interpersonal relations as well as science fiction, mystery, sports, and humor. Also one-acts plays, 450 to 550 words. Payments starts at $75.

STRAIGHT–8121 Hamilton Ave., Cincinnati, OH 45231. Mrs. Bee Nelson, Editor.
Character-building stories, about 1,500 words, with teen-age characters, on Christian athletes, church work, school incidents, family situations, teen problems, mystery, etc. Feature articles, 1,000 to 1,200 words. Magazine is correlated with international Bible school lessons. Pay varies.

'TEEN MAGAZINE–8831 Sunset Blvd., Los Angeles, CA 90069. Roxanne Camron, Editor.
Fiction, 2,500 to 4,000 words, on relevant subjects, depicting today's teen-age girl. Pays $100 and up. Query Kathy McCoy, Feature Editor.

TEENS TODAY–6401 The Paseo, Kansas City, MO 64131. Roy F. Lynn, Editor.
For grades 10 to 12. Contemporary, realistic fiction, to 2,500 words, and articles, to 1,500 words, on central truths of Christian faith. Profiles of Christians; some poetry. Pays 2¢ a word, 25¢ a line for poetry, on acceptance.

UNION GOSPEL PRESS–See *My Delight.*

VENTURE–Christian Service Brigade, P.O. Box 150, Wheaton, IL 60187. Don Dixon, Editor.
Fiction for boys 8 to 18. Feature articles, 1,000 to 1,500 words, to help boys develop Bible-based life style. Biographical stories and incidents of Christian men and/or boys considered. Pays $25 to $100 per article, on publication.

WIND–Box 2000, Marion, IN 46952. David L. Keith, Executive Editor.
Newspaper published by The Wesleyan Church. Religious or educational articles, to 1,000 words, for teens. Pays 2¢ a word, $2.50 each for photos and cartoons.

WORLD OVER–426 West 57th St., New York, NY 10019. Ezekiel Schloss, Editor.
Fiction of Jewish interest, historical or contemporary, for children 9 to 14. Jewish content (holidays, etc.) essential. Pays 4¢ to 5¢ a word, on acceptance, for story of 600 to 1,200 words; $175 to $225 for serial (5 chapters, 1,200 words per chapter); more for exceptional material. Query.

YOUNG AMBASSADOR–Box 82808, Lincoln, NE 68501. Robert H. Sink, Managing Editor.
Fiction, nonfiction, 2,000 words, spiritual tone, but not preachy, for young teens. Pays to 3¢ a word.

YOUNG JUDAEAN–817 Broadway, New York, NY 10003. Barbara Gingold, Editor.
Monthly magazine for children 8 to 13, and members of Young Judaean. Articles, 500 to 1,500 words with photos or illustrations, about Jewish-American life, subjects of Jewish historical and international interest, Israel, and Zionist-oriented material. Fiction, of Jewish interest, 800 to 2,000 words. Humor, travel, reviews, fillers. Poetry, from 8 lines. Pays in copies or small token payment.

YOUNG MISS–52 Vanderbilt Ave., New York, NY 10017. Rubie Saunders, Editor.
For girls 10 to 14. Realistic stories, 2,000 to 2,300 words, on contemporary problems of young people. Articles on sports, careers, crafts, personal problems, 1,000 to 2,000 words. Query. Novelettes, 6,000 to 6,500 words. Pays $50 to $100 for short fiction, $100 to $150 for novelettes, $50 up for articles, on acceptance.

YOUTH ALIVE–1445 Boonville Ave., Springfield, MO 65802.
For mid- and late teens. Photo features, photos, interviews, forums, biographical features, reports on outstanding Christian youth, how-to-do-it features, some fiction, satire, humor, anecdotes, poems, news, motivational articles, seasonal material, personal experiences, 800 to 1,000 words. Pays about 2½¢ a word, on acceptance. Free sample copy and writer's guide.

YOUTH IN ACTION–Winona Lake, IN 46590.
Official publication of Free Methodist Youth Ministries. Articles, 500 to 1,500 words, on activities of youth in churches and conferences, and on guidance for Christian living. Poetry. Buys good quality, black-and-white or color photos. Pays 1½¢ a word.

REPRINT MAGAZINES

If a writer has sold an article or story to a magazine and retains the reprint rights, he may submit the piece to a reprint publication. The following list gives a few of these reprint or digest magazines.

Many of the smaller and more specialized magazines listed elsewhere as markets for unpublished material occasionally buy reprint rights. A writer can submit a copy of a published article or story to another magazine, together with information about when and where the material has been published, if he is certain that he has the permission of the original publisher.

CATHOLIC DIGEST—P.O. Box 3090, St. Paul, MN 55165.

CHILDREN'S DIGEST—52 Vanderbilt Ave., New York, NY 10017.

READER'S DIGEST—Pleasantville, NY 10570.

TELEVISION AND PLAYS

This section includes markets for dramatic material: television, publishers of plays for the amateur stage, community and college theatres, and literary magazines that occasionally buy plays.

Changes are taking place continually in the television world. New shows are always being tried out; old shows go off the air or become inactive script markets. Therefore, the following list of programs should not be considered complete or permanent.

If the address of a particular program is not available, write to the program's Script Editor, in care of the local television station program director, or to the story editor of the national network televising the program. It is always wise to query first, especially in the case of a new program or a program that has not definitely stated it is buying free-lance scripts.

There are relatively few markets for free-lance material in radio at the present time. For full information, write to the major networks listed below.

Publishers of plays for school, community, and church groups offer a hospitable market for free-lance writers. This field has rewards and pleasures of its own, and playwrights who are interested in writing for television and the professional theatre will find the amateur stage a good proving ground.

A number of community theatres, college dramatic groups, and little theatres are actively in the market for plays be free-lance writers for stage production. Payment is seldom great, but usually college and community theatres buy only the right to produce a play and all further rights revert to the author.

As a rule, Broadway producers will not read plays sent in by an unknown playwright. Writers with plays they wish to have considered for Broadway production should query one of the recognized literary agents listed at the end of this book.

Several literary, university and "little" magazines are occasionally interested in publishing plays. They are not an active play market because of space limitations; dramatic material can appear only infrequently if at all. However, they may be good markets for experimental drama, or plays which have little chance of appearing in more popular media.

MAJOR TELEVISION AND RADIO NETWORKS

AMERICAN BROADCASTING CO., INC.—1330 Avenue of the Americas, New York, NY 10019.

COLUMBIA BROADCASTING SYSTEM—51 West 52nd St., New York, NY 10019.

NATIONAL BROADCASTING CO.–RCA Bldg., 30 Rockefeller Plaza, New York, NY 10020.

PUBLIC BROADCASTING SERVICE–955 L'Enfant Plaza North, S.W., Washington, DC 20024.

TELEVISION PROGRAMS

ALL IN THE FAMILY–*Network:* CBS-TV. *Length:* 30 minutes.
Script: Situation comedy series about opinionated middle-class husband and father and his family. Scripts through recognized agents only. *Contact:* Don Nicholl, Executive Producer, or Michael Ross and Bernie West, Producers, Tandem Productions, CBS Television City, 7800 Beverly Blvd., Los Angeles, CA 90036.

BARETTA–*Network:* ABC-TV. *Length:* 1 hour.
Script: Police drama about imaginative detective who uses colorful disguises to pursue criminals. Scripts through recognized agents only. *Contact:* Jo Swerling, Jr., Producer, Public Arts at Universal Studioes, 100 Universal City Plaza, Universal City, CA 91608.

CBS RADIO MYSTERY THEATER–*Network:* CBS. *Length:* 1 hour.
Contact: Himan Brown, Producer. Himan Brown Studio, 221 West 26th St., New York, NY 10001. Not a free-lance market.

CBS PLAYHOUSE 90–*Network:* CBS-TV. *Length:* 90 minutes.
Script: Occasional presentation of plays by both well-known and new writers. Scripts through recognized agents only. *Contact:* Robert Markell, CBS-TV, 51 West 52nd St., New York, NY 10019.

CBS PROGRAM PLANNING AND DEVELOPMENT–CBS-TV, 51 West 52nd St., New York, NY 10019. Robert Goldfarb, Director of Program Development.
New program ideas. Scripts or queries through recognized agents only.

CANADIAN BROADCASTING CORPORATION–National Script Dept., P.O. Box 500, Postal Terminal A, Toronto, Ont. Canada.
Quality TV drama and radio drama, 30 and 60 minutes in length.

CANNON–*Network:* CBS-TV. *Length:* 1 hour.
Script: Suspense drama about former police lieutenant, now private investigator handling major cases with variety of interests. Scripts on assignment through recognized agents only. *Contact:* Leigh Vance, Associate Producer, QM Productions, Samuel Goldwyn Studios, 1041 North Formosa, Los Angeles, CA 90046.

CHICO AND THE MAN–*Network:* NBC-TV. *Length:* 30 minutes.
Script: Situation comedy about elderly, embittered garage owner who finds new values and sometimes stormy relationship with energetic Chicano youth who works way into job at garage. Scripts through recognized agents only. *Contact:* Robert Hilliard or Michael Morris, Script Supervisors, Komack Co., Inc., with Wolper Productions, c/o NBC Television City, 3000 West Alameda Ave., Burbank, CA 91503.

COLUMBO—See *Sunday Mystery Movie.*

DIRECTIONS—*Network:* ABC-TV. *Length:* 30 minutes.
Scripts: Programs to be endorsed by all religious faiths: can be religious, presenting perspectives of the faiths and how they affect people today; or can deal with any current social problems of concern to various faith groups. Scripts on assignment only. *Contact:* Sid Darion, Manager of Public Affairs, ABC-TV News, 1926 Broadway, New York, NY 10023.

EMERGENCY:—*Network:* NBC-TV. *Length:* 1 hour.
Script: Dramas about Los Angeles hospital emergency unit and L.A. County Fire Department's Paramedic Unit. Scripts on assignment through recognized agents only. *Contact:* Mr. Robert A. Cinader, Executive Producer, Mark VII, Ltd., with Universal Television, Universal City Studios, Universal City, CA 91608.

GOOD TIMES—*Network:* CBS-TV. *Length:* 30 minutes.
Script: Situation comedy about life, joys, sorrows of black family in Chicago high-rise ghetto. Scripts through recognized agents only. *Contact:* Allan Manings, Executive Producer, Tandem Productions, c/o CBS Television City, 7800 Beverly Blvd., Los Angeles, CA 90036.

GUNSMOKE—*Network:* CBS-TV. *Length:* 60 minutes.
Script: Western adventure series, Dodge City in 1870s, using period drama with straight story lines. Scripts must be accompanied by standard release form. Market is closed until April 1, 1975. *Contact:* Earl W. Wallace, CBS-TV at Studio Center, North Hollywood, CA 91604.

HAPPY DAYS—*Network:* ABC-TV. *Length:* 30 minutes.
Script: Family situation comedy recreating 50's and 60's. Scripts through recognized agents only. *Contact:* Ed Scharlack, Story Consultant, Paramount TV, 5451 Marathon, Los Angeles, CA 90028.

HARRY O—*Network:* ABC-TV. *Length:* 1 hour.
Script: Suspense drama about tough yet compassionate private detective, who attracts people in trouble. Scripts through recognized agents only. *Contact:* Robert Dozier, Producer, Warner Brothers Television, 4000 Warner Blvd., Burbank, CA 91505.

HAWAII 5-0—*Network:* CBS-TV. *Length:* 1 hour.
Script: Police adventure, set in Hawaii. Scripts on assignment through recognized agents only. *Contact:* Curtis Kenyon, Story Consultant, Leonard Freeman Productions, CBS Studio Center, 4024 Radford, North Hollywood, CA 91604.

THE JEFFERSONS—*Network:* CBS-TV. *Length:* 30 minutes.
Script: Comedy about Lionel, Louise and George Jefferson (of *All in the Family*) living in a Manhattan high-rise. Scripts through recognized agents only. *Contact:* Lloyd Turner and Gordon Mitchell, Story Editors, T.A.T. Communications Company, NRW Productions, c/o CBS-TV Center, 7800 Beverly Blvd., Los Angeles, CA 90036.

BARNABY JONES—*Network:* CBS-TV. *Length:* 1 hour.
Script: Suspense drama about veteran private investigator working in Los Angeles and Southern California. Scripts on assignment through recognized agents only. *Contact:* B. W. Sandefur, Associate Producer, QM Productions, Samuel Goldwyn Studios, 1041 N. Formosa, Los Angeles, CA 90046.

KOJAK—*Network:* CBS-TV. *Length:* 1 hour.
Script: Police drama about Lieut. Kojak. Scripts through recognized agents only. *Contact:* Matt Rapf, Executive Producer, or Gene Kearny, Story Editor, Universal Television, Universal City, CA 91608.

KUNG FU—*Network:* ABC-TV. *Length:* 1 hour.
Script: Drama about Chinese-American who uses knowledge of kung fu, oriental philosophy which combines inner serenity with discipline of mind and body, to relate to people in frontier West. Scripts on assignment through recognized agents only. *Contact:* Ed Waters, Executive Story Consultant, Warner Brothers TV, 4000 Warner Blvd., Burbank, CA 91505.

LITTLE HOUSE ON THE PRAIRIE—*Network:* NBC-TV. *Length:* 1 hour.
Script: Family pioneer drama set in southwestern Minnesota, 100 years ago. Scripts through recognized agents only. *Contact:* John Hawkins, Producer. Paramount Studio, 5451 Marathon St., Hollywood, CA 90038.

M*A*S*H—*Network:* CBS-TV. *Length:* 30 minutes.
Script: The high jinks of two accomplished Army surgeons between duty hours of combat surgery; based on movie and book of same name. Scripts on assignment through recognized agents only. *Contact:* Larry Gelbart, Co-Producer, 20th Century-Fox TV, 10201 W. Pico, Los Angeles, CA 90064.

MAUDE—*Network:* CBS-TV. *Length:* 30 minutes.
Script: Comedy series about Maude, who thinks of herself as a liberated woman, able to manage problems of a modern marriage and a grown-up daughter. Scripts on assignment through recognized agents only. *Contact:* Budd Grossman, Tandem Productions, CBS Television City, 7800 Beverly Blvd., Los Angeles, CA 90036.

McCLOUD—See *Sunday Mystery Movie.*

McMILLAN AND WIFE—See *Sunday Mystery Movie.*

MEDICAL CENTER—*Network:* CBS-TV. *Length:* 1 hour.
Script: Strong emotional dramas involving medical personnel, patients, and students at large university medical center. Scripts on assignment through recognized agents only. *Contact:* Jack Guss, Story Editor, Alfra Productions, MGM Studios, 10202 West Washington Blvd., Culver City, CA 90230.

THE MARY TYLER MOORE SHOW—*Network:* CBS-TV. *Length:* 30 minutes.
Script: Situation comedy about 30-year-old career woman working in television. Original scripts on assignment through recognized agents only. No assignments open at this time. *Contact:* Ed Weinberger, Producer, CBS Studio Center, 4024 Radford Ave., Studio City, CA 91604.

NBC WORLD PREMIER MOVIE— *Network:* NBC-TV. *Length:* 90 minutes.
Script: Original movie dramas and adaptations. Scripts through recognized agents only. *Contact:* Story Consultant, NBC Television, 3000 West Alameda Ave., Burbank, CA 91523.

PETROCELLI—*Network:* NBC-TV. *Length:* 1 hour.
Script: Drama abcut Harvard-educated lawyer who takes practice to Southwestern cattle town. Scripts through recognized agents only. *Contact:* Paramount TV, 5451 Marathon, Los Angeles, CA 90038.

POLICE STORY—*Network:* NBC-TV. *Length:* 1 hour.
Script: True stories drawn from files of nation's police departments. Scripts on assignment through recognized agents only. *Contact:* Mark Rodgers or Liam O'Brien, Executive Story Consultants, Columbia Pictures Television, Colgems Square, Burbank, CA 91505.

POLICE WOMAN—*Network:* NBC-TV. *Length:* 1 hour.
Script: Police drama about women officers in law enforcement. Scripts from

recognized agents only. *Contact:* Edward DeBlasio, Story Editor, David Gerber Productions/Columbia Pictures Television, Colgems Sq., Burbank, CA 91505.

RHODA–*Network:* CBS-TV. *Length:* 30 minutes.
Script: Comedy about modern marriage, a woman who works, and her family. Script through recognized agents only. *Contact:* MTM Enterprises, c/o CBS Studio Center, 4024 Radford Ave., Studio City, CA 91604.

SANFORD AND SON–*Network:* NBC-TV. *Length:* 30 minutes.
Script: Situation comedy about aging black junk dealer and his son. Scripts on assignment through recognized agents only. *Contact:* Saul Turteltaub and Bernie Orenstein, Producers, Tandem Productions, NBC Television, 3000 West Alameda Blvd., Burbank, CA 91532.

THE SIX MILLION DOLLAR MAN–*Network:* ABC-TV. *Length:* 1 hour.
Script: Action-adventure stories with melodramatic or science fiction slant about Steve Austin whose body was recreated after crash by cybernetic medical science, and who now has incredible powers which he uses in doing governmental assignments. Scripts through recognized agents only. *Contact:* Lionel E. Siegel, Co-Producer, Universal City Studios, Universal City, CA 91608.

THE STREETS OF SAN FRANCISCO–*Network:* ABC-TV. *Length:* 1 hour.
Script: Human dramas about people whose problems bring them in contact with San Francisco Police Department. Scripts on assignment through recognized agents only. *Contact:* William Robert Yates, Producer, Quinn Martin Productions, 1014 N. Formosa, Los Angeles, CA 90046.

SUNDAY MYSTERY MOVIE–*Network:* NBC-TV. *Length:* 90 minutes.
Script: (Three police dramas in rotation: COLUMBO is about police lieutenant, McCLOUD is New Mexico lawman in New York City; McMILLAN AND WIFE is about San Francisco Police Commissioner; scripts on assignment through recognized agents only. *Contact:* Executive Producer, Universal City Studios, 100 Universal City Plaza, Universal City, CA 91608.

S.W.A.T.–*Network:* ABC-TV. *Length:* 1 hour.
Script: Police drama about commander of five-man special force assigned to handle dangerous missions beyond capability of regular police. Scripts through recognized agents only. *Contact:* Robert Hamner, Producer, 20th Century-Fox Film Corp., 10201 West Pico, Los Angeles, CA 90064.

TUESDAY MOVIE OF THE WEEK–*Network:* ABC-TV. *Length:* 90 minutes.
Script: Drama anthology series, original productions: suspense-drama, action-adventure, comedies, westerns, science fiction. Scripts through recognized agents only. *Contact:* Maggie Duffy, Executive Story Editor, 9255 Sunset Blvd., Los Angeles, CA 90069. Same address and requirements for *Wednesday Movie of the Week.*

WEDNESDAY MOVIE OF THE WEEK–See *Tuesday Movie of the Week.*

MARCUS WELBY, M.D.–*Network:* ABC-TV. *Length:* 1 hour.
Script: Medical dramas about general practitioner and his associate, Dr. Stephen Kiley, in Santa Monica, Calif. Scripts on assignment only, through recognized agents. *Contact:* Story Editor, Universal City Studios, 100 Universal City Plaza, Universal City, CA 91608.

THE WONDERFUL WORLD OF DISNEY–*Network:* NBC-TV. *Length:* 1 hour.
Script: Variety of subject matter with elements (not juvenile) to appeal to all age groups: suspense, adventure, nature, comedy. Free-lance and staff-written; agent contact required. *Contact:* Frank Paris, Executive Story Editor, Walt Disney Productions, 500 South Buena Vista St., Burbank, CA 91521.

PLAY PUBLISHERS

ART CRAFT PLAY COMPANY–Box 1058, Cedar Rapids, IA 52406.
Plays for production by high schools, colleges, and little theatres; one set best. One-act dramas for contest use. Write for free leaflet, "Pointers to Writers of Amateur Plays."

WALTER H. BAKER COMPANY (BAKER'S PLAYS)–100 Chauncy St., Boston, MA 02111.
"You will always find us ready and willing to read any manuscript that is submitted ... provided it is in the field of dramatics."

CHILD LIFE MAGAZINE–1100 Waterway Blvd., P.O. Box 567B, Indianapolis, IN 46206. Jane E. Norris, Editor.
Short plays, 300 to 700 words, for classroom and living room production, suitable for children 7 to 11. Pays about 3¢ a word, on publication.

CHILDREN'S PLAYMATE MAGAZINE–1100 Waterway Blvd., P.O. Box 567B, Indianapolis, IN 46206. Beth Wood Thomas, Editor.
Short plays, 200 to 500 words, for children ages 3 to 8. Pays about 3¢ a word, on publication.

CONTEMPORARY DRAMA SERVICE–Box 457, Downers Grove, IL 60515. Arthur L. Zapel, Editor.
Easy-to-stage comedies, skits and one-act plays for schools and churches. Documentaries, adaptations of classics and improvisational material for classroom use. Current needs include: storyteller collections for one or two narrators, chancel drama for Christmas and Easter church use, scripts for synagogue use; to 4,000 words. Include synopsis. Pays by fee arrangement or royalty basis.

THE DRAMATIC PUBLISHING CO.–86 East Randolph St., Chicago, IL 60601.
Full-length and one-act plays, musical comedies for amateur and stock groups: children's theatre, high schools, colleges, clubs, churches, summer and community theatres. Pays by royalty contract, on acceptance. Free catalog on request.

DRAMATICS–College Hill Station, Box E, Cincinnati, OH 45224. Dennis Klasmeier, Editor.
One-act plays for high school production. Running time under 30 minutes. Pays $40 on publication.

ELDRIDGE PUBLISHING CO.–Franklin, OH 45005.
Three-act and one-act plays for schools, churches, community groups, etc. Need Christmas comedies, one-act Christmas sacred plays and pageants. Best to submit material in summer. Address: Kay Myerly, Editorial Dept.

SAMUEL FRENCH, INC.–25 West 45th St., New York, NY 10036.
One- and three-act plays for nonprofessional market: stock, community theatre, colleges, high schools, children's theatre, churches, organizations; Broadway and off-Broadway productions. Contracts usually on royalty basis.

HEUER PUBLISHING CO.–Drawer 248, Cedar Rapids, IA 52406. Edward I. Heuer, Editor.
Three-act plays for school, church, and general community groups. Pays on acceptance. Prompt reports.

INSTRUCTOR–Dansville, NY 14437.
Limited number of plays for elementary schools, around 2,000 words. Prefers plays for very young children and for grades 3 through 6; considers very few for grades 7 and 8. "Each month we try to emphasize holidays, special weeks, and occasions. Play frameworks or stories which children can dramatize creatively are desired." Pays from $15 to $50.

JACK AND JILL—P.O. Box 567B, 1100 Waterway Blvd., Indianapolis, IN 46206. William Wagner, Editor.

Plays for children; humor desired. Pays on publication.

DAVID McKAY COMPANY, INC.—750 Third Ave., New York, NY 10017. Gail Sloan, Play Dept. Editor.

Three-act and one-act adult comedies and dramas of good quality which have been tried out first in local production or have gained favorable recognition in playwriting contests. One- or three-act plays for children ages 3 to 13. No musicals. One set plays preferred. Payment varies.

PERFORMANCE PUBLISHING—976 North McLean Blvd., Elgin, IN 60120. Virginia Butler, Editor.

One- and three-act plays. Pays by royalty contract.

PIONEER DRAMA SERVICE—2172 South Colorado Blvd., Denver, CO 80222. Shubert Fendrich, Publisher.

Scripts of produced plays in three categories: Children's Theatre Plays (to be performed by adults for children), about one hour in length; "old time" melodramas, 15 to 90 minutes in length; small cast musicals for amateur production. Outstanding one-acts, under 30 minutes. Cast should be balanced or lean favorably towards roles for women. Submission should include production history as well as a stamped, self-addressed envelope. Free catalog on request. Pays 50% of production royalties and subsidiary sales.

PLAYS, THE DRAMA MAGAZINE FOR YOUNG PEOPLE—8 Arlington St., Boston, MA 02116. Carol Kountz, Managing Editor.

One-act plays, simple settings, suitable for production by young people from seven to seventeen. Casts may be mixed, all-male or all-female. Plays with one set preferred. Subjects: holidays, historical, dramatized classics, biographical, patriotic, comedy, skits, puppet plays, farces, etc. Maximum lengths: lower grades, 8–10 double-spaced typewritten pages; middle grades, 15 double-spaced typewritten pages; junior high and older groups, 25 double-spaced typewritten pages. Manuscript specification sheet available on request. Pays good rates, on acceptance.

TEACHER—1 Fawcett Place, Greenwich, CT 06830. Claudia Cohl, Editor.

Tested school entertainment material—assembly programs, seasonal celebrations, plays with plot and emotional appeal. Especially welcome are incomplete plays that set up a situation, start dialogue, and then suggest ways in which children and teachers can complete them; also plays allowing children to improvise (rather than memorize) lines. Plays should have flexible cast, preferably ten or more characters. Pays $25 minimum, on acceptance.

REGIONAL AND UNIVERSITY THEATRES

ACADEMY THEATRE–3213 Roswell Rd., N.E., Atlanta, GA 30305.
Plays of highest quality: full-length, experimental, drama, comedy, musical, etc. Writer-in-residence program, with emphasis on working closely with company. Address New Scripts.

ALPHA-OMEGA-PLAYERS–Repertory Theatre of America, P.O. Box 8192, Dallas, TX 75205.
New plays for repertory, with small casts and simple production style. Stage adaptations of works by famous authors, preferably American. A popular play will be kept for several seasons, at about 200 performances per season. Royalty negotiable. Query first.

AMERICAN THEATER–106 East 14th St., New York, NY 10003. Richard Kuss, Artistic Director.
Americana: dramas, comedies, musicals; traditional or experimental. No payment.

BOWIE STATE COLLEGE THEATRE–Bowie, MD 20715. Address Carole Singleton, Speech and Theatre Department.
Black plays of all types, and children's plays. Pays on royalty basis.

CENTER THEATRE GROUP OF LOS ANGELES–135 North Grand Ave., Los Angeles, CA. Lawrence S. Mirkin, Literary Manager.
Plays of all types and lengths considered for production. Payment negotiated.

CHELSEA THEATRE CENTER–Brooklyn Academy of Music, 30 Lafayette Ave., Brooklyn, NY 11217.
Full-length (occasionally one-act) plays, saying something new or using theatre in new way, for full production. Payment is based on Standard Dramatists Guild contract, as applied to off-Broadway productions.

CIRCLE REPERTORY THEATRE COMPANY–2307 Broadway, New York, NY 10024. Marshall W. Mason, Artistic Director.
Drama, comedy, musical; traditional or experimental. Allow six months for report.

THE CLEVELAND PLAY HOUSE–2040 East 86th St., Cleveland, OH 44106. Robert Snook, New Script Department.
Plays for possible production. Manuscripts should be clean and securely bound, and stamped, self-addressed envelope must be included.

COURTYARD PLAYHOUSE–46 West 85th St., New York, NY 10024. Ken Eulo, Artistic Director.
All types of plays including poetry and experimental.

THE CUBICULO–414 West 51st St., New York, NY 10019. Elaine Sulka, Managing Director.
Small cast, non-musical, non-monumental plays. No payment. Takes long time to report.

EARPLAY–WHA Radio, Vilas Communication Hall, 821 University Ave., Madison, WI 53706.
Project sponsored by the University of Wisconsin-Extension and Corporation for Public Broadcasting. Radio plays of literary quality, all lengths, with strong character treatment, bold sound backgrounds, and clear plot lines. Purchases and produces plays for three years unlimited use on 500 public radio stations in U. S. Pays from

$200 for 10-minute scripts to $500 for 30-minute scripts, on acceptance. Manuscripts without stamped, self-addressed envelopes will not be returned.

HONOLULU THEATRE FOR YOUTH–Box 3257, Honolulu, HI 96801.
Good, intelligently written children's plays by new or established playwrights, one hour in length, for presentation to school-age audiences (pre-school to high school) by predominantly adult casts. Authors should write to Managing Director for detailed information about requirements. Royalties paid by arrangement.

HOPE COLLEGE–Dept. of Theatre, Holland, MI 49423.
Regular and experimental productions on small scale. Proscenium, thrust and arena-studio stages. Pays on royalty basis.

THE PLAYWRIGHTS' LAB (formerly *Minnesota Playwriting Lab*)–1788 Hennepin Ave., #4, Minneapolis, MN 55403.
One-act, full, or experimental plays. Playwright should be in residence for productions, so authors from upper Midwest preferred. Query first if script is needed back immediately. Payment is extremely variable.

NEW HERITAGE THEATRE–Box 2781, San Diego, CA 92112.
New, full-lenth plays, musicals on any subject. "Theatrical" plays preferred to naturalism or absurdism. No payment.

NORTH CAROLINA SCHOOL OF THE ARTS–School of Drama, P.O. Box 4657, Winston-Salem, NC 27107.
Full-length and one-act plays for possible production, especially contemporary themes, multi-racial casting, musical plays (school has composers), experimental styles, and plays for elementary school audiences. Roles for young actors, females, desired. Possible residency during production.

OFFICE FOR ADVANCED DRAMA RESEARCH–3526 Humboldt Ave., South, Minneapolis, MN 55408. Arthur H. Ballet, Director.
Unproduced plays; no adaptations or musicals accepted. Recommends and underwrites several plays each year for production in theatres throughout U.S. Transportation, expenses and royalty paid. Write for "Prospectus."

EUGENE O'NEILL MEMORIAL THEATRE CENTER–Suite 1012, 1860 Broadway, New York, NY 10023 and 305 Great Neck Rd., Waterford, CT 06385.
New plays by new playwrights for production during annual National, Playwrights Conference in Waterford, Conn., during summer season. Scripts of previously unproduced plays (one play per playwright) may be submitted between September 15 and December 31 only, to New York office. Two copies of the script are required with stamped envelope for return of scripts. Pays stipend; room and board provided at Conference.

PLAYERS' WORKSHOP–83 East 4th St., New York, NY 10003. Clay Stevenson, Artistic Director.
Dramas, comedies, musicals; experimental or traditional. No payment.

RALEIGH LITTLE THEATRE–Box 5637, Raleigh, NC 27607.
New full-length plays, especially comedies, dramas and musicals. Pays $25 to $40.

MARK TAPER FORUM–Center Theatre Group, 135 North Grand Ave., Los Angeles, CA 90012.
Plays on any subject, of any length. Reports in about six weeks. Send only one play.

THEATRE AMERICANA–Box 245, Altadena, CA 91001.
Three-act comedies, tragedies, farces, musicals (accompanied by piano arrangements), for production in community theatre. One-set plays preferred. Award of $300 is made for play judged best of season's four productions. Wants Bicentennial themes. Address Play-Reading Chairperson.

THEATRE AT ST. CLEMENT'S–423 West 46th St., New York, NY 10036. Kevin O'Connor, Artistic Director.
Dramas, comedies, musicals; traditional or experimental.

THEATRE GENESIS–St. Mark's Church, Second Ave. at 10th St., New York, NY 10003. Walter Hadler, Artistic Director.
Experimental dramas, comedies, musicals. Some payment.

THEATRE REPORT–1023 North La Brea Ave., Los Angeles, CA 90038.
Produced plays never performed on West Coast; well-written, dynamic, contemporary, with point of view. Payment for rights negotiable.

UNIVERSITY OF ALABAMA THEATRE–Box 1965, University of Alabama, Tuscaloosa, AL 35486.
Full-length plays. Pays author's expenses to attend rehearsals, or standard catalog royalty. Address Director of Theatre.

UNIVERSITY OF DENVER–Dept. of Theatre, Denver, CO 80210.
Comedies, dramas, musicals, adaptations and new types of plays. No payment.

WPA THEATRE–333 Bowery Ave., New York, NY 10003. Harry Orzello, Artistic Director.
Dramas, comedies, musicals; traditional or experimental. Small fee.

LITERARY MAGAZINES

CHELSEA–Box 5880, G. C. Station, New York, NY 10017.
Occasional short plays of high quality. Pays in copies.

THE DEKALB LITERARY ARTS JOURNAL–DeKalb College, 555 Indian Creek Dr., Clarkston, GA 30021. Gayle Goodin, Editor.
One-act plays. Pays in copies.

THE FAULT–41186 Alice Ave., Fremont, CA 94538. Terrence Ames, Editor.
Short plays. Pays in copies.

FICTION–193 Beacon St., Boston, MA 02116. Vincent McCaffrey, Editor.
Drama, any length, all genres, of readable format. New authors emphasized. Pays about 1¢ per word.

THE LITERARY REVIEW–Fairleigh Dickinson University, Rutherford, NJ 07070. Charles Angoff, Editor.
Literary plays, radio and television plays. Pays in copies. Reports in three months.

THE NEW RENAISSANCE–9 Heath Rd., Arlington, MA 02174.
One-act, quality and/or off-beat plays, primarily for reading. Will accept submissions March through June. Manuscripts without self-addressed, stamped envelope will not be returned.

PRISM INTERNATIONAL–Creative Writing, University of British Columbia, Vancouver, B.C., Canada V6T 1W5. Michael Bullock, Editor-in-Chief.
Short plays. Pays $5 per magazine page, on publication.

PROTEUS–1004 North Jefferson St., Arlington, VA 22205. Frank Gatling, Editor.
Plays, any length. Pays in copies. Reports in one to six weeks.

QUARTERLY REVIEW OF LITERATURE–26 Haslet Ave., Princeton, NJ 08540.
Publishes verse plays occasionally, when exceptionally good. Several issues should be studied before material is submitted.

WIND–RFD Rte. No. 1, Box 810, Pikeville, KY 41501. Quentin R. Howard, Editor.
Uses one one-act play each year. Pays in copies.

BOOK PUBLISHERS

Three lists are included here: general book publishers, who publish primarily hardcover editions; firms that accept original manuscripts for paperback editions; and university presses, which usually publish specialized books or books by authorities in a given field.

Royalty rates usually start at about ten per cent of the retail price of the book, and increase after a certain number of copies have been sold. The publishing company usually pays the author an advance against royalties when the book contract is signed or when the finished manuscript is received.

Book manuscripts may be sent by Railway Express or by first-class mail, but the most inexpensive and commonly used method at present is by "Special Fourth Class Rate—Manuscript." For a summary of postal regulations for the "Special Fourth Class Rate—Manuscript," see Chapter 100, *Manuscript Preparation and Submission,* and for complete details of this postal rate, insurance, etc., inquire at your local post office.

HARDCOVER BOOK PUBLISHERS

ABBEY PRESS—St. Meinrad, IN 47577. John J. McHale, Editor.
Nonfiction of a religious nature; some books on family relationships. Pays advance against royalties. Query with table of contents and writing sample. Include stamped, return envelope.

ABELARD-SCHUMAN LIMITED (Division of *Thomas Y. Crowell Co.,*—666 Fifth Ave., New York, NY 10019.
Fiction, nonfiction, science, biography, garden, cookbooks, mysteries, children's books. Query.

ABINGDON PRESS—201 Eighth Ave. South, Nashville, TN 37202. Emory S. Bucke, Senior Editor.
Religious books, juveniles, college texts, general nonfiction: biography, Americana, marriage and family, social issues and recreation. Reports on juveniles in two months, on all others in one month. Query with outline and sample chapters.

HARRY N. ABRAMS, INC. (Subsidiary of *Times Mirror Co.*)—110 East 59th St., New York, NY 10022.
Art, photography, illustrated trade books. Query.

ACADEMIC PRESS, INC. (Subsidiary of *Harcourt Brace Jovanovich*)—111 Fifth Ave., New York, NY 10003.
Scientific, technical, medical, behavioral and social science books. Query.

ACROPOLIS BOOKS LTD.—Colortone Bldg., 2400 17th St. N.W., Washington, DC 20009.
Books on current issues, family and leisure, contemporary education. Query.

ADDISON-WESLEY PUBLISHING CO.—Reading, MA 01867. Juvenile Division. Addisonian Press Books, Young Scott Books. Ray Broekel, Editor-in-Chief.
Picture books and nonfiction for 4- to 16-year-olds. Especially interested in school-oriented enrichment books in social studies and language arts curriculum areas.

AERO PUBLISHERS, INC—329 Aviation Rd., Fallbrook, CA 92028.
Illustrated nonfiction on aviation and space. Pays on royalty basis. Query.

ALLYN AND BACON, INC.—470 Atlantic Ave., Boston, MA 02210.
Textbooks and professional books in education, business, drama, and computer science. Philip Parsons, Editor-in-Chief, elementary-high school texts; Wayne Barcomb, Director, college texts; John Gilman, Director, professional books. Pays on royalty basis.

AMERICAN BOOK COMPANY (A division of *Litton Educational Publishing, Inc.*)—
Litton Industries, 450 West 33rd St., New York, NY 10001.
Textbooks and educational materials for schools.

AMERICAN HERITAGE PRESS—Incorporated into *McGraw-Hill.*

AMERICAN WEST PUBLISHING CO.—599 College Ave., Palo Alto, CA 94396. Patricia
Kollings, Editor of Books.
Specialized, high-quality nonfiction on the West, both natural and human history.
Pays standard royalty rates. Query first.

AMPHOTO (American Photographic Book Publishing Co., Inc.)—East Gate and
Zeckendorf Blvd., Garden City, NY 11530.
Books on photography. Query.

ARBOR HOUSE PUBLISHING CO., INC.—641 Lexington Ave., New York, NY 10022.
General fiction and nonfiction. Query.

ARCO PUBLISHING CO.—219 Park Ave. South, New York, NY 10003. David
Goodnough, Editor.
How-to books; how to pass tests of all types; tests and testing; books on business,
sports, hobbies, health and nutrition; general nonfiction. Prefers queries or outlines
first. Pays outright and by contract.

ARKHAM HOUSE—Sauk City, WI 53583.
Macabre fiction and verse, 50,000 to 80,000 words. Pays by standard royalty rates.
Query.

ARLINGTON HOUSE, INC.—165 Huguenot St., New Rochelle, NY 10801. Robert
Markle, Editor.
Nonfiction. Mail order self-help books, books for political conservatives, and
nostalgic books on the 1920–1950 era. Query first.

ASIA PUBLISHING HOUSE, INC.—Graybar Building, 420 Lexington Ave., New York,
NY 10017.
Textbooks, reference and scholarly books in social sciences, humanities and
engineering. Query.

ASSOCIATION PRESS—291 Broadway, New York, NY 10007. Robert W. Hill,
Director.
General nonfiction: recreation, group leadership, sports, social and behavioral
sciences, family life and marriage education, adult education, sex education, religious
and ethical subjects. Royalty basis. Query.

ASTOR-HONOR, INC.—48 East 43rd St., New York, NY 10017.
General trade and nonfiction books. Juvenile line, *Astor Books,* and quality
paperback line, *Honor Books.* Query.

ATHENEUM PUBLISHERS—122 East 42nd St., New York, NY 10017. Alfred Knopf,
Jr., Chairman; Simon Michael Bessie, President.
Quality fiction and nonfiction, including biography, history, books on current affairs,
belles-lettres, juveniles, and books for a general audience. Also quality paperbacks
(reprints only). Pays on royalty basis.

THE ATLANTIC MONTHLY PRESS—8 Arlington St., Boston, MA 02116. Peter
Davison, Director.
Fiction, biography, history, social sciences, belles-lettres, poetry, general nonfiction,
juveniles. The editorial board often tries to link part-serialization in *The Atlantic* with
book publication. Publishes books in association with *Little, Brown.*

AUGSBURG PUBLISHING HOUSE—426 South Fifth St., Minneapolis, MN 55415.
Roland Seboldt, Director of Book Development.
Fiction and nonfiction on Christian themes or related topics; juveniles. Pays on
regular royalty basis.

AURORA PUBLISHERS, INC.–118 16th Ave. South, Nashville, TN 37203.
General hardcover and paperback publishers; juveniles (from earliest ages through young adult). Send query or sample chapters. Pays standard royalty rate.

BAKER BOOK HOUSE–1019 Wealthy St., S.E., Grand Rapids, MI 49506. Daniel Van't Kerkhoff, Editor.
Nonfiction from 30,000 to 60,000 words: Bible study aids, homiletic literature. Novelties, inspirational. Pays on royalty basis.

BARLENMIR HOUSE, PUBLISHERS–413 City Island Ave., New York, NY 10064.
Books on the fine arts, painting, dance, music, poetry, graphics, film, multi-media, crafts; also on psychology of human interest, psychology of art, etc. Standard royalty contract. Query first with biographical material and short paragraph on manuscript; include stamped return envelope.

A. S. BARNES & CO., INC.–Box 421, Cranbury, NJ 08512.
Books on sports, outdoors, cinema, art, crafts, horses, recreation, general nonfiction. Pays on royalty basis. Query.

RICHARD W. BARON PUBLISHING CO., INC.–201 Park Ave. South, New York, NY 10003.
Contemporary fiction and nonfiction. No unsolicited manuscripts accepted. Query.

BASIC BOOKS, INC. PUBLISHERS–10 East 53rd St., New York, NY 10022.
Books on behavioral, and social sciences; belles-lettres; history; and general nonfiction. Query first.

THE BEACON PRESS–25 Beacon St., Boston, MA 02108.
General nonfiction with emphasis on current events and major problems of American society. Also, scholarly works supporting this interest in contemporary affairs, and liberal religious works. Pays on royalty basis. Always query first.

THE BETHANY PRESS–Box 179, St. Louis, MO 63166.
Protestant. Well-researched book manuscripts on biblical, religious, and humanitarian themes in lay language. Query.

BETTER HOMES AND GARDENS BOOKS–See *Meredith Corporation.*

BINFORD & MORT–2536 S.E. 11th Ave., Portland, OR 97202. L. K. Phillips, Editor.
Books about the Pacific Northwest, preferably nonfiction, about 70,000 words. Pays on royalty basis.

BLOCH PUBLISHING CO., INC.–915 Broadway, New York, NY 10010. Charles E. Bloch, President.
Books of Jewish content.

THE BOBBS-MERRILL CO., INC.–4 West 58th St., New York, NY 10019. Eugene Rachlis, Publisher and Editor-in-Chief, Barbara Norville, Mystery Line, Evelyn Gendel, Craftsline.
Novels, mystery and suspense, biographies, autobiographies, popular science, history and crafts. No poetry. Juvenile fiction or nonfiction for all age levels, all lengths. Pays by royalty contract. No unsolicited manuscripts. Query J. J. Fleckner, Associate Editor.

BOOKS FOR BETTER LIVING–21322 Lassen St., Chatsworth, CA 91311. Hedy White, Editor.
Nonfiction book manuscripts on self-improvement, how-to, health, food, the occult, popular psychology and sociology, consumer-interests. Pays by three-part advance against royalties.

THOMAS BOUREGY & CO., INC.–22 East 60th St., New York, NY 10022. Ellen LaBarbera, Editor.
Light, wholesome romances, modern Gothics, westerns, 50,000 words. Pays on royalty basis.

BOWMAN—622 Rodier Drive, Glendale, CA 91201. K. E. Lindstrom, Executive Editor.
Educational manuscripts on elementary school disciplines. Pays by advance against
royalties or by outright payment. Query.

CHARLES T. BRANFORD CO.—28 Union St., Newton Centre, MA 02159. Ilse F.
Jacobs, Editor.
Nonfiction books on art, antiques, dolls, how-to, hobby, crafts, gardening, and
needlework. No fiction or verse. Pays on royalty basis. Query.

GEORGE BRAZILLER, INC.—One Park Ave., New York, NY 10016.
Literature, history, philosophy, science, art, social science books; exceptional fiction.

BROADMAN PRESS—127 Ninth Ave. North, Nashville, TN 37234.
General religious nonfiction; William J. Fallis, Editor. Inspirational and fiction; J. S.
Johnson, Editor. Usually pays on royalty basis. Query.

BRUCE (A division of *Benziger Bruce and Glencoe. Inc.*)—8701 Wilshire Blvd., Beverly
Hills, CA 90211. Chester C. Lucido, Jr., Editorial Director.
Textbooks, workbooks in the areas of vocational, industrial and career education for
secondary, college and adult training. Books on electricity, electronics, sheet metal,
pipefitting, woodworking, drafting, upholstery, metalworking and career guidance.
Pays on royalty basis. Query.

CAHNERS BOOKS—89 Franklin St., Boston, MA 02110.
Books and information for business and industry, vocational education, cookbooks.
Query.

CANFIELD PRESS—850 Montgomery St., San Francisco, CA 94133.
Educational books for junior college audience. Query.

THE CAXTON PRINTERS, LTD.—Box 700, Caldwell, ID 83605.
Most interested in authentic Americana, with emphasis on frontier and Western
materials, but considers other types which are authentic and outstanding. No fiction.
Pays on royalty basis. Query.

CHARTERHOUSE BOOKS—Incorporated into *David McKay Co.*

CHATEAU PUBLISHING, INC.— Box 20432, Herndon Station, Orlando, FL 32814.
Marcia Roen, Editor.
General nonfiction. Query. Rate of payment by agreement.

THE CHATHAM PRESS—143 Sound Beach Ave., Old Greenwich, CT 06870. Christopher Harris, Editor.
Illustrated nonfiction; encourages regional books. Pays by standard royalty rates.

CHILDRENS PRESS—1224 West Van Buren St., Chicago, IL 60607. Mrs. Joan F.
Downing, Editor.
Juvenile books, in line with primary and elementary school curriculum. More
nonfiction than fiction.

CHILTON BOOK COMPANY—201 King of Prussia Rd., Radnor, PA 19089. John Kelly,
Editor-in-Chief; Benton Arnovitz, Senior Editor, trade books; Crissie Lossing,
Senior Editor, arts and crafts; Paul Driscoll, Senior Editor, automotive.
General nonfiction: how-to, biography, history, popular music, games, recreation,
sports, nature, travel, popular psychology, sociology, religion, occult, popular
science, current events, reference, business, arts and crafts, automotive. Reports in 2
to 8 weeks. Pays by standard royalties, advance negotiable. Query with outline and
sample. Enclose return postage.

CHRONICLE BOOKS—870 Market St., San Francisco, CA 94102.
General nonfiction, some with photos and drawings. Pays standard royalty rates.
Query.

THE CITADEL PRESS—120 Enterprise Ave., Secaucus, NJ 07094. Allan J. Wilson, Editor-in-Chief.
Nonfiction, some fiction. Paperbacks.

CONCORDIA PUBLISHING HOUSE—3558 South Jefferson Ave., St. Louis, MO 63118.
Fiction and nonfiction with moral or religious tone, for adults. Also juvenile and teen-age books. Royalty payments.

CONTINUUM BOOKS—See *Seabury Press.*

CORNELL MARITIME PRESS, INC.—Cambridge, MD 21613. Mrs. Mary Jane Cornell, Editor.
Maritime technical, professional and how-to books. *Tidewater Publishers* – Books on Chesapeake Bay, Maryland, Virginia. Royalty basis. Query with outline.

COWARD, McCANN & GEOGHEGAN—200 Madison Ave., New York, NY 10016. John J. Geoghegan, President and Editor-in-Chief.
Fiction, quality suspense. All types of nonfiction, no purely technical books. Juvenile fiction and nonfiction for nursery school age to teen-age. "If you do not have an agent, and wish to submit your manuscript to us, write us a letter first describing its nature and general content." Pays on royalty basis.

CREATIVE HOME LIBRARY—See *Meredith Corporation.*

CRITERION BOOKS—666 Fifth Ave., New York, NY 10019.
Fiction and nonfiction, children's books. Query.

THOMAS Y. CROWELL CO.—666 Fifth Ave., New York, NY 10019.
Adult fiction and nonfiction books, reference books and children's books. College and secondary school textbooks. Regular royalty payments. Do not send manuscripts; always query first.

CROWN PUBLISHERS, INC.—419 Park Ave. South, New York, NY 10016. Herbert Michelman, Editor-in-Chief; Norma Jean Sawicki, Juveniles.
All types of fiction and nonfiction. Query.

THE DARTNELL CORPORATION—4660 Ravenswood Ave., Chicago, IL 60640.
Loose-leaf manuals on business topics, from 60,000 to 100,000 words. Royalty basis.

JONATHAN DAVID PUBLISHERS, INC.—68-22 Eliot Ave., Middle Village, NY 11379. Alfred J. Kolatch, Editor-in-Chief.
General nonfiction. Royalty or outright purchase. Query ideas with detailed outline and sample chapter.

JOHN DE GRAFF, INC.—Clinton Corners, NY 12514.
Nonfiction, particularly pleasure boating.

DELACORTE PRESS—1 Dag Hammarskjold Plaza, 245 East 47th St., New York, NY 10017.
Fiction, nonfiction. "All manuscripts that arrive without a query answered in the affirmative by a member of our staff are returned unread. It has always been our policy to encourage new authors, however, and we welcome queries. Address Mr. Frank Wilkinson."

THE DEVIN-ADAIR COMPANY—143 Sound Beach Ave., Old Greenwich, CT 06870.
Serious nonfiction. Politically conservative, Irish, and nature and popular health topics. Has an Ecological Book Club and a Veritas Book Club. Royalty basis. Always query.

THE DIAL PRESS—1 Dag Hammarskjold Plaza, 245 East 47th St., New York, NY 10017. Richard Marek, Editor-in-Chief; Phyllis Fogelman, Editor, Children's Books.
General fiction and nonfiction. No mysteries, westerns, verse, romances, or highly

technical works. Pays in regular royalties and advances. Send query letter or sample chapter rather than complete manuscript.

DIMENSION BOOKS, INC.—P.O. Box 811, Denville, NJ 07834. Thomas Coffey, Editor. Nonfiction, Catholic books.

DIPLOMATIC PRESS, INC.—P.O. Box 593, Times Sq. Sta. New York, NY 10036. Nonfiction on every field of human interest, to 100,000 words. Pays on royalty basis. Unsolicited manuscripts not returned unless accompanied by self-addressed, stamped envelope.

DODD, MEAD & COMPANY, INC.—79 Madison Ave., New York, NY 10016. Limited fiction list. General nonfiction. Seldom publishes verse. Juveniles. All types and all lengths. Pays on royalty basis. Query first.

DOUBLEDAY & CO., INC.—245 Park Ave., New York, NY 10017. "Interested in good books of all types by writers, published and unpublished. Will accept complete manuscripts in fields of Mystery, Science Fiction and Western only; these should be addressed to appropriate department. All other writers are invited to write for free one-page instructions on 'How to Submit Your Book to Doubleday.' Pays on royalty basis."

DOW JONES-IRWIN, INC.—1818 Ridge Rd., Homewood, IL 60430. Ralph Rieves, Editor. Business books only. Pays by royalty rates.

DRAKE PUBLISHERS, INC.—381 Park Ave. South, New York, NY 10016. General nonfiction: hobby, crafts, biography, history, 50,000 to 90,000 words. Pays flat fee or on royalty basis. Query with outline, contents.

DROKE HOUSE/HALLUX—116 West Orr St., Anderson, SC 29621. S. G. Hall, Editor. Fiction and nonfiction. Royalty payment varies. Usually reports within 6 to 8 weeks. Query first.

E. P. DUTTON & CO., INC.—201 Park Ave. South, New York, NY 10003. General nonfiction of all kinds, fiction, children's books, quality paperbacks. Pays on royalty basis.

WM. B. EERDMANS PUBLISHING CO.—255 Jefferson Ave. S.E., Grand Rapids, MI 49502. Marlin VanElderen, Editor. Predominantly nonfiction of a Christian theological (usually Protestant) character. Some Great Lakes regional. Pays on royalty basis.

ELK GROVE PRESS—P.O. Box 1637, Whittier, CA 90609. Mrs. Ruth Shaw Radlauer, Editor. Fiction and nonfiction. Pre-school, kindergarten concept books under 1,000 words. Middle grades and up, under 10,000 words. Outright purchase or royalty contract. Query with statement of word length and reading level.

EMERSON BOOKS, INC.—Reynolds Lane, Buchanan, NY 10511. Interested in how-to, puzzle, and math books with popular appeal. Self-help books, collecting books, and books on crafts and martial arts. Reference books. Royalty payment.

PAUL S. ERIKSSON, INC.—119 West 57th St., New York, NY 10019. Adult fiction, general nonfiction, biography, etc. Pays by usual royalty agreement. Query first.

M. EVANS & CO., INC.—216 East 49th St., New York, NY 10017. General fiction, nonfiction, juveniles. Query.

FARRAR, STRAUS AND GIROUX—19 Union Square West, New York, NY 10003. Fiction and nonfiction, also list of *Hill and Wang. Noonday Press,* paperbacks. *Octagon Books,* scholarly reprints.

FREDERICK FELL PUBLISHERS, INC.–386 Park Ave. South, New York, NY 10016.
Book Shelf, business and finance. *Fell's Better Health Series,* physical and mental health. Also nonfiction on current social topics, mysticism and the occult. Query Charles Nurnberg, Vice President, with outline and sample chapters. Royalty basis.

FIDES PUBLISHERS, INC.–Notre Dame, IN 46556. James F. Burns, Editor.
Religious-oriented books, and books on modern education, Montessori applications. Royalty basis.

FLEET PRESS CORPORATION–160 Fifth Ave., New York, NY 10010. D. Schiff and Susan Nueckel, Editors.
Nonfiction, excluding scientific and technical manuscripts. No fiction or poetry. Query first. No unsolicited manuscripts. *Fleet Academic Editions, Inc.* – Humanities and social sciences. Query first.

FOLLETT PUBLISHING COMPANY–1010 West Washington Blvd., Chicago, IL 60607.
Quality juvenile fiction and nonfiction, adult reference, general nonfiction and sports. Children's book department overstocked; will not read manuscripts or queries at present. Address sports, popular reference, current affairs to John Hess.

FORTRESS PRESS–2900 Queen Lane, Philadelphia, PA 19129. Norman A. Hjelm, Director and Senior Editor.
Books on theology and general religion for the layman, the student, the minister, the scholar. Pays by standard royalty agreement.

THE FREE PRESS (A division of *Macmillan Publishing Co., Inc.*)–866 Third Ave., New York, NY 10022. Mr. Edward W. Barry, President.
Nonfiction: college-level texts and professional books in the social sciences and humanities. Pays by royalty.

FRIENDSHIP PRESS–475 Riverside Drive, New York, NY 10027.
Nonfiction, social issues from religious perspective, ecumenical. Query a must.

FUNK & WAGNALLS (A division of *Thomas Y. Crowell Company*)–666 Fifth Ave., New York, NY 10019.
Adult nonfiction, reference books, current affairs, science, biography, how-to and handbooks. Query first with outline. Address Trade Editorial Dept. Pays on royalty basis.

GAMBIT, INC.–306 Dartmouth St., Boston, MA 02116.
General fiction and nonfiction.

GARRARD PUBLISHING COMPANY–1607 North Market St., Champaign, IL 61820.
Juvenile and supplementary books for elementary classes. Query.

BERNARD GEIS ASSOCIATES–128 East 56th St., New York, NY 10022.
General nonfiction, fiction. Publishes a limited number of titles per year. Query first.

K. S. GINIGER CO., INC.–225 Park Ave. South, New York, NY 10003.
Trade, juvenile, reference, religious. No unsolicited manuscripts. Query.

GOLDEN BOOKS–See *Western Publishing Company, Inc.*

GOLDEN PRESS–850 Third Ave., New York, NY 10022.
Fiction and nonfiction for children, reference books, adult nonfiction. See also *Western Publishing Co., Inc.*

THE STEPHEN GREENE PRESS–Box 1000, Brattleboro, VT 05301.
Quality nonfiction; general Americana, specializing in New England; also country living, horses, conservation, natural history, individual and outdoor sports, trains, popular transportation, building technology, lively history and social commentary. Query first with complete outline and at least one sample chapter.

GROSSET & DUNLAP, INC.—51 Madison Ave., New York, NY 10010.
History, biography, literature, science, fine arts; also practical and self-help nonfiction, cookbooks, reference books and general nonfiction for adults. No fiction, poetry. Not accepting unsolicited manuscripts at present.

GROSSMAN PUBLISHERS (Division of *The Viking Press, Inc.*)—625 Madison Ave., New York, NY 10022.
General fiction and nonfiction. Query.

GROVE PRESS, INC.—53 East 11th St., New York, NY 10003. Barney Rosset, Editor and Publisher.
General high-quality fiction and nonfiction. Also *Evergreen Books,* paperback series. Pays on royalty basis. Must query first.

HARCOURT BRACE JOVANOVICH, INC.—757 Third Ave., New York, NY 10017.
General adult fiction and nonfiction, 60,000 words and up. Fiction and nonfiction, 5,000 to 60,000 words, for beginning readers through young teen-agers. "More nonfiction than fiction ... fewer picture books." Query first or send sample chapters for nonfiction. Fiction may be submitted in entirety. Enclose return postage.

HARPER & ROW, PUBLISHERS—10 East 53rd St., New York, NY 10021.
Address manuscripts of fiction, nonfiction, biographies, social and economic, etc. to Trade Dept., college texts to College Dept., books for boys and girls from picture and story books for the youngest up to fiction and nonfiction for teens to Junior Books Dept., books of religion, theology, etc. to Religious Books Dept., paperback, originals and reprints, and Barnes & Noble College Outlines, Everyday Handbooks and British Imports to Paperback Dept. Pays by royalty contract.

HARPER'S MAGAZINE PRESS—2 Park Ave., New York, NY 10016. Lawrence Freundlich, Editor.
Fiction and nonfiction. Standard royalty contract. Query first.

HART PUBLISHING CO., INC.—15 West 4th St., New York, NY 10012.
Adult nonfiction. Query.

HARVEY HOUSE, INC.—20 Waterside Plaza, New York, NY 10010. Jeanne Gardner, Editor.
Picture books, fiction and nonfiction. Strong on science and/or informational books.

HASTINGS HOUSE, PUBLISHERS, INC.—10 East 40th St., New York, NY 10016. Walter Frese, Editor.
General nonfiction; Americana, biography, travel, guide and photographic picture books, books on cooking and wines. Juveniles: Miss Judy Donnelly, Editor. Communication arts (including films, television and radio), graphic and visual arts: Russell F. Neale, Editor. Pays on royalty basis.

HEARTHSIDE PRESS, INC.—445 Northern Blvd., Great Neck, NY 11021. Nedda C. Anders, Editor.
Home, needlecraft, antiques, food and garden books.

D.C. HEATH AND COMPANY (Division of *Raytheon*)—125 Spring St., Lexington, MA 02173.
Textbooks, audio-visual materials for schools and colleges; spoken-word records (Caedmon Records); research monographs and professional studies (Lexington Books).

HERDER & HERDER—See *Continuum Books.*

HILL AND WANG (Division of *Farrar, Straus & Giroux, Inc.*)—19 Union Square West, New York, NY 10003. Arthur W. Wang, Editor-in-Chief.
Nonfiction: history, social history and drama. Standard royalty contracts. Must query first.

HOBBS/CONTEXT CORPORATION (formerly *Hobbs, Dorman & Co.*)—Rm. 1505, 52 Vanderbilt Ave., New York, NY 10017.
Educational texts and supplementary reading; technical reports; how-to material; instructional cassettes. Query first.

HOLIDAY HOUSE—18 East 56th St., New York, NY 10022. Margery Cuyler, Editor.
General juvenile books of high merit, including science and nature books for kindergarten to teen-age.

HOLT, RINEHART AND WINSTON, INC.—383 Madison Ave., New York, NY 10017.
General fiction and nonfiction; also juveniles. Pays royalties twice yearly. Query first with outline and sample chapters. Write to General Book Division.

HORIZON PRESS—156 Fifth Ave., New York, NY 10010. Ben Raeburn, Editor.
General trade books, nonfiction, art, architecture, science, and reference books; some fiction. Standard royalty agreement.

HOUGHTON MIFFLIN CO.—2 Park St., Boston, MA 02107.
Fiction: stressing contemporary themes and issues, American or foreign background; historical; suspense; general. Nonfiction: cooking and crafts; history, natural history, and important biography; books on socio-political subjects; reference; general. Literary Fellowship to finance work in progress. General juvenile and teen-age books.

HOWELL BOOK HOUSE, INC.—730 Fifth Ave., New York, NY 10019.
Nonfiction, informative works on care, training, breeding, etc., of pure-bred dogs. How-to books, histories, behavior and other aspects of dog knowledge. Minimum length about 20,000 words. Pays by standard royalty rates.

HOWELL-NORTH BOOKS—1050 Parker St., Berkeley, CA 94710. F. D. North, Editor.
Specialized—railroad histories, Western Americana, pictorials mainly. Pays royalties, no advance. Query.

HUMANITIES PRESS—Atlantic Highlands, NJ 07716.
Scholarly books on academic subjects. Query required.

INTERNATIONAL MARINE PUBLISHING CO.—21 Elm St., Camden, ME 04843. Roger C. Taylor, President; Peter Spectre, Editor.
Marine subjects, including practical manuals on commercial and pleasure boating, boat building, boat design, commercial fishing and studies in maritime history. Pays standard royalty rates.

JEWISH PUBLICATION SOCIETY—1528 Walnut St., Philadelphia, PA 19102. Maier Deshell, Editor.
Nonfiction, fiction and juveniles. All material must have a bearing on Jewish life, literature, history, biography, etc. Frequently publishes translations. Pays on royalty basis. Query first.

JOHNSON PUBLISHING COMPANY—820 South Michigan Ave., Chicago, IL 60605.
Nonfiction, children's, scholarly books, primarily about black people. Query.

JOSSEY-BASS, INC., PUBLISHERS—615 Montgomery St., San Francisco, CA 94111.
Professional and advanced trade and textbooks. Query.

JUDSON PRESS—Valley Forge, PA 19481. Harold L. Twiss, Editor.
Religious. Current moral and social issues, inspirational and devotional material. Pays by royalty rates.

JULIAN PRESS, INC.—150 Fifth Ave., New York, NY 10011. Arthur Ceppos, Editor.
Nonfiction; psychiatry, philosophy, education. Standard royalty contract. Query first.

KEATS PUBLISHING, INC.—212 Elm St., Box 876, New Canaan, CT. An Keats, Editor.
General nonfiction, natural health, inspiration, how-to. Query. Pays on standard royalty basis.

ROBERT R. KNAPP, PUBLISHER—Box 7234, San Diego, CA 92107.
Professional reference, and textbooks: the humanities and social sciences, especially education, psychology, psychiatry, and statistics. Query first. Pays on royalty basis.

ALFRED A. KNOPF, INC.—201 East 50th St., New York, NY 10022. Mr. Ashbel Green, Vice-President and Senior Editor.
High quality book-length fiction. Nonfiction: not too technical. Prefers letters describing subject matter and qualifications of author. College texts in humanities and the social sciences. Juveniles: picture books, 3,000 to 5,000 words, fiction and nonfiction. Pat Ross, Juvenile Editor. Royalty basis.

JOHN KNOX PRESS—341 Ponce de Leon Ave. NE, Atlanta, GA 30308. Richard A. Ray, Editor.
Books on the ethical, social, and cultural dimensions of religion, the relation of science and religion, biblical studies, counseling, and inspirational. Pays on royalty basis. Query first with outline or sample chapter.

LANTERN PRESS—354 Hussey Road, Mt. Vernon, NY 10552.
Juvenile fiction and nonfiction; adult nonfiction. Query first.

SEYMOUR LAWRENCE, INC.—90 Beacon St., Boston, MA 02108.
Works of fiction of literary distinction; books on child care and child development; children's books. Pays standard royalty rates. Query first on nonfiction; submit completed manuscript on fiction.

LENOX HILL PRESS—419 Park Ave. South, New York, NY 10016. Alice Sachs, Editor.
Gothic and light romances, westerns, 55,000 to 60,000 words. No manuscripts with an emphasis on sex and violence. Pays $250 for romances, $200 for westerns, on receipt of signed contract.

LERNER PUBLICATIONS CO.—241 First Ave. North, Minneapolis, MN 55401.
Fiction and nonfiction for children from preschool through high school. Send complete manuscript with return postage enclosed rather than query. Current catalogue and author guidelines available upon request. Send all manuscripts to Ms. Jennifer Martin. Reports in 10 to 12 weeks.

LION BOOKS—111 East 39th St., New York, NY 10016. Sayre Ross, Editor-in-Chief.
Young adult, nonfiction, sports, history, personality, diet and nature. Royalty and flat fee basis.

J.B. LIPPINCOTT COMPANY—521 Fifth Ave., New York, NY 10017. Edward L. Burlingame, Editor-in-Chief.
Adult and juvenile fiction and nonfiction. Submit juvenile manuscripts to Dorothy Briley, Editor, Books for Young Readers. Include return postage. Contracts and royalty payments competitive with other major publishers.

LITTLE, BROWN & CO.—34 Beacon St., Boston, MA 02106. Roger Donald, Editor-in-Chief. John G. Keller, Children's Book Editor.
Fiction, general nonfiction, sports books, juveniles, law, medical and college texts.

LITTLE GOLDEN BOOKS®—See *Western Publishing Company, Inc.*

LIVERIGHT PUBLISHING—500 Fifth Ave., New York, NY 10036.
Interested in nonfiction and good fiction; books on art and architecture, literary figures, biography; politics and current affairs, 50,000 words and up. Submit synopses and biographical sketches in advance for nonfiction, query and synopsis for fiction. Advances depend upon the book; standard royalties.

ROBERT B. LUCE, INC.—2000 N St. N.W., Washington, DC 20036. Robert D. Van Roijen, President. Joseph J. Binns, Managing Editor. Sarah Banks Forman, Assistant Editor.
Prefers nonfiction, public affairs books, but will accept a limited amount of fiction. Pays by usual royalty agreement with an advance.

McGRAW-HILL BOOK CO.—General Book Div., 1221 Ave of the Americas, New York, N.Y. 10020. Jon Gillett, General Manager, General Books.
Fiction and general nonfiction, including biography, history, education, popular science, business, reference. No verse or plays. Payment on royalty basis. 6 week response. *McGraw-Hill Junior Books*: fiction and nonfiction in the fields of history, biography, science, guidance and related subjects for younger readers.

DAVID McKAY CO., INC.—750 Third Ave., New York, NY 10017. James Louttit, President, Grace Shaw, Wallace Exman, David Currier, Senior Editors.
Contemporary adult novels with appealing characters, strong story line, pace, tension; Gothics; romantic suspense; occult; occasional innovative fiction. Nonfiction of contemporary interest in fields of human behavior, popular history, social commentary, etc. How-tos; books by experts. Mature fiction, nonfiction for young adults. Prefers complete manuscripts. Reports in about three weeks. Pays by royalty contract.

MACMILLAN PUBLISHING CO., INC.—866 Third Ave., New York, NY 10022.
Fiction; general nonfiction; children's books; religious, medical and health, business, technical, and textbooks on all levels. Address fiction and general nonfiction to Trade Department; children's books to Children's Book Department; textbooks to the College or School Departments. Query first.

MACRAE SMITH CO.—225 South 15th St., Philadelphia, PA 19102. Donald P. Macrae, President. Ruth Miner, Editor.
Adult trade books, and juvenile and young adult, ages 8 to 11, 12 to 16: nonfiction, reference, and fiction.

MASON/CHARTER PUBLISHERS, INC. (formerly *Mason & Lipscomb*)—384 Fifth Ave., New York, NY 10018. O.R. Petrocelli, Executive Vice President and Publishers. Margaret B. Parkinson, Executive Editor.
General trade books: stresses fiction, biography and history, but also interested in travel, social and behavioral sciences, politics, etc. Query with outline or synopsis.

MEREDITH CORPORATION, CONSUMER BOOK DIVISION (*Better Homes and Gardens Books* and *Creative Home Library*)—1716 Locust St., Des Moines, IA 50336. Don Dooley, Editorial Director.
Books on: sewing, crafts, health, decorating, gardening, money management, home entertainment, cars in the family, building and home improvement. Study other BH & G books. Query first with outline and sample chapter. Address the Editors. Pays flat fees and/or royalties.

JULIAN MESSNER (A division of *Simon and Schuster*)—1 West 39th St., New York, NY 10018. Lee M. Hoffman, Executive Editor, Books for Young People.
Nonfiction, 50,000 to 58,000 words, for teen-agers 12 to 17 (address Iris Rosoff, Assistant Editor). Curriculum-oriented nonfiction, 10,000 to 15,000 words, for grades 4 to 6: social studies, science, ethnic backgrounds.

MOODY PRESS—820 North LaSalle St., Chicago, IL 60610. Mr. Leslie H. Strobbe, Editor.
Evangelical publishing house associated with Moody Bible Institute. Religious fiction and nonfiction only, reflecting conservative doctrinal position. Pays standard royalties.

MOREHOUSE BARLOW CO., INC.—14 East 41st St., New York, NY 10017.
Nonfiction, especially curriculum-oriented texts, adult and children's religious books. No fiction or poetry. Pays on fee/royalty basis. Query first with outline and sample chapter.

WILLIAM MORROW & CO., INC.—105 Madison Ave., New York, NY 10016. John C. Willey, Editor-in-Chief. Constance C. Epstein, Editor of *Morrow Junior Books*.
General adult fiction and nonfiction. Juvenile books for all ages except pre-school. Pays on royalty basis.

NASH PUBLISHING–1 Dupont St., Plainview, NY 11803. Cynthia Swan, Editor.
Controversial nonfiction books on current issues; how-to titles; self-improvement; psychological subjects. Pays by flat fee or standard royalty rates. Queries only. Include stamped, self-addressed envelope to expedite reply.

THOMAS NELSON, INC.–30 East 42nd St., New York, NY 10017. Mrs. Gloria R. Mosesson, Editor.
Adult nonfiction, biographies, books on the arts, religion, history. Adult mysteries and gothics. Juvenile and young adult fiction and nonfiction.

NELSON-HALL PUBLISHERS–325 West Jackson Blvd., Chicago, IL 60606. V. Peter Ferrara, Editor.
General nonfiction trade books, with emphasis on applied psychology, sociology, anthropology. Scholarly books in the behavioral sciences. Authors must be recognized authorities on the subjects about which they write. Length, 50,000 to 100,000 words. Query with outline. Pays by standard royalty contract.

NEW DIRECTIONS PUBLISHING CORP.–333 Ave. of the Americas, New York, NY 10014.
Modern literature, poetry, criticism, belles-lettres. No unsolicited manuscripts. Query first.

NEW VIEWPOINTS (A division of *Franklin Watts, Inc.*)–730 Fifth Ave., New York, NY 10019. Will Davison, Editor.
College-level, adult nonfiction, especially history and the social sciences. Query first. Pays on royalty basis.

NEW YORK GRAPHIC SOCIETY (A subsidiary of *Time, Inc.*)–11 Beacon St., Boston, MA 02108.
Illustrated books on film, photography, Americana, crafts, and general adult subjects. Send query or outline, with writers biography and credits.

W. W. NORTON & COMPANY, INC.–500 Fifth Ave., New York, NY 10036.
Fiction and nonfiction. Pays on royalty basis.

OCEANA PUBLICATIONS, INC.–75 Main St., Dobbs Ferry, NY 10522. W. W. Cowan, Managing Editor.
Law and public policy. Query first. Pays flat fee for small titles, standard royalty contract for others.

OCTOBER HOUSE, INC.–Box 454, Stonington, CT 06378.
Not in the market for manuscripts at present. Manuscripts returned only if return postage is provided.

ODDO PUBLISHING, INC.–Storybook Acres, Beauregard Blvd., Fayetteville, GA 30214.
Juveniles for school and library use, kindergarten to junior high, on reading, speech improvement, conservation, Indian heritage, basic science, and American history, preferably in series type. Remedial reading series for grades 2 to 6 with 10- to 16-year-old interest level. Royalty and outright purchase considered. Query first.

OHARA PUBLICATIONS, INC.–1847 W. Empire Ave., Burbank, CA 91504.
Prefers nonfiction subjects on the Orient and Pacific, but will consider fiction, on a limited basis. Query first with synopsis or description of manuscript, plus resume of published books or articles. Pays standard royalty rates.

ONTARIO PRESS–61 West Ontario St., Chicago, IL 60610.
Novels and collected short stories. Pays on standard royalty basis.

OPEN COURT PUBLISHING COMPANY–Box 599, LaSalle, IL 61301. Miss A.K. Turley, Senior Editor, General Books Division.
Nonfiction: education, philosophy, religion, history, biography, general interest; juveniles. Query.

OXFORD UNIVERSITY PRESS—200 Madison Ave., New York, NY 10016.
Authoritative books on literature, history, religion, philosophy, biography, government, economics, science, art, music; college textbooks, medical books, etc. No fiction. Query before submitting.

PACIFIC BOOKS, PUBLISHERS—P.O. Box 558, Palo Alto, CA 94302. Henry Ponleithner, Editor.
Nonfiction general interest books. Specialties include Western Americana and Hawaiiana. Royalty schedule varies with book.

PANJANDRUM BOOKS—99 Sanchez St., San Francisco, CA 94114. Dennis H. Koran, Editor.
Short stories, poetry, special-interest nonfiction. Query.

PANTHEON BOOKS—201 East 50th St., New York, NY 10022.
Primarily nonfiction, academically-oriented trade books on Asian studies, history, political science, economics, medicine, law, sociology, psychology, anthropology, education, and Black studies. Separate juvenile division.

PARENTS' MAGAZINE PRESS—52 Vanderbilt Ave., New York, NY 10017. Selma Lanes, Editor.
Picture books, 500 to 2,500 words, for children 4 to 8. Simplicity of style, originality of concept. and possibilities for illustration essential.

PARKER PUBLISHING CO., INC.—West Nyack, NY 10994.
Practical, self-help, how-to books: popular health, mystic and occult, inspiration, in-service teaching and education, secretarial, selling, personal and business self-improvement, money opportunities, 65,000 words. Pays on royalty basis.

PARNASSUS PRESS—4080 Halleck St., Emeryville, CA 94608.
Adult and children's books, fiction and nonfiction. Juveniles from pre-school picture books to teen-age novels. Query. Pays by advance and royalties.

PAULIST PRESS—1865 Broadway, New York, NY 10023. Kevin A. Lynch, C.S.P., Editor.
Catholic book publishers interested in religious education materials, theology, philosophy, liturgical and spiritual writing. Welcomes and gives prompt attention to unsolicited manuscripts.

PETROCELLI/CHARTER (Division of *Mason/Charter*; formerly *Petrocelli Books*)—384 Fifth Ave., New York, NY 10018.
Technical, scientific and business books. Pays on royalty basis.

PFLAUM/STANDARD—2285 Arbor Blvd., Dayton, OH 45439. John M. Heher, General Education Editor. Rod Brownfield, Religious Education Editor.
Books, especially texts, and filmstrips on film study, mental health, personal guidance, religious education, teacher training. Pays on royalty basis.

S.G. PHILLIPS, INC.—305 West 86th St., New York, NY 10024. Sidney Phillips, Editor.
Fiction and nonfiction with contemporary themes relevant to the interests and concerns of today's young people. Especially interested in biographies, politics, history, archaeology, anthropology, social sciences, architecture, city planning, as well as outstanding fiction on all subjects for all age groups. No unsolicited manuscripts—query the editor.

PLATT & MUNK—1055 Bronx River Ave., Bronx, NY 10472. Leslie McGuire, Editor.
Mass-market juvenile books for ages 1-10. Division of Questor Education Products Company.

PLAYBOY PRESS—747 Third Ave., New York, NY 10017. Bill Adler, Senior Editor.
High-quality, book-length fiction and nonfiction. Query first.

CLARKSON N. POTTER, INC.—419 Park Ave. South, New York, NY 10016. Clarkson N. Potter, Editor-in-Chief; Mrs. Jane West, Senior Editor.
General trade books and nonfiction; especially on Americana, science, art, antiques, folk art, the contemporary scene. Pays on royalty basis. Query first.

PRAEGER PUBLISHERS, INC.—111 Fourth Ave., New York, NY 10003. Arnold Dolin, Editor-in-Chief.
Nonfiction on international relations, history, social sciences, economics, art, architecture, design, archaeology, reference, contemporary issues, urban affairs, education, biography, music, quality paperbacks. Pays on royalty basis. Query first.

PRENTICE-HALL, INC.—Englewood Cliffs, NJ 97632.
Fiction and nonfiction. Special interest in biography, history, politics, sports, juvenile. No westerns, poetry. Other book publishing divisions are College Books, Educational Textbooks, Business and Professional Books. Query first.

PRICE/STERN/SLOAN PUBLISHERS, INC.—410 North La Cienega Blvd., Los Angeles, CA 90048.
Short, humorous "non-books." No fiction, poetry, or juveniles. Query first.

PRUETT PUBLISHING COMPANY—3235K Prairie Ave., Boulder, CO 80301.
Books about the history and development of American West; railroads; outdoor books for Rocky Mt. region. Special education materials and some college level texts. No fiction or poetry.

PUBLIC AFFAIRS PRESS—419 New Jersey Ave. S.E., Washington, DC 20003.
Nonfiction: current affairs and social sciences. Payment varies.

G.P. PUTNAM'S SONS—200 Madison Ave., New York, NY 10016. Walter J. Minton, President. Harvey Ginsberg, Editor-in-Chief. Clyde Taylor, Publisher. Marcia Magill, Executive Editor. Charles Mercer and Margaret Frith, Co-Directors, Juvenile Department.
Fiction and nonfiction for adults and children. Royalty basis. Queries only.

QUADRANGLE/THE NEW YORK TIMES BOOK CO.—10 East 53rd St., New York, NY 10022. Herbert Nagourney, President. Roger Jellinek, Editor-in-Chief.
Serious nonfiction by recognized authorities. Query first.

RAND McNALLY & COMPANY—Box 7600, Chicago, IL 60680. Address the Editorial Dept., Trade Publishing Division.
Adult nonfiction on exploration, adventure, travel, Americana, history, world environmental problems, nature, etc. Juveniles, both fiction and nonfiction.

RANDOM HOUSE, INC.—201 East 50th St., New York, NY 10022.
High-grade fiction and nonfiction including reference and college textbooks. Juveniles: fiction and nonfiction, profusely illustrated picture books, easy-to-read material. Catalogues available on request. Also *Vintage Books,* a paperback series. Query first.

HENRY REGNERY CO.—180 North Michigan Ave., Chicago, IL 60601. Dominick Abel, Editorial Vice-President.
General nonfiction. Query first.

FLEMING H. REVELL COMPANY—Old Tappan, NJ 07675. Dr. Frank S. Mead, Editor-in-Chief. Richard Baltzell, Editorial Director.
Revell Books—Inspirational and devotional religious books, self-help, personality biographies. Reports after at least one month. Pays on royalty basis.

THE WARD RITCHIE PRESS—474 South Arroyo Parkway, Pasadena, CA 91105.
General interest nonfiction, cookbooks, Americana, and travel and history guidebooks. Standard royalty rates. Query.

RODALE PRESS BOOK DIVISION—33 East Minor St., Emmaus, PA 18049. Charles Gerras, Executive Editor.
Nonfiction for general readership, on health, food, nutrition, specific diseases and nutrients, etc., by authors with credentials in these fields. Query.

RICHARDS ROSEN PRESS, INC.—29 East 21st St., New York, NY 10010. Ruth C. Rosen, Editor.
Nonfiction books on guidance, journalism, theatre, social problems, for the young adult, to 40,000 words. Payment arranged.

ROY PUBLISHERS, INC.—30 East 74th St., New York, NY 10021. Hanna Kister, Editor.
General fiction, nonfiction and juveniles, with emphasis on international interests. Overstocked; manuscripts sent without permission will be refused.

RUTLEDGE BOOKS, INC.—25 West 43rd St., New York, NY 10036.
All types of unusual adult nonfiction of high quality. Cookbooks and sportsbooks a specialty. Query first with outline. Pays in advance and royalties.

SAGE BOOKS—1139 South Wabash, Chicago, IL 60605.
Nonfiction books about the American West. Pays regular royalty rates. See *Swallow Press*.

ST. MARTIN'S PRESS, INC.—175 Fifth Ave., New York, NY 10010.
Fiction, general nonfiction and juveniles. History, political science, biography, music and reference books, college textbooks. Pays on royalty basis.

SATURDAY REVIEW PRESS—201 Park Ave. South, New York, NY 10003.
General adult fiction and nonfiction, especially contemporary and historical fiction, social issues, history, biography, popular science. Pays by advances and standard royalty rates.

SCHOCKEN BOOKS—200 Madison Ave., New York, NY 10016. Chris Kuppig, Editor.
Nonfiction: history, education, sociology, religious thought, Judaica, women's studies. Pays standard royalty rates.

SCHOLASTIC BOOKS—50 West 44th St., New York, NY 10036. Mrs. Norma Ainsworth, Editor of Manuscript Dept.
Book clubs for grades 1-12 use picture books, science, biography, mystery, how-to, teen-age interests, beauty and grooming, young adult mystery and suspense. Also fiction for teenagers who read at 2nd to 4th grade level. Query.

CHARLES SCRIBNER'S SONS—597 Fifth Ave., New York, NY 10017.
Books of all kinds, including juveniles. Query first.

SCRIMSHAW PRESS—149 9th St., San Francisco, CA 94103. Frederick Mitchell, Editor.
Fiction and nonfiction, usually illustrated. Pays on royalty basis.

THE SEABURY PRESS—815 Second Ave., New York, NY 10017.
Continuum Books: Justus George Lawler, Senior Editor. General interest books of literary, behavioral, social, and educational concern. *Crossroad Books:* F. Reid Isaac, Senior Editor. Religous books. *Clarion Books:* James C. Giblin, Editor-in-Chief. General books for juveniles from preschool through young adult. Pays by royalty contract.

SHEED & WARD, INC.—6700 Squibb Rd., Mission, KS 66202. James F. Andrews, Editor-in-Chief.
General nonfiction and fiction; also philosophy, theology, psychology, sociology, and history, with religious interest.

SHERBOURNE PRESS—1640 South La Cienega, Los Angeles, CA 90035. Mr. Gil Porter, Editor.

General nonfiction, with emphasis on self-help, consumer protection, diet, health, wealth, sex, etc.

SIERRA CLUB BOOKS—1650 Mills Tower, 220 Bush St., San Francisco, CA 94104.
Specialized conservation, natural history, outdoor guidebooks, recreation, etc. Query.

SIMON & SCHUSTER—630 Fifth Ave., New York, NY 10020. Michael V. Korda, Editor-in-Chief. Henry Robbins, Executive Editor. Phyllis Grann, Jonathan Dolger, Dianne Harris, Julie Houston, Alice Mayhew, Nan Talese, Barbara Wyden, Editors.
General fiction, nonfiction, mysteries. "We now return unread all unsolicited manuscripts not addressed to an editor by name." Pays standard royalty rates.

STACKPOLE BOOKS—Cameron and Kelker St., Harrisburg, PA 17105.
Nonfiction, 30,000 words and up, on the outdoors, guns, sports, camping, Americana, current affairs, leisure-time pursuits, and general nonfiction. Pays on royalty basis. Query.

STECK-VAUGHN COMPANY—Box 2028, Austin, TX 78767. Paul C. Craig, Vice-President, Editorial; Joel L. Pyland, Executive Editor.
Textbooks and other educational materials.

STEIN AND DAY—Scarborough House, Briarcliff Manor, NY 10510. Renni Browne and George Caldwell, Editors.
Quality fiction, including mysteries. All types of nonfiction except technical material. No unsolicited manuscripts will be considered. Nonfiction authors should first submit a summary or outline and sample chapter of their work; novelists should submit first chapter only. Stamped, return envelope must accompany submissions. Pays on royalty basis.

STERLING PUBLISHING CO.—419 Park Ave. South, New York, NY 10016. Burton Hobson, Editorial Director.
How-tos, general information, science and sports books for adults and young people. Pays sometimes on royalty basis, usually by outright purchase. Must query first.

STONE WALL PRESS, INC.—19 Muzzey St., Lexington, MA 02173.
Books on outdoor and leisure-time activities in New England and eastern U.S.; hunting, fishing, camping, nature, conservation, with photos or drawings. Royalty rates. Query.

SUNSTONE PRESS—Box 2321, Santa Fe, NM 87501.
Primarily Southwestern nonfiction, some fiction. Poetry, craft and cookbooks. Query. Pays standard royalty rates.

SWALLOW PRESS—1139 South Wabash, Chicago, IL 60605. Durrett Wagner, Editor.
General nonfiction. Pays regular royalty rates. Publishers of *Sage Books*. Query.

TAPLINGER PUBLISHING CO., INC.—200 Park Ave. South, New York, NY 10003.
Nonfiction, especially natural history, crafts, psychology and literary biography. Query.

J. P. TARCHER, INC.—9110 Sunset Blvd., Los Angeles, CA 90069.
General nonfiction: psychology, self-help, current biography, etc. No fiction or poetry. Must query first with outline and sample chapter. Pays on standard royalty rates.

TRANS-ANGLO BOOKS—P. O. Box 38, Corona del Mar, CA 92625. Spencer Crump, Editor.

Nonfiction, 10,000 to 50,000 words with photos, on Americana and Railroadiana. No family histories or poetry. Pays 5% to 10% royalty, on publication. Reports in three to six weeks. Catalog sent on request. Query.

TROUBADOR PRESS—126 Folsom St., San Francisco, CA 94105.
Coloring books, cookbooks, game, cut-out, craft, and activity books; general adult nonfiction; quality, illustrated trade paperbacks. Pays by royalties with advances or by outright purchase. Query first with outline and/or sample illustrations, to Brenda Shahan, Reading Department. Include stamped return envelope.

FREDERICK UNGAR PUBLISHING CO., INC.—250 Park Ave. South, New York, NY 10003.
Reference, nonfiction, literature (especially in translation) and criticism. Must query first.

UNION OF AMERICAN HEBREW CONGREGATIONS—838 Fifth Ave., New York, NY 10021. Abraham Segal, Director of Education.
Texts and instructional materials in all media combinations, for students and/or teachers at all age-levels on Jewish values, concerns, content, experiences, for classroom, home, camp settings. Queries, outlines, samples preferred.

UNITED CHURCH PRESS—1505 Race St., Philadelphia, PA 19102. Theodore A. McConnell, Editor-in-Chief.
Nonfiction, primarily religion, theology, and ethics; also, social sciences, humanities and current affairs in relationship to ethical and value issues. Pays standard royalty rates. Query first with sample chapters and complete outline.

THE VANGUARD PRESS, INC.—424 Madison Ave., New York, NY 10017. Bernice Woll, Editor.
Fiction and nonfiction, about 50,000 words and up. Large juvenile list of all categories, emphasizing nonfiction in new fields. Occasional special books. Pays on royalty basis. Particularly interested in new writers of promise and ability. Query first with sample chapters. Submit to Dana Randt, Editor, Manuscript Dept.

THE VIKING PRESS, INC.—625 Madison Ave., New York, NY 10022.
Book-length novels of literary quality. Biography, general works on history, science, sociology, etc., for the layman. Art and travel (*Studio Books*). Higher type of juveniles (*Junior Books*). Paperbound (*Viking Compass Books, Viking Seafarer Books, Viking Portable Library*). Pays usual royalty rates. Query first.

HENRY Z. WALCK, INC.—750 Third Ave., New York, NY 10017.
Juvenile books. Query first.

WALKER AND COMPANY—720 Fifth Ave., New York, NY 10019.
Nonfiction, fiction, mystery. Uses occasional drawings or photographs in conjunction with text. Standard royalty schedule.

FREDERICK WARNE & CO., INC.—101 Fifth Ave., New York, NY 10003.
Books for children and young adults. Enclose stamped, return envelope with submission. Reports in four to six weeks.

IVES WASHBURN, INC.—750 Third Ave., New York, NY 10017. James Louttit, Juvenile and Trade Editor.
A selected small list of fiction, nonfiction and junior books. Query first.

WATSON-GUPTILL PUBLICATIONS—1515 Broadway, New York, NY 10036.
How-to books for artists, art teachers, art students and hobbyists. Subjects include painting, sculpture, printmaking, drawing, commercial art, crafts, art education. Books emphasize techniques, step-by-step demonstrations. Pays on royalty basis.

FRANKLIN WATTS, INC.—730 Fifth Ave., New York, NY 10019. Kathryn Ernst, Editor-in-Chief.
Fiction on contemporary themes, and nonfiction for elementary and secondary school levels. Query.

WESTERN PUBLISHING COMPANY, INC.—Juvenile picture-storybook division, 1220 Mound Ave., Racine, WI 53404.
Picture-storybooks under 800 words; childhood experiences, early learning concepts, animal stories, mechanical subjects. Humor welcomed. Novels 35,000 words and up, for pre-teen and early-teen readers; query with synopsis. Reports in two to five weeks. Manuscripts purchased outright. Same address and requirements for *Whitman Tell-a-Tale*® books and novels, *Little Golden Books*®, and novelty *Golden Books*.

THE WESTMINISTER PRESS—902 Witherspoon Bldg., Philadelphia, PA 19107. Barbara Bates, Children's Book Editor.
Juvenile fiction and nonfiction for age 9 and up. Payments on royalty basis.

WEYBRIGHT AND TALLEY—750 Third Ave., New York, NY 10017. Truman M. Talley, President.
Largely nonfiction. Major business, corporate, and Wall Street books for the general public; books on Washington high-level and power politics; outstanding nature narratives and science explorations. Query first with brief outline or table of contents and sample chapter.

ALBERT WHITMAN & CO.—560 West Lake St., Chicago, IL 60606. Caroline Rubin, Editor.
Overstocked at present.

WHITMAN TELL-A-TALE BOOKS—See *Western Publishing Co.*

WHITMORE PUBLISHING CO.—35 Cricket Terrace, Ardmore, PA 19003. Blair Simon, Managing Editor.
Nonfiction on education, ethics, politics, international economics, evolution, science, career planning, counseling, communications, and models for social or personal creativity. Fiction and poetry relating to these themes. Also paperbacks. Standard royalty contract. Query.

WILDERNESS PRESS—2440 Bancroft Way, Berkeley, CA 94704. Thomas Winnett, Editor.
Guides to Western outdoor areas; books on outdoor, self-powered activities. Pays royalties of 8% to 10% semiannually. Query.

JOHN WILEY & SONS, INC.—605 Third Ave., New York, NY 10016. Robert B. Polhemus, Manager, Book Dept., Wiley-Interscience Division.
Technical, scientific, and business books. Pays on royalty basis. Query first.

WINCHESTER PRESS—205 East 42nd St., New York, NY 10017. Robert Elman, Editor.
Nonfiction books; how-tos, sports, conservation. Standard royalty schedule. Query first.

WORD BOOKS—4800 West Waco Drive, Waco, TX 76703. Floyd W. Thatcher, Editor.
All types of religious nonfiction, 160 to 200 typed pages. Standard royalty payments.

PETER H. WYDEN, PUBLISHER—750 Third Ave., New York, NY 10017.
General book publishers. Nonfiction. Query.

YOUNG SCOTT BOOKS—See *Addison-Wesley.*

ZONDERVAN PUBLISHING HOUSE—1415 Lake Drive S.E., Grand Rapids, MI 49506. T. Alton Bryant, Editor.
Protestant religious subjects. Inspirational and devotional themes for young people

and adults; textbooks and handbooks for schools and clergymen; adult biography with moral and religious content; church renewal. Books on religious subjects from a psychological orientation.

PAPERBACK BOOK PUBLISHERS

ACE BOOKS—A Division of Charter Communications, Inc., 1120 Avenue of the Americas, New York, NY 10036. Mrs. Evelyn B. Grippo, Editor-in-Chief.
Science fiction and western novels, nurse romances, women's suspense novels, Gothic romance-suspense, occult nonfiction; modern novels, and nonfiction: up to 75,000 words. Original and reprint. Include one-page synopsis of plot or idea with all material. Advance flexible. Standard royalties.

ANCHOR PRESS/DOUBLEDAY—245 Park Ave., New York, NY 10017.
Adult trade books in sociology, modern lifestyles and philosophy, psychology, para-psychology, for the sophisticated reader.

ARCHWAY PAPERBACKS (Published by *Pocket Books*)—630 Fifth Ave., New York, NY 10020. Patricia MacDonald, Editor.
Fiction, mysteries, animal stories, adventure, young romance, humor, sports, etc., and nonfiction (biographies, science, hobbies, crafts) for young readers, 8 to 14. Might be interested in original manuscripts. Must query first.

ARCO BOOKS, INC.—219 Park Ave. South, New York, NY 10003. David Goodnough, Editor.
Nonfiction originals and reprints, 50,000 words and up. Outright purchase and standard royalty payment.

AVON BOOKS—959 Eighth Ave., New York, NY 10019. Peter M. Mayer, Editor-in-Chief.
Modern fiction with commercial slant; educational nonfiction; 60,000 to 200,000 words. Prefers works by previously published writers, but looks at all. Query first. Good royalties against an advance.

AWARD BOOKS—235 East 45th St., New York, NY 10017.
Fiction, with emphasis on adventure, espionage, suspense, Gothics, westerns. Nonfiction books for women; sports and games; reference books on business, money and investments, hobbies and collecting (antiques). Do-it-yourself and how-to books. Some off-beat cookbooks, diet, health, physical fitness books. Query with outline preferred. Reports within 8 to 10 weeks. Payment rates vary.

BANTAM BOOKS, INC.—666 Fifth Ave., New York, NY 10019.
Accepts material through agents and publishers only.

BRANDON BOOKS—21322 Lassen St., Chatsworth, CA 91311.
Fiction. Query.

CAMELOT BOOKS (A division of *Avon Books*)—959 Eighth Ave., New York, NY 10019. Nancy Coffey, Editor.
Fiction and nonfiction for young readers, ages 8 to 14. Uses originals. Payment is negotiable. Query first.

COLLIER BOOKS—866 Third Ave., New York, NY 10022.
Wide variety of nonfiction of any length. No original fiction. Royalty basis. Query.

CORNERSTONE LIBRARY, INC.—630 Fifth Ave., New York, NY 10020.
Basic books in the leisuretime fields (chess, tennis, golf, bridge), guide books to various subjects and how-tos; originals as well as reprints. No fiction. Royalty basis.

DAW BOOKS, INC.–1301 Ave. of the Americas, New York, NY 10019. Donald A. Wollheim, Publisher.
Paperbacks covering entire field of science fiction/fantasy novel. Pays $2,000 advance and up, against royalties of 6%, 8%, and up.

DELL BOOKS–1 Dag Hammarskjold Plaza, 245 East 47th St., New York, NY 10017. Ross Claiborne, Executive Editor.
Fiction and nonfiction, 60,000 words and up. Query.

DELTA BOOKS–Dell Publishing Co., 1 Dag Hammerskjold Plaza, 245 East 47th St., New York, NY 10017. Richard Huett, Editor-in-Chief.
Selected fiction. Nonfiction of general and academic interest, especially in history, psychology, science, literature, philosophy, sociology, economics, anthropology, archaeology. Query first. Similar requirements for *Laurel Editions.*

FAWCETT WORLD LIBRARY–1515 Broadway, New York, NY 10036.
Fawcett Crest Books: Fiction and nonfiction reprints. Pays in royalty basis. Query first. *Fawcett Premier Books:* Reprints and originals for secondary schools and colleges; supplementary readings. Pays on royalty basis. *Gold Medal Books:* Original paperback fiction and nonfiction for mass market. Pays on royalty basis. Query first; reports on manuscripts in three to six weeks.

GOLD MEDAL BOOKS–See *Fawcett World Library.*

GROSSET "SPECIALS"–Grosset & Dunlap, Inc., 51 Madison Ave., New York, NY 10010.
Broad range of nonfiction, original and reprint, for mass distribution. Not accepting unsolicited manuscripts at present.

LASER BOOKS–See *Harlequin Romances.*

HARLEQUIN ROMANCES–Harlequin Enterprises, Ltd., 240 Duncan Mill Rd., Don Mills, Ont., Canada M3B 1Z4.
Queries or manuscripts for romance novels with mass appeal. Pays by royalty contract. *Laser Books:* science fiction with element of human adventure.

MANOR BOOKS–432 Park Ave., South, New York, NY 10016.
Fiction and nonfiction reprints and originals. Query.

MERIDAN BOOKS–See *New American Library.*

NEW AMERICAN LIBRARY–1301 Ave. of the Americas, New York, NY 10019.
Signet Books: Popular fiction; topical nonfiction, self-help, how-to, biographies, popular psychology and sociology, etc. *Plume Books:* General nonfiction on current topics (e.g., feminism), hobbies, crafts, outdoor life, etc. *Meridian Books:* For undergraduate, college market. Surveys of current thinking in given academic area, especially in liberal arts and social sciences. *Mentor:* Original nonfiction for high school and college levels on history, film, women's studies, psychology, anthropology, ethnic studies, media and urban studies. Standard royalty contract. Query with outline and sample material for nonfiction.

101 PRODUCTIONS–834 Mission St., San Francisco, CA 94103.
Cookbooks, home, travel manuscripts, 200 pages and up. Standard royalties after publication.

PAPERBACK LIBRARY–See *Warner Paperback Library.*

PENGUIN BOOKS, INC.–7110 Ambassador Rd., Baltimore, MD 21207.
Adult nonfiction only. Reprints and originals.

PINNACLE BOOKS, INC.–275 Madison Ave., New York, NY 10016. Andrew Ettinger, Editor.
Topical nonfiction, popular sociological issues, fast-moving fiction, adventure, espionage, historical intrigue and romance, etc. Originals, translations, and reprints.

Pays by standard royalty contract. No unsolicited manuscripts. Query first. Send stamped, return envelope for brochure and requirements memo.

PLUME BOOKS—See *New American Library*.

POCKET BOOKS (A division of *Simon & Schuster, Inc.*)—630 Fifth Ave., New York, NY 10020.
Chiefly reprints. Some originals published. Query.

POPULAR LIBRARY, INC.—600 Third Ave., New York, NY 10016. Patrick O'Connor, Editor-in-Chief.
Reprints and few originals. General fiction, Gothics, westerns, science fiction. Pays on royalty basis. Query first.

PYRAMID COMMUNICATONS, INC.—757 Third Ave., New York, NY 10017.
Fiction: historical romances, mammoth Gothics, family chronicles, suspense. No westerns, science fictions, mysteries. Originals and reprints. Query first.

REGAL BOOKS—Box 1591, Glendale, CA 91209. David A. Stoop, Managing Editor.
Evangelical Christian. Fiction, nonfiction, poetry. Pays on standard royalty basis. Query.

REWARD BOOKS (A subsidiary of *Prentice-Hall, Inc.*)—Englewood Cliffs, NJ 07632. William Costello, Editor-in-Chief.
Nonfiction manuscripts, 60,000 words, on: self-help, inspiration, the occult, money-opportunity, popular health, dieting, beauty, folk remedies, sports, various areas of popular psychology. Pays 10% of net trade sales.

SIGNET BOOKS—See *New American Library*.

SPECTRUM BOOKS (A subsidiary of *Prentice-Hall, Inc.*)—Englewood Cliffs, NJ 07632. Paperbacks.

TEMPO BOOKS—51 Madison Ave., New York, NY 10010. Harriet McDougal, Editor.
Fiction and nonfiction for children and young adults. Reprints; some orignals, especially puzzles and sports. Pays standard advance against royalties on nonfiction and fiction; fees on puzzles. Prefers query and outline first.

TOWER PUBLICATIONS, INC.—185 Madison Ave., New York, NY 10016. Publishers of *Belmont Tower Books.* Peter McCurtin, Editor-in-Chief.
Mysteries, westerns, Gothics, general modern novels, series packages, 40,000 to 50,000 words. Query first with outline and sample chapter. Pays standard royalties.

UNIVERSAL LIBRARY (A division of *Grosset & Dunlap, Inc.*)—51 Madison Ave., New York, NY 10010.
Not issuing new titles at present.

VINTAGE BOOKS (A division of *Random House*)—201 East 50th St., New York, NY 10022.
Paperbacks. Query.

WARNER PAPERBACK LIBRARY—75 Rockefeller Plaza, New York, NY 10019. Bob Abel, Executive Editor.
Romantic historical novels, mystery-adventure series with continuing hero, Gothic novels, novels that reveal inner workings of an industry, profession, lifestyle, etc. Controversial nonfiction. Length: 50,000 to 125,000 words. Query first with three sample chapters. Pays standard publishing practice of advance against royalties.

WASHINGTON SQUARE PRESS (A division of *Simon & Schuster, Inc.*)—630 Fifth Ave., New York, NY 10020.
Specializes in books of educational interest for high school market and the general public. Mostly nonfiction and anthologies. Query first.

WILSHIRE BOOK CO.–12015 Sherman Rd., North Hollywood, CA 91605.
Specialized. Tennis, inspirational, psychological, self-help books (e.g., Psycho-cybernetics), horse instruction and training books, 35,000 to 70,000 words. Query with synopsis or outline. Pays standard royalties.

UNIVERSITY PRESSES

BRIGHAM YOUNG UNIVERSITY PRESS–209 University Press Bldg., Provo, UT 84601.

BROWN UNIVERSITY PRESS–129 Waterman St., Providence, RI 02912.

BUCKNELL UNIVERSITY PRESS–Lewisburg, PA 17837.

CAMBRIDGE UNIVERSITY PRESS–32 East 57th St., New York, NY 10022.

THE CATHOLIC UNIVERSITY OF AMERICA PRESS–620 Michigan Ave., N.E., Washington, DC 20017.

COLUMBIA UNIVERSITY PRESS–562 West 113th St., New York, NY 10025.

CORNELL UNIVERSITY PRESS–124 Roberts Pl., Ithaca, NY 14850.

DUKE UNIVERSITY PRESS–Box 6697, College Station, Durham, NC 27708.

DUQUESNE UNIVERSITY PRESS–Pittsburgh, PA 15219.

FORDHAM UNIVERSITY PRESS– Box L, Bronx, NY 10458.

HARVARD UNIVERSITY PRESS–79 Garden St., Cambridge, MA 02138.

INDIANA UNIVERSITY PRESS–10th and Morton Sts., Bloomington, IN 47401.

IOWA STATE UNIVERSITY PRESS–Ames, IA 50010.

THE JOHNS HOPKINS PRESS–Baltimore, MD 21218.

KENT STATE UNIVERSITY PRESS–Kent, OH 44242.

LOUISIANA STATE UNIVERSITY PRESS–Baton Rouge, LA 70803.

LOYOLA UNIVERSITY PRESS–3441 North Ashland Ave., Chicago, IL 60657.

THE M.I.T. PRESS–28 Carleton St., Cambridge, MA 02142.

MICHIGAN STATE UNIVERSITY PRESS–1405 South Harrison Rd., East Lansing, MI 48824.

NEW YORK UNIVERSITY PRESS–21 West 4th St., New York, NY 10003.

NORTHWESTERN UNIVERSITY PRESS–1735 Benson Ave., Evanston, IL 60201.

OHIO STATE UNIVERSITY PRESS–Hitchcock Hall, 2070 Neil Ave., Columbus, OH 43210.

OHIO UNIVERSITY PRESS–Athens, OH 45701.

OREGON STATE UNIVERSITY PRESS–101 Waldo Hall, Corvallis, OR 97331.

OXFORD UNIVERSITY PRESS–200 Madison Ave., New York, NY 10016.

THE PENNSYLVANIA STATE UNIVERSITY PRESS–215 Wagner Bldg., University Park, PA 16802.

THE PRESS OF CASE WESTERN RESERVE UNIVERSITY–Quail Bldg., Cleveland, OH 44106.

PRINCETON UNIVERSITY PRESS–Princeton, NJ 08540.

RUTGERS UNIVERSITY PRESS–30 College Ave., New Brunswick, NJ 08903.

ST. JOHN'S UNIVERSITY PRESS–Grand Central and Utopia Parkways, Jamaica, NY 11432.

SOUTHERN ILLINOIS UNIVERSITY PRESS–Carbondale, IL 62901.

SOUTHERN METHODIST UNIVERSITY PRESS–Dallas, TX 75222.

STANFORD UNIVERSITY PRESS–Stanford, CA 94305.

SYRACUSE UNIVERSITY PRESS–Box 8, University Station, Syracuse, NY 13210.

TEMPLE UNIVERSITY PRESS–Philadelphia, PA 19122.

UNIVERSITY OF ALABAMA PRESS–Drawer 2877, University, AL 35486.

UNIVERSITY OF ARIZONA PRESS–Box 3398, College Station, Tucson, AZ 85722.

UNIVERSITY OF CALIFORNIA PRESS–Berkeley, CA 94720.

UNIVERSITY OF CHICAGO PRESS–5750 Ellis Ave., Chicago, IL 60637.

UNIVERSITY OF GEORGIA PRESS–Athens, GA 30601.

UNIVERSITY OF ILLINOIS PRESS–Urbana, IL 61801.

UNIVERSITY OF IOWA PRESS–Iowa City, IA 52242.

UNIVERSITY OF MASSACHUSETTS PRESS–Munson Hall, Amherst, MA 01002.

UNIVERSITY OF MIAMI PRESS–Drawer 9088, Coral Gables, FL 33124.

UNIVERSITY OF MICHIGAN PRESS–Ann Arbor, MI 48106.

UNIVERSITY OF MINNESOTA PRESS–2037 University Ave., S.E., Minneapolis, MN 55455.

UNIVERSITY OF MISSOURI PRESS–Columbia, MO 65201.

UNIVERSITY OF NEBRASKA PRESS–Lincoln, NE 68508.

UNIVERSITY OF NEW MEXICO PRESS–Albuquerque, NM 87106.

UNIVERSITY OF NORTH CAROLINA PRESS–Chapel Hill, NC 27515.

UNIVERSITY OF NOTRE DAME PRESS–Notre Dame, IN 45556.

UNIVERSITY OF OKLAHOMA PRESS–Norman, OK 73069.

UNIVERSITY OF PENNSYLVANIA PRESS–3933 Walnut St., Philadelphia, PA 19104.

UNIVERSITY OF PITTSBURGH PRESS–127 North Bellefield Ave., Pittsburgh, PA 15260.

UNIVERSITY OF SOUTH CAROLINA PRESS–USC Campus, Columbia, SC 29208.

UNIVERSITY OF TENNESSEE PRESS–Publications Bldg., Knoxville, TN 37916.

UNIVERSITY OF TEXAS PRESS–Box 7819, University Station, Austin, TX 78712.

UNIVERSITY OF UTAH PRESS–Bldg. 513, Salt Lake City, UT 84112.

UNIVERSITY OF WASHINGTON PRESS–Seattle, WA 98105.

UNIVERSITY OF WISCONSIN PRESS–Box 1379, Madison, WI 53701.

THE UNIVERSITY PRESS OF HAWAII–535 Ward Ave., Honolulu, HI 96814.

THE UNIVERSITY PRESS OF KANSAS–358 Watson, Lawrence, KS 66044.

THE UNIVERSITY PRESS OF KENTUCKY–Lafferty Hall, Lexington, KY 40506.

THE UNIVERSITY PRESS OF NEW ENGLAND–Box 979, Hanover, NH 03755.

THE UNIVERSITY PRESS OF VIRGINIA–Box 3608, University Sta., Charlottesville, VA 22903.

THE UNIVERSITY PRESS OF WASHINGTON, D.C.–University Press Bldg., Delbrook
    Campus, C.A.S., Riverton, VA 22651.

THE UNIVERSITY PRESSES OF FLORIDA–15 N.W. 15 St., Gainesville, FL 32601.

VANDERBILT UNIVERSITY PRESS–Nashville, TN 37203.

WAYNE STATE UNIVERSITY PRESS–5980 Cass, Detroit, MI 48202.

WESLEYAN UNIVERSITY PRESS–356 Washington St., Middletown, CT 06457.

YALE UNIVERSITY PRESS–302 Temple St., New Haven, CT 06511.

SYNDICATES

Syndicates are business organizations which publish nothing themselves, but buy material from writers, artists, etc., and sell it to newspapers throughout the country and the world. Authors are then paid a percentage of the gross proceeds, or, in some cases, an outright fee.

The following list includes major syndicates in the market for free-lance material at the present time. For a complete list of all syndicates, see the *Editor and Publisher Annual Directory of Syndicated Features,* available from *Editor and Publisher,* 750 Third Ave., New York, N. Y. 10022. It is always best to query syndicates before sending manuscripts, as their needs change frequently.

B P SINGER FEATURES INC.—3164 West Tyler Ave., Anaheim, CA 92801. Jane Sherrod, Editor.
Fiction, all lengths, previously published and on universal themes; biography and woman interest material, all lengths. Illustrated columns and short humor. Books for foreign reprint. Color transparencies, cartoons, comic strips. Buys outright or pays on percentage basis.

CHICAGO TRIBUNE-NEW YORK NEWS SYNDICATE, INC.—220 East 42nd St., New York, NY 10017. Thomas B. Dorsey, Executive Editor.
Topical, exclusive one shots, 1,500 to 2,000 words. Series, 5-6 parts, 7,500 words.

ENTERPRISE SCIENCE NEWS—Newspaper Enterprise Assn., 230 Park Ave., New York, NY 10017. David Hendin, Editor.
Science feature material with high reader impact, 800 to 1,000 words, by experienced, established science and medical writers. Photos necessary. Pays $75 and up, on publication.

THE HOLLYWOOD INFORMER SYNDICATE—Box 49957, Los Angeles, CA 90049. John Austin, Director.
Feature material, 1,000 to 1,500 words, on TV and motion picture personalities, knowledgeably written. Pays on percentage basis. Open for suggestions on 3- to 4-part (15,000 to 20,000 words) life story ideas on major personalities. Negotiated payment, on acceptance.

INTERCITY NEWS SERVICE—103 Park Ave., New York, NY 10017. John Kelly, Editor; Ed Nassauer, General Manager.
Business, financial and trade press articles, and special correspondence, by staff writers and special assignment only.

KING FEATURES SYNDICATE—235 East 45th St., New York, NY 10077. Neal Freeman, Editor.
Columns, comics, features of all types, photos. Most contributors are on contract. Payment varies.

LOS ANGELES TIMES SYNDICATE—Times Mirror Square, Los Angeles, CA 90053. Patrick McHugh, Chief Editor.
Features on long-range program basis: comic strips, panels, daily columns, etc. No short stories or spot releases.

McNAUGHT SYNDICATE, INC.—60 East 42nd St., New York, NY 10077. Anne Rickey, Editor.
Humorous material; drawings and ideas for syndication. Pays on acceptance.

NATIONAL CATHOLIC NEWS SERVICE—1312 Massachusetts Ave. N.W., Washington, DC 20005. James E. Fiedler, News Editor. Mrs. Angela Schreiber, Feature Editor. Thomas N. Lorsung, Picture Editor.
Serves Catholic diocesan weekly newspapers in U.S. and Canada. Articles about

Catholic Church or issues of special interest to Catholics, and photos. Pays up to 5¢ a published word, after publication.

NATIONAL NEWSPAPER SYNDICATE–National Newspaper Syndicate, Inc., of America, 20 North Wacker Dr., Chicago, IL 60606. John Hickey, Editor.
Permanent features only.

NEWSPAPER ENTERPRISE ASSOCIATION, INC.–230 Park Ave., New York, NY 10017.
News features, background material, feature stories on current news. Submit to Robert Cochnar, Executive Editor. Most material staff written, or done by writers under contract.

NORTH AMERICAN NEWSPAPER ALLIANCE–220 East 48th St., New York, NY 10017. Sheldon Engelmayer, Editor.
News and feature stories of nationwide interest, to 750 words. Special Sunday articles, to 1,500 words. Series of two to five articles. Decision within a few days. Pays from $25, immediately after distribution.

PUBLISHERS-HALL SYNDICATE, INC.–401 North Wabash Ave., Chicago, IL 60611. Robert Cowles, President. Richard Sherry, Executive Vice President and Editor.
Columns, comic strips, panel cartoons, serializations.

THE REGISTER AND TRIBUNE SYNDICATE–715 Locust St., Des Moines, IA 50304. Dennis R. Allen, President.
Ideas for regular newspaper columns, comic strips, and any continuing features for newspapers. Decision based on 6 or 12 releases and explanatory outline. Pays percentage of collections. Query.

RELIGIOUS NEWS SERVICE–43 West 57th St., New York, NY 10019. Lillian R. Block, Managing Editor.
Nonfiction only; spot religious news stories and features. Pays 2¢ a word, beginning of each month. Good, clear, glossy photos on religious subjects. Pays $5 and up for photos, on acceptance.

TRANSWORLD FEATURE SYNDICATE, INC.–141 East 44th St., New York, NY 10077. Mary Taylor Schilling, International Manager.
Feature material for overseas markets. Query first.

UNITED FEATURE SYNDICATE–220 East 42nd St., New York, NY 10017. Sidney Goldberg, Managing Editor.
Comics, columns, occasional special series of articles. Pays on 50-50 basis.

UNIVERSAL TRADE PRESS SYNDICATE–37–20 Ferry Hts., Fair Lawn, NJ 07410. Leon D. Gruberg, Director.
Services trade papers with spot news and feature articles. Pays 65 to 80 percent of receipts. Query first in 50 words.

THE WASHINGTON STAR SYNDICATE–444 Madison Ave., New York, NY 10022. Harry Elmlark, Editor.
Features of various kinds. Most material handled under long-term contract.

WOMEN'S NEWS SERVICE–220 East 42nd St., New York, NY 10017. Sid Goldberg, Editor.
Trendy articles with photos, 300 to 700 words, on style or leisure; interviews with newsmakers; news-features of national interest. Pays $25 to $50 after acceptance.

LITERARY PRIZE OFFERS, GRANTS AND FELLOWSHIPS

Each year many important prize contests are open to free-lance writers. Some of these are conducted regularly. Others are one-time competitions, and writers should watch the newspapers and magazines, including "Prize Offers and Awards" column in *The Writer,* for announcements of these special contests.

The short summaries given below are intended merely as guides. Closing dates, requirements, and rules are tentative. No manuscript should be submitted to any competition unless the writer has first checked with the Contest Editor and received complete information about a particular contest.

Also included here are a number of fellowships and grants available to free-lance writers. Authors should write to the addresses given for complete details for making application.

Send stamped, self-addressed envelope with all requests for contest rules and applications forms.

ACADEMY OF AMERICAN POETS—1078 Madison Ave., New York, NY 10028.
Offers the Walt Whitman Award of $1,000 and publication for a book of poetry by an unpublished poet. Closes in December.

THE ATLANTIC—8 Arlington St., Boston, MA 02116.
Offers continuing awards for *"Atlantic Firsts,"* outstanding stories by new writers, 2,000 to 10,000 words. These stories are purchased at the magazine's top rates, and judged at the end of the year for a first prize of $750 and a second prize of $250.

COUNCIL ON INTERRACIAL BOOKS FOR CHILDREN—1841 Broadway, New York, NY 10023.
Offers five prizes of $500 each for children's book manuscripts by previously unpublished African American, Chicano, Puerto Rican, American Indian and Asian American writers. Closes in September.

E.P. DUTTON & CO., INC.—201 Park Ave., South, New York, NY 10003.
Offers the Dutton Man in His Environment Book Award for a full-length nonfiction work dealing with past, present or future of man in his environment. The award is a $10,000 advance against royalties. Closes in December.
Also offers the Dutton Animal Book Award for an adult fiction or nonfiction book relating to animals. The award is a $10,000 advance against royalties. Closes in December.

FOLLETT PUBLISHING CO.—1010 West Washington Blvd., Chicago, IL 60607.
Offers the Charles W. Follett Award for fiction and nonfiction book-length manuscripts for young people. The award is $3,000, plus publication. Closes in June.

HARPER & ROW, PUBLISHERS—10 East 53rd St., New York, NY 10022.
Offers the Harper-Saxton Fellowship to aid talented new writers. The fellowship consists of $7,500, of which $2,500 is an outright grant, and $5,000 is an advance against royalties. No closing date.

HOUGHTON MIFFLIN CO.—2 Park St., Boston, MA 02107.
Offers the Houghton Mifflin Literary Fellowships to help promising authors who need financial assistance to complete literary projects in fiction and nonfiction. The award is $7,500, of which $5,000 is an advance against royalties, and $2,500 is an outright grant. No closing date.

INTERNATIONAL POETRY FORUM—University of Pittsburgh Press, Pittsburgh, PA 15260.
Offers the United States Award of $2,000 plus publication for a first book of poetry by a U.S. citizen. Closes in April.

IOWA SHORT FICTION AWARD–English-Philosophy Bldg., The University of Iowa, Iowa City, IA 52240.
Offers $1,000 plus publication for a book-length collection of short fiction by a writer who has not published a volume of fiction. Closes in September.

THE MACDOWELL COLONY–Peterborough, NH 03458.
Offers fellowships for room and board to provide professionals in the arts freedom to concentrate upon creative work. Apply four to six months in advance.

MADEMOISELLE MAGAZINE–350 Madison Ave., New York, NY 10017.
Conducts College Writing Competitions in Fiction and Poetry, open to women college undergraduates. Cash prizes and publication in the magazine are awarded to the winning works. Contests usually close in February.

NATIONAL ENDOWMENT FOR THE ARTS–Washington, DC 20506.
The Literature Program of the NEA offers non-matching fellowships of $6,000 to published writers of exceptional talent. To be eligible, a writer must have published short stories, a novel, poems, essays or a play. Closes in September.

NEW ENGLAND THEATRE CONFERENCE–50 Exchange St., Waltham, MA 02154.
Offers the John Gassner Memorial Playwriting Awards of $150, $100, and $50 for unproduced, unproduced one-act plays. Open to New England playwrights. Closes in April.

O'NEILL FOUNDATION AWARDS–O'Neill Theatre Center, 1860 Broadway, New York, NY 10023.
$150 stipend plus production of winning plays at the annual National Playwrights Conference in Waterford, Conn. Open to unproduced plays only. Opens in September and closes in December.

POETRY SOCIETY OF AMERICA AWARDS–15 Gramercy Park, New York, NY 10003.
The Poetry Society of America offers a number of awards for unpublished poems in various forms: John Masefield Memorial Award ($500) for a narrative poem in any form to 200 lines; Celia B. Wagner Memorial Award ($300) for the best poem worthy of the tradition of the art, any style and length; Elias Lieberman Student Poetry Award ($100) for a poem by a high school or preparatory school student. Contests close in January. Other prizes offered during the year.

MARY ROBERTS RINEHART FOUNDATION GRANTS-IN-AID–The Mary Roberts Rinehart Foundation, Room 504, 516 Fifth Ave., New York, NY 10036.
Provides financial assistance to help creative writers complete work definitely projected. No closing date.

SEVENTEEN–850 Third Ave., New York, NY 10022.
Offers prizes of up to $500 for short stories by teen-agers. Closes in July.

THE SONS OF THE REPUBLIC OF TEXAS–2426 Watts Rd., Houston, TX 77025.
Offers the Summerfield G. Roberts Award of $1,000 for a book or manuscript of creative writing pertaining to the Republic of Texas events and personalities. Closes in January.

THEATRE AMERICANA–Box 245, Altadena, CA 91001.
Offers the C. Brooks Fry Award of $300 for the best full-length play of four plays chosen for production during the season. Closes in April.

VIRGINIA QUARTERLY REVIEW–One West Range, Charlottesville, VA 22903.
Awards the Emily Clark Balch prizes in creative American writing. The annual awards are given in alternate years for short stories and poetry. The first prize for short stories is $1,000 and the first prize for poetry is $500. There are additional prizes and the winning works will be published in the magazine. Closing date is usually in March.

826 THE WRITER'S HANDBOOK

WILMETTE CHILDREN'S THEATRE—Seventh and Laurel, Wilmette, IL 60091.
Sponsors annual playwriting contest for plays for children. Two prizes of $300 and $200 plus production are awarded annually. Closes in May.

THE YALE UNIVERSITY PRESS—92A Yale Station, New Haven, CT 06520.
The Yale Series of Younger Poets awards are made for manuscripts of poetry by poets under forty who have not had a volume of verse published. The winning manuscript will be published by Yale University Press. Competition opens in March and closes in May.

ORGANIZATIONS FOR WRITERS

AMERICAN TRANSLATORS ASSOCIATION
Box 129,
Croton-on-Hudson,
NY 10520
Rosemary Malia, *Staff Administrator*
American Translators Association is a professional society concerned with the interests of practicing translators, and serves as a forum and clearing house to advance the standards of the profession and to promote the intellectual and material interests of translators and interpreters in the United States. Its publications contain material useful to professionals and to aspirants for a career as translators.

Membership is open to any person actively engaged in translating, interpreting, or professionally related work (*Active Member*), or to any person or organization interested in the objectives of the Association *(Associate Member)*. Dues for individuals are $20 annually.

THE AUTHORS LEAGUE OF AMERICA, INC.
234 West 44th St.
New York, NY 10036
Mills Ten Eyck, *Executive Secretary*
The Authors League of America is a national organization of authors and dramatists, representing them on matters of joint concern, such as copyright, taxes, and freedom of expression. Since reorganization in 1964, an author or dramatist automatically becomes a member of the League upon joining The Authors Guild, Inc., or The Dramatists Guild, Inc., which are themselves corporate members of the League, but are concerned with the protection and promotion of the professional interest of their respective memberships, including contract terms. Because the Dramatists Guild is concerned with playwrights and authors writing for the musical stage, the material presented here deals only with the Authors Guild.

Who is eligible to join The Authors Guild? By resolution of The Authors Guild Council, any author who shall have had a book published by a reputable American publisher within seven years prior to his application; or any author who shall have had three works, fiction or nonfiction, published by a magazine or magazines of general circulation, either national or local, within eighteen months prior to his application; or any author whose professional standing, in the opinion of the Membership Committee, shall entitle him to membership whether or not he shall have had work published as defined above, shall be eligible to join The Authors Guild as an *active* member with voting rights.

The Authors Guild Council has also provided that the Membership Committee may give permission to an author with work in progress but not yet meeting the specifications for active membership to enroll as an *associate* member with all rights except voting rights. The circumstances of such permissions are left to the discretion of the Membership Committee. Many authors become associate members when they are offered a contract by a publisher for their first book.

Both active and associate members pay annual dues of $35.

MYSTERY WRITERS OF AMERICA, INC.
105 East 19th St.
New York, NY 10003
Gloria Amoury, *Executive Secretary*

Mystery Writers of America, Inc., exists for the purpose of raising the prestige of mystery and detective writing, and of defending the rights and increasing the income of all writers in the field of mystery, detection, and fact crime.

There are five chapters of the MWA in the United States: New York, New England, Midwest, Northern California and Southern California, and an At Large membership for those living in the United States but not conveniently near one of the chapters. As of 1975, membership totaled approximately 700 members.

There are four classifications of membership in MWA: 1) *Active*—for anyone who has made a single sale in the field of mystery, suspense, or crime writing (book, magazine, newspaper, motion picture, radio, television). Only *Active* members may vote or hold office. 2) *Associate*—for non-writers who are allied to the mystery field—editors, publishers, critics, literary agents, motion picture, radio or television producers. 3) *Corresponding*—for writers living outside the United States. *Corresponding* members do not need to be American citizens. 4) *Affiliate*—for new writers who have not as yet made a sale, or non-writers who are mystery enthusiasts.

Annual dues for *Active* members are $30; for *Associate* members, $30; for *Corresponding* members, $8; and for *Affiliate* members, $30.

P.E.N. AMERICAN CENTER
156 Fifth Ave.
New York, NY 10010
Kirsten Michalski, *Executive Secretary*

P.E.N. American Center is an independent association of writers—poets, playwrights, essayists, editors and novelists—that promotes and maintains intellectual cooperation among men and women of letters in the United States and abroad in the interest of literature, exchange of ideas, freedom of expression, and good will.

The P.E.N. American Center sponsors literary symposiums, panels, and workshops; grants literary prizes; provides services and aid for imprisoned writers; operates an extensive program for translators, including conferences, prizes, and fellowships.

The criteria for membership are the publication of two books of literary merit in the United States, and nomination by a P.E.N. member. There are three classifications for dues, although no special privileges go with the higher amounts, which simply constitute contributions to P.E.N. *Regular:* $20 per year; *Contributing:* $35 per year; *Sustaining:* $50 and up per year.

THE POETRY SOCIETY OF AMERICA
15 Gramercy Park
New York, NY 10003
Charles A. Wagner, *Executive Secretary*

The purpose of The Poetry Society of America is to secure fuller recognition for poetry, to kindle a fuller and more intelligent appreciation of poetry, especially of the work of living American poets, and to encourage and foster American poetry and aid and assist American poets.

Members of the Society are elected by the Executive Board. Persons in sympathy with the general purposes of the Society, including poets and students and lovers of poetry, are eligible for membership. Members are divided into three classes: *Members, Associate* members, and *Honorary* members, all of whom are qualified to vote in the elections of officers and of members of the Executive Board or upon a proposed amendment to the Constitution of the Society.

To qualify as *Members,* applicants must submit five short poems, published or unpublished. Poets of standing qualify for membership without the need to submit work. *Associate* membership includes critics, educators, librarians, teachers of English, etc. All such individuals qualify automatically. *Honorary* membership is strictly limited to outstanding poets by invitation of the Executive Board.

Dues for all classes of membership are the same— $18 annually.

SOCIETY OF AMERICAN TRAVEL WRITERS
1120 Connecticut Ave., Suite 940
Washington, DC 20036
Ken Fischer, *Administrative Coordinator*

The Society of American Travel Writers is a professional association of writers, photographers, editors, broadcasters, and public relations representatives with an ultimate aim to serve the traveling public. Through magazine and newspaper articles, travel books and guides, and radio and television programs, its members strive to provide travelers with accurate reports on destination, facilities and services.

Membership in the Society of American Travel Writers is by invitation of the Board of Directors. Active Membership is limited to salaried travel editors, writers, broadcasters, or photographers; and to those who are employed as free lancers in any of the above areas and with a sufficient steady volume of published or distributed work about travel to satisfy the Board of Directors. Associate Membership is open to persons regularly engaged in public relations within the travel industry. Initiation fee for Active members is $50, for Associate members, $100. Annual dues for Active members are $35, for Associate members, $75.

SOCIETY OF CHILDREN'S BOOK WRITERS
P.O. Box 296
Los Angeles, CA 90066
Lin Oliver, *Executive Director*

The Society of Children's Book Writers is a national organization of authors, editors, publishers, illustrators, librarians, educators and agents, that offers a variety of services to people who write for or share an interest in children's literature.

The functions of the Society of Children's Book Writers are (1) to serve as a network for the exchange of knowledge—providing, through its publications, market, workshop, contest, grant and scholarship information; (2) to serve as a voice for its membership, aiding writers of children's books to effect necessary changes within the fields; (3) to stimulate, through sponsorship of conferences, workshops and awards, creation of the finest books for young people.

Full memberships are open to those who have had at least one children's book or story published within the last six years. Associate memberships are open to all those with an interest in children's literature, whether or not they have published. Yearly dues are $20 for both full and associate members.

AMERICAN SOCIETY OF JOURNALISTS AND AUTHORS
(formerly SOCIETY OF MAGAZINE WRITERS)
123 West 43rd St.
New York, NY 10036
Dorothea Lobsenz, *Administrative Secretary*

The American Society of Journalists and Authors attempts to secure for the free lancer a respected place in American letters, and has over 350 members, who meet exacting standards of achievement in nonfiction writing. It has established a recommended rate schedule and a code of ethics and good practices for writers and editors. Other services for members are: monthly newsletter; monthly dinner meetings with speakers; Dial-a-Writer Referral Service; all-day workshops and craft sessions.

Membership is open to qualified professional free-lance writers of nonfiction; qualifications of applicants are judged by the Membership Committee. Initiation fee is $25 and annual dues range from $45 to $60, depending upon location.

SOCIETY FOR TECHNICAL COMMUNICATION
1010 Vermont Ave., N.W.
Washington, DC 20005
Curtis T. Youngblood, *Executive Director*

The Society for Technical Communication is a professional organization dedicated to the advancement of the theory and practice of technical communication in all media. The membership represents virtually every discipline associated with technical communication, including technical writers and editors, publishers, artists and draftsmen, researchers, educators, and audio-visual specialists. There are about 50 chapters in the United States and Canada.

There are four classifications of membership: *Senior Member, Member, Affiliate Member,* and *Student Member.* Each grade requires certain experience in some phase of technical communication.

Annual dues are $20 (Student Members, $10).

SCIENCE FICTION WRITERS OF AMERICA
c/o Andrew J. Offutt, *Membership Chairman*
Haldeman, KY 40329

The purpose of the Science Fiction Writers of America, a professional organization of science-fiction writers whose works have been published in the United States, is to foster and further the interests of writers and publishers of science fiction.

The Science Fiction Writers of America presents the Nebula Award annually for excellence in the field, and publishes the *Bulletin* and *Forum* for its members.

Any writer who has had a work of science fiction published, performed or broadcast is eligible for membership in the Science Fiction Writers of America, either as an active or associate member. For membership information and applications, writers should apply to the Membership Chairman at the above address. Dues are $12.50 per year.

WESTERN WRITERS OF AMERICA, INC.
1505 West D Street
North Platte, Nebraska 69101
Nellie Yost, *Secretary-Treasurer*

Western Writers of America, Inc., is a non-profit organization of professional writers of fiction and nonfiction pertaining to the traditions, legends, development and history of the American West. Its chief purpose is to promote a more widespread distribution readership and appreciation of the literature of the West.

Awards of merit—WWA Spur Awards—are given each year to the authors of the best Western material in five categories published during the past year.

There are two types of membership: *Active* and *Associate.* To be eligible for an *Active* membership, a writer must have either three Western books published, or twenty-five Western short stories or articles sold and published, or have credit for twenty original Western teleplays or five original Western screenplays actually produced and presented. Only active members can hold office or vote for officials or changes in the constitution. *Associate* membership is open to writers with one published Western book or five magazine stories or articles. *Associate* membership may also be granted to other persons active in the field of Western literature, such as editors, publishers, literary agents, literary critics, and motion picture and television producers and directors. Dues are $25 a year.

WRITERS GUILD OF AMERICA, EAST, INC.
22 West 48th St.
New York, NY 10036
Leonard Wasser, *Executive Director*

The Writers Guild of America (East and West) represents writers in the fields of radio, television, and motion pictures. For jurisdictional purposes, there are two separate corporations—Writers Guild of America, East, Inc., and Writers Guild of America, West, Inc. (see below). However, in actual operations, as far as contracts, dues, membership, etc., are concerned, the two corporations function together to create a national organization.

The purpose of the Guild is to promote and protect the professional interests of all creators and adaptors of literary, dramatic, and musical material in the radio, television, and motion picture industries, and to represent its members for the purpose of collective bargaining.

In order to qualify for membership, a writer must be presently employed in one of the three fields or have had material produced in one of these three fields within the past two years.

The basic dues are $12.50 a quarter. In addition there are quarterly dues based on a percentage of the writer's earnings in any of these fields over which the Guild has jurisdiction. The initiation fee is $300.

The Writers Guild has basic agreements with the producers and employers in all of these fields covering free lance writers and also, in some instances, staff writers.

WRITERS GUILD OF AMERICA, WEST, INC.
8955 Beverly Blvd.
Los Angeles, California 90048
Michael H. Franklin, *Executive Director*

The Writers Guild of America, West, Inc., represents all screen, television and radio writers in Hollywood (some 3,000 of them) with respect to their contractual relationship with producers, agents and their fellow writers.

The writer's remuneration, rights, and working conditions are all of concern to the Guild, which seeks always to spell them out by legal agreement, and also to further his or her general ascendancy in the industry. Contracts are held by the Guild with practically every producer in Hollywood in all three media.

For this service the writer pays to the Guild $40 annual basic dues and a percentage of his earnings.

Entrance requirements for membership are sale of original literary material to radio, screen, or television within the preceding two-year period, or employment as a writer, in any one of these three fields during the same period of time.

Writers Guild of America, West, is affiliated with the Writers Guild of America, East, which performs the same functions under the same conditions of membership requirements and dues for screen, television, and radio writers east of the Mississippi.

AMERICAN LITERARY AGENTS

Most literary agents do not usually accept new writers as clients. Since the agent's only income is a percentage—usually 10%—of the amount he receives from the sales he makes for his clients, he must have as clients writers who are selling fairly regularly to good markets. Always query an agent first. Do not send any manuscripts until the agent has asked you to do so. The following list is only a partial selection of representative agents. Addresses given are in New York City. (Zip codes are given in parentheses.)

Maxwell Aley Associates, 145 East 35th Street (10016)
American Play Company, Inc., 52 Vanderbilt Avenue (10017)
Julian Bach Literary Agency, Inc., 3 East 48th Street (10017)
Bill Berger Associates, Inc., 535 East 72nd Street (10021)
Lurton Blassingame, 60 East 42nd Street (10017)
Georges Borchardt, Inc., 145 East 52nd Street (10022)
Brandt & Brandt, 101 Park Avenue (10017)
The Helen Brann Agency, 14 Sutton Place South (10022)
Curtis Brown, Ltd., 60 East 56th Street (10022)
James Brown Associates, Inc., 22 East 60th Street (10022)
Collins-Knowlton-Wing, Inc., 60 East 56th Street (10022)
John Cushman Associates, Inc., 25 West 43 Street (10036)
Joan Daves, 515 Madison Avenue (10022)
Candida Donadio & Associates, Inc., 111 West 57th Street (10019)
Ann Elmo Agency, Inc., 52 Vanderbilt Avenue (10017)
Frieda Fishbein, 353 West 57th Street (10019)
Barthold Fles Literary Agency, 507 Fifth Avenue (10017)
Harold Freedman, Brandt & Brandt Dramatic Dept., Inc., 101 Park Avenue (10017)
Samuel French, Inc., 25 West 45th Street (10036)
Sanford Jerome Greenburger, 757 Third Avenue (10017)
Blanche C. Gregory, Inc., 2 Tudor City Place (10017)
International Famous Agency, 1301 Avenue of the Americas (10019)
Nannine Joseph, 200 West 54th Street (10019)
Lucy Kroll Agency, 390 West End Avenue (10024)
The Lantz Office, Inc., 114 East 55th Street (10022)
Lenniger Literary Agency, Inc., 437 Fifth Avenue (10016)
The Sterling Lord Agency, 660 Madison Avenue (10021)
McIntosh, McKee & Dodds, Inc. 22 East 40th Street (10016)
McIntosh & Otis, 475 Fifth Avenue (10017)
Elisabeth Marton, 96 Fifth Avenue (10011)
Harold Matson Company, Inc., 22 East 40th Street (10016)
William Morris Agency, Inc., 1350 Avenue of the Americas (10019)
Harold Ober Associates, Inc., 40 East 49th Street (10017)
Paul R. Reynolds, Inc., 599 Fifth Avenue (10017)
Flora Roberts, Inc., 116 East 59th Street (10022)
Maria Rodell, 141 East 55th Street (10022)
Russell & Volkening, Inc., 551 Fifth Avenue (10017)
Leah Salisbury, Inc., 790 Madison Avenue (10021)
John Schaffner, 425 East 51st Street (10022)
Ad Schulberg Agency, 300 East 57th Street (10022)
Seligmann & Collier, 280 Madison Avenue (10016)
Gunther Stuhlman, 65 Irving Place (10003)
A. Watkins, Inc., 77 Park Avenue (10016)
W B Agency, Inc., 156 East 52nd Street (10022)
Mary Yost Associates, 141 East 55th Street (10022)

INDEX TO MARKETS